D0345685

John Hogue is considered a world authority on Nostradamus and millennium prediction. He is the author of several best-sellers, including the *Millennium Book of Prophecy* and *Nostradamus: The Complete Prophecies*. His work has brought him international acclaim, and he has appeared on over 200 radio and television shows on three continents. He was been widely praised for his ability to cut through the social, religious and nationalistic projections of prophets and their interpreters to find what visions of the future are shared by the world's past and present prophetic traditions. For more information contact John Hogue at his website: hogueprophecy.com.

THE LAST POPE

The Decline and Fall of the Church of Rome

THE PROPHECIES OF ST. MALACHY FOR THE NEW MILLENNIUM

John Hogue

ELEMENT

Shaftesbury, Dorset • Boston, Massachusetts • Melbourne, Victoria

© Element Books Limited 2000
Text © John Hogue 2000

First published in Hardback in 1998 by
Element Books Limited

This edition first published in the UK in 2000 by
Element Books Limited
Shaftesbury, Dorset SP7 8BP

Published in the USA in 2000 by
Element Books, Inc.
160 North Washington Street
Boston MA 02114

Published in Australia in 2000 by
Element Books and distributed
by Penguin Australia Limited
487 Maroondah Highway, Ringwood,
Victoria 3134

John Hogue has asserted his right under the
Copyright, Designs and Patents Act, 1988
to be identified as the author of this work.

Cover design by Mark Slader
Design by Roger Lightfoot
Illustrations by Pete Welford
Typeset by Intype London Ltd
Printed and bound in Great Britain by
Caledonian International Book Manufacturing Ltd, Glasgow

British Library Cataloguing in Publication
data available

Library of Congress Cataloging in Publication
data available

ISBN 1 86204 732 4

To that Blessed One beyond all dogmas and Mafias of the soul.

Acknowledgments

Over four decades ago a little babe found his bottom uncomfortably moistened in a baptismal bowl and the oil-smeared thumb of a Catholic priest dabbed him right between the eyes.

I guess this book is that little baby's answer.

One of the most cherished persons who made that rendezvous with the oil possible – and all the other incidents in what so far has been an eventful life – is my mother and best friend, Irene Hogue. Thank you for your love and help in assisting me to close the holy book on this Catholic chapter in my life.

To all those who were not at my baptism (but encouraged and assisted my submersion into the historical depths of the papacy), I wish to thank my beloved woman-friend Ashika Jenua Kennedy, my agent from down under, Ronald S. Tanner, my publisher Michael Mann, his secretary Sue James, John Baldock, Florence Hamilton and all the people at Element Books Ltd. for burning the midnight holy oil and suffering the stigmata of deadline stomach ulcers to see this book to the printers before we ran out of time in the Second Christian Millennium. I also wish to thank the inter-library loan department of King County Library in Seattle, and especially the Library of the Episcopal Divinity School of Weston Jesuit School of Theology in Cambridge, MA, for loaning me their very fragile, flaking and rare copy of *Histoire de Papes* by Abbé Joseph Maître. A big thank you also goes to Suzanne Thackeray for her research leads.

Finally, this book could not be possible if it was not for the loving and critical care of the Writer's midwife, Linda Obadia. Thank you for your conceptual and line editing! Thank you for your spiritual sychronicity and friendship.

Contents

THE FUTURE

Plate Illustrations

Colour Plates

1. Arms of Callistus III, copied from Hans Ingeram's book of arms, 1459 (see pages 125–8).

2. Arms of Paul II from the St. Gall book of arms, 1466–1470, displaying the lion described in the prophecy (see pages 129–30).

3. Candidates likely to succeed John Paul II: Cardinal Carlo Martini, Archbishop of Milan; Cardinal Jean-Marie Lustiger, Archbishop of Paris; and Cardinal Francis Arinze of Onitsha, Prefect for the Council of Inter-Religious Dialogue (see pages 332–7).

4. Pope John Paul II celebrating mass at Immaculate Conception Cathedral, Denver, Colorado, August 1993 (see pages 298–321).

5. Irish singer Sinead O'Connor on the American *Saturday Night Live* television show, tearing up a picture of John Paul II in protest at his stance on abortion (see pages 308–10).

6. Arms of Paul VI showing the three fleur-de-lis "A Flower of Flowers" on a red chevron (see pages 274–87).

7. Arms of John XXIII (see pages 266–74).

Black and White Plates

1. Stone sculpture from Rheims Cathedral, showing the head of a pope adorned in the sugar-loaf style of papal headwear usual until the beginning of the 14th century.

2. Sketch by 18th-century French artist David, showing Napoleon as a "rapacious eagle" in the prophecy. Napoleon is seizing the

crown from Pope Pius VII's hands during his coronation, a gesture to show that his was a superior power to that of the Vicar of Christ (see pages 220–4).

3. Arms of Alexander VII in Santa Maria del Popolo, Rome. Note the stars as "guardians" over the six-mounts symbols in the lower left and upper right of the armorial bearing (see page 192).

4. Arms of Alexander VI showing the bull to the left (see pages 135–40).

5. An imaginary portrait of Innocent II by J. B. de Cavelleriis, from Ciccarelli, *Vite de'Pontefici* (1587). The portrait is suggestive of the appearance of the pope met by St. Malachy in 1140.

6. Arms of Calistus III showing the bull in the centre shield (see pages 125–8).

7. Pastiche based on original photomontage depicting Nazi persecution of the Church. c. 1935 (see pages 254–5).

8. Artist's impression of a woodcut depicting the pope as the Antichrist. This shows how the excesses and corruption of the Church fostered waves of distrust and suspicion from the Renaissance onward.

Picture Credits

The author and the publisher would like to thank the following for their kind permission to use color illustrations for which they hold the copyright: Gamma Press/Frank Spooner Pictures for 3 (Cardinal Jean-Marie Lustiger); Hemsey/Frank Spooner Pictures for 5; Heraldry Today for 1, 2, 6 and 7, are reproduced from *Galbreath PapalHeraldry*, 2nd edn, revised by Geoffrey Briggs 1972, Heraldry Today, Ramsbury, Wiltshire SN8 2QH, UK; Liaison/Frank Spooner Pictures for 4; Michael Pett/Frank Spooner Pictures for 3 (Cardinal Carlo Martini); Reuters/Archive Photos/ The Image Bank for 3 (Cardinal Francis Arinze); and to the following for permission to reproduce black and white illustrations: Antiquariat/Marco Pinkus for permission to recreate 7; Heraldry Today for 1, 3, 4, 5, 6, reproduced from *Galbreath PapalHeraldry*, 2nd edn, revised by Geoffrey Briggs 1972, Heraldry Today, Ramsbury, Wiltshire UK SN8 2QH; Musée du Louvre, Paris for 4.

During the last persecution of the Holy Roman Church, there shall sit Peter of Rome, who shall feed the sheep amidst many great tribulations, and when these have passed, the City of the Seven Hills shall be utterly destroyed, and the awful Judge will judge the people.

St. Malachy
The final coda to his prophecies
Either written by Malachy in 1140,
or attributed to him c.1595

PREFACE

A Past and Future History
of the Popes

As WE APPROACH the year 2000, the Holy Church begins to shiver
with the first waves of millennial fever. The time for a fresh and
insightful examination of the prophecies attributed to St. Malachy
concerning the near-future end of the papacy is needed.

The Last Pope is a unique and unorthodox past and future
history of the Roman Catholic Church. Prophecies critical to the
understanding of the Church are not repressed here but are
intended as compassionate guidelines to help it undergo its ultimate transformation.

We begin with the personal history of St. Malachy and examine
to what extent his medieval Church and mindset were products
of pagan Rome's transubstantiation of Christianity over the pre-
ceding 11 centuries.

After that we follow the evolution of the Church into modern
times and then into the future, using St. Malachy's 111 Latin
mottoes and doomsday coda to tell the story of the grand succession of popes unto Judgment Day. In unrolling the succession
we will inject Catholic visionaries of doom and revelation in the
order of their appearance in history. Among them you will see
the approved and disapproved auguries of St. Hildegard von
Bingen, Joachim de Fiore and the parallel vision of the papal
succession from Catholic prophecy's most controversial seer, Nostradamus.

Side by side with the chronological milestones of Catholic
prophecy will be the first comprehensive examination of the love/
hate, admission/denial relationships that popes have had with
their own legacy (or plague) of Catholic seers.

Roughly halfway through the succession, the mottoes of St.
Malachy suffer a credibility crisis. We scrutinize the skeptical view
that the Latin mottoes are forgeries from the High Renaissance

and then we put these arguments to the test with a continued examination of the succession of popes up to and beyond our times.

As we approach the new millennium the prophecies of St. Malachy and the Catholic seers take on greater urgency. We will investigate Pope John Paul's obsession with the prophecies of chastisement and salvation coming from apparitions of the Virgin Mary at Fátima, Garabandal and Medjugorje.

The *Last Pope* climaxes with a foretaste of the tribulation and apocalypse expected for the remaining two popes on St. Malachy's list, called Glory of the Olive and Peter of Rome.

The final words to the prophecy of St. Malachy are hopelessly doom-laden, but is its author able to see only the darkness left after the door slams on his own age? We will unlock the final seal, if you will, of other Catholic visionaries introduced earlier and compare their warnings of doom and religious rebirth to St. Malachy's final terrifying testament.

INTRODUCTION

Are We Two Popes Away from Judgment Day?

ON AN EARLY summer's eve in the year 1140, an Irish bishop and his attendant monks climbed Janiculum Hill on the western edge of Rome. They ascended the vista to pray in thanksgiving for the safe completion of their 16-month pilgrimage. Afterward they sat upon the hill's ancient brow to marvel at the many churches and magnificent pagan ruins that stood high enough among the tired, tiled and stucco urban jumble below to catch the final blush of the setting sun.

Bishop Malachy, reclining on Janiculum Hill with his flock of Irish monks, relaxed against the sensation of the earth exhaling the heat of the day. The wrinkles around his pale eyes softened as the glare of sun-reflected stone surrendered to the cool colors of the approaching night. As he watched the great city slip behind the bed sheets of its lengthening shadows, his attendants saw him begin to cry.

Just as Jesus once wept before Jerusalem, a future saint now washed his vision of Rome. But unlike the Messiah who had been the Irish bishop's reason for dedicating his life to monastic discipline and the mortification of the flesh, Malachy's tears were the overflow of an inner ecstasy.

The bishop cried himself to sleep. His monks stood watch in the darkness over their master, not daring to disturb his motionless form which seemed cast in a palpable silent presence. Not long after the stars defined the shadow spires of Rome and the trees of Janiculum Hill vibrated with the rhythmic mantras of cicadas, a voice called out within their midst. It was as though a loving finger carefully and softly tapped each man on the shoulder of their contemplation, making them startle.

"Rome . . ."
The bishop's scribe drew close to his master's face.
"Rome . . ." whispered Malachy again.

The scribe could barely make out the movement of his master's lips. The white crescent moons of the bishop's eyes caught the starlight just as his eyelids closed to a trance. For a time his dream gaze moved rapidly, dancing over the topography of some fantastic inner sight. Then they relaxed, and an unknown presence within the man descended to work his lips, letting pass a Latin phrase. Normal sleep seemed to return for a time before the eyes of the bishop would rove across the inner screen of a new vision and the lips would deposit another phrase.

By daybreak the weary scribe smothered the last of several candles and witnessed the ascension of the rising sun casting its first blush on the drying quill strokes of 111 Latin phrases on yellow parchment.

The bishop, now awake from his dream, explained that God had given him a vision of every pope to reign after the current pontiff (Innocent II) until the end of time when God would judge the world.

Some will say that the facts of this medieval story come to us clothed in the fantasy weave of an apocryphal Renaissance gown. Critics agree that St. Malachy and his monks mounted Janiculum Hill, but claim that no prophecy was uttered there. They say that the scribe who wrote down his ecstatic outpourings did so with fresh Renaissance ink on old medieval parchment four and a half centuries later. But as we will see, the truth of these prophetic assertions can still cause the whispering cloth of fable to rustle as she strides into our time. And if we can investigate the naked essence of these prophecies without being distracted by the covering of potential myth, we could find before us an authentic and powerful list of predictions chronicling the decline and fall of the Church of Rome.

Whether these Latin phrases were composed in 1140 or by someone in the 1590s under the pseudonym of a medieval saint, their author is a prophet. If his assertion is true and the papal succession is finite, then we who are alive in the final few years of this second millennium after Christ – we who mark its

sun-setting decade in the reign of the frail and aging Pope John
Paul II – are but two popes away from Judgment Day.

THE TOMORROW THEY WANT TO SELL

We are told that before Malachy and his monks returned to
Ireland they presented Pope Innocent II with a manuscript containing these prophecies. The document passed from his hand to
the Vatican's subterranean archives where it remained forgotten
for over 450 years. In the early 1590s Dom Arnold Wion, a
Benedictine historian, discovered the 111 mottoes and their coda
of doomsday at the end of the reign of the last pope and inserted
them in his famous work on Catholic history *Lignum vitae*, published in 1596.

For the next few hundred years the inserted list attracted much
attention and controversy, essentially because it dared to rub the
Church's nose in a prophetic faux pas. Whoever the author is,
church authorities considered it spiritually incorrect for any Catholic seer to begin a countdown to the end of the Catholic Church.
Given a pope's average life expectancy, the last pope depicted in
these Latin mottoes will sit on St. Peter's throne sometime around
– or shortly after – the year 2000.

Any document that predicted an end to the Catholic Church
and the final destruction of Rome would certainly warrant the
launching of an anti-information campaign. Enter the Jesuits,
the harshest critics of these prophecies. When the phrases were
rediscovered near the close of the 16th century, the priests of the
Society of Jesus acted as a papal secret service to defend the faith
and sustain orthodoxy.

Imagine if operatives in the CIA had uncovered a prophetic
document in the Library of Congress containing an accurate prediction of the succession of US presidents up to the final overthrow
of the US? Would not the CIA declare it a forgery to protect
national security? And if these prophecies were already in the
public domain, would not they promote a set of approved visions
that contradicted them and painted a rosy future for the US
presidency?

I say that is precisely what the defenders of the Vatican's future have done and continue to do.

In my quarter-century study of the world's prophetic traditions, I have never encountered a more diligent board of censors for its prophets than that of the Roman Catholic Church. You will not find St. Malachy on the bookshelves of Church-run bookstores. Nor will you chance upon books by visionaries who even imply that the Church as it exists today might not be around in the coming millennium.

The answer why can be found at the beginning of books by Vatican-approved Catholic authors, which display the *Lumen Gentium*. This proviso in essence instructs the Catholic faithful to remain open to private revelations. However, *Lumen Gentium* adds that "Judgments as to their genuineness and their correct use lie with those who lead the Church and those whose special task is not to extinguish the spirit but to examine everything and keep that which is good."

"Good" is defined by the Vatican censors, not by you or me. You will therefore find accounts only from seers that do not put into question the eventual survival and triumph of the hard-pressed Catholic Church during the coming century.

The Holy Father's homogenized prophecies generally march into the future in the serried ranks in the following chronological expectations:

- *The Warning.* These are signs from "approved" seers that the tribulation and Second Coming of Christ, the "Bridegroom" of Mother Church, are at hand.
- *The Miracle.* The visitations and mass healings of Christ's mother, the Blessed Virgin Mary, the rash of divine stigmata and other portents all direct people's attention to a coming miraculous sign from the heavens which will be seen by everyone on Earth. After the Miracle, many people will atone and convert to Catholicism, but the majority of humanity will tune it out and be seduced by the Antichrist.
- *The Chastisement.* God sends two final prophets, Elias and Enoch. They are martyred by the Antichrist. The Virgin Mary can no longer stay the angry hand of her son in Heaven, and humanity is punished for its sins. The Church and the faithful

are sorely tested by the Antichrist, natural disasters and Armageddon.
* **The Era of Peace.** A millennium of peace begins. Christ returns
and upon his divine authority, the Catholic Church, albeit bat-
tered and bruised, is restored. The Catholic Church becomes
Christ's "only" Church on Earth. All survivors are converted
to Catholicism, even the remaining errant Jews.

A Catholic bookstore stocking its shelves according to the dictates
of Rome will not represent digressions to the above prophetic
dogma. At best you will see books that question the exact time
sequence and degree of guilt and punishment forewarned, but
essentially the above scenario gets the Vatican's seal of approved
futures. It is the tomorrow they want to sell.

LOOKING AHEAD THROUGH THE REAR-
VIEW MIRROR

Neither John Paul II nor his censors deny that the coming decades
of the 21st century will confront the Church with its greatest
tests of faith and survival. Cracks in the edifice of the Roman
Catholic Church are spreading. The largest religious sect in
Christendom, which claims a population of faithful sheep
exploding beyond the 1 billion mark, is seeing a rapid decline in
its attendant army of shepherds and shepherdesses: the 4,000 or
more bishops, 400,000 priests and 1 million sisterly supernumer-
aries, the nuns. A schism is growing among the priesthood and
laity which could dwarf the one endured during the Protestant
Reformation. Then, as now, many Catholics believed their leaders
in Rome to be out of touch with the times or with their needs.
Pope John Paul II and his hierarchy resist mounting pressures for
the doctrine of the Church to enter at least the 20th century
before the 21st century begins. As personable as he is, John Paul
is a pope cut in the cloth of centuries of tradition. He is trained
to drive the Holy See into the future by looking through the rear-
view mirror reflecting the past.

In such a climate, we see millions leaving the Church, even in
the Catholic bastions of South America. They can no longer see

their faith sustained by the medieval wafer and wine-turned-vinegar of medieval religious views and rituals.

The future, by its very nature, brings every human being into an encounter with the unexpected. History gives us many examples of individuals and organizations which tried to impose their past-oriented will on the new and unwanted directions in destiny's current. Rather than relax and adapt themselves to meet fresh directions, those who held on to their prophetic expectations drowned. Consider the political hierarchies which lost World War II. Imperial Japan and Nazi Germany suppressed all mention of the signs that the tide had turned. All critical views were censured as defeatism or lack of faith. The closer the end came, the more fantastic were the predictions of ultimate and miraculous success from the Imperial Palace in Tokyo and the Führer's bunker in Berlin.

What is the pattern here?

A religious organization secure about its destiny does not waste time censuring doomsday prophecies. Nor does it need to bring to bear its official support for predictions which see its eventual triumph over all other religions of the world.

If truth abides, no apocalypse can destroy it. Did Christ's teaching come to an end on the cross? Did the words of Buddha die on his lips when he expired on his last full-moon night?

Four hundred years after the rediscovery of the prophecies of St. Malachy, time judges their official rejection by Church authorities as suspect because the mottoes remain remarkably and even chillingly accurate in describing the natures, family arms and fates of popes up to the current Vicar of Christ and perhaps beyond.

The days of John Paul II are numbered.

After he departs there remain only two more successors until these prophecies attributed to St. Malachy reach their forbidding coda of a Catholic apocalypse.

THE LIFE OF ST. MALACHY

And How His Church Became Roman

PRIDE AND PIETY: THE EARLY YEARS

THE LIQUID SUNLIGHT of medieval Ireland nurtured the flowering of a number of canonized Christian seers. Chief among these Gaelic oracles was Mael Maedhoig Ua Morgair, known in English as Malachy O'Morgair. He was born in Armagh, 94 years after most first-millennium Christian seers had miss-shot their doomsday bolt, on targeting the year 1000 as the time of the apocalypse and Christ's Second Coming. He was the child of northern Irish nobleman and chief, Lector of Armagh, and his equally learned wife, who came from a well-to-do family of Bangor, County Down.

The future saint would grow up in the shadow of Armagh Cathedral in an urban outpost of civilization and Catholic faith in northern Ireland, receiving his education from his devout and lettered father. Outside of Armagh, Christians often suffered confusion and spiritual depravation from priests who purchased their posts and recited slipshod sacraments, or ad-libbed their own illiterate renditions of the Lord's Prayer. Some of the once great seventh-century monasteries had fallen into simony and other financial and spiritual states of corruption. But these iniquities were over the horizon, for the time being, out of the short and innocent sight of a young boy in Armagh passing through an uneventful childhood.

In 1102, while on his way to Munster and having a particularly bad day enduring the harsh and often dangerous conditions of medieval travel, the good Lector of Armagh suddenly died.

Malachy's widowed mother was a stout-hearted and sharp-witted woman who handily managed her new role as a single parent bringing up Malachy, his brother Christian and their baby sister. "A dutiful Christian woman," writes Malachy's sympathetic biographer, his friend St. Bernard de Clairvaux. She was careful not to spoil her children, instilling in them a fear of God and a love for His commandments. Malachy in particular was a diligent, well-behaved, and even promising student. A slip of St. Bernard's quill leaves little recorded about Malachy's rebellious sister.

It is said that the depth and intensity of spiritual desire within a seeker can attract the appropriate teacher. Sometime in his early teens Malachy perplexed his more worldly school chums with his magnetic attraction to the hermit Imar O'Haglan, a hard-core renunciate who sequestered himself away from the world in a dingy cell a few lonely steps behind the cathedral at Armagh.

In O'Haglan the teen found the teacher of his dreams. His mentor rose to the occasion, teaching his novice the joys of hard labor while fasting and helping him discover the pious ache of self-denial in the face of all things worldly. Inside O'Haglan's cell one could hear prayers punctuated with the snap of the lash as the master instructed his neophyte in the art of mortifying the flesh to save his soul. Many of his fellow monastic inmates considered O'Haglan a saint. They judged the young Malachy to be in good hands. His brother, Christian O'Morgair, would be inspired to join the monastery and earn respect as a devout and loving abbot.

The regular sessions of self-flagellation, however, turned the stomach of Malachy's sister. She is said to have urged Malachy to try on every argument against the life of a renunciate. Her reasons did not fit.

His school friends also begged him not to abandon his noble class. "Honor your father's profession," they pleaded. "Don't squander an assured career as a brilliant professor." But they too found a wall rising behind the God-struck eyes of this saint in training.

O'Haglan taught Malachy more than penance and pain. Besides the flesh-splitting revelation of the whip, he taught his disciple how to sing Gregorian chants. He also inflamed the young man with a righteous calling for Church reform.

O'Haglan's praise for the devotions and spiritual intensity of the young monk reached the ears of his good friend, the arch-bishop Cellach of Armagh, who in 1117 waived canonical law and ordained the 22-year-old as a deacon three years under the age limit. Deacon O'Morgair tried unsuccessfully to refuse the appointment. He preferred the life of a hermit to that of a pastoral deacon, who would be forced to get his hands dirty encountering the daily dramas of the laity. Once ordained, however, he surrendered to God's will, plunging wholeheartedly into his new responsibilities.

Around this time Malachy and his sister had an ugly confrontation. The new deacon was overseeing the burial of a parishioner when his "sinful" sister approached the grave site and gave him a piece of her immoral mind. "Don't you know that the Bible says, 'Let the dead bury the dead'?" she taunted.

He looked down his deaconed nose at her and sternly replied, "You recite scripture well, but you are ignorant of its spirit."

Ms. O'Morgair was reciting words spoken ten centuries earlier by Christ to a disciple (who some believe was Simon Peter) on the shores of Galilee. Upon his first brief meeting with the Son of God the man dropped fishnet and family to follow the fisher of souls. But as they departed town a relative came running up with news that the initiate's father had suddenly died. The relative urged him to postpone his disciplehood long enough to perform his duty as a son at the funeral. The new disciple asked Christ if he could go and bury his dead father first.

"Let the dead bury the dead," dismissed the gentle Christ, "Come follow me."

The deacon of Christ knew well enough the ammunition his sister was attempting to use. It backfired. He merely glowered at her and said, "I make this sacred vow: I will never speak to you again!"

Malachy always kept his promises.

Up to now, his biographers gloss over this encounter between estranged siblings. Perhaps an investigation along male-chauvinist lines can summon some insight into his character.

First off, it must be remembered that historical accounts are generally written by the victors of wars and arguments. It is Malachy's biographer, St. Bernard, who has recorded this event. St. Bernard, a celibate monk famous for judging women as the doorway to original sin, is the recorder of Malachy's reflections. It is no surprise that his sister's side of the story never sees the light of day. We are never even told her name.

Maybe she had come to the grave site to rebel against the pallid and anti-life creature her brother had become. Perhaps she viewed her brother as a hypocrite, hiding a life-negative and self-torturing existence under the mask of saintliness. History's fragments tell us that the male children of the late Lector of Armagh and his intelligent wife were sharp-witted, but what about the female child? Perhaps she was heretically progressive in her views on love: that it was not a thing of duty and obedience, whips and fear.

And what about Malachy's rebuke? Consider what soon transpired.

A few years later when Malachy was living in Lismore, news reached him of his sister's sudden death. Malachy's biographers hasten to point out the many months of long prayer vigils he dedicated to the salvation of his sister's immortal soul. Once satisfied that he had done his holy duty, he stopped his memorial masses, believing that she had been redeemed and sent to heaven.

Four weeks later he saw her staggering in his dreams.

He was plagued by her starving apparition complaining that she had eaten nothing for a month. Upon waking, Malachy remembered that his last memorial mass for her had been exactly one month before. He resumed his long prayer sessions and masses dedicated to her. After a time she appeared in his dreams in successive states of healing. He recalled seeing her entering a church dressed at first in black, then walking halfway down the hall in gray, and at last, lying on the altar dressed in the purity of white, ready to be consecrated by Christ. Malachy divined this to mean that she had come to rest in peace in heaven.

I believe that Malachy, although later made a saint, was as frail a human being as any less holy than he. Hiding behind his beatified-to-be actions to save the soul of his sister lurks a brother suffering remorse, asking for forgiveness. Perhaps all the prayers and disturbing dreams were percolating with repressed feelings of guilt for closing his heart and finding no closure.

THE RELUCTANT PRIMATE OF IRELAND

Not long after Malachy severed relations with his sister, Cellach made him his vicar-general and the archbishop gave him the task of reforming the diocese of Armagh in his absence. Upon his return the archbishop found a very different diocese, one where the laity flocked to church in the proper sequence of the canonical hours, their ears ringing with Malachy's message of the virtues of matrimony and penance.

The archbishop was quite satisfied with what he saw, but the renunciate in Malachy was not. New temptations to escape the pastoral life were rubbed hot inside by this overtly social and political job. With the blessing of Cellach, he traveled to Lismore to study under a noted canon scholar named Malchus, who was bishop of Lismore and Waterford.

In 1123, Malachy's uncle – an abbot though not an ordained priest – appointed him as his successor to the decrepit but famous ruin of an abbey at Bangor, County Down. Malachy set to work restoring the church with a construction crew of ten monks from Lismore. It is at this time that the first of many miraculous acts occurred for which Malachy would later be canonized.

The moss gorging on Irish winter rains had scarcely made a roothold on the fresh pine beams of the new church when Malachy had to abandon the peace of abbey life and surrender to another demand for promotion. In 1124 – now 30 years of age – he reluctantly accepted the notorious bishopric of Down and Connor. The bishopric was considered one of Ireland's blackest holes for the faith. Malachy would face a moratorium on church tithes, a shortage of priests and an even greater shortage of celibate clerics; he would wince at the improvised perform-ances of the sacraments based on the rejection of canon law in favor of native and often semi-pagan Irish rituals.

One custom most vexing to the new bishop was the age-old convention of married Irish priests. Peter de Rosa reminds us in *Vicars of Christ* that even St. Patrick, the founder of Irish Christ-ianity, was quite proud of being a descendant of several generations of priests who "knew" their wives in the biblical sense. Even Archbishop Cellach, Malachy's greatest ally and promoter, was himself the eighth premarital successor of married arch-bishops of Armagh.

Malachy struggled for three years to instigate reform. The measure of his success can be gauged by the ire of the local chieftain, Conor O'Louglin, whose soldiers drove Malachy and his monks out of Down and Connor and even beyond his abbey outside of Bangor. One could see the monastic refugees scam-pering on the road to Munster, cast in the apocalyptic light of their torched wooden church.

Malachy and his monks found shelter and protection in the person of King Cormac McCarthy, whom the bishop had sheltered a year earlier at Bangor during the king's own brief exile. King Cormac gave Malachy land, sheep, and the material means to construct and found the monastery called Ibracense (also called Iveragh) in Ballinskelligs, County Kerry. Ibracense became an important mecca for the spread of the Order of Austin Canons across Ireland.

One night in 1129 Malachy is said to have had a visionary dream. He was handed the crosier of Archbishop Cellach. It was therefore not a great surprise to him or his community of monks when they received news of Cellach's death and his last request that Malachy be his successor.

The appointment of Malachy was a big fly in the beer of Cellach's blood relations. A local chieftain and ally of the late archbishop's clan put his sword and shield of support behind a rival candidate, a clansman named Muirchetrach.

Malachy spent the next three years avoiding bloodshed by making no attempt to occupy the see until the papal legate became so disgusted with the unpleasing Muirchetrach that he ordered Malachy to take over his bishopric, plunging Malachy head first into an encounter. Or, putting it another way:

> Gilbert of Limeric, the papal legate,
> Saw that the bishopric was ruled by an ingrate.
> He plucked Malachy from Bangor,
> And earned him much rancor,
> By attempting a canonical update.

Malachy preferred compromise to confrontation. Living outside the cathedral city of Armagh he watched over the members of the diocese, not daring to set foot in the city or cathedral, as this would certainly provoke a bloodbath. He let time and faith be his weapons. In 1134 the formidably named Muirchetrach died, after nominating Niall, the brother of Cellach, as his successor. With time Niall capitulated but grabbed the symbolic Armagh crosier staff of Jesus and the holy book of Armagh as trophies in a last-minute act of pious pique. Because holy objects often ranked higher in the medieval minds of the laity than the ordained priests who used them, this plunder gave Niall some religious clout with petitioners living in the northernmost regions of northern Ireland. However, the central and southern counties of Ireland by now were firmly in Malachy's camp and he was appointed primate of the entire Irish Church.

He eventually retrieved the objects; then in 1137, after reigning for three years as primate, he retired to Bangor.

A PILGRIMAGE TO ROME

It was after a short period of relaxing in the solitude of a monastic schedule that Malachy reasoned he must go to Rome and seek out Pope Innocent II for official recognition for the newly reformed sees of Armagh and Cashel. He must not return to Ireland without the symbol of papal approval, a pair of pallia to be reverently lowered upon the shoulders of the archbishops of Armagh and Cashel. (The pallium is a circular band of white wool decorated with six crosses and other religious symbols signifying a bishop's direct jurisdiction over an ecclesiastical province.)

His brethren at Bangor were against the harrowing journey and pressured him to decide on a throw of the dice. Malachy could not abide trusting a holy pilgrimage to chance, but all the same, he had faith that the dice would roll in his favor. They did.

With the issue settled, the archbishop of Bangor picked a handful of companions, and with three pack animals in tow they boarded a ship in late 1139, heading for Rome via Scotland, England and France. After passing through Paris, the little band turned down the rutted dirt track heading to the southeast, pushing sandaled feet off pot-holed roads for another 100 miles or so to cross the threshold of the most talked-about monastery of the day, the Cistercian Abbey of Clairvaux. There Malachy would meet the most influential and beloved friend of his life, the future saint Bernard.

The early to mid-12th century saw a great movement for religious reform in Western Europe, expressed in part by the spread of new ecclesiastical orders. A collective desire had swelled to discard the time-worn and corrupted mores of the Benedictines, which had so dominated Christian life. The new wave of monastic lifestyles in the 12th century was like rock 'n' roll breaking free from mainstream music in the 20th century. Ye, verily, I say unto you, Bernard and Clairvaux were to the monastic craze of the 1130s what Elvis Presley and Memphis were to the 1950s. If you were a priest looking for a new rock of ages, Bernard was your holy roller. This charismatic monk, known for his charm, wit and religious eloquence, was "the king," and his "Memphis" of a monastic retreat at Clairvaux was a must-see on your medieval pilgrimage.

It all started when Bernard, aged 22, led an entourage of 34 friends and nobles, including some of his congenital brothers, to stop their jigglin' and sinnin' and enter the monastery at Cîteaux. In the Middle Ages dedicating your life to poverty and seclusion from hound-dog worldly cares was cool. But a life of humility could not keep a charismatic gospeler down, and brother Bernard would become one of the most influential voices for Church reform of his day. Thanks to his golden-tongued evangelism, he flooded the nearly extinct monastery with new monks and resources, making it once again a thriving monastic center. For this achievement he was appointed abbot of a new foundation at Clairvaux, "thank-you-v'ry-much."

By the time Malachy and his band entered the cloister at Clairvaux, Abbot Bernard had several hundred monks in tow and had already established numerous foundations in France and England. By then the abbot of Clairvaux had become an ecclesiastical king-maker: the power of his voice and pen was enough to convince the cardinalate to uphold the pontificate of Innocent II against the Antipope Anacletus during a disputed papal election.

Elvis Presley loved martial arts. So did Brother Bernard. At the Synod of Troyes, he enticed the church authorities into recognizing the Order of the Knights Templars. It was his pet vision of a monastic and militaristic organization aimed at collecting well-armed and pure-at-heart knights pledged to fight the Church's battles in the Crusades. Bernard's holy hawkishness was later applied through the evangelical seductiveness of his letters that promoted his greatest mistake, the disastrous Second Crusade. Many blamed him for the debacle.

Malachy's attraction to Bernard was immediate and deep. Bernard's severe poverty and devotion to fasting no doubt impressed Malachy. At one time Bernard expected his monks to fulfill their harsh labors on a subsistence diet of beech leaves on a barley bread shingle. Just the man who could replace the void left in Malachy's heart by the death of whip-snapping O'Haglan.

Although Malachy rested at Clairvaux for only a few months, he was completely smitten by the place and its abbot. Upon resuming his pilgrimage to Rome, with the warmth of Bernard's parting embrace and blessings still upon him, Malachy secretly resolved to ask the pope if he might resign his bishopric so he could live out his days in the silence and seclusion of Clairvaux.

By the summer of 1140, and after a journey of 16 months, Malachy passed over the malarial Pontine marshes which imperceptibly sponged away the foundations of the ancient ivy-bearded city walls surrounding the Eternal City of Rome. During the 12th century *mirabilia Urbis Romae* bulged from its cracked classical seams with a huge influx of pilgrims, visitors and tourists picking their way though the labyrinth of streets running through a maze of medieval buildings pressed tightly together by the expansive foundations of hundreds of churches. The Irish bishop could crimp his weathered neck to peer with satisfaction at the holy cathedrals and basilicas marking Christ's triumph over ancient Rome. His heart rose, as did the spires climbing out of the squalor and up to heaven thanks in part to the masonry and stone robbed from the crumbling magnificence of Rome's numerous pagan ruins.

Some might say that much more than the stones from Imperial Rome supported the churches of Rome. It has been argued that the spiritual lifeblood of Christ's Church had not only converted the pagan world's capital city, but Rome had returned the favor. She had tainted much of the purity of the Galilean's simple faith and theology with the imperiousness of a fallen Antichrist empire.

In other words, the religion of Jesus of Nazareth becoming the "Church" of Rome is akin to Luke Skywalker's religion of "The Force" becoming the "Church of Darth Vader."

After 11 centuries, the sacred Rome that Malachy first set his joyful eyes upon was a ruin of pagan grandeur as well as early Christian innocence.

Rome was now a glorious contradiction: the capital of "Roman" Catholic Christianity – not Judean, not Galilean, not even the Church of the Nazarene as some biblical scholars believed it was named by its founder, the Messiah Y'shua bar Yoseph.

As China is known for absorbing invaders into its culture, ancient Rome was notorious for Latinizing and Romanticizing religions. By the fourth century "Y'shuanity" had become a state religion of Rome. The priests of the new Roman Church shaved their pates and wore "pontifical" robes like those of the pagan Mythraic cult. Representations of Y'shua on the cross showed a loincloth over his private parts so as not to expose the savior's all-too-Jewish lack of a foreskin. The Yid name also had to go. The Christian "pontifex" (which is Latin for priest or "pontiff") sanitized his savior, giving him a de-Semited name, Jesus Christ, of "Christ"-ianity.

A NEW CULT OF "BABY EATERS" INFESTS ANCIENT ROME

Between AD 61 and 64, and 11 centuries before Malachy's weary feet passed through the dilapidated gates of medieval Rome, the sore, besandled bony feet of an old Jew named Simon Peter shuffled through the sturdy Western gate of the pagan world capital.

Rome with its million citizens was a dirty sea of tangled tenements flowing over the Pontine plain around seven magnificent marble-covered islands of ivory-white palaces and temples. Upon these seven hills of Rome circled the mist of burnt offerings and the sewer-blotting aroma of incense. The Rome that shriveled the Jewish nostrils and appeared before the failing eyesight of Y'shua's "sent man" (which is what "apostle" means) was a microcosm of the entire empire. All the races, religions, cults and creeds walked over its dirty doormat, staking their place in its urban labyrinth.

Peter entered Rome as one of the early Church's most important heirs, and became bishop of the illegal cult's largest underground community in the Roman world.

A less dogma-bound re-examination of language and historical data about the earliest Christian era has prompted some modern scholars to revise their conception of the historical Jesus (Y'shua) and his sect of the Nazarenes, redefining them as the spiritual terrorists of their day. Y'shua was a Jewish revolutionary come like a whirlwind upon the spiritual as well as political arena. He was born a Jew, preached as a Jew of a reformed Jewish faith and was martyred as a Jew. Y'shua, before his name was Hellenized by the gentiles into Jesus, staked his claim to the title *Messiah*, defined in Jewish theology as the spiritual as well as hereditary king of Israel descended by blood from King David.

In effect Jesus declared himself the Jewish Dalai Lama or the Jewish people's pope.

How did it happen that a movement so self-contained within its own race and culture became, by the days of Bishop Malachy, the all-powerful medieval religion of the Western European gentiles?

Rabbi Saul of Tarsus happened.

The 13th apostle was not part of the inner circle of Jesus' 12 disciples. He never stood face to face with him to be corrected when he went astray. Saul was a Jewish agent working for the Roman government; he was a violent man on a crusade to weed out and destroy followers of the heretical Jewish sect that we call Christians.

One day his hate turned into love. Call it an act of divine vision, or a case of sun stroke, Saul was smitten by a vision and voice of the crucified Christ while traveling on a desert road on his way to root out Christ's followers in Damascus.

The champion of orthodox Judaism became the Christian faith's first great evangelist. For 20 centuries we have all had to take it on faith that Y'shua, in spirit, blinding Saul with his light in the Syrian desert, had changed his mind and deemed it right that his Church should be adapted any which way Saul could to make it attractive to the gentiles. Y'shua would use him to build a bridge to the gentile world with the cosmopolitan language of Saul's fluent Greek.

Rabbi Saul did not need to consult the apostles or Jesus' successor to the claim of Messiah, his brother James. *Christos* had spoken to him directly. Paul (his new name) was the founder of Christianity's more universal or "catholic" outreach to the world beyond God's chosen people.

The Nazarene hierarchy labeled Paul its first heretic. To the Nazarenes, the message of Jesus was more important than the martyred man. Paul used his formidable eloquence to change the focus back to the departed Messiah, or *Christos* – the new Greek label he helped to promote. Paul is also responsible for planting other un-Nazarene dogma: the Holy Eucharist, the crucifixion and resurrection and the kingdom of Christ being "not of this Earth."

Paul's oratory was compelling enough that he received support from a key insider, Simon Zelotes (Simon the Zealot), whose name was handed down to us thanks to incorrect translations from Aramaic to Greek to Latin as Simon Peter, the Canaanite, son of Jonah.

Since the 1980s a new understanding of early Christian history relying on a better examination of pre-gentile Cabalistic and Aramaic documents and the Dead Sea Scrolls has sent an earthquake through Christianity. Scholars like Michael Baigent, Richard Leigh and Henry Lincoln – authors of *The Messianic Legacy* – have revised the history of the first important years of Christianity. Their far more accurate translations of early Greek and Aramaic records put traditional views about the lives of the Apostles into question. In one case they reveal Jesus allowing at least one politically extreme zealot into his inner circle and upon this spiritual terrorist would be the responsibility to build his Church. This was the Apostle Peter, "the Canaanite." (Canaanite is a corruption of the Aramaic word for zealot, *qannai*, which was rendered into the Greek *kananaios*.) Bar Jonah – one of the two names the Bible gives for Peter's father – is another translation error for the Aramaic *barjonna* which, like *kananaios*, means "outlaw," "anarchist" or "zealot." A proper reading of Aramaic would further alter the way the Bible describes him: from Simon Peter to Simon *called* Peter (the rock). Peter or "Rocky" was his nickname in the Nazarene sect. It is a sobriquet for being rock-like or tough. Thus Jesus has rendered the responsibility of building his

Church on the "rock"-like man who would later become the first bishop of Rome, Pope Peter I.

Paul's triumph of will stirred the zealous Simon to join his ambitious crusade to catholicize the Nazarene movement for all people on Earth. With Peter's shift in allegiance a majority of Nazarenes moved away from Jesus' brother and heir, James, to support the more fiery and reformed Rabbi of Tarsus.

In the coming decades both Paul and Peter would travel across the Roman world finding thousands of gentile converts flocking to their novel monotheistic cult. The creed and vision of early Christianity was far less complicated and far more straightforward than the brand practiced by Malachy and the laity of medieval times.

There were no celibate popes or priesthoods overlording early Christian communes. There were nearly as many Church "mothers" as Church "fathers." The record of women's significant contributions to the early Church was systematically expunged from the medieval history accounts that Malachy would read in Malchus' library in Lismore.

There was certainly no love of opulence, peacock thrones, pallia, triple-tiara crowns or bejeweled crosiers. Early Christians did not gather in huge cathedrals or pay heavy taxes to construct papal palaces. They lived a mostly modest communal lifestyle, sharing what little they had. Only towards the end of the first century would there arise an obsession with doomsday doctrine and Christ's return. For now, talk of the crucifixion was in the footnotes. The main message taught in the early days was to trust in Jesus, to love one another and to love even one's enemies, and live each day with totality and care as if it were the last.

"Repent" in those days meant to "re-member" or to become one with the spirit once again through Christ's grace. To "sin" meant you had "forgotten" your connection with God. A sinner was not to be judged or made guilty for his or her transgressions. A Christian sheep losing his way was not to be tortured and burned at the stake but shepherded back to the fold. A sinner should be loved and forgiven. It was this compassionate message and the loving deeds of Christians that attracted so many converts. The early Church fathers and mothers had power to convert others not by promises of bread or threats of the sword, but through their example of faith. There were no papal armies, Albigensian massacres or Jewish pogroms initiated by these Christians. Rather, it was the Roman society that felt threatened and therefore decided that this new monotheistic religion was dangerous and should be repressed.

The label "cult" was originally used in ancient Rome to describe a religious system or community of religious worship and ritual, especially one focusing upon the novel idea of a single deity or spirit. There was little or no difference between the zealous devotion of a mainstream Roman pantheist and his monotheistic "cult" counterpart except that the former did his worshipping to a plurality of Gods and Goddesses. They both gave veneration, but a cultist was obsessed about only one founder and one God and doctrine when he joined his or her exclusive group of followers sharing an esoteric interest. The term "cult" was used then as it is now – as a contradiction in terms. A little more "respect" (which means "looking a second time") at the definition of cult would make it hard for any religion to avoid being labeled with this four-letter word for a number of fear-motivated reasons. Often a religion finds itself no longer called a cult after it has become a majority religion with political power in a society. Any new religions considered a threat to the religious status quo are called cults, and with good reason. Rumor-mongers of ancient Rome (the yellow journalists of the day) had as many far-fetched and fear-fed images of Christian cultists as misinformed and frightened people today have of the novel doctrines of Scientologists, Ramthers and Rajneeshees. Certainly the vast majority of strange new sects never evolve as far as supplanting the mainstream religion of their day, but history has shown us that it is equally certain that all respected religions of today once began as cults.

As medieval and mainstream Christians would later tag all woes and ills of their society on the Jews, your average pantheistic Roman pagan blamed the "baby-eating" Christ followers for every owlish ill omen befalling ancient Rome.

BORN-AGAIN ROME

Such was the climate of feelings when Simon the Zealot, called Peter, entered the catacombs of Roman "Babylon" to become the first bishop of the underground Christian community. It was somewhere down in a dark corner of the Roman catacombs that he wrote his first Epistle.

If there was a prophetic angle to the early Christian faith, it defined the current Emperor Nero of Rome as the Antichrist, especially after he was moved to embark on a drastic spring cleaning of the fetid slums of Rome by setting them on fire in AD 64. Just as the arsonist Hitler blamed the burning of the Reichstag on an innocent, Nero blamed his torching of Rome on the Christians.

The Roman mob set upon them. Peter, along with Paul, was seized and executed. Paul was beheaded. Peter was taken to a spot outside of the city – a hillock upon which Christianity's greatest cathedral and the Vatican City complex would later be built. Where the dome of a canonized Peter would rise 16 centuries hence, the feet of Simon Zelotes were hoisted into the air in his infamous upside-down crucifixion.

The martyrdom of Peter in Rome established the Petrine diocese of that city as the prime center of early Christianity. Thus each successor after Peter was expected to bear the same mantle of Christ's authority to build the rock of the Christian Church upon what was once the very corrupted hole of pagan Babylon.

Over the next two centuries the cult of the canonized St. Paul and St. Peter spread more rapidly than any other religion partly because most of the early Christian fathers took St. Paul's lead and gained converts by matching Christ's feats to those of other Roman gods, miracle to miracle, virgin birth to virgin birth. The Gospels were soon pockmarked by a number of non-Judaic aspects from the popular Roman cults of Attis, Adonis, Dionysos, Osiris and especially Zoroaster. Indeed much of the New Testament's basic doctrines of good fighting evil, Satan, salvation and the resurrection of Christ all sound suspiciously similar to the Zorastrian sect of Persian Mithraism, which was the most popular Eastern religion in pagan Rome at that time. The "Roman" Catholic robes, the swinging censers, the choice of incense and the crosier of the bishop of Rome all have pagan origins. Even the cult of the Virgin Mary can find its source from Mithras, who, like Jesus, was born of a sanctified virgin. Mithraism also forecasts a final battle like Armageddon in which good triumphs over satanic evil. Even the Church's long marriage to doomsday prophecies may have its origin in the very popular end-time prophetic traditions of Mithras.

As Malachy rested and prepared for his audience with Pope Innocent II, he might not have been aware that he had a pagan cult to thank for the term "pontiff," which he would use in his salutation to the bishop of Rome.

Most Christians would recognize the following words as an important cornerstone of their religion:

> "He who shall not eat of my body nor drink of my blood so that he may be one with me and I with him, shall not be saved."

Do you think this is Jesus talking?

No way, Hosea!

These words are from the Mithraic communion.

One of the early Christian Fathers, Tertullian, upon reading St. Paul's similarly worded description of the Christian communion, damned him as the Devil's agent for smuggling heathen rites into Christianity.

After St. Paul, the next great Roman mutation of Christianity can be credited to the pagan Roman Emperor, Constantine the Great.

Constantine ruled between AD 312 and 337. Without him St. Paul's dream of a universal outreach to the gentile world would never have happened. Constantine, a political animal if there ever was one, could see that the new faith had become the largest minority sect in the Roman world. If he were to legalize and institutionalize the cult as one of Rome's state religions he might bring half of the Roman world over to his side in the struggle to become emperor. He was a politician who remembered his friends. After winning his battle to become emperor he legalized Christianity and spread it throughout the Roman world as the faith adopted by its leaders.

Constantine was never a Christian. Only on his deathbed did he hedge his eternal bets and allow himself to be baptized.

Constantine was the chief priest (*Pontifex maximus*) of the pagan Sun God, the Sol Invictus cult. He deemed it politically expedient to bring the two monotheistic religions of Sol Invictus and Christianity closer together in doctrine and organization. This could not be achieved until he marshaled Christianity's generally independent and freestyle communities and bishoprics under Imperial Rome's bureaucratic control. To this end Constantine gathered the Church bishops together at the Council of Nicaea in AD 325. Its chief goal was to tame divergent Christian beliefs and fashion the doctrine that would best serve the majority faction of Catholic bishops he supported. Thanks to Constantine's bishops, much of what is known of the historic Jesus was censored. Even the degree of the Messiah's divine genealogy as the Son of God had to be established by ballot. Constantine officially deemed himself to be the savior of Christianity as foretold in its Second Coming prophecies. As long as he lived the Church all but ignored the Son of God and revered the Sun God's Pontifex Maximus as the Messiah of the Second Coming.

The Council of Nicaea blurred the distinction between Christian and other pagan rites and celebrations even further than St. Paul intended. Christianity adopted such ideas as celebrating Christ's birth on the pagan Yuletide celebration day around the winter solstice, which was celebrated as the annual rebirth and "resurrection of the Sun." After the Council of Nicaea paintings of St. Paul, St. Peter, Jesus and all the other saints adopted the aura of light around their hallowed heads – the nimbus of the God Sol Invictus. The soul's immortality was promoted, and the doctrine so cherished by Mithraic and Sol Invictus cultists of a final judgment and resurrection of the dead from their graves found its way into Christian prophetic tradition.

Nicaea is responsible for establishing the vow of celibacy as a prerequisite for the Christian priesthood, even though the first pope, the Apostle Peter, lived and died a married bishop of Rome. The bishops at Nicaea established a double standard which would lead to centuries of hypocrisy and cupidity in the priesthood. Bachelor priests were ordered never to marry, but priests who were already married could keep their wives. Because celibate priests and nuns were given wide ranging financial privileges and tax relief, the duplicity of Nicaea later led to greedy and unscrupulous men and women taking vows of priesthood and celibacy in name only. Over time the institution of celibacy was used by male church leaders to set themselves above women as cleaner and closer to God and therefore better qualified to run the Church.

A century before the bishops redesigned Christianity at Nicaea, Jews had been granted full citizenship in the Roman Empire by the Edict of Caracalla. The new Church of Rome after Nicaea initiated the beginning of the persecution of the Jews as the "killers of Christ."

When Constantine divided the Roman Empire into Eastern and Western halves and moved the imperial capital to Constantinople in the Eastern half, the bishops of Rome enjoyed much more civil power than ever before. Over time the popes became ever more influential in sustaining the bureaucracy and state institutions of the Western Roman Empire, as well as in the performance of the role of patriarch of the Western Churches. In the coming centuries the pontiffs began assuming the role of Christian Caesar.

IMPERIAL ROME IS DEAD.
LONG LIVE THE ROMAN CHURCH

The Dark Ages descended roughly two centuries after Constantine. The Rome of the pagans had fallen by that time, yet the Church of Rome gained more central control of its theocratic spread through Western and Northern Europe. The dogmatic shape of Constantine's reforms was well entrenched. Because this religious imperium had withstood the breakdown of society and because it was one of the few organizations keeping records and copying historical and religious manuscripts, much of the knowledge of the past which did not jive with its orthodoxy was easily lost or destroyed in the chaos of the times. The many pre-Constantine documents supporting an earlier, less Romanized view of Christianity were rapidly being misplaced and burned throughout the fifth and sixth centuries.

The Dark Ages also saw the Church of Rome's spiritual imperium glorified by the pontificate of Gregory the Great (AD 590–604), the first monk ever elected. This Alexander the Great of pontiffs conquered the minds and hearts of a spiritual empire that established the medieval papacy in Rome that so magnetically attracted Malachy. Thanks to his reorganization and support of monastic orders, the medieval countryside became dotted with hundreds of monasteries, creating havens for men like our good Irish bishop.

Gregory revitalized the civil administration of the Church while civil order in the secular world waned and reorganized the territories of his spiritual empire in what would become the Holy See, or *Patrimonium Petri* (Patrimony of Peter). Imperial Rome had fallen and the people of Western Europe turned to the Church, not only for the holy wafer but, thanks to this brilliant civil organizer, to fill their bellies. With barbarian kingdoms often in disarray and rising and falling upon the corpse of the Roman Imperium, the church remained one of the few social and civil constants.

It was Pope Gregory's literal interpretation of St. Augustine (AD 354–430) and St. Paul on original sin that created the Christian cult of shame around the body and all things natural, which Gregory as Caesar of the Roman Church endorsed as a code that all Catholics must obey. The pope who made himself sick to death by fasting and mortifying his flesh made the anti-life and anti-sex philosophy of St. Augustine the cornerstone to the Catholic doctrine of Malachy's day. Our good bishop was indoctrinated to consider sex with a woman sinful, even in relationship to pregnancy. Malachy no doubt wandered his parishes preaching this Augustinian dogma. One can imagine him compelling husbands to do penance after having intercourse with their wives, in the form of taking a bath – a punishment to make one flinch in the down-and-dirty medieval era.

PUT YOUR FAITH IN FORGERIES

One last milestone remained before Christ's Church of the spirit kingdom could become a secular and political power on Earth. Someone had to find documentation proving what the New Testament forgot to declare: that the Church had authority to enter the arena of power, politics and the exploitation of the coin.

In the year 752 Pope Stephen III was sorely vexed by the

Lombard kingdom plundering Church properties in northern Italy. He called upon King Pepin (714–68) of the Franks for military aid. To buttress his request he presented a document, dated AD 315, purportedly written by Emperor Constantine. Fortunately for the pope, the Frankish warlord did not know the difference between classical and medieval Latin. (Pepin never did learn how to read.) The state of historical scholarship was so wretched that the Frankish notaries and scholars overlooked its factual errors. The paper looked ancient enough, and who had the technology in those days to test how fresh a stain of the ink was upon the crumbling parchment?

The document contained Emperor Constantine's description of his miraculous healing from leprosy by Pope Sylvester (actually Pope Miltiades was ruling in 315 – mere details!). In gratitude for his healing and conversion to Christianity, the document states that Constantine grants the bishop of Rome "all the palaces and districts of the city of Rome and Italy and the regions of the west." He grants all of St. Peter's successors political powers above and beyond those of secular monarchs throughout the Christian regions of Western Europe.

Pepin was impressed enough to flood northern Italy with soldiers and defeat the Lombards for their secular and religious lord and successor to St. Peter. In return, Pope Stephen made Pepin, and later his son and heir, Charlemagne, "patricians of the Romans."

Thanks to this bald-faced forgery known as the Donation of Constantine, the life of humble poverty lived by Jesus and the first pope was replaced by a claim for future successors of Peter to inherit all the worldly power, palaces and wealth that were once the property of pagan Roman emperors west of Greece and the Middle East.

Through the Donation, Stephen would crown Charlemagne Emperor of a Holy Roman Empire, subservient to the pope. This uneasy marriage of Caesar popes and imperial emperors would beset Europe with many wars and miseries. Politics and temporal power struggles would dominate the thoughts and actions of most pontiffs until all claims to secular control were finally stamped out with the extinction of the Papal States in 1870.

The document's glaring errors were exposed by a papal aide, Lorenzo Valla, in 1440. Eleven pontiffs in a row made sure his findings would not be published. Finally they were leaked in 1517 and used by Martin Luther to strengthen his case for the Protestant Reformation against papal excesses and indulgences. But no concession of error would be issued from Rome for centuries to come. The humility that would allow an admission of error was impossible, especially after another set of forgeries were released by the formidable Pope Gregory VII (1073–85) less than two decades before the birth of our Irish prophet.

For seven centuries after Christ walked on the Earth the Greeks had called the imperial pagan capital turned Holy City of Roman Christendom the home of forgeries. Honoring this tried and true tradition since the Donation of Constantine, Gregory VII appointed an army of scribes to produce any forgery that would solidify his absolute power in the Western Christian world.

De Rosa aptly describes this crime as anticipating George Orwell's *1984* by 900 years "not in some godless state at the behest of Big Brother, but in the heart of Roman Catholicism in favor of the pope."

Without the slightest blush Gregory proclaimed that his *Dictatus papae* was based on the discovery in the papal archives of ancient Roman records dating back to St. Peter's ministry in Rome. Upon their spurious authority Gregory redefined the powers of the pope, which included the following:

> The pope can be judged by no one on Earth. The Roman Church has never erred, nor can it make mistakes. Only the pope can depose bishops. He alone is entitled to Imperial [Roman] insignia. He alone can dethrone emperors or kings, and absolve their subjects from allegiance. And last but not least, a righteously elected pope is automatically a saint, made so by the merits of Peter.

It is hard for me to imagine such imperious salvoes coming from the mouth of an apostle who, according to the documentation within the New Testament, was notorious for being all too human and fallible.

Gregory then "discovered" the Pseudo-Isidorian Decretals which falsely attributed to the early Christian fathers the edict that condemned all business with an excommunicated person. Gregory would extend this lie to excommunicated emperors and kings. This forced an emperor off his throne and out of his royal clothes and crown to wade through the Alpine snows in mendicant rags to do penance before the pope. Thus was the Holy Roman Emperor Henry IV brought to his knees by a forgery.

Of the 324 passages of Gregory's *Decretum*, the penultimate Catholic document on the code of canon law, his forgers inserted 313 passages falsely attributed to early Christian fathers. Many of the canon laws established by the *Decretum* that defined a "Roman" Catholicism in Malachy's day survived into modern times. From counterfeiters we get the assignation of clerics as humans a cut above the Catholic laity, deserving more sacred and political rights than common Catholic folk. We find that excommunicated Catholics are now judged as heretics, worthy to be tortured and burned to death. The pope now is equal to the Son of God, which allowed every future curia (the pope's cabinet ministers and their civil servants) to act in the pontiff's name with no questions asked. The great Christian theologian Thomas Aquinas (1224–1274), in his classic *Summa Theologica*, duped by Gregory's simulated infallibility based most of his quotes of early Christian leaders on the lies of the *Decretum*.

Thanks to Gregory, the Church of Rome beheld in an ecstasy by Malachy on a warm summer's eve finished its conversion from a Jewish revolutionary sect to an imperial and "Holy" Roman state religion.

A PAPAL AUDIENCE AND A RETURN TO IRELAND

Following a few days' rest after entering Rome, Malachy was led by friendly priests and guides to stand before the solemn edifice of the Lateran Basilica, the official papal residence. There Malachy had his audience with Pope Innocent II. Innocent gladly welcomed him as a friend of Bernard de Clairvaux, who was indeed the pontiff's staunchest ally.

Innocent's tempestuous reign was always in need of allies. He had already survived challenges to his elevation to supreme priest of the Church by two antipopes. Exactly one year before the audience with Malachy, Innocent was captured and his papal armies routed by the Norman forces of King Roger II. He was released only after he officially acknowledged Roger's supremacy in southern Italy.

At the time of Malachy's audience, the inner circle of the papacy was enjoying a lull in the ongoing disasters. But that would soon end. The pope who smiled down on the bowed bishop from Ireland would sit for only three more years on the throne of St. Peter. He would lose his ally Louis VII of France, and the crowds of thankful pilgrims filling the Roman streets would soon be replaced by rioters establishing a republican commune against the papacy.

Malachy first put before Innocent the subject of the Irish sees. The pope was happy to approve of them and granted the creation of documents and pallia to be carried back to Ireland by Malachy as official sanction for his see authority and reforms. But his request to retire to the Abbey of Clairvaux was firmly denied. Innocent would not release such a valuable pastor whose dedication to the Church could spread the Cistercian order throughout Ireland. Instead he promoted Malachy to papal legate (the pope's ambassador) in Ireland.

Malachy left the Eternal City (Rome) with the treasured pallia in hand. He retraced his steps through Piedmont and entered France, spending a precious and all-too-short interlude at the Abbey of Clairvaux, where he would leave four of his monks with brother Bernard to learn the Cistercian discipline. He returned to Ireland by 1141 and dove into his new duties as prelate with his customary zeal.

The new prelate got himself into a controversy over religious architectural reform when he ordered the construction of an oratory of stone, rather than the customary lath, wood or plaster design. The local laity were worked up into open rebellion by a man we are told was once helped by Malachy in his time of need. The ringleader demanded that the construction be stopped and Irish religious tradition be supported or else he might be compelled to incite the people into tearing down the offensive structure.

Hell hath no fury like a saint-to-be who has God, the pontiff and Brother Bernard on his side. "Wretched man!" he roared, "the building you have seen begun shall most certainly be completed, but its completion you shall not see!"

Once again we see the persuasive power of Malachy's holy

mojo. As the walls of the oratory kept rising to completion the health of the man kept failing. He died before the last stone brick was placed.

Some of Malachy's episodes of prophetic vision can be excused as coincidence, but the next prophecy attributed to him is not so easily explained. At some point in his travels as the papal legate he was purported to have logged this prophecy for the distant future of the Emerald Isle:

> Ireland will suffer English oppression for a week of centuries [700 years], but will preserve her fidelity to God and His Church. At the end of that time she will be delivered, and the English in turn must suffer severe chastisement. Ireland, however, will be instrumental in bringing back the English to the unity of Faith.

Complete Anglo-Norman domination of Ireland was achieved a century after Malachy's prediction. Independence for the southern part of Ireland came 700 years later in the early 20th century. If this utterance is not apocryphal, then it predates the schism between the Church of England and the Catholic faith by four centuries and implies that Anglicanism will falter sometime in our near future when the final pope finishes his reign.

PROPHECIES, MIRACLES AND MALACHY'S FINAL JOURNEY

Bernard de Clairvaux chronicles a flurry of miraculous acts punctuating the final years of Malachy's life. Our prophet is said to have walked with bishop's crook in hand between two gathering armies and kept them apart by causing a stream to flood through the chosen battlefield at the peak of dry season. Where Moses parts the Red Sea and makes the land dry, it appears that our Irish Moses parts the warring armies by making their battlefield all wet. On another occasion he pulled a Mahatma Gandhi on King Turlough Mor O'Connor. He threatened to fast unto death until a certain innocent nobleman was finally released. It is said that Malachy could even bring salvation to a certain man who suffered from the blue tongue of his nagging wife.

In 1148, at the ripe old medieval age of 54, Malachy sensed

that his corporeal dissolution was at hand. Around this time he was asked where and when he would like to die. "I would prefer to expire on All Souls Day in Ireland. However, if the Lord chooses that it be not Ireland, then I would like to die at Clairvaux."

In that same year, while conducting a synod in Inishpatrick, off Skerries, Malachy offered to deliver the official documents on the sees of Armagh and Cashel to the new pope, Euguenius III, who was at the time nearby touring France.

While preparing to embark on the journey his brethren, heavy with concern for their ailing prelate, begged him not to go. Finally the day came when Malachy bade farewell to his tearful monks standing on the docks of Bangor. Two of his devotees, mixing tears with wet kisses upon his outstretched hands, implored him to agree to one last request – that he promise to return to Ireland.

As Malachy made his way to the gangplank he was followed by the most pitiable of their spiritual family, the young monk Catholicus, who for the last six years had been plagued by epileptic fits.

Catholicus fell to his knees before Malachy, sobbing. "Alas, my father, are you then going to leave us? And although well aware to what almost daily afflictions you are abandoning me, you have no compassion on my misery?"

Malachy cradled the monk in his arms and softly replied, "Rest assured, my child. You shall not be troubled again until my return."

Not long after his ship put to sea, a strong headwind drove the vessel back to the shore. Malachy must have quietly smiled to himself and praised the Lord, for he took this surprise twist of fate as a sign that his promise to return to Ireland was fulfilled. The winds were more agreeable the following day, and the tattered square sail of the stout-hulled ship soon disappeared out of view over the horizon. From that day on Catholicus never suffered another fit. Maybe because Malachy never returned.

Malachy passed through Scotland but was prevented from his rendezvous with the pope in France by King Stephen of England, who delayed the band from crossing the English Channel until suspicions of intrigues between the prelate and the rival Scottish king were put to rest. As the autumn chill began bruising the trees with orange across the French countryside, Malachy's little band received a warm welcome from Abbot Bernard and his community at Clairvaux.

These last days of Malachy's were some of the happiest of his life. His entourage must have noted their master's revived health and spirit. They planned for a long and happy winter stay at Clairvaux, to let Malachy rest and gain strength for the final pilgrimage to Rome the following spring.

After celebrating Mass on 18 October 1148, in honor of the Feast of St. Luke, Malachy admitted to Bernard that he was feeling ill. In the late afternoon of 2 November (All Souls' Day) it was clear to all that he was dying. Malachy gently refused Bernard's offer to have the Last Sacraments delivered to him at his bedside and managed to walk to the church to receive extreme Unction.

Towards midnight the entire community gathered around his cot, where brother Bernard tenderly held the dying bishop and Irish legate of the Holy See in his arms.

Malachy was buried at Clairvaux where, thanks to the influence of Bernard, his saint-cult spread over the next several decades. In 1170 his name was placed in the Irish Martyrology of Gorman. Twenty years later Pope Clement III sanctioned the cult among the Cistercians and he was canonized. His feast day was moved from the 2 November to 3 November to avoid All Souls' Day.

At the dawn of the next century St. Malachy's skull was exhumed and placed as a relic in the Cathedral of Troyes in France. The bleached Cathedral dome of his long-departed brain was reunited with the exhumed head of the now-canonized St. Bernard, whose skull later formed a companion piece at Troyes. Today the rest of their skeletons are still mixed in a collective grave with three other saints as part of a cost-saving scheme of the priests at the parish of Ville-sous-la-Ferte.

THE
GRAND SUCCESSION
OF PONTIFFS

(AD 1143–2020s?)

A Note on St. Malachy's Latin Mottoes

THE III MOTTOES and doomsday coda attributed to St. Malachy were first published in the year 1595 by the Dominican researcher Dom Arnold Wion (b. 1554). They appear as a segment in his famous ecclesiastical tome *Lignum vitae*. Wion relies heavily on Father Alphonsus Ciaccionius (b. 1540) for most of his interpretation of the mottoes. A full account of the history of believers and debunkers of these prophecies appears in the segment following the life of Pope Clement VIII (see p. 175).

The 111 mottoes and doomsday coda attributed to St. Malachy were written in a blend of medieval Latin and Latinized Italian. These cryptic phrases are rarely more than three words in length and are believed to contain a number of clues to the reign of each pope until doomsday. The themes can be categorized as follows:

- *Coat of arms.* The coat of arms depicts the paternal armorial bearings held by the pope. For instance, FLOS FLORUM (A Flower of Flowers) describes the fleur-de-lys design on the arms of Paul VI. The mottoes sometimes will depict variations or additions to the family arms during a pope's career as bishop or cardinal. In rarer cases the maternal arms are described or the arms of the pope's chief nemesis are inserted, as could be the case of Pius IX, whose motto CRUX DE CRUCE (The Cross from a Cross) better describes the armorial bearings of his enemy, King Victor Emmanuel of Savoy.
- *The theme or deeds of a pontificate.* PEREGRINUS APOSTOLICUS (An Apostolic Wanderer) foresees the tragic pontificate of Pius VI, who was arrested by soldiers of the French Revolution and forced from Rome to house arrest in Turin and then across the

Alps to his new prison lodgings in France – first at Briançon and finally at the citadel in Valence. It was here that he died.

- *The pope's new name.* An inscription such as CONCIONATOR PATAREUS (A Patarean Preacher) reminds us that Benedict XI's namesake – St. Benedict – was a native of Patara, and might readily be called PATAREUS, the Patarean.

- *Milestones in the pontiff's life before his election.* The motto DE CAPRA ET ALBERGO (From a She-goat and a Tavern) names two cardinals served by the future Pius II: Cardinal Caprancia (CAPRA) and Cardinal Albergati (ALBERGO).

- *The cardinal title or posting of the pope before his election.* The motto LUX IN OSTIO (A Light in the Door) connotes Lucius III's term as cardinal bishop of Ostia, the "door" or port at the mouth of the Tiber which serves Rome.

- *An important historical influence or event.* The pope who saw the beginning of the Thirty Years War (1618–48), Paul V, is called GENS PERVERSA (A Perverse People). This insinuates the religiously heretical Protestants fighting the Catholic pope in what would become Europe's most devastating religious war in history.

- *A chief nemesis.* AQUILA RAPAX (Rapacious Eagle) identifies Pius VII's formidable tormentor, Emperor Napoleon Bonaparte, who used an eagle as his symbol and who would arrest the pope, disband the Papal States and pillage Rome's papal treasures.

- *The pope's Christian name.* Pius III is called DE PARVO HOMINE (From a Little Man) after his family name Piccolomini (little man). The compound rubric EX UNDARUM BENEDICTIONE (From a Blessing of the Waves) describes the wavy armorial device of Cardinal Benedetto (Benedict) Gaetani, who became Boniface VIII.

- *The town or province of birth.* ABBAS SUBURRANUS (A Sub-urran Abbot) describes the Roman suburb where Anastasius IV was born. EX MAGNITUDE MONTIS (From the Greatness of a Mountain) stands for Eugenius III, who was born in Grammonte, which is Italian for *Mons Magnus* (great mountain).

- *A key geographic location in the pontiff's life.* EX ANTIQUITATE URBIS (From the Oldness of a City) implies Cremona, the district of the future Gregory XIV's birth as well as the name of its district capital, the city wherein he served as bishop. The city of Cremona is the most ancient Latin settlement in the Po River Valley.

- **Combinations of the above.** Two or more aspects are blended together to make a complex pun or layered message. For example DE INFERNO PRÆGNANI (The Pregnani from Hell) blends Urban VI's Christian name with a prophetic editorial against the Great Schism he would inflict on the Church during his reign. SIGNUM OSTIENSE (A Sign of Ostia) combines the family name Segni (sign) with Cardinal Segni's posting as cardinal bishop of Ostia before becoming Alexander IV.

Note: the spelling of the Latin mottoes follows Wion's Renaissance representations as they appeared in 1595 for *Lignum vitae.*

ONE

Ex castro tiberis
(From the Castle on the Tiber)

CELESTINE II
(1143–1144)

WITHIN THE COOL confines of the Church of San Florido in the Umbrian town called Città de Castello there stands a fine silver altar-frontal piece which remains one of the town's proudest medieval treasures. The altar, along with the yellowed paper and wrinkled covers of 56 priceless volumes, was donated "for the ransom of his soul" more than 850 years earlier by the first pope in St. Malachy's papal succession.

Guido of Città di Castello (Castle) would come to the throne of St. Peter from the "castle" city on the upper Tiber River three years after St. Malachy delivered his papal prophecies to his predecessor, the much-harried and embittered Pope Innocent II.

Cardinal Castello was a noted scholar and long-time friend to the controversial theologian Peter Abelard (1079–1142). He remained fond of what remained of Abelard even after his mentor's well-known and scandalous love affair with his student, Heloïse of Canon Fulbert, led to his castration. He held fast to his association even after Abelard's revolutionary doctrinal insights earned him the official condemnation by the Council of Sens in 1140. Cardinal Guido walked a tightrope with heresy when he warmed to such Abelarian heresies as the new-fangled concept of seeking truth through carefully weighing the opposing positions of authorities. Even St. Bernard de Clairvaux took the cardinal to task in a letter for defending Abelard.

Though the cardinal's loyalty endangered his promotion, in September 1143 he was quickly elected pope a mere two days after the passing of Innocent II. He took the name Celestine II. Already old and ailing, he would survive for only six months. It turned out that St. Bernard's concerns were unfounded. Celestine toed the religiously correct line.

TWO

Inimicus expulsus
(The Enemy Driven Out)

LUCIUS II
(1144–1145)

IN MARCH 1144, rumors of war with Norman-controlled southern Italy and an open rebellion of the citizens of Rome against papal authority overshadowed the election of a new pope. A time of war required a warrior pope who could repress the rebellious citizens of Rome and stamp out their sinful demands for freedom and democracy. He also needed the savvy to drum up the will, wealth and weapons to thwart the Norman menace gathering on the southern borders of the papal dominions.

The Sacred College of Cardinals therefore voted that the mitered crown be placed upon the worthy head of Cardinal Gheraldo Cassianemici of Bologna. This noble, whose family name means "drive out the enemy," had a well-respected resumé as a canon lawyer before entering the Lateran Basilica, where he vigorously worked for several popes before his near-unanimous election.

There was little time for celebration. This pope, who named himself after his ancient martyred predecessor, St. Lucius I, began gathering his troops soon after he was elected. The people of Rome sided with a gaggle of ambitious nobles who had established a self-governing commune in the senate halls, in defiance of the theocracy of the new pontiff. They had chosen Giordano Pierleoni, the brother of the late, great heretic Antipope Anacletus II, as their spokesman. The communards were ill disposed towards a parlay and more than likely would enjoy doing unto Lucius II what was done to his third-century namesake – banish him from Rome – or worse, dispatch him post-haste to God.

Lucius had to swallow his pride and seek an enemy of his enemy as a friend. He turned to Roger II of Sicily for military assistance. The Norman king had once been his friend when Lucius was the rector of Benevenuto, but Roger had shut his helmet visor steadfastly against any of the pope's written requests. The Norman king could profit only from a Holy See eating itself with civil strife. He chose to wait, holding the pope to a seven-year armistice agreement which allowed Roger to retain possession of papal territories he had already invaded, in return for a promise not to seize Benevenuto or any other papal dominion. Lucius next tried to garner mercenaries and money from the north. The new German king, the Hohenstaufen Conrad III (1138–1152), could send only his regards, as he was hard pressed at home with his own wars.

Lucius had one last option: to discard the role of pontiff as general peacemaker for the role of pontiff as General Patton. He latched on leather buckler and armor over his pallium and robes and led what remaining papal forces he could muster into a charge on the Capitol. Pope Lucius, the bishop of Rome, had declared war on his own parishioners. In early 1145, in the most-Christian city ruled by the Vicar of the Prince of Peace, the faithful slaughtered the faithful in a bloody urban battle. Lucius' attack was eventually checked, but not before great loss of life. During the mêlée he was struck by several stone missiles shot from the roof of the senate building. His broken and bleeding body was carried out of Rome to the monastery of San Gregorio, where he soon died.

The enemy in this case seems to have been the pope himself, who is *driven out* of Rome by its people.

THREE

Ex magnitudine montis
(From the Greatness of a Mountain)

EUGENIUS III
(1145–1153)

THE ELECTING CARDINALS' choice for the third contemporary of St. Malachy to rule the Church surprised even his biographer, St.

Bernard de Clairvaux, for it was one of his own disciples, the simple Cistercian monk from Pisa named Bernardo Pignatelli. He had studied under the charismatic saint for the bulk of the 1130s before he was ordained Abbot of SS. Vincenzo and Anastasio outside Rome. It was while praying at this latter location that Pignatelli received the shocking news that the electors had chosen him as pope, the very day that his predecessor, Lucius II, died from his mortal wounds.

Pignatelli was born in Grammonte, which is Italian for *Mons Magnus* (great mountain). There is no record that Eugenius was even aware of the Irish saint's Latin mottoes, although his mentor, St. Bernard, advised him to "study the life and follow the example of St. Malachy, and all would be well."

One could argue that the man hastily brought into Rome to be crowned as Eugenius III would prove himself to be a mountain rather than a molehill of a pope. No sooner was he enthroned in the Lateran than he threw fuel on the fire of Roman sedition by invoking his right assigned by the Donation of Constantine to dictate temporal as well as religious authority over Rome. He fled Rome before sundown to avoid being torn to pieces by the angry Roman mob. His consecration took place in exile at Farfa. From there, cooling his Constantinian passions, he negotiated with the Roman senators to re-establish his suzerainty over the Eternal City after agreeing to recognize the new Roman commune.

He was forced to flee town again by the heretical Roman senator Arnold of Brescia, who continued to oppose Eugenius' intervention in secular Roman politics. The pope and his curia toured France, where he drummed up support for the Second Crusade. He employed his mentor, St. Bernard, as chief spokesman for a holy war against the Saracens. The Second Crusade proved to be a disaster. Rather than uniting Eastern and Western Christendom against a common enemy, Eugenius had to use all his influence to prevent his crusaders from sacking the Eastern Orthodox capital of Constantinople.

He convened synods in France at Paris and Reims and in Germany at Trier where he promoted stronger theological discipline and dogma for the dissemination of the faith. His passion for the straight and narrow was reflected in his daily habits. Offered the usual papal perks of fine robes and opulence, he chose instead to retain his simple monk's robe and continue his Cistercian disciplines of fasting and long periods of solitude and prayer.

In 1148, as the earth lay fresh over Malachy's grave, Eugenius did come down *from . . . the mountains* when he crossed the Maritime Alps in the wake of gathering Christian forces heading to the Middle East. He returned to Italy, where he eventually had Arnold of Brescia excommunicated, after the radical reformer had declared the pope a "man of blood." But it took many years of hard negotiation and the cultivation of a political alliance with the Hohenstaufen tyrant, the powerful, red-bearded Holy Roman Emperor, Frederick I Barbarossa (1123?–1190), before Eugenius could safely return to Rome. Soon after ratifying the Treaty of Constance with diplomats of the German Emperor, he died in Tivoli.

HILDEGARD VON BINGEN: CHAMPION OF ORTHODOX CATHOLIC PROPHECY

Eugenius was the first of four popes who would correspond with one of the Catholic faith's chief seeresses, St. Hildegard von Bingen (1098–1179). She was born at Bermersheim, Germany, just four years after the birth of St. Malachy. She entered a Benedictine convent near Diessenberg, of which she became Mother Superior in 1136. Hildegard is considered one of the most notable (as well as one of the few) learned feminine minds of the medieval era. She spent much of her life in the solitude and quiet of the convent writing treatises on a wide array of subjects, from interpretations of the Gospels, to chronicles on the lives of local German saints, to long and highly detailed tracts on anatomy and the natural sciences.

Around 1147, at the age of 42, she moved her convent to Rupertsberg, near Bingen. As Malachy was taking his last steps through a turbulent life on the way to his final resting place at Clairvaux, St. Hildegard, living several hundred miles to the northeast, was halfway through composing and illustrating her oracular masterpiece *Scito vias Domini* (Know the Ways of the Lord), or *Scivias* for short. Her call to prophesy came in 1141 with the first of what would be ten years of prophetic episodes. She described them as a "fiery light" that washed clean her whole heart and brain, giving her direct insight into God's mysteries hidden in his Holy Scriptures.

The decision to reveal her prophecies to the world had not come easily. The confessions of this staunchly orthodox and zealous abbess clearly imply that she believed the male priestly hierarchy so remiss in their duty to sustain Mother Church that a man's job had to be taken on by a mere woman. She seems to be saying, between the lines, that in God's plan even though women are lesser human beings than men, the priesthood's lack of diligence was so severe that it forced God to use one of Eve's sinful descendants to spread his prophetic message.

Scivias was completed in 1151. It consists of three marvelously illustrated books containing over 200,000 words. Book One unlocks the secrets of God's creation of Heaven and Earth; Book Two plots out the road to redemption through Christ; and Book Three – the most famous – brings us up to the present and future evolution of the Church and history. The climax is the world's apocalyptic end, the binding of Satan and the eradication of evil. Heaven and Earth are transformed through the salvation and sanctification of true believers in God and Christ. The epilogue, "The Symphony of Praise," consists of a number of innovative Gregorian songs composed by St. Hildegard, many of which became number-one hits on the classical billboard charts of the final decade before the year 2000. Ironically the CD's cover depicts the hooded face of the pious and celibate Hildegard modeled after the libertine actress, Drew Barrymore. The opening songs of Hildegard's *Symphony* mourn the eternal damnation of sinners but are soon followed by songs that celebrate the eternal timelessness of the blissful post-apocalyptic universe where the forgiven forever sing praise of God.

St. Hildegard's most famous vision was recorded in Chapter 11 of Book Three: "The Last Days and the Fall of the Antichrist." The skeptics who observed the fiery psychic tendrils in paintings of Hildegard offer a theory which effectively denies any serious consideration of her visions. They maintain that the fiery psychic tendrils which symbolize the divine light of God's prophetic gift were no more than the byproduct of the abbess's physical affliction: a migraine condition known as scintillating scotoma. Perhaps the doctors have got it backwards. What if scintillating scotoma was a physical byproduct of her mind's eye scrying God's messages off the synaptic screen of her inner sight?

She records a vision strongly rooted in medieval apocalyptic dogma, similar to predictions promoted by the tenth-century monk Adso.

Thanks to St. Hildegard's holy headache she saw "five ferocious epochs" to come before Judgment Day. They are represented by animal archetypes which stand for future rulers that come out of Satan's kingdom in the frigid north. The first four are a fiery dog "who does not burn," a yellow lion, a pale horse, a black pig and a gray wolf. For all one knows the final animal comes to her mind in part from her Rhineland background, for it parallels the Teutonic and Viking heathens' predictions for the final battle between good and evil called Ragnarök. This Norse–Germanic Armageddon takes place in the epoch of a gray wolf. The image brings to mind the gray military greatcoat of a future Catholic-born tyrant in the 20th century whose first name is derived from the ancient German "adolphus," which means "wolf."

These five evil rulers are precursors to a Dopplegänger Christ to come, the Antichrist. In St. Hildegard's vision, Christ is a virgin. In contrast the Antichrist, pretending to be the Second Coming of Christ, is a lusty and sex-crazed usurper, born of a harlot, who seduces people into thinking that he is the chaste son of a virgin who can even rise from the dead. His scam is put under scrutiny by two end-time prophets called Enoch and Elijah, whom God plans to send to Earth just as the Antichrist is about to become ruler of God's Church and all political states. These two prophets give people one last chance to see the Antichrist as he truly is, before the son of evil, mascarading as the Son of God, has them martyred.

St. Hildegard warns the clerics of her day that the Antichrist will come from inside the Church. She thrusts this scenario home with the lurid vision of the Church as an allegorical crowned and glorified woman named Ecclesia who offers her outstretched arms in flowing golden sleeves. But lo! our Mother Church stands before St. Hildegard without her holy knickers. Then with all the delicacy of a Middle Ages sanitation manager, St. Hildegard describes and later illustrates the corruption of Ecclesia from within, with the help of her now famous drawings. What is displayed sprouting from between her legs could be characterized as the worst case of clap ever seen. The Mother Church's maiden hairs and labia have transformed into the hairy face and locked-jaw and saw-toothed grimace of a singularly foul beast of an Antichrist.

But fear not, St. Hildegard's doomsday rant of migraine fires has a happy ending. Ecclesia the Church is Christ's one true bride, and she will survive her terrible ravaging and her lapse from the right path to enjoy a second and eternal honeymoon with the triumphant and true return of her bridegroom. When this happens, the son of perdition springs free from Ecclesia's sore and pock-marked loins to rise upon a huge shit pile. Another illustration shows the beast worshipped by a spiritually deceived humanity as he stands atop his nose-shriveling throne. Christ, we are promised, will fatally knock him off his putrid pedestal with a thunderbolt.

After the Antichrist is zapped, the Judgment Day comes with all its Book-of-Revelation intensity of Earth changes, catastrophes and fighting. History then comes to a complete end. God unleashes his medieval justice on good and evil alike. The souls rising from their graves will clearly show the marks of either the black or white state – literally it seems. St. Hildegard sees the naked sinners shaking in their painted black skin. There are no lawyers for the doomed, no defense. In fact the heathens populating regions beyond Christendom do not even get the chance to face their accusers – they are immediately thrown into the lake of eternal fire and damnation. Those at least who heard of Christ in their lifetime but remained unbelievers go through the motions before receiving the pre-ordained verdict of eternal doom.

After that the redeemed live in a New Heaven and Earth where time, the firmament, moon and planets, the oceans and the seasons stand forever frozen in a picture frame of eternity. There will be no need for weathermen in St. Hildegard's paradise, nor will the blessed ones need a candle to dispel the night: the atmosphere will neither be hot or cold and it will always be daytime.

Just what will people do in God's eternal permanence? They will sing. Forever. They will be cloistered in one huge medieval monastery of eternal joy. You might call it a perfect vision of what St. Hildegard saw as a pious life.

Hildegard's endorsement of St. Bernard and, later, Pope Eugenius, who had a draft of her *Scivias* prophecies while presiding over the Synod of Triers, ensured that her critics would be for the most part powerless in forestalling the wide spread of her writings. The visions in *Scivias* and later elaborations about the latter days would bias future Catholic visionaries and their doctrinaire interpreters up to the year 2000.

FOUR

Abbas Suburranus
(A Suburran Abbot)

ANASTASIUS IV
(1153–1154)

THE FUTURE ANASTASIUS was born Corrado di Suburra, or "Corrado from the Suburran quarter" in Rome. He was elected the same day that Eugenius died outside of Rome in Tivoli. Unlike his predecessor, Anastasius got along remarkably well with his fellow Romans and enjoyed his brief days as pope, renovating and beautifying the Lateran Basilica and restoring the ancient Pantheon. The plaster and paint of the initial stages of restoration had scarcely dried when the tomb of the aged pontiff was added to the renovation of the Lateran on his death after only one year in office, in December 1154.

FIVE

De rure albo
(From a White Country Place [England])

ADRIAN IV
(1154–1159)

THE IRISH PROPHET makes one of his more notable complex puns with this motto. Breakspear, the son of a priest, was born near the Abbey of St. Albans, England. The ancient Roman name for Great Britain was *Albion*, from the Latin word for white (*albus*) – as the white cliffs of Dover were described by the first Roman conquerors who laid eyes on them. Therefore our first and probably last English pope comes *from a white country place*. Furthermore Breakspear served the Church as papal legate to Denmark, Sweden and Norway; all three snow-covered northern realms were figuratively known as *white countries*.

Pope Eugenius made Breakspear a cardinal in 1144 for two reasons: the first was his reputation as a spiritual martinet. But these same qualities made him so unpopular as abbot of the Augustinian monastery of St. Rufus in Avignon that the pope had to forestall an open rebellion from his monks by dismissing Breakspear through promotion. He proved himself later as a brilliant papal legate of Scandinavia. His abilities as a harsh disciplinarian and reformer got him unanimously voted as pope by the Sacred College of Cardinals. It was hoped that he would be a no-BS bishop of Rome and put the Roman communards and the Norman rulers of Sicily in their place.

Adrian placed the whole city of Rome under interdiction after one of his cardinals was stabbed to death in broad daylight on the Via Sacra. The following papal edict which prohibited all Romans from receiving the holy sacraments and a Christian burial only aroused them again into open rebellion. Adrian had to leave town, and he re-established the papal government in nearby Viterbo. Once there he sought the favor and military support of Emperor Frederick Barbarossa, who by chance had just visited the seditious streets of Rome and had the chief ringleader of the

Roman senate, Arnold of Brescia, arrested, tried, hung and burned at the stake.

Adrian's holy strong-arming eventually pushed Frederick Barbarossa the wrong way when he reminded Barbarossa that according to the Donation of Constantine the imperial crown was a *beneficium* or gift of the pope. Their disagreement would grow, spanning many decades and papal and imperial successors to come.

St. Malachy's homeland was the next target. Adrian granted his countryman King Henry II of England the right to subjugate Ireland, using the counterfeit Constantinian decree as justification once again.

A recorded conversation between Adrian and his close friend John of Salisbury, later bishop of Chartres, reveals the state of the Church of Rome's popularity among the medieval laity.

"What do people really think of the pope and the Church?" asked Adrian.

John of Salisbury, noted for his compassionately blunt tongue replied, "People are saying that the Church behaves more like a stepmother than a mother; that in it is a fatal vein of avarice, scribes and Pharisees laying grievous burdens on men's shoulders, accumulating precious furniture, covetous to a degree. And that the Holy Father himself is burdensome and scarcely to be borne."

SIX

Ex tetro carcere
(From a Harsh Prison)

VICTOR IV, ANTIPOPE
(1159–1164)

In 1159 a band of soldiers led by Cardinal Ottaviano di Monticelli broke into the gathering of papal electors to rend the purple mantle from the shoulders of Cardinal Orlando Bandinelli, just as he was being enthroned as the successor to Adrian IV. Cardinal

Ottaviano had the authorized pope pushed out of the hall by sword point, while a small minority of armed cardinals saw to it that Ottaviano himself was enthroned as pope. This incident triggered a bitter schism of 18 years between Bandinelli as Alexander III against Ottaviano (who was consecrated as Antipope Victor IV) and three other antipopes backed by the Holy Roman Emperor Frederick I Barbarossa.

Shortly after Victor's consecration in Farfa, outside of Rome, the kings of France and England scorned Barbarossa's protégé. Soon most of Europe followed, repudiating the revival of imperial manipulation of the papacy. After wandering with his anti-curia from town to town in northern Italy, Victor suddenly died on 20 April after a short and painful illness at Lucca. He was buried in the crypt of an impoverished monastery outside the walls of the city.

Ciaccionius believes the motto Ex TETRO CARCERE describes Victor's full title as a cardinal, which was *cardinalis Sancti Nicolai in carcere*. Other interpreters read TETRO CARCERE to mean *foul cell* rather than *harsh prison*. Perhaps the inscription uses poetic license to predict the final sad act of Victor's legacy. Twenty-three years later Pope Gregory VIII, while passing through Lucca, ordered the crypt broken open. He had Victor's moldy remains thrown out from the *foul prison* of his tomb.

SEVEN

Via Transtibernia
(The Way beyond the Tiber)

PASCHAL III, ANTIPOPE
(1164–1168)

VICTOR IV WAS quickly succeeded by Guido of Crema, cardinal priest of San Callisto, as a second pro-imperialist antipope, Paschal III. He was chosen and consecrated in a fashion totally contrary to canonical law, by Rainald von Dassel, Emperor

Frederick Barbarossa's chancellor. His birthplace 270 miles northeast of the headwaters of the Tiber River geographically makes Paschal's origins *beyond the Tiber.* Ciaccionius reminds us that TRANSTIBERNIA stands for one of his cardinal titles: *Cardinalis St^{ae} Marinae Transtiberinae.* Victor's respectability was an even harder sale than the struggle on behalf of his predecessor. It took Barbarossa and an imperial army encamped outside Rome to ensure that Frederick's second protégé was (grudgingly) enthroned in St. Peter's on 22 July 1167, while Alexander III went into hiding. Paschal then crowned Barbarossa Holy Roman Emperor a second time.

The emperor soon grew disenamored with his choice and publicly declared that both Paschal and Alexander should abdicate so that a new election could choose a fresh pope. Shortly afterwards a plague of malaria beset Rome and decimated the imperial army. Barbarossa, seriously ill, returned to Germany with Paschal in tow. Paschal would return to Rome the following year protected by a bodyguard of thousands of imperial troops. In September 1168, Paschal locked himself inside the *harsh* or *foul* prison fortress, Castel Sant'Angelo, for his own safety. A new Roman senate was scheduled for 1 November 1168. It was expected to support the return of Alexander III. Paschal died before the elections were convened.

EIGHT

De Pannonia Tuscæ
(From the Hungary of Tuscia)

CALIXTUS III, ANTIPOPE
(1168–1178)

LITTLE IS KNOWN about the life of the third antipope set against Alexander III except that his name was Giovanni and that he could have been a native of the Balkans or Hungary. Emperor Frederick I Barbarossa warmed to the choice of the abbot of the

Tuscan monastery at Strumi as Calixtus only as a device to put political pressure on Alexander when negotiations with the authentic pope broke down. Beyond that, Antipope Calixtus had even less support than his two predecessors. The German emperor finally made peace with Alexander in 1176, making Calixtus irrelevant. In 1177 he renounced his antipope, proposing to Alexander that Calixtus be given an abbey as a condolence. Calixtus annoyed the emperor by lamely holding on to his legitimacy until Alexander assured him that if he abjured his schism with the Mother Church and took a post as rector of Benevento he would not be harmed.

The fourth and last antipope, Innocent III (1179–1180), does not appear on St. Malachy's list. Perhaps this stems from him being so discredited that it took little effort for Alexander to have him arrested and imprisoned in the Abbey of SS. Trinità of La Cava in the province of Salerno for the rest of his life. The date of his death is unknown.

NINE

Ex ansere custodi
(From the Custodian Goose)

ALEXANDER III
(1159–1181)

WE RETURN TO the legal inheritor of Peter's throne, who was run out of the Sacred College of Cardinals by sword point. Orlando Bandinelli was born in Siena around 1100. Little is known of his family except that they were well respected. Onofrio Panvinio, a noted Roman antiquary of the 16th century, believed that his family name was actually Paparone, which in Italian means "gosling," (*paparo*), but this fact is widely disputed. A goose is displayed on the Bandinelli/Paparone coat of arms. Paparone was considered one of the finest authorities of his day on canon law and was quickly promoted to the curias of Eugenius III and Adrian IV. He earned a reputation as a zealous enemy of Emperor Frederick I Barbarossa.

After the minority of sword-wielding cardinals supporting Cardinal Ottaviano (Antipope Victor IV) ran the properly elected Cardinal Paparone out of the Lateran Basilica, our custodian goose sought refuge behind the stout walls of the Castel Sant'Angelo until he could sneak away to Ninfa to be consecrated as Alexander III.

Alexander found some prophetic solace in St. Hildegard. She had been a close friend and confidante of Frederick Barbarossa until he promoted a second antipope, Paschall III, to succeed Victor IV, rather than seek reconciliation with Alexander. St. Hildegard, with all righteous and oracular authority, declared the German emperor "a madman." Ever the feisty doctrinaire, she openly opposed him when he named a third antipope, Calixtus III, in 1168. She side-stepped any pressure from Barbarossa to water down her spiritual support of Alexander III. In the end Alexander either outlived or prevailed over all four antipopes and forced Barbarossa to acknowledge his authority as Vicar of Christ two years before the emperor's death.

In 1179 he was forced out of Rome a second time by the Roman commune. Upon his death at Città Castellana, his body was taken back to Rome to be buried in the Lateran Basilica, where the citizens of the Eternal City covered his tomb with insults.

Although history considers him to be one of the greatest popes, some of his legal decisions as an infallible representative of Christ on Earth remain an embarrassment to the Church even to this day. In the Third Council of the Lateran (1179), Alexander codified all previous enactments against Jews. Our watchful goose played his part in nourishing anti-Semitism in Europe for centuries to come, and must be held partly responsible for contributing to the evil

delusions of a future Catholic in the 20th century named Adolf
Hitler.

TEN

Lux in ostio
(A Light in the Door)

LUCIUS III
(1181–1185)

UBALDO ALLUCINGOLI, A native of Lucca (*Lux*), succeeded Alexander III. Prior to this holiest of appointments he had been
cardinal bishop of Ostia, the *door* or port at the mouth of the
Tiber which served Rome. Also Ubaldo's family name – meaning
"entranced one" in Italian – hints at an aspect of *light* (Lux).
Allucignoli was the second Cistercian disciple of St. Bernard de
Clairvaux to become a pope. Historians describe this aged renunciate as honest, good intentioned, but essentially weak. He was
crowned at Velletri outside of Rome and chose to stay away
from the rebellious Roman citizenry during the early part of his
pontificate.

The future Lucius III had been the late Pope Alexander's chief
advisor at the Peace of Venice in 1156 at which the Holy Roman
Emperor at last accepted Alexander III as the true pope. Lucius
would crack the door a little further to the light of peace in his
short reign by gaining further concessions from Emperor Frederick, including a promise to join King Richard the Lionheart
of England (1157–1199) and King Philip II Augustus of France
(1165–1223) on a third crusade to the Holy Land. Perhaps he felt
that the papacy was safer and better served by such ambitious
kings and emperors venting their spleen on the infidels of Islam
rather than upon the Church's religious and secular authority. The
launching of the crusade was delayed, and eventually relations
between a pope and the imperial court were once again strained
to breaking point, just before Lucius died.

One of his chief actions was to convene the Synod of Verona, chiefly to redouble the Church's efforts to stamp out heresy. He declared that all differences and criticisms held by Catholics against their pope undermine his God-given authority and are therefore grave sins.

ELEVEN

Sus in cribro
(A Sow in a Sieve)

URBAN III
(1185–1187)

A DECODING OF the above inscription applies a tale of classical legend to the successor of Lucius III, the Milanese native Umberto Crivelli. Because *Sieve* is their name, the Crivelli arms display a silver one in front of quarterly gold and gules (red); however, there is no sow to be seen. The motto implies a mixed heraldic metaphor of the arms of Crivelli and the city of Milan, a city which derived its name from the discovery of a creature that was half pig and half sheep. He was archdeacon of Milan when he was unanimously voted as Urban III, successor to Lucius III. The cardinal electors chose him because they believed that he would stubbornly resist the imperial designs on the papacy by Frederick I Barbarossa.

Twenty-three years earlier Urban had witnessed the sack of Milan by Frederick's mercenaries. Several members of his own family were butchered before his eyes. This representative of

Christ's message of forgiveness could never pardon his enemy and he dedicated his pontificate to the curtailment of Frederick's stranglehold on Italy and the papacy. He began by withholding payment of the annual *regalia* tax to the imperial treasury for one year. He resisted the marriage of Frederick's son Henry to Constance, the Norman heiress of Sicily, to forestall any attempt to completely surround the papal dominions by hostile imperial vassal states.

Urban spent most of his reign in Verona because of the seditious mood of the Roman senate. By 1187 the city fathers of Verona, who were sympathetic to imperial persuasion, demanded that he leave the city. He would set out on horseback from there in October 1187 on a mission to excommunicate Frederick in Venice, but he caught a cold from the autumn chill and died in Ferrara on 19 October. It is said that he died of a broken heart upon hearing news that Jerusalem had fallen to Islamic forces led by Saladin.

TWELVE

Ensis Laurentii
(The Sword of Lawrence)

GREGORY VIII
(1187)

THE DAY AFTER Urban's death the cardinals in his entourage at Ferrara elected Cardinal Alberto de Morra, a Cistercian, to become Gregory VIII. They had grown disenchanted with Urban's intransigence with Emperor Frederick I Barbarossa. They chose among their number someone who was on good terms with the German emperor yet seemed able to stand firm for the papacy.

While a cardinal he was posted at S. Laurent, in Lucina. Thus we have a motto implying the two swords of St. Lawrence on his coat of arms. This widely popular deacon and martyr from third-century Rome was a patron saint of medieval soldiers. They believed that the prayers addressed to St. Lawrence on the naked blades of their swords could ensure victory against the infidels of Christendom.

Gregory preached that the Holy City of Jerusalem had fallen as God's punishment to Christians for their sins. He led a mission to Pisa to negotiate peace between the Pisans and the Genoese, to better facilitate the rapid embarkation of crusaders on ships to the Holy Land. The pressures of promoting the Third Crusade took their toll on the aged pope, who was in his mid-70s. While in Pisa he fell ill and died.

THIRTEEN

De schola exiet
(He Will Come Out of a School)

CLEMENT III
(1187–1191)

IN PISA THE cardinals gathered once again after the brief two-month pontificate of Gregory VIII to elect Paolo Scolari, the cardinal bishop of Praeneste (Palestrina). The motto makes a pun on his birth name Scolari by hiding it in the Latin SCHOLA, although he was noted neither for scholarship nor for coming from a prestigious school. He was a native Roman and quite popular with its commune, which permitted him to return to the Eternal City and reside in the Lateran Basilica. One of his first acts was to draw a costly peace treaty with the Holy Roman Empire. This freed him to devote his attention to launching the Third Crusade.

The enterprise never took Jerusalem and stalled before Acre, where Richard I and Philip II Augustus of France quarrelled until the French king withdrew his troops and Richard was forced to make a truce with Saladin and leave the Holy Land. But months before the mess at Acre an even greater disaster befell the papacy when Frederick I Barbarossa suffered an apparent heart attack while the crusader army was crossing a river in Turkey. He fell off his horse and drowned under the weight of his armor. This released his ambitious son, Henry VI (1165–1197), to pursue his dream of imperial control over the Italian peninsula.

A third blow to Pope Clement came with the news that William II, king of Sicily, had died without leaving a male heir. Henry VI made his claim to the throne based on his Norman wife's blood ties to William. If he succeeded, Henry could unite the empire and bring the papacy to its knees. Clement chose Tancred of Lecce, a grandson of the late King Roger II of Sicily (d. 1154), to be crowned king at Palermo. Enraged, Henry invaded Italy but stopped near Lake Bracciano when word arrived that Clement had died.

FOURTEEN

De rure bovensi
(From the Cattle Country)

CELESTINE III
(1191–1198)

GIACINTO BOBO (Bovensi) was the first of four popes to come from the House of Orsini. He served for more than four decades as a cardinal and agent of popes Celestine II and Alexander III until he was elected pope at the age of 85. Although he had been one of the few papal supporters well respected by the late Frederick I Barbarossa, he did not enjoy the same relationship with Frederick's son, Henry VI. The day Orsini was chosen as pontiff, Henry was sitting on horseback at the head of his army outside Rome, waiting to be crowned Holy Roman Emperor. Orsini, as Celestine III, embarked upon a political policy of turning the other cheek, thus paving the way for imperial domination of Italy through his "bovine" passivity. He meted out no criticism to Henry for imprisoning Richard the Lionheart and was agreeable to crowning Henry emperor. Although it bothered him, Celestine did not mention the matter of the Sicilian succession and looked in the other direction when Henry's army marched south to claim Sicily. The invasion collapsed before Naples and Henry retreated to Germany.

Celestine could also give Henry something he desperately wanted. If Celestine baptized his young son Frederick II (1194–1250), the imperial crown would become hereditary. Henry pledged to shower the Middle East with Islamic and Jewish blood in a fourth crusade if the pope would sprinkle some holy water on his son. Celestine was agreeable but forever non-committal. He kept delaying an answer until Henry died in September 1197. Celestine died four months later in January 1198.

Historians often debate whether the first Orsini pope's eccentric politics of vacillation were accidental or a shrewd bit of calculation. The motto poetically described this pope's slow-to-decide nature as *bovine*. Indeed the patience of the stolid cow outlasted the formidable imperial cow driver.

One could also apply the motto to Clement's herd of relatives grazing off papal funds. He was not against rewarding many of his Orsini relations with titles and lands, much of this being pasture land for cattle, i.e. *bovine country*.

In 1190 Clement sanctioned the cult of St. Malachy among the Cistercians, thus canonizing him.

FIFTEEN

Comes signatus
(A Signed Count)

INNOCENT III
(1198–1216)

IT SEEMS THAT St. Malachy accurately foresaw the man who would officially incorporate, for the first time, family arms with the ecclesiastical arms of the pope, a custom that would be followed by each successive pontificate. Lothair of Segni was born in Gavignano Castle in Campagna di Roma, the son of the Count of Segni and nephew of Clement III. The Italian word *segni* means *sign*.

Count Segni possessed great political acumen and a sharp intellect. He was educated at the universities of Paris, Rome and Bologna, and was elected pope at the age of 37. Innocent declared himself the Vicar of Christ, or better, God's direct channel to Christians and therefore holier than normal men. But he did concede that he was less holy than God the Father and than Christ the Son, who had been seeded into being by the Holy Ghost.

During Innocent's pontificate the papacy reached the peak of its secular power. He nurtured the division between rival claimants to the throne of the Holy Roman Empire, and drove out the German nobles who held Italian fiefs under the empire, until most of Italy was consolidated under the papacy. He vigorously preached for a fourth crusade, which, to his horror, captured and sacked the greatest Christian capital of the day, Constantinople, instead of liberating Jerusalem from the Muhammedans. Seeking advantage, he appointed a Latin patriarch to the ruined Byzantine capital and sanctioned the so-called Latin Empire of Constantinople in the hope that it might in some way lead to a reunion of the Latin and Greek Orthodox Churches. The Byzantines were thoroughly disgusted with their new Latin overlord, and the actions of the pope only deepened the centuries-long rift in Christendom. Innocent rationalized that the rape of Constantinople was God's retribution for the Eastern Church's refusal to submit to the Vicar of Christ on Earth.

By 1207, and after attempting to bring the Cathars of Southern France back to the Mother Church, God apparently had inspired Innocent to throw Christian patience aside and unleash the Albigensian Crusade. What followed was one of the greatest massacres in history in the name of religion, and the wholesale annihilation of a truly progressive medieval community. The Cathars lived in Languedoc, a region which Helen Ellerbe in her book *The Dark Side of Christian History* claimed was a rare medieval province that tolerated people's differences.

"Many races lived together harmoniously," says Ellerbe, "Greeks, Phoenicians, Jews and Muslims. Jews were not only free from persecution, but held management and advisory positions with lords and even prelates. There was less class distinction, a milder form of serfdom, freer towns and a judicial system based upon Roman law. Nowhere were citizens as educated. Culture and commerce flourished, making it one of the most prosperous regions in Europe."

To this oasis of forbearance Pope Innocent aimed thousands of armored knights, armed with the promise of indulgences and salvation for their sins if they would pluck out the living light of as many Cathars, Jews and Muslims as possible. Thanks to the pope's Christian generosity, the property of the dead was granted to the crusaders as blessed loot. Pope Innocent's final solution for the Cathars took three decades, killing an estimated one million people and decimating much of the population of southern France, leaving it a desert ruin for many more decades.

While the massacre of Cathars was in full swing, Innocent turned his divine displeasure towards King John of England for allowing himself to sign and ratify what has become one of the founding documents for democracy, the Magna Carta. In 1215 Innocent also oversaw the Fourth Lateran Council, which is most notable for its renewed holy terror against Muslims and Jews. Innocent declared that the Muslim infidels and the people responsible for the death of Christ should be concentrated into ghettos and wear yellow hats and other forms of distinctive clothing that would mark them as separate from the God-forgiven Christian majority.

In 1216, at the age of 65, Innocent set forth from Rome on a mission to compel the city-states of Pisa and Genoa to open their ports for a fifth crusade. While in Perugia he suddenly succumbed to one of his usual bouts with fever. This time he quite unexpectedly died.

Innocent was at times moved beyond his understanding to establish new monastic orders, even though he admittedly determined that some of their mystic founders, such as St. Francis of Assisi, were hard for him to fathom. Along with the Franciscan order he saw fit to accept the request of St. Dominic to establish the order of Black Friars, although he was probably at pains to comprehend why St. Dominic held on to the idea of peaceful resolution of the heresies of the Albigensians when the pope had written them off to hell by holy crusade. It might have pleased Innocent to know that a few decades after his passing, the majority of monks chosen to direct the Inquisition would come from the Franciscan and Dominican orders.

JOACHIM DE FIORE: CHAMPION OF UNORTHODOX CATHOLIC PROPHECY

In 1204 Innocent would earn his place in Catholic prophetic controversy with a flourish of his busy pen by signing a papal bull reconfirming the monastic order of Joachim de Fiore.

Joachim de Fiore (c.1135–1202) was a Cistercian monk and hermit who lived in Calabria, Italy. He was five years old when St. Malachy had his purported vision of the papal succession unto doomsday. He spent much of his early adult life as a hermit in the rocky hills of Calabria. A pilgrimage to the Holy Land would set him on a course which would eventually make this mystic a prophet. Upon his return to his hermit's cell in Calabria he eased himself out of a life of total solitude to join the Cistercian order and become a noted scholar and commentator on biblical and Sibylline prophetic works. His predictions of the future rely heavily on these traditions and also reveal a novel and even reformist view of Augustinian dogma concerning the end times and the Second Coming.

Delno C. West and Sandra Zimdars-Swartz, in *Joachim of Fiore: A Study in Spiritual Perception and History,* make some insightful observations about what made Joachim unique for his time as an apocalyptic seer. A chief reason was that he considered inquiry into history as another path to understanding God. The authors remind us that medieval theologians and intellectuals of western Europe tended to place faith and divine propaganda above historical inquiry into the past. Historical facts were overlooked in favor of the certainty of biblical dogma. A medieval thinker had no qualms about the Bible not jiving with historical fact. Instead, as West and Zimdars-Swartz point out, the Bible was "a drama of salvation; the scenes paradigms of Christian life applicable to any age."

A curious mind was a fly in the holy ointment of biblical dogma. The Bible was God's Word, was it not? Therefore that article loved by the lower caste of man's mind – mere historical fact – was only valuable if and when it provided foundation for the faith.

Joachim de Fiore, like St. Hildegard before him, believed that God graced him with prophetic powers which gave him the key to unlock the symbolism of the Bible. But unlike his Benedictine predecessor his divinely graced visions told him that insights into God should be in balance with historical inquiry. He saved himself from being staked out as a heretic by obeying enough of the basic dogma of Christian prophecies about the end times to be respectable. But unlike Hildegard he sees St. Augustine's disclaimer, that no one can know the exact manifestation and sequence of future events in the final days, as a good reason to polish and update St. Augustine's interpretations. In other words, he applied historical inquiry to understand the past so one could better foresee the future.

His theories bore fruit. By injecting historical inquiry he gained notoriety in his time for untangling the labyrinth of numerous biblical scriptures which had heretofore pained the pates of religious pedagogues. With the "new eyes" he believed God had given him as a divine gift, Joachim dispensed with the 700-year-old Tichonian–Augustinian dogma that the time cycle of the Christian Millennium had begun with Christ's life on Earth and would last until doomsday and the Second Coming. Joachim did not subscribe to their belief that any freeze-framed "new age" after the end times was in eternity and outside of normal time.

One of his more original interpretations of the future of the Catholic Church and Christianity organizes the historical evolution of the faith into a "Trinity" of epochs. The first epoch is dominated by the Old Testament and is known as the Age of the Father: a time of obedience and fear, slavery and tradition. The first coming of Jesus Christ marked the Age of the Son: an epoch of faith, symbolism, youthfulness and liberty. According to some Joachite interpretations, the third and final Age of the Holy Spirit, which will blossom after a brief and violent apocalyptic period, is at hand sometime shortly after the year 2000.

This final epoch of the Holy Spirit will be a time when humanity is governed by the wisdom of contemplative monks. (I might add that a modern interpretation would define them as meditative visionaries.) The Age of the Holy Spirit will be a time of mutual love and the brotherhood of man. The world will know complete freedom, resurrection, meditation and, ultimately, spiritual transcendence.

Joachim made it clear before his death in 1202 that he believed the Antichrist was already lurking in the world. He expected that the sixth trumpet blast described in the Book of Revelation (9:14–21) would signify the time when the world would recognize him. Unleashed from the Euphrates River four angels are due to destroy one-third of humankind with squadrons numbering 200 million that vomit plagues of fire, smoke and sulfur.

Joachim was certain that the apocalypse described in the Bible's final testament would bring forth the Age of the Holy Spirit. He dared go against the traditional interdiction against calculating the advent of the latter days quoted in Matthew 24:42[1] and proclaimed the year 1260 as the year of Armageddon and the beginning of his third epoch of the Spirit. Some of Joachim's disciples even believed that the Antichrist was the royal tyke that the late Pope Celestine III had delayed baptizing: Frederick II, son of Holy Roman Emperor Henry VI.

The tribulations to come during the reign of the adult Frederick II only strengthened their belief.

SIXTEEN

Canonicus ex Latere
(A Canon from the Side)

HONORIUS III
(1216–1227)

CENCIO SAVELLI CAME from a powerful Roman family. He would rise through the papal government to become one of the medieval Roman Catholic Church's most efficient bureaucrats and reformers. Just prior to his compromise election as pope he had obtained wide-ranging notoriety for compiling the first complete financial register of the Roman Church, the *Liber censuum*. His election as pope was no doubt influenced by his close association as tutor and friend to the new heir to the Holy Roman Empire,

---

[1]*Keep awake, then; for ye do not know on what day your Lord is to come.*

the future Emperor Frederick II. Although quite old and in failing health, Cencio as Honorius III would find one last surge of power in his fading candle of life to propel him through an active and diligent pontificate of ten years. During that time he crowned his pupil Frederick II twice – as German king and then as Holy Roman Emperor. He pressed the young monarch to mount a crusade, but the dispute between them over the management of the Kingdom of Sicily would delay Frederick setting sail for the Holy Land so many times that Honorius threatened to excommunicate him. A renewed war between the papacy and the Holy Roman Empire was forestalled by the pope's death.

Honorius was a zealot for papal reform and the further expansion of the Franciscan and Dominican orders. He reconfirmed the monastic order of Joachim de Fiore in two papal bulls in 1216 and again in 1220. Here we see that St. Malachy's motto is hiding "Lateran" behind one of Honorius' pre-pontifical titles. He was once canon of St. John Lateran.

Growing tensions between the pope and the young German emperor fed a number of pseudo works depicting Frederick II as the Antichrist, which are presumed to be penned by forgers of Joachim de Fiore. Few of these doomsday watchers were aware that Honorius himself was a reputed sorcerer, dabbling in the occult arts.

St. Malachy clearly foresaw in his motto one of Honorius' most important literary contributions to the Church. A dedicated workaholic, Honorius managed to find the time *from the side* to compile the first complete reference to canon law, the *Compilatio Quinta*.

SEVENTEEN

Avis ostiensis
(The Bird of Ostia)

GREGORY IX
(1227–1241)

UGOLINO OF SEGNI, son of the count of Segni, was the nephew of Innocent III and his coat of arms displayed the same checkered gold eagle and sable of the House of Segni. He briefly served Ostia as its cardinal bishop in 1206. We can safely conclude that the inscription pins this checkered *bird* as the future Gregory IX.

By the time he was chosen pope he was already a highly respected expert in canon law and theology. He would prove to be as forceful and self-righteous a pope as his uncle. His rule was overshadowed by a struggle with Emperor Frederick II over the papacy. No sooner had his posterior warmed the throne of St. Peter than he demanded that Frederick fulfill his vow to wage a sea invasion of the Holy Land. Where Honorius only threatened, Gregory hurled a declaration of excommunication at the vacillating Holy Roman Emperor, even after Frederick II had negotiated a treaty with the Saracens to win back Jerusalem without bloodshed. After a brief reconciliation in 1230 relations between emperor and pope soured once again. One of the last things the pope would see before he died on 22 August 1241 were imperial troops surrounding the walls of the Eternal City, preparing for a siege of Rome.

Many prophecy watchers within the Lateran Basilica of the late 1230s and early 1240s thought that the end times were at hand. In his final years, intelligence reports reached Gregory about

Mongolian hordes, riding from the East on horseback, who had annihilated large Hungarian and Russian Christian armies with relative ease. Maybe the pope listened to doomsday interpreters who believed that these Asiatic barbarians were the first vanguard of the expected 200 million horsemen foreseen in Revelation 9:16. Had not Joachim de Fiore expected these horse-riding hordes to invade Europe before doomsday in 1260? Certainly Frederick II and his menacing imperial troops outside the city gates looked ever more like the foreseen Antichrist of the end times who would put Rome under his metalled heel.

These and other signs of threats to the faith by anti-Christian forces moved Gregory to issue decrees stating that it was every Catholic's duty to persecute heretics. He published a bull that gave birth to an ecclesiastic Gestapo which would spread one of the darkest stains on the legacy of the Roman Catholic Church for centuries to come. Anyone who did not submit to any papal edict sanctioned by the pope was to receive torture until they confessed. Gregory, Vicar of Christ and earthly representative to the Prince of Peace and forgiveness, officially upheld what the early Church had condemned: that heretics had no rights, that they would receive no representation by legal counsel. Thus began the Inquisition.

Whoever Gregory's inquisitors suspected to be a heretic was as good as fodder for the flames. The process of agonizing torture, mutilation and death by fire of a suspect usually proceeded whether the victim confessed to his or her sins or not. Two years before Gregory died he punctuated the edict by sending the Inquisition to bleed a small town in Champagne. He had appointed the Dominican Robert le Bougre to investigate a certain Bishop Moranis, who was accused of permitting heretics to fester and spread unbelief throughout his diocese. Le Bougre's answer was to have the bishop and the whole town put on trial. On 29 May 1239 he sent the bishop and 180 men, women and children to the stake.

EIGHTEEN

Leo Sabinus
(The Sabine Lion)

CELESTINE IV
(1241)

ST. MALACHY PINPOINTS Gofredo Castiglioni (Castle-Lion) who was appointed cardinal of Sabina (SABINUS) as the successor of *The Bird of Ostia* (Gregory IX). His coat of arms displays a silver lion holding a golden castle.

Gregory's death during the crisis of 1241 produced one of the more memorable papal elections. Only 12 cardinals were left to choose his successor. Frederick II held two of them in a dungeon while he and his army waited outside the city walls for the remaining ten cardinals to pick a suitable, imperially friendly pontiff. Within Rome itself the cardinals had to satisfy another tyrant, the effective dictator of the Roman commune, Matteo Orsini, who had them locked up in a refuse-laden, dreary wreck of a palace. Orsini demanded that the cardinals choose someone from their own sweating, famished and imprisoned group. Soon their number dwindled to nine. After two months of subsisting on maggot-ridden food and fetid water the survivors picked Castiglioni to be Celestine IV on 25 October 1241. His reign would go down in history as one of the shortest in papal history. He died 16 days later from complications of heat exhaustion and diarrhea contracted during his incarceration.

NINETEEN

Comes Laurentius
(Count Lawrence)

INNOCENT IV
(1243–1254)

AFTER NEARLY TWO years of imperial and papal influence-trading and lobbying, the electing body of cardinals finally cast their votes for Cardinal Sinibaldo Fieschi to succeed the hapless Celestine IV as Innocent IV. It was hoped that his friendship with Antichrist-candidate Emperor Frederick II would ease papal and imperial tensions.

The news of his election produced an ominous observation from Frederick: "My friendship with a cardinal is ever possible; with a pope, never!"

Innocent Number IV, like his predecessor, Number III, made it clear that once a cardinal becomes Christ's middleman on Earth you had better submit to his will, whoever you are. Innocent could not back his bark with enough iron bite from mercenary pikes – he was run out of Rome soon after his election. He moved his curia to France, where he excommunicated Frederick from a safe distance at the Council of Lyons in 1245. He proved he could adequately lead the Church far away from Rome and imperial strangleholds. The death of Frederick II took him out of the Joachite sweepstakes for Antichrist, but very soon got Innocent bogged down in the tarpool politics of imperial succession.

The inscription COMES LAURENTIUS covers the fact that our pope was the son of *Count* Hugo of Lavagna and a cardinal of St. Lorenzo (*Lawrence*) in Lucina. It also is a good example of a relatively obscure event in a pope's life getting a priority mention. Innocent had initiated an inquiry into the life and miracles of Lawrence Loricatus, who was being considered for sainthood in 1244. Lawrence, a hermit of Subiaco, had died the previous year and was already a popular candidate for sainthood because of his book of prayers and his zeal in mortifying the flesh. Rather than wear a hair shirt, Lawrence chose to do lifetime penance for accidentally killing a man by wearing chain mail over his bare skin and a heavy breastplate. But he did not receive formal canonization until 1778.

Another potential doomsday threat was nullified by the death of a Mongol Khan and the deft negotiations of Innocent. In 1241, during the short reign of Celestine IV, the Mongol armies led by Batu had crushed a German–Polish army in the battle of Legnica, near Breslau, Poland, and made raids on Kiev, Buda and Pest. Batu was poised to ride over the city of Vienna and plunge deep into Europe when news came of the death of Ghengis Khan's son and successor, Ogodei. Rather than bring an apocalypse upon western European civilization, Batu turned his forces back to the Asian steppes so that they might elect a new khan at the Mongol capital of Karakorum. In the following years, Innocent sent missions to Karakorum and successfully established an alliance with the Mongols against the Muslims, even though he failed at his ambition to convert the Khan to Christianity. Nonetheless doomsday was postponed for the time being by an unholy alliance of strange political bedfellows.

Innocent injected more power into the Inquisition by officially sanctioning the use of torture. He ordained that even bad thoughts threatened the Church and were punishable by torture and being fried at the stake.

He died in Naples on 7 December 1254.

TWENTY

———>| |<———

Signum Ostiense
(A Sign of Ostia)

ALEXANDER IV
(1254–1261)

RINALDO, COUNT OF Segni (meaning *sign*), was the third member of the House of Segni to become a pope. The inscription above does not overlook the fact that the future Alexander IV would be made cardinal bishop of Ostia by his uncle. He was elected pontiff upon the merit of his family ties and his staunch resistance to Hohenstaufen designs on the papacy. Alexander excommunicated the bastard of Frederick II, Manfred, who was regent to the young Conradin (d. 1268). Condradin was the son of Frederick's chosen successor, the late Conrad IV (1237–1254), who had died the year Alexander became pontiff.

Alexander's military efforts against Manfred met with defeat in Sicily, allowing the imperial bastard's troops to methodically occupy much of central Italy and most of the Papal States. Alexander was forced to retreat from Rome to reside in Viterbo, as Manfred was elected a senator by the Roman commune. The ailing pontiff died soon after, leaving only a paltry eight cardinals to choose the next successor because he had not appointed any replacements.

SPIRITUALLY INCORRECT:
THE *ETERNAL GOSPEL*

During the reign of Alexander, the Joachite cult of doomsday prophecy reached its zenith. Alexander had become pope six years before the expected dawn of Joachim de Fiore's third epoch of the Holy Spirit scheduled for 1260. Discussion of Joachim's prophecies and their credibility passed from the lips of even Alexander himself. News had reached the pontiff of a disturbing revelation volunteered by Gerard di Borgo San Donnino, a Franciscan theologian teaching at the University of Paris in 1254–1255.

Gerard had declared that Joachim de Fiore's writings were something akin to a Third Testament from God!

He proclaimed that the Old and New Testaments should be disregarded and replaced by the scriptures and prophecies of the great late Calabrian abbot, who he believed had received a new dispensation from God via the same angel described in Revelation 14:6–7.

The passage reads: "Then I saw an angel flying in mid-heaven, with an eternal gospel to proclaim to those on Earth, to every nation and tribe, language and people. He cried in a loud voice,

'Fear God and pay him homage; for the hour of his judgment has come!' "

This rubbed orthodoxy raw, and with 1260 so near at hand Alexander appointed a special commission to meet at Anagni to carefully study Joachim's prophecies and investigate Gerard di Borgo's compilation of Joachite interpretations in a new "Eternal Gospel." Mainstream accounts are at best sketchy concerning the content of Gerard di Borgo's *Eternal Gospel*. West and Zimdars-Swartz believe that he had published Joachim's *Liber Concordie novi ac veteris Testamenti* prefaced by his own *Liber Introductorius*. The pope followed the commission's recommendation and had Gerard's scandalous interpretations burned. The Franciscan was condemned to life in prison for heresy and plagiarizing Joachim's works.

Strangely enough the reputation of Joachim's prophecies survived the scandal.

Perhaps Gerard di Borgo's real sin was to dare an interpretation which went against the very heart of approved Catholic prophetic dogma. His interpretations of Joachite prophecy put into question the survival of the Church at the dawning of the coming new age of the Holy Spirit. It was always assumed that after the warning, chastisement and tribulation of the Antichrist, the Roman Church would rise phoenix-like from the ashes of doomsday to rule the world for a 1,000 years after Christ's Second Coming. How dare this Franciscan scholar-mendicant interpret Joachite prophecy to imply that the Church hierarchy would no longer be needed in the beatific age to come? How could he even conceive of normal people having an intimate and direct contact with God without popes or priests!

Gerard was effectively censured and no record of his replies to the commission at Anagni remains. For all we know he was himself a visionary, using the works of Joachim just as the latter had used the Holy Scriptures to reinterpret the Bible. Either he was very brave or a very naive interpreter of prophecy, ignorant of the age-old downfall of seers who do not cook their prophetic food to satisfy the intolerant tastes of the day.

Joachim de Fiore, like another controversial Catholic seer three centuries later, Michel Nostradamus, may have protected the body of his prophetic works for future generations by obscuring a vision of a new religious revolution to supplant the Catholic faith. It is better to write a politically correct and general statement that during the third epoch of the Holy Spirit a 'special understanding of the existing Scripture' would come to pass. He saves his legacy by not telling just what kind of revelation this will be. Perhaps Gerard di Borgo was unwise enough to read between Joachim's lines and say the intended secret out loud.

ANOTHER CHRISTIAN DOOMSDAY MISSED

As the year 1260 arrived there were certainly indications that Bible prophecy and especially the current Joachite interpretations of such might be fulfilled. The Mongol horde descended on the Holy Land from the north with all the fury of the foretold Gog and Magog. Manfred (c.1232–1266), the bastard regent of the Holy Roman Empire, fitted the bill for the Antichrist of obscure lineage, dominating Europe in a new Roman tyranny and putting the squeeze on God's Church and Vicar in Rome. The repugnant, though accepted, interpretation that the final pope would abandon Rome to the Antichrist seemed to be fulfilled with Alexander's departure to Viterbo.

The year 1260 passed with Manfred still not controlling the Christian world like a good Antichrist should. The Mongol Gog-and-Magogian horde rode through the plains of Mediggio without incident only to suffer their first major defeat 50 miles farther south. They were cut to pieces at Ain Jalut by Mameluke cavalry who chased them out of the Holy Land.

By 1261 neither Joachim de Fiore's apocalypse nor the age of the Holy Spirit descended on Earth, and his reputation plummeted. But as we will see, he, like many good Christian seers before him, may have correctly foreseen the potentials of the future, even if his own hopes for a rapid appearance of the Golden Age made him jump at the temptation to incorrectly date the advent near his own time. It must be remembered that greater and more respected giants of Christian prophecy made the same mistake. St. John the Divine, who wrote the Book of Revelation, clearly intended doomsday and the Second Coming to take place in his own lifetime. Even Christ incorrectly implied his speedy return to the embraces of his apostles.

Twenty centuries later, we still await the Second Coming.

TWENTY-ONE

Hierusalem Campaniæ
(Jerusalem of Champagne)

URBAN IV
(1261–1264)

JACQUES PANTALÉON, A cobbler's son from Troyes in Champagne, France, would rise within the Church hierarchy to become patriarch of Jerusalem. Fate would have him passing through Viterbo in 1261 at the time when the eight surviving cardinals of the late Alexander's pontificate were deadlocked on who to elect as the new pope. They chose the patriarch. He proved himself to be an able pontiff, reforming the finances of the Church and laying the foundations for the eventual overthrow of the Hohenstaufen dynasty of the Holy Roman Empire. He curried the ambitions of Charles d'Anjou (1226–1285), the brother of King Louis IX of France (1226–1270), by sanctioning his usurpation of the throne of Sicily. Anjou became the pope's first move in the final chess game for domination of the Italian peninsula between the Hohenstaufen emperors and the papacy.

TWENTY-TWO

Draco depressus
(A Dragon Pressed Down)

CLEMENT IV
(1265–1268)

AFTER THE FIRST move against the Hohenstaufens the papal chess
player suddenly died. It took four months for the divided cardinals
to elect his successor. He would bear arms depicting a red eagle
standing atop a green dragon. The next pope would be another
Frenchman, Guy Foulques, a noted lawyer at the court of King
Louis IX of France. He was also a family man with two daughters.
Upon the death of his wife in 1256 Foulques was ordained a
Carthusian monk. Five years later he was promoted to cardinal
by Urban IV. Four years after that he was summoned by the
cardinal electors to Viterbo, where he could be seen tearfully
pleading with them to reconsider their vote. They eventually convinced him to mount the throne of St. Peter and he took the
name Clement IV in honor of his favorite saint, Pope Clement I
(martyred c.100) – the fourth successor to the first pope, the
Apostle Peter.

The new pope had a unique problem. Suitors began arriving at
Viterbo asking for the hand of his two daughters. He had the
young women sent to convents to spare the embarrassment of a
celibate pontiff being called father-in-law or grandfather.

By the second year of his pontificate he set up his papal headquarters in the Dominican convent of Santa Maria in Gradi,
outside of Viterbo. There he resumed playing the end game with
the Hohenstaufen dynasty. In 1266 he crowned Charles d'Anjou

as king of Naples and Sicily, stressing the papal coffers to the breaking point to arm him with enough mercenaries to prosecute his holy crusade against the advancing imperial forces of Manfred and Conradin. Anjou defeated and killed Manfred at the battle of Benevento (1266) and routed Conradin's forces at Tagliacozzo (1268). Conradin was captured by Anjou at Tagliacozzo and later beheaded on 29 October of that year.

Heraldry expert Donald Lindsay Galbreath believes in a variation of the Villani story (*Cronica*, Lib. VII, CAP. 2) that the pope sent his adherents in Florence a banner with symbolic charges depicting an eagle pouncing with clutched talons upon a serpentine dragon. It would therefore seem that St. Malachy foresaw the great papal victory and extinction of the Hohenstaufen menace 128 years before with his motto *Dragon Pressed Down* or *Crushed*. Conradin's great grandfather, Frederick I Barbarossa, was called an evil *Dragon* by the anti-imperialist cardinals. No doubt many priests who dabbled in Bible prophecy believed that the red-bearded Frederick and his rusty-haired heirs were candidates for the title 'great red dragon' of Revelation 12:3.

With one menace defeated, Clement had filled the void in Italian politics with a new dragon threatening the papacy, Charles d'Anjou.

TWENTY-THREE

Anguineus vir
(A Snake-like Man)

GREGORY X
(1271–1276)

Incorrect   *Correct*

TEOBALDO VISCONTI HAD been a well-respected student at the University of Paris, where he became a close associate of St. Thomas Aquinas and St. Bonaventure (1218–1274). Although historians agree that he belonged to the Visconti family of Piacenza, the arms of the more well-known Milanese noble house have frequently been attached to Teobaldo Visconti: a shield depicting a man being devoured by a serpent.

He had helped to organize the Council of Lyons in 1245. By 1271 he was archdeacon of Liège and rubbing chain-mailed shoulders with crusader knights garrisoned at Acre in the Holy Land when the shocking news arrived from Viterbo that he had been chosen pope. The cardinals huddled in Viterbo had been deadlocked for three years over who should succeed Clement IV. They picked Teobaldo because he was anything but a snake-like or slippery man. Teobaldo dutifully returned to Viterbo and later was consecrated in Rome at St. Peter's as Gregory X. His short and vigorous pontificate was dominated by attempts to garner support from European royalty for another crusade in the Holy Land. This effort came to naught. His diplomatic campaign to unite the Eastern and Western Churches soon fell flat on its face. His most lasting legacy was issuing the decree *Ubi periculum* (1274), which established the conclave system for the election of popes. Rather than being remembered as a cunning snake, he was beatified in 1713.

TWENTY-FOUR

Concionatur Gallus
(A French Preacher)

INNOCENT V
(1276)

THE FRENCHMAN PIERRE DE TARENTAISE would be the first Dominican pope. He had learned his preaching skills while studying at the University of Paris with St. Albertus Magnus (1206–80) and Thomas Aquinas. This *French Preacher* joined the order of *Preaching* Friars in Provence, France. He applied his noted oratory and writing skills to author the famous commentary on the *Sentences* of Peter Lombard (c.1100–1160), one of the most significant theological textbooks used during the medieval period. He was the first pope elected by Gregory's stringent rules of the conclave which had been fashioned to prevent protracted interregnums of the Holy See. The new rules dictated that the Sacred College of Cardinals must gather at the place of death of a pontiff within ten days of his passing and be sealed into their place of voting with no contact with the outside world. The longer the voting took, the more austere their living and eating conditions would become.

Pierre de Tarentaise was 52 and apparently vigorous when he took the papal throne as Innocent V. He tried applying his noted speech-making skills to sustain the faltering reunion of Eastern and Western Churches, while seeking to diplomatically soften the roughened egos of French and German rulers. He also preached for their participation in a new crusade. Six months and a day after his consecration he suddenly died of a fever.

TWENTY-FIVE

Bonus Comes
(A Good Count)

ADRIAN V
(1276)

As a SENATOR of the Roman commune, Charles d'Anjou had the political influence to stringently apply the conclave's rules on the cardinals sealed inside the St. John Lateran. When the voting dragged on in the dog days of early summer, he cut the cardinals' rations of food and water. Soon a number of the older cardinals were faint with hunger and heat exhaustion. Finally the 70-year-old Cardinal *Count Ottobonus* Fieschi was chosen to become Pope Adrian V on 4 July 1276. The first order of papal business was to escape the oppressive heat of Rome for the more pleasant climate of Viterbo. Upon his arrival he dropped dead without ever being ordained, consecrated or crowned pontiff.

His one official administrative act upon accepting the pontificate was to suspend Gregory X's conclave degree, promising to create a new one.

TWENTY-SIX

Piscator Thuscus
(A Tuscan Fisherman)

JOHN XXI
(1276–1277)

THE CONCLAVE IN Viterbo for the successor of Adrian V started with a riot of angry cardinals. The mayor of the town had endeavored to seal the cardinals in their electoral conclave, only to find out at the last moment that the late pope had suspended Gregory

X's conclave decree. The contentious election finally climaxed with Pedro Juliao, a native of Lisbon, Portugal, taking the numerically flawed title Pope John XXI. Perhaps it was the heat, but some papal scribe somewhere had miscounted the succession and overlooked John number XX. Rather than lose papal face and infallibility, the newly elected pope allowed the error to remain. The hapless Pope John saw his short reign come to a dramatic end when he was crushed by the collapsing ceiling of the papal palace in Viterbo.

The Latin epigraph reminds us that the Portuguese pontiff had once been appointed to Tuscany as cardinal bishop of Tusculum (TUSCUS) in 1273. He is poetically called *fisherman*, alluding to his Christian name and his being successor to St. Peter, the fisherman of souls.

TWENTY-SEVEN

Rosa composita
(A Composed Rose)

NICHOLAS III
(1277–1280)

THANKS TO THE political clout of the Roman Giovanni Cardinal Gaetano of the House of Orsini, John XXI was chosen pope. After the broken body of the late pope was buried – not far out of earshot of the carpenters' hammers and saws rebuilding the fallen roof of the Viterbo palace – Gaetano, as a member of the new conclave of a mere seven cardinals, was to choose a successor. They were deadlocked for six months until Gaetano emerged as Nicholas III. The new pope would be a nagging thorn in the ambitions of Charles d'Anjou, the king of Naples and Sicily. By meeting with the emissaries of Byzantine Emperor Michael VIII Palaeologus (1259–1282), Nicholas would put his papal crook in the machinations of Charles' plan to invade Constantinople.

Nicholas openly flaunted nepotism; of the six cardinals he would appoint, three were fellow Orsinis. He reasoned that he must surround himself with family members and Romans to curb the growing influence of Charles and the French on the papacy. His main passion was spending huge sums of Church money to restore and beautify Rome, especially the Lateran Palace and St. Peter's Cathedral. He also constructed an opulent summer palace (with solid ceilings, no doubt) for himself at Viterbo.

The armorial bearings of this Orsini pope display a rose. He was the son of Matteo Rossi (Rose) and therefore one could figuratively say he was a created or *a composed Rose* through the husbandry of his father. The noted Catholic prophecy scholar Abbé Joseph Maître thinks that he was also known for his serious or *composed* nature.

TWENTY-EIGHT

Ex telonio Liliacæi Martini
(From the Receipt of Custom of Martin of the Lilies)

MARTIN IV
(1281–1285)

AFTER THE DEATH of Nicholas the cardinals gathered at Viterbo for six months of intriguing before the Angevin puppet Cardinal Simon de Brie became Pope Martin IV. He took his new name from the patron saint of France (the *lilies* are its symbol). The inscription may also apply itself to Simon de Brie's role as Church treasurer of St. Martin's, in Tours, where he recorded the donations (that is, receipts of custom) of patrons to the cathedral.

His Gallic sympathies with the policies and ambitions of Charles d'Anjou, king of Naples, made it certain that the Italian citizens of Rome would never welcome him within their walls. He supported Charles' intention to unite the Western Church with the Eastern Orthodox, by force if necessary, and excommunicated the Byzantine Emperor Michael VIII Palaeologus. The threat proffered in Pope Martin's outstretched hand effectively killed the attempted reunion which had been negotiated at the Council of Lyons over a decade earlier. He died in Perugia a few weeks after his master, Charles d'Anjou (king of Sicily).

TWENTY-NINE

Ex rosa Leonina
(From a Leonine Rose)

HONORIUS IV
(1285–1287)

DESPITE THE SUSPENSION of conclave rules, the Sacred College of Cardinals gathered at Perugia wasted little time in picking Giacomo Savelli as successor to Martin IV. Savelli came from a noble Roman family whose family shield displayed two lions holding a rose. He took the name Honorius IV in honor of his grand-uncle, Honorius III. His brief two-year reign saw the material and political expansion of the mendicant Dominican and Franciscan orders, to which he gave exclusive control of the Inquisition. He encouraged the study of oriental languages in the futile hope for a reunion of the Eastern and Western Churches.

Though he had been a good friend of the late Charles d'Anjou, king of Sicily, he distanced the papacy somewhat from Angevin manipulation. Honorius, however, would divert the funds collected for a planned crusade against the Muslims in the Holy Land into the military money pit for a crusade against fellow Christians. He could not resist making an attempt to return the oppressive Angevin rulers to Sicily. His efforts met with disastrous failure.

THIRTY

Picus inter escas
(A Woodpecker among the Food)

NICHOLAS IV
(1288–1292)

AFTER THE PASSING of Honorius the throne of St. Peter remained empty for over 11 months. During that time six cardinal electors had died from the summer heat. The deadlock was finally broken in February 1288. The heat and later the winter's chill had finally sapped the ambitions and pride out of the cardinals and in exasperation they endeavored to choose the least egoistic among them. The vote was unanimous for Girolamo Masci, the first Franciscan to become pontiff.

The reign of Nicholas IV was shadowed by his slavish support of one of Rome's most powerful families, the Colonnas. During Nicholas' reign the last crusader possession in the Holy Land, Acre, fell to the Saracens. His calls to Christian princes for a crusade were ignored. He even tried to negotiate an alliance with the Mongol Emperor Kublai Khan (1216–1294) for the same ends, but came up empty. He did enjoy some success in establishing far-ranging missions to Africa and China.

Ciacconius' interpretation supposes that the names of his birthplace and native province are hidden in the Latin. Nicholas came from the town of ASColi or ESColi (ESCAS) in PICenum (PICUS).

THIRTY-ONE

Ex eremo[1] *celsus*[2]
(From the Lofty Hermit)

ST. CELESTINE V
(1294)

TWENTY-SEVEN MONTHS AFTER the death of Nicholas IV a procession of several cardinals, dignitaries and their attendants could be seen laboriously making their way up the side of Mt. Morrone. The red robes of the cardinals stood out in sharp contrast to the barren and rocky wilderness of the Abruzzi region of the Apennine mountains. They met the disbelieving eyes of hermit monks who dwelled in the pile of rocks along the mountainside known as the monastery (and future prison) of San Spirito – a bleak place for those in desperate need of escape from the temptations of worldly life.

The cardinals demanded that the monks produce their abbot, Pietro del Morrone. One managed to clear his throat – tightened by the paralysis of vows of silence and fasting – to say that Brother Morrone had abandoned the monastery and retired farther up the mountain to his cave more than 1,000 feet above sea level. An uncounted number of tortuous steps later, the papal party stood at the end of their 150-mile journey from the conclave at Perugia to gaze for the first time upon the hollow eyes and gaunt face of their new pope, who blinked in disbelief behind the bars of his cell.

It took a moment for Cardinal Peter Colonna, the leader of the papal mission, to catch his breath and get used to the smell of

---

[1]EREMO = a play on the Latin *eremita* (an ecclesiastical hermit); *eremo* = Italian for hermitage, a place of retreat.
[2]CELSUS = appraised, high, lofty, elevated, i.e. holy.
Ciacconius believes that St. Malachy's gift of prophecy transcends language barriers. He thinks he is hiding the Italian clue behind the Latin. For example, *celsus* in Italian is *celso*, and its soft c is pronounced very similar to the soft g of *gelso*, which is a synonym in Italian for *moro*, or *morone*, a mulberry tree. Celestine was a hermit living on Mt. Morrone.

the unwashed Holy Father-to-be, whom Peter de Rosa described as a man "peering through the bars of his home-made cell like a bewildered monkey." A moment later this 85-year-old devout hermit watched Cardinal Colonna and the others all bend a knee to him, summarily ending his peaceful prison-cell lifestyle. After one of the longest and most contentious interregnums of the papacy, a prophecy about the Church attributed to Pietro del Morrone opened the door to its author becoming the next pope.

"No, this is not a joke," Colonna explained, and went on to fill the hermit's prayer-numbed mind with images of 27 months of political maneuvering by powerful families, Angevin sympathizers and the traffic jam of personal vendettas and colliding ambitions which had kept the 12 cardinals of the conclave in gridlock on a choice for Pope Nicholas' successor.

By the spring of 1294 the deadlock had produced chaos and rioting in Rome. It was around that time that Cardinal Latino Malabranca revealed a prophecy attributed to Pietro del Moronne that "divine retribution" would befall the Church if a new pope was not soon chosen. And it was understood that this pope must be a lofty and religious man, humble and beyond worldly reproach. Once again the Church leaders were moved by crisis to look towards prophecy for the salvation of the Church. They turned to interpretations of the prophecies of Joachim de Fiore for an answer, just as they had done over three decades before. When the end of the world and time expected in 1260 passed without as much as a doomsday adieu, his prophecies were generally discarded, only to be resurrected because of the current crisis. Now Joachite and pseudo-Joachite prophecies fed the fuel of a 13th-century expectation still popular with Catholics today: You will know that the end times and the redemption of the Church are near when the papacy elects a line of "angelic" popes. Thanks to Cardinal Malabranca's evangelism and his pivotal power as the dean of the conclave, he managed to convince first two-thirds and later the entire body of cardinal electors that the papacy needed a pope as excessively devout and lofty as the well-known hermit, healer and prophet of Mt. Morrone.

Morrone accepted a bath, a miter cap and the fresh robes of a pontiff only under great protest. The ascetic was taken from his mountain cell and was guided on a donkey by the hand of Charles d'Anjou's heir, Charles II of Naples (1246–1309), down the mountain to Aquila, where he was consecrated as Celestine V.

The papacy of this "angel pope" was a catastrophe.

Charles II never let go, figuratively speaking, of the pontiff's donkey leash. Celestine was taken to Naples where he became Charles' puppet, meekly acceding to the appointment of 12 pro-Angevin cardinals, of which seven were French.

Prophecy aside, it soon became apparent that angels do not make good leaders of the papacy. Celestine may have been holy, but he was wholly ignorant of politics and even the cross-and-wafer basics of daily church duties. His Latin was atrocious, forcing the pontificate to write his edicts in Italian. And his commands only fouled the church machinery and brought more chaos and crisis. After four disastrous months Celestine – seeing what harm he was doing to his beloved Mother Church – locked himself away in his apartments, turning them into a monk's cell.

The naive pontiff was tricked into abdicating St. Peter's throne through the unorthodox counsel of the treacherous and ambitious Cardinal Benedetto Gaetani. Celestine had asked the cardinal, a noted expert on canon law, to find a holy loophole to get him back into his tattered and dirty habit and back up Mt. Morrone into his barred cave as soon as possible. Gaetani, under cover of darkness, drilled a hole into the wall of the pope's cell, twisting a speaking tube into it. For several nights the hermit pope curled upon the stone floor was awakened by a voice calling out to him in the darkness:

"Celestine . . . Celestine . . . lay down your office. It is too great a burden for you to bear . . ."

The pope became convinced that the Holy Spirit was calling upon him to abdicate. Celestine retired soon after and was succeeded by none other than Gaetani as Boniface VIII. His successor kept Celestine under lock and key and would not grant his simple wish to return to the rocky wilds of Mt. Morrone, fearing that his own pontificate might be threatened by radical Catholic doomsday cultists and other papal enemies who might climb the mountain and pluck the former pope from his cell to lead a schism.

Boniface finally had Celestine locked behind bars in the tower of Castel Fumone, east of Ferentino. The old hermit resigned himself to his new lodgings, saying, "I have desired nothing in my life save for a cell, and a cell they have given to me." He would live within his its confines for two more years before finally passing away in 1296. Historians claim that he was not harshly treated. Certainly a fanatic mendicant who abstained from the rich bounty of papal banquets, and preferred to munch in seclusion on dry bread crust and water, would find prison life in Fumone more to his tastes. Still, an argument could be made that he died of starvation and general neglect. Clement V had him canonized in 1313.

Before passing away, Celestine did a little prophesying himself, accurately predicting the fate of his successor: "You leaped on the throne like a fox, you will reign like a lion, you will die like a dog."

THIRTY-TWO

Ex undarum benedictione
(From a Blessing of the Waves)

BONIFACE VIII
(1294–1303)

THE INSCRIPTION CORRECTLY alludes to the lateral wave designs rolling across the coat of arms of the next pope, Cardinal Benedetto Gaetani. It also gives us his Christian name, *Benedict*, before the sly fox discarded it – and his predecessor – to become Boniface VIII.

His pontificate was anything but a blessing. Boniface would take the medieval Holy See to its zenith only to see its secular power weakened beyond repair by his intolerance of the rise of monarchical and national power in Europe. He sought to repress political change by making himself God's holy Caesar and demagogue. In 1302 he published *Unam Sanctam* wherein he defined a pope's power as two swords in the world, one spiritual and the other temporal. The spiritual sword was wielded directly by the Vicar of Christ, whereas the temporal power of monarchs and civil authority could be wielded only under the direction of the pope. *Unam Sanctam* punctuates this claim with the following: "Now, therefore, we declare, say, determine, and pronounce that for every human creature it is essential for their salvation to be subject to the authority of the Roman Pontiff."

For a time the cold-eyed Pope Boniface made good his predecessor's prediction. Like *a lion* he turned on his enemies, the Colonna, ransacking their properties and leveling their home town of Palestrina. His favorite epitaph, hurled in a shower of spittle through the gaps in his teeth on his cardinals and enemies alike, was: "I am *Pfss*-Caesar, I am em-*pfth*-peror!"

He struck out against the European monarchs who disobeyed *Unam Sanctam*, pouncing on King Philip IV of France in particular because he was the chief ally of the Colonnas. The Colonna had spread the rumor that Boniface had seized the papacy under false pretenses and had tricked his predecessor, Celestine V, into abdicating. They also circulated the story that Boniface had had Celestine murdered in prison.

In September 1303 Boniface was captured by forces of Sciarra Colonna and King Philip's lieutenant, Guillaume de Nogaret (c.1260–1313), at the pope's opulent palace in his home town of Anagni. Nogaret stopped Sciarra from beheading the 85-year-old pontiff, but allowed the head of the Colonna family to take his revenge. He knocked off the pontiff's mitered hat and cut away his garments with his stiletto until Boniface was stripped down to his loin cloth and a multitude of hopping lice. Most of Nogaret's mercenaries then proceeded to ransack the sizable plunder collected by the pope in his short reign. Once satisfied with their spoils, most of the mercenaries left. This allowed the townspeople of Anagni to free their native son and bring him back to Rome and safety.

The ordeal had broken the leonine pontiff, who seemed to become a blubbering and senile old man after only three days of incarceration. While in confinement he had refused all food and drink, fearing that his enemies would poison him. Once returned to Rome he locked himself away in his apartment in the Lateran Basilica for over a month. Priests outside his door could hear him banging his head against the wall. He was seen gnawing at his arm like a dog worrying a bone. In the end Celestine's prophecy was fulfilled. The "fox" who had tricked his way into St. Peter's chair, and ruled like a lion – calling himself Lord and master of the Universe – in the end died like a dog, alone and insane.

THIRTY-THREE

Concionator patareus
(A Patarean Preacher)

BENEDICT XI
(1303–1304)

As FAR As I understand it Patara was a bishopric in the Eastern Orthodox Church in the Byzantine Empire and had no connection with Niccolo Boccasini, the Dominican friar who later became Benedict XI. On the other hand Ciacconius reminds us that the pope's namesake, St. Benedict, was a native of Patara, and might readily be called PATAREUS, the Patarean. Before becoming pope our candidate was a member of the Order of *Preaching* Friars.

Cardinal Boccasini was one of two popes who stuck by their nearly naked and lice-ridden pontiff during Boniface VIII's three days and nights of brutalization at Anagni. His courage earned him consecration as Benedict XI. During his brief eight-month reign this generally timid and pacific pope softened the papacy's rocky relationship with France. He found it politically expedient to absolve Philip IV and the French people from censures placed on them by his predecessor. He forgave the Colonna cardinals, but his amnesty did not extend to returning the confiscated property of the Colonna family or absolving Nogaret and Sciarra Colonna for their actions at Anagni.

In July 1304 Benedict summoned Nogaret and Sciarra to face a pontifical tribunal. A few days later the pope sat down for his evening meal and was offered a pile of figs on a silver platter by a sister of the Order of St. Petronilla. His passion for figs dulled his awareness to anything else; he never caught on that the good sister was a male assassin in drag. That night after gorging himself the pope suffered an attack of severe dysentery and soon was dead.

THIRTY-FOUR

De fessis Aquitanicis
(From the Ditches of Aquitaine)

CLEMENT V
(1305–1314)

THE SUDDEN DEATH of Benedict XI drew the cardinals together to meet at Perugia to wallow in a bitter 11-month deadlock between pro-French and pro-Bonifacian factions. The former group sought the rehabilitation of the Colonna cardinals and appeasement with the French king Philip IV. The latter faction was in the majority and sought a candidate who would take revenge on Philip IV and the Colonna for the persecution of Boniface VIII at Anagni.

The French faction suggested that since no one could be chosen who was agreeable to all the factions, why not pick someone outside of the cardinals – for instance someone like the Aquitainian Bertrand de Got, the archbishop of Bordeaux, who despite his friendship with Philip IV of France had thrown his full support to Boniface. No sooner had Bertrand de Got been voted and consecrated as Pope Clement V did the pro-Bonifacian faction see that they were victims of French intrigue. A puppet of Philip IV was now sitting on the throne of St. Peter. The man with the armorial three gold bars and gules representing the *fesses* (ditches) of Aquitaine would move the papacy headquarters out of Rome for what has been called the Second Babylonian Captivity (1309–1377) – in this case, Babylon is Avignon, in the south of France.

One of Clement's first acts was to order the curia and offices of the Church to pack their bags and come with him across the Maritime Alps into France. For the next few years Clement and the papal leadership moved its headquarters through Provence and Gascony, finally settling, with king Philip's blessing, in Avignon in March 1309. At the time it was thought to be temporary. But as the years piled up and Clement injected the swelling body of cardinals with French appointments, it was clear that an effort was being made by the French pontiff and his king to purge the influence of Italians from the papacy for a very long time. The savaging of the king's hated enemy, Boniface VIII, was forgiven, the Colonna family was restored and financially compensated and the late pope's edicts were overthrown. Clement also had Celestine V canonized as revenge for Boniface's intrigue with a speaking tube.

During the Avignon papacy Clement set the precedent for excessive opulence. Those who sought the pontiff's blessing knew to lay their petition on the ample bosom of the pope's mistress, the lovely Comtesse de Foix of Perigord. The coffers of Avignon and the king of France were filled to bursting when Clement surrendered to the king's lust for the wealth and property of the Knights Templars and had them disbanded, their leaders tortured and their properties confiscated.

Malachy's term *ditches* might also imply his condemnation of Clement's amoral pontificate and his extreme nepotism. He made five members of his family cardinals and showered so many gifts on his mistress, relatives and political and religious cronies that the papal treasury was nearly bankrupt by the time of his death.

THIRTY-FIVE

De sutore osseo
(From a Bony Shoemaker)

JOHN XXII
(1316–1334)

CARDINAL JACQUES DUESE was born in Cahors, France. Modern scholars are in dispute as to whether his father was a shoemaker or the head of a wealthy burgher family who made his way into the lower nobility, thanks to his brother's elevation to blue-bloodhood by the king of France in 1316. Whether Dad was a knobby-kneed and ossified fellow named *Ossa* is not recorded by historians, but his sickly son's singular ugliness was well known. Peter de Rosa in *Vicars of Christ* puts all political correctness aside to describe the future John XXII as a "fragile little monster" with a laugh "that cackled with unimprovable malice."

It took his fellow cardinals over two years to pick a new pope. Finally they threw up their hands in exasperation and agreed on Duese as their candidate. At best he was considered an inter-mediate choice; aged 72 and in terrible health, he would, they figured, limp along for long enough to buy some time for a better choice of pope to surface. But John XXII would cheat the tomb longer than anyone expected. And like a frayed and bent Energizer bunny he would keep going and going and going . . . running on his old and rusty battery for 18 years.

De Rosa adds that he "was to prove a harsh and durable pontiff, ambitious, full of avarice, [and] more worldly than a pimp."

Finance was his main focus. And to that end he did some little good by reorganizing the papal curia and instituting a number of far-reaching changes in ecclesiastical money management.

Although frugal in his private affairs and simple lifestyle, his nepotism far exceeded that of his hedonistic predecessor, Clement. He used his ingenious, if not unscrupulous, financial acumen to fill the coffers, emptied by Clement, with the proceeds from sham indulgences. Any sin could be forgiven by this pope if the sinner offered the right price. He even encouraged Catholics to sin again, or break their vows, as long as they could pay for continued forgiveness. It seemed that the biggest sin was being in arrears with the pontiff. In one day John excommunicated 1 patriarch, 5 archbishops, 30 bishops and 46 abbots for not paying their taxes to the Church on time. One of the reasons John lived frugally was that 70 per cent of his plundering of simple plowshare-pushing and pruning-hook-carrying Catholics was used to fashion the swords and pikes to arm his mercenary hosts for a bloody string of wars in Italy.

His greed went as far as to revise the dogma of Christ's poverty and declare heretical the idea that Christ and his Apostles had no property. For a time the hardest-core mendicant order of the Spiritual Franciscans were branded heretics and 114 were burned alive. The rest had fled north from their monasteries to Germany, where they sought the protection of John's chief nemesis, the Holy Roman Emperor Louis of Bavaria (1287?–1347), who had labeled the pope of Avignon an antichrist.

The end of John's reign was marred further by his heretical view of life in heaven before and after doomsday. In brief he declared that the dearly departed saints and the Virgin Mary were "under the altar of God"; in other words, they were not in heaven and would not bathe in the ecstasy of God's vision until after Judgment Day. He also added that neither were the damned dwelling in hell until after doomsday dawned.

His views caused an uproar in Christendom and many theologians agreed with the German emperor in declaring him a heretic. John offered enormous sums to anyone who could find a quote from St. Augustine supporting the pope's view. None were found. Historians are not sure whether John made a public retraction. Some believe that he held onto his heresy unto death at age 90.

At the time of his death the papal treasury exceeded anything that the Florentine bankers sent to assess it had ever seen. They catalogued 25 million gold florins and an equal number of precious stones and objects.

I leave the final observation to de Rosa: "The real heresy of John XXII, Christ's vicar and successor of St. Peter, was that he burned the poorest of Christ's poor [the Franciscans] and died the richest man in the world."

THIRTY-SIX

Corvus schismaticus
(A Schismatic Raven)

NICHOLAS V, ANTIPOPE
(1328–1330)

BORN IN CORVARO, a town named after a raven, Pietro di Corbario abandoned his wife and children to become a Franciscan monk in 1310 and for a number of years resided in their house of Santa Maria in Aracoeli, Rome. In 1328 he was singled out by the Holy Roman Emperor, Louis IV of Bavaria, to serve as antipope to the legitimate, albeit heretical, John XXII residing in Avignon.

It appears that Corbario was presented to Emperor Louis as a near saint and ascetic. In fact he was something of a hypocrite with a dark secret which surfaced only after Louis crowned him Antipope Nicholas V on 15 May 1328. Not long after Nicholas had established himself in Rome, an old crow of a lady came knocking at the Lateran Basilica door, announcing herself to be Mrs. di Corbario. Apparently Mr. Corbario had committed a major faux pas in canon law. He had abandoned his wife and family to join the Franciscans without receiving her permission. This meant that deadbeat daddy Nicholas V had not been an authentic monk, let alone qualified to be a pontiff, whether pope or antipope. Louis IV was philosophical about the matter. He had Mrs. di Corbario paid off and was later heard to say, "At least *my* pope is a Catholic."

When Louis IV left Rome in August 1328, he was forced to take his antipope in tow. They were both hounded by the jeers and catcalls of the Roman citizenry. For the next two years support for his anti-pontificate rapidly dwindled. Finally Nicholas was handed over to John XXII at Avignon where he bowed before the legitimate pontiff. He was restored to his former life and tattered gray habit as Friar di Corbario after publicly avowing himself as "a *schismatic* pope." John forgave him and he spent the last three years of his life in honorable confinement in the papal apartments.

THIRTY-SEVEN

Frigidus Abbas
(A Cold Abbot)

BENEDICT XII
(1334–1342)

JACQUES FOURNIER, born in the province of Toulouse, was a Cistercian abbot of Fontfroide in 1131 before he succeeded John XXII in 1334. Fontfroide means "*cold* spring" in French; thus the motto makes a word-play out of *cold Abbot*. The motto lays on further twists of pun-ishment with the different Latin applications for *frigidus*. One could say that *Abbot* Fournier was *cold*-hearted when, as bishop of Pamiers, he was responsible for rubbing out the last surviving Albigensians. For this and other noble deeds John XXII made him cardinal in 1327. Five years later he succeeded John as Benedict XII, the third Avignon pope.

His pontificate was notorious for its austerity (cold atmosphere) and edicts. Rather than wallow in luxury and nepotism like his Avignon predecessors, Benedict, who had no surviving family, was a real holy kill-joy. He wore a simple habit, proclaiming that a pope must live like Melchizedek the priest-king of Genesis, to which even Abraham had to bow down and give his tithe. It can be gathered from reading biblical references to Melchizedek, that Benedict saw himself as an equally stern critic of his priests in the curia and cardinalate. He felt compelled to teach the priestly teachers of the laity the ABCs of Christianity.

His pontificate was noted for its strict and wide-ranging reform of the Roman clergy and curia. Free-wheeling monks were ordered back behind the walls of their monasteries. The mendicant orders of Dominicans and Franciscans were burdened with new and severe rules intended to bring them closer to God via a state of primal poverty.

Benedict was unsuccessful in forestalling the Hundred Years War between the English and the French. His reign also saw the Papal States of Italy fall into sharp decline. He sent aid to the citizens of Rome to soften the deepening economic depression but chose not to return the pontificate to the empty Lateran Basilica. For this he suffered a number of satires by Petrarch, who labeled him as a drunk and unfit helmsman of the Church for coldly refusing to return his pontificate to Rome.

He died on 24 April 1342 after a rule of eight years.

THIRTY-EIGHT

De rosa Athrebatensi
(From the Rose of Arras)

CLEMENT VI
(1342–1352)

AFTER THE LONG cold winter of Benedict's pontificate, the cardinals gathering at Avignon desired a rosier successor. Their unanimous vote fell on the eloquent, easy-going and debonair former bishop of Arras, Cardinal Pierre Roger, son of Guillaume Roger, Lord of Rosiers (Roses). The family coat of arms has six rosettes.

The inscription *Rose* could also signify an important event during his reign. The red boils and pustules of the Black Death which spread across Europe during the fifth and sixth year of his pontificate were called *roses* by the common people. The catastrophe gave Clement yet another chance to demonstrate his rosy, life-affirming attitude. When the plague broke out in Avignon in 1348 nearly half the city's people died. Rather than lock himself away in the safety of his palace, Clement ordered his papal curia to follow his example and continue to perform their ecclesiastical duties among the sickened laity.

He was a rare *rose* among popes when it came to the care of the Jews. He boldly stopped the Catholic citizens of Avignon from making them scapegoats for the plague and put an end to riots in the Jewish quarter.

The Black Death would eventually kill one-third of Western Europe's people and coincidentally fulfill in part the prophecy of the seven final plagues in the Book of Revelation (chapters 15 and 16) through which one-third of humanity was required to die as God's chastisement. Many good Catholics wondered whether the pestilence was the beginning of the expected Chastisement and return of Christ foreseen by St. Hildegard and other Catholic seers.

The life-loving pope in Avignon apparently gave little energy to the doomsday fever. In fact by 1350, when the plague had run its course, he was of the mind to ease the suffering of his stricken flock. For instance, Clement was happy to rescind Benedict's harsh edict and grant the deputation of the Roman senate their request to cut the time between jubilee years celebrated in Rome from 100 years to 50. This change definitely improved the welfare of the common Roman and made the economy of the faltering Eternal City far rosier as Rome filled to its walled brim with pilgrims coming to give thanks in Roman churches for surviving the Black Death and a brush with the apocalypse.

"My predecessor didn't know how to be pope!" said Clement about Benedict. He dug into the deep pockets of the papal treasury to shower wealth on his cardinals and his flock to make them happy, especially those sheep nearest the shadow of the great stone walls of the Avignon papal residence. The citizens of Avignon, from the highest born to the whores, were buried in the moneys collected from Catholic Christendom. As De Rosa observed: "Few complained that Bacchus and Venus were more honored than Jesus Christ in Avignon."

The pope had a long line of rosy-cheeked little boys and mistresses who took part in his special "plenary indulgences" consecrated on the altar of his bed. He would later legitimize all of his children seeded beneath the sheets of such sacramental acts.

On two occasions he felt obligated to leave his pleasures and ascend through the vast labyrinth of the Avignon palace to the Hall of Torture. There he would stand – with pained eyes and his mouth and nose covered by a handkerchief to shield him from the stench of feces, fear and blood – to pump up the morale of the Franciscan and Dominican friars of the Inquisition with his presence as they went about their grim work shaving the hairs, grinding the bones and slashing the flesh of screaming heretics.

He also made efforts to resurrect a crusade against the Muslim unbelievers, but it came to naught and he had to please himself with a few devastating raids on Muslim ports.

As far as money and favors can supply, Clement earned his reputation as a pope loved by all the classes. He died on 6 December 1352 from a sudden illness after a pontificate of ten years. The later canonized Catholic seeresses Bridget of Sweden (d. 1373) and Catherine of Siena (1347–1380), had both corresponded from Rome, pleading that the pontiff end his licentious life and return to Rome or suffer death. Three days before his passing, Bridget relates, the bell of St. Peter's Basilica in Rome was melted by a lightning bolt during a violent thunderstorm. She says that crowds in the market quarter began celebrating because they believed it was a sign that the pope had died and gone to hell.

THIRTY-NINE

De montibus Pammachii
(From the Mountains of Pammachius)

INNOCENT VI
(1352–1362)

THE AVIGNON SUCCESSION once again replaced licentiousness with repression when cardinal bishop Etienne Aubert gained the throne as Innocent VI by promising to strengthen the power of the Sacred College of Cardinals over future popes. He took back his promise after his first taste of the sacred and autocratic powers of Christ's Church. What the chief prince of the Church had promised the cardinals he took away, down sizing the papal household and the powers of the cardinalate and curia via wide-ranging reforms. His severity of rule, especially in the torture and burning of a number of Spiritual Franciscans, was cause for Bridget of Sweden, residing in Rome, to declare him a persecutor of Christ's sheep.

Innocent was the first Avignon pope to sincerely desire the return of the papacy to Rome, but the general civil unrest in the Eternal City made this impractical. He did appoint the warrior cardinal Gil de Albornoz (c.1295–1367) as vicar-general of the Papal States. Albornoz unleashed war throughout central Italy for years to come in order to restore the pope's secular control. Innocent could not achieve a lasting peace between France and England, but his Treaty of Brestigny in 1360 would at least bring a ten-year breather in the hostilities of the Hundred Years War (1337–1453). He passed away in 1362, disappointed that his most cherished desire, a return to Rome, went unfulfilled.

The motto is a play on Innocent's birthplace of *Monts*, near Pompadour (Limousin), France and his posting as bishop of Clermont. One of his cardinal subtitles when posted at SS. Giovanni à Paolo was "*Pammachius* of the Heavenly *Mountain*."

FORTY

Gallus Vicecomes
(A French Viscount)

URBAN V
(1362–1370)

THE BLACK ROBE of the otherworldly Benedictine Guillaume de Grimoard of France would wrinkle on the seat of the throne of St. Peter when the Sacred College of Cardinals in Avignon elected him in a second ballot to become Urban V. He was born in Languedoc of a noble family, and after joining the Benedictine order became a noted lecturer in canon law. He was chosen pope primarily for his reputation as a shrewd politician while serving as papal legate of Italy. When he was summoned to Avignon to take the newly conceived triple-tiara crown, the new pontiff rejected fancy raiments for his simple black Benedictine robe. Though never appointed a cardinal, it is said that he was deeply religious and, no matter how hectic his schedule, Urban's curia were compelled to allow him time each day for prayers and scriptural study. By taking the name Urban he had it in mind to be remembered as a holy pope because so many earlier Urbans were believed to have been saintly pontiffs. He continued his predecessor's efforts to strip the indulgent Avignon court of its King Herodic and hedonistic opulence and restore it to the austerity of anti-sinful life. He had many spiritually ambitious desires: among them was the reunification of the Eastern and Western Churches, to be accomplished after his triumphal return to Rome.

Only in the latter desire was he momentarily successful. He returned the Holy See to Rome in 1367, although the general unrest and political volatility of the Italian peninsula made his stay there untenable after only three years. Hidden in St. Malachy's motto is a reference to *French* Pope Urban's chief nemesis, Bernabò Visconti (*viscount*) of Milan (1323–85), the man most responsible for impeding the pontiff's return to Rome. As a former legate to Italy, Urban had been a *French* nuncio at the Court of Visconti (VICECOMES). It was the threatened invasion of Visconti's forces which compelled the pope with deep regret to remove his curia back again to Avignon, despite the prescient warnings of St. Bridget of Sweden. Ever the seeress to pack punishment for the disobeyance of her predictions, she warned Urban that death would meet him in Avignon if he did not return to Rome. Three months after his return to Avignon he fell seriously ill and died in December 1370.

FORTY-ONE

Novus de virgine forti
(A New Man from a Strong Virgin)

GREGORY XI
(1370–1378)

ON FACE VALUE the motto constitutes praise for the merits of Pierre Roger de Beaufort's mother, *Marie* du Chambon, prior to her marriage, but we must look elsewhere for a virginal candidate. One holy virgin hides in his title as Cardinal of *Sanctae* Mariae *Novae*. Indeed the future Gregory XI would be influenced by the words of two future women saints, Bridget of Sweden and Catherine of Siena. Because the former was married with children, the motto is probably zeroing in on Catherine of Siena who never was deflowered by either libertines or legal marriage. A *strong virgin* is also figurative in the broader sense, representing Catherine in her future canonization as a Marian cultist; in other words, she was often visited, so she claimed, by apparitions of the Virgin Mary.

Pierre Roger de Beaufort would come to the saintly virgin's attention after his unanimous election in Avignon and succession after Urban V as Gregory XI. One of his earlier actions was to invite Catherine of Siena to Avignon. The saint-to-be turned her righteous nose up at the offer, replying that she did not need to visit the papal court to smell it: "The stink of the curia, Holiness, has long ago reached my city." All the same she did submit to the pope's invitation, consulting with him in Avignon for three months. Her visit encouraged the chief ambition of Gregory's eight-year reign: to drag the grumbling curia and court of the papacy back to the Eternal City where it belonged. From 1375 through 1378 he received morale-boosting letters from Catherine of Siena supporting him in prosecuting his war with Florence to win back the Papal States.

At last he had obtained his goal, riding into Rome by January of 1377, but his sojourn there was painfully short. The atrocities committed at Cesena by his military commander (and future antipope), Cardinal Robert of Geneva, reverberated in the streets of Rome. The angry Roman mob forced Gregory to retreat to Anagni from the new papal residence established in the Vatican. The written condemnations by his saintly and virginal patron, Catherine of Siena, stung far worse than the catcalls of Romans in the streets. She condemned the pontiff for his hard-line insistence on harsh peace terms against Florence, which had contributed to the volatile political climate in Italy and finally led to the massacre at Cesena and the pontiff's exile from Rome. Just before he left for Anagni he received a prophetic threat from Catherine: disaster both personal and for his pontificate was assured if he left Rome. Her words worked to feed psychic lead into his burdens and nourish Gregory's apocalyptic forebodings of the schism to come once he was no more.

Catherine saw her prophecy fulfilled in March 1378 when the exhausted and care-worn pontiff died.

FORTY-TWO

De cruce apostolica
(From an Apostolic Cross)

CLEMENT VII, ANTIPOPE
(1378–1394)

THE NEXT THREE mottoes examine the succession of Antipopes in what was called the Great Western Schism (1378–1417). The coat of arms of Robert of Geneva is dominated by a large gold *cross* with azure quarter pieces. He was made cardinal priest of the Basilica of the Twelve Apostles by Gregory XI. The cardinal priest also served as cardinal general commanding the forces of Gregory XI in the War of the Eight Saints (1375–1378) – a conflict designed to bring back papal dominance to Italy. When Gregory died Robert voted for Urban VI (1378–1389) to replace him, and had been one of the first in line to pay him homage. Shortly afterwards, when the new man on St. Peter's chair became an erratic monster, Cardinal Robert on one occasion was seen holding back Urban's arm, which was ready to strike the face of the cardinal of Limoges. Later when he tried to reason with him and prevent his excommunicating yet another cardinal, the pontiff shouted in his high and piercing castrati voice, "I can do anything, absolutely anything I like!"

Cardinal Robert was soon leading a faction of cardinals to have the new pope retired on a charge that he was insane. Like fallen angels vacating the Heaven of a mad God, most of the Sacred College of Cardinals fled to Fondi, where they chose Robert of Geneva to become Antipope Clement VII. Thanks to his political skills and aided by the truculent nature of Pope Urban, Clement gathered support for his pontificate from most of Spain, France, Burgundy, Naples and Scotland. He appointed his own college of cardinals and curia and set up his headquarters at Avignon, in a style redolent of the opulence and sensuality of the more hedonistic Avignon popes. He survived his nemesis by five years but never attained full legitimacy. Upon Urban's death the conclave in Rome ignored his claims and elected Boniface IX, who pressured Clement to abdicate in the interest of healing the Great Western Schism. Up to the last breath Clement refused to budge from his claim, although he did go as far as to order the reciting of prayers and the celebration of masses praying for the removal of the schism. He finally died from a massive stroke in 1394.

FORTY-THREE

Luna Cosmediana
(The Moon of Cosmedin)

BENEDICT XIII, ANTIPOPE
(1394–1417)

THE SECOND ANTIPOPE of the Great Western Schism, and successor to Clement VII, was the Spanish "Moonie" born Pedro de Luna (*moon*). He had been the cardinal deacon of Santa Maria in Cosmedin before his election as Antipope Benedict XIII. His arms display a prominent silver reverse-crescent moon. He was one of the last cardinals to abandon the rabid Urban VI and join the rebel conclave led by Robert of Geneva (Antipope Clement VII), whom he later served as legate to Spain. He was pivotal in swinging Aragón, Castile, Navarre and Portugal into Clement's anti-papal camp.

When Clement died the anti-Sacred College of Cardinals chose Pedro chiefly because of his promise to abdicate if some agreeable resolution to the schism could be made with the Roman pontiff, Boniface IX. But once the anti-tiara burdened his schismatic head he suddenly developed an allergic antipathy to his promises.

It could be said that Benedict XIII did more than any other antipope to drag the schism deeper into Satan's abyss. He hid his obstinacy behind the appealing mask of negotiating a settlement with three legitimate popes for 15 long years. By 1409 most members of the anti- and legitimate-cardinalates of both camps were so fed up with their popes that they gathered for a council at Pisa, where they condemned Antipope Benedict and Pope Gregory VII as heretics and decided to try their luck with a third pontiff, Alexander V.

Ever the anti-papal and anal-retentive pontiff, Benedict held on to his conviction that he alone was the true Vicar of Christ, even after the Council of Constance (1414–1417) resolved the Great Western Schism. He retreated to Castile and held modest court and curia within the impregnable fortress of Peñiscola; his College of Cardinals consisted of a mere four appointees. Benedict, who would rather excommunicate the entire Church than give up the struggle, died an unforgiven heretic on 23 May 1423. To this day the citizens of Peñiscola remember him as Papa Luna (Pope *Moon of Cosmedin*). His bones were crushed and thrown out with the trash by marauding French soldiers in 1811.

FORTY-FOUR

Schisma Barchinonium
(A Schismatic of Barcelona)

CLEMENT VIII, ANTIPOPE
(1424–1429)

THE LEGITIMATE POPE Urban was followed by Boniface IX (1389–1404) and then Innocent VII (1404–1406); then he was succeeded by Oddone Colonna as Martin V (1417–1431). A little more than halfway though Martin's papacy, Antipope Benedict XIII gave up his schismatic ghost within the stone bowels of the impenetrable fortress of Peñiscola on the Spanish Riviera. His passing and the ascendancy of his replacement, Gil Sanchez Munoz, the arch priest of Teruel and former canon of *Barcelona*, was a religious joke ordained by a pitifully small college of three cardinals. Munoz accepted their unanimous vote, becoming Antipope Clement VIII – honoring the name of the man who had started the Great (and now late) Western Schism over four decades before.

The walls of Peñiscola effectively blocked out from mind and from view the forces of Queen Maria of Aragón blockading Clement's pitiful pontificate from the world. Upon hearing about the farce, Martin V instructed the bishops of Barcelona and Tortosa to either bring the little schismatic band to trial or bring them back to their senses.

The chief legacy of Clement's reign was his use by King Alfonso as political leverage to squeeze some concessions out of Martin. Once exploited, Clement was compelled by Alfonso to step down. The last act of his play as pope was to assemble his little band of cardinals and dignitaries to officially elect Oddone Colonna as Pope Martin V. After Clement discarded his papal costume to return to being Gil Sanchez Munoz, he was treated kindly by the real pope, who appointed him bishop of Majorca. He held this post until his death 17 years later in 1446.

It appears that the mottoes of St. Malachy completely overlook Antipope Benedict XIV. This schismatic piccolo pope was a certain Bernard Garnier, a simple sacrist of Rodez, France. He was nominated by Jean Carrier, the black sheep who had abandoned Clement VIII's four-man sacred college, reducing it to three. Apparently Cartier could not bring himself to uphold the election of Clement because of the man's weakness for simony, so he diced the schism at Peñiscola into even smaller silly bits. Soon after his elevation Benedict disappears from historical record.

FORTY-FIVE

De inferno prægnani
(The Pregnani from Hell)

URBAN VI
(1378–1389)

NOW THE MOTTOES switch their narrative focus to the four legitimate popes of the Great Western Schism.

Until I came in contact with the Indian mystic Osho (1931–1990), I had always taken it for granted that power can corrupt good people. But he had lowered the gauntlet by presenting a new point of view that challenged my thinking. He proposed that corruption is already hiding inside the repressed minds of so-called good people and that power in itself is neutral. Once ordinary people are given power, their repressed corruption comes to the surface.

It can be argued that Bartolomeo Prignano, the archbishop of Bari and future Urban VI, gives us a fine example of Osho's theory in action.

When the Sacred College of Cardinals met in the Vatican Basilica, just outside the angry streets of Rome, they confirmed the 60-year-old Bartolomeo Prignano as their pontiff. He was a respected authority in canon law and was widely regarded as a stable and efficient administrator. Prignano was expected to make a solid pope because of his conscientiousness, bureaucratic efficiency and love of spiritual austerity.

But once the heavy tiara crown pressed down upon his aged head the holy Papa Jekyll became a pontificating Mr. Hyde.

Behind the mask of conscientiousness hid what Peter de Rosa in *Vicars of Christ* described as one of the "most spiteful and vile-tempered of pontiffs." Once he was handed the shaft of St. Peter's crook, the sober and moderate administrator and negotiator wielded its power like the sharp end of Odin's spear, pontificating his autocratic and holy rights above all other mortals with a truculence and self-righteous obstinacy rarely bettered by the most sour popes of any era. His tirades, hurled at curia and cardinals alike, soon made his supporters fear that the sudden elevation to the highest powers of the Church had addled his mind. His violent and blistering criticisms and pronouncements also made powerful enemies of his secular supporters, such as the Holy Roman Emperor Charles IV (1355–1378), and served to alienate most of his cardinals, who abandoned him in Rome to gather at Anagni. There the French delegation declared that Urban's election had been coerced by the Roman mob under threat of death and was therefore illegitimate. Most of the members of the Sacred College of Cardinals reconvened at Fondi and proclaimed Robert of Geneva as Clement VII, the true pontiff.

The first order of business for the two popes was to excommunicate each other. For the next decade Europe drew its lines of faith between them. Burgundy, France, Naples, Savoy and Scotland sent their prayers to God through Clement VII, and England, Germany, central and northern Italy and central Europe offered obedience to Urban as their divine go-between to the Lord.

Urban could also rely on the support of Catherine of Siena, who publicly put her visionary weight behind his pontificate while she privately issued letters calling upon him to wield his new powers wisely and temper his erratic and inflammatory behavior with the monarchs of Europe.

St. Malachy's epitaph, *Pregnani from Hell*, clearly plays with this pope's Christian name *Prignano*. His birthplace was Pandino, which we are told is in the district of Naples, known as the *Inferno* because of its close proximity to Vesuvius. Abbé Joseph Maître in *La Prophétie des Papes attribuée à St. Malachie* reminds us the Prignani was archbishop of Acerenza, a place that the ancients named for its lava flows or *infernal rivers* (of Hell). The motto may have also foreseen the fire-and-brimstone bombasts of

Prignano (Urban VI) as the infernal cause of what would later be called the Great Schism of the West (1378–1417).

Throughout most of his reign Urban, convinced that he was the one God had chosen to be pontiff, did little to heal the rift splitting the Church apart. He remained in Rome while the second Church and curia of Antipope Clement VII set up court back in Avignon. Urban appointed a new curia and Sacred College of Cardinals, stuffing its chairs with 29 new men in purple. Of this number, six were later arrested, tortured and put to death when he discovered they were plotting with his one-time ally, the Holy Roman Emperor Charles IV, to convene a special council of regency to debate his sanity and ability to rule.

For most of his pontificate he focused a prodigious amount of bile and energy on retaking Naples from the supporters of Anti-pope Clement. In this obsession to seize the city of his birth his caustic tongue and unstable nature left him, by the last year of his reign, deserted by all but his most thick-skinned cardinals. Gone were the mercenaries he did not pay, and he was universally hated by the citizens of Rome. He was most likely poisoned to death in October 1389, leaving the Papal States in anarchy and the Roman Church in one of its darkest hours.

Once again Catholic prophecy watchers began reading their copies of Joachim de Fiore and St. Hildegard's *Scivias* and wondered if the Church had entered the Chastisement stage before the Second Coming. A contemporary Catholic reformer, John Wycliff (c.1330–1384), in *The Last Age of the Church* would be bold enough to use quotes from Joachim de Fiore (or pseudo-Joachite sources) to support his indictments against Urban's Church as being that of the Antichrist.

FORTY-SIX

Cubus de mixtione
(The Square of Mixture)

BONIFACE IX
(1389–1404)

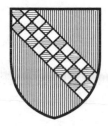

THE ARMS OF Urban VI's successor, Pietro Tomacelli of Naples, display a mixture of light and a diagonal bend of checkered silver-and-azure squares across the shield. He was voted in as the second legitimate pope of the Great Schism by the conclave made up of 14 Roman cardinals. Not much is known today about his background except that this scion of a noble but impoverished Neapolitan family was not well educated and had a sunny and affable personality which countered the well-educated and dark-tempered Urban. What he lacked in learning was compensated by his skill in political maneuvering and manipulating people. He replaced Urban's autocratic pontificating and eccentricity with articulate words and stable actions.

His rule was marked by efforts to solidify his legitimacy against Antipope Clement VII in England, Germany, Hungary and all but the southern one-third of Italy. His honeymoon with the citizens of Rome soon soured, and Boniface left the Vatican to reside first in Perugia and then in Assisi. An exposed plot to assassinate him gave Boniface the excuse to exterminate the Roman republic and return to the city as pontiff and Roman dictator. The citizens, for the most part, surrendered to his benevolent autocracy and were heartened by the pope's efforts to repair the Castel Sant'Angelo and strengthen the bridges of Rome.

When Antipope Clement VII died, Boniface excommunicated

his successor Antipope Benedict XIII. Boniface would never consider making any serious effort to negotiate with such a schismatic renegade. He did acquiesce to two perfunctory meetings with Benedict's envoys to discuss the schism. After their violent exchanges the ailing pontiff soon died. Benedict's envoys were blamed for his death and thrown into the dungeon as punishment, only to be released after the antipope paid a huge ransom.

While we are on the subject of money, Boniface goes down in papal history as one of the worst nepotists to sit as Christ's chief representative on Earth. With the Church divided he was desperate for money and sold appointments to the highest bidder; he burdened the laity with oppressive taxes and attained a new low in the excesses of indulgences – the selling of salvation for the right price.

FORTY-SEVEN

De meliore Sydere
(From a Better Star)

INNOCENT VII
(1404–1406)

IN A TURN from correct medieval superstition, the motto describes the coat of arms of the third legitimate pontiff of the Great Schism as a *better* star. Actually the celestial body in question is a golden-bearded star, or comet, drawn across the oblique of the shield of Cardinal Cosmo Gentili de' Migliorate from Sulmona, Italy. *Migliorate* in Italian means *better*.

Upon Boniface's death de' Migliorate was one of eight cardinals gathered to pick a successor. Like his antipapal opponent, the "luney" Benedict XIII, he took the pre-election pledge to do all that was morally and spiritually possible to end the schism, even if it meant stepping down from St. Peter's chair. The council he arranged with Antipope Benedict at Rome was postponed until Benedict and his anti-cardinals set sail for Genoa, in 1404, only to learn that their invitation to the council at Rome had been withdrawn.

Malachy might call the quiet and humble Innocent a *better star*, but to the common Roman citizen the pontiff with the armorial bearing of a snaking comet was as big a starry disaster as the word "comet" originally signified: an evil omen from a malevolent bearded star. Rioting plagued the city once again. Innocent was forced to flee for his life with his curia to Viterbo after the pope's brutal nephew, Ludovico Migliorati, tried to restore order by slaughtering 12 Roman civic leaders.

The pope was allowed to return in March of 1406 only because the citizens of Rome preferred the lesser of two evils. Innocent was better than the dictator that replaced him, Ladislas, king of Naples (1386–1414). Innocent had to excommunicate Ladislas before he and his mercenaries would depart the Castel Sant'Angelo.

Three months before he died in November 1406, he ordained the expansion and reorganization of the University of Rome, and laid the foundation of new faculties for the study of Greek, medicine, logic, philosophy and rhetoric.

FORTY-EIGHT

Nauta de Ponte nigro
(A Sailor from a Black Bridge)

GREGORY XII
(1406–1415)

THE FOURTH LEGITIMATE pope in the Great Western Schism was born in Venice, the city of sailors. *Black Bridge* (Negrepont) was the name of a Venetian colony on the Aegean island of Evvoea in which Angelo Correr served as a papal commendatory.

The first order of business for the decrepit octogenarian as Gregory XII was to clutch bony fingers upon the golden dome of his oversized crown and take it to be pawned off for outstanding gambling debts.

To the people of Christendom he announced his willingness to give away his title if it would bring an end to the schism. In private he made arrangements to move his curia to Rimini, where he attempted to give away Rome to the tyrant Ladislas, king of Naples, and sell off anything not bolted down in the Eternal City.

It soon became clear that the last thing Gregory would give up was the power of the pontificate. His promise to meet with Anti-pope Benedict XIII went nowhere, and his intractable stance and flagrant simony eventually compelled most of his cardinals to abandon him and meet in Pisa, in 1409, to negotiate with the equally disgusted band of anti-cardinals of Benedict XIII. By the 16th session of the Council of Pisa the cardinals had deposed both Gregory and Benedict as schismatics, obdurate heretics and perjurers. The Holy See was declared vacant. They soon filled it with the pontifical posterior of Alexander V.

Gregory's position was much weakened but he persevered, sur-viving Alexander's brief reign and that of his notorious successor, Antipope John XXIII. Gregory tenaciously held on to life and his claim as St. Peter's true successor until well into his 90th year, when he agreed to the terms of the Council of Constance (1414–1418) and resigned as pope on 4 July 1415. His pontifical acts were formally ratified and he was appointed cardinal bishop of Porto. He died near Ancona, Italy, two years later, and three weeks before the election of Martin V, who ended the Great Schism.

FORTY-NINE

Flagellum solis
(The Scourge of the Sun)

ALEXANDER V, ANTIPOPE
(1409–1410)

IT IS STILL debated today whether the Greek Cardinal Pietro Philarghi was an antipope or a true pontiff. He was chosen at the Council of Pisa to replace antipope Benedict XIII and Pope Gregory XII, who were both requested to retire and bring an end to the Great Western Schism.

Prior to his consecration as Alexander V, Philarghi, a one-time street urchin and orphan roving the streets of the Venetian colony of Candia, on the island of Crete, rose from the ranks of the Franciscans. He performed missionary work in Bohemia, Poland and Russia, finally holding a chair in theology in Pavia, where he began writing works on theology which are considered medieval classics to this day. He became archbishop of Milan in 1402, a cardinal in 1405 and his eloquent pen and tongue played an important role in preliminary negotiations to set up the Council of Pisa in 1409. Thus Philarghi was chosen as Pope Alexander V of the Pisan gathering of cardinals and for the next ten months, until he unexpectedly died, the Christian world had to choose between three Vicars of Christ.

Alexander's short reign began with much hope for reform, but ultimate power placed in the hands of even this gifted and literate theologian hatched a repressed lust for showering lavish gifts to his political and theological bedfellows and other cronies.

The theological reformer John Wycliffe was condemned by Alexander for his teachings and his unapproved interpretation of Joachim de Fiore. Wycliffe depicted the pontificate of Alexander as the expected Antichrist foreseen to threaten and destroy the Church from within before the end of the world.

Alexander was pressured by his friend, the seductive and ruthless Cardinal Baldassare Cossa, to set up his papal headquarters in the cardinal's city of Bologna while the cardinal strapped on his armor and buckler to lead papal armies in a protracted siege of Rome. Once the Romans submitted to Cossa, Alexander received their invitation to bring home his pontificate.

But this was not to be. Alexander suddenly died. Rumors spread around Bologna and Rome that Cardinal Cossa had poisoned him so that as his successor he could take the prize of Rome.

Perhaps the *scourge* of an ill-starred anti-pontificate was foreseen in the motto's metaphor for Alexander's coat of arms – an azure shield dominated by a gnarly gold star with eight twisted tongues of flame surrounded by eight smaller stars. These may have appeared to the author of these mottoes like balls of fire falling from heaven like an evil omen.

FIFTY

Cervus Sirenæ
(The Stag of Syrenæ)

JOHN XXIII, ANTIPOPE
(1410–1415)

THIS LATIN MOTTO packs cardinalate titles and poetic twists which can describe Baldassare Cossa, one of the most dashingly brutal and godless antipopes to ever raid the succession of St. Peter. After Baldassare's stint as a pirate fighting in the naval war between Louis II d'Anjou (1377–1417) and Ladislas of Naples, he raided the priesthood, rising to the rank of papal legate and deacon cardinal of St. Estachio in Naples. From *Parthenope* (the ancient name of Naples taken from a mythical siren) we get SYRENAE. The emblem of St. Estachio is a stag (CERVUS). By using CERVUS, or *stag*, the motto represents this adventurer's nature and his virility with the "hinds" at court. The antlers of the stag represent military prowess, a talent that the late Boniface IX noticed in his fellow Bolognian when the latter laid down his pirate sword to fight with subtler weapons of mind and faith as a newly ordained priest. Boniface made him archdeacon of the city and later his papal treasurer, and this fiercely ambitious and amoral political animal assisted the pope in his unscrupulous money-raising schemes.

In 1404 Boniface made him cardinal deacon of San Eustachio and sent him charging into Romagna and Bologna as his legate to ruthlessly restore them to the Papal States. It was rumored that Cossa mounted 200 women during his legation.

This brings us to another poetic layer of the motto's use of *Cyrenæ*. Ancient Libya was the home of the Cyrenaic philosophy, a minor school of ancient Greek thinking which believed that knowledge is unreliable and useless; that a man should try to control his circumstances rather than be controlled by them. They believed that the path of immediate pleasure in the moment was preferable to the pursuit of intellectual contemplation. Thus Baldassare Cossa could be characterized as hedonistic Cyreniac in all of its darker aspects. Gossip had it that he never took confession or partook of the sacrament of Holy Communion. Privately he admitted that he did not believe in the soul's immortality or in the resurrection of the dead at Judgment Day. Many of his intimates suspected that he was an atheist.

Baldassare Cossa was instrumental in arranging the Council of Pisa. Ostensibly he sought to bring an end to the Great Western Schism, but secretly he calculated that any good merit earned there would lay a carpet for him as close to the chair of St. Peter as possible. With Pope Gregory XII and Antipope Benedict XIII deposed he was instrumental in seeing his friend, Cardinal Pietro Philarghi, consecrated at Pisa as Antipope Alexander V.

In poetic Latin the plural form of CERVUS describes stakes stuck in the ground to form a palisade for military defense. After influencing Alexander to make his headquarters within Cossa's political territory, the city of Bologna, our ambitious *stag* was commanded by the new antipope to set his armies in a ring of palisade *stags* around Rome in a protracted siege. When the citizens of Rome submitted to his forces Alexander suddenly and suspiciously died and Cossa rode into Rome as his successor, John XXIII.

In 1411, the year Christendom had three popes, he took charge of the Eternal City, assured of the most support and political clout of the three Vicars rutting for St. Peter's chair. He summoned a reform council in 1412, but after two years of discussion and condemnations no solid progress towards ending the schism was made. With his political capital stuck on the greater horns of the unresolved schism, John finally yielded to pressure from his cardinals and the future Holy Roman Emperor, Sigismund of Germany (1368–1437), to convene a general council at Lake Constance. When the council voted that all three popes should abdicate to end the schism, John maneuvered and resisted abdication for a week. After escaping Constance in the hope that he could disrupt the council, he was eventually hunted down. The bagged Stag of Cyreniac manners, disguised as a page, was brought back to Constance to stand trial. He was accused of being a libertine, perjurer and a bald-faced practitioner of simony. He was reduced to a de-horned, broken buck, eager to submit to their judgment and proclaim their infallibility. He renounced his rights to the papacy for life and became Baldassare Cossa once again.

The new pope, Martin V, had him thrown into a posh prison in Germany for three years until the elector Ludwig III of Bavaria, in 1419, purchased his freedom from Martin with a vast sum. After Cossa's submission Pope Martin apparently looked the other way and had the notorious rapist of court ladies and the murderer of Alexander V appointed cardinal bishop of Tusculum. He died in Florence at the end of that same year, a spent and burned-out man at age 59.

FIFTY-ONE

Corona veli auri
(The Crown with the Golden Veil)

MARTIN V
(1417–1431)

THE LATIN PHRASE correctly describes the cardinalate post of the first universally recognized Holy Father after the Council of Constance resolved the Great Western Schism. Cardinal Oddone of the powerful Colonna family would serve as deacon cardinal of S. Giorgio in Velabro (*Velum aureum* – VELI AURI). The Colonna arms display a pillar topped by a *crown*. His reign began with much expectation and hope for reform. The Council of Constance had established that such gatherings of Church leaders had, like the pope, a direct line to Christ. According to the new arrangements in the post-schismatic Church, a pontiff must pledge to continue to convene regular gatherings of Holy Councils. He was to act less like an autocrat of Christ and more like a collaborator in governing Christ's Church; in other words, he should be more like a papal president contending with a congress of cardinals.

He united cardinals from the Avignon and Roman cardinalates and his reforms did much to bring order and discipline to the curia and the priesthood at large. But it could be said that the *veil of gold* would also pass before his eyes: he stubbornly held on to a pope's right to abuse benefices.

Once Oddone had been ordained as Martin V he made haste to put himself spiritually and geographically as far away from the constraints of Constance as he could. He would postpone and derail future councils and effectively stifle the Church of Rome's experiment in spiritual democracy.

Martin, the harsh martinet, is defined by history as the founder of the monarchical papacy. He fought a bloody war to bring the Papal States back into his control and effectively brought the cardinals under his will, successfully nullifying most of the reforms arranged at Constance and the council at Pavia (1423). He was forced to accede to the wide-ranging demands for a council to be held at Basel in 1431, but he picked his own president, Cardinal Cesarini, and gave him autocratic powers to suspend or dismiss their resolutions.

Martin died of a sudden stroke, little more than three weeks after Cesarini was sent off with the Holy Father's blessing to throw his staff, as it were, in the council's machinery.

FIFTY-TWO

Lupa cœlestina[1]
(A Celestinian She-wolf)

EUGENIUS IV
(1431–1447)

THE MOTTO GIVES us a subtle riddle for the successor of Martin V. Cardinal Gabriello Condulmaro took vows as an Augustinian

[1]CŒLESTINA = from *cælestin*: lofty, heavenly, from heaven.

monk, and not as a Celestinian as Ciacconius believed. Abbé Maître points out that as bishop of Siena he adopted the arms of the city, which are those of a she-wolf.

Cardinal Condulmaro participated in the Council of Constance. He apparently was little affected by the council's experimentation with more democratic forms of governing the Church. The many rain drops of its revolutionary reforms were just so much water falling off a wolf's thick coat of fur – such as putting an end to simony, banning concubinage in the clergy and allowing ecclesiasts in each country more administrational and financial independence from Rome. The bishops and cardinals of the new conciliarism movement at Constance had declared an end to the abuses of ban and anathema by popes and ordained that from now on the pope and his curia could no longer demand or receive any fees for ecclesiastical offices. The pope was obliged to turn his mind and energies away from obsessing over worldly treasures and turn his prayers and attention to the spiritual needs of Christians as they prepare for the world to come.

At the conclave to elect the next pope, Cardinal Condulmaro was the top candidate because he had played such an influential role at the Council of Constance. He had also made a big show of publicly promising to nurture conciliarism's chief edict: to oversee the new reforms that allowed the council of cardinals to regularly meet and share the administration of the Church. He was therefore elected to St. Peter's throne to become Eugenius IV.

What strange magic does the papal crown have on the pious heads of those men chosen to wear it? No sooner is it mounted upon the bony temple of a human ego than its weighty pressure pinches off all promises for temperance, then it presses hard to conjure the hidden lusts for absolute power. Not long after the crown had creased the forehead of the new pope, Eugenius shape-shifted into a protective predator werewolf defending Church autocracy. In his troubled reign he would eventually crush the reforms of Constance and all other councils convened during his pontificate and effectively kill the brief and promising experiment in Church democracy.

Many historians believe Eugenius' impulsive actions and political naïvety made him the pawn of history's events rather than the pawnbroker. He had a chance to revolutionize the Church, and if he had had the courage perhaps the Protestant Reformation of the next century and the ruinous religious wars which killed off half of central Europe's population and forever undermined the Church's credibility in world history may have never happened. By censuring the best chances for authentic reforms which could have led to a more "Christian" rather than "Roman" Church, Eugenius is responsible for the papacy's descent into its darkest and most unholy succession of pontiffs by the end of the 15th century.

FIFTY-THREE

Amator crucis
(A Lover of the Cross)

FELIX V, ANTIPOPE
(1439–1449)

THE COUNCIL OF CONSTANCE (1414–1418) ordained that regular meetings must be convened by the pope with the cardinals and bishops of the Church. The next reform meeting was sanctioned by Martin V and further confirmed by Eugenius IV to take place in Basel, Switzerland, in July 1431. But Eugenius soon showed his true colors when he declared the gathering of Church leaders as a "beggarly mob, mere vulgar fellows from the lowest dregs of the clergy, apostates, blaspheming rebels, men guilty of sacrilege, gaolbirds, men who without exception deserve only to be hunted back to the devil whence they came."

Sparse attendance and ample paranoia from Eugenius resulted

in the dissolution of the council of Basel six months later in December 1439. The pope promised to reconvene a new council with himself as its director (or rather, dictator) in 18 months' time. His actions were met with rebellion at Basel. The council declared his pontificate null and void, and a rump council of 1 cardinal and 32 electing abbots and bishops nominated a layman known for his deep love of the Church, Amadeus VIII, duke of Savoy, to replace Eugenius as Antipope Felix V.

There are a lot of pun-pushing word-plays with AMATOR CRUCIS. For one thing the Christian name "Amadeus" essentially means AMATOR – "one who has a passionate love of God." This *lover of the cross* had a large silver one on a gules background on his coat of arms.

Amadeus began his journey towards the cross deeply saddened by the loss of his beloved wife in 1422 and his son in 1431. He retired to a life of seclusion and prayer and established a spiritual order of knights (the Order of St. Maurice) along the shores of Lake Geneva at Rapaille. It was there that a delegation from Basel came to announce his election as antipope. He at first resisted, but his deep concern for the Church's future and hope for a return to its earlier, less political and pontifical roots compelled him to accept their offer.

As Felix V he ruled over the council but his authority had little influence beyond his own lands. In the decade of his anti-pontificate Eugenius, who held far more political clout with the monarchs of Europe, effectively isolated Felix. These rulers felt more comfortable dealing with (and sometimes fighting with) an autocratic pope from Rome than with a more democratically elected pontiff directly answerable to the priesthood of his Church.

After overseeing the Council of Basel for seven years Felix became disenchanted with the chaos of democracy and the quibbling of the council. He moved his curia back to Savoy but soon surrendered to reality and the counsel of his secretary, Aeneas Sylvius Piccolomini (the future Pope Pius II). All evidence pointed to the fact that Eugenius' successor, the more tactful Nicholas V, was too powerful and the schism must be negotiated to a conclusion. On 7 April 1449 Felix abdicated as antipope. Nicholas

V, who was more tolerant and forgiving than his predecessor, had him appointed cardinal and apostolic vicar-general of Savoy.

Amadeus, the last of the antipopes, died on 7 January 1451.

FIFTY-FOUR

De modicitate Lunæ
(From the Temperance of the Moon)

NICHOLAS V
(1447–1455)

CARDINAL TOMMASO PARENTUCELLI, the former humanist tutor of Italian royalty, would succeed the contentious *she-wolf* Eugenius IV as Nicholas V. Born at Luna, near La Spezia, this intellectual and passionate lover of books founded the Vatican Library and would be remembered as the first Renaissance pope. The motto may imply two things: Parentucelli's humble birthplace named *moon* and the *temperance* of his pontificate. Nicholas had humanist sympathies and he encouraged the general openness of the new era of learning and love of the arts. Nicholas was pivotal in making the papacy a direct collaborator in the Italian Renaissance. His court in Rome was filled with scholars, humanists and artists. He dug deep into the Church coffers to finance the restoration of Rome's dilapidated bridges, churches, palaces and other important buildings. He reasoned that these improvements in the stone facades of Rome, plus the Church's patronage of arts and letters, enhanced the city and the papacy's merit as a leader of culture as well as of the faith.

His *temperance* of mind fashioned a few tactful concessions to achieve a peaceful resolution of the schism of Felix V and the rump council of Basel.

Nicholas' temperance would wane when he became more paranoid in his final years, after discovering and liquidating a band of conspirators preparing to assassinate him. Next came the loss of Eastern Christendom's ancient capital to the *moon* soldiers of

Islam. In 1453 the crescent-moon flags of the Ottoman Turks rose over the great churches of Constantinople after a long and bloody siege. Malachy's term MODICITATE can also stand for "littleness" or "pettiness" as in the pettiness of the European monarchs who did not soldier their finances and forces to the pontiff's call for a crusade to deliver Constantinople from the Turks.

Nicholas died a disheartened man in March 1455. He had hoped to be remembered as the pontiff who restored Rome to its architectural glory, established the papacy as the patron of the Renaissance and delivered Constantinople back to Christ. The strains of the latter ambition overwhelmed his physical and financial resources and significantly drew his energies away from his humanist ambitions. The most important issue left unresolved by his death was the urgent need for Church reform.

FIFTY-FIVE

Bos pascens
(A Bull Browsing)

CALLISTUS III
(1455–1458)

NICHOLAS' SUCCESSOR WOULD come from Valencia, Spain. At the advanced age of 77, Cardinal Alfonso de Borgia was chosen by the conclave as a compromise between two unacceptable candidates: one favored the Colonna family and the other, John Bessarion (1403–1472), a noted humanist and theologian, was a Greek. Anyway, no one expected the creaking and gout-ridden cardinal from Spain to be anything more than a short-lived care-taker pope.

The papal oddsmakers were partially correct. The new Callistus III's coat of arms of a red bull browsing in a field adorned the churches of Rome for a brief three years. But in that time he would become a diligent bull in the china shop of Church reform, shattering any porcelain-thin hope that the discarnate soul of his predecessor had for a political and spiritual renovation of the Church.

Callistus would push the foot of the papacy deeper into the cow patty of nepotism. Although he was at face value austere, pious and retiring, his psychological release valve for corruption tempted him to spew honors, titles and wealth over his relatives. He promoted two young nephews, still in the blush and debaucheries of their early 20s, to the cardinalate. Callistus went as far as to appoint one of them, the ruthless and murderous Rodrigo Borgia, to be vice chancellor of the curia, setting the stage for his future advent as one of the papacy's most anti-Christian pontiffs.

The aged Callistus showed surprising energy when lobbying Christian monarchs to collect moneys and mercenaries for a crusade against the Turks. The venture drew lukewarm support. Some islands in the Aegean were retaken by a crusader fleet more modest than expected.

He was a major disappointment to the humanist movement cultivated by his predecessor. But the free thinkers and artists of the Renaissance could find solace in papal disinterest; at least it was better than censure.

Before he died Callistus reopened the investigation of Joan of Arc and declared her innocent of witchcraft. His most noted reform effort was to direct the Church policy against Jews towards a new low in Christian and Semite relations: banning all social interaction of Christians with "those who killed the Christ."

The day Callistus died the citizens of Rome rose up to over-throw his universally hated Spanish relatives and appointees.

FIFTY-SIX

De capra et albergo
(From a She-goat and a Tavern)

PIUS II
(1458–1464)

OUT WENT THE rampaging bull of Valencia and in came one of the greatest humanist popes of the Renaissance. Enea Silvio (or Aeneas Sylvanus) Piccolomini, the son of impoverished royalty, knew the humble life of a farmer. As a boy he tilled the fields at Corsignano, near Siena.

The sermons of the later-canonized St. Bernard of Siena (1380–1444) set his heart afire with the desire to become a monk. His intellect and literary gifts were not destined to mold away in a secluded cell, nor was his brilliance fated to grow anemic in the dark shadows of monastic halls. He remained a lay Catholic and academic, studying in Florence with the famous humanist Francesco Filelfo (d. 1481). His eloquence and diplomatic skills fostered Aeneas' rapid ascent in the ranks of the Church to become secretary to a number of bishops and prelates present at the Council of Basel (1432–1435). The motto DE CAPRA ET ALBERGO alludes to his roles as diplomatic errant of Cardinal Niccolò Albergati (ALBERGO), and later as secretary to the influential Cardinal Caprancia (CAPRA). His missions to Germany also made a powerful supporter out of the Holy Roman Emperor, Frederick III (1440–1493), who would award him the status of poet laureate and invite him to become his own diplomat.

For the next ten years he enjoyed a hedonistic life, siring several bastard children and two literary Renaissance classics: the popular amorous adventure novel *Lucretia and Euryalus* and the erotic comedy *Chrysis*. The deaths of his children, compounded by a serious illness and the final sputtering flame of a dissolute mid-life crisis, compelled Aeneas to enter the priesthood. In his new calling he convinced his friend, Emperor Frederick, and the German electors to abandon their neutrality in the Great Schism and recognize Eugenius IV. For this deed he was rapidly promoted to bishop by Nicholas V and to cardinal by Callistus III. At this time he wrote the renowned biography of Frederick III.

His own deft negotiations during the conclave of 1458 maneuvered him into election as successor to Callistus III. He chose the name Pius more for literary than pious reasons, out of love for one of his favorite classical literary heroes, Virgil's *pius Aeneas*.

The weighty metal dome of his crown cooled his humanism. The powerful heights of being St. Peter's successor on Earth made him look down his nose at fellow humanists: he became a distant if not cordial critic rather than their hoped-for patron. The Catholic layman who once worked so hard to promote the equality of councils to the pontificate reversed himself as pope, ordering that his earlier anti-papal writings be ignored.

"Believe the old man and not the youth," he ordered. "Reject Aeneas and accept Pius."

In 1460 he slapped the last ladle of cement against the tomb door of his progressive youth when he issued the bull *Excerabilis*, denouncing all appeals to a pope from future councils.

His six-year pontificate was overshadowed by the advance of the Turks into the Mediterranean and Eastern Europe. He promoted further crusades against the invading Muslims with mixed success. He even wrote a letter to Sultan Mehmet II, using his literary skills to try to convince the infidel to abandon the Koran and become his baptized emperor and ally of a new Christian Eastern Empire.

As it turned out, Pius never sent the letter. Frail and prematurely aged by his eventful life he died at age 59, at Ancona, on the day a pitifully small Venetian fleet arrived to embark a pitifully smaller army of mercenaries in the harbor in answer to one of his calls for a crusade.

FIFTY-SEVEN

De Cervo et Leone
(From a Stag and a Lion)

PAUL II
(1464–1471)

THE VENETIAN CARDINAL Pietro Barbo, nephew of Eugenius IV, who once was bishop of Cervia (CERVO), chose an ostentatious lion-emblazoned coat of arms to decorate the Vatican.

No Renaissance pontiff endured more literary cuts and slashes to his ego than Pope Paul II. His relationship with priests and learned laymen turned sour when he backpedaled on promises to purge the Church of the corruption and nepotism of his two predecessors, the Borgian pope Callistus III and Pius II.

Pietro as Paul II was physically attractive and certainly vain. The cardinals who cast their ballot for him had to dissuade Pietro from adopting the title Pope Formosa ("handsome" in Greek).

He had a schizophrenic relationship with Renaissance artists and thinkers. On the one hand he was their patron, but he closed the Roman Academy in 1468 in a fit of paranoia, believing that the school's faculty were secretly polluting the Roman youth with pagan ideas. When one of the faculty members, Bartolomeo Platina (1421–1481), openly condemned the pope's predecessor, Pius II, as a tyrant, Paul had him thrown into the dungeons of Castle Sant'Angelo to do penance.

When Bartolomeo protested, the pope ordered the historian tortured. Such actions, added to Paul's dilettantism and awkward Latin, made him hated by intellectuals though they did accept his lavish contributions of silver and gold to the arts. This avowed hater of paganism did support other aspects of humanism. He also restored the ancient pagan Arches of Titus and Septimius Severus and, like pagan emperors of yore, won the common citizens of Rome over to his camp by staging public games and epic entertainments.

He had exceedingly favorable relations with the Holy Roman Emperor Frederick III, although the emperor would not go to war with the Turks even after the pope spent a fortune on an extravagant banquet in his honor when he visited Rome.

Speaking of food, Paul died of a stroke three years later after gorging on one too many melons at another sumptuous repast.

It is fair to say that he missed the opportunity to implement the reforms necessary to temper the growing excesses of the Renaissance papacy. But his true legacy suffers from the facts and traumas stitched together in ink from the quill of Bartolomeo Platina who, once released from his dungeon, would be appointed as the Vatican's new biographer four years after Pope Paul's death.

FIFTY-EIGHT

Piscator Minorita[1]
(A Minorite Fisherman)

SIXTUS IV
(1471–1484)

How WOULD St. Francis of Assisi consider the earthly development of Francesco della Rovere, the poor man's son from Celle, near Savona, who would later become a pope?

Would not his spirit smile upon the nine-year-old, seeing him stripped of his worldly raiment to be dressed in the tattered gray and threadbare badge of the saint, the robe of the Franciscan order? And if the spirit of St. Francis descended to this sinful

---

[1]MINORITA = from *Friars Minor*, the name given to the Franciscan order by its founder, St. Francis of Assisi.

Earth, would he not find a safe haven behind the luster of eyes so pious?

Forty-eight years pass, and if St. Francis descended again from heaven to check on the progress of the boy his spirit would behold a middle-aged cardinal sitting in the midst of the conclave held after Paul II's death. The boy who had become a respected theologian and general of his own Franciscan Order, was about to ascend to St. Peter's chair as Pope Sixtus IV.

St. Francis preserve him! What has happened to his piety?

The once chaste child has grown to sire a number of bastard children, whom he calls his "nephews." He awards chamber pots made of gold to his stable of mistresses for easing the pressure of his vow of celibacy with their carnal arts.

After Francesco della Rovere became Pope Sixtus IV it would take the patience and depth of compassion of a great soul like St. Francis to endure what was done in his and Christ's name.

Sixtus would license brothels in Rome and earn himself 30,000 ducats a year. Not a peddler of bogus parts of saints was he. Sixtus would exploit the simple souls of Christendom by selling indulgences to the dead. Ladies and gentlemen, step right up and save your dearly departed, sweltering in Purgatory. Submit yourself to a vow of financial ruin and the Franciscan pope promises to deliver straight to heaven, by means of your livelihood yard sale, the soul of your departed father, your dead mother, your stillborn children, your expired wife, your husband; yea, even the nagging ghost of your mother-in-law!

In place of the pious prayers of a nine-year-old was a pope scheming a litany of larceny. Prayer cannot save you; only money can – that was his secret motto. And if a priest let his saintly peter slip outside his vow of celibacy, Sixtus was forgiving as long as the backside-slider paid the tax leveled on tens of thousands of priests with wives.

And then there was the matter of the Spanish Inquisition.

Sixtus blessed and set it into motion in 1478 to investigate the Christian credentials of newly baptized Jews and Muslims after most of Spain was reconquered from the Moors. To this day the Spanish Inquisition remains an unhealed stigmata wound on the reputation of the Roman Church. Sixtus appointed the infamous Tomàs de Torquemada (1420–1498) as grand inquisitor.

Within three years this Reinhard Heydrich[1] of the Holy Father burned two thousand Jews and Muslim citizens in Andalusia alone; in a decade Torquemada had condemned hundreds of thousands of men, women and children to rot in dungeons across Spain. He also had 114,000 people tortured to death, including 10,200 who were burned alive simply because their conversion to Christianity was under suspicion.

The boy who had pledged to suffer like Christ on the cross crucified the Church. Once Sixtus held power he waved off his oath to reform the Church and canceled all decrees of the Council of Constance (1414–1417), effectively making the pope God's holy autocrat on Earth, without any checks and balances from ecumenical councils. He made cardinals out of his two bastards Pietro Riatrio and Giuliano della Rovere (the future Julius II). It must be noted that it was popular in the days of the debauched Renaissance popes to say that their bastard child was the Holy Father's "nephew." Sixtus advanced more relatives to positions of power and stuffed their coffers full with more Vatican gold than any nepotistic pontiff before him.

What words of eternal condemnation would reach the grieving soul of St. Francis from Earth in the days following the death of Sixtus?

"He waded miter-deep in crime and bloodshed."

"He laid waste to Italy with his wars."

"He embodied the utmost possible concentration of human wickedness."

"He lowered the moral tone of Europe."

If St. Francis could have endured one last descent to sinful Earth to say farewell to the corpse of a hell-bound pope, he might have taken pity on his final mortal indignity. In the Holy Father's apartments he would have found the corpse of Sixtus lying inside a bedroom stripped clean of all valuables. He would watch John Burchard, the pope's German chaplain, looking furtively from side to side to be sure that no one sees him strip off his master's death-soiled nightshirt, his only remaining garment, using it to wash the body.

Perhaps St. Francis would think: there he is, a Franciscan at

---

[1]Reinhard Heydrich, second in command of the SS Gestapo, assassinated 1943.

last, without a possession, nor even a thread to wear, just as a Franciscan friar should meet his maker.

FIFTY-NINE

Præcursor Siciliæ
(A Forerunner from Sicily)

INNOCENT VIII
(1484–1492)

NOT LONG AFTER Burchard searched through the remains of the late pope's sacked apartments to find a simple cassock and a cast-away pair of slippers to clothe his corpse for burial, the conclave convened to seek God's help, bribes and any other political ploy to elect a new pontiff.

The "nephew" of the dead pope, Cardinal Guiliano della Rovere (Julius II), knew he could not swing, promise or pay off enough cardinals to win the pontificate this time, so he backed someone he could manipulate. His calculating eye fell on the sickly and anemic Cardinal Giovanni Batista Cibò, the son of Neapolitan nobles. His father, Arano Cibò, was the viceroy of Sicily and he was named after Christ's *forerunner*, John the Baptist. The cardinal hoped that the influence he applied to elect his favorite as Innocent VIII would lead to Cibò becoming the *forerunner* of Rovere's own pontificate.

Innocent's eight-year rule mirrored the debaucheries, atrocities and corruption of Sixtus. He had his own gaggle of bastard children, whom he promoted to high rank. Cardinal Guiliano manipulated him into marrying off his favorite son, Franchesch-etto, to the Medicis of Florence, setting the stage for future catastrophes for the Church. The cardinal also convinced him to wage a ruinous war against Ferdinand I of Naples (1423–1494). Afterwards the peace treaty sealed the papacy's loss of L'Aquila as well as most of its political clout on the Italian peninsula.

Innocent entered an insolvent pontificate thanks to the excesses of his predecessor, so he continued to promote indulgences and sold fabricated bureaucratic positions to the highest bidder. He earned a further 40,000 ducats per annum by keeping the wayward brother of Sultan Beyezid II (1481–1512) under luxurious house arrest in Rome.

When Granada, the last Moorish stronghold in Spain, fell in 1492 a jubilant Innocent pressed the grand inquisitor, Torquemada, to intensify his purge of Moors and Jews. Those who would not convert were swept clear of Spain, resulting in what Peter de Rosa called "a wave of emigration not matched until the 1930s in Nazi Germany."

He drove the papacy to a new low in religious atrocity by issuing the bull *Summis Desiderantes* in 1484, declaring war against witches. Thus began centuries of persecution by the Inquisition in central Europe to rival the terror of Hitler and Stalin. No one knows how many women were arrested on rumors and hearsay alone, and then sent to investigations without legal counsel. Over the next 300 years hundreds of thousands – perhaps even millions – of women disappeared in the middle of the night never to return from God's gulag. The women were dragged down into dungeons to be stripped naked, then shaved clean of all their body and head hair before they were tortured and mutilated until they confessed whatever the brooding Franciscan and Dominican brothers wanted them to say. The survivors of the ordeal were summarily hung or burned to death whether they confessed or not.

When Innocent, at age 60, was wracked with his final sickness, it is said that he drank nursemaids' milk and had his doctors bleed several boys to death to supply transfusions of youthful blood to replace the exhausted corpuscles in his collapsing veins.

When his chaplain came to give him his last rites he saw the pope in bed, his radiant face, body and bedclothes soaked with the spilled blood of his last transfusion victim. The pope was convinced that he was forgiven of any sin.

"I come to You, Lord, in my *Innocence*," he said, breathing his last.

No pope before him had left papacy in such a state of anarchy and violence. The prayers of many ordinary Catholics across Europe were pleas to God to send a pontiff who could save the

Church from its descent into anti-Christianity. What came next made many Christians lose heart and believe that God's light had gone out in Rome.

SIXTY

Bos Albanus in portu
(An Alban Bull in the Port)

ALEXANDER VI
(1492–1503)

IT HAS BEEN said that Cardinal Rodrigo de Borgia was no hypocrite. He did not act holier than thou and did not put on any airs of piety by day while pumping mistresses by night. He knew he was a predatory wolf in the Lamb of God's clothing. To him, being Holy Father – God's ultimate servant of the servants of Christ on Earth – was good business, a stroke of luck not to be wasted by a false front of saintliness. Being pope gave him and his family the unique advantage of exploiting secular and spiritual power over Europe's Christians.

Rodrigo could thank his maternal uncle, the late Callistus III, for expanding his appetite for wealth siphoned off the collection plates of the Church. When growing up at Játiva, near Valencia, he witnessed the Borgia family being transformed by the magic wand of nepotism from small landowners to well-laced and ruffle-collared ruffians. Money sent home by a papal patriarch gave their passions license. If young Rodrigo at age 12 could disembowel a playmate by repeated thrusts of his child-sized sword, who dared protest when his uncle was chief priest of Catalan? And when the unatoned young man had found something else to poke indiscriminately, this time at the ladies and harlots of Spain, he became a religious prince of the most powerful see in Spain, becoming archbishop of Valencia in 1456 at the age of 25.

Did the husbands and brothers of raped and ravaged girls and women avenge their honor? Who would have the nerve to question the actions – or tempt the wrath – of the secret agents of the archbishop's uncle, the pope?

Within a year Archbishop Rodrigo is named a cardinal deacon. He is beckoned by his uncle to ride, as it were, the papal *bull* of his family's coat of arms up the ladder of titles, receiving along the way gifts of politically significant bishoprics and abbeys – including the bishoprics of Albano and Porto (ALBANUS IN PORTU) – until he is appointed vice chancellor of the Holy See itself by 1547. Once positioned with his meaty hands on the Vatican's purse strings, Rodrigo became fantastically wealthy, holding on to his position through the reigns of four popes.

The new vice chancellor set down to bed his beloved mistress, Vannozza Catanei, and spawn a herd of bastard children the likes of which Italy would wish to forget. Little Juan de Borgia, his favorite son, would be brutally murdered by his brother, Cesare Borgia. His father would find his dagger-perforated corpse floating in the Tiber River. Cesare would step in to fill the void he created and become his father's evil conscience as well as Machiavelli's model of political calculation and ruthlessness in his classic *The Prince*.

Rodrigo loved his daughter, the fetching Lucretzia, enough to occasionally be her lover. Later, when he became pope, she acted as his virtual regent in Rome when he was away on papal business or visiting one of his mistresses in other Italian cities.

Only one of the three successors to his uncle dared to do anything more than verbally chastise the vice chancellor of the church for his vices. Even then Pius II broached the subject with care, as he had a few bastards in his own closet.

The man who fathered Machiavelli's favorite political animal had his own street smarts and a whole grab-bag of political talents. He had the high energy, patience and an authentic genius for administration to pave the way to his ultimate ambition.

The death of Innocent VIII gave him his chance. Rodrigo had amassed the second-largest fortune held by any cardinal in Christendom just for the day he could bribe the conclave to vote him in as St. Peter's successor. It is said that he gave four mule-loads of silver to his chief rival, Cardinal Sforza, to step aside. Despite this he was still one vote short. Once his wealth was exhausted the famous Borgia luck came to the rescue. All that remained between him and his goal was the ballot of one senile 96-year-old cardinal, who happened to cast his ballot for Rodrigo without receiving even a ducat.

The conclave gave praise to God for helping them choose a new successor to St. Peter. He took the name Alexander VI and could not care less that the name was held last by an antipope. His chief rivals, Giovanni de Medici and Cardinal della Rovere, fled Rome. The future Leo X and Julius II understood too well that an avaricious wolf had been crowned shepherd to Christ's sheep, and they wisely removed themselves from the reach of his jaws.

The year the papacy elected its most secular pope was 1492, the same year Christopher Columbus (1446?–1506) discovered the New World. What is less well known is that these two acts play an important role in the progress of Catholic prophecy towards doomsday. Alexander's assault on the virtues of the Catholic Church no doubt influenced the spiritual direction of Martin Luther, who at the time of the pope's ordination was a boy. He would later terminate the Church of Rome's spiritual autocracy over Western Europe by becoming the prophet of the Protestant Reformation.

It is not widely known that Columbus was inspired to discover an Atlantic route to India in part because he was an avid reader of the controversial prophecies of the Joachim de Fiore cult. He saw himself as God's instrument to spread the Gospel to all the inhabitants of Earth. He believed that this act must precede Joachim's foreseen advent of the Age of the Holy Spirit. In 1493, when Columbus returned on a second voyage and began to spread the gospel – and the plague – to the natives of the New World, the new pope contributed to Columbus' interpretation of prophecy by issuing a bull dividing between Portugal and Spain the spoils of native slaves and wealth expected from the New World.

The reign of Alexander VI did produce some positive accomplishments. The Castel Sant'Angelo was refurbished and Alexander built the marvelous 11,000-thousand room Borgia Palace at the Vatican. He encouraged and financed the studies of the astronomer Copernicus and was also a lavish patron of some of greatest artists of the Renaissance, such as Pinturicchio and Michelangelo. The latter could be seen next to the tall and broad-shouldered *bull* of a pontiff bending over the legendary sculptor's plans for the creation of a new St. Peter's Basilica. Without the Borgia pope's help, the most inspired paintings and sculptures of Michelangelo and many other artists depicting what is noble in the human spirit would never have graced the world. Thanks to Alexander's visionary plans the great dome of St. Peter's – the very symbol of the grandeur of the Catholic Church – would eventually rise to dominate the Roman skyline a century later.

When he first became pope, Alexander had promised Church reform. He gained respect for enforcing harsh and swift edicts to end the civil violence plaguing Rome, but nepotism, bodice-busting and booty hunts – be it of the flesh or the coin – postponed the pledged Church reform. Until, that is, one terrible morning five years into his reign when the waterlogged body of his favorite son, Juan, was fished out of the fetid brown waters of the Tiber.

"At last our pontiff truly is a fisher of men," observed the average Roman wag.

Alexander sincerely grieved the loss and vowed to God that he would clean up his act, get himself and the entire priesthood on the good side of celibacy and dedicate their lives to Christ and Church reform. The Holy Father's hand drafted a papal bull chock full of far-reaching reforms.

It never saw the light of day.

Cesare Borgia, Juan's suspected murderer and his father's new chief family advisor, made sure that it remained stuffed away somewhere in bureaucratic limbo.

The quill itching to scratch out its revitalization of Christ's Church found its feathered tail plucked out of the pontiff's hand by the sensuous fingers of Julia Farnese, the teenage wife of Orsino Orsini – better known by all as the pope's new whore. She had slipped behind the satin curtains to hold the props of the pope's

(Left) Stone sculpture from Rheims Cathedral, showing the head of a pope adorned in the sugar-loaf style of papal headwear usual until the beginning of the 14th century

(Below) Sketch by 18th century French artist David, showing Napoleon as the 'rapacious eagle' of the prophecy. Napoleon is seizing the crown from Pope Pius VII's hands during his coronation. Napoleon made this gesture to show that his was a superior power to that of the Vicar of Christ

Arms of Alexander VII in the church of Santa Maria del Popolo, Rome. Note the stars as 'guardians' over the six-mounts symbols 'guardian of the mountain' in lower left/upper right of the armorial bearing

Arms of Alexander VI showing the 'Alban bull' to the left

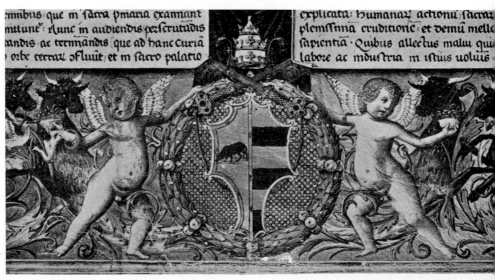

INNOCENTIVS · II · PP · ROMA ·

Imaginary portrait of Innocent II illustrates the appearance of
the pope St Malachy met in 1140

Arms of Callistus III showing the bull in the centre shield

(Right) Pastiche based on original photomontage depicting Nazi persecution of the Church, circa 1935

(Below) Artist's impression of a woodcut depicting the pope as Antichrist. This shows how the excesses and corruption of the Church fostered waves of distrust and suspicion from the Renaissance onward

lusts after the faded rose, Vannozza Catanei, had been married off.

Reform forgotten, in the second half of Alexander's reign he became ever more drawn into the political intrigues and blood lusts of Cesare Borgia, who desired to use the papal stamp of his father to subjugate the Roman nobility and usurp the Papal States for himself.

Alexander is perhaps the only pope in history who had carnal relations with three generations of his own family: his daughter, her mother and her grandmother. His most notorious orgy, called the Joust of the Whores, took place late on an October night in 1501. Burchard describes in his diary how the pope, invited by Lucrezia, entered a banquet hall with Cesare crowded with 50 of Rome's finest whores. The strumpets were made to dance before them. As the honored guests dined, stripping meat off the bone and munching it down with a wine chaser, the whores began carefully stripping off their clothes, until they were draped completely naked about the table of the pope and his son, as "dessert." With passions dissipated, all around the reverent hussies bent naked knees to the floor as the Borgia pope cast showers of chestnuts, like holy water, upon the groveling mass of squealing woman flesh.

Two years later Alexander, ever energetic even while entering his seventh decade, died unexpectedly, a victim of his own favorite weapon, cantarella, the white powder of death. For years he had appointed cardinals after the candidates paid a vast sum and promised that all their family's possessions and wealth would be donated to the Church upon the cardinal's death. Sometime after their ordination Alexander would see to it that one of the many criminals he pardoned would "do him a favor" and sprinkle white arsenic into the new cardinal's wine glass. During the eleven years of his reign a great many cardinals mysteriously died in agony from something they ate or drank, and their lands and possessions soon became those of the Church or, better still, possessions of Alexander.

In 1503 Cesare and the pope sat to dine and kill some enemies at dinner; however, Cesare's servants had mixed up the wine glasses and both father and son fell desperately ill. The son would recover and die bravely on a battlefield in Spain three years later, punctured in 33 places by pike and sword. But his father, at age 73, had not the strength to survive the fire of poison eating away his stomach. Before his soul exited his body, he endured watching the latter literally rot around him. The poison turned the fat in his belly to liquid and his skin began to peel off from his bones. He received last rites within the famous tower of the Borgia Apartments, designed by Pinturicchio. Soon his apartments were ransacked for loot by the bodyguards of his bedridden son. Fate once again gave the stoic chaplain Burchard the onerous task of searching the burglarized apartments for the proper attire and utensils to wash and clothe the naked corpse of a pontiff.

It is said that the corpse quickly began to decompose and soon appeared more monstrous than the worst frog-faced demon painted by Bosch. One saw foam bubbling out between a gaping mouth stretched wide open by the swollen satanic finger of a blackening tongue. Guistiniani, the ambassador of Venice, had the distinct displeasure of witnessing poor Burchard and servants manhandle the shapeless mass which hissed gases as it was hoisted down and forced into a narrow coffin.

Guistiniani would later write home to his prince that Alexander's corpse was "the ugliest, most monstrous and horrible dead body that was ever seen, without any form or likeness of humanity."

SIXTY-ONE

De parvo homine
(From a Little Man)

PIUS III
(1503)

FRANCESCO TODESCHINI of Siena was officially a nephew of Pius II and thus was permitted to adopt Pius II's Italian family name, Piccolomini, which means *little man*. Therefore it is apt to describe him prophetically as *from a little man*.

This was not the first time Cardinal Francesco Piccolomini was considered as a candidate for pope. This time around he was elected Vicar of Christ, but not for his skills as cardinal protector of England, or for his fluent German and excellent term as legate of Germany. Nor was he chosen for refusing to be bribed by Charles VIII of France to influence the last conclave. He was not chosen because he was the only cardinal in the Sacred College brave enough to stand up to Alexander VI and protest his proposed transfer of much of the Papal States to his son, Juan, duke of Gandía.

Culture was not the reason either, even though Piccolomini had earned respect for founding the Libreria Piccolomini at Siena to house his uncle's (father's?) library. The deadlocked conclave of 1503 chose Piccolomini more for his tenuous health and prematurely aged body. In the short term his compromise election would prevent Cesare Borgia from dominating the papacy, and in the long term (hopefully not too long, as many hoped) his ill health would make his reign as Pius III short enough to be that of an interim pope.

The *little man* would exceed expectations and deliver a pontificate of scarcely "little time." Pius would die 26 days after his election as Holy Father.

SIXTY-TWO

Fructus Jovis juvabit
(The Fruit of Jupiter Will Help)

JULIUS II
(1503–1513)

IF THE CATHOLIC Church had identified itself for more than 1,000 years as being "Roman" I guess it had to happen that one day it would attract the pontificate of a truly Jovian pope. Once the fuming remains of Alexander VI were safely stuffed away in his tomb, Cardinal Giuliano della Rovere felt it safe to return from exile to Rome. Upon his elevation as pope after the brief reign of his predecessor, Rovere as Julius II soon displayed a number of attributes of pagan Rome's king of the gods, Jupiter.

Like Jupiter, Julius was tall and athletic. A long and luscious Jovian beard roiled about his chin. You can see just how God-like he must have appeared when contemplating the stormy beard tresses and eagle eyes of Michelangelo's Moses. Apparently the sculpture is modeled after Julius. (Did I forget to mention his Jovian excess of pride and pretense?)

King of the gods and Vicar of Christ both possessed thunderous and intense natures. They carried a staff – and Julius was not averse to slamming it over the head or shoulder of servants, artists or cardinals. Jupiter is an amorous deity, and certainly Julius contributed his part to the legacy of papal cupidity, fathering three daughters as a cardinal.

Both the pagan god and Christian God's representative on Earth were known to throw thunderbolts. In the pontiff's case these were shot out of rows of cannons setting aflame a number of besieged

Italian cities or flung as artillery bolts of iron and fire carrying off the heads of enemy soldiers during the Italian War of Louis XII (1499–1503) and the War of the League of Cambrai (1508–1514).

Pope Julius was a soulmate of another Jove-worshipping pagan, Julius Caesar. A brilliant tactician and general, Julius would spend most of his tempestuous reign buckling sword and armor beneath his pontifical robes, eventually restoring most of the lost political prestige and territories of the Papal States. He earned the name the Warrior Pope, preferring a sword rather than a Bible in his hand.

"Let's see who has the bigger balls, the king of France or the pope!" he shouted during the Italian Wars with a classic flair of Jovian bravado. Clearly he was describing something other than cannon shot.

Now let us talk about acorns.

Julius, as it happened, squirreled away enough of them to bribe the conclave and seize the chair of St. Peter. And what does this have to do with Jupiter? Jupiter's sacred tree is the majestic oak. Julius' coat of arms displays oak branches flush with a rich bounty of acorns. Acorns are Jupiter's sacred *fruit*.

The motto matched the man because the *fruit of Jupiter* did help. When not hurling lightning bolts he represented the higher aspects of the god Jupiter by promoting expansion, higher mind-edness (in the pontiff's case, the new humanism of the Renaissance). Jove and Julius were patrons of the arts. The *fruit* of Julius' coffers would *help* to finance the creation of a number of Renaissance painting masterpieces by Raphael and architectural designs by Bramante. It was Julius who used his God-like will to tame his own rebellious Titan, Michelangelo, compelling him to paint the ceiling of the Sistine Chapel. It is believed that many of the pope's ideas were incorporated in the epic painting of scenes from Genesis, including perhaps the very Jovian image of God reaching out to touch life into Adam.

When he died of fever he was praised as the liberator of Italy from foreign invaders. The power of the Papal States was secure. The Roman Church lurched slightly towards reform after he declared simony illegal. Thanks to his administrative skills the Vatican's empty treasury filled to overflowing, despite his expensive building projects and wars.

Jupiter in his darker aspect is the god of bigotry and religious fanaticism. The war-like, Jovian pope also supported the spread of the Inquisition and financed much of his ambitions with indulgences. He seemed too uninterested in the approaching storm of Protestantism to aspire to achieve the higher-mindedess of Jupiter and offer the Church the *fruits* of true reform.

SIXTY-THREE

De craticula Politiana
(From the Politian Gridiron)

LEO X
(1513–1521)

THE MOTTO DESCRIBES Angelo Ambrogini (1454–1494), known as *Poliziano* (Politian), the name of his birthplace. He was the tutor of the future Leo X, born Giovanni de' Medici. The gridiron was the symbol of the namesake of his famous father, St. Laurence.

It could be safely said that this second son of Lorenzo the Magnificent was a pampered child. Powerful Florentine family connections through his mother, an Orsini, assured a rapid climb on a path of gold to whatever position of power and influence his father might choose. For Giovanni the target was God's Church, and little time was wasted. He was tonsured and ordained a priest at age seven. He was summoned from Florence at age 37 by the conclave in Rome in 1513 to succeed the dead Julius as Leo X.

Leo was a good administrator, a shrewd politician and at first it appears he was even chaste, until he revealed his fondness for little boys. He furthered the work of his predecessor, pushing the invading French almost completely out of Italy. This allowed the pope to spend the bulk of his seven-year pontificate lavishing millions of ducats on the arts, legendary banquets and his grandiose building projects. After years of delays Leo began work in earnest on the construction of a new St. Peter's Basilica, which he intended to be the greatest church in Christendom. The pope's ears were deaf to the protests of his priests as he blessed the demolition of old St. Peter's with all of its priceless early Christian art treasures.

Bramante's design for the new St. Peter's soon became Leo's greatest money pit. Julius' treasury was emptied, and even the booming business from 10,000 whores servicing a citizenry of 50,000 in the papal brothels of Rome could not finance the raising of St. Peter's great dome closer to heaven.

Leo pulled the keys of the Vatican out of the gates of Heaven, as it were, and tried to jimmy the locks of bank vaults and the treasuries of noble families willing to buy posts. He coveted the money boxes of simple Christians desperate to ensure a place in heaven and turned the keys to Christ's kingdom in the lock of any cash-making scheme.

He borrowed from the banking houses of Gaddi and Salviati. The bank of Chigi charged him 40 per cent interest. He outdid Sixtus IV in the sale of holy offices. He pushed his record of 650 offices to 2,150. In one year alone (1517) he created 30 cardinals and raked in 500,000 ducats. Eventually a cardinal's hat came to cost you on the average 30,000 ducats.

He even tried to profit from an exposed assassination attempt. Several cardinals led by Cardinal Petrucci of Siena, disgusted with Leo's excesses and broken promises, planned to have a bribed doctor pass poison through the pope's posterior while treating his legendary case of piles. Letters about the plot were intercepted. The doctor was hung, drawn and quartered. Cardinal Petrucci was strangled by a Muslim, as it would be bad form for a Vicar of Christ to execute one of his cardinals by means of a Christian executioner. The families of the surviving conspirators had to pay huge ransoms, often exceeding 50,000 ducats per head, to receive a pope's pardon.

And still it was not enough money.

Leo had gained the pope's crown through a solemn vow to discontinue Pope Julius' use of usury and indulgences. But the new basilica built in the Apostle's name could not be finished unless he expanded the indulgence scheme beyond all previous excesses of Sixtus IV. An army of Christian priestly soldiers was issued from Rome, not to gather souls, but to bankroll a crusade to hoodwink the simple people throughout Europe into thinking that they could purchase themselves and their dearly departed a bargain ticket to Heaven.

Salvation on the cheap.

Leo expected that volume rather than a high retail price for fewer indulgences would haul in a Calvary-sized mountain of money to burn off the bills of his lavish life and projects in Rome.

What it did instead was incite the Protestant Reformation.

The Church authorities across the German states, you could say, ran a syndicate over the sinful laity. Taxes imposed by this papal Mafia of the German soul had already collected half the wealth in Germany. One more indulgence-fleecing from the pope broke the camel's back of the Church's credibility. For centuries Christians had endured spiritual neglect from the popes of Rome until the climate was right for one Augustinian monk named Martin Luther to galvanize the resentment of millions of average Christians into a spiritual rebellion.

In 1517 Luther wrote a pamphlet on indulgences and other essays critical of papal abuses followed. Luther believed that salvation could not be obtained by hopscotching one's way through a series of elaborate rituals; nor could one be forgiven of sins by paying for them in gold – retail or wholesale. Luther dared proclaim what early Christians accepted as fact long before the advent of Constantine, popes and theocratic syndicates: that faith in the gospel of Jesus Christ was the one and only way to salvation.

Three years later, in 1520, Leo X brushed Luther off with a condemnation of heresy, thinking that it would put the errant priest and his movement in its place. Even Niccolò Machiavelli (1469–1527), one of the pope's advisors, did not take Martin Luther's cult seriously.

The final years of Leo's reign would see the Reformation gain momentum thanks to the pope's alienation of the Holy Roman Empire in favor of stronger ties to the French king. Awakening to the danger of Lutheranism too late he reversed his policies and accepted the election of Charles V (1500–1555) as Holy Roman

Emperor and expanded his order of excommunication to anyone who followed Martin Luther.

Many Protestant leaders countered by using renegade interpretations of Catholic seers like Joachim de Fiore to support their view that the pope was an agent of the Antichrist. This forced Leo to write an official admonition at the Fifth Lateran Council against all those who would popularize interpretations of the prophecies of St. Hildegard or any other Catholic seers who implicated Protestantism as a sign of the final days before the return of Jesus Christ. Leo quoted Matthew 24:13, First Corinthians 13:13 and Timothy 6:14 to remind doomsday-mongers that no one can be certain when the apocalypse or the final days will happen.

Young for a pope, Leo was expected to reign a very long time. Perhaps the flush of youthfulness made him postpone taking seriously the growing dissatisfaction in Christendom with the Roman Church. He died suddenly from malaria in 1522 at the age of only 47, leaving a great schism spreading in the Church and the renewed threat of political turmoil in the Papal States and Italy.

The fairest epitaph may come from the contemporary historian Sarpi, who wrote, "He would have been a perfect pope, if to these [artistic] accomplishments he had added even the slightest knowledge of religion."

SIXTY-FOUR

Leo Florentinus
(A Lion of Florence)

ADRIAN VI
(1522–1523)

THE CONCLAVE AFTER Leo's departure from this world chose a Dutch carpenter's son from Utrecht, Holland – Cardinal Adrian Florenz Dedal. He was a devout ascetic and professorial in nature. The first non-Italian in centuries, he won the papal succession in part because of the influence he might bring to bear on his one-time pupil, Charles V, the rising powerhouse of Europe and Holy Roman Emperor.

No sooner had plans been initiated to adorn the papal offices and livery with his family arms with their poised lions than Pope Adrian initiated reforms, especially in regard to indulgences. He met heavy resistance. His own curia and church administrators sabotaged his plans to inject religion and ethics back into the oversecularized machinery of the Church. To pay off Leo's criminally large debts Adrian cut off financial support for artists and put construction projects on hold. This only increased the hatred of Renaissance artists and thinkers as well as the Roman mob, for this "northern barbarian" who dared sit on St. Peter's throne. *Their* throne!

He unsuccessfully pursued military alliances to thwart the growing threat of the Turkish juggernaut rolling over Eastern Europe and the eastern Mediterranean.

The Reformation widened.

The *lion* of "Florenz" ended up a tragic and isolated figure.

History would never hear his roar or applaud him for saving the Roman Church from its spiritual decline. In September 1523, exhausted, disillusioned and unacquainted with the oppressive summer heat of Rome, he fell ill and died in the eighth month of his pontificate.

SIXTY-FIVE

Flos pilæ ægri
(From the Flower of the Ball)

CLEMENT VII
(1523–1534)

GIULIO DE' MEDICI, the bastard son of Giuliano de' Medici, would be sprung in the pinball machine of the family's ambitions towards the bell-ringing conquest of the seat of St. Peter. And it seems that St. Malachy catches his hometown, heritage and posting as a cardinal all within his brief Latin motto. As a Medici he is a Florentine, the city named after a flower. His cousin, Leo X, appoints him archbishop of Florence in 1513, using his power to brush aside Giulio's illegitimacy. A decade later – and for a second time in as many years – a Medici becomes pope. Once again the Medici arms with their distinctive five red balls (representing the physician's pill) topped by an azure and beflowered ball can be seen on the chevron and keys of the Vatican emblem.

Clement VII, the reformed bastard Medici pope, would dive into his job by emulating the excessive habits of his departed cousin, promoting the arts and the lavishness one expects from Renaissance popes. At first his pontificate showed promise, but it was soon overwhelmed by a number of political scandals and military disasters leading to the sack of Rome in May 1527 by an army of Spanish Catholics and German Lutheran mercenaries. The troops of Charles V rampaged through the streets of Rome for five months, plundering a century of Renaissance art, raping nuns and slaughtering priests. Clement just missed being run through by a German pike when his Swiss Guard fought off the invaders torching the Eternal City. They died to a man for their pope, buying him time with their spilled blood to run from the Vatican and hide within the walls of Castel Sant'Angelo.

Soon after the initial wave of violence was satiated Clement surrendered himself and the papacy to the power of the Holy Roman Emperor. Charles V would restore most of Clement's lost secular holdings and the Papal States at the cost of Clement's promise to toe the emperor's line as his puppet.

What Julius II had built, the Lord of Europe – Charles V – hath taken away. The papacy would never hold that much temporal power again.

While Rome smoldered, Clement moved his administration first to Orvieto and later to Viterbo, where he would reside for two years. During that time he wrestled with the difficult issue of Henry VIII of England's request for a divorce from Catherine of Aragon. Such requests for annulment because of a barren womb had been easy for popes to grant, but Queen Catherine had Charles V as her nephew. Rather than see Viterbo sacked like Rome, Clement rejected Henry's request. Come hell or the pope's high decree of excommunication, Henry would divorce himself and England from the Roman Church and join both to the hip of the Protestant Reformation sweeping across Germany, Holland and Scandinavia.

Catholic Europe was unraveling, yet Clement in his final days could look with satisfaction on the advance of Catholicism in Central and South America.

SIXTY-SIX

Hyacinthus medicorum
(The Lily Physician)

PAUL III
(1534–1549)

THE MOTTO IMPLIES the family arms of Alessandro Farnese and poetically describes his mission as the first pontiff of the Counter-Reformation. The Farnese clan displays six gold hyacinths – lilies – on their azure coat of arms. Alessandro was not a doctor (MEDICORUM) but he was cardinal of SS. Cosmas and Damian, and both saints were doctors.

Thanks to the sexual skills of his sister, Giulia Farnese, the mistress of Alexander VI, he would be awarded a cardinal's hat and henceforth have to endure the nickname Petticoat Cardinal. As a cardinal of a Borgia pope he would make his own sorties beneath petticoats. He and his mistress bore three sons and a daughter. But he got religion during the reign of Leo X, renounced his mistress and sinful life and was ordained a full cardinal by 1519. Born again to the path of celibacy he led the reform movement in the sacred college. Under Clement VII he became the dean of that body and gained a reputation for courage, staying at Clement's side throughout the purgatory of their incarceration after the sack of Rome in 1527. He was elected to succeed Clement in October of 1534 at the age of 66.

Malachy's motto waxes metaphorical – Paul III became a *physician* pope intent on doctoring the ailing Church with a strong dose of reform.

His relatively long reign of 15 years marked the beginning of the Counter-Reformation – an attempt to improve and revitalize the Roman Church in response to its past excesses while restructuring itself politically and theologically to successfully wage a counter-attack on the Protestant Reformation. Paul established new and militant religious orders such as the Jesuits and developed other new congregations such as the Theatines, Barnabites, Somaschi and Ursulines. He established the Congregation of the Roman Inquisition, better known as the Holy Office, granting its inquisitor-generals central authority in the war against heresy. He gave its agents sweeping powers of censorship and permission to imprison anyone on suspicion of heresy, confiscate their property, use any means of torture to gain confession and execute the wicked.

While the dungeons of the papacy were filled to capacity, and the Jesuit agents of the pope prowled throughout Catholic lands to check the spread of free thought and restore the dogma, Paul III indulged in nepotism. He expanded the estates of the Carafa clan and his own bastard children and passed out cardinal hats to his grandson and his 14- and 16-year-old "nephews."

Papal wealth from indulgences once again flowed towards the reconstruction of St. Peter's Basilica, with Michelangelo appointed its new architect after the death of Bramante. Paul commissioned Michelangelo to paint the *Last Judgment* on the altar wall in the Sistine Chapel. He also did much to restore the damage done to the Vatican Library during the sack of Rome in 1527, and commissioned Sangallo to construct the vast and opulent Farnese Palace.

Upon seeing Michelangelo's completed *Last Judgment* fresco the pope fell onto his knees and begged the stern image of Christ to forgive him for all of his transgressions.

To block the leak of deserting laity in Germany he agreed with the request of Charles V to hold the Council of Trent (1545–1563) to regalvanize and reform the Church. The councils would span the reigns of three popes. During Paul's pontificate Catholic theology was revitalized. Sacred tradition was put on an equal basis with scripture. The Vulgate Bible, along with its Apocrypha section, was proclaimed the true Word of God. In 1547 the council tackled defining the doctrine of Justification, which led to the absolute condemnation of Lutheranism.

Paul blessed Charles V's war against the German Protestants of the Schmalkaldic League (1546–1547) and encouraged Francis I to isolate and repress the spread of Huguenots (French Protestants) in France. He suffered further setbacks in England when he was forced to excommunicate Henry VIII a second time, which effectively placed an interdict on the English. But the growing weakness of Rome's pontiffs was exposed when Paul's order for sanctions against England by the Catholic continental powers went nowhere.

Family troubles compounded the agony of his gout-ridden joints, hastening his death at 81.

The tomb of Paul III is adorned with a number of voluptuous ladies, one of them modeled after his sister Giulia, the mistress of Alexander VI, posing as Justice with her scales. If you chance upon it today in St. Peter's you will not find the girls blushing in the pale glow of their marble birthday suits, for the Victorian era's pope, Leo XII, had them adorned with metal Grecian dresses, painted over to look like marble.

SIXTY-SEVEN

De corona montana
(Of the Mountain Crown)

JULIUS III
(1550–1555)

THE SUCCESSOR OF Paul III was Giovanni Maria Ciocchi del Monte (*of the mountain*). His family arms display two golden laurel wreaths, implying the *mountain crowns* of pagan Roman gods who dwelled on Mt. Olympus.

The conclave voted him onto St. Peter's chair as a compromise to break the deadlock between French and Farnese cardinals. News of del Monte's ascendancy as Julius III angered Charles V, who remembered how this stubborn and dedicated co-president of the Council of Trent had driven him to distraction.

History depicts Julius as the usual High Renaissance pope with the customary contradiction of reform and piety by day and hedonism and financial excess by night. Like the others he was a well-read student of the humanities, a patron of the arts and a disciple of the senses, hunting and the theater. Michelangelo continued his labors on St. Peter's, and choir music from the great Renaissance composer Palestrina kissed the incomplete walls of the Basilica after Julius appointed him chief choir master.

The corpulent and fun-loving pontiff was a little eccentric in his carnal pleasures. Rather than deflower maidens and breed the usual gaggle of "nephews" who later could enjoy the golden gifts of nepotism, Julius caused a bit of a scandal by frolicking with a 15-year-old youth whom he saved from the streets of Parma, Innocenzo. He would later adopt his lover as his "brother" and make him a cardinal.

He was devoted to the Counter-Reformation, expanding the authority of the Society of Jesus (the Jesuits) to save souls throughout Christendom and the New World. He reconvened the Council of Trent in 1551, but all efforts there were hamstrung by political conflict. Finally, the outbreak of war forced him to cancel the council in 1552 after 16 sessions.

In the year Julius became pope one of the English Reformation's most outspoken thinkers, John Bale, dug up prophetic passages of medieval Catholic seer Joachim de Fiore as his "ancient" authority foretelling the doom of the papist Church. In his *Images of Both Churches*, published in 1550, he interprets the mathematical prophecies of Joachim as dating the rise of the Protestant Reformation, which is itself synonymous with the advent of Joachim's "Age of the Holy Spirit." Rome therefore is Babylon; and Julius and his successors, the Antichrist. As evidence, Bale adds a suspicious quote attributed to the Calabrian hermit:

The church of Rome shall be destroyed in the Third State [Age of the Holy Spirit], *as the Synagogue of the Jews was destroyed in the Second State* [Age of the Son – Christ], *and the spiritual church shall from thenceforth succeed, to the end of the world.*

The fire and brimstone salvoes of dead Catholic seers aside, Julius III in his brief five-year reign enjoyed rekindled hope for the return of the Christian sheep of England to the Catholic fold when the fanatic Catholic, Mary Tudor, became Queen of England in 1553.

Julius died of complications from gout shortly after he sent Cardinal Morone on a hopeless mission to bring Charles V and the German states back into allegiance with Rome on the model of England. A few months after the dead pontiff was secured in his tomb, Queen Mary – also called Bloody Mary – began the first mass burnings of Protestants in Europe.

SIXTY-EIGHT

Frumentum floccidum
(Hairy Grain)

MARCELLUS II
(1555)

NEXT IN LINE was Julius III's right-hand theologian and Vatican librarian, Cardinal Marcello Cervini, who served with him as co-president as they opened the first sessions of the Council of Trent in 1545. We can gather from the cryptic phrase *hairy grain* that the author of these prophecies was privy to knowledge of his family coat of arms. They display a fan of ripe and hairy-seeded wheat stocks set behind a stag.

Pope Marcellus is chiefly remembered for being one of the few pontiffs to retain his baptized name, no doubt because he wished to honor and emulate the early Christian pope St. Marcellus I (AD 308–309). The first Marcellus, like the latter, was dealing with a crisis in faith among Christians, in which both desired to restore discipline to their flocks. Where St. Marcellus was successful, Marcellus II, already sick and infirm, would work himself to death, suffering a massive stroke on May Day 1555, just 22 days into his reign.

Around the time of Marcellus' lavish funeral in Rome, Catholic prophecy would pass another milestone when a publisher in Lyons, France, would begin selling the first three volumes of a planned ten-volume set of four-line predictions. The series, called *Les Prophéties*, was by the devout Catholic and former Jew, Dr. Michel Nostradamus (1503–1566). Within Nostradamus' proposed history of the future were the seeds of one of the Church's sorest prophetic controversies. Dozens of his obscurely written quatrain poems can be applied to a number of future popes into the 20th century, and in most cases these interpretations were negative towards the Roman Church. Thanks to Nostradamus the prophecies of St. Malachy would gain new and – in the case of the Vatican Inquisitors – unwanted attention. They seem to possess parallel visions leading to the same conclusion: the last pontiff before doomsday will be named Pope Peter.

SIXTY-NINE

De fide Petri
(Of the Faith of Peter)

PAUL IV
(1555–1559)

THE NEXT POPE would rise to the blessed chair of St. Peter from the dark and infernal torture chambers of the Holy Offices of the Roman Inquisition.

Of the faith of Cardinal Giampietro (John-*Peter*) Carafa, much has been said and little of it is flattering. I might strain myself by stretching the language of apologists to the brain-breaking point. At least I could say that his faith in Peter's Church and orthodoxy was as straight and narrow as the executioner's stake. Or, I might say that his passion to save the Church from the heresies of witchcraft, Jews, Protestants, sodomites and women in general was as single-pointed as thumb screws. After surviving four years of his grim pontificate, the citizens of Rome believed that if his mother could have seen the future man her son would become, she would have strangled him to death as he gurgled and cooed in his crib. To them, and to the thousands he mercilessly tortured and burned, and to the Jews of the Papal States whom he condemned to wear yellow hats and forced to stay within the confines of ghettos, the Carafa pope was God's wrath incarnate.

"Were my father a heretic, I would gather the wood to burn him," said the future Paul IV, reflecting on his family origins. He was born a scion of the Carafa Neapolitan baronial family living under the shadow of Mt. Vesuvius. While studying in Rome, under the protective eye of his uncle Oliviero Carafa, he cultivated a solid grounding in humanism and scholarship, which he combined with a strict discipline of asceticism. Through his uncle's offices he rose rapidly in the theocratic ranks and gained the reputation as a passionate and uncompromising reformer, desirous to purge St. Peter's Church of its secular and hedonistic abuses and promote the virtue of Christian poverty and the apostolic way of life.

Paul III appointed him general of the newly reorganized Roman

Inquisition in 1542. He soon became something of a Heinrich Himmler of the Inquisition, whipping it into shape as an efficient secret Gestapo for God. He gained the admiration of Julius III who named him dean of the Sacred College of Cardinals in 1553.

After the brief reign of Marcellus II the 79-year-old dean received the majority vote of reform-minded cardinals in the conclave. As Paul IV, Carafa had long abandoned the humanist ideas of his youth and the path of diplomacy and moderation. He would guide the Church like a medieval autocrat, spicing his proclamations with southern Italian epitaphs that would make a Marine drill instructor blanch.

Peter de Rosa, in *Vicars of Christ*, makes a clever, if unflattering, comparison between the new pontiff and the volcano on whose blackened ridges he was born: "His massive head was shaped like Vesuvius. . . . He, too, erupted without warning, spewing out destruction and death. His shaggy beard and craggy brow gave him a savage look; his cratered eyes, red and blotchy, shone like burning lava. His cracked voice, seldom free from catarrh, rolled and thundered, demanding instant, blind obedience."

One of his first bulls was *Cum nimis absurdum*, one of the most notorious examples of papal anti-Semitism. It defines Jews as Christ-killers and therefore in part to blame for the rise of Protestantism. As such they should be treated as slaves. Thanks to Paul IV we get the term "ghetto," the name taken from the Venetian Foundry, for the urban concentration districts where all Jews were to be confined in every city of the Papal States. He forced the Jews to sell their belongings and businesses for next to nothing and be herded into the squalor of their new lodgings. Commerce of any kind was forbidden. They could sell only food and second-hand clothing and each crowded, disease-infested ghetto was granted only one synagogue.

The pope ordained that all their holy books should be burned, forbade them to speak or teach Hebrew and prohibited Christians from seeking employment or medical attention from Jews.

The Roman ghetto was a malarial stink hole not fit for human habitation. From the Vatican Paul could view the riverside district stretching along the often-flooded shores of the open sewer that was the Tiber River.

Pope Paul, dedicated to the liquidation of Protestantism,

declined to resume the Council of Trent, which had been stalled since 1553. He alienated the Spanish and pontificated his way out of any reconciliation with Mary Tudor's successor, the Protestant Queen Elizabeth I, ensuring that England would remain a bastion of Protestantism. He overlooked the flagrant corruption and abuses of his own bloodthirsty relatives until their political blunders forced a ruinous war upon the papacy and he had to contain their excesses.

In his final years Pope Paul withdrew most of his remaining energies from politics and consoled himself by showering his attention on the business and torture chambers of his beloved Roman Inquisition.

When he died in the sweltering summer of 1559 the citizens of Rome broke into the headquarters of the Inquisition and set it on fire. Thousands of wretched Jews and Christian prisoners of Paul's holy terror were released from the dungeons of Rome and other papal cities. The rioters also pulled down and destroyed Paul's statue on the capitol. Among them were the people of St. Peter's race, some of the Jews freed from the confines of their ghetto, who placed a yellow hat on the statue's broken-off head lying on the square.

SEVENTY

Esculapii pharmacum
(The Medicine of Aesculapius[1])

PIUS IV
(1559–1565)

THE FIRES IN the Holy Offices of the Inquisition were dowsed and the wreckage of Paul's statue was soon cleared away. But the task of choosing his successor would not be so easy. The conclave was deadlocked for four months due to bickering of three factions: the French, Spanish, and the Italians led by the late pope's nephew, Cardinal Carlo Carafa. The latter group persevered and placed the coat of arms of Giovanni Angelo Medici, now Pius IV, on the Vatican banner.

The arms of this Medici matched the illustrious Florentine family in appearance only. The Milanese Medicis were no relation to the Florentine power house. This pope was born a Milanese tax collector's son. His brother was the well-known Gian-Giacomo, known as *Il Medichino* (the doctor).

The motto supplies a hint that "Medici" is the name and quality of this pope. He is *medicina* – the Italian root for "medicine" – for an ailing Church. A "drug" or "medicine" in Malachy's medieval Latin is also called *pharmacum*.

Pius IV would indeed be something of a healer. He was everything his predecessor was not – open, endearing, approachable, easy-going. Six decades of good living had produced a corpulent

---

[1]Aesculapius = Roman god of medicine and healing; identified with the Greek Asclepius. His statue is in the Vatican Museum.

old man in need of exercise. Pius waddled to the challenge and upset his curia by making a Stairmaster of Rome's seven hills. One could find this affable pope walking and talking with the simple Christian citizenry of Rome. They fell in love with him. His presence healed the psychic wounds inflicted upon Romans by Paul IV. He eased the terror and suffering of Christendom by curtailing the powers of the Inquisition and ordained a more liberal application of Paul's Index of Forbidden Books. Thousands were released from prisons across the Papal States. He delivered the noted theologian Cardinal Giovanni Morone (1509–1580) from the dungeons of Castel Sant'Angelo to which he had been condemned for heresy by Paul. He abolished the ban on vagrant monks which Paul had used to send thousands of sincere priests to the slave galleys.

Thanks to Pius the Church became a little less Roman and a little more Christian. His chief medicine for the Protestant question was to reconvene the Council of Trent (1560–1563) and bring it to a successful conclusion. Thanks to his *medicine* the council set the standard of Roman Catholic faith and practice until John Paul II published a new Catechism in 1994.

He was also a generous patron to artists and scholars, and oversaw a number of notable building renovations and the strengthening of Rome's fortifications. But the heavy taxes required to finish these projects brought his honeymoon with the Romans and citizens of the rest of the Papal States to an end: he was nearly assassinated towards the close of his reign.

Pius spent the last two years of his pontificate striving assiduously but with mixed success to implement the Church reforms proposed at Trent.

SEVENTY-ONE

Angelus nemorosus
(A Woodland Angel)

ST. PIUS V
(1566–1572)

ST. MALACHY MAY have crafted this motto out of this pope's childhood background and his enduring legacy as a Church reformer. Michele Ghislieri was born of poor parents from Bosco, Italy (whose ancient name was *Bois Nemus*). He was named after the Archangel Michael. People there recall him as a very pious and saintly boy who staffed out a living as a shepherd along the woodlands and meadows of the Ligurian Apennine hills of Alessandria province before he was ordained a Dominican monk at the age of 14. His religious zeal and mastery of Catholic dogma so impressed Cardinal Giampietro Carafa that he had Michele take his place as Grand Inquisitor when Carafa was promoted to Pope Paul IV in 1555.

On 7 January, after a 19-day conclave, Michele became the surprise choice for pope, thanks to the weight of the rigorist party led by Paul IV's nephew, Cardinal Carlo Carafa (the future St. Borromeo [1538–1584]). News of the election of another Church Inquisitor and darling of the dead Carafa pope blew like the cold January winds across Rome and the citizens of the Papal States. Would the winter of religious terror return? Jews and gentiles alike held their breath.

Aware of the anxiety, the new Pius V made great and saintly efforts to be as fair-minded as a former torturer of heretics and Jews and shaver and mutilator of women could be. He dedicated his pontificate to initiating all the reforms decreed at the Council of Trent. He would see to it that reform spread across the Catholic dominions, from the cathedrals built over the ruins of the pagan Aztec temples of Mexico to those dotting the palm beaches of Goa, reaching as far as the Catholic outposts which brought orthodoxy to the green and steamy chaos of the Congo.

He put an end to the Vatican's brothel business, demanded

celibacy from the priesthood and threw every prostitute out of Rome. Taverns were closed. Bullfighters in Italy were out of a job – gored by the paper horns of a papal bull. The Roman senate protested that he was turning Rome into a monastery. Others complained that once the sexual release valve of prostitutes was miter-capped by the pope, no lady of virtue within Rome would be safe from the revamped "celibate" priests.

Pius V would hear nothing of it. He talked and listened to God.

At least he lived by his own edicts. He retained his renunciate life, wearing the hairy underwear and black threadbare robes of a Dominican under his luxurious pontifical robes. Pius heard God tell him to abolish nepotism, but only after he appointed his grand-nephew, the Dominican Michele Bonelli, as cardinal and his secretary of state. To his credit, unlike his predecessors he gave his relations the bare minimum of favor and finances.

God told him to review the status of all religious orders, banning some of them. The Lord told him that henceforth all candidates for cardinal should undergo close moral and spiritual examination by a commission. The abuse of dispensations and indulgences was put under control. Cardinals, bishops and priests who slid back into the sensuous sins of the Renaissance were sent to Jesuit monasteries for cult-of-the-body deprogramming.

God told him to step up the persecution of the Jews.

Those who would convert to Christianity could remain in the Papal States. The pope rammed this edict home by publicly baptizing a Jewish couple and their three children, with five cardinals acting as godfathers. Then Christ's representative godfather on Earth expelled almost every Jew from the Papal States, except for a concentration of much-needed skilled laborers living in the ghettos of Ancona and the Roman malarial sink hole next to the Tiber.

The Lord told him to stamp out blasphemy.

He built a new palace for the Inquisition on the site of the one that the citizens of Rome had burned, and directed his saintly zeal to the enhancement of its powers. One often found the pope showing up at the Holy Offices, seeking release from his mundane duties at the Vatican by watching suspected heretics admit their transgressions under torture. One might imagine that such a saintly pontiff, left alone on the uncomfortable monk's pallet of his bed, might disturb the feast of his body lice as he tossed and turned feeling some pang of remorse for those poor people that dogma or even torture could not save from Satan. Actually he often complained to his associates in tones of sterling piety that he was far too lenient. And yet, towards the end of his life he must have felt some satisfaction for effectively repressing thousands of printers and publishers and torturing enough critical intellectuals, Christ-killing Jews and free-thinking heretics to keep God's Italy free of all taint of Protestantism.

His political achievements were mixed. His excommunication of Queen Elizabeth and all English people who supported her did not bring England back to Catholicism but only showed how far the influence of the Roman Church had fallen since medieval times. He directed financial and clerical support to the Queen Regent Catherine de' Medici (1519–1589), to curtail the rise of Huguenots in France, only to see her sin on the side of humanism and the devil by granting Huguenots freedom of religion in 1570.

On one point his psychodramas with God must have had him hearing the Lord's praise: his organization of the powerful Holy League of Venice and Spain. The league checked the advance of Islam into the Mediterranean with the rout of the Turkish armada at the battle of Lepanto in October 1571.

Seven months later his talks with God ended on May Day 1572. For his piety and diligence in promoting the reforms of the Council of Trent, Pius V was beatified exactly a century after his death by Clement X on 1 May 1672 and canonized on 22 May 1721 by Clement XI.

SEVENTY-TWO

Medium corpus pilarum
(A Half Body of the Balls)

GREGORY XIII
(1572–1585)

THE BOLOGNIAN, Ugo Boncompagni, the future Gregory XIII, had half the body of a dragon in his estrutcheon. He added the Medici balls to his arms when Pius IV appointed him a cardinal.

History describes him as privately kind and pleasant. He had risen in the papal ranks as a distinguished jurist and diplomat. After his election as pope he continued to promote the reforms of the Council of Trent. He formed a number of seminaries and financed the creation of 23 colleges in Rome alone. Gregory enhanced the powers of the Jesuits and also promoted the spread of Catholic missionaries in the Far East and the New World. The priests from his seminaries in Germany and Hungary helped slow the spread of Protestantism there.

Gregory had a far more liberal stance on abortion than the "infallible" popes of the late 20th century. He proclaimed that a fetus less than 40 days old was not human and therefore aborting it was not a crime. Although he considered it murder to kill a fetus alive longer than 40 days, Gregory still believed that abortion was not as terrible a sin as killing someone already born; unlike murder, abortion does not include the sinful motivations that we usually attribute to those who survive their first birthday, such as anger, hatred or revenge.

The pope seemed blindly, if not divinely, unaware of any motivation for revenge when he led *Te Deum*s in Rome to celebrate the murder of several thousand Huguenots in Paris on St. Bartholomew's feast day – 24 August 1572. The killings eventually spread across France in subsequent weeks, and Gregory's joy swelled to greater heights of thanksgiving to God as Catholics dipped their swords in the blood of 50,000 Huguenot men, women and babes – some cut out of their mothers.

Gregory's hatred for the Jews was right with God, so he believed. In 1581 he wrote a line which one might find in the pages of a future Catholic-born Messiah against international Jewry, Adolf Hitler: "The guilt of the Jews in rejecting and crucifying Christ only grows deeper with successive generations, entailing perpetual slavery."

Under Gregory, synagogues in the Romagna were desecrated by detachments of ex-Jewish Catholic priests. All remaining Jewish citizens in the Papal States were put under surveillance. Their synagogues could be closed for months on end. Heads of families in the Roman ghetto were dragged out of bed in the middle of the night to suffer mind-control torture at the House of Catechumens.

The price of Gregory's war of education and re-education drained the papal coffers. To sustain his ambitious building programs and bankroll the numerous foundations and hundreds of missionaries and colleges around the globe, he squeezed the Papal States' economy to breaking point. Papal nobles who could not pay his heavy taxes were forced to relinquish all their lands and properties to the Church. When he finally passed away much of the papal nobility was forced into banditry. He left central Italy and the city of Rome in the embrace of chaos and crime.

SEVENTY-THREE

Axis in medietate signi
(An Axis in the Midst of a Sign)

SIXTUS V
(1585–1590)

THE MOTTO ACCURATELY describes the diagonal line of bend gules set across the arms of Felice Peretti as an *axis* dividing the estrutcheon or *sign* of a lion holding a branch of a pear tree.

Felice Peretti was born in Grottammare, near Ancona, Italy, in 1520, the son of poor farm laborers. Through the help of a Franciscan uncle he was plucked from the pigsties, where he worked as a swine herder, to join the order at the age of 12. He began his indoctrination as a novice at Montalto. Sometime just prior to his ordination in 1547, it is said that the young novice was walking in the wake of other Franciscans along a muddy road on a mission to the nearby city of Ancona. They chanced upon a dusky-bearded traveling physician, a foreigner, walking his way out of town. The man guided his heavily loaded mule off the path to allow the friars access. His penetrating gray eyes smiled at the passing friars until they fixed themselves on Brother Peretti. As Peretti passed, the traveler slowly bowed on his knee into the mud in reverence as if he were gazing upon the vision of a passing saint. The friars turned back to regard the lunatic soiling his breeches and stockings in the muck. Perhaps the addled physician had heard the young friar preach, for Peretti was already locally famous for his brilliant evangelism.

When asked why he was gazing with adoration at Peretti the doctor replied – either in Latin or Italian but undoubtedly in words laced with a strong French Provençal accent – "I must yield myself and bend a knee before His Holiness."

That did it. The man must be a kook. No friar, least of all someone as humble as the former swineherd from Grottammare, deserved to be addressed with the salutation reserved only for a pope. Amused, Peretti and the friars walked on, leaving the kneeling Frenchman in the mud.

The details of this story come from the biographers of one of the greatest and most controversial Catholic seers of this millennium, Dr. Michel Nostradamus (1503–1566). It seems that the Frenchman had perceived a *sign* that Peretti would later become a pope. Several years after this chance meeting Brother Peretti's golden tongue and theological scholarship would usher him into the chief Inquisitor's chair in Venice. After assuming his post, this man of leonine energy was such a formidable predator of heretics that Paul IV had to recall him back to Rome to forestall rioting.

Two decades after he met Nostradamus, Peretti became vicar-general of the entire Franciscan order. In 1571 – five years after Nostradamus had been laid to rest – Peretti, now called Cardinal Montalto, retired from public life. The chances of his becoming a pontiff were slim. He was entering his second decade since the *sign* of Nostradamus had been delivered. His rival, Gregory XIII, was now the pontiff, and the cardinal's retainers had let it slip around the Sacred College of Cardinals that their leonine master had become a sickly lamb with one hoof in the grave.

As a member of the college, Cardinal Peretti da Montalto dragged himself from his villa on the Esquiline to attend the conclave. All cardinals attending could not forget his constant coughing throughout the proceedings. He did indeed look like death warmed over, and his dark wrinkles twisting around a face contorted with a consumptive cough evidently made his influential friends reconsider him a great candidate as a short-lived caretaker pope.

According to his biographer, Levi, the moment after he received the unanimous vote of the cardinals, Peretti stopped coughing, unbent his bowed shoulders, threw his crutches away and roared like a lion: "Now I am Caesar!" On that day, 40 years after Nostradamus had seen the sign, Peretti wiped the painted wrinkles off his face to become Sixtus V.

For the next five years Rome and Christendom would have an energetic, violent and often inflexible lion perched on St. Peter's chair. He ruthlessly hunted down the brigands terrorizing the Papal States and had 10,000 thieves publicly executed. He censured his critics in the priesthood with a wave of his paw and contended that he could appoint or dismiss anyone, be he a respected theologian like the Jesuit, Robert Bellarmine (1542–1621) or the Holy Roman Emperor. Sixtus had stubborn faith that he was the king of the secular and well as the religious jungle.

He initiated more building projects in his short five-year reign than had been undertaken in the last 50. Like a pharaoh he put the citizens of Rome to work on vast edifices. The dome of St. Peter's was completed and the Egyptian obelisk was moved by thousands of straining laborers and animals to its present location in the Vatican piazza. New aqueducts stretched to Rome. The Vatican Library was built, where Malachy's prophetic document would be moved and soon rediscovered. His reconstruction of Rome marked the beginning of the Baroque period in the history of Roman architecture.

Sixtus, who suffered from bouts of malaria, partially drained the marshes of Rome, reformed the economy, raised new taxes, sold only secular papal offices to the highest bidder and filled the Vatican coffers to overflowing. The poor Franciscan swine farmer became the richest prince in Europe.

Not only was he the fulfillment of Nostradamus' *sign*, but his papacy could be called an *axis* in the spiritual history of the papacy. His reign is the dividing line, signifying the high-water mark of the Counter-Reformation. After his passing, the Church of Rome's central administration would enjoy his lasting reforms. The Sacred College of Cardinals would be limited to 70, and remain so ordained for centuries to come until it was increased by John XXIII. He remodeled the secretariat of state, established 15 permanent congregations of cardinals and instigated other reforms in the curia and spiritual administration of the Church which would last until Vatican II in 1962. The last reforms of the Council of Trent were achieved when Sixtus ordered a commission to revise the Latin Vulgate Bible used in every Catholic church.

On a more sour note, his reign marked one of the Church of

Rome's greatest theological embarrassments. Thinking himself to be a first-rate translator, the impatient pontiff – an insomniac – filled most of his nights composing a shockingly second-rate translation of the Vulgate. His lion-sized ego would not suffer any criticism or delay of publication, and he expected his mangled edition of God's word to replace all the better translations throughout Catholic Christendom, under threat of excommunication. One did not dare question Christ's perfect Vicar, and as long as Sixtus lived the Roman Church lay exposed to theological attacks by the Protestants.

Four months after butchering the Vulgate another attack of malaria laid low the papal lion. Upon hearing the church bells of Rome marking his passing the Roman mob ventured forth and toppled his statue on the capitol. That night Rome endured a singularly violent August thunderstorm. The violet salvoes of lightning illuminating the completed dome of St. Peter's were believed to be a sign that the tempestuous soul of Sixtus was stirring the skies with his passage to heaven – or to hell. The opinion depended on whether one had read his bastardized Bible.

SEVENTY-FOUR

De rore cœli
(From the Heavenly Dew)

URBAN VII
(1590)

CARDINAL GIAMBATTISTA CASTAGNA, a former archbishop of Rossano in Calabria, was a reformer of great promise. He was elected Pope Urban VII on 15 September 1590. The following day he was struck down by malaria. He died on 27 September 1590, from the same fevers that carried off Sixtus.

The motto cues us in to Cardinal Castagna's posting as cardinal of Rossano, a region which medieval myth depicts as the place where manna from heaven is collected.

SEVENTY-FIVE

Ex antiquitate Urbis
(From the Oldness of a City)

GREGORY XIV
(1590–1591)

THE MOTTOES set their Latin sights on Cardinal Niccolò Sfondrati, a member of one of the principal families of Cremona, whose ancient capital city of the same name was one of the first Latin colonies established in the Po Valley in 218 BCE. Thanks in part to his family's influence, he was ordained bishop of that *old* city at the age of 25. He attended the reconvened Council of Trent (1562–1563) where he established a reputation as a zealous reformer.

After an intrigue-ridden two-month conclave to replace Urban VII he surfaced as the most tolerable candidate for pontiff. As Gregory XIV he would show himself to be spiritually humble and self-deprecating to a fault, and a mediocre administrator. To shore up his governmental and political failings he made his ambitious nephew, Paulo Emilio Sfondrati, a cardinal and his secretary of state. The 26-year-old knew little more than the pope about how to run the Roman Church. He drained Sixtus' hard-won treasury to finance an army sent to France to assist the Catholics against the Huguenot king Henry IV (1553–1610). Henry would soon prove the investment irrelevant when he won moderate Catholics to his banner by converting to Catholicism, ending four decades of religious civil war in France. He had been heard to say, "Paris is well worth a mass."

Gregory's reign is best remembered for its charity to the citizens of Rome who were suffering from outbreaks of plague and malaria. He also helped to salvage the Vulgate Bible from the literary mangling it received from Sixtus V, wisely appointing the noted Jesuit scholar and theologian Robert Bellarmine to the task.

Once Bellarmine had corrected its errors the pontiff had a ticklish problem. The act of replacing the Sixtus Vulgate with a corrected version would imply that the late Vicar of Christ, who could not make errors, screwed up. Do nothing and the Word of God would remain riddled with errors. The question of whether to give an honest explanation or wage a cover-up was left to Gregory's successor. He died in October 1591 in the tenth month of his pontificate, four months after Bellarmine had finished the monumental job of correcting the Vulgate Bible.

SEVENTY-SIX

Pia civitas in bello
(A Dutiful State in War)

INNOCENT IX
(1591)

THE NEXT POPE would be the Bolognian Cardinal Gian-Antonio Facchinetti, whose name is derived from a family of humble porters or *facchino*, of which he was a scion. His two-month pontificate as Innocent IX left little time to achieve more glory for (or damage to) the Church. The motto does accurately describe his chief life accomplishment. In 1571, while papal nuncio of Venice, his deft negotiations brought the city-state into a powerful anti-Turkish alliance. Venice would indeed be a *dutiful state in war*, combining its powerful fleet of galleys with those of Spain, Monaco, Malta and the Papal States to destroy the Turkish fleet in the Gulf of Corinth in the Battle of Lepanto.

SEVENTY-SEVEN

Crux Romulea
(A Roman Cross)

CLEMENT VIII
(1592–1605)

IPPOLITO ALDOBRANDINI WAS destined to become Clement VIII, the last pope of the Counter-Reformation. With him the *Roman cross* was clearly on the rebound. The spread of Protestantism was checked. Armies of Jesuit priests, armed with a revitalized and reformed dogma to match the righteousness of their Protestant enemies, reconverted and reclaimed large tracts of Germany and Eastern Europe for the pope in Rome.

Cardinal Aldobrandini swayed the votes for his election in the fourth conclave after he pledged to free the papacy of Spanish domination since the reign of Gregory XIV. In other words he promised to make the *cross* of Christ Roman once again and not an agency of the powerful King Philip II of Spain (1527–1598). He was for the most part successful in removing Spanish cardinals and purging the Papal States government and policies of Spanish influence. He restrained Philip II by establishing good relations with the reconverted and forgiven Catholic King Henry IV of France.

One of his first acts was to publish the corrected version of Sixtus' Vulgate Bible which the Jesuit theologian, Robert Bellarmine, had restored. Clement had the awkward problem that the Roman See must not show itself to be contradictory. Clement issued his "Clementine" edition of the Vulgate Bible, making the flimsy excuse that the printers were responsible for the "Sixtine" edition's thousands of errors. He then issued orders for Jesuits to comb the households, printing shops and bookstores of Europe – especially in the German states of the Holy Roman Empire – to buy back the highly expensive first editions. This still did not save the Roman Church from the bad press of Protestant scholars pointing out the wide difference of infallible opinion between the "Sixtine" and new "Clementine" editions of the Vulgate.

The pontiff who would stiffen the severity of the Inquisition, ban all Jewish books and publicly burn more than 30 prominent heretics at the stake was also the first pontiff to sanction the marriage of a Catholic prince to a Protestant princess. No explanation for this reversion of divine Roman Catholic law was given other than Clement saying that it was done for "the common good."

The chief carrier of the *Roman cross* lashed out at the democratic heresies of the Edict of Nantes, which was issued by Henry IV in 1598. Clement was horrified that a Catholic king would give equality of citizenship to all, regardless of their religion. But complaint was all he could afford because Henry had helped Clement to expand the properties of the Papal States at the cost of the Spanish.

On New Year's Eve 1599, eight thousand specially invited guests gathered in the Vatican Piazza to witness Clement's opening of the Holy Door of St. Peter's, marking the final stage of the death and resurrection of the Basilica. Some would say that the moment Clement carried the Roman Catholic cross through the hallowed portal also marked the conclusion of a turbulent era for the Church of Rome.

A century before, when plans were freshly drawn to rebuild St. Peter's, the credibility of the Church had been strained to the limit by the anti-Christian and pro-secular libertine pope Alexander VI. His successor, Leo X, began tearing down St. Peter's church for the new edifice just as the pope's taxes and indulgences helped to demolish Catholicism's hold on Western Christendom, precipitating the Protestant Reformation. As the walls and art of the old church steadily fell to the workman's sledgehammer, it looked as if the Roman Church was also dwindling in numbers as Protestantism increased.

But by mid-century, architects and papal augurs could discern the signs of the glory to come. Mother Church began to rise, counter-reformed, like the newly and resurrected St. Peter's climbing steadily out of the ruins. Pillars of stone like the new dogma, along with fresh walls of brick as strong as the intolerance to heretical thinking, rose ever so slowly to dominate the Roman skyline. The Counter-Reformation popes began recovering lands and Christians lost to the Protestants. As the new century drew near, Sixtus V, the lion of the Counter-Reformation, completed

St. Peter's dome, leaving Clement to impose his final touches to the theology and dogma of the reformed Roman faith and likewise complete the exterior of the greatest cathedral in the world.

Although Clement would rule for another five years, the opening of the great doors of St. Peter's on the last day of the 16th century was the high point of his pontificate. In the following Jubilee year of 1600, millions of pilgrims from all over Christendom would file inside her vast interior, to behold in awe the renewed glories of the triumphant Roman Catholic cross.

THE WION DISCOVERY

The reign of Clement VIII marks the time the purported manuscript of St. Malachy's papal succession prophecy surfaced for public scrutiny.

The Benedictine historian Dom Arnold Wion sandwiched the 111 mottoes and prophetic coda attributed to St. Malachy in his work entitled *Lignum vitae*, which was published in Venice in 1595. Skeptics like to point out that Wion staked his faith on an undocumented claim. He certainly shows the era's state of loose research by putting his foot in the ink bottle of a serious historical gaffe. He lists Malachy incorrectly as one of the noted Benedictine bishops of medieval times (he was a Cistercian). After giving a brief account of the Irish saint's life and miracles he adds: "Malachy is said to have written some treatises, none of which I have come across except a prophecy concerning the sovereign pontiffs. As it is short and, so far as I know, has never yet been printed, and because many desire to see it, I insert it here."

Wion includes the heretofore unpublished Latin interpretations that he attributes to the papal heraldic historian, Ciacconius, for the first 74 mottoes. The rest are listed without comment. Ciacconius himself never referred to these prophecies in any of his prodigious works prior to Wion's published claim. Nor does a single motto surface in his vast opus on the history of the popes and cardinals published six years later in 1601.

Mottoes and rumors of mottoes from Malachy apparently were

the rage in scholarly trash talk of the 1590s. Clearly someone was spreading the rumor around for years prior to their publication, as Wion's statement shows. Although the little Malachy list appears only on pages 307–311 of *Lignum vitae* – a mammoth 1,800-page tome – the interest and impact it had in Catholic prophecy circles of the High Renaissance was significant. In reality *Lignum vitae* is, for the most part, remembered today because it introduced the world to the prophecies of St. Malachy. The motto list began inking the pages of a number of historical works throughout the next half century before more skeptical scholars rolled up their ink-stained ruffled sleeves to take a few devastating quill swipes at their authenticity.

Time helped to bring the scholars out for a brain brawl, because the post-Wion mottoes (namely for popes logged "after" Wion's 1595 publication) began to betray a dramatic change in interpretive focus from the pre-Wion list of 74. As we have already seen, pre-Wion mottoes seem to fire off impressive hits on a pope's heraldry, family or Christian name, his birthplace, his episcopal sees or his titles as bishop, canon or cardinal. But the first several post-Wion mottoes swing south to describe more abstract issues, which are open to interpretation, such as a pope's deeds or events during his pontificate (see tables opposite).

This departure in device prediction led a number of mid-17th century Jesuit scholars, including Francisco Menestrier and Juan Planella, to lay the groundwork for the centuries-old argument against these prophecies being authentic medieval predictions. Some of their criticisms are well founded, while others betray an agenda.

SOME SKEPTICAL CLAIMS OPEN TO INTERPRETATION

It is certainly hard to imagine that such a sensational document of doomsday predictions could be kept under wraps in the prophecy-struck medieval era. On the other hand, it is not the first time that the Church has kept a secret. There could have been far fewer witnesses to St. Malachy passing his predictions to Pope Innocent than were involved in the creation of Pope Stephen's fraudulent

Last five pontiffs before Wion's publication

Pope motto numbers	70	71	72	73	74
Church posting/Church titles					
Heraldry/symbols	x		x	x	
Christian name/papal name	x	x			
Birthplace					
Family titles and facts		x			x
Nationality					
Key geographic location					
Chief nemesis/outside influence					
Character implied					
Deeds, events of pontificate					

First five pontiffs after Wion's publication

Pope motto numbers	75	76	77	78	79
Church posting/Church titles	x?				
Heraldry/symbols					
Christian name/papal name					
Birthplace					
Family titles and facts					
Nationality					
Key geographic location	x?				
Chief nemesis/outside influence					x
Character implied					
Deeds, events of pontificate		x	x	x?	

Note: x? mean that it is far more open to interpretation than a pre-Wion application.

Donation of Constantine. As many as 100 scribes and associates of Gregory VII knew that his Isidorian Decretals were forgeries, yet centuries passed without one dissenting voice recording the crime.

Many wonder how St. Malachy's biographer, St. Bernard, overlooked the pope's predictions when he wrote the praises of other prophetic events in the saint's life. Well, St. Bernard's writings can be very selective. He never mentioned the name of St. Malachy's sister in his writings. Are we to assume that he did not have one?

His biography of Malachy is a homily. He has carefully edited his subject so that it appears he can do no wrong. Maybe that also includes censoring heretical mottoes. To endorse such would reflect on St. Bernard's saintliness as well, and go against his own recorded belief that the end of the world was at hand, not centuries later.

Then there is the disquieting fact that Arnold Wion inserts these mottoes into his book in 1595 but cannot provide any background regarding either their creation or their discovery by Ciacconius. We have to wait 276 years for the details to surface about St. Malachy's prophetic episode on Janiculum Hill and his gift of the prophecies to Innocent II. The stories first arrive in 1871 in Abbé Cucherat's *Revue du monde catholique*. His source was probably second-hand information from a manuscript that was said to have been destroyed 74 years before. There once was a work entitled *Profezia de'Sommi Pontefici Romani* published in Ferrara in 1794 by an anonymous author. It claimed to trace back the original paper trail to the time before Wion and Ciaconnius discovered St. Malachy's original manuscript. Unfortunately the last copy of *Profezia* was destroyed when the convent at Rimini, where it was preserved, was ransacked and shut down by French revolutionary forces in 1797. If it had survived we might have objective evidence supporting Ciacconius' or Wion's role as recorders rather than presumed forgers.

Sometimes the Jesuit researchers of the 17th century expected the mottoes to assume the position of their expectations. The Jesuits believed that God's prophecies to a saint would be fulfilled without error. But no one is perfect. It must be remembered that around the time these researchers were writing their denouncement of the Malachy prophecies, their colleagues in Rome were trying to repress Galileo for exposing an imperfection in the Word of a perfect God – the scriptural claim that the sun orbits the Earth.

Prophecy scholars of the 20th century, such as Herbert Thurston and Aible Luddy, say that the pre-Wion mottoes do not focus on abstract issues such as the deeds or general events of a pope's life as they do in the post-Wion mottoes. (Actually, I came across mention of such in mottoes 2, 16, 19, 27, 31, 34, 37, 44, 45, 49, 50, 53, 54, 62 and 70 of pre-Wion). The same observation is leveled at abstract themes such as a chief nemesis or an important outside influence. (I found these in mottoes 22, 38, 40, 41, and 54 in the pre-Wion list.)

Thurston and Luddy say that the armorial bearings of antipopes are missing in pre-Wion mottoes. They overlooked mottoes 42, 43 and 53.

A devout Catholic skeptic might wonder why antipopes are mentioned with respect by a pro-Roman pontifical saint while respected popes are derided.

This is a matter of opinion rather than evidence. In one case Thurston broaches this question in relation to a generally respected post-Wion pope, Innocent XI (d.1689), dubbed BELLUA INSATIABILIS (*Insatiable monster*). As you will later see, this nasty epitaph could stand for the good Pope Innocent's chief nemesis, Louis XIV.

SKEPTICAL CLAIMS BASED ON HARDER EVIDENCE

Skeptics often cite the genealogical goof of Ciacconius depicting number 35, DE SUTORE OSSEO (John XXII), as the son of a bony shoemaker named Ossa rather than the son of a blue-blooded French burgermeister, Arnaud Duèze. Mollat in *Les Papes d'Avignon* (Paris, 1912) categorically disputes the shoemaker story, whereas Peter de Rosa in *Vicars of Christ* (1988) does not. De Rosa's account is in agreement with Mollat that John XXII's Christian name was that of the nouveau lesser noble Jacques Duèze, but he does not contradict the story that he was a cobbler's son.

Botched heraldry provides skeptics with significant ground for their assertion that these mottoes were not authored by St. Malachy. Herbert Thurston (*The War & The Prophets*, 1915), in his excitement to undermine the mottoes, likes to cite number 22, DRACO DEPRESSUS (Clement IV), as an instance of confirmed mistaken heraldry, but in this case he is grudgingly contradicted 15 years later by Donald Lindsay Galbreath, an even more formidable Malachy prophecy critic. Galbreath points to Villani's account that the pope gave Florence a banner of an eagle perched on top of a serpent, which became his family's new armorial bearings.

"Doubtful though the Villani's story appears to be," says Galbreath, in his *A Treatise on Ecclesiastical Heraldry*, "until an authentic example of the coat of the Foulques family is found, the eagle and dragon shield must be taken to represent Clement IV's arms."

Galbreath pokes the best damning finger at pre-Wion mottoes. He thinks a forger has exposed himself by relying on a pirated edition of Panvinio's *Epitome* published by the Mantuan publisher Jacobus Stradus sometime after 1557.

On page 68 of *A Treatise on Ecclesiastical Heraldry*, Galbreath says, "The unknown fabricator's erudition was mediocre. He generally depends on Panvinio's *Epitome*, that is on [Stradus'] series of arms, confused the two Milanese Popes Alexander II and Urban III, attaches Gregory X to the better-known Visconti of Milan instead of the Piacenza family, and attributes totally incorrect arms to Innocent VI; these last two were mistakes of the *Epitome* which were avoided by Ciacconius."

Let us take a second look at Galbreath's criticisms.

Alexander II (d. 1021) is not even on St. Malachy's list. His coat depicts a boar. Perhaps Galbreath's testimony is suffering from an editorial error and he really means Alexander "III" of motto 9 (Ex ANSERE CUSTODI – *From the custodian goose*). If so then he probably adds his weight to claims that Paparone (which means "gosling" in Italian) was definitely not a family name of Alexander "III"; therefore, the goose on his arms is wrong.

Galbreath is not correct about Urban III. Urban is definitely not confused with someone else. Galbreath's own depiction of the Crivelli family "sieve" on his coat of arms supports the motto's contention that Umberto Crivelli was meant to be number 11 (Sus IN CRIBRO – *A sow in the sieve*). The motto supports the use of *sow* as a mixed heraldic metaphor of the arms for Crivelli and the city of Milan, a city which derived its name from the discovery of a creature that was half pig and half sheep.

As for Gregory X, Galbreath makes his strongest argument for forgery. He calls to notice the general agreement of historians that Tedalbo Visconti belonged to the Visconti family of Piacenza and would therefore not bear arms of the more famous Milanese house which were often mistakenly attributed to him. Motto number 23 (ANGUINEUS VIR – *A snake-like man*) should therefore depict a crenelated gold parapet on an azure field and not a man being devoured by a snake.

Galbreath's criticism about Innocent VI is groundless. Motto number 39 (DE MONTIBUS PAMMACHII – *From the mountains of Pammachius*) describes details of the pope's birthplace and cardinal title, not his heraldry.

It is regrettable that Galbreath's first criticism is thrown into doubt by his or his editor's inability to count their Alexanders. Nevertheless, as I am also sometimes a victim of editorial errors in my books, I support his claim to ungoose motto number 9 for Alexander "III" and use it as an exhibit supporting a forgery.

The snake in the grass of Gregory X's heraldry is Galbreath's best shot. Someone who believes that these mottoes are from St. Malachy would have few excuses for Gregory's Piacenzan arms being supplanted by the Visconti *snake*, especially since this was a well-known error in the popular heraldry sources that a forger from the latter-half of the 16th century might use.

Still, to me, the dramatic shift in focus of the prophecies after their discovery is the most compelling evidence that St. Malachy did not write these mottoes because there is no logical reason for him to change prophetic perception after motto number 74.

FORGER OR FORECASTER?

If St. Malachy did not write this prophecy, then who did? Some historians believe Wion was the author of this fabrication; however, it cannot be ruled out that the far more substantial knowledge of popes pouring from the fertile brain of Ciacconius makes him an even stronger suspect, though he shows no hint of being a flim-flammer in his other works. Moreover, the Visconti mix-up was avoided by Ciacconius in all of his heraldic opuses, before and after 1595.

The Jesuit scholars tend to promote these prophecies as merely the spawn of a forger intending to cash in on some short-term objective. Thurston supports Menestrier and Harnack's theory that the fabrication had its origin during the long and contentious conclave which preceded the election of Gregory XIV in 1590. They believe that the mottoes were devised as divine evidence to sway the Sacred College of Cardinals to vote Cardinal Simoncelli, bishop of Orvieto, into the papacy. Even the least etymologically informed cardinal in the conclave could apply the name Orvieto to motto 75 (EX ANTIQUITATE URBIS) because Orvieto is derived from the Latin

Urbs vetus. On the other hand the motto can equally apply to the ancient city of the man who did become Pope Gregory, as I have already explained. If this is a mere forgery then the mottoes following *Urbs vetus* should fall flat on their false projections of the future.

They do not. As we will see.

The label "forger" may not be completely fair. There is no denying that the motto themes do make a dramatic change in focus to more abstract themes for the final 36 inscriptions remaining in the succession. But a closer and less emotionally charged examination beyond the rigidity of hard-line Jesuit detractors may reveal not only a forger but a forger who was himself a prophet.

This would not be the first time in Judeo-Christian prophetic tradition that an authentic seer hid behind the reputation of a dearly departed and respected prophet. For example, the byline of the Old Testament prophet Isaiah was used by several people whose works were later consolidated, giving the illusion of one author. "First Isaiah" is primarily responsible for chapters 1–39, though changes in narrative style hint that some passages were penned by his disciples. This Isaiah of Jerusalem, as he is called, was an advisor to four kings of Judah between 783 and 687 BCE Chapters 40–55 could be the work of an unknown author generally identified as the Second Isaiah, who made his prophetic mark toward the close of the exile to Babylon (587–539 BCE). The final chapters (55–65) are descriptions from diverse authors using the Isaiah pseudonym during the post-Babylonian exile period. Biblical scholars believe that the prophet Daniel is a composite of several people covering a period as wide-ranging as the 14th to the 1st century BCE. There seem to be two Ezekiels as well.

The practice of hiding behind the pseudonym of a great master was a respected custom of anonymous authors outside the Judeo-Christian tradition as well. Many writers secret themselves behind the illustrious names of Hindu rishis, and a number of philosophers and prophets stand behind the name of the neo-Platonist seer Hermes Trismegistus.

Just as Gerard di Borgo may have been crouching behind the writings of Joachim de Fiore, so might a mystery forger conceal his authentic prophecies by warming up with mottoes attributed to St. Malachy.

Mystics and prophets use all kinds of devices to attract attention. If these mottoes were not written by St. Malachy, it was undeniably unorthodox for the real author to make up so many trick mottoes before launching into his own prophecies.

There is some logic to it.

The first 74 Latin devices are a means to get our attention. It is also a good way to avoid the rack of the Roman Inquisition on charges of heresy. If Pope Stephen could put words in Constantine's mouth, and if Gregory VII could get people's attention by putting new words of wisdom in the mouths of the early Church fathers, then why could not an anonymous Catholic seer insert his heretical vision into the legacy of a dead saint who can tell no tales to the contrary?

So let us now resume our pope-by-pope examination to the end of the list to see if the suspected forger is a prophet in disguise. After that we can examine my final assessment of the post-Wion mottoes in a closing appendix section to ascertain whether St. Malachy or someone else has seen the future of the Vatican to its final hour.

SEVENTY-EIGHT

Undosus[1] vir
(A Surging Man)

LEO XI
(1605)

THANKS TO Gregory XIII's patronage, Alessandro Ottaviano de' Medici would rise rapidly in the ranks to become bishop of Pistoia in 1573, archbishop of Florence in 1574 and crest to the heights of full cardinal by 1583.

His diplomacy during Pope Clement's reign helped the pontiff to absolve Henry IV from excommunication, effectively turning the tide of the long and bloody religious civil wars in France. As the papal legate to France (1596–1599) he successfully revived

[1]UNDOSUS = full of waves, wavy, surging, billowy.

Church discipline and was in charge of the negotiations which finally led to the Peace of Vervins between France and Spain.

At the conclave following Clement VIII's death the force of his popularity and reputation surged too strongly for the Spanish cardinals to prevent de' Medici's rise at age 70 on the big wave that washed him up onto God's throne on Earth. He adopted his uncle's name, becoming Pope Leo XI on 1 April 1605, no doubt hanging ten on the dizzy white water of popular expectations that he could more than adequately fill the papal slippers of his famous predecessor.

Twenty-seven days later he was wiped out by a common cold.

The motto attributed to St. Malachy is an accurate description of Leo XI's brief passage on the papal throne. His reign surged, crested and exhausted itself with the speed of a wave's collapse on a beach.

SEVENTY-NINE

Gens perversa[1]
(A Perverse People)

PAUL V
(1605–1621)

CAMILLO BORGHESE, the cardinal vicar of Rome, was well placed to become Leo's successor. He had come up slowly through the ranks and was universally considered one of the finest experts on canon law of his day.

Paul V defined his policy, and that of the Roman Church, as a neutral arbiter between political and religious factions of the day. Regrettably his perception of canon law and papal supremacy over secular rulers was not in keeping with the changing times. War in central Europe was on the horizon and he could do little

---

[1]PERVERSA = perverse; directed away from what is right or good; persisting in error; to turn the wrong way.

to stop it. For over half a century the inevitable clash of Protestant and Catholic factions in central Europe had been postponed by the compromises agreed to in the Peace of Augsburg in 1555. The agreement permitted German princes the freedom to choose the religion of their subjects, allowing Protestant princes the right to introduce the Reformation into their principalities. Then came the Counter-Reformation and the triumph of Catholic princes, who regained much lost territory through marriage and political maneuver. By the end of Paul's reign the Treaty of Augsburg was being used as a legal ploy to usurp what had been lost to the *perverse* and heretical Protestants.

One can imagine the animosity and religious tensions created when a new Catholic prince, assuming the throne of a formerly Protestant-ruled principality, would demand by right of the treaty that all Protestants either convert to Catholicism or leave his lands. Their freedom to worship was restricted and hundreds of Protestant churches were destroyed. These measures and atrocities had the effect of pushing the remaining Protestant territories and their princes into a defensive alliance called the Evangelical Union. The Catholic princes and the German emperor countered this move by establishing the Catholic League.

In 1618, a full 63 years after Augsburg was signed, the battle lines were drawn. All eyes turned to the pope to see what he would do. Paul delayed declaring his allegiance to the Catholic League, turning over and over in his lawyer's mind what possible legal consequences might arise from putting the Church of Rome's weight behind an alliance that violated the Peace of Augsburg.

He would delay his support for the first two years of a conflict that would become the bloodiest religious conflict in European history, the Thirty Years War (1618–1648).

At last he put legal ruminations aside and flooded the Catholic League's war chest with vast subsidies from the Vatican treasury. Thanks in part to his financial support, the armies of the *perverse* Protestants were thrown out of Bohemia after the Catholic League's victory at the battle of White Mountain near Prague on 8 November 1620. Paul celebrated the victory by leading a procession in Rome, but the exhausting proceedings brought on a stroke. His body was carried back to his apartments where the

68-year-old pontiff suffered a second and fatal stroke shortly after the New Year.

EIGHTY

In tribulatione pacis
(In Tribulation of Peace)

GREGORY XV
(1621–1623)

THE MAN TO earn this motto was Alessandro Ludovisi of Bologna, the first Jesuit-trained pope. He was a zealot Christian soldier in an army of priests marshaled forth to revive and spread the "true faith" across the world. It is safe to say that in his heart of hearts Alessandro viewed any *peace* with the devil-deceived deacons of Luther's heresy as an onerous *tribulation*.

As Gregory XV he pressured France to promote anti-Calvinist policies and therefore weaken the *tribulation* of peace between the Christian communities decreed by the Edict of Nantes.

Rather than be an arbiter of peace and Christian temperance, Gregory pledged himself and the Church of Rome to the annihilation of the Protestants during the opening phase of the Thirty Years War. The Holy Father showered papal money as payment for the Catholic League's cannonballs and musketry and the torrents of blood rent forth by money-sharpened seas of pikes. During his reign vast sums from the Vatican ensured that Catholic armies could massacre what remained of the Protestant presence in Bohemia while also re-establishing Catholic domination of the Protestant hotbed of the German Palatinate.

Half the population of central Europe was destined to be consumed in a battle of Armageddon fought by Protestants and Catholics over whom Jesus loved better. To many who endured its horror the Thirty Years War was the apocalyptic tribulation foretold in the Bible. In three decades' time the raping and rampaging mercenary Protestant and Catholic armies would turn vast areas of Germany into a desert pockmarked by the craters of burned villages and forested by the skeletal remains of victims hanging from stakes.

Pope Gregory succeeded in ending the tribulation of another peace – a 12-year truce between the Protestant Dutch and the Spanish. Thanks to papal pressure, the agony of a 50-year war would become the Eighty Years War in the Spanish Netherlands (1568–1648).

Halfway through his short two-year pontificate Gregory threw himself into waging a psychic war against heresy and sin around the world. He created the Sacred Congregation for the Propagation of the Faith, responsible for directing the spread of missionary Catholicism beyond Europe and across the heathen world. His intentions were in harmony with the belief in Catholic prophetic interpretation that the Second Coming of Christ and the day of judgment of humanity could not happen before every corner of Earth had heard the "good news" of Christ's "Catholic" mission.

Gregory's industrious efforts are largely credited for establishing Catholicism as the largest Christian sect in the world.

EIGHTY-ONE

Lilium et rosa
(The Lily and the Rose)

URBAN VIII
(1623–1644)

THIS ONE IS as clear as any pre-Wion motto attributed to St. Malachy. The man who would succeed the Jesuit pope came from the city which bears a red lily as its symbol: Florence. He would also gain prominence as the cardinal bishop of Spoletto, guiding the faithful in Umbria, the central Italian province which takes the rose as its symbol. Maître believes that the inscription implies the papal name because the lily and rose decorated the armorial bearings of an earlier Urban the IV.

Cardinal Bishop Maffeo Barberini was the first elected pontiff to enjoy the suspense of a secret ballot. In the deadlocked conclave to pick Gregory XV's successor he won 50 out of 55 votes. As Urban VIII he would manage Church financial business like a son of one of Florence's rich and influential commercial families should – with no hand but his own upon the papal purse strings. He has been called the typical Baroque pontiff: a promoter of the Counter-Reformation and the spread of missionaries to conquer the hearts (and tax base) of distant lands, while being a worldly sophisticate and a lavish patron of the Baroque arts, architecture, music, literature and nepotism.

The second phase of the Thirty Years War cast a shadow on his reign. At this time the Protestant cause was on the rebound with the introduction of Swedish forces led by King Gustavus Adolphus (1594–1632). Urban swung his money and influence to another *lily*, the French monarchy. German imperial setbacks on the battlefield were in part responsible for Urban switching his allegiance to the French King Louis XIII (1610–1643) who was, for all intents and purposes, a puppet of his chief advisor, Cardinal Richelieu (1585–1642). The cardinal was a man to match the pontiff's cynicism and worldliness. Later, when word reached Rome of Richelieu's death, Urban was reputed to have reflected, "If there's a God, the Cardinal de Richelieu will have much to answer for. If not . . . well, he had a successful life."

The ease with which this Baroque Vicar of Christ could question the existence of God did not prevent him in 1633 from trying and condemning his friend, Galileo Galilei (1564–1642), for daring to use science to prove that God's Holy Bible was in error. It would not do to have someone prove that the creator of Heaven and Earth did not know that the Earth rotated around the sun and not vice versa. Only the aged astronomer's friendship with his fellow Florentine saved Galileo from being tortured by the Inquisition before his trial. Galileo was ordered to recant his scientific findings. It would take the Roman Church 359 years and the succession of 29 popes before a pontiff found the courage to concede the error in 1992.

Urban lavished – and nearly exhausted – papal fortunes on architectural projects by Giovanni Lorenzo Bernini (1598–1680). You might say he did this by robbing the City of Peter's pagan Roman monuments to pay St. Paul. Much of the bronze in the famous Bernini altar within St. Peter's was stolen from the Pantheon. This act of pillage, and the crushing taxes levied on Roman citizens to pay for Urban's nepotism and military blunders, turned the citizens of Rome against their pontiff.

By the early 1630s the flow of Vatican treasure to promote the Thirty Years War had slowed to a trickle. When asked by the desperate Holy Roman Emperor for financial aid, Urban pleaded hardship. By the conclusion of his reign he had squandered the equivalent of 30 million imperial thalers on his three nephews. With such an investment, the Catholic League could have won the Thirty Years War in half the time.

On the day of Urban's death the streets of Rome filled with spontaneous and festive celebration for the passing of one of the Church of Rome's most excessive nepotists.

EIGHTY-TWO

Jucunditas crucis
(The Pleasure of the Cross)

INNOCENT X
(1644–1655)

NEXT IN LINE was the Roman Giambattista Pamfili, who tendered a dedicated career as a lawyer for the curia of several popes. He was elected Innocent X after promising the Spanish faction of cardinals that he would curb the effects of his successor's pro-French policies.

As pope he would appoint a commission to investigate the financial excesses of his patrons. The embezzling Barberini nephews avoided punishment thanks to the political pressure of Richlieu's successor as France's prime minister, Cardinal Mazarin (1602–1661).

It turned out that Innocent was not innocent of his own unique form of nepotism. He would appointed his shrewish and insatiably greedy sister-in-law, Donna Olimpia Maidalchini, to the role usually occupied by a pope's befrocked bastard nephew. It came to pass that Donna Olimpia, the pope's rumored mistress, functioned as the de facto "Popessa," running the Church. Every decision he made in his pontificate had to pass her private approval.

Innocent's 11-year reign would intersect with the final stages of the Thirty Years War. What began three decades before as a battle to determine who was fighting on the right side of God evolved into a more cynical war of dynastic rivalries between German princes. It also developed into a battle for dominance in central

Europe between greater powers, including France and Sweden, at the expense of the war-torn and exhausted Holy Roman Empire.

Innocent and the Catholic *cross* would have the *pleasure* of seeing the war finally come to an end in 1648, along with the 80-year religious conflict in the Netherlands. An engraved medallion was issued by the pontiff with a caption commemorating the *joy* and triumph of *the cross*. It portrays two angels on bended knee on heavenly clouds above the Earth, worshipping the exalted cross of Christ glowing with rays emanating from its apex.

But what was *joy* to the *cross* would not turn into a political advantage for the pope. Innocent opposed the Treaty of Westphalia following the Thirty Years War because it overlooked most of the political and religious interests of the Church. He was horrified to read a clause that granted citizens of the Holy Roman Empire the freedom to choose their own religion even if their ruling emperor or prince followed a different faith. And if that was not rubbing enough grime of democracy into the divine dogma of the Church, the treaty gave everyone religious equality whether they were Protestant heretics or true Catholic believers.

His protests and his bulls were all but ignored by the rulers of Europe. The Treaty of Westphalia rammed it home to the papacy that its triumphal days in secular politics had pretty much come to an end outside of its own territories.

When the 82-year-old pontiff was at death's door, his prima Donna nipped her nepotistic earnings and ran from the Vatican. The body of her henpecked pontiff was left in his bedroom unwashed and unprepared for his funeral for three days. When papal officials demanded that she pay for the pontiff's funeral she protested that as an impoverished widow she could not pay a ducat.

EIGHTY-THREE

Montium custos
(Guardian of the Mountains)

ALEXANDER VII
(1655–1667)

WHEN YOU VISIT the Vatican you cannot enter the St. Peter's Square without passing through the broad stone arms of the Bernini colonnade which contain it. If you look closer you will find the family arms of Fabio Chigi (Alexander VII) decorating the colonnades. The Chigi family crest displays a gold sextuple mount (*mountains*) watched over by an eight-pointed *custodian* star.

In 1648 we find Chigi in his role as a papal legate of Cologne representing Innocent X at the negotiations and bringing a conclusion to the Thirty Years War. The infirm and irascible negotiator would not speak directly to Protestant heretics. The final draft of the Treaty of Westphalia shook violent protests from his fragile frame. He declared the treaty too lenient for allowing the heretics too much equality with Catholics. Though his protestations would bring admiration from Rome, Chigi could do little more than vent his spleen. The treaty was ratified by a majority of princes and dignitaries who, unlike Chigi and the pontiff he served in distant Rome, never lived through the horrors of religious warfare nor tasted the blood of its futility.

When he became Pope Alexander VII seven years later, Chigi would feel the sting of powerlessness when dealing with the powerful Cardinal Mazarin, regent of Louis XIV of France during the king's minority. When Mazarin met his maker in 1661 Louis dismissed the legate of Paris and sent troops to seize the papal enclaves of Avignon and Venaissin in southern France on the flimsiest of pretexts. He had acted on a rumor going around Rome that his papal ambassador might lose his diplomatic immunity. He then threatened to march on the Papal States and Rome if he did not get satisfaction.

The "barque" of St. Peter's See had little political bite. Alexander was powerless. No help surfaced from Spain or the exhausted Holy Roman Empire, nor did anyone else care to come to his aid. To preserve the existence of the papacy Alexander had to make copious apologies and surrender to Louis' will on every episcopal appointment in France.

Alexander, like the popes who would succeed him, could sustain papal authority only as long as he aimed his bulls at moral, social and spiritual matters. He gained the ecclesiastical high ground by condemning the heretical teachings of Jansenism and resolving the controversy of Probabilism. He showed marked success in extending the reach of Catholic missionaries throughout the world, especially in the Far East. Alexander also welcomed the learned of the Baroque era to Rome, revitalizing the intellectual climate of its university and that of the Vatican Library.

EIGHTY-FOUR

Sydus olorum
(A Constellation of Swans)

CLEMENT IX
(1667–1669)

ABBÉ MAÎTRE SAYS that the hall used in the conclave to pick the successor to Alexander was called the Chamber of the Swans.

If this be true then a constellation of stellar cardinals picked Cardinal Giulio Rospigliosi, Alexander's secretary of state, as his successor because his good past relations with France might ease the tensions isolating the papacy from Europe's rising power-house. His brief reign as Clement IX did gain the papacy some independence from the manipulation of Louis XIV. A compromise was reached over Jansenism, though Clement lost additional ground to the French monarch when he was forced to give Louis a free hand in appointing whoever he chose for church positions in France.

Clement would watch the attempt of his Christian naval alliance to save the Venetian colony in Crete come apart when the French fleet abandoned the assault, leading to the fall of the last Venetian stronghold on Crete to the Turks in September 1669. Clement took the failure of this venture very hard and his health rapidly failed. He died of a stroke three months later, leaving the papacy deep in debt to Venice and her allies.

EIGHTY-FIVE

De flumine magno
(From a Great River)

CLEMENT X
(1670–1676)

WHEN EMILIO ALTIERI, the future Clement X, was an infant the great river Tiber flooded its banks and poured into the Altieri household. It is said that the flood waters could have cast babe and cradle Moses-like down the "Italian Nile" if it were not for the quick thinking of his wet nurse.

Some St. Malachy watchers tell us that the Altieri family identify their coat of arms with its six silver molets (of eight-pointed stars) in an azure background as the cosmic *magnum flumen*, the great river of stars flowing through the heaven as the Milky Way.

His concern about his advanced age of 79 played a factor in Clement X stepping off on the wrong foot by choosing his cardinal nephew, Cardinal Paluzzi degli Albertoni, as his chief advisor and assistant. Paluzzi was soon to become the pope's puppet master, running the Roman Church in his name. In four years he so alienated papal diplomats by abolishing their tax immunities that the aged pontiff had to sack him.

Clement's reign was also overshadowed by worsening relations with Louis XIV over Gallicanism in the French Church. Louis claimed divine right as king to confiscate Church property to finance his wars and to choose his own appointments to French ecclesiastical offices, vacant sees and abbeys without prior approval from Rome. Taking Louis' lead, other monarchs of Europe exerted unprecedented pressure on the pope to allow them to choose their own candidates as cardinals and bishops. Clement's protests were all but ignored when they went ahead without his permission.

On the crusading front he had a little more luck. He created a successful alliance to protect Poland from Turkish invasion. This even included an invitation to the Protestant king of Sweden, Charles XI, to join.

Prior to meeting his maker Clement launched a flurry of canonizations which included South America's first native saint, Rose of Lima (d. 1617), in Rome's ever-expanding religious empire in the New World.

EIGHTY-SIX

Bellua insatiabilis
(Insatiable Beast)

INNOCENT XI
(1676–1689)

SKEPTICS OF THE mottoes point out the extremes to which pro-Malachy prophecy scholars will go to find something – anything – that explains a motto which appears to be going nowhere except in the file of evidence supporting a forgery from the 1590s. On page 152 of his *Life of St. Malachy*, Luddy writes: "Thus *Bellua Insatiabilis* (insatiable beast), which designates Innocent XI . . . has been understood to refer to the insatiable avidity wherewith he used to consult an unfortunate cardinal of the name Cibo [food]! Be these thy prophets, O Israel?"

I would like to give some "Cibo" for thought. On some occasions the mottoes describe a dominant figure other than the pope, casting a shadow or some light over his pontificate. In this case it may not be Cardinal Benedetto Odescalchi (the future Innocent XI) who is the *insatiable beast*, but his chief rival for Church power in France, Louis XIV.

But if that still seems to be a stretch for some skeptics, the motto for Innocent is as on target for his coat of arms as pre-Wion mottoes. The Odescalchi arms are dominated by a lion (*an insatiable beast*). His outstretched paw and stance is in the position of what is called, in heraldry, *passant in chief*. In other words he is a kingly lion, ready to honor and allow you to pass uneaten.

The heraldic poetry aptly describes Innocent XI's vigorous

13-year feud with the formidable king of the monarchical animals of Europe, Louis XIV.

Innocent was the first pope to gain any kind of concession from Louis. This came in the form of his revocation of the Edict of Nantes on 18 October 1685. At first the pope celebrated the revocation of equal rights to the French Huguenot Protestants as a gift from God. But he soon fell suspicious of Louis' motives. Suspicion turned to horror as Louis' hunger for religious persecution and violence was unleashed on the Huguenots. Innocent was not sympathetic to the Protestant heresy, but enough blood and devastation had been unleashed on religious grounds in the last two centuries to convince even a pope to publicly abhor persecution of heretics on such a mass scale. He was at least able to express some pity for the more than 50,000 Huguenot families who in the next three years would be cast out of France like the Jews had been.

By 1688 the religious tug-of-war of wills between pope and king threatened an open schism. The Protestant overthrow of the Catholic English King James II the following year brought Louis and Innocent back from the brink and probably forestalled a return of antipopes, residing in Avignon and appointed by a French king.

Innocent did strike a successful blow for Christendom against the Ottoman Empire when his Holy League (*sans* France) relieved Vienna from a Turkish siege and pushed the infidels out of large areas of Eastern Europe.

Innocent was celebrated for his unbending piety. A zealous celibate, he decreed that sex for pleasure's sake was a sin. It was only allowed by Christ's Vicar as a necessary – though original – sin, in exchange for making more redeemable Catholics. His edicts abolishing carnivals and public indecency were generally ignored. He died in his 78th year and was regarded as one of the best 17th-century popes.

EIGHTY-SEVEN

Pœnitentia gloriosa
(Glorious Penance)

ALEXANDER VIII
(1689–1691)

"MY TWENTY-THIRD hour has struck," declared the conclave's 79-year-old pope-elect, Cardinal Pietro Otoboni. He knew he would have to work fast.

His brief reign as Alexander VIII would witness this noted canon judge reconciling the Roman Church with the now aged French lion, Louis XIV. He would pluck the papal enclaves of Venaissin and Avignon out of the king's graying paws and file down his claws with a condemnation of the Gallican Articles of 1682, which Louis had used to promote his authority over the French Catholic Church.

Maître tries on the vague idea that the motto describes the stellar penance of the pope's favorite saint (St. Bruno, c.1032–1101). Thanks to Alexander's initiative, the next pope would watch with satisfaction as penitent schismatics in the French Catholic Church return to the mainstream and bow down to the *glorious* control of Rome.

EIGHTY-EIGHT

Rastrum in porta
(The Rake at the Door)

INNOCENT XII
(1691–1700)

SCORE ONE FOR the pro-forgery critics if this motto was meant to refer to the arms of St. Malachy's presumed 29th pope before doomsday. No rakes are there – three golden pignate jugs to be exact. In other words the papal cape and cope go to coat of arms of the jugs of Cardinal Antonio Pignatelli. Abbé Maître, however, does point out that his full Christian name was Antonio Pignatelli *del Rastello* (RASTRUM).

We might have another papal-deed motto here, for Pignatelli's reign as Innocent XII did *rake* in a whole leaf-pile of reform. After a five-month marathon conclave, the oppressive Roman summer heat cast its sultry ballot for a resolution of the deadlock. Pignatelli took the name Innocent as a message to expect his pontificate to be as reform minded and tenacious as the 11th Innocently named pontiff.

He immediately launched reforms of the curia and demanded fairness in the governing of the Papal States. Nepotism was abolished with the decree *Romanum Decet Pontificem* (1692), significantly raking away all abuses – on behalf of the self-aggrandizement of a pope's greedy relatives – from pocketing the papal treasury to pilfering the tithe of poor Catholics.

"If the leader of the Church has poor relations, let him give them the same charity as he gives other needy people," said the new pontiff.

Innocent did finish the work that Alexander VIII began, putting to rest the long-standing religious battle that the Roman Church waged with Louis XIV over Gallicianism. Innocent's *Cum alias*, a decree of only 23 sentences, effectively raked away most of the remaining support for Jansenists and Quietism. There would, however, still be a few sticky and stubborn leaves piled up at his successor's door.

EIGHTY-NINE

Flores circumdati
(Flowers Set to Surround)

CLEMENT XI
(1700–1721)

GIOVANNI FRANCESCO ALBANI, who became Clement XI, was born an Umbrian. Umbria chooses a rose flower as its symbol. Moreover he was born at Urbino, which has as its ancient coat of arms a garland of flowers. Abbé Maître points out that during his pontificate an engraved medallion was fashioned commemorating his birthplace. It shows the coat of arms and papal tiara of Innocent IX surrounded with a garland of luscious flowers. At the base of the medallion is the Latin inscription: 'FLORES CIRCVM DATI'!

All floral salutations aside, many critical papal watchers, including a number of Catholic historians, view his long 21-year pontificate as a great leap backwards for the Roman Church. Clement's new Church bull, *Unigenitus*, is a hallmark of unbending Catholic fundamentalism and reaction to the changing times of the dawning 18th century.

In brief this is what he ordained: No lay Christian man or woman can read the Holy Scriptures at any time, nor can any Catholic religious book be read by rank-and-file Christians on Sunday, the Lord's Day. Only priests can read and instruct from the Bible according to the dictates of the pontiff.

This edict came as a reaction to the laity's misinterpretation of the Vulgate Bible during the Counter-Reformation. Rather than correct their errors Clement plucks the Bible and the good works of Catholic theologians out of their hands. To Clement the highest spiritual love of Christ requires a Catholic to grant his pope unquestioning obedience. He is the Spiritual "Führer" of Christ on Earth.

In 1715 he issued *Ex Illa Die*, which erased a half century of hard missionary advances by the Jesuits in the Far East.

By 1692 the Jesuits had at last gained Chinese imperial permission to allow the Catholic Bible to be read all over the Chinese Empire. Then Clement became pope. He condemned the tolerance of Jesuit missionaries, who for decades had allowed Chinese converts to continue to pay respect to the wooden tablets and shrines of their departed ancestors. The Jesuits reasoned that these Chinese rites – as they were called – were harmless, because it was understood in China that no spirit of an ancestor actually lived in the tablets or shrines. They were used only as a means of showing respect and gratefulness to one's departed ancestors.

Clement did not see this the same way. To him it was all pagan idolatry and he would put an end to it.

Not only did Clement's *Unigenitus* and *Ex Illa Die* knock the Bible out of hands of Catholic Christians – Chinese or otherwise – but his condemnation of the Chinese rites burnt the bridge between cultures after hundreds of thousands of Chinese had crossed into Christendom's arms.

The pope's iron piety was like an unyielding door slammed shut in the faces of billions of Chinese to come. Apparently the unerring pope forgot the tolerance of St. Paul, who bent the rigid dogma of early Jewish Christianity to allow gentiles into the new cult of Christ.

If he had acted more like the Apostle and less like a Church Inquisitor, Clement could have turned China into a Christian state by the 20th century, saving billions of souls from dying without chance of salvation.

To be fair to Clement, I must paraphrase one of Peter de Rosa's ironic points on page 235 of *Vicars of Christ*. Certainly a Catholic China would not have supported any birth control. By the year 2000 there would have been two to three billion starving and breeding believers there. Clement, claims De Rosa, "arguably saved the world from catastrophe."

I would add that Clement helped postponed a third world war

in our century, fought over food and water resources. We might be able to hang on for a few decades after the current anti-contraceptive pope, John Paul II, gives up his ghost.

NINETY

De bona religione
(Of Good Religion)

INNOCENT XIII
(1721–1724)

THE MOTTO CONCERNS itself with the religious credentials of this future pontiff, Cardinal Michelangelo of the illustrious Conti family. The Conti are descendants of an illustrious Roman family of *good religion* who gave the papacy three popes: Innocent III, Gregory IX and Alexander IV. The father of Cardinal Michelangelo, the duke of Poli, certainly gave him a powerful religious name, for he was named after the Archangel Michael. The archangel's appellation in its Hebraic roots means "Who is like unto God?" In Bible lore Michael first appeared in the Book of Daniel as one of the chief princes of the angelic hosts of the Lord. The archangel is invoked in the Roman Catholic liturgy for the dead: "May Michael the standard bearer lead them into the holy light, which you promised of old to Abraham and his seed."

No doubt Cardinal Michelangelo was chosen pontiff for his sterling religious service with the curia and as governor of several Papal States. He combined a redoubtable diplomatic skill with a passion for the quiet life of a religious renunciate. Upon his election he adopted the name of his ancestor Innocent III (d. 1226).

The secular policy of his brief three-year pontificate was to restore the papacy's political credibility with the major powers of Europe.

The chief religious challenges of his reign concerned the two Js – Jansenism and the Jesuits. He would contradict his own earlier views against Clement's anti-Jansenist bull *Unigenitus*. As pope he would confirm the bull and censure the seven French bishops who wrote an open letter to him requesting that he rescind Clement XI's draconian religious constitution. For all his life the theology of the Jesuits went against the grain of Innocent's religious convictions. When spies discovered that Jesuit missionaries in China were disobeying his predecessor's ban on Chinese rites, Innocent pontificated like an avenging Archangel Michael, demanding that the Jesuits obey Clement's ban, or else.

In the final days of his reign he elevated his brother Bernard to the cardinalate, fostering fears that Innocent would act like other righteous popes in the past: commanding moral strength and piety from others while overlooking their own nepotism. As it turned out Innocent lived up to his motto of *good religion*. He made sure that the ban on nepotism was religiously obeyed. Cardinal Bernard only received the modest income stipulated by the ban.

NINETY-ONE

Miles in bello
(A Soldier in War)

BENEDICT XIII
(1724–1730)

THIS SCION OF the Orsinis, the ancient Italian family known for its illustrious line of papal warriors and two popes (Celestine III and Nicholas III), would resist his family's protests and seek the path of religion.

With his election at age 75, Cardinal Pietro Francesco Orsini declared himself Benedict XIV, until someone pointed out that the last man to hold that title was a heretic and an antipope. The faux pas corrected, onward went a Christian soldier to rule the

Roman Church as Benedict XIII.[1] He abandoned the luxury of the Vatican apartments for a more monkish abode.

History records that Benedict was a devout and religious pope, who generally neglected to manage or even understand his secular duties. He took a hard line toward resistance in the French clergy to the bull *Unigenitus*, which they believed went counter to the teachings of St. Augustine and St. Thomas Aquinas on grace and predestination. In more important matters, he banned the wearing of powdered wigs by the cardinals and banned the popular Roman lottery.

If the Roman citizens lost their favorite pastime the pope apparently did not mind if they entertained themselves by hurling filth at crowds of Jews forced to attend church. Nor did the piety of Benedict soften of other repressions against the race from which Christ had come. Jews sitting in church were often struck by priestly proctors slapping iron rods on their palms while monitoring whether the Jews were attentive to the mass. The ghetto's cemetery had few tombstones. Nor did one see a funeral procession lit by tapers during Benedict's reign: both sacred rites of the sons of Abraham remained forbidden on his watch.

Benedict passed away after six years, leaving few Roman citizens to mourn his loss. The papacy's finances were a shambles, and Rome was cast in the gloom of his piety and an economic depression due to the unworldly pontiff's faith in the rascal Cardinal Niccolò Coscia, who as his chief advisor isolated the pontiff from his cardinals and the laity while he pilfered the Vatican treasury.

[1]The fact that this title was used by yet another antipope did not seem to phase anyone.

NINETY-TWO

Columna excelsa
(A Lofty Pillar)

Clement XII
(1730–1740)

CARDINAL LORENZO CORSINI, the scion of a wealthy Florentine family, received the triple-tiara crown at the age of 79. As Clement XII he would make his mark on the succession of St. Peter in the one last and bed-ridden decade of life left to him. Two years into his pontificate the light in his old and tired scholar's eyes was smothered by blindness. Soon feeble health and the onset of gout forced him to move from St. Peter's throne to pontificate from his bed. Old age and blindness did not keep him from fighting a heroic battle to balance the papal treasury's books. The embezzler Cardinal Coscia and his lieutenants in crime were brought to trial. Coscia was billed a huge fine and languished for ten years in the dungeons of Castel Sant'Angelo. The Papal State lotteries were put back in business. Clement rescinded his unworldly predecessor's ban on paper money and his moratorium on the export of valuables and taxes on imports.

The history of those times wove a cruel irony. The Roman Church, like its enfeebled and blind Vicar of Christ, entered the rapidly changing social era known as the Enlightenment broke, bedridden and politically – and almost financially – bankrupt. Spanish forces invaded the Papal States and pressed thousands of its male citizens into military service, feeling not the slightest concern for their immortal souls when Clement condemned their actions.

Despite these setbacks Clement spent some of his family's fortunes to elevate the Eternal City's reputation as a center of art,
architectural grandeur and literature. The Vatican library received
thousands of manuscripts, medals and vases during his papal
tenancy. He embellished Rome with beautiful buildings and
restored the Andrea Corsini chapel and the lofty pillared faɛades
of St. John Lateran. Page 260 of Abbé Maître's *La Prophétie
des Papes* (1901) illustrates two medallions commemorating the
renovation; one of them depicts the *lofty pillars* and high columnar facade of St. John Lateran.

NINETY-THREE

Animal rurale
(A Rustic Beast)

BENEDICT XIV
(1740–1758)

WHAT A PROPHET condemns in the future is often better understood, and even blessed, by the people of the future. Thus St.
Malachy – or the seer using his pseudonym – may have viewed
the pontificate of Benedict XIV as that of a theologically ignorant
peasant beast. Historically popes have not viewed the progressive
ideas of democracy and religious freedom as good for religion. It
is therefore possible that the seer of these Latin mottoes might
tag this deprecating motto on a pontiff who at last accepted the
political realities of his day, rather than sustain the moldy medieval
view that the pope was a secular as well as spiritual dictator of
God's vision for Earth.

During the longest deadlock ever endured by a conclave in
modern times (six months), Cardinal Lambertini let fly the wit
and humor that would sweeten his pontificate.

"Well, if you ask me," reflected the cardinal with his tongue in
his cheek, "if you wish to elect a saint, choose [Cardinal] Gotti;
a statesman, [Cardinal] Aldobrandini; an honest man, elect me."

Apparently the joke was taken seriously by enough cardinals – the 65-year-old Cardinal Lambertini was chosen pope as a compromise. His 18 years as Benedict XIV saw the papacy through the high summer of the historical era known as the Enlightenment – a period of unprecedented gains made in scientific, social and philosophical thinking.

Benedict would prove to be a pope of his times.

A medieval seer or Counter-Reformation forecasting forger might call him a *beast* for suspending rulings from the Council of Trent which prevented mixed marriages between Catholics and Protestants. Benedict reduced the number of holy days in many Catholic countries and called for the humane treatment of native Americans. Although he finally repressed the Chinese rites he did moderate the suppression of the Malabar rites in pantheistic India. Benedict liberalized the Index of Forbidden Books, requesting more scholarly guidelines for censure. He softened some of the righteously sharp edges of the *Unigenitus*. As an "Enlightenment pope" he established a number of academies for literary and philosophical discussion, along with academies for higher mathematics and the sciences of chemistry and surgery.

He was the first pontiff to command wide respect from the Protestants and had magnificent relations with the Turkish Sultan. For a time Benedict enjoyed an intellectual honeymoon with French philosophers, but the speed of their free thinking forced him later – and regretfully – to declare a ban on the works of his friend Voltaire and to repress Freemasonry.

His rule was marked by hundreds of Jewish families mourning the loss of their children who were kidnapped, baptized and forbidden to return on threat of charges of heresy and torture by the Inquisition. But Benedict's Catholic anti-Semitism had its limits. The Jews of the Roman ghetto saw some easing of their lot as second-class humans. And he tolerated the abuse of Church law to save a Jew for Christ.

His papacy would end with dark clouds settling on the Society of Jesus. A month before his death at age 83, he launched an investigation into complaints from Portugal and other lands that the Jesuit order was neglecting its duties and indulging in trade.

NINETY-FOUR

Rosa Umbriæ
(A Rose of Umbria)

CLEMENT XIII
(1758–1769)

VENETIAN CLERIC Carlo della Torre Rezzonico received his first education and indoctrination into the Catholic Church through the grace of Jesuit teachers. He later performed his duties in a number of posts, including a brief stint as governor of Rieti in Umbria.

Jesuits and Umbria would play an important role in this man's legacy as pope: his pontificate would be overshadowed by those who wished to use his divine authority to destroy the Society of Jesus. And the province of Umbria uses the rose as its symbol, forever ensuring that Clement XIII is a favorite proof for the authenticity of these mottoes as prophecies.

No sooner had Cardinal Rezzonico exited the conclave in full pomp as Clement XIII, than this meek Christian lamb of a pontiff was slapped with rumors and attacks from all fronts about the Jesuits. It was a time when absolutist rulers made papal bulls secular bullocks. One obstacle remained to be tamed – the international powers of the Society of Jesus. First came charges (mostly lies) from Portugal and its far-flung colonies that the Jesuits were neglecting their spiritual work and lusting after illegal trade and free-enterprise schemes. For a decade the pope resisted the collective pressure of Portugal, Spain and France until an official request to abolish the Jesuit order in January 1769 was waved in his face.

Clement bought some time by summoning a special consistory in the following month. But the culmination of stress and old age brought on a fatal stroke the day before it was convened.

NINETY-FIVE

Ursus velox
(A Swift Bear)

CLEMENT XIV
(1769–1775)

YOU WILL ELECT an anti-Jesuit pope – or else!

That was the bottom line of the French and Spanish ambassadors' diplomatic volleys to the cardinals gathered in the volatile conclave to choose a successor to Clement XIII. D'Aubeterre, the French ambassador, rubbed further salt into the wafer of St. Peter's representative voting body. He demanded that they choose from his little list of candidates or else the Church would suffer dire consequences. Furthermore, he insisted that their candidate sign a promise to disband the Society of Jesus once and for all! The Franciscan Cardinal Ganganelli, the son of a village doctor of San Archangelo near Rimini, was on the list. Of all the candidates on the French short-list he apparently was the least insulted by the impertinence of the demand and found himself chosen as pope.

Ganganelli adopted the name of his predecessor and one soon beheld the paternal arms of Clement XIV on official papers and coins. No bears here; however, Maître relies on the revelation of the canon Ginzel to tell us that Ganganelli was born a short distance from Rimini. The arms of Rimini display a bear!

The Bourbon Spanish and French ultimatum only strengthened with time. If the Jesuits remained, then Spain and France would leave the Roman Church! Any hope that Clement had of Empress Marie Thérèse of Austria (1717–1780) budging from neutrality on the matter seemed futile. Clement at last surrendered to the demands and disbanded the Society of Jesus in 1773.

The Church's loss was celebrated throughout Europe as a victory for humanism and the so-called Age of Enlightenment. Clement's cave-in significantly harmed the worldwide Catholic school and missionary system. Jesuit priests received a first-hand object lesson in being singled out, like the Jews, for varying degrees of persecution. A Jesuit Diaspora ensued, and many impoverished monks could be found crowding pro-Jesuit enclaves of England, Prussia and Russia for many decades to come.

One can only imagine the inner reflections of this ever more gloom-laden pontiff while he sat listening to the lyrical and festive music of his favorite composer, Mozart, in papal concerts. On his holy watch as successor to St. Peter he had been a partner in bringing the Roman Church to its lowest status as a political power in many centuries. In effect the claims outlined in the bull *In Coena Domini*, which had been upheld by every pope since 1372, were officially dropped by Clement. Without any explanation he had abandoned the often-used declaration which had essentially defined the pope as the religious and secular ruler and dictator of the entire Christian world. His predecessor had recited it for the last time against the Spanish Bourbons, and thus triggered the ultimatum against the Jesuits.

Actions rather than claims now shaped the papal reality of the second half of the 18th century. Clement, if he was anything, was a political realist. Still it was undeniable that his final days were cloaked in a deepening depression as he contemplated the future. He was powerless to stop the unprecedented secular-mindedness of his times. He could not do anything more than watch helplessly as Prussia and Russia partitioned and eliminated the Catholic bastion of Poland.

There was also the renaissance of heathen democracy, rising in America from its Freemason founding fathers and whispered in the parlor rooms of the French middle classes. Democracy and republicanism were poised to defy ancient traditions of absolutism – be they of a prince of the blood or of the faith.

Where would it all lead? What the French monarchy did to the Jesuits today could be performed against every holy order, nunnery and church by a republic tomorrow. Could any insightful Catholic prophecy watcher not think that the days of the Antichrist were at hand, perhaps coming as soon as in the pontificate of Clement's successor?

When Clement suddenly died, a year after he disbanded the Jesuits in 1774, the rapid, almost *Alban Bull*-Borgian decomposition of his corpse fueled rumors that he had been poisoned. His body was examined by doctors and the rumor was proved to be groundless. Even in his post-mortem existence he was violated by

modernism. To this day he remains the only pope to have under-
gone an autopsy.

NINETY-SIX

Peregrinus apostolicus
(An Apostolic Wanderer)

PIUS VI
(1775–1799)

HISTORY HAS ITS seasons. Times of lent follow the days of fes-
tivity. One knows it is Renaissance breeding season when new
ideas, religions and cultures crowd out the old growth of traditions, dogmas and civilizations blushing with the last
fundamental fire of their resistance to change. The new alpha
male and female eras rut for dominance over the old. In the
process individuals are carried off by the passions. Individuals,
whatever their merits, can be crushed like vulnerable lion cubs
and fawns when history's passions rut and roll over their hiding
places.

In the ancient prophetic tradition of predictive astrology it is
believed that the cosmos influences humankind's unconscious will.
The gifted astrologer can probe the patterns of stars and planets
like cosmic Braille to read and interpret Earth's invisible future
bumps with destiny as she passes through the dark universe.
History's collective trends influencing every individual can be
revealed to us.

The astrologers speak of a "Cosmic Year," which lasts roughly

26,000 solar years. This year is divided into 12 chapters, or constellations. Each of these "months" forms a human era lasting a little more than 2,000 years. This is the time it takes one zodiac constellation to transit over the skies in a precession of equinoxes. Every year the sun passes entirely around the zodiac and returns to the point from which it started, the vernal equinox – and every year the sun falls slightly behind the spot in a constellation where it started the year before. This creates the appearance of the sun moving backwards over roughly 2,000 years' time across one constellation after another.

Two thousand years ago, the Piscean astrological age began when the star of the Magi (described in Matthew 2) was most likely created by a conjunction of Jupiter and Saturn in Pisces, the sign of the fish. It was predicted in the Bible that a Messiah figure would come preaching the sign of Jonah who was devoured by a great "fish" (Matthew 12:40, Luke 11:29). Christian mystics would claim that as Jonah endured three days in the belly of a fish, Jesus would rise after three days from death. Other references in the Bible depict a fish-signed Messiah who would become a fisher of souls and establish the era's dominant religion. As per the cosmic permutations of the era, this religion would be an otherworldly cult in which superstition would be its negative potential and faith its positive potential. It would spread across the world because it was most in sync with the amoral momentum of its age.

I say "amoral" because astrology dictates that unconscious forces affect us whether we judge them as right or wrong, good or evil. The mystics of astrology tell us that the stars will continue to influence us until we reawaken to our lost enlightenment and stand as a center of consciousness and light in the unconscious cyclone of the surrounding universe. Until that reawakening comes we all are like semiconscious paddlers, swimming in history's dark cosmic currents.

These currents are arbitrary, neutral. They do not care about our egoistic identifications. They push along or drown the poor, the pontiff, the pious or the pernicious alike.

Consider this.

If you are caught in dangerous river rapids, do you think the river cares about whether you are a good person or bad? Does it respond to your judgments, moralities and expectations, or does it simply go on "rivering" along the mountainside, randomly saving you from – or savaging you on – the rocks and whirlpools of its mindless whim?

Our story about St. Malachy's prophecies began when the Piscean Age was in its heyday. It could be said that this paternalistic era fed the unconscious will of the masses who needed a father-pontiff figure – a middleman to the only begotten Son and his Father God – who is linked to the hearts of their followers by that classic Piscean Age mystical concept of a Holy Spirit. This dreamy and mystical era sees people surrender themselves to worshipping a Holy Spirit who is invisible, who works in mysterious and irrational ways. The Holy Ghost is as tangible as the Kingdom of Heaven, which in classic Piscean Age dogmadreaming is "not of this Earth."

During the High Middle Ages, when our first papal motto was purported to have been logged, the Piscean flow of history nourished people's need to follow blindly the eloquent dictates of those who claimed to have the keys to this invisible, otherworldly paradise. The medieval Europeans were ripe fruit to harvest for a banquet of fear concerning the other invisible fate in the otherworld, Satan's inferno. All minor divergences and contradictions aside, the general flow of history's current in medieval Europe supported the pope being a power above secular monarchs. An age so blinded by belief could easily give rise to a pontiff like Gregory VII spending his reign overseeing an army of scribes concocting false documents. At high Piscean noontime, when there is no legitimate way to support one's claims as secular and spiritual overlord of Christendom, it is the Piscean thing to do to dream up some illusory evidence.

Have faith, forget the facts.

Myth and the propagation of belief was king. Hard data to the contrary was demonic.

Time never stands still, and ages, like flowers, must see their colors fade. The seasons change and new ages of green growth crowd out the brown and dried dogmas of the old. The Piscean Age is dying out, but hold onto your spades – it is not time to bury her just yet. In astrology a great 2,000-year age does not suddenly end. Just as we cannot define the moment when childhood turned into youth and youth flipped suddenly into adulthood, so too does an age ascend and pass away in steady glacial movement. But as each century passes in an astrological age, we experience more strongly the influences of the new age to come. The slowly eroding influence of the Piscean Age undermined the authority of her greatest religious expression, the Roman Church.

What follows Pisces is the Age of Aquarius, the Water Bearer. This new age is not dominated by faith. It will turn the collective current of humanity towards revolution, science and a hunger for a higher consciousness beyond dogma as the new virtues. You can begin to witness the assault of Aquarian thinking on history's rutting grounds about 500 years ago, when the pontiffs were in the thrall of the Renaissance, and their Piscean Age faith was seduced by an unprecedented level of licentiousness and love of things secular. You have the Borgia and Medici popes, rampant nepotism and corruption. But you also have a freeing of minds, the pursuit of art and literature and new thinking. These are the signs of Aquarius rising.

"Freedom" by the way, is the motto of the Aquarian Age. The Piscean Age chastity belt of obedience and fear of authority is supplanted by Aquarian "free" love; in other words, from repression and blind faith, Aquarius swings history's pendulum towards the abuse of freedom, namely licentiousness, or it swings us collectively towards a rendezvous with the response-ability necessary to be free.

The first tender growth of a new age will often be contained by the old growth. The Counter-Reformation popes are a good example. They restored much which was lost to the free thinking and excesses of the Renaissance popes, but as time went by even their reforms were subconsciously influenced and colored by the new currents of the Aquarian water bearer.

The Piscean "good old days" of secular and religious infallibility are definitely beginning to slip from the hands of popes entering the 18th century. Another powerful surge of the new age tests their view of morality and orthodoxy during the Age of Enlightenment. Can one imagine a free thinker like Voltaire being friends with a medieval pope? Can one imagine a medieval pope's censuring of Voltaire's person and works having so little effect?

The currents indeed have changed.

Beginning with the year 1775, which marked the election of Cardinal Giovanni Angelo Braschi to St. Peter's ancient throne as Pius VI, the world would see the rebellious waters of the Aquarian Age inflict the first of a series of tsunami assaults on the old Piscean world order.

The waves of Aquarius continue to gain strength and frequency to the present day.

Braschi was chosen after a conclave of 134 days. This handsome (and a little vain) political promise-balancer satisfied both pro- and anti-Jesuit factions that he would uphold their views as the new pope.

By the second year of his pontificate American colonialists had fired their first shot across the bow of authoritarian monarchies and state-controlled religion by launching the American Revolution. Pius would show little interest in distant guerrilla conflicts pitting mostly Protestant against Protestant. He was not a man of vision, and lacked a weatherman's sense of the changing winds of history. He had not the capacity to see how the little squall of democracy on the fringes of civilization could cross the Atlantic and bear down on Europe as the hurricane of the French Revolution 14 years later.

In the meantime he basked in fair-weather memories of papacies past. He closed off the increasing winds of reform with a warm winter coat of old-fashioned protocol, orthodoxy and excessive nepotism. Rather than rebuild his Church to withstand the coming storm he added his grand architectural touches to Rome. The decrepit roads to the Eternal City were rebuilt during the quiet first half of his reign, better facilitating the march of invading French Republican armies into the Papal States during the second half of his near-quarter century pontificate. And he would evoke a lasting admiration from the citizens of Rome for his costly and ultimately quixotic attempt to drain the Pontine Marshes.

At the onset of the 1780s the fortunes of that little rebellion of pagan, Pericles-loving democrats in America were turning against the armies of Britain. But that was of little concern for now. Pius could enjoy the support of like-minded and slack-visioned secular

Catholic rulers in France, Portugal and Spain as long as he kept his foot on the throats of the Jesuits.

Things were not so peaceful in the Austrian Empire. Emperor Joseph II (d. 1790) blessed the creation of a new system of religious freedom in his realm. This Josephism, as it became called, proclaimed full religious toleration for all subjects of the emperor. His Toleration Edict in 1781 limited the power of the Roman Church in Austria to spiritual matters alone. All other church matters, including church properties, were now subject to the state and to the decisions of local diocesan bishops.

By 1782, Pius made the long journey (unprecedented for a pope) to Vienna to talk some sense into the Austrian Emperor, but to no avail.

This would not be the first time that Pius would fulfill his destiny as the tragic *Apostolic wanderer*. An engraved medallion commemorating the pope's unique journey was foreseen in the motto of St. Malachy. Beneath the profile of Pius VI, reads the caption:

PEREGRINVS APOSTOLIC
VIENNE · MENSE MART
1782

Then the French Revolution came in 1789.

By 1792 republicanism and atheism were paramount in France. Now every other priest, nun and cleric found themselves banished from their churches and monasteries in a worse condition than the Jesuits before them. Soon hordes of refugee priests and nuns crowded the streets of Rome, living like beggars.

It had all been witnessed before, by a controversial Catholic seer who had found his works of prophecy blacklisted in the Index of Forbidden Books by Pius in 1781. In a letter written in 1557 to the then king of France, Henry II, Nostradamus proclaimed the coming of a revolution of the common people to take place by 1792. By then the Church would experience its greatest persecution so far. Nostradamus describes the "headless idiots" who would form their own religion based on reason rather than faith (in fact many were decapitated by their own guillotines).

Nostradamus also believed that the revolutionaries would create a new calendar in 1792 because they saw their overthrow of the French monarchy and the Church as the advent of a new age.

All of these visions did transpire by the year 1792.

It would be easy enough to brush off any rush of revolution and its leaders as "anti-Christ." Excesses were certainly many during the decade of revolution (1789–1799), but during that time millions of people in France, Holland, Belgium and Italy experienced a level of political and religious freedom never seen before. It must be remembered that the pontiff and his Church, as the defenders of orthodoxy, would condemn equally the good and the evil excesses of people rebelling against state and church control of their religious lives. It would condemn as Satanic the overthrow of a feudal system which kept people chained like slaves to the lands of aristocrats and priestly overlords alike.

Medieval definitions of rigid religion, unquestioning obedience to the pope and love as a thing of penance, guilt and duty could no longer be taken for granted with the onset of the first powerful waves of the Aquarian Age. Freedom to vote for your government, freedom to worship as you choose, freedom to rise beyond your class through the merit of your talents was the new and "Anti-Christian" way. The medieval sanctity of class systems and the Inquisition were doomed.

To Pius the Antichrist had arrived.

Nostradamus called him Napaulon Roy, or Neapaluon – clear word-plays for Napoleon Bonaparte. He was the first of three Antichrists that the French seer expected would walk the Earth before the final Judgment Day.

All the following extracts from his prophecies, written in 1555–1557, marked Pius' fate as a refugee, or better, St. Malachy's *Apostolic Wanderer* of the 1790s.

In Nostradamus' vision the First Antichrist was a "simple soldier" who would "attain to empire." He would have a ferocious name never held by any French king (Napoleon Bonaparte). He would be "brave in arms" and do "the very worst towards the Church," vexing priests "as water does the sponge."

Once General Bonaparte came into Italy, his Republican armies would "assault Rome." Bonaparte would refuse entry to the Eternal City to Pius and his successor. Nostradamus calls the popes "the Piuses." (Pius VI and his successor Pius VII). The "depraved ones" of anti-Christian France will keep them both "imprisoned."

You would know the beginning of Pius' tribulation when a French army bivouacked "all around the environs of the city [of Rome]" with "soldiers lodged throughout the fields and towns." Expect "great pillage" to be "inflicted upon the pontiff." Finally the pope, "the great Fisherman," would be "in ruinous trouble."[1]

Nostradamus then called out from the past to Pius with this final warning:

> Roman Pontiff, beware of approaching,
> Out of the city which the two rivers water,
> In that place you will come to spit your blood,
> You and your friends when the rose will blossom.
> (2 Q97)

And this is what did transpire:

In 1795 Napoleon Bonaparte led a French republican army into Northern Italy. The French Directory (the government ruling at the time) demanded that the pope drop his rejection of the Civil Constitution of the Clergy and the Revolution. The Civil Constitution had reorganized the French church so that priests were now salaried employees of the government who must pledge their allegiance to the Revolution and not to the pope. The pope remained defiant. After Napoleon had defeated the Austrians and their northern Italian allies in a brilliant military campaign, Napoleon was ordered to set his soldiers loose on the Papal States. By 1797 Pius could do nothing but recognize the French Republic and order his papal subjects to obey the French Directory's peace terms. The Papal States were greatly reduced and incorporated into France, and Napoleon plundered Rome of many of her transportable artifacts and manuscripts.

At the commencement of the new year the French general Duphot was murdered in a riot on the streets of Rome. By February the French army camped around the city marched within its walls to take command of the Castle Sant'Angelo. Its commander,

---

[1] All quotes from Nostradamus are derived from the following four-line poems in his work *Les Prophéties*, with the index numbers: 5 Q (quatrain) 57, 8 Q1, 5 Q30, 6 Q25 and 2 Q97. For more elaboration, read my book *Nostradamus: The Complete Prophecies* (Element Books, 1997).

General Berthier, proclaimed Rome a republic and Pius was arrested and deposed. It is said that Pius stood up to his captors with quiet defiance. Berthier demanded that he relinquish the ring of the Fisherman. He refused. Crowds of Roman citizens gathered under the driving winter rain to watch as the carriage of their beloved "papa" pulled out of Rome into exile, under military guard.

He was now the *Apostolic Wanderer* of St. Malachy's motto. He was placed under house arrest in a charterhouse in Florence. There he was cut off from his curia and had but a handful of retainers and advisors sharing his incarceration. By 1799 war once again broke out and, fearing his potential deliverance, the French Directory forced the sick and aged pontiff to "wander" across the Alps via Turin to his new prison lodgings in Briançon, France. This was at the end of April, around the time the first roses were in bloom – just as Nostradamus had predicted. Then Pius was moved in July to a citadel in the southern French city of Valence with his entourage of 32 priests (his *friends*).

True to Nostradamus' prophecy Pius VI would die in Valence, which sits between the confluence of two rivers, the Isère and the Rhône. He succumbed to an attack of acute gastroenteritis on 29 August 1799. Witnesses say that he was vomiting blood while he endured his final agony (*he will spit his blood*).

To prophecy watchers living in the final months of the 18th century it looked as if the Church of Rome was effectively destroyed and the great Chastisement of Christianity had begun.

Not long after Pius' death Napoleon would return to France and overthrow the French Directory, becoming First Consul (dictator). By 1804 he would proclaim himself emperor of the French and do much to fulfill most orthodox views of Catholic medieval prophecies concerning the Antichrist.

The time is coming when princes and people will renounce the authority of the pope. Individual countries will prefer their own Church rulers to the pope. The German Empire will be divided [Napoleon terminated the Holy Roman Empire in 1808]. *Church property will be secularized. Priests will be persecuted. After the birth of the Antichrist heretics will preach their false doctrines undisturbed, resulting in "Christians having doubts about their holy Catholic faith."*

St. Hildegard (d. 1179)

NINETY-SEVEN

Aquila rapax
(Rapacious Eagle)

PIUS VII
(1800–1823)

THE DEFIANT AND doomed Pius VI had a few surprises hiding up his cassock sleeve. When he died many in Europe believed that for all intents and purposes the succession of St. Peter died with him. But early in 1797 Pius had begun to suspect that the French might seize and arrest him, so he started passing on secret instructions to his cardinals so they could form a conclave to choose his successor in case he died in prison.

The conclave did proceed under Austrian protection at Venice seven months after his death. The Sacred College of Cardinals got itself mired in a Venetian bog of a deadlock for four and a half months until Cardinal Luigi Barnabà Chiaramonte was at last elected as a compromise choice.

Taking his name after his martyred predecessor, Pius VII flexed the muscles of his papal authority by ignoring the urgings of the Austrians to stay in their territory (where they hoped to control him) and headed for Rome by the first July of the new century.

The motto for Pius VII clearly does not describe this quiet, politically progressive, patient and long-suffering pontiff. Just as the pre-Wion motto *Dragon Pressed Down* describes the chief nemesis of Clement IV, the Hohenstafen Emperor, the phrase *rapacious eagle* identifies the chief nemesis of Pius VII, Napoleon Bonaparte, who would adopt the imperial eagle of the classical fascist dictators of Rome as his symbol. Brass eagles could be seen on the standards of Napoleon's irresistible armies as they conquered most of continental Europe during the first nine years of Pius VII's reign.

Pius chose Ercole Consalvi (1757–1824) to be his secretary of state and spokesman for his pontificate. He would be a man to match the wits and political genius of Napoleon's foreign minister, the defrocked priest Talleyrand.

Slowly, carefully, Pius and Consalvi initiated modest reforms in the Papal States, achieving the evacuation of occupying forces of the Neapolitans and Austrians, if not the French. Pius, a man sympathetic to many aspects of democracy, wished to impress upon Napoleon that he was a Vicar of Christ willing to accept realities in revolutionary France as long as essential Catholic beliefs were not rejected. His concordat with the French dictator in 1801 restored Catholicism in France; however, by the following year Napoleon issued the Organic Articles which pinched off most papal control of the French Church.

In 1804 Pius sought to further ease relations by offering to officiate at the coronation of Napoleon and his wife Josephine as emperor and empress of France. Napoleon topped a week of snubs against the pontiff and his entourage by seizing the crown out of Pius' hands and placing it on his own head. Pius returned to Rome, embarrassed and without any of the Organic Articles modified. He waited for developments, keeping the papacy neutral as Europe's crowned powers went to war against the upstart emperor of France.

One by one the Catholic powers fell to Napoleon, and political and secular realities that had defined the world in which the Roman Church had lived were no more. By 1808, Austria, Prussia and Russia were defeated and Catholic Spain was occupied, and Napoleon saw fit to send armies with their rapacious eagle standards swooping down on the Papal States. The pretense was the pope's resistance to supporting Napoleon's continental blockade of England.

By the following year the Papal States ceased to be. Napoleon's talons snatched them and carried them off into the greater French Empire. The papal army was incorporated into Napoleon's legions, and the pope's personal bodyguard was dissolved. The emperor demanded and received Consalvi's resignation. A number of cardinals were sent packing as the new puppet master in Paris deemed one candidate after another for the head of Pius' curia unacceptable. By May 1809 Napoleon fell on the helpless prey of ancient laws which had defined the Church of Rome's power for a millennium. He decreed the Donation of Pepin (based on the fraudulent Donation of Constantine) abolished and thus put an end once and for all to the pope's temporal power.

The following day Pius issued a bull of excommunication to "all robbers of Peter's patrimony," not daring to mention Napoleon outright. Within a few weeks soldiers and police from the French garrison in Rome barged into the Quirinal palace, the papal summer residence, and arrested Pius.

This event, like so many others, was foreseen by Nostradamus two and a half centuries earlier.

A pestilence to the Church, from the king newly united . . . (1 Q52) *The great pontiff seized while navigating* [in other words, navigating the barque of St. Peter the fisherman]. *The great one* [Pius VII] *thereafter to fail, the clergy in tumult. The second one elected* [the second Pius], *absent* (his power) *declines* [the second pope "Pius" afflicted by Napoleon is now forced to leave Rome under arrest] (5 Q15).

From 1809 to 1811 the pope remained under arrest in Savona and would suffer as a prisoner in virtual isolation. He endured psychological torture for resisting Napoleon's demand to invest the emperor's choice of bishops. By 1811 Napoleon moved his prisoner closer to home, placing him under house arrest at Fontainebleau outside of Paris. There the emperor could apply more direct pressure to bend the pope to his will.

In Quatrain 77 of Century (Volume) 5 of his history of the future *Les Prophéties*, Nostradamus clearly has Pius in his future sights when he writes:

> *All the degrees of Ecclesiastical honor,*
> *Will be changed to Jupiter Quirinus:*
> *The priest of Quirinus* [Pius] *to one of Mars* [Napoleon the warrior]:
> *Then a king of France will make him one of Vulcan.*

Nostradamus uses one of his famous word-plays to call Pius VII the *priest of Quirinus* after the French secret police arrest the pope at his summer palace, which is also called *the Quirinal*. Napoleon is the *one of Mars*, the neo-Roman Caesar, ever modeling himself after them. He drags his prisoner pope to Fontainebleau, near Paris, Napoleon's new Rome. There he will be the new head *priest* of his neo-Roman state religion. The pagan Romans called such a priest *Quirinus*. Pius will be *one of* (or rendered by the patron of artificers into) *Vulcan*; that is, Pius becomes a figurehead manufactured by the *king of France*.

Nostradamus' first Antichrist explained his actions later in his memoirs:

I was in a position to exalt the pope beyond all bounds and to surround him with such pomp and ceremony that he would have ceased to regret the loss of his temporal power. I would have made an idol out of him. . . . Paris would have become the capital of Christendom, and I would have become the master of the religious as well as the political world. . . . my Church councils would have been representative of all Christendom, and the popes would have been mere chairmen. I would have opened and closed these assemblies, approved and made public their decisions, as did Constantine and Charlemagne.

Ironically some elements of Napoleon's anti-Christian dream are accepted as reality by the modern Church. Whether one agrees with his tyrannical motives or actions to achieve his goals, Napoleon, more than most rulers in modern times, brought the Roman Church, albeit kicking and screaming, into the modern world. Although Pius and his successors would later try to restore their secular authority over the Catholic world, Napoleon effectively destroyed it. Pontiffs thereafter had to surrender to the reality that they were a power to be reckoned with only in spiritual matters.

It is easy to forget the many good reforms Napoleon created when one is faced with his terrible treatment of Pius and the Church. But as we have seen, 700 years of papal abuses that go around do indeed come around when the common people of Europe, the chief victims of the Roman Church's many excesses, demand their freedom in the French Revolution.

True, Napoleon stopped their revolution, but his dictatorship served to spread many of the virtues inherent in the first revolution to blossom in Europe under the light of the awakening Aquarian Age. Napoleon's legal code is the basis for modern democracy in France and he is responsible for giving Jews religious and secular equality with Christians throughout his empire.

Jews still languished in ghettos in the Papal States until French soldiers liberated them.

Napoleon also disbanded the Inquisition. The same troops that occupied Rome also delivered thousands of tortured wretches from the dungeons of Pius' priests. And when Napoleon was finally overthrown in 1815 and Pius was reinstated as the pope and ruler of the restored Papal States, one of his first actions was to reinstate many of the restrictions placed on the movement of Jews and bring the Inquisition back!

The torture chambers in the Vatican would resume their fearful work well into the 1830s, even though Pius, to his merit, publicly forbade the use of physical torture machines back in 1814. He also did not demand that the Jews return to their fetid ghettos.

It sometimes takes an Antichrist to make a Vicar of Christ more humane.

Pius by 1816 was soon to reap the rewards of his heroic resistance against and persecution by the deposed Antichrist. Pius had nearly all the territories of Papal States (*sans* the French papal enclaves of Avignon and Venaissin) and his temporal powers returned by the sympathetic Congress of Vienna (1814–1815) which was involved with redrawing the map of a Europe that Napoleon forever changed.

The Jesuits were reinstated and the pope could once again call upon his right-hand man, Consalvi, as curial secretary of state. Pius' final years were spent in a partially unsuccessful attempt to exorcise the Antichrist's legacy of liberalism and religious tolerance from the Catholic Church. Pius did exude an ample portion of Christian forgiveness by harboring members of Napoleon's family in Rome after they were denied a place to live anywhere else in Europe. He would also officially request that the British government ease the hardships of his tormentor, languishing away in exile on the island of St. Helena.

The *rapacious eagle* died there in 1821. Pius followed two years later. He left a religiously resurgent though politically weakened pontificate for his successors, whose challenge would be to keep under tight control the reforms injected into the Catholic Church and Papal States by the spirit of the French Revolution.

NINETY-EIGHT

Canis et coluber
(A Dog and a Snake)

LEO XII
(1823–1829)

TO MANY INTERPRETERS of these Latin epigraphs CANIS ET COLUBER is an adequate epithet for the negative character of Cardinal Annibale della Genga, the successor to the long-lived Pius VII.

Humorless and zealously orthodox, Genga was elected pope by a swing vote of conservative cardinals who envisioned him as their savior from the infestation of liberal ideas into the Church.

As Leo XII he would not disappoint them.

His grim six-year pontificate tried to turn the Catholic clock back to the days before the French Revolution. He had only limited success outside of the Papal States, but inside its borders he created a theocratic police state. A blackout curtain of decrees threw a smothering weight over liberal ideas, the sale of wine outside taverns and the spread of Freemasonry. Those marble ladies and gentlemen who adorned the Vatican tombs and art galleries of Rome and who wore only the Roman air were locked away inside storage crates. Those which could not be moved were properly dressed by papal command. Once again Rome's many artisans applied mock metal dresses painted over to look like marbled cloth to cover their stony private parts.

Leo felt that Christians were backsliding in their punishment of the Christ-killing Jews. Where his predecessor adapted to the times Leo had no problems issuing orders for the Jews to return to their ghettos. When an epidemic of smallpox spread through the Roman ghetto he banned the use of vaccinations because it went against "natural law." And if a Christian doctor felt compelled to tend to sick Jews, papal law forbade him from remaining unless he first tried to convert them to Christianity. If that failed he was to grab his medicine bag and leave them to fate or face charges of heresy.

Thanks to a doctor of questionable skill Leo died from complications during a surgical operation. He left the Papal States a European social and political backwater with a moribund economy. He did re-establish generally good relations with conservative sovereigns, and his pontificate helped to steer future popes away from politics towards their modern role as the spiritual pastors of humanity. After Leo (the 13th pope before doomsday), the chair of St. Peter would be used as the bully pulpit to remind Christians and heathens alike – for better or worse – that the popes are the moral and spiritual conscience of Earth.

NINETY-NINE

Vir religiosus
(A Religious Man)

PIUS VIII
(1829–1830)

A SKEPTIC OF the post-Wion mottoes – or worse, a post-Wion wag – might crow that any pope worth his holy wafer is a *religious man*. Defenders of the post-Wion prophecies might put on their thinking-Maître caps to hunt for any acts of particular piety and religiousness to be found in Cardinal Francesco Saverio Castiglione's life before and after he was elected as Pius VIII.

He was an expert in canon law before taking the cloth. He was imprisoned by Napoleon for six years for refusing to swear his allegiance to the usurping Antichrist's Italian regime. Then there was Pius VII's high and religious regard for Castiglione. Pius could not resist spicing his words of wisdom to Castiglione by saying from time to time, "When you are Pius VIII, you will settle this affair." The good cardinal did do a bang-up job defending the faith from free-thinking authors as the prefect of the Congregation of the Index (of forbidden books). Through censoring many books he did his religious best to make the faith secure from the doubts of intelligent examination and reasoning.

Later as pontiff he decreed that anyone who even kept a book by a heretic should be treated like a heretic. And if someone overheard criticism of the Inquisition and did not report it to the papal police, he was to consider himself as guilty as the malcontent and to have the devil beaten or thumb-screwed or rack-stretched out of him, for his own salvation.

Castiglione did not succeed Pius VII, but had to wait through the reign of Leo XII before securing St. Peter's throne in 1829. During his brief and delayed reign, the Papal States enjoyed some respite from the Stalinist sanctity of his hard and autocratic predecessor.

Pius VIII could be thought a *religious man* for the passing of the Roman Catholic Relief Act in Great Britain in 1829, and establishing the first strong ties with Roman Catholics in Armenia and the USA in the following year.

His authoritarian curia viewed Pius as religious for allowing Cardinal Albani, his secretary of state, a free hand in officially condemning the rising tide of democracy and national emancipation movements which broke out in Belgium, Ireland and Poland in 1830.

And what could be more religious than his bull *Litteris alto*? It proclaimed mixed marriages between Catholics and Protestants as a grave crime, a sin against God's law and a horror which assuredly produces physical deformities and "spiritual dangers."

ONE HUNDRED

De balneis Etruriæ
(From Balnea in Tuscany)

GREGORY XVI
(1831–1846)

THE NEXT PONTIFF would come from the strict Benedictine religious Order of the Camadolese, whose main headquarters was at Balnea, a town in the Tuscan hills a short distance from Florence.

The reputation that Cardinal Alberto Cappellari had for arch-conservatism had already preceded him when he joined his fellow cardinals in the conclave of 1830. When Napoleon's soldiers had dragged Pius VI off the chair of St. Peter, Cappellari defiantly published the book *The Triumph of the Holy See and the Church against the Attacks of Innovators*. The book upheld the infallibility of Christ's Vicar on Earth and his divine right to wield temporal power over Napoleon or any other mere secular ruler.

As prefect of the Congregation for the Propagation of the Faith (1826), Cappellari injected new blood into the dogma preached in missions overseas. His supporters knew that Cappellari, if he were pope, could shove an iron crook into the machinery of liberalism overtaking the faith.

The prime minister of the Austrian Empire, Prince Klemens von Metternich (1773–1859), endorsed Cappellari as just the kind of absolutist-loving, anti-modernist needed to guide the Roman Church beyond "the political madness of the age."

As Gregory XVI he waged a 15-year theological war against all things new and liberal. The new technology of steam trains and railways was abolished from the Papal States because it produced "pathways to the devil." His election as pope immediately caused a revolt across the Papal States which required Gregory to request Austrian armies to repress his citizens. To restore peace to the streets of Rome he grudgingly conceded limited reforms, but he would deny anything as overtly democratic as requests to grant elected assemblies or allow state councils to be composed of mere laymen. This predictably caused a second rebellion of the papal citizenry, requiring a second invasion of Austrian troops to crush dissent.

France deemed the Austrian occupation a ruse to grab up the Papal States and sent an army to occupy Ancona. Thus the first seven years of Gregory's reign ceded all the Papal States to Austrian and French occupation.

To the former chief propagandist of the Roman Church occupation was a better evil than granting democratic reform, freedom of thought, freedom of the press and the separation of Church and state – all of which were soundly condemned in his encyclical *Mirari vos* (1832).

Gregory would also condemn slavery and be responsible for the reconstruction and revival of Catholic missions around the world, especially in Canada and the USA.

As patron of the arts and archaeology Gregory added more prophetic merit to his motto DE BALNEIS ETRURIÆ by sponsoring the study of the ancient Estruscan baths (the *Balnea*) in that area. He also founded the Gregorian-Egyptian and Gregorian-Etruscan museums in the Vatican and the Christian Museum in the Lateran Basilica.

His righteous intransigence to change earned him an unflattering role in books by Protestant prophecy watchers like Edward Bichersteth, who in his *Practical Guide to Prophecies* (1836) dug up prophecies attributed to Joachim de Fiore as prescient evidence that Gregory was the potentate of an anti-Christian Babylon. He even had his part to play as the forewarned antipope of the Final Days, as interpreted by the Protestant cult of the Millerites who, in 1844, pulled on their white ascension robes to await the end of the world.

Gregory survived "doomsday" and the Millerite movement by two years.

ONE HUNDRED AND ONE

Crux de cruce
(The Cross from a Cross)[1]

PIUS IX
(1846–1878)

The Cross of Savoy

AFTER GREGORY CAME Giovanni Mastai-Ferretti, a man who many believe was one of the most significant popes of modern times.

Between his ordination as a priest in 1819 and his election as pope in 1846, he moved rapidly through the hierarchy, leaving behind a reputation as a progressive and liberal pastor as he accomplished his duties as a missionary in Chile (1823–1825) and managed the Hospice of St. Michele in Rome (1825–1827). While serving as archbishop of Spoleto (1827–1832) and as bishop of Imola (1832–1840) the cardinalate became aware of his pontiff potential and his cautious sympathies for Italian nationalism. He became a cardinal in 1840 and it took only two days for the conclave of 1846 to elect him as a moderate successor to Gregory XVI.

At the age of 54 Cardinal Giovanni, now Pius IX, began the longest reign from St. Peter's chair in papal history. His 34-year reign would see the termination of the Church of Rome's last vestiges of secular power. But before his body was laid to rest in 1878 he would leave the barque of St. Peter firmly set on its modern course as a superpower of the otherworldly realm of the spirit.

[1]Alternative: Cross upon a Cross.

His Latin motto, *the cross from a cross*, is rich in the metaphorical layers of St. Malachy's prophetic cake. It foresees *the cross* that Pius would bear from being the chief victim of history's march into nationalism. He would suffer his own Pontius Pilate, King Victor-Emmanuel (1820–1878), from the House of Savoy – whose coat of arms is dominated by a large white cross in a red chevron with a blue border. In 1870 the cross of Savoy centered in a green, white and red tricolor would fly over Castel Sant'-Angelo in place of the crosses, keys and triple tiara of the yellow and white papal banner. In that year Victor-Emmanuel's modern Italian state would annex the Papal States, bringing to a close its 1,116-year existence.

Upon Pius' election the Austrian prime minister, von Metternich, reflected that here was a pontiff who was "warm at heart, weak of head, and lacking utterly in common sense."

Pius would move through revolutionary times tripping over the contradictions of his character. He had the irrational reasoning of a sincere man of heart who believed that the people should be free to nourish their democratic and nationalistic desires – as long as they did not establish anything objective and legally binding not to the pope's liking, i.e. anything such as transforming his police "Papal" State into a constitutional democracy.

Pius began his reign as a kind of Gorbachev pontiff. There was a feeling of new openness emanating from St. Peter's throne. Pius freed and forgave thousands of political and religious prisoners in a general amnesty. He distinctly implied his support of Italian nationalist desires. The papal government was injected with a number of democratic reforms which dispelled much of the darkness of his predecessor's anal-retentive reign. But like Gorbachev, the avowed Marxist-Leninist, Pius as the avowed orthodox Vicar of Christ believed that he could deconstruct some of the authoritarian controls on his society and install democracy into the Papal States in order to save them. In the end both men miscalculated the response to their tinkering with the system. In both cases slightly cracking open the floodgates on the repressive dam of the people's desire for freedom and change unleashed a flood of revolution.

Pius differed from Gorbachev when the dam burst. Where the future and final premier of the Soviet Union passively allowed the communist empire to unravel, Pius fought tenaciously to plug the leak in his absolute and temporal authority which he himself had sprung.

In 1848–1849, two years into his reign, Europe was overwhelmed by a series of Aquarian Age revolutions. Pius faced a rebellion in Rome and had to escape the Vatican, in disguise, and spend two years in the Kingdom of Naples. When he returned in the wake of a French army of occupation the chastened liberal had converted into one of the most reactive pontiffs of the 19th century.

For the next 30 years the Papal States became the North Korea of the 19th century – a closed and repressive backwater out of touch with the times. Pius became another Kim Il Sung, a kind of saintly Stalinist overlording a totalitarian theocratic state. With the bayonets and cannon of his French garrison he could back up his bulls and edicts, effectively ending freedom of thought.

By the 1840s most European Jews had been freed from their ghettos and received an unprecedented measure of equal rights and freedom to practice their religion.

Not in the Papal States.

Jews were squeezed back into their urban concentration camps. Jewish children were regularly snatched from families to be baptized. In general the race which had given Christians their beloved Christ was repressed with a virulence that would make other anti-Semitic popes of the 19th century blush. A Jew could even be sent to prison for employing a Christian to clean his linen.

Pius employed his own Gestapo who infiltrated the citizenry with spies. People were tortured and executed for minor offenses. Thanks to Pius IX the Inquisition continued its barbarities in the name of Christ within the Papal States up to 1870. Torture had been disavowed since 1830s, but defendants during Pius IX's reign were tried without legal representation and the tribunal of priests sitting in judgment had unlimited power. You would not be sent to the rack to confess your sins, but you could end up tortured by neglect and locked away and forgotten in the dungeons. Descriptions recorded in 1870 by troops of Victor-Emmanuel who were liberating the Papal States describe the survivors of the dungeons in terms reminiscent of death-camp survivors from the 20th century.

Pius seemed not to notice.

He lived above it all, attending to his spiritual duties to Christ. His devotion to increasing the glory of the Church throughout the world was as total and dedicated as his political reign of terror. The repugnant means which were used to justify their absolutist temporal ends became the responsibility of his sole advisor, the secretary of state, Giacomo Antionelli (d. 1876). This Beria of the papacy was the spawn of a Neapolitan bandit. Behind his priestly robes hid a rapist and an adulterer in the tradition of the Borgias who would run the pope's fascist dictatorship and steadily bleed it of funds for his own pleasure.

Up to 1870, when the rest of Italy was united, Pius stubbornly held on to his papal territories, brushing off overtures from Victor-Emmanuel for the pope to accept the reality of Italian unification and save the papacy. His promises to secure the spiritual power of the pope were rejected. Catholic rulers and theologians outside of the Papal States corresponded with Pius, reminding him that Christ's kingdom was never intended to be secular. His kingdom was "not of this Earth." They pointed out that no pope had ruled as a secular king until the Papal States were established 700 years into the ministry of Christ. And this Patrimony of Peter had existed only by grace of a forgery, the Donation of Constantine.

It is said that the jubilation in the streets of Rome in 1870 at the time of its liberation by Italian troops rivaled the celebrations of 1944, when Allied troops liberated the Eternal City from Nazi German occupation.

As the pope smoldered with rage in the Vatican, Victor-Emmanuel – whom the pope judged as the "Prince of Darkness" – made Rome the capital of a unified Italy. He freed thousands from the dungeons of the Inquisition and by royal decree gave Jews the freedom that the papacy had denied them for more than 1,500 years.

Because of him, the last ghetto in Europe was abolished.

Victor-Emmanuel made sensitive and patient efforts to bring the medieval mind-set of Pius around to the 19th century. When his armies entered Rome he was careful not to allow a single artillery shell to hit the Vatican. The pope was not to be harmed or arrested. Victor-Emmanuel honored his promise to protect the pope's religious powers with his Law of Guarantees (1871). These established the 108.7 acres of the Vatican complex as the inviolable property of the pontiff. It granted other properties in and around Rome as part of a new Vatican State, free of any control from the new Italian government.

Pius' thank you was to reject the terms and excommunicate the king. He also threatened the same for any Italian citizen who served Victor-Emmanuel's government. His excommunication had next to no effect.

Pius would spend the last eight years of his reign denying the loss of his temporal powers. He would bear his cross as the self-proclaimed "prisoner of the Vatican." He successfully propagated the image of a persecuted pope to the Catholic laity around the world. The cross bearer against the modernism of the holder of the Cross of Savoy circulated around Germany, Ireland and much of the Catholic world pictures of himself lying on filthy straw in a dungeon. In response poor Catholics dug deeper into their threadbare pockets to pay the tax of Peter's pence. Pius saw the coffers of his Vatican "prison" overflow.

Peter de Rosa reminds us that Pius' "prison" had more acreage than did all the Jews who ever lived in the Roman ghetto down the centuries. Our holy prisoner had the finest of beds, and luxurious apartments with thousands of rooms. I would like to add that he enjoyed a "prison" library containing thousands of the finest books – many of them from the best banned authors – in the world. He could leave his "cell" to exercise in dozens of acres of the luscious Vatican gardens or, as de Rosa said, "play the occasional game of billiards with Cardinal Antonelli."

Thus Pius ended his life as a Jacobite poet observed, as a "prisoner of himself."

APPARITIONS OF MARY

Where his political rule was an unmitigated disaster, his reign as a politician of the spirit had far more impact on the future of the Church.

Pius IX was the first modern pontiff to significantly encourage and spread the Marian cult of devotion. It is clear from his own writings that he took to heart the Virgin Mary sightings and their collective message of the coming tribulation. Centuries of Catholic lore stressed that if the Mother of Christ appeared with ever increasing frequency to the simplest and most humble Catholics, it was a sign that the final days were at hand.

The number of apparitions of the Blessed Virgin had suddenly jumped since the 1830s. In 1846, Pius' first year as pope, the first significant sighting of the Virgin Mary in modern times took place near La Salette in the French Alps.

Sometime in the early afternoon of 19 September Mélanie Calvat, a 14-year-old shepherdess and stonemason's daughter, along with her companion, an 11-year-old son of a wheelwright named Pierre-Maximin Giraud, descended the meadows of Mt. Planteau with their eight cattle, a dog and a goat to refresh them at the "beast's spring." While resting there they ate their lunch and fell asleep for about an hour. When they awoke the animals were gone. They ran to a vista point to see where they had wandered, then walked back to the spring to pick up their knapsacks.

Someone or something was sitting there.

At first Mélanie thought that the sun had fallen next to the creek. The two beheld a glowing ball that opened and issued forth "a beautiful lady, all light and flowers," said Mélanie. The lady sat on some stones lining the creek; she was hunched forward, her face buried in her hands. Her luminous frame shook silently. Mélanie and Maximin watched, speechless, as the lady suddenly floated into the air.

Throughout her life Mélanie would add more details about what the entity said. These statements and prophecies would later find themselves embellished and published around the world as messages from the Virgin Mary. It is important to remember that neither Mélanie nor Maximin at first identified this spectral messenger as the Blessed Virgin. It was their family members and farm employers who convinced them.

Whoever this being from La Salette was, she in essence conveyed a prophecy which bemoaned the decline of spirituality in the world and the loss of direction of the Catholic church. In later years more information was published which revealed a dire forecast implying the advent of civil strife and wars. The words attributed to the Lady of the Beast's Spring could also describe the present-day dangers of the greenhouse effect and a coming global paroxysm of seismic and volcanic activity which other seers, like Edgar Cayce (d. 1945), believe will begin after 1998.

The bishop of Grenoble believed their story and sent word of Mélanie Calvat's vision to Pope Pius IX. Some biographies say that he even sent her in person to relate everything that she and Maximin Giraud had heard and seen.

In 1854, eight years after the visions of La Salette, Pius, while enduring his exile from Rome at Gaeta, redefined the Catholic doctrine by proclaiming the Immaculate Conception of the Virgin Mary. Pius' revelation brushed aside the up-to-then errorless assertions against the immaculate conception from dozens of Christianity's saintly thinkers. St. Malachy's beloved friend, St. Bernard de Clairvaux, considered the thought of Mary as being free of sin at conception an aberration.

St. Bernard believed that people are conceived out of lust, period. Mary was free from sin once she was born, not before.

That line of perfect dogma remained essentially uncontradicted until Pius IX began riding the modern wave of the Marian cult. With his declaration of Mary's immaculate conception, she was henceforth cleaned of sin even *before* her birth; otherwise one must assume that God through the holy spirit was caught contributing to the original sin of sex.

Critics of Pius' definition of Mary's freedom from original sin believe that it was an act of spiritual politics. The Church, navigating through the treacherous waters of the ever more atheistic and skeptical modern era, needed a spiritual shot in the arm to renew the faith. Pius' detour on the infallible march of Christian doctrine was a beatific boost of vitamin B into the arm of the Marian cult. Through a revitalized worship of Mary, nearly two millennia of the feminine spiritual virtues of patience, compassion and love repressed by the patriarchal popes finally had their official outlet for full expression.

Through the spread of the Mary cult Pius renewed the spiritual, if not the political, faith of millions in the Roman Church. In 1858 the 19th century's most significant Mary sighting took place 18 times at Massabielle, at a grotto near Lourdes. The catalyst of these sightings, the simple peasant and future St. Bernadette, said that the Blessed Virgin identified herself as the Immaculate Conception (a term Pius already had made public four years before the first vision). The grotto of Lourdes remains one of Catholicism's most sacred places of pilgrimage to this day.

In 1864, ten years to the day after he pronounced Mary's conception as immaculate, Pius would try to retain his hold on slipping absolutes with the encyclical *Quanta cura* and its controversial addendum, the *Syllabus of Errors*.

Among the 80 declarations of the *Syllabus of Errors* was Pius' proclamation that the Church of Rome is the alpha and omega of truth on Earth. In short, all things new and progressive were judged as evil. Freedom of thought – evil. Freedom of worship – evil.

For the most part the minions of Catholicism dutifully obeyed. Many of Pius' reactionary declarations on sex, democracy and evolution hamstring the Catholic Church to this day. Many historians believe that Pius forever retarded the Church of Rome's ability to adapt to the modern era. It could be said that he, more than most pontiffs of the 19th century, added fuel to the self-fulfillment of prophecies which could threaten an end of an anachronistic Church in the 21st century.

But Pius' counter-spiritual revolution did not stop with the *Syllabus of Errors*. The closer the armies of Italian liberation came to Rome the more desperate and fantastic became Pius' pronouncements.

At the First Vatican Council (1869–1870) Pius rose to new heights of absolutism by declaring himself infallible.

Before 1870 an ordinary Catholic believer could choose in the privacy of his own heart whether a pope in matters of doctrine and morality was perfect. But Pius' *ex cathedra* statement – that is, from the throne of St. Peter's – spiritually bound every Catholic heart to obey his edict without question. It no longer mattered that the first pope, the Apostle Peter, was fallible, or that early Christian fathers never imagined they had the right to define the doctrines and spiritual beliefs of the entire Church.

Now the spiritual vision of *Cross from a Cross* demanded that all Catholics bear his *cross* of absolute belief in the perfection of the pope.

Such a pronouncement had the effect of nailing the hands and feet of a pontiff's secular power to the cross of Savoy.

Strangely enough it gave the Roman Church a new lease on

religious life. Some wags might say that when papal secular politics was crucified it rose again – beyond the reach of objective and legal criticism and beyond the checks and balances of reason – to become a thing beyond reason.

ONE HUNDRED AND TWO

Lumen in cœlo
(A Light in the Sky)

LEO XIII
(1878–1903)

THE COAT OF papal arms had not been changed for 32 years. After the second month of 1878, the crown and gold and silver keys of the Vatican would decorate the beautiful arms of the House of Pecci. These happen to be dominated by the *light* of a great comet.

Cardinal Giocchino Vincenzo Pecci was chosen in the third ballot as a compromise successor. The scholarly and moderate Pecci's delicate 68-year-old frame teetered under the weight of the triple tiara crown as the first pontiff of a Holy See to be toothless in the realm of secular power. Many of the cardinals who chose him predicted that the new Leo XIII would not long survive the rigors of his holy office.

How wrong they were.

Leo would summon his waning life force for another 25 years, making his reign the second longest in history.

He softened or overturned many of his predecessors' inflexible policies and used his formidable political skill to empower the spiritual influence of the Roman Church around the world outside of Italy.

Through Leo the Church met the closing years of the 19th century with its most rapid global expansion, founding 248 sees, 48 vicarages and 2 patriarchates, plus new hierarchies in North Africa, India, Japan and Scotland and as many as 28 new dioceses in the USA. He helped to spread the Marian cult by designating 11 February as a feast day for the Immaculate Conception of the Blessed Virgin Mary.

At home, Leo would not accept modern Italy, its government or its terms limiting the papacy to the confines of the Vatican compound. Leo cut off his contacts with the Italian churches for decades to spite his loss of the papacy.

His efforts to reconcile the Vatican papacy with England and France were unsuccessful, and he censured the Catholic "Americanism" movement which sought to make an amalgamation of Catholic faith with modern ideas and democratic practices.

In 1883 he opened the doors of the Vatican library to all scholars who wished to examine them, saying "the Church has no secrets." This must have been news to them, for many secular scholars flocked to examine which books prior pontiffs had banned as being religiously incorrect.

His pontificate ended with much of the Church's reputation as a spiritual conscience and authority renewed and globally respected. Malachy motto watchers like to add that Leo's *light* is not only that of a heraldic bent-wise comet but describes his character as well. He was said to have a profound spiritual charisma. Many believers would like to observe – and perhaps a few actually did see – the light of his saintly Sol Invictus aura.

The more doom-laden interpreter might say that Leo's light, being that of a comet, is a foreboding omen for the waves of apocalyptic turbulence that the barque of St. Peter was about to navigate down the white-water rapids of the 20th century.

ONE HUNDRED AND THREE

Ignis ardens
(Burning Fire)

ST. PIUS X
(1903–1914)

There will be signs in the sun, moon, and stars. . . . Men will faint from terror, apprehensive of what is coming on the world, for the heavenly bodies will be shaken.
Luke 21:25–6

[IGNIS ARDENS] may either symbolize the zeal and charity of the pontiff to be elected, or may depict the violence of the sufferings and trials he is to endure, perhaps from a terrible war, perhaps from a general conflagration or cataclysm in the moral or physical order.
Abbé Joseph Maître (1902),
Les Papes et la Papauté d'après la Prophétie attribuée à St. Malachie

The *burning fire* of a six-pointed star dominates the coat of arms of Guiseppe Melchior Sarto, who replaced the long-lived and vital Pope Leo after his sudden and unexpected death.

In 1903 the cardinals of the sacred college showed a collective desire to pick a man made of a different cloth than Leo XIII. This first pontiff chosen in the new and final century of the Second Christian Millennium, they reasoned, should be a religious leader. So they elected a man who had distinguished himself through his lengthy life in the priesthood as a pastoral rather than political figure. Staunchly orthodox, pure to a fault, Cardinal Sarto only encouraged his supporters when he tried to dissuade them from choosing his name.

Gone was Sarto; in his place arose Pius X. He was the most recent pontiff to be canonized (in 1954). One could say that his pontificate was a *burning fire* of religious zeal, attempting to shine a light on a world lurching towards the rolling thunder of its first taste of Armageddon.

It suited his reality to define himself a "prisoner of the Vatican" as Pius IX and Leo XIII had. Unlike his predecessors he would do more to open relations with the Italian government and, as his own official motto implied, tried to "restore all things in Christ," by at least establishing a cautious détente between the isolated Vatican and the leaders of Italy. He also lifted the ban on Catholics voting in Italy's elections.

Still, Pius was overwhelmed by modern times. Sincere as he was, he could not snap out of the traditional perception of popes, who saw the future as good only if it resembled the past. Pius sought to restore all things to a concept of Christ that was more than 19 centuries old. Yet when his master walked the Earth he brushed aside the 15-century-old dogma of Moses to establish "a new law." Perhaps if Pius had been pontiff of the Sanhedrin when the cult guru from Galilee was making spiritual revolution, he would have faced the future like Caiaphas did – with his backside – and navigated tomorrow's waters by the lost currents of yesterday's dogmas.

In his decree *Lamentabiliti* (1907) Pius fired off an assortment of backward-blasting salvoes. For example the laity and backsliding theologians were told to cease their efforts to find common ground with Catholic faith and objective science. Attempts to find harmony between piety and the politics of socialism and democracy were forbidden. Narrations of the apostle John were to be once again viewed as historical fact and not mystical contemplation. According to Pius the Catholic Faith does have a right to pass judgment against the assertions of science – even though the Bible contains only revealed truths. Jesus cannot be viewed as being in error, even if his Second Coming was not as immediate as he had promised. And most important, Pius announced that Catholic society is *not* subject to perpetual evolution as is human society-at-large.

On the short summer night of 30 June 1908, one year following Pius' attack on liberalism, millions of people across Europe thought they saw the *burning fire* of an orange light rising in the northern and northeastern skies. Many people in the English countryside cranked up their new-fangled communication device called the telephone to call relatives in London and ask if the city was on fire. Newspapers across the Northern Hemisphere reported this "false dawn" and related disquieting stories of queer changes in atmospheric pressure. People gaped in disbelief as their compasses spun out of control and their suddenly perplexed horses and animals lost their balance. Many cities in the Russian empire noted the passing seismic waves of some distant earthquake, but no epicenter could be discovered.

A sign of evil to come?

Perhaps.

Such a conclusion would have remained untested – and uncontested – in a more backward era. But scientists would, within 20 years', discover that the strange light had been a reflection of the sun's rays off a gigantic mushroom cloud of some cosmic phenomenon exploding a few miles above the vast taiga forests near the Tunguska River region of Siberia. Whether the object was a meteor, extraterrestrial ship, comet or even a wandering black hole is still unknown, but it is estimated that its detonation was equal to a nuclear explosion of more than 30 megatons – which is enough explosive punch to obliterate 1,500 cities the size of Hiroshima. But the Tunguska region is one of the most remote areas on Earth so the burning fire flattened hundreds of thousands of acres of forest instead.

Only a few Tunguska aboriginal natives were later interviewed by the scientists, but they all described a huge column of fire rising to the heavens, and being buffeted by deafening tattoos of thunder and rolling earthquakes. For the Tunguska natives the explosion was the fulfillment of their prophecy that the end of the world was nigh.

Another *burning fire* would put the fear of end times into many of the so-called civilized peoples of Europe. In the year 1912 (the eighth year of Pius' reign) the Holy Father, like millions of other Christians in America and Europe, witnessed an unusually dramatic passing of Halley's Comet in the sky. Prophetic folklore viewed these bearded stars as omens of revolutionary convulsion, general war and catastrophe. The great comet of 1812, for example, had been identified as an omen forecasting Napoleon's greatest military catastrophe later that year when he invaded Russia.

A century later, Halley's Comet only added to the general fear that a terrible war was coming. Pius had no doubt that a global war was about to divide and devastate the Christian world. His final years found him desperately firing off letters to the saber-rattling, Christ-loving monarchs of Europe, urging them to seek peace.

World War I commenced on 1 August 1914, just three days short of Pius' 11th anniversary as pope. He viewed the world war as the beginning of the end times. On his anniversary he predicted many of the war's apocalyptic consequences for Christianity, warning that the "present wickedness of the world" was only a precursor to far more dreadful tribulations to come before doomsday.

Seeing his efforts to prevent the war come to naught, it is said that he fell into a profound depression which hastened his death on 20 August 1914.

ONE HUNDRED AND FOUR

Religio depopulata
(Religion Depopulated)[1]

BENEDICT XV
(1914–1922)

ST. MALACHY PROPHECY watchers waited in suspense for the man who would acquire this dreadful motto for his destiny.

Some of the cardinals gathering for the conclave to elect Pius X's successor held in September 1914 probably were aware of the renewed interest in this predicted papal succession unto

---

[1] Alternative translations: a) *Religion laid waste*; b) *Christendom depopulated* [Dupont].

doomsday, an interest which had been fanned by the publication of the Abbé Joseph Maître's classic on St. Malachy's predictions, *La Prophétie des Papes* (1901). At least a handful of cardinals who assembled to cast their ballots might have read it. Some would be aware that someone among them – a friend, a political foe or even they themselves – might win destiny's lottery and be chosen as the seventh pope before the terrible day of the Lord's Judgment of the Earth.

It took no prophet, nor even an extremely lucky forgery, to recognize that the new pope's reign would be overshadowed – if not overwhelmed – by the hecatomb of world war. Therefore the Sacred College of Cardinals chose the newly ordained cardinal Giacomo della Chiesa to be Pope Benedict XV. He was a staunch conservative against the so-called "progress" of modern times who might apply his long service in the diplomatic corps of the Church to undertake a negotiated peace between God's warring Christian children.

The new pope would immediately find himself faced with a perplexing spiritual dilemma. He was pastor to ten million baptized Catholic soldiers fighting for Germany, Austria Hungary and other allies of the Central Powers. He was also Vicar of Christ for the 19 million French, Italian, English and other European – and later American – Catholics who fought for the Allied side.

Just whose prayers for victory should the pontiff send to heaven?

It was necessary that he become God's neutral diplomat. He could not – or would not – explain why one set of Catholic Christians could send another set of "enemy" Catholic Christians to meet their same God.

Many people were perplexed by his lack of action.

A "heathen unbeliever" like Benedict's Hindu contemporary, Mahatma Gandhi (1869–1948), was ready to put his life on the line for peace and non-violence. On more than one occasion Gandhi, in his passive revolution against British rule of India, had threatened to stop violence by doing violence to himself. In 1947 he would even undertake a fast unto death to end the riots and wholesale slaughter being committed by Hindus and Muslims during the Indian Partition.

If Christ was ready to die for the sins of the world, why could not Benedict expose himself to war's deadly and satanic hand to stop Christian from butchering Christian?

Imagine, if you will, a different Benedict XV – one who announces that he will carry Christ's cross into the no man's land of the trenches and stand between the warring Christian armies. We see Christ's representative on Earth threatening to expose himself to bullets and artillery shells until both armies cease fire. He would stand in the lunar landscape of death, asking all combatants to remember that they are brothers in Christ's love and demanding that they go home and make peace.

Benedict could have embarked on a pilgrimage to the nearest front in northeastern Italy. He could have taken his cross and wandered into the valley of death and carnage in a battle like Caporetto, or come forth at any one of the 11 battles fought along the Isonzo River. If an army of simple Christians could march into the jaws of lions in the Roman Colosseum and Circus Maximus, what was stopping the "Roman" pontiff or a dozen successors from marching one after the other to be martyred in World War I? The sight of one courageous pontiff after another giving his life for peace may have inspired Christian soldiers the world over to put down their guns.

There is every chance that they would have been killed, just as there was every chance that Jesus entering Jerusalem would be crucified. But consider how Christ's martyrdom changed the world.

There was no reason for the Vicar of such a Christ to fear death. His berth in heaven was assured. And certainly there were hundreds of cardinals who could fill his mitered cap if he did not return.

Such a Christ-like act of courage was not possible for Benedict. He was characterized by unsympathetic critics as an intellectual and spiritual featherweight who failed dismally to referee the most brutal global boxing match yet waged by man. He chose to write declarations for peace – which were generally ignored – in the safe and far-off confines of the Vatican rather than facing the lions of war.

In his defense, I must say that Benedict did go far in mobilizing the Church to succor the wounded and prisoners of war from both sides. And some believe that his seven-point peace plan came close to bringing an end to the killing in 1917. The German Christians approved of Benedict's plan, but the Allied Christians were more keen for fighting it out. By then they were receiving an influx of fresh Christian blood to spill in the trenches from four million recently drafted American Protestants and Catholics.

When the war ended, Benedict was snubbed by the victorious Allies at the Versailles Peace Treaty talks: he was not being invited. Some historians, however, believe that the Protestant American President Woodrow Wilson's 14-point peace plan submitted at Versailles was based on Benedict's seven-point plan.

A number of gifted Catholic seers, such as Pastor Bartholomeus (1613–1658) and the 18th-century Bavarian cowherd Stormberger, are among the first prescient gentile pathfinders to side with the Jewish cabalistic interpretation of Old Testament prophecy about God's final battle on Earth. The cabalists believe that the battle to end all battles, Armageddon, will be a conflict fought in three installments. These are generally interpreted to be a first, second and a third and final world war.

This grim motto falling upon Benedict could clearly apply to Armageddon: Part One. His eight-year pontificate saw the Christian religion *depopulated* by nearly a quarter-billion souls. He was elected pope one month into the four-year carnage of World War I. Approximately 19 million soldiers and 10 million civilians died during the war. At least 99 per cent of these 29 million souls were Christians.

As the war ground to a halt in 1918 Pope RELIGIO DEPOPULATA looked out over a world suffering the scourge of the Spanish influenza. This pandemic raged for two years and carried off 21,500,000 people. Most of the victims were in Asia and Africa but at least five million European and American Christians were consumed. At the close of World War I the Christian bulwark of the Russian Empire fell into the hands of the atheistic Communist Bolsheviks. Civil war and famine carried off two million Orthodox Russian Christians. By the time Benedict lay on his deathbed in 1922 the communists had won the civil war and stole away 200 million Orthodox Christians into the cult of atheistic communism. During Benedict's reign Christianity was depopulated by a total of 235 million believers.

THE LADY OF FÁTIMA

In the fourth year of Pope Benedict's pontificate, towards the end of World War I, three shepherd children were tending their sheep in the fields near the Portuguese village of Fátima. Their visitation by a spectral entity identified as the Virgin Mary has become one of the most famous prophetic events in history. The messages coming from the mysterious "Lady of Fátima" would influence the lives and policies of the next four popes; it is expected that her prophetic warnings will significantly affect the policies of the two future popes remaining to complete St. Malachy's doomsday succession list.

On one fine spring day in 1917, the three children – Lucia, ten; Francisco, nine; and Giacinta, seven – heard claps of thunder roll across the blue, cloudless sky. Soon afterwards they witnessed the luminous form of a lady, brighter than the sun, standing upon a cloud above a little evergreen tree. Only Lucia, the oldest child, heard the apparition speak to them, for several minutes. The apparition asked the children to return to the tree on the 13th day of each month from 13 May to 13 October 1917, at which time she would reveal who she was. She then vanished.

As the children faithfully returned each month to the site at Cova da Iria word got around of the event. Soon the 13th day of each month saw larger and larger throngs of the curious coming from far and wide to watch, pray and wait as the children stood in silence in front of the tree.

Apparently no one else saw the strange apparition. Some people later related hearing a subtle buzzing in their ears and said that they felt cloaked in a blanket of peace. Others remember seeing only a bright cloud floating above the little pine tree.

The skeptics saw nothing, and soon the government and police decided to put an end to what they considered to be childish and unlawful gatherings. The civil prefect of Outrem seized the children at their appointed rendezvous with the apparition on 13 August. He interrogated and threatened the children with torture for two days. The traumatized children stuck to their story. The resplendent lady reappeared to them six days later at Valinhos, not far from the original sight of the first apparition. She blessed them for keeping their faith and promised to appear one more time on 13 October and present a miracle that would prove to all people that she was real.

On that date a crowd 50,000 strong gathered at Cova da Iria and stoically waited in a driving rainstorm for "the happening." Among them were the civil prefect of Outrem and many skeptical journalists, unbelievers and political radicals waiting to be the first to howl at what they were convinced would be the biggest spiritual hoax of the century.

The children knelt before the little pine tree and were the only witnesses to a shining figure who told them she was the Lady of the Rosary. She imparted three prophecies, or "secrets," regarding the "latter days" before the apocalypse.

No one else saw a thing. The soaked crowd and numerous cripples waiting to be healed began to murmur impatiently for a sign. Soon all would be shaken by either one of the greatest mass illusions in history or one of the greatest mass experiences of the unknown.

The rain stopped and the clouds parted to reveal the sun. Witnesses say that the glowing orb spun rapidly and descended towards the earth three times like a top out of control. Published accounts tell of mass healings and the crowds' rain-soaked clothes miraculously drying during the sun's UFO-like dance in the sky. Apparently, skeptic and zealot alike bowed down and prayed.

Word went around that the Lady of Fátima had predicted that the great war would soon after be over and Christian Russia might fall into the hands of some kind of Antichrist-like government. They also heard the tearful Lucia relate that the Blessed Virgin apparition had said that the two younger children, Francisco and Giacinta, would soon come home to heaven. In fact they did die the following year in the great Spanish influenza pandemic of 1918.

Lucia later became a nun and was taught how to write so that the three "secrets" of the Virgin could be recorded during the reign of the next pope, Pius XI.

ONE HUNDRED AND FIVE

————————>( )<————————

Fides intrepida
(Intrepid Faith)

PIUS XI
(1922–1939)

CARDINAL RATTI, THE passionate mountain climber and highly respected chief librarian of the Ambrosian and later the Vatican Library, was next in line to sit on St. Peter's Chair. Multilingual and scholarly, this former archbishop of Milan had been appointed a cardinal only seven months earlier, after serving as a staunch anti-communist apostolic visitor to Warsaw (1921) during Poland's war of independence from Soviet Russia. He gained merit among voting members of the sacred college for remaining in the Polish capital despite the risk of being shot if a Bolshevik force had succeeded in taking the city.

On 6 February the relatively young and athletic 54-year-old pontiff was ordained Pius XI. He defined his new pontificate with the intrepid motto, "To seek the peace of Christ in the reign of Christ." Much of his energies and diplomatic skills during his 17-year rule were used to navigate the Church through the darker Aquarian Age waves of change.

Nine months into his reign, the Italian nation surrounding his little Vatican enclave became a Fascist republic under its new prime minister, Benito Mussolini (1883–1945). The pope and *Il Duce* were both dedicated anti-communists and would manufacture a good working relationship, primarily through the intellectual skill and diplomacy of Pius' two secretaries of state, Cardinal Gasparri (d. 1930) and Cardinal Eugenio Pacelli (the future Pius XII). Thanks to them, Pius XI ended the nearly 60-year political limbo of Vatican statelessness by negotiating the Lateran Treaty in 1929 with fascist Italy, thus creating the modern-day Vatican City-State. The treaty in effect ended the symbolic and self-imposed "house arrest" of every pontiff since 1870, the year when Pius IX had refused to officially acknowledge the loss of the Papal States.

Mussolini granted Pius and all future popes their rights as

absolute temporal and spiritual sovereigns of the 108.7 acres of the Vatican complex. Fascist Italy would respect the independence of the Holy See in international affairs and honor the borders of the Vatican City-State as a sovereign nation enjoying diplomatic and political independence.

Mussolini, eager to gain political capital with the Italian people, signed generous agreements with Pius which proclaimed Fascist Italy a Catholic country, with a mandatory Catholic-run school system. An organization named Catholic Action was granted all powers to reindoctrinate the Italian laity, and Catholic youth groups such as the Jocists were permitted. Mussolini granted the pope absolute spiritual authority over his Italian subjects. The country governed by a blackshirt dictatorship would pay the Vatican City-State 750 million lire in cash and another billion lire in negotiable bonds. Throughout Mussolini's long tyranny Fascist Italy would pay the salaries of all priests within its borders. The payments were continued by post-war democratic governments until 1985.

"Mussolini has given God back to Italy and Italy back to God," declared Pius. He would later add that Mussolini was a "gift from Providence, a man free from the prejudices of the politicians of the liberal school."

One began seeing the rosaries and crosses of Italian priests jiggle as men of the cloth snapped to attention and gave Mussolini the customary stiff-armed Fascist salute as a gesture of good will and warmer relations.

One could imagine that a medieval seer or a Renaissance forger of these prophecies of St. Malachy would be well pleased to call this pontiff *intrepid* in his faith, for many of Pius' views seemed to be medieval rocks churning white water in the river of progress. For instance he imperiously decreed that Christian unity could only happen if all Christians returned to the one and only "true" Catholic faith. Between 1925 and 1933 he issued a number of encyclicals concerning issues of marriage, education, economy and birth control which promoted a great leap backwards to earlier, less secular times.

Pius' answer to the advances of contraception was to publish the encyclical *Casti connubii* (1930) which only toughened the

Roman Church's policy on marriage and stated that contraception was sinful.

"No reason, however grave, may be put forward by which anything intrinsically against nature may become conformable to nature and morally good. Since, therefore, the conjugal act is destined by nature for the begetting of children, those who in exercising it deliberately frustrate its natural power and purpose sin against nature and commit a deed which is shameful and intrinsically vicious."

The pope's conscience was clear. If he had anything to do with it, the overpopulated future would be like the underpopulated past, whatever the cost.

Pius flexed his intrepid faith when he promoted the spread of Catholic Action groups around the world. He commanded Catholics everywhere to resist socialist and communist persecution, first in Mexico during its civil war in the 1920s, later in the 1930s when Josef Stalin (1879–1953) unleashed communist purges against Ukrainian Catholics in the Soviet Union and yet again when the Republican government of Spain persecuted priests and Catholics during its fight with the pro-Catholic Spanish fascist dictator, Francisco Franco (1892–1975), during the Spanish Civil War (1936–39).

In his *intrepid faith* he would put his trust in a Catholic layperson from Linz, Austria who, prior to World War I, lived in that "blessed" state of the poorest when he was a hobo ekeing out a wretched existence on the streets of Vienna. Two decades later the bum had risen from obscurity to become Chancellor of Germany in 1933. Adolf Hitler (1889–1945) then saved his adopted country from the evils of communism.

Certainly Pius, a Vicar of Christ, must have recognized a greater good hidden behind the evil of Adolf Hitler. Did he not send Cardinal Pacelli to negotiate a concordat with the National Socialist dictatorship in 1933, effectively silencing protests of danger coming from German priests and laity alike? What could they know about the good of Hitler if the keeper of the keys to God's paradise could so easily brush aside their protests and bless the Führer? Did Pius not know that such an act enhanced Hitler's political powers, making it easier to begin arresting all communists – along with free thinkers, critics (a number of them priests and good Catholics), Jews and anyone else who did not fit in Catholic Hitler's Third Reich?

One needs a good dose of intrepid faith in the mysterious ways of an infallible pontiff who, in 1933 can trust that the black-shirts of Mussolini and the black uniformed secret police of Adolf Hitler are doing right by Christ, yet be shaken in his faith in Nazism and Italian fascism a mere four years later.

God moves in mysterious ways when Pius in his encyclical *Mit brennender Sorge* ("With burning sadness") condemns Nazism as a vehicle of the Antichrist.

This might have been a good time to lift the ban on the writings of Catholic Nostradamus to read his warnings that Adolf Hitler (whom he called "Hister") would become the second of three Antichrists before doomsday. He had warned that this man, a "Captain of Greater Germany," armed with the sign of a "crooked cross," would break peace unions in the years "thirty-seven" as well as in "forty" and "forty-five."

The nagging words of Catholic prophetic tradition were once again whispered across the Catholic world as it seemed that God was about to unleash another installment of Armageddon upon the Earth.

In January 1938 the "signs in the sky" warned by the Christ in St. Matthew's gospel appeared to be dancing with coruscating vibrancy all across the northern skies of Europe. As the winter skies over Portugal filled with unholy light, the surviving child responsible for keeping the three secrets of the Fátima prophecy – now a full-grown woman at age 29 in a nun's habit – was gazing out the small window of her convent cell at the lurid northern lights.

Lucia dos Santos was now known as Sister Marie dos Dores (Sister Mary of the Sorrows). She had entered the College of Sisters of St. Dorothy at Vilar do Porto in 1921, becoming a nun in their Carmelite order by 1925. In the following years Lucia had had further paranormal encounters with what she believed to be Jesus Christ and the Blessed Virgin. These led her to apply her new skill of writing to record all of her visions for posterity.

In 1927, the Virgin is said to have requested that the first two secrets given at Fátima ten years before be revealed to the public at large. In the next few years Sister Marie submitted two letters, each containing one of the first two secrets, to her spiritual directors and confessors. Her uncorroborated report claims that her confessor, Fr. José Bernardo Gonçalves, passed the information all the way to Pius XI.

If this is true here is what the pontiff may have been told. In her first secret back in 1917 the apparition at Fátima revealed to the three children all the horrors of hell. The second secret may have read thus: (The text below was published in 1941 with further clarifications received in visions during 1929.)

God wishes to establish in the world devotion to my Immaculate Heart. If what I say to you is done, many souls will be saved and there will be peace. The war is going to end; but if people do not cease offending God, a worse one will break out during the pontificate of Pius XI.

[The war ending is the First World War. The new war therefore would be the Second World War, which did begin seven months after the death of Pius XI.]

When you see a night illumined by an unknown light, know that this is the great sign given you by God that He is about to punish the world for its crimes, by means of war, famine, and persecutions of the Church and of the Holy Father.

[During the Second World War, when the prophetic accounts of Sister "Lucia" were widely published, she reflected that the strange spectral lights dancing in the northern skies of Europe and America on the night of 25 January 1938 were not simply a strong display of the aurora borealis but a sign from God that a greater world war was about to begin.]

The second secret continued with the Virgin's request that Russia be consecrated to her Immaculate Heart or else great tribulations would come. These tribulations have been described as the five scourges.

The first would be the outbreak of World War II, following the phantom lights in the northern skies. The second was the rise of worldwide communism, which could cover the entire Earth if the Blessed Virgin's requests went unheeded. The third and fourth scourges would fall on Catholics and the Church and followed the traditional themes of other seers concerning the Chastisement prophecies: The faithful would be martyred as well as a future pope. The fifth and final scourge implied the gruesome themes of the third secret from Fátima, which Lucia had been instructed by the Virgin Mary to keep sealed in an envelope until the year 1960. It was rumored that the fifth scourge described the Third World War of Armageddon.

To prevent these scourges the Virgin Mary requested that Russia be consecrated to her Immaculate Heart. She says:

> *If my requests are heeded, Russia will be converted, and there will be peace; if not, she will spread her errors throughout the world, causing wars and persecutions of the Church. The good will be martyred; the Holy Father will have much to suffer; various nations will be annihilated. In the end, my Immaculate Heart will triumph. The Holy Father will consecrate Russia to me, and she will be converted, and a period of peace will be granted to the world.*

Pius XI would not officially consecrate Russia to Mary's Immaculate Heart, and, either by coincidence or by divine retribution, war did come and the prophecies of the spread of communism out of Russia during the resultant Cold War were generally fulfilled. But communism would not conquer the world. And even Russia herself would cast off its Marxist chains and find millions returning to the Christian faith.

What had happened to change the course of destiny?

Many Catholic prophecy watchers like to believe that what Pius XI ignored in the Virgin Mary's request, his successor, Cardinal Pacelli, obeyed. Pacelli was a devotee of the Fátima secrets and as Pope Pius XII he would belatedly dedicate the entire world (including Russia of course) to the Virgin Mary's Immaculate Heart. For all we know, the Holy Mother put in a good word with her Son to bless Perestroika in the late 1980s.

The rapid breakdown of good relations with Hitler's Germany and Mussolini's fascist Italy was of more immediate concern to Pius XI than a simple Portuguese sister's purported apparitions of the Virgin Mary. In his final year of life he used his spiritual influence as chief Pastor of the Church to pressure German Catholics, Nazi and otherwise, to come back to God. *Mit brennender Sorge* was smuggled into Germany and read in every Catholic pulpit. Protests by the more vocal Catholic priests and laity got these courageous ones box-carred away to Hitler's newly constructed concentration camps. In Italy Mussolini aped Hitler's anti-Christian and anti-Semitic policies, to the horror of the pontiff.

When the year 1939 began Pius was composing a new encyclical which was expected to vent his full and eloquent denouncement of Nazi anti-Christian philosophies, as well as condemn the persecution of the Jews within fascist lands. While in the midst of his writing the pontiff, who had always been physically vigorous, suddenly fell ill and died in February. Conspiracy buffs might claim that cardinals sympathetic to the Nazi cause hastened his ascent to St. Peter's audience in heaven, but their theories are not backed by hard evidence.

Although Pius' encyclical was virtually complete, his successor mysteriously made a point not to have it published. It would remain hidden from public view for over half a century, as all requests by scholars to see the text were doggedly resisted by Vatican authorities until 1996. Apparently the Vatican preferred a policy of preventing the embarrassment of Pius' successor, who withheld an encyclical which would have conclusively staked the Church's position as anti-Hitler at the onset of World War II.

This repression and other policies of silence in the face of the horrors unleashed by Hitler and Mussolini would forever cast a shadow on the legacy of the next pope whom the mottoes describe as an Angelic Pastor.

ONE HUNDRED AND SIX

Pastor angelicus
(An Angelic Pastor)

PIUS XII
(1939–1958)

The time has come when Germany will be called the most belligerent nation of the world. The period has arrived when out of her bosom will come the terrible warrior who will undertake to spread war in the world. The men in arms will call him the Anti-Christ. . . .

The conqueror will come from the banks of the Danube. [Hitler grew up on the banks of the Danube in Linz, Austria].

He will be a remarkable chief among men. The war that he will make will be the most terrifying that men have ever undertaken. His arm will be flamboyant and the helmets of his soldiers will bear points darting flashlights, while their hands will carry lighted torches. [The *points* could be the glinting spikes of pre-Nazi German helmets worn by Hitler as a soldier in the First World War. The lighted torches of Nazi night parades are also implied.]

It will be impossible to calculate the number of cruelties committed. He will be victorious on land, sea, and even in the air because one will see winged warriors, in these unbelievable attacks, mounting to the heavens to seize the stars and throw them on the cities . . . in order to start gigantic fires. . . . Future generations will be astonished to see that his powerful and numerous enemies will not have been capable of stopping the march of his victories.
St. Odile (d. 740)

We believe that the present hour is a dread phase of events foretold by Christ. It seems that darkness is about to fall on the world. Humanity is in the grip of a supreme crisis.
Pius XII (24 November 1940)

The prophecies of the abbess of Odile, St. Hildegard, and pseudo-Joachite writings attributed to Joachim de Fiore all share a collective vision popular in orthodox Catholic prophecy: that during the time of the Warnings, before the coming Chastisement of the Church, there would be a series of "angelic pontiffs." It is therefore not surprising that one would find a pope *angelicus* near the end of St. Malachy's list – whether the author is an Irish saint or a good forger who has done his prophetic homework.

To a majority of Catholics Cardinal Euguenio Maria Giuseppe Giovanni Pacelli, who rose from his position as secretary of state of the Vatican to become Pius XII in March 1939, was an *angelic* pastor. He was regal, his aquiline face divinely impassive.

The Pacelli coat of arms displays an angelic tableau of the dove of the Holy Spirit clasping an olive branch in its beak. The name "Pacelli" might take its origin from the Italian *pace*, meaning "peaceful, silent, calm, or tranquil" – all were aspects of Pacelli's character and deportment. Pius was an ardent disciple and scholar of the teachings of the 13th-century Christian philosopher St. Thomas Aquinas, who was labeled the *Angelic* doctor.

Pius' critics and supporters are as passionate as those still arguing the merits and demons of America's 37th president, Richard Nixon – a man who once observed that he would have made "a good pope."

It can be argued that Pope Pius was the closest the Vatican ever came to having a Nixonian pontiff. Like Richard Nixon he was a man of potential genius and greatness, overshadowed by darkness. Pius was a complex Vicar of Christ of intellectual brilliance and unquestionably sincere religious piety who was trying to find a diplomatic way to sustain medieval views of religion and morality or at least adapt them to the 20th century. An ardent anti-communist, like Nixon, he was ahead of his time in warning the world of the dangers of this atheistic, materialistic movement. Yet his legacy will be forever overshadowed by his own Watergate scandals: his sympathy for Nazi Germany, his official silence about the Holocaust and his post-war protection of Nazi and other fascist war criminals as long as they were church-going Catholics and dedicated anti-communists.

Pius is the compassionate holy man who gave all the Church could spare to war relief through the Pontifical Aid Commission. One saw him in dusty and bloodstained robes, administering last rites to dying civilians after an Allied bombing raid on Rome in 1944. He is also the Holy Father who publicly praised the soldiers of the Third Reich for their invasion of Russia. He is the pontiff who managed to save an estimated 400,000 Jews from the gas chambers, but never officially or publicly condemned the slaughter of six million Jews. He is fondly remembered by the Jewish community of Rome for harboring hundreds of its citizens within the walls of the Vatican. This is the same man who after the war would use the Vatican's properties to hide hundreds of Nazi war criminals from judgment at Nuremberg for their crimes against humanity.

The Sacred College of Cardinals had chosen Pius XII in 1939

because of his sterling reputation as the finest diplomat in the Vatican – exactly what was needed to help sustain the Church through the coming war. His long service as nuncio of the post-World War I German Weimar Republic and his adept and skillful negotiations concerning the concordats with Mussolini's Fascist Italy (1930) and Hitler's Nazi Germany (1933) gave him a certain advantage and direct knowledge of how to deal with the dictators who directly ruled over tens of millions of Catholics.

When war broke out a little over six months after his election, Pius fashioned a policy similar to Benedict XV's: professing papal neutrality in the face of so many Catholics fighting on Axis and Allied sides. He allowed priests on both sides to interpret his words as Christ's blessing for their cause, be it fascist or demo-cratic.

Like a dispassionate angel above the fray of human sinners, Pius skirted condemning Nazi Germany for its brutal invasion and conquest of the 30 million Catholics of Poland. "There are forty million Catholics in the Reich," he explained. "What would they be exposed to after such an act by the Holy See?"

He avoided pronouncing Nazi Germany as an aggressor after its invasion of Belgium and Holland in 1940. Pius said nothing when Italy joined the war, even though he privately disapproved of it. Too many of his Nazi-saluting Italian bishops supported Mussolini. His silence was taken as support for the Italian view that Fascism was in harmony with Catholicism.

After the fall of France in 1940 Pius urged the French to work in harmony with the Nazi occupation. He urged British prime minister Winston Churchill (1874–1965) to take Hitler's peace offer after the defeat of France.

He could not understand why his proposal was shunned by the British government.

Where most of the world saw defiant Britain's lonely and cour-ageous defeat of the German Luftwaffe over its skies as the first significant check of Nazi world dominance, Pius believed that the English bore the blame for continuing the war.

When Nazi Germany invaded the atheist Soviet Union in June 1941, Pius' staunch anti-communist instinct felt compelled to bless the Nazi invasion as a "holy crusade." He privately admitted that he preferred Germans over Russians, and prayed for Germany's victory against communist Russia. He even gave comfort to the Catholic German soldiers on the Eastern front when he declared on Vatican Radio that the Nazi exploits in Russia were "magnanimous acts of valor which now defend the foundations of Christian culture." This papal approval no doubt inspired those Catholics in SS special action units in Soviet occupied territories to step up their torching of Russian villages by the thousands – citizens included – and their slaughter of Jews by the millions.

Other "magnanimous acts" of the Nazi iron "Christian" cross crusade would include the killing of 2.5 million German soldiers, 2 million German civilians and 28 million Soviet soldiers and citizens in a little over three years. Beside the killed there were 14 million injured and wounded Soviet citizens and over 25 million people were left homeless. In their zeal to make the world a better place without communists, the Nazi crusader destroyed nearly 2,000 Russian cities and towns and 70,000 villages and hamlets. Included in this toll is the spilled blood of ancestors of the crucified Christ – two million Jewish Soviet citizens annihilated.

Pius' words could only vindicate the actions of a former Jesuit novice priest named Heinrich Himmler, who had fashioned the fearsome black uniforms of his Gestapo and SS soldiers after the black robes of the Jesuit order. If the devil's godless commies used red as their color, Himmler wanted the black color of priestly robes to adorn the backs of his anti-communist, anti-kike SS crusaders.

Pius would keep his official lips shut as tight as a gas-chamber door when reports of Hitler's campaign to exterminate the Jews found their way to his office in the Vatican.

The secretariat of Pius' reign also hid behind iron silence when Catholics killed non-Catholic Christians. No Vatican protest came when 700,000 Orthodox Christian Serbs were systematically liquidated in the new fascist and arch-Catholic state of Croatia. Apparently the executions were enthusiastically supported by the Catholic priesthood there. Orthodox Christians were given the choice: conversion to the "true" Catholic faith or their blood-soaked faces pushed into the dirt of a trench by the recoil of a pistol shot. After the war Pius' curia would later hide the fugitive Croatian dictator, Ante Pavelic, from justice in the pope's summer residence of Castelgandolfo.

After 1942 Pius warmed to the idea, professed in his correspondences with American president Franklin Delano Roosevelt (1882–1945), that Germany would lose the war. His official Vatican policies became – with delicacy – more friendly to the Allied cause as their victories increased. Still he remained adamantly against Allied demands for Germany and Italy's unconditional surrender. He preferred the Allies to seek a negotiated peace with the dictators.

As the war came to an end Pius was downright perplexed by Britain and America allying themselves so completely with Stalinist Russia. To him the Yalta and Potsdam accords granting vast portions of Catholic Eastern Europe to communist jurisdiction was setting the stage for a greater evil than Hitler to threaten Christendom.

Even Pius' harshest critics generally agree that he privately agonized over the ever more dreadful reports of the deportation and execution of the Jews. He knew what was happening. Six years of Armageddon: Part Two was waged and not a single public protest or encyclical was issued from his pen as Jews were tortured and died in the millions. Throughout the war he resisted worldwide pressure to excommunicate Mussolini and Hitler for their crimes against humanity.

I cannot condemn this man as a coward, as others have done. I see him as a victim of centuries of Catholic conditioning.

Pius, like so many popes before him, was responsible for sustaining the momentum of over a millennium of anti-Semitic policy. The pope as an individual must submit to the pressure of 19 centuries of doctrine. Even if the heart of this man was willing to protest the Holocaust, his mind could not. Even his great mind was that of a programmed Catholic, stuffed with the Pavlovian reactions instilled by 1,600 years of the papacy's anti-Semitic policies.

The same brainwashing by the Church of Rome shaped the minds of millions of Catholics to behave like their pontiff and look the other way as other lay Catholics took their revenge against the Jews. Catholics like Adolf Hitler, Josef Goebbels, Heinrich Himmler, Reinhard Heydrich and lesser Catholic numeraries of the Final Solution, like Dr. Joseph Mengele and Adolf

Eichmann, followed their childhood indoctrination from baptismal tub to catechism on a quest for a final solution.

I am at pains to point out that fascism was born mostly out of Catholic lands. The first fascist government was established in Catholic Italy. Catholic Austria, where Hitler was born, produced the most Nazi war criminals per capita. Next in line is Catholic Bavaria – hate's harvesting ground for the National Socialist Party and most of the non-Austrian Nazi war criminals like Catholic Dr. Mengele.

Hitler, the author of the "big lie," was himself a victim of the ancient "big lie" of the official Roman Church – that Jews were subhuman and their guilt in the murder of Christ warranted their collective punishment.

But in his defense I will say that Pius' sin of silence was based on sound political reasons. The Vatican State was an island in a fascist sea, in a Europe dominated by Hitler's terror troops. He knew that the days when a pope's bull of excommunication could bring a German emperor to his knees were long gone.

When Hitler occupied Italy after the fall of Mussolini's government in 1943 he might have made good his threat and sent SS paratroopers into the Vatican to arrest Pius and place a Nazi puppet on St. Peter's chair. Nostradamus' forewarned Second Antichrist may have forced Pius to suffer the same exile and incarceration that other Piuses (VI and VII) endured from the soldiers of Nostradamus' First Antichrist, Napoleon. Pius could not speak out against the killing of Jews or the evils of fascism without risking the confiscation of the wealth and destruction of the power remaining to the Vatican State.

I do not think it is unfair of me to expect the Vicar of Christ to possess some of the virtues of the Christ he claims to represent. When faced with a challenge as grave as World War II, I expect his actions to be like those of his master.

Imagine Christ standing before Jerusalem contemplating the consequences that his entry into the Holy City would bring upon his person and upon his little flock of followers. If Pius' actions represent Christ on Earth then I should expect Jesus would turn his back on the Holy City and say to his disciples, "Oh, let's not go into Jerusalem. Let's not do anything that might break up my flock. I'll stay silent about the money changers defiling my Father's temple. I won't cause a riot there, because what will happen to my followers if I make a fuss?"

If Pius could not represent the fearlessness of Jesus, then what about representing at least St. Peter? The first pope gladly went to his crucifixion on the very same hill where the Vatican City-State of Pius XII stood. Not only did the first bishop of Rome go to his death, but he encouraged his imprisoned followers to go singing into the jaws of lions in the Circus Maximus. Did he hold himself back and stay silent because he feared Christ's Church would be destroyed?

The brave acts of Christians in those dark days enhanced the credibility of Christianity. Their martyrdom spread the faith around the world.

The early pontiffs and Christians had guts. Their courage and faith stood the tribulation of lions and innumerable persecutions.

It seems that prophecies forewarning of a more cowardly Christianity before the end times are true.

If 40 million German Catholics, with Pius at their lead, had gone singing into the jaws of Nazi lions and the purgatory of concentration camps, it could have changed history. Real Christian sacrifice and courage might have ended the Holocaust, and certainly atoned for two millennia of Christian anti-Semitism.

ANTI-COMMUNISTS FOR CHRIST

The result of Pius' inaction was the preservation of the Vatican State. World War II finally burned itself out and the 50 million slaughtered were soon buried. Catholic aid organizations heroically saved as many Jews and refugees as they could from the horrors of Hitler's industrial death incorporated.

Before blowing his brains out Hitler had fulfilled one of his prophecies: that he would destroy the old world order. Now Catholics could see a clearer shape of things foretold in their doomsday prophecies – a world divided by East and West, religion versus anti-religion, capitalist democrat versus proletariat communist. The atomic bombs and missiles were stockpiled on both sides. The black swastika scare was replaced by the red scare.

Only recently has information come to the public channels

regarding what lengths Pius was ready to go to stop the spread of communism during the opening phase of the Cold War. In *Unholy Trinity* (St. Martin's Press, 1992) Mark Aarons and John Loftus' definitive study of US and Vatican espionage, we see a desperate pontiff making pacts with British and American intelligence agencies to locate and squirrel away hundreds of Nazi war criminals to be utilized in the fight against the spread of communism. Pius, with the help of men like Monsignor Montini (the future Paul VI), blessed the use of embassies and diplomatic offices and powers of the Vatican to establish "rat lines" to ferry former Nazis and their collaborators out of Germany and Eastern Europe. The Eichmanns and Mengeles would find new homes and new careers in Argentina, Canada and the US as anti-communist spies, scientists and rocket designers serving their new Western and Christian masters.

I for one can understand how Pius "the man" would be tempted to use a lesser evil to fight a greater evil. But Pius as the "Vicar of Christ," a pope who made many of his own prophetic pronouncements apparently could not foresee communism not overtaking the world, or dropping dead by 1990.

Events have shown Hitler – not Stalin or world communism – to be the greater threat all along.

Most historians believe that if Hitler's "crusade" against communism in Russia had been successful he could have won the war. All the Jews remaining in Eurasia would have died and Hitler would have proceeded with his planned depopulation of the Slavic race by 40 million. Once Eurasia was dominated by his "Greater German Reich" our anti-communist dictator would have initiated his peacetime plan to dismantle the Catholic and Protestant churches over a generation.

If we look at the prophetic angle one could argue that if Pius' prayers for Hitler's victory against communism had been heeded, then history would have followed a new timeline that perfectly fit the dire warnings of the Chastisement prophecies.

Hitler would become the Antichrist, who dominates the Eastern Hemisphere. America would rule the Western Hemisphere. Hitler as Antichrist would then initiate his systematic persecution of Christians of the "only true Catholic church" and place his own puppet pope on St. Peter's chair as his false prophet. Hitler's

European Union would have fulfilled both Catholic and Protestant interpretations of the book of Revelation for a resurgent Roman Empire.

This timeline did not happen.

Communism survived Pius' prayers to Christ, and Hitler did not win in Russia.

Catholic prophecy watchers might come to Pius' defense and say that the timeline was altered because the pope fulfilled one of the requests of the apparition of the Virgin Mary at Fátima. Pius was an avowed Marian pope and promoter of the Fátima secrets. There are reports, denied by the Vatican, of Pius opening the envelope containing the third secret of Fátima. What he read made him weep. A more sensational rumor had him afterwards falling into a faint, unable to leave his bed for three days.

It must be remembered that the apparition of Mary told Sister Lucia that Russia would be returned from its atheism if it was consecrated by Pope Pius XI to the Immaculate Heart of the virgin. He did not follow her instruction, but his successor did: Pius XII entrusted the whole world to her Immaculate Heart (including Russia) in 1942.

After the war the spread of communism across Eastern Europe and Asia only galvanized interest in the Fátima prophecies and increased sightings of the Virgin Mary The most significant visitations just after the war came between 1945 and 1949 to a Dutch woman named Ida Peerdeman of Amsterdam. She discoursed on numerous occasions with an apparition who called herself the Lady of All Nations. The astral Virgin promised world peace if Ida would petition the pope to fulfill the "last dogma in Marian history." In short, Ida was told to ask the pope to make Mary, Mother of God, the Co-Redemptrix, Mediatrix and Advocate with Christ. Needless to say, this visitation was not recognized by Pius or by the Church even to this day, but it did set into motion copycat and perhaps some authentic visionary requests for the Roman Church to make Mary one in stature with her son.

By 1950 Pius would make the only official *ex cathedra* declaration since Pius IX when he settled the issue of Mary's Assumption into Heaven. He alleged that Mary was indeed taken up, body and soul, to paradise. Strangely this infallible message coming to the pontiff from the perfect dimension of divine grace did not enlighten Pius about whether Mary had died or been carried off alive into heaven.

In his waning years Pius carefully gardened a small bud of openness to change that would later flower in his successor John XXIII's short, though revolutionary, reign. One issue in particular – contraception – is examined in more detail here because of its importance in the future destiny of the Roman church during the reign of the last pope.

In 1951 Pius reversed the ancient Augustinian dogma which made the safe-period or rhythm method of birth control a sin. Pius was the first pope to officially allow sexual intercourse in a marriage to be something more than mere procreation. But contraception of any other kind was still evil. Abortion, even if it was necessary to save a mother's life, was condemned.

From the late 1940s through till his death in 1958 Pius became an ever more vocal proponent of large families at a time when many in the world at large began to recognize the real danger of the population explosion. Pius in 1958 attacked planned parenthood as a device of the devil. From his lofty position as Vicar of Christ, the priest, who spent most of his religious life serving as a Vatican bureaucrat who never dealt, as a pastor in a parish, with the day-to-day trials of men and women rearing large families on dwindling incomes, asserted:

> Wherever you find large families in great numbers, they point to the physical and moral health of a Christian people. . . . Virtues flourish spontaneously in homes where a baby's cries always echo from the crib. . . .

The Vicar of Christ's belief is not backed by the realities of fetid and overcrowded Catholic barrios of South America, or even in the Christian slum holes in Calcutta administered by the sisters under the guidance of the late Mother Teresa. I for one have passed through these and numerous other slums of the Third World during the 1980s and 1990s. I witnessed the breakdown of families because they are too large. I for one heard more unhappy than delighted cries from babes suffering in hunger and with disease because of their exploding numbers.

Pius' dream is our nightmare. The gaping eyes and underfed faces of parents aged far beyond their years, often strained and sickened, toting a gaggle of six to a dozen swollen-bellied children, do not invade Pius' utopia.

"Their [parent's] youth," he says, "never seems to fade away, as long as the sweet fragrance of a crib remains in the home . . ."

Pius at 82 would carry this dream to his deathbed when he passed away on 9 October 1958 at Castlegandolfo.

Pius was the last of the Church-triumphant and dictatorial pontiffs. Some say that by the conclusion of his tumultuous 19-year pontificate he was more loved and respected by people outside of the Catholic Church than within. His conservative grip on the hearts and minds of the Roman Church set the pendulum swinging for an era of unprecedented Church reform.

ONE HUNDRED AND SEVEN

Pastor et nauta
(A Shepherd and a Sailor)

JOHN XXIII
(1958–1963)

The sacred union will be of short duration,
Some changed, the greater part reformed:
In the ship [of the Holy See] *will be the enduring race,*
When Rome will have a new leopard.
Nostradamus (1557) 6 Q20

[A *leopard* in heraldry is depicted sometimes as a winged lion, as in the arms of John XXIII.]

Arms of Callistus III from Hans
Ingeram's book of arms, 1459

Arms of Paul II from the St
Gall book of arms, 1466–70,
displaying the lion described
in the prophecy

CANDIDATES LIKELY TO SUCCEED
POPE JOHN PAUL II

Cardinal Carlo Martini,
Archbishop of Milan

Cardinal Jean-Marie Lustiger,
Archbishop of Paris

Cardinal Francis Arinze of Onitsha,
Prefect for the Council of
Inter-Religious Dialogue

Pope John Paul II celebrating mass at Immaculate Conception Cathedral, Denver, Colorado, August 1993

(Below) Irish singer Sinead O'Connor on the American 'Saturday Night Live' television show, tearing up a picture of John Paul II in protest at his stance on abortion

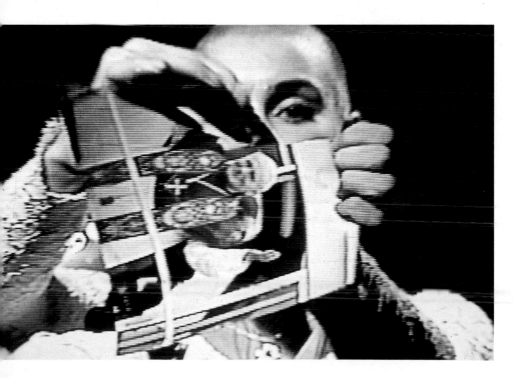

Arms of Paul VI showing three
silver fleur-de-lis – 'A Flower of
Flowers' – on a red chevron

Arms of John XXIII

Some people expect the pope to be a statesman, a diplomat, a scholar and an administrator – a man who understands all forms of progress in human life, without exception. But such people make a great mistake, for they misunderstand the true function of the papacy. To Us, the function of the pope is to be a Shepherd to the whole of his Flock.

John XXIII shortly after his election in 1958

Maybe the mottoes missed *Pastor Angelicus* by one succession.

Nineteen days after the death of Pius XII the Sacred College of Cardinals in the 12th ballot chose the 77-year-old Cardinal Angelo Giuseppe Roncalli as a compromise successor. Rumors of his infirmities from advanced age and poor health presaged a brief and unremarkable pontificate during which cardinals would have breathing space to redress political and spiritual alliances for the election of a more suitable pope. What they really wanted was a man made more in the cloth of a Pius XII, someone experienced in the workings of the Vatican bureaucracy, like Archbishop Montini of Milan. Montini could have become pope in 1958 had not Pius delayed appointing him a cardinal.

On 4 November the rustic Cardinal Roncalli, son of peasant farmers from the Italian north, near Bergamo, was officially ordained. Taking the name John XXIII he declared his wish to be a good shepherd of the church. Harmless enough! But this warm-hearted and good-humored pontiff packed a formidable intellect which included a command of several languages. His first two months in the driver's seat of St. Peter's Church made it clear to the world that his grandmotherly, florid face and kind eyes did not equate similar driving instincts. This pope pressed his slippered foot on the pedal and pushed it to the metal, commencing his five-year race against age and time to help the Roman Church catch up with the 20th century.

By the end of January 1959 he had already thrown out Sixtus V's limit on the Sacred College, increasing it from 70 to 89 members. He had injected into its membership the fresh blood of dozens of non-European cardinals, making its demographics more in harmony with the international nature of modern Catholicism. He had also held the first synod in Rome's history to revitalize the city's religious life. The first month of the new year ended with a proposal to further revolutionize the Church and rewrite canon law in the first Vatican Council since 1870.

The motto PASTOR ET NAUTA corresponds well with John's ministry as pope. He defined his pontificate as that of a good *shepherd*, an affectionate appellation for a beloved or Christ-like pastor who, like Jesus, is a good shepherd tending his Christian flock. Even the black sheep are loved. A pope with such a name would naturally be a compassionate, down-to-earth and rustic man. John drew pride and strength from being the son of a "humble but robust and honest laborer."

He believed that it was every Christian's duty – from pope to priest to laity – to imitate Christ and to aspire to establish "fraternal harmony among nations" by means of peaceful solutions and the abandonment of war. To him every sheep in Christ's flock has its small and important contribution to make in the establishment of the kingdom of Christ on Earth. Nations were defined by this pope simply as "communities of men" – that is, "of brothers" – who are to seek cooperation and work for the "common prosperity of human society, not simply for their particular needs."

His view of humanity's place in God's universe was not medieval. It was not even 20th century. John envisioned a humanity that has yet to walk this Earth:

> Human society must primarily be considered something pertaining to the spiritual. Through it, in the bright light of truth, men should share their knowledge; be able to exercise their rights and fulfill their obligations; be inspired to seek spiritual values; mutually derive genuine pleasure from the beautiful, of whatever order it be; always be readily disposed to pass on to others the best of their own cultural heritage; and eagerly strive to make their own the spiritual achievements of others.

In John the Roman Church had a *shepherd* who has been called the most 'Catholic' (that is, catholic, or universal) and least bigoted pontiff in history. This pope so loved his Church and the world that he would find the courage to put centuries of dogma under fresh scrutiny, and be the first pontiff to expose many of the Church's ancient crimes to the healing air.

The motto for John matches a number of objective details of

his life. Before becoming pope he was patriarch of Venice, an ancient maritime city famous for its sailors. He was Venice's PASTOR or *shepherd* and its NAUTA – its *sailor*. NAUTA also implies John's role as the spiritual *sailor* guiding the barque of St. Peter, the symbol of the Holy See. It implies that his spiritual nature is like the first bishop of Rome, who was Peter, the fisher (*sailor*) of souls.

Pope John opened the Second Vatican Council on 11 October 1962. John had stated that, in a moment of ecstasy, he felt an inspiration from the Holy Spirit to arrange the gathering meant to be a new Pentecost. Vatican II was to regenerate all policies, doctrines and organizational aspects of the Catholic Church, bringing them up to date to serve humanity's spiritual needs in modern times.

The badge of Vatican II displayed a cross and a ship (PASTOR ET NAUTA).

John invited leaders from 18 non-Roman Christian sects to oversee the proceedings. He urged the Catholic Church hierarchy to deliver God's message in a positive and human manner without condemnatory language or stern anathemas. To make its sacred meaning accessible to ordinary Catholics, mass could be held in the vernacular rather than in Latin. Until John's watch as Vicar of Christ, theologians were generally expected to endorse a pope's decisions without question. Now a theologian's religious duty was to "evaluate and interpret" all papal decisions, without threat of condemnation. After Vatican II, no theologian was censored or dismissed for sharing his insights until the reign of John Paul II.

In his opening address for Vatican II in St. Peter's, John invited the Roman Church to rise above its fear of other Christian churches and to settle what Peter de Rosa called the Cold War of Churches.

In the coming days the pope was able to watch the proceedings by remote television. The expected power struggle between reformers and dogmatists in the council ensued. He must have curled one of his inscrutable smiles as a majority of clerics and church leaders voted in favor of reform and effectively proved that the real power of the Church over doctrine no longer lay with the curia. In essence, by convocating the Vatican Council John had restored the dream of forging a balance between the priesthood and the pontiff and his curia similar to that which was attempted in the Council of Constance back in 1417.

Traditionalist clerics quietly bristled at the presence of so many lay men and women and non-Catholic religious leaders present to watch the proceedings. Who was John to invite worldwide Christendom and delegates from Islam, Buddhism and other faiths to St. Peter's pews? Before John the word "ecumenical" stood for unity of the Christian faiths dictated from afar by Rome.

Many celibate cardinals were miffed at his appointment of so many Catholic laypersons to the commission examining birth control. What do non-celibate Catholics know about raising children and having sex! John would approve the commission's findings for Catholics to use "responsible parenthood" when planning their families. This was the first admission in 2,000 years by the Church of Rome that bringing as many children into the world as biologically possible was not always a "blessed event" no matter what state of poverty the family found itself in.

The conservatives in the Catholic hierarchy soon found themselves politically isolated. Many of the hallmarks of reaction to modern times were abandoned. The cornerstones of reactionary policies such as Pius IX's *Syllabus of Errors* and St. Pius X's *Lamentabili* were voted out of favor. John's policy of *aggiornamento* (renewal) would have been condemned by Pius IX as heresy. John's official observation on papal infallibility demonstrated his shrewd peasant's wit: he could only make an infallible statement, he pointed out, if he were speaking *ex cathedra* – a thing, he added, he never intended to do.

News of perestroika in the papacy made many Jewish leaders wonder if John would – or could – push the envelope of Catholic glasnost far enough to address the Church's crimes against the Jewish people. Pope John, the venerable former apostolic delegate to the Balkans, Turkey and Greece during the years of the Final Solution, was remembered as a hero by Jews for issuing false baptismal certificates to 4,000 descendants of Abraham so that they could avoid deportation to the death camps.

In 1960, the year he proposed Vatican II, Pope John published the following prayer of atonement for 16 centuries of anti-Semitic Catholic polices. To popes and priests alike he said, "The mark of Cain is stamped upon our foreheads. Across the centuries, our brother Abel was lain in blood which we drew, and shed tears we caused by forgetting Thy love. Forgive us, Lord, for the curse we falsely attributed to their name as Jews. Forgive us for crucifying Thee a second time in their flesh. For we knew not what we did."

When John was elected pontiff he quickly cast out the adjective "perfidious" used to describe the Jews in the Good Friday liturgy. He appointed Cardinal Bea to prepare a document on Catholic persecution of the Jews for Vatican II, but the pope died before it was published.

In his closing address at the first session of Vatican II on 8 December 1962 he stated that he was not happy with the speed of renewal and urged the bishops to continue their reforms.

A THIRD SECRET OF FÁTIMA FOR A CUBAN MISSILE CRISIS

John's revolutionary spirit also disturbed the orthodox interpretation of Catholic doomsday prophecies. From 1960 onwards he distanced himself from Pius XII's stance on Marian worship.

The year arrived when Catholic prophecy watchers expected the pope to publish the third secret of Fátima. But John kept it locked away. A source reported that he confided to a few friends that he had read its contents and had nearly "fainted with horror."

A German reporter claims to have a copy of this leaked document. It was first printed in the German magazine *Neues Europa* on 15 October 1963. It is generally believed to be an authentic overview of the actual letter written by Lucia (Sister Marie dos Dores), the eldest and surviving child who had experienced the apparitions of the Virgin Mary in Fátima in 1917.

In the purported extract the apparition stated that the third secret would meet strong resistance. The Lady of Fátima was pleased that her miracle, the "Prodigy of the Sun," was believed and accepted by so many worshippers standing in the fields of her final visitation at Fátima. She also claimed to be the same apparition who visited "Mélanie and Maximin at La Salette." The Holy Mother warned that sin and wickedness had grown and reached all the way to the highest leaders in governments and

God's holy church since she had appeared. If this document is true then Catholic schisms, nuclear explosions, ecological disasters, earthquakes and a final global catastrophe would come any time after 1960. Death, it seems, will be "everywhere" because of the "mistakes" and insensitivity of those who do not care for themselves or God's Earth.

"For the Church, too, the time of its greatest trial will come," professed the letter. The arms race is forewarned, as are veiled prophetic threats that could be interpreted as supporting the coming schism between liberal and conservative factions of the Catholic Church in the reign of the next pontiff after John. There are also hints of the coming scandal in the Vatican Bank and prophetic fuel to fan stories that a future pope after John would be assassinated because Satan "will effectually succeed in bringing his influence right up to the top of the Church."

"A great war," she says, "will break out in the second half of the 20th century." Death will be everywhere all over the world, cutting down high and low, and "heads of the Church with their faithful." And finally, as with many Christian versions of the end of time, those who survive are promised a better and more innocent world to come from the ashes of our present world, when God will be proclaimed again in his Glory and humanity will serve and praise him "as in the time when the world was not so perverted."

Pope John preferred to disagree with the prophets of doom by promoting global peace and brotherhood. He added a carefully worded critique on the popular interpretation of Fátima and other Catholic prophecies at Vatican II, urging all humanity to trust in "divine providence" that would lead them to "a new order of human relations" directed towards the actualization of the Lord's "superior and inscrutable designs." He implied that God's divine plan for the future is beyond our expectations or projections – Marian, doomsday or otherwise.

John put his vision into practice.

Ten days after he opened Vatican II, the Cold War experienced its closest brush with a sudden thermonuclear warm-up, the Cuban Missile Crisis. On 22 October 1962 the American (and first Catholic) president, John F. Kennedy (1917–1963), revealed to the world a Soviet build-up of offensive nuclear missiles in

Cuba. He ordered a naval and air embargo on all Soviet ships carrying offensive military equipment or missiles to that island nation. As Soviet ships bore down on the American naval pickets in the Caribbean, Pope John publicly urged both Kennedy and Premier Khrushchev of the Soviet Union (1894–1975) to exercise caution. By 2 November the two leaders finally stepped back from the brink of a Marian-style Armageddon, agreeing to a formula which designed the withdrawal of Soviet missiles from Cuba along with American missiles from Turkey.

Pope John had gained the respect of both world leaders. In the following year he received the International Balzan Foundation's Peace Prize in 1963. In that year he also raised the eyebrows of anti-communist cardinals and laity and received wide approval in the communist nations as the first pope to initiate a dialogue with communist leaders. He wrote an encyclical *Pacem in terris* (Peace on Earth) dedicated to "all" mankind. It focused on the aspirations of every citizen of the Earth to move beyond their political ideologies and work towards the recognition of human rights and duties as the foundation for world peace. Unlike Pius XI and XII, who promoted nothing less than a theological and ideological holy war against communism, John preached the peaceful coexistence between the Western and the Eastern blocs. Shortly after releasing *Pacem in terris* he chased his words with actions by receiving Nikita Khrushchev's son-in-law in a private audience. In the coming months the Cold War between pontiffs and Soviet premiers thawed through John's redesign of a more open Vatican policy.

It is believed that through such audiences with Khrushchev's relations and with the Kennedys he contributed his indirect influence in promoting détente between the Cold War superpowers. This led to the USSR and the USA signing with Great Britain a limited nuclear test-ban treaty on 25 July 1963, a month after the pope died.

By April 1963 while John was composing *Pacem in terris* he was aware that his 82-year journey on Earth was near its end. Although his body suffered acutely from internal bleeding and peritonitis, he lay in his deathbed happy to be treated as just another member of his family surrounded by his beloved brothers and sister Assunta, and also satisfied that future sessions and the work of his Second Vatican Council would continue. On 3 June

1963, a bright sunny late spring day, the bells of St. Peter's announced the death of one of history's most beloved popes. As thousands bent a knee in the sun-soaked palazzo of St. Peter's to say a prayer for their departed pontiff, few could deny that they had lost a Vicar of Christ who unconditionally loved them in return.

In effect the bells also tolled for the termination of the Vatican's all-too-brief spring of reform. On 21 June, in the fifth ballot of the largest conclave assembly in history, John's confidant, Cardinal Montini of Milan – the cardinal he jokingly called Hamlitico because of his Shakespearian brooding over reform and reaction to Vatican II – was chosen as his successor.

ONE HUNDRED AND EIGHT

Flos florum
(Flower of Flowers)

PAUL VI
(1963–1978)

THE ARMS OF Giovanni Battista Montini display three fleur-de-lys. This *flower* of the three-flowered coat of arms tried to accomplish a contradiction: revolutionary change through orthodox decrees and control. Pope Paul wanted to produce more of John's reform wine, but he thought that he could press the juice of revolution's grape without breaking the dogmatic confines of the grape skin.

It is not unusual for a mystic to effectively contain contradictions.

But to do so one must really be catholic, in the original definition of that lovely Greek word, and be universal enough to embrace the totality of God's paradoxical and contentious creation. One polarity cannot force the other to submit. Revolution does not flourish when chained by orthodoxy.

Paul's predecessor seemed aware that orthodoxy and revolution had to learn how to dance together. And their dance of reform required a fluid and adaptable mind, or better yet, a man of heart to choreograph their two-step from St. Peter's chair. A man of heart knows when it is time to switch and let one's partner take the lead in the dance – this moment it is orthodoxy, the next it is revolution.

Paul was not a man of heart but a man guided by thinking, thinking . . . and more thinking. Some would say that he thought far more than he could act. And when he acted on his thoughts he could never cut his moorings to them completely free, leaving the acts of his pontificate tied to the apron strings of his worrying and vacillating mind.

He did not have John's down-to-earth peasant wisdom. He was far more refined and sophisticated, perhaps to the extreme.

Some say he was a sophist.

A good heart-sense grows in the earthy genetics and atmosphere of an itinerant laborer's son like Pope John. A good intellect often grows in the bodily desert of a boy of fragile health like Pope Paul.

Giovanni Montini never knew robust health. He was the bookish and often bedridden son of a pious mother and a prosperous lawyer and parliamentary deputy of Concesio, near Brescia. His tenuous health kept Montini mostly at home, away from childhood's necessary heart-shaping encounters. He even studied for the seminary at home until he was ordained in 1920 at the age of 23.

Obviously the new priest was too frail to take on the heartful challenges of a parish. His intellect received most of his attention, and the brilliance he displayed in mind naturally led to his posting to the Vatican secretariat of state. He taught papal diplomacy and got involved in the intellectual playground of Catholic student movements. By 1937 he became assistant to Cardinal Eugenio Pacelli, the secretary of state to Pius XI, and through his offices traveled the world, perceiving sinful lay life as interpreted by the straight and narrow, pop-bottle spectacles of Pacelli's vision. And when Pacelli became Pius XII, Montini remained one of his closest aides and disciples throughout the purgatory years of World War II, taking on assignments as the administrator of the Church's internal affairs.

After the war he declined the post of cardinal and became archbishop of Milan, where he worked diligently to repair the diocese after the ravages of war and political and social turmoil. His success as a missionary in renewing Catholic faith in the Milanese laity was less than hoped for. Perhaps the lack of social connection with the people was the price paid by the sickly boy sequestered away in his room. Life's fortunes shaped a man for whom it was easier to have relationships with books than with people.

Where Pius XII ignored, the new pope John listened. One of his first acts was to heed the popular cry of the Milanese to make Archbishop Montini a cardinal. Soon Montini and his 90 crates of books were back in Rome, helping John with the preparations for Vatican II.

Upon John's death in 1963 Montini was elected in the fifth ballot, taking the name Paul as a sign that his pontificate would be like that of the first great Christian missionary, one of pilgrimage around the world spreading the renewed and reformed Roman Catholic "good news."

Paul did his best to implement John's vision, and many of his reforms were moved through the council in four sessions of Vatican II held between 1963 through 1965. Still, something of John's fire and shepherding was missing.

Paul's command of Vatican II lacked the hands-on, day-to-day custodianship of a real visionary. The first session of Vatican II had been so successful because John knew when to lovingly nudge the council in the right direction. A man guided from the compass of authentic vision can keep tightening the leash of his curia to keep them from wandering back to the old trees of dogma and traditional interpretation.

Paul did at least prune the leaves of Roman Catholic doctrine to effect a new shape in canon law, promote procedural reforms and invite lay Catholic men and women to be auditors of Vatican

II's proceedings. Four centuries of banning books through the Index came to an end. Paul pushed through Pope John's resisted reform of mass performed in the vernacular and did much to re-establish dialogues with other Christian religions as a part of his favorite ambition of restoring unity to world Christendom.

But some of Pope John's reforms required more than a re-shaping of the outer foliage of the Roman Church. Hard and controversial issues such as the Church's policy on sex, celibacy and contraception, or Catholic anti-Semitism, required courage and decisiveness to cut them at the root. These qualities were lacking in John's successor.

Paul allowed the council to water down John's apology and prayer of atonement to the Jewish people. Though the abuse of the Jews was judged as terrible, the wording of the final draft showed the deft smokescreen of a good diplomatic servant of Pius XII: by not directly implicating the Church in any crime against Jews, or even addressing the encyclicals of past infallible popes who labeled Jews as Christ-killers, he effectively accomplished nothing.

Paul let slip his own anti-Semitic conditioning when he made the following public statement in 1965 while preaching at Passion Sunday: 'Jews were predestined to receive the Messiah and had been waiting for him for thousands of years. When Christ comes, the Jewish people not only do not recognize him, they oppose him, slander him and finally kill him.'

In short, Paul is still calling Jews Christ-killers.

This comes from the man who defended the policy of silence of his late boss, Pius XII, saying that any public protest against the Holocaust "would not have only been futile but harmful."

John's short pontificate spared him from an encounter with the sexual revolution of the latter-day 1960s. The pill that liberated women from their traditional role as breeding factories through most of their adult lives allowed their natural creative powers to rise up and make them equally unique members of the hu-"man" or better "huwoman" race. "Barefoot and pregnant" would soon become bare-womb and pregnant-with-energy-to-spare for other pursuits. The Vatican's stance on birth control had to at least find a new and compelling argument to ram home its case, otherwise the pill and pressure to control the population explosion from overtaking the world would make an unfertilized egg out of Catholic sex doctrine.

To conceive or not to conceive, that was the question agonized by Paul VI between 1966 and 1967 as he pondered over his long-awaited encyclical, *Humanae vitae*. Like Hamlet he brooded and turned the flower bed of his mind again and again, sifting through ideas, never letting the soil of his thoughts stand still long enough in silence to grow new flowers of insight.

Alas, poor Yorik's bones of intolerance were all he could find, for he knew them well, Horatio, too well.

When at last his encyclical was unleashed on the world in July 1968, *Humanae vitae* abruptly discharged a reactionary response against all forms of birth control and contraception. It spilled the seed of reform promoted by a majority of the Vatican II Council, who had voted for some easing of the frigid stance of the Church against "all" contraception.

Women would have to bring their babies into the world even if it killed them. Rape victims too. The Catholic poor would have to praise the Lord and pass on the contraceptives.

Humanae vitae had become the worst blunder of the Roman church since Galileo was censured. It put the Church of Rome squarely in the way of progress in easing the rising tide of misery and danger of catastrophic wars and ecological disasters breeding in the overcrowded and underfed and underwatered nations of the future. I look back at the same United Nations reports on overpopulation from the late 1960s which Pope Paul had agonized over, and they almost seem modest to my late 1990s eyes.

The dire prophecy of the World Population Data Sheet of those days was generally correct. The increase of 500 million souls on the planet between 1958 and 1968 and the dramatic climb of birth rates in Asia and Catholic-dominated regions such as Central and South America presaged a doubling of the then 3.5 billion people of planet Earth in just over 25 years. If all Catholics had slavishly obeyed Pope Paul, that deadly goal may have been reached even earlier. Thanks in part to those Catholics and non-Catholics who took the curbing of an apocalyptically steep birthing curve seriously, contraception has helped to slow the birth rate. In 1998, a full 30 years after the publication of *Humanae vitae*, we are still around one billion below the 1968 projection.

Pope Paul's attack on contraception helped to spur the silent rebellion of priests supporting their parishioners to follow their own conscience – not the pope's – on the matter of using birth control. Paul only added more fuel to the lay belief that celibate popes, especially those with little pastoral experience like himself, were out of touch with the caresses and cares of sexual life and parenthood.

Rather than bring priests together behind the pontiff *Humanae vitae* became the papal wafer that broke the back of many a priestly oath of celibacy. Over 30,000 priests requested to be freed of their frocks and celibacy during his pontificate. Paul's remaining ten years in office were the beginning of today's mass exodus of priests from their religious duties.

Millions of educated Catholic women in America and Europe were dismayed: the pope just didn't get it. In 1977 he upheld 20 centuries of the Christian dogma established by St. Paul that the Lord intended woman to be created for man's sake. He argued that women could not be priests because "the Lord was a man."

The sexual controversies stirred by *Humanae vitae* let loose speculation by the Italian press about the sexual life of Paul VI. Rumors were rampant that he was a homosexual and therefore the issue of contraception was not something that concerned him personally because of his "unnatural" sex life. So pervasive were the rumors that Paul, in a public audience, raised the blood pressure of his aides by openly denying that he was having an affair with his lifetime male secretary. Paul thrust this home by condemning homosexuality and masturbation as mortal sins.

Humanae vitae was the last encyclical he ever published. In the next decade remaining in his pontificate Paul's eyes were veiled by hesitancy and hurt.

His sympathetic biographers like to argue that despite the great divisions that *Humanae vitae* and other edicts caused amongst Catholics, Paul's diplomatic skills prevented a full-blown schism during his reign in the socially turbulent 1960s and 1970s. He guided the ship of the Holy See through the Vietnam years and the civil rights movement, both of which overshadowed Catholic American life. He was the first pontiff to visit the Holy Land and establish ties with the race of Christ in their resurrected and besieged state of Israel.

Paul did try to emulate his namesake as a missionary to the world. He traveled more than any pope in history up to that time, to promote Christian unity and to calm growing tensions during the Cold War.

Try as he might, he could never earn the love and popularity of his predecessor. His brilliant and doubt-ridden mind, his lack of humor and habit of frigid formality and aloofness may have gone unnoticed in earlier times. But in a jet-set pontiff, such a traditional holier-than-thou aura injected too much sulfite in the wine of his sacred memory.

Pope Paul died from a heart attack while resting at his retreat at Castelgandolfo on 6 August 1978, which by coincidence was the 33rd anniversary of America's atomic attack on Hiroshima. He had retreated there to nurse his grief after presiding over the funeral of his lifelong friend Aldo Moro, the Christian Democrat political leader abducted and killed by communist terrorists.

Paul, like his mentor, Pius XII, was a Marian disciple. In later sessions of Vatican II he overturned Pope John's policy of retreat from Marian cultism and promoted the Blessed Virgin to "Mother of the Church."

Prophecies of repentance or doom follow every believer in the Mary sightings like the aroma of her spectral roses. The pope would have his day with the third secret of Fátima. Millions of Marians still waited for some official word from Christ's Vicar concerning its message. John's official silence and words of caution against locking horns on doomsday interpretations meant that the cult of Mary had to wait for further enlightenment to come out of the mouth of his successor. A full seven years after the expected release of the third secret in 1960, Paul yielded to pressure and, through a spokesman, announced in early 1967 that now was not the time to reveal the secret to the world.

The decision, like so many others in his life, did not come lightly or without some mental torture. The pope had met the 53-year-old Sister Lucia in 1967. No record of their meeting exists. Witnesses say that she was requested to whisper the third secret into the pontiff's ear. It is said that his eyes clouded with terror and the blood in his face drained away as his mind was filled with horrors coming to the world. Suddenly he pulled away from her. The audience was over.

THE LADY OF GARABANDAL

With the official door shut on the Fátima prophecies, one might reason that the Apparition of Mary had to find a new set of messengers.

On the evening of 18 June 1961, in the third year of John XXIII's reign, four young girls (three of them 12 and one 11 years of age) were playing in the fields not far from their small northwestern Spanish mountain village of San Sebastian de Garab andal when they heard a rumbling in the sky which sounded like thunder. First Conchita (Maria Concepcion) Gonzalez and later Loli (Maria Dolores) Mazon, Jacinta Gonzalez and the 11-year-old Maria Cruz Gonzalez witnessed a luminous apparition of a nine-year-old boy who Conchita later described as "a most beautiful figure with a great deal of light, which did not at all tire my eyes."

They ran home in great excitement telling their parents that 'an angel' had visited them.

Over the next week the girls ventured out of the village every evening to meet the "angel." Of the fifth encounter on 1 July Conchita, who was setting down her experiences in her diary, reported that the angel had many things to say. Most important, he announced that on the following evening the girls would be visited by the Virgin Mary.

At dusk on Sunday, 2 July, Garabandal was packed with hundreds of people drawn by news reports about the apparition. By 7 p.m. they had gathered around the children who, upon reaching the place of their visitations, dropped to their knees and lifted their heads heavenwards, their eyes sparkling in transfixed delight at some invisible splendor that no one else could see. What they saw was apparently shared by each girl in the inner fire of her mind's eye. The angel materialized within an aura of multi-solar brilliance as before, but he was not alone. Beside him was another angelic being of exactly the same size and appearance. They stepped aside to allow a figure to walk forth out of the brilliant light. She was a young woman between 16 and 18 years of age, dressed in a brilliant white robe. Long tresses of nut-brown hair were covered by a blue mantle and a crown of golden stars. The girls knew her to be the Mother of Jesus Christ.

Thus began hundreds of visitations by the 'Lady,' as the girls called her, over the next four years, drawing thousands of people to Garabandal. The Lady frequently visited one, two or all the girls – the remarkable events did not require all of them to be present. Her appearances were far more spontaneous than at Fátima or Lourdes.

Back in 1994 I saw movies of the girls in their ecstasies when filming a segment as a guest expert on the prophecies of St. Malachy and Nostradamus for NBC's *Ancient Prophecies* series. The girls had their heads thrown backwards, their backs and limbs erect and rigid, their eyes, smiles and bodies locked as if suspended by some blissful otherworldly force. Pinpricks could not disturb their reverie, nor did their bodies suffer stiffness and pain from the unusual positions they assumed, sometimes for hours on end, as they gazed and spoke to their blessed Lady. Witnesses who had moved their rigid bodies remarked how they were sometimes heavy as stone and at other times as light as a pillow. At times the girls would get up and walk backwards with their heads whiplashed heavenwards, gazing at the invisible apparitions. They would step swiftly with complete trust, some-times walking backwards up the sides of rocky hills without ever stumbling.

Ray Stanford in *Fátima Prophecy* (Ballantine, 1987) points out that their paranormal behavior was not indicative of hysteria, "which is characterized, in part, by a *loss* of bodily coordination." I for one can appreciate their physical states and bodily coordi-nation, as I have had frequent episodes of ecstasy as a practitioner of Eastern meditation techniques for over a quarter of a century.

Their experiences remind me of one of my own episodes of bliss while living at the spiritual commune city of Rajneeshpuram in the mid-1980s. It was evening and I was descending from my little pup-tent home on the side of a steep desert mountain to go to the commune cafeteria for supper. I did not see any angels or the Virgin Mary in the paling evening sky. In fact I did not see anything at all but the endless burning blue of no-thing-ness. As early as I can remember, God to me was an endless sky, an emptiness which contained all contradictions. God was a void filled to overflowing with something unnamable, unchanging – a pure eternity untouched by good and evil.

That evening, as I walked down the dirt path between clumps of range grass I gazed into the sky and felt the emptiness descend into my body. My head moved backwards and I began to run for joy off the path and down the steep face of the mountain. I hurtled over rocks and grass mounds, never looking where I was going but never tripping, running at breakneck speed. In that state my body had "eyes" nourished by a trust in that divine and unexpected delight.

I therefore have no doubt about the girls at Garabandal and that, whatever their vision was – be it an authentic visitation from the Virgin, an extraterrestrial visitation masquerading as the Virgin, or even their Catholic indoctrination projected upon the vault of eternity – it is possible to run off mountainsides, forwards or backwards. Your total trust in an authentic ecstasy will guide your feet safely.

On 8 August 1961 the girls were informed by the Lady of a "great miracle" which would someday descend on Garabandal, healing many gathered there and leaving physical evidence behind so that skeptics could not deny it had taken place.

The following night, the hale and hearty 36-year-old Father Luis Andréu, who was one of the few people outside of the four girls who apparently saw the apparitions and got a glimpse of the Miracle to come, dropped dead from joy. The autopsy could not find a cause. In later visits the girls related intimate details from the Lady of the departed padre's life to his brother, Father Ramon Andréu, which could only be known by him. It seems that the spirit of Father Luis sometimes came along with the Lady, and these virtually uneducated girls did a lot better than jabber nonsense in tongues like televangelists. They would recite complex phrases from the departed priest in Greek and several other languages unknown to them.

At the time of writing (February 1998) this miracle has yet to happen. Conchita says that the Lady will warn the world eight days before the event. This will allow people to gather at Garabandal at 8:30p.m. on some future Thursday evening coinciding with the feast day of a martyred saint who is associated with the Holy Eucharist. When the miracle descends on Garabandal, Conchita says, it will be so great that "Russia will be converted."

In October 1961 the Lady bade the girls to warn humanity that we must "do much penance and make many sacrifices."

"We must often visit the Blessed Sacrament," continued the apparition through Conchita's written account, "but, above all, we must be very good, for, if we are not, we will be punished. The cup is already filling and if we do not amend our lives there will come a great chastisement."

The year 1961 had already opened with ominous signs that the Cold War was lurching towards a hot and thermonuclear finale. America broke off diplomatic relations with Castro's newly formed government in Cuba. Soviet military and political aid to the island nation was countered by a CIA-backed anti-communist invasion force which was annihilated in Cuba's Bay of Pigs. In June, the month of the first apparitions at Garabandal, President Kennedy and Premier Khrushchev endured a rocky summit in Vienna. By August, when the Lady promised a great miracle, the East German government – with the blessings of the Soviet Union – closed the borders to West Germany and began to construct the infamous Berlin Wall. NATO and the USA responded by beefing up the garrison in Berlin. In October, four days after the warning of a coming Chastisement, the Chinese broke their alliance with the Soviet Union. Nine days later the Soviets detonated a large hydrogen bomb in their testing grounds at Novaya Zemlya. The year ended with renewed efforts by Soviet and American military complexes to manufacture more atomic weapons and the intercontinental ballistic missiles to carry them.

On the evening of 19 June 1962 Soviet nuclear missiles were in cargo ships heading for Cuba. In Rome John XXIII was finishing work on preliminary plans for the Second Vatican Council. In Garabandal, Spain, a crowd of pilgrims followed Mari Loli and Jacinta up the *calleja* (a dried-out river wash strewn with stones) for another expected meeting with the Lady. The crowds were surprised when the girls turned and bade them wait outside the grove of pines, which was the usual meeting place, and let them enter the grove alone.

Not long after the girls disappeared underneath the trees the crowd heard the mountainsides reverberate with terrible shrieks and tearful pleas to invisible apparitions.

"Let the little children die first!" cried one sobbing voice, "Please, please, give the people time to go to confession before it happens!"

The pilgrims rapidly fell to their knees in prayer. The gathering gloom witnessed the rustle of hands gliding like lusterless fireflies over chests and foreheads as people made the sign of the cross. The shrieks would begin again and again, softened and silenced only by renewed fervent prayers of the crowd.

The same terrible vision visited Conchita, Mari Loli and Jacinta on the following night. Afterwards the tearful children would relate little of what the Lady had shown them, leaving witnesses to surmise that the girls must have seen a vision of the great Chastisement to come. Witnesses present would never forget the horror of those cries in what later became known as "the nights of the screams."

In July 1963 Conchita relates in her diary a conversation she had with Jesus Christ during her ecstasies. He spoke about the promised miracle and how it would help convert the whole world to Christianity.

The following summer, the first for Giovanni Montini as Pope Paul VI, Conchita received more details about the great miracle to come, predicting that the famous stigmatist and Catholic seer Padre Pio would see it and that a blind American boy, Joey Lomangino, would be healed. She later added that the body of Father Luis would be discovered uncorrupted.

The skeleton of Father Luis was exhumed in 1976 and Padre Pio died in September 1968, to the dismay of Conchita.

Whenever a prophetic "sign" goes wrong you can expect the mental balm of a rationalization to ease the discomfort of the faithful. When the miracle happens, believers of Garabandal say, Father Luis should be exhumed once again. This time you will find his bones surrounded by his uncorrupted flesh. As for Padre Pio's unexpected departure, a month after he was laid to rest a close friend of his, Father Bernardino Cennamo, met Conchita while she was making a pilgrimage to Lourdes. Cennamo told her "Padre Pio saw the miracle before he died. He told me so, himself." It was reasoned that Fathers Pio and Luis had received the blessing of a preview of miraculous things to come.

*

Sympathizers lobbied all the way to Rome for acknowledgment of the Garabandal apparitions. In January 1966 Paul VI invited the seers for an audience in the Vatican. He warmly received Conchita, her mother and Father Luna, a priest of Zaragosa who had witnessed some of the apparitions. In their private meeting it is said that she revealed the date of the Miracle to Paul VI. The pope is said to have given her a special blessing.

"I bless you," he said, "and, with my blessing the whole Church blesses you."

Skeptics of the Garabandal cult of Mary within the halls of the Vatican refute this account, saying that Conchita's request for an audience was canceled. The doubters say that another purported interview with Luna, Conchita and Aniceta – by members of Paul's curia – did not compel Cardinal Ottavaina, the prefect of the Congregation for the Doctrine of the Faith, to tag the Garabandal visions as the most significant visitation since Fátima. Skeptics claim that when interviewed the three girls only smiled at the questions.

On the fourth anniversary of the first sighting at Garabandal, 18 June 1965, roughly six months before Conchita went to Rome, she received the final public message (delivered, she says, by the Archangel Michael) before 2,000 pilgrims at Garabandal:

> Since my message of 18 October [1961] has not been complied with and has not been made known to the world, I am advising you that this is the last one. Before, the cup [of wrath] was filling up. Now, it is overflowing. Many cardinals, many bishops, and many priests are on the road to perdition and are taking many souls with them. Less and less importance is being given to the Eucharist.
>
> You should turn the wrath of God away from yourselves by your efforts. If you asked Him for forgiveness with sincere hearts, He will pardon you. I, your mother, through the intercession of Saint Michael the Archangel, ask you to amend your lives. You are now receiving the last warnings. I love you very much and do not want your condemnation. You should make more sacrifices. Think about the passion of Jesus.

After her purported meeting with Paul VI Conchita explained that the final message was a warning of an event in the future. It would be Mary's wake-up call to the entire world, and would be seen across the planet. This warning would be God's church bell to wake up the wicked and believers alike to get right with his divine (and Catholic) program.

No fires from the sky would come to kill millions; this warning was more existential in nature. Conchita explained it as a warning that would take place in the hearts of good and bad people alike, giving them an inner experience of their sins. Mari Loli and Conchita later related that this warning would precede the miracle. Finally the Chastisement would be delivered after the miracle and be meted out by the Lord with the degree of horror equal to humanity's degree of sinfulness at that end time.

At the time of this writing Conchita is 46. She waits, as does the Catholic world, for the apparition of Mary to give the faithful and unbelievers alike an eight-day advanced warning for the expected "Miracle."

ONE HUNDRED AND NINE

De medietate lunæ
(From the Half Moon)[1]

JOHN PAUL I
(1978)

PRIOR TO PAUL'S demise, most St. Malachy prophecy watchers expected things to turn apocalyptically sour when a moon-monikered pontiff followed the pope called *Flower of Flowers*.

Among the more interesting interpretations of just who this would be is that of Yves Dupont (*Catholic Prophecy*, p. 19). His speculation, recorded eight years before the death of Paul VI, best embodies all the positive and negative potentials contained in this motto. He brushes aside the obvious interpretation of it representing a coat of arms and sees *moon* standing as biblically symbolic for a worldly, as opposed to spiritual, "kingdom." Thus

---

[1] This motto is rich in alternative interpretations: a) *Of the Middle Moon*; b) *From the Center of the Moon*; c) *From the Midst of the Moon*.

we expect a pope who will either be elected out of a gathering of cardinals who are for the most part creatures of worldly concerns and ideas, or the pope himself will be influenced by temporal rather than spiritual concepts.

He may be a pontiff of his times – a man elected when the "forces of Satan" have "virtual control of the world via their secret government," warns Dupont. On the other hand, Dupont muses, the pope could simply be a good though mediocre priest, a weak man easily influenced and "dominated by worldly ideas, and thus do great havoc to the Church."

Now, with hindsight blinking through the horn-rimmed time frame of the 1990s, we can examine the life of the one who did become the *half moon* pontiff and determine just how sharp Dupont's foresight was.

THE WAXING "GOOD MOON"

The fourth from the last pope in Malachy's list was born in 1912 in the northern Italian hill village of Forno di Canale. His parents were poor peasants. His father, an itinerant laborer, and his mother both had keen interest in "worldly" socialist causes. They named the child Albino Luciani ("white light") – certainly a spiritual-sounding name, or at least one that can allude to the "white light" of the *moon*. Early on Albino Luciani showed an interest in becoming a priest of Christ's communism – an equal sharing of love rather than an equable distribution of poverty and hardship among the soulless proletariats.

The nearby town of Belluno ("good moon") would play an important role. After being schooled in local seminaries and completing his military obligation, Luciani was ordained priest in Belluno in 1935 at the age of 23. He went to Rome to finish his doctrinal studies at the Gregorian University, but did not embark from there upon the usual road traveled by those who end their careers as popes. Rather than joining the Vatican diplomatic corps to seize his place in Rome's sacred centers of power and worldliness, Luciani's burning desire was to return to his native parish and become a simple curate tending to the day-to-day life of lay Catholics.

By 1937 he was appointed vice-rector to the bishop of Belluno and ten years later was nominated vice-general for the entire diocese. There he wrote his first book, *Crumbs from the Catechism* (*Catechesi in Briciole*), and his reputation as a quiet and humble man, whose positive and loving presence had a powerful impact on everyone he met, began to spread, reaching all the way to the top of the Church hierarchy. He also gained a more dubious reputation from Catholic conservatives for forging a good working relationship with communists in his diocese. In 1958 the new pope, John XXIII, named him bishop of the mountain diocese of Vittorio Venetto, where Albani served up his brand of grass-roots pastorship for a little over a decade.

The bishop was an unassertive participant of the Second Vatican Council (1962–1963). For much of the time he listened, learned and quietly considered how he would explain to his parishioners back home that the traditional concepts he taught them one day could become "errors" the next.

His report to the people of his diocese reflects his innocent intelligence and the common and tender touch of his pen: "If you come across error, rather than uprooting it or knocking it down, see if you can trim it patiently, allowing the light to shine upon the nucleus of goodness and truth that usually is not missing even in erroneous opinions."

He was eventually noticed for his active role as a member of the doctrinal commission of the Italian Conference of Bishops. When the commission was studying birth control Albino strongly advised that the Roman Catholic Church sanction the use of the anovulant pill for contraception. He balanced his defense of it by supporting individualist right of conscience. Bishop or not, Albino – praying and meeting in the hallowed and ivory-towered capital of the Roman Church – was ever the parish priest. He could not just brush aside the real problems of poor people dealing with the burden of growing families and shrinking financial and physical resources.

In 1969 John's successor, Paul VI, impressed with "Don Albino's" pastoral heart and intelligence and inspired by popular demand, appointed him patriarch of Venice.

Venice enjoyed a pastoral patriarch with a Teflon purity, simplicity and common touch impervious to the ornate clothing and powers of his lofty position. People of that canaled city could enjoy seeing their great patriarch, who sneaked out of his offices by night, dressed in a simple cassock, to bicycle his way to a restaurant and eat his favorite seaweed pizza. A high priest of the Church usually turned up his righteous nose at divorcees, socialists and those who had sex out of wedlock. Patriarch Luciani walked the streets and mingled with sinners in their public places – like the man who had once walked the shores of Galilee and was Luciani's raison d'être.

In Venice he made his reputation as a liberal though obedient servant of Paul VI. Much as he might disagree with Paul's declarations if the pope made them public, Luciani obeyed and never contradicted his master. Luciani was clearly leaning towards a more liberal view on artificial birth control, but when *Humanae vitae* was published he publicly declared, "Rome has spoken. The case is closed." However, his private actions and statements show that the controversy was very much alive in him.

Author David Yallop, in his book *In God's Name*, gleaned some intimate insights into the private views of Luciani from Father Mario Senigaglia. Where the Church publicly condemned the divorced or those who sinfully copulated without marriage vows, Luciani accepted them.

"He was a very understanding man," related Senigaglia. "Very many times I would hear him say to couples, 'We have made of sex the only sin, when in fact it is linked to human weakness and frailty and is therefore perhaps the least of sins.' "

The patriarch of Venice was not only a man of meek and mild humility. He fired off bold statements about white racism against African-Americans and Native Americans. He asked people to recognize the accidental good in Russia and America's nuclear standoff – that the fear of Armageddon had at least prevented a world war for decades. Out of this irony of mutually assured destruction he looked for the positive opportunity that it presented: "A gradual controlled, and universal disarmament is possible only if an international organization with more efficient powers and possibilities for sanctions than the present United Nations comes into being and if education for peace becomes sincere."

He was not just a simple priest with a simple intellect. In 1976 he published an unusual book called *Illustrissimi* ("The most illustrious ones"), which contained a number of whimsical yet sharp-witted letters to authors and figures in fiction and history such as Figaro, Pinocchio, Charles Dickens and St. Malachy's biographer, Saint Bernard. The book is unique in the history of important church leaders. I cannot find any other priest, patriarch or pope who could so effectively use his sense of humor as a device to share serious insights in print.

In the letter addressed to Christ, Luciani writes: "I have been criticized. 'He's a bishop, he's a cardinal,' people have said, 'he's been writing letters to all kinds of people: to Mark Twain, to Peguy, to Casella, to Penelope, to Dickens, to Marlowe, to Goldoni, and heaven knows how many others. And not a line to Jesus Christ!' "

Dupont's prediction of an anti-Christian pope awaiting this motto goes afoul with Luciani's growing stance against communism, which the pontiff-to-be concluded was incompatible with Christianity. Luciani, like Pope Paul, was passionately interested in striving for unity between all Christian sects. In nine years as patriarch he hosted five ecumenical conferences. One of these was a meeting of the Anglican–Roman Catholic International Commission, which published a list of mutually-agreed statements that brought the severed churches dramatically closer to an understanding.

Luciani did not sit easy with wealth, extravagance or ecclesiastical pomp. As the new patriarch of Venice one of his first orders of business was to sell Pope John's gift of a bejeweled cross and gold chain which had once belonged to Pius XII.

"It is very little in terms of the money it would produce," he reasoned, "but it is perhaps something if it helps people to understand that the true treasures of the Church are . . . the poor, the weak who must be helped not with occasional charity but in such a way that they can be raised a little at a time to that standard of life and that level of culture to which they have a right."

He went ahead and sold other church valuables in Venice to the highest bidders and encouraged parish priests to do the same to help the poor. In 1971 Luciani proposed that the wealthy churches of the West give a 1 per cent tithe to the impoverished churches of the Third World.

He explained his charity in a letter to Pope Paul, citing the views of two Indian "heathen" thinkers – Mahatma Gandhi and Sandhu Singh. The latter had described men of Europe as akin to a round stone which had sat in the river of Christian love for many centuries. If you break the rock open, Singh asserted, you will discover that the wetness of Christianity has not penetrated its dry and cold heart and "does not live within . . ."

The future pontiff wished to bring water to the rock-like dogma that put more focus on pomp than on piety in the Church of Rome.

"I am first a bishop among bishops, a shepherd among shepherds, who must have as his first duty the spreading of the Good News and the safety of his lambs."

THE SMILING POPE

In 1978 Pope Paul died. With the third ballot the conclave of cardinals voted Luciani as his successor. A majority of the cardinals desired a completely fresh style for the next pope – one that was more in touch with the needs of modern, ordinary Catholics. One free of the traditional constraining hold of the curia establishment.

John Paul appeared for the first time in a window on St. Peter's columned facade to give the thousands gathered in St. Peter's Square and the millions at their televisions sets around the world his first blessing. Many were at once captivated by his innocence and heartfulness and his winning smile. This was not the evil, worldly pope foreseen by Dupont. Luciani's election was met with unrestrained celebration. People began comparing him with the beloved Pope John and called him God's candidate.

Immediately after his election Luciani demonstrated the new papal style – not autocratic and remote but down-to-earth and approachable. He immediately broke with tradition by becoming the first dual-named pope in history. The choice of name expressed his aim to combine the reformer's heart of John XXIII with the traditional temperance of Paul VI. The new pope's idea of revolution was indeed revolutionary. He wished to promote Vatican II while preserving the "great discipline of the Church in the life of priests and of the faithful." In other words, rather than instigate the violent and extreme changes that most revolutions are known for, he would strive for something truly revolutionary: balanced transformation.

In his first speech he dispensed with the customary royal "we" to refer to himself, and he rejected the traditional pomp and ceremony during his papal inauguration. In place of the papal crown he wore a simple cap, and instead of being carried on the elaborate peacock-feathered throne designed for the ceremony he chose to go on foot.

He defined himself as a "poor man accustomed to small things and silence" who sought to take the Church back to its early purity. His balanced spiritual revolution strove to slim down a big-business religion of vast material wealth and turn its attention back to being God's chief pastoral agent of the gospel's "good news" for humanity. John Paul's vision of a pastoralization of the Earth by means of the catholic – with a small *c* – Church, whether he was aware of it or not, was a vision in sync with that of Joachim de Fiore's "universal" theocracy which he prophesied would guide the Earth during the Third Era of the Holy Spirit.

John Paul punctuated his wish for reform by saying, "The world awaits this today [the pastoralization of the entire Catholic Church]; it knows well that the sublime perfection it has attained by research and technology has already reached a peak, beyond which yawns the abyss, blinding the eyes with darkness. It is the temptation of substituting for God's one's own decision, decisions that would prescind from moral laws. The danger for modern man is that he would reduce the Earth to a desert, the person to an automat, brotherly love to a planned collectivism, often introducing death where God wishes life."

In his first 30 days he paved the way for the re-examination of many traditional Church convictions. He once remarked that "God is not only your father but your mother" – not a statement guaranteed to find favor with the existing Vatican hierarchy. He also angered the curia and worried Church conservatives with his support of women's rights and his readiness to take a new look at the Catholic Church's opposition to artificial means of birth control.

Early on he made clear his concern for overpopulation and its role in nurturing crushing poverty. He wanted to promote the evangelical and ecumenical spirit rather than orthodoxy. "We intend to dedicate our prayerful attention to everything that would favor union."

He wished to teach through love and caring – not by infallible edicts.

John Paul received more attention in a few weeks and won even more hearts than John XXIII. He held a press conference before a gathering of over a thousand journalists and held them enthralled with his warm and simple wit. Photographs of the session show the pope with his shining eyes and smile – dressed in his white moon-like and simple finery – bracketed by the dark robes and black looks of two members of his papal cabinet, both of them being appointees of the humorless Pope Paul curia. One of the scouring faces belonged to Cardinal Villot, the pope's secretary of state and second in command of the Church.

It must be remembered that curias have been the theocracy within the theocracy – always preparing, guarding and ultimately isolating their popes from the outside world. By the second week of his pontificate the cheerful John Paul was distanced from his adoring laity by increasingly numerous security guards and a screen of curial officials. Villot and other curia members tried to monitor his every movement and apply their diplomatic and sometimes authoritative skills to take control over the pope. But "Gianpaolo" still followed his spontaneous habits, pushing the buttons of curia protocol freaks by slipping away by himself into the labyrinth of the Vatican palaces.

At dawn one day, the pope took a walk to a point just a few feet beyond the Vatican border. He stood outside the Porta Sant'Anna, his feet on Italian soil, looking up and down the deserted street. He then turned back through the gate and wished the dumbfounded Swiss Guards a good morning. Another morning dawned with him standing at his window in the Apostolic Palace at 5:15a.m. waving at the Vatican policemen down on the square below, grinning warmly as they waved back. Such moments were inevitably followed by a hushed lecture from the perplexed secretary of state: Really! A pope should not be seen at the window. Someone might assassinate him!

The incident at Porta Sant'Anna earned the pope smoldering rebukes from the prefect of the pontifical household, the chief security officer and Monsignor Noé, the master of ceremonies. John Paul gently replied to them that he did not wish to hurt anyone. Then he broke his luminous-Luciani smile and added that, anyway, no harm was done and some good had been achieved.

"Achieved?" stammered Noé in disbelief.

"Yes, achieved," said the beaming pontiff, who added that he doubted any of them had been out of bed that early for a very long time. He suggested that they should see the positive side of this encounter – that it was a "perfect start to their day."

REFORM MISSED BY A HEARTBEAT

John Paul I was determined to examine the Vatican's financial affairs. Since 1974 the former patriarch of Venice had been following news reports suggesting that the Vatican Bank was being used as a front for criminal behavior. The relatively young institution had been founded by Pius XI after he and Benito Mussolini agreed to establish the Vatican City-State through the Lateran Treaty of 1929. Pope Paul had chosen an old friend, Michele Sindona – a Sicilian banker with close ties to the Mafia and neo-fascist organizations – as a financial advisor to the Vatican Bank. Sindona in the coming years would draw the financial lifeblood of the Church's flush coffers to support a huge network of money laundering, corruption, murder and fraud.

John Paul was aware of these accusations and had voiced his desire to Villot that an investigation be made. He also indicated his readiness, if need be, to relocate several Vatican insiders who were major players in the operations known as Vatican, Inc. No doubt his investigation would have uncovered the Vatican connections with the Mafia and with the right-wing Freemason's group known as P2. But before he could set the plans for his investigation in motion, Pope John Paul I died from a heart attack.

The night before the pope planned to start his reformation of the Vatican Bank and make changes in other key posts, he retired for bed at 9:30p.m. His servants found him at 4:45a.m. dead in his bed, with the papers listing who was to be dismissed scattered over the covers and the floor. As soon as Cardinal Villot was summoned to the bedroom he pocketed the papers, along with the pope's last will and testament (which had been on his desk in his study). John Paul always had a bottle of Effortil at his bedside to regulate his low blood pressure. Witnesses testified that Cardinal Villot had the bottle immediately cleared from the bedroom. Then he issued false statements to the police and the press about the circumstances surrounding the death of the pope. The controversial list has never been publicly disclosed.

In Florence, Cardinal Benelli emerged for a press conference on the morning the pope's death was announced. With tears in his eyes he said, "The Church has lost the right man for the right moment. We are very distressed. We are left frightened."

Villot's suspicious behavior immediately attracted the press, who clamored for an autopsy. Villot declined, giving the excuse that there was no precedent for such a request. He either did not know – or did not want the press to know – that an autopsy had been performed on Clement XIV back in 1775. Before anyone could counter his objection Villot had the pope's body carried off to the Vatican coroners to be embalmed.

To this day the Vatican angrily denies any foul play. Certainly there is a chance that John Paul died from the strains of his job. People do die from low blood pressure, although not as frequently as they do from hypertension and high blood pressure – a condition the pontiff definitely did not suffer.

Twenty-three days before John Paul's death, he was having tea with the 49-year-old Metropolitan Nikodim, patriarch of the Russian Orthodox Church in Leningrad (St. Petersburg). Out of politeness John Paul let the metropolitan sip his tea first. The pope then raised his own cup to his lips but suddenly lowered it, staring with concern at Nikodim's contorted face. The metropolitan's tea and saucer fell to the floor, and he dropped dead from a massive coronary.

It must be pointed out that Metropolitan Nikodim did suffer from severe heart disease and his death could be nothing more than a dreadful coincidence. Still, there was no thought to examine the contents of the tea. Any accusations of a botched assassination attempt on John Paul could be easily ignored if it were not for the fact that the Church of Rome bears the heavy historical burden of the murder of up to 40 popes – many of them by poison.

Other developments after John Paul's sudden death add to the suspicion that he was assassinated. Not long after the pope died, a succession of suspicious deaths and murders took the lives of investigators and the investigated surrounding the Vatican's ties to Sindona's dirty money accounts. The efforts of John Paul's successor to suppress evidence and prevent agents of the Vatican Bank who were under suspicion from delivering any depositions to the Italian government only strengthens the accusations of papal murder.

Dupont believed that a shadow world government guided by the forces of the Antichrist could exist by the reign of DE MEDIETATE LUNÆ. He expected this government to pick their man as pontiff after they had infiltrated the highest echelons of the Vatican hierarchy.

Perhaps Dupont got it backwards.

Rather than a shadow government of the Antichrist choosing John Paul I, an authentic and sincere pope stood in the way of their plans and was isolated and destroyed by dark forces hiding behind priestly robes of the Vatican hierarchy.

Forger or not, the author of this motto, *from the half moon*, can claim a true predictive success by tagging this tragic pontiff with this phase of the moon. John Paul was discovered lying in his bed without a pulse on 29 September at 4:45a.m. (Italian time) by his veteran servant, Sister Vincenza. The waning moon moved into its third quarter at 5:20a.m. Ten minutes later the pope's death was confirmed just as the world saw another *half moon*, in the heavens.

ONE HUNDRED AND TEN

De labore solis
(From the Sun's Labor)

JOHN PAUL II
(1978–)

WITH THIS MOTTO we enter the present day to examine one of the most significant popes in history. Many believe that his long pontificate, entering its 20th year, stands on the threshold of the end of history.

Karol Wojtyla from Wadowice, near Cracow, Poland, would become the first non-Italian pope in 456 years. He was the son of a retired Polish army officer living on a modest pension. Karol developed a deep attachment to his father after his mother died when he was only nine. He would make a reputation for himself as a brilliant student and high school athlete with a passion for poetry, soccer, swimming, mountain hiking and canoeing. In 1938 his father moved to Cracow so that his son could pursue a university degree in Polish literature and explore what many of his friends and acquaintances believed would be a notable career as a thespian.

In 1939 his secular ambitions had a fatal collision with World War II and the Nazi occupation of Poland. Karol's beloved father died in 1942, leaving him without any family, and he was forced to seek hard labor to get by. Common laborers rarely reached St. Peter's chair; thus the inscription *from the sun's labor* may signify the stamina of the Polish pontiff-to-be who toiled in a limestone quarry and later worked at a water purification plant.

After surviving two near-fatal industrial accidents Karol Wojtyla studied to become a priest in the Church's underground seminary. Some have depicted the young novice priest as a kind of spiritual resistance fighter against the Nazis. After the war he returned to finish his university studies, and was awarded a doctorate in philosophy. By 1946 he completed his seminarian courses with distinction and was ordained a priest. He was sent to Rome where he earned a doctorate in theology in 1947. During the 1950s he spent time as a diligent and caring pastor as well as a formidable professor of ethics in Lubin. Becoming a man of the cloth did not lessen his passion for vigorous sports such as canoeing, hiking and a newfound love of skiing. During the 1960s and 1970s he earned distinction when assisting the Polish primate, Cardinal Wyzynsky, in resisting Polish communist authorities. He rapidly rose through the Church ranks, first becoming auxiliary bishop of Cracow in 1958, then archbishop in 1963 at the relatively young age of 45.

His participation in Vatican II (1962–1965) gained him his first international notice. In the 1960s and 70s he traveled all over the world as a Vatican representative to various synods and ecumenical gatherings. Paul VI made Wojtyla a cardinal in 1967 and used his pastoral treatise on sexuality (*Love and Responsibility*) as the basis for his encyclical *Humanae vitae*. In 1976 Paul VI honored Cardinal Wojtyla with the gift of delivering a series of Lenten sermons for the pope and his private papal household. Wojtyla also heard pope "Hamlitico's" brooding confessions.

By high summer of 1978, when the world celebrated and lost the smiling pope John Paul I, Cardinal Wojtyla was a widely honored and respected figure in the Vatican hierarchy. When the Cardinals once again gathered for a conclave in October, their former ardor for a completely fresh papal style was cooled by the splash of the late Gianpaolo's revolutionary zeal. Their prayers and ballots revealed, however, that there was still some room for the unorthodox. It took them eight ballots to pick someone far more mainstream in his beliefs but far more removed from the tradition of choosing Italians as pope. The sudden death of John Paul I also influenced their choice of the youngest man to sit in St. Peter's chair since Pius IX in 1846. Many prayed that his reign would be as long. Thus, at the age of 58, Cardinal Wojtyla became John Paul II, adopting the name of his predecessor.

On 21 October he officially inaugurated his reign with the novel title Universal Pastor of the Church. Soon it was understood that this new pope was an orthodox priest in revolutionary's clothing. His first pronouncements reinstituted the papal "we," dropping the more approachable "I" of Gianpaolo. The new John Paul made clear that he would interpret the reforms of Vatican II to the "exact" letter – in other words, as straight and narrow as possible – to control what the Polish pope believed were the many dangerous "innovations" and misinterpretations which tore apart Paul's ministry after Vatican II.

With the new pontiff firmly in control the Malachy prophecy watchers began to disseminate their interpretations of his motto. This post-Wion inscription follows the usual abstract theme of deeds and pontifical themes rather than lightly hiding the heraldry, birthplace or Christian name behind its word-play. Still, St. Malachy or his forger can be praised for stacking a lot of meaning in a few Latin words. The *labor* or "toil" of the sun could describe this hard-working pope's incredible regimen of globe trotting, tarmac kissing and masses under the hot suns of temperate and tropical climes over the past two decades. At the time of writing (January 1998) the pope is about to embark on his 80th trip from Rome. In 19 years this jet-setting pontifex maximus has kissed the ground of 102 countries, and it is estimated that he has traveled as many miles around the world as it would take to travel back and forth two and a half times to the Moon.

In medieval Latin poetry a "laboring" sun is one which rises in the East or is darkened in the travail of an eclipse. J. R. Jochmans, author of the prophetic classic *Rolling Thunder*, reminds us that John Paul II, like the sun, comes from Eastern Europe, and therefore from the East.

Astrologer Doris Kay thinks that the motto should read, *To Enter from the Eclipsing Sun*. She reminds us that John Paul II was born on 18 May 1920 – the date of a total eclipse.

John Paul himself declares his official motto to be *Totus tuus*, which means "All thine." This is the opening words to a prayer to the Virgin Mary, signifying his deep lifetime devotion to the patron saint of Poland.

The motto that he is best known for is his religious battle cry, "Be not afraid," first uttered on St. Peter's Square during his inauguration as pope.

To many still frightened by rumors of the last pontiff's poisoning and to those grieving the unexpected death of John Paul I, the declaration was a powerful balm for their pain.

John Paul reflected on this exhortation 16 years later in his best-selling book *Crossing the Threshold of Hope*. He said "be not afraid" was addressed to all people to "conquer fear in the present world situation."

He believes that the source of his declaration was "from the Holy Spirit, the Consoler, promised by the Lord Jesus to His disciples than from the man who spoke them."

"Have no fear", John Paul admonishes us all, "of that which you yourselves have created, have no fear of all that man has produced, and that every day is becoming more dangerous for him! Finally have no fear of yourselves!"

Why does John Paul believe that living without fear is possible? Because, he says, "Man has been redeemed by God." He believes that the power of Christ's cross and resurrection "is greater than any evil which man could or should fear."

"THE CHURCH HAS NO SECRETS"
(LEO XIII: 1883)

Four centuries before John Paul told us not to be afraid, the Catholic seer Michel Nostradamus apparently foresaw the poisoning of a reform-minded pope by the twelve red-robed cabinet members of his own curia:

> *He who will have government of the great cape* [the Holy See]
> *Will be led to investigate in certain cases:*
> *The twelve red ones will spoil the cover,*
> *Under murder, murder will be perpetrated.*
> (4 Q11)

Since the mysterious death of John Paul I and the suspicious actions of his curia under the temporary command of Cardinal Villot, many Nostradamus scholars have attributed this prophecy to the *twelve red* cardinals who *spoiled* the first John Paul's semi-secret investigation into the infiltration of the Mother Church by the Mafia and neo-fascist elements of secret societies. The late pope wanted to find out if the accusation was true that God's bank was being used as a safe haven for the laundering of heroin money at an annual rate of 600 million US dollars per year. The cases of corruption in the Vatican Bank and elsewhere would not be *investigated*. After the pope's sudden and unexpected death many of the perpetrators and the investigators into Vatican Inc. would die in what looked like an orgy of Mafia murders to silence instigators of, and witnesses to, the crime.

Between January and March 1979 the magistrate of Milan and an investigative reporter, who were both actively probing the sinister schemes of Michele Sindona and his banking associates' Vatican connection, were murdered. Leading members of the Bank of Italy who were pressing for action on the financial dealings of Sindona were arrested on false charges.

Six months into the new pope's reign Cardinal Villot, the man who destroyed evidence and saw to the Holy Father's swift embalming before an autopsy could be arranged, died, it was said, from chronic bronchitis. By July 1979 Giorgio Ambrosioli was murdered shortly after he testified in court about the links between Sindona and Roberto Calvi's Ambrosia Bank of Milan as well as with Bishop Paul Marcinkus, the head of the Vatican Bank. Ambrosioli also divulged a sophisticated network of money-and-influence mongering between the three and P2 – a neo-fascist Freemason group with powerful connections in the Italian and Vatican governments.

July 1979 did not end without the assassination of the chief of Rome's security service, Lt. Col. Antonio Varisco, who had spoken with Ambrosioli two days before his death.

By October a bomb had exploded in the apartment of the managing director of Mediobanca, Enrico Cuccia – a man who testified that he heard Michele Sindona threaten to kill Giorgio Ambrosioli.

The new year of 1980 began with the pontiff who said "Be not afraid" making no comment to the press or the government of Italy when the Vatican suddenly withdrew its agreement that Cardinals Guiseppe Caprio, Segio Guerri and Bishop Paul Marcinkus would provide videotaped depositions on behalf of Michele Sindona in his US trial on charges of fraud, conspiracy and misappropriation of funds in connection with the collapse of Franklin National Bank.

In May Sindona attempted suicide in jail. In June he was sentenced to 25 years in a US federal penitentiary. His accomplice, Roberto Calvi, also attempted suicide while in jail awaiting charges of fraud. Calvi was later released on bail and reconfirmed as chairman of Banco Ambrosiano. In September Calvi requested and received "letters of comfort" from the Vatican Bank. In other words the bank of the Church of Rome went on record declaring its controlling interests in, and assuming responsibility for, more than one billion dollars of debt incurred by a number of banks controlled by Calvi.

By January of 1981 a group of shareholders in Banco Ambrosiano (one of the "comforted" and controlled holdings of the Church) sent a letter to John Paul II, outlining the sordid connections between the Vatican Bank, Roberto Calvi, P2 and the Mafia.

The pontiff who said "Be not afraid" and who boldly declared that "the power of Christ's cross and resurrection is greater than any evil which man could or should fear" never acknowledged their letter.

Murder keeps precipitating murder. In April 1982 Roberto Rosone, general manager and deputy chairman of Banco Ambrosiano, fearlessly went where no pontiff would tread and tried to clean up the bank's operations. Someone attempted to murder him. In June Roberto Calvi was found dead at the end of a rope supended from a bridge in London. A few days later a one-billion-300-million-dollar "hole" was discovered in Banco Ambrosiano, Milan. Four years to the month when John Paul II was made pope, Guiseppe Dellacha, an executive at Banco Ambrosiano, "fell" out of a window in Banco Ambrosiano in Milan. In 1986 Michele Sindona was found dead of poisoning in the Italian jail to which he had been extradited on charges of ordering the murder of Giorgio Ambrosioli.

When John Paul II took office he was briefed about the revelations contained in the reports found spread across the bed of his dead predecessor. Instead of dismissing Bishop Paul Marcinkus, the man in charge of the Vatican Bank and a prime suspect for masterminding the scandal and participating in the conspiracy to kill the pope, the new pontiff had promoted him to archbishop.

John Paul II, who would later utter another famous phrase, "The truth will set you free," kept Marcinkus in firm control of the Church's finances throughout the rest of the 1980s. He made sure that Marcinkus was never "set free" for questioning by Italian authorities.

The Vatican succeeded in its tried-and-true tradition of waiting out a controversy.

Throughout the rest of the 1980s the Italian police authorities held to their long-standing threat to detain Marcinkus if he put one foot outside the Vatican compound. By 1990 the ban was finally lifted and Marcinkus was allowed to retire to America, showered with praise and honors by his pope.

By 1990, we are told, John Paul commanded the Vatican to initiate some reforms pertaining to papal finances. No one outside the Vatican was allowed to examine the process or see what was discarded in the way of potentially incriminating documents or evidence.

To this day the pontificate of John Paul II has not answered the allegations against the Vatican Bank. No documents or objective evidence are provided which could once and for all reveal the truth and set John Paul's church free from the shadow of a Borgian-pope-style conspiracy.

THE MOST ADMIRED, THE LEAST OBEYED

John Paul is not the first pope to focus his attention on the broader issues of his role as Vicar of Christ at the cost of leaving scandals and rumors of scandals for lesser functionaries to clean up. I can understand how the sins and Mafia murders of a half-dozen Catholics do not weigh as equally important against the salvation of the entire world. American president Nixon in 1972 put Watergate low on his laundry list while bringing to bear his political genius and attention to establishing diplomatic relations with China and détente with the Soviet Union. These actions may have prevented a third world war. What president would have had the time in October of 1973 to obsess about a few bungling burglars caught stealing papers from the Democratic party offices in Washington DC when the Yom Kippur War threatened a Soviet intervention which could escalate into World War III? Who can even remember one's part in the illegal scams of Ollie North and Iran Contra when you are President Ronald Reagan in 1986–1987, locked in hard negotiations for a zero option of nuclear disarmament with Soviet premier Gorbachev?

Clearly this pope believes that his investigation into the spiritual sins clouding the heart of modern man transcends all secular criminal investigations. A pope, in his view, must be a moral force. The future and salvation of humanity's collective soul is at stake. He has no time for papal Watergates and Whitewaters or banking bishops in hot water with mere Italian law. A pope should concern himself only with the message of Christ's gospel to bless the world.

A detailed account of this pope's labors to prepare humanity for the Third Christian Millennium would take too long to detail. It can be safely said that no pope has physically, and perhaps even intellectually, worked harder for his flock. In 19 years John Paul II has expanded and injected the Sacred College of Cardinals with new candidates to better represent the Church's demographic axis shift to the Third World. He has rewritten the code of Canon Law, reformed the curia, streamlined the Vatican's civil and banking services and expended titanic efforts to bolster ecumenism and interfaith dialogue, especially with the Anglican and Easter Orthodox Christian religions. His eloquent and powerful pen has composed more encyclicals than the last four popes put together.

No pontiff has tackled a wider-ranging set of complex and contentious issues such as human sexuality, abortion, technology and science, capitalism and labor, capital punishment, euthanasia and fetal research. This pope played a major part in fulfilling Marian prophecy by using the weight of his experience as a pastor in the communist bloc to bring down that atheist empire. He even spilled his own blood for the cause of anti-communism when on 13 May 1981 he survived an assassination attempt by Mehmet Ali Agca in St. Peter's Square.

Investigations into the plot to kill the pope implicate the KGB and other communist-bloc secret services. Agca, who is now in prison, is not talking, but he did receive a special visit. The victim prayed with his assassin and forgave him. John Paul rose again from near death to witness Christ's victory against communism, but his vigorous athletic body never was the same. It appears that the three bullets which mangled his stomach, colon and small intestines and drilled his right hand and arm like nails pounded into a cross have drained him of 20 years of life.

As I am writing this on 21 January 1998, John Paul is in his special Alitalia jet en route to communist Cuba to bring his message of a "Culture of Life." He is expected to deliver his unique blend of secular and religious testimonies defending the human and religious rights of Cuba's people suffering under communism. At the same time he is expected to launch an attack against what he views as a cruel economic and social embargo of ordinary Cuban people by the USA.

Millions of excited Cubans will add their numbers to the multitude who have prayed in mass with this physically bent and aged but spiritually unbending pope. No pontiff in history has been seen by more people and held more masses under the sun which orbits Galileo's Earth than John Paul II. Conversely there has never been a pontiff who has seen his encyclicals and commands selectively altered and left on the cutting room floor of more Catholic minds than he. John Paul believes that his issued commands must be obeyed in an era when a large number of Catholics believe that persuasion rather than pontificating is needed.

John Paul adds his contradictions to the long tradition of popes who praise human freedom and demand blind obedience to dogma. He is joined to the pallium of his theological soulmate, the Vatican's chief enforcer of doctrine, Cardinal Ratzinger, Prelate of the Congregation of the Doctrine of the Faith. If we might serve this title raw, this well-cooked modern-day euphemism makes Ratzinger the direct descendant of men who oversaw the anti-Semitic policies of the Church, burned witches and heretics and tortured countless millions under the auspices of the Spanish, Roman and Universal Inquisition.

Papal conservatives believe that Ratzinger will someday be remembered as a saint. Liberal and progressive Catholics call this German-born Archbishop of Munich Panzer Kardinal because he figuratively runs a tank over many a Catholic's hope for a reformed and more progressive church during John Paul's rule. Others whisper that Ratzinger is the other piece in John Paul's theological puzzle and is considered by many in and outside of Rome as the most despised and feared member of the pope's curia.

"In fact we do agree completely on all essentials of Church doctrine and order," admitted Ratzinger in a 1993 *Time* magazine article, "Keeper of the Straight and Narrow," by Rome corespondent Richard N. Ostling.

"We arrive at the same conclusions," continued Ratzinger, "and our differences of approach, where they do exist, stimulate discussion."

Over the last 19 years liberal bishops and cardinals have been systematically purged from the Vatican inner circle, and many a theological career outside of Rome is crucified by innuendo rather than nails. Ratzinger was instrumental in John Paul's move to have Swiss theologian Hans Küng fired from his professorship at the University of Tübingen for criticizing the doctrine of papal infallibility. Other priests and nuns must mark carefully what they say against John Paul's encyclicals or else suffer his Inquisitor's secret investigations, or be summoned to interrogations such as the one endured by Reverend Leonardo Boff, Brazil's founder of liberation theology, who has since abandoned the priesthood.

The exodus of priests from their vows since the reign of Paul VI has only increased in the Ratzinger–John Paul era, and it could be counted on that their theology will in the future stand as hard as panzer steel for celibacy as it does against abortion, premarital sex and extramarital sex. Prodigal priests and nuns are compelled to hold to their celibacy vows or stay defrocked, even though the first pope, the Apostle Peter, was married and not a celibate. Ratzinger, who Ostling's insiders in the Vatican say is not John Paul's moral and theological equal but his superior, seems more than happy to shake out the weak in doctrine to preserve the strong. He appears serenely unconcerned that upholding his absolutist spiritual stance is bleeding the priesthood as white as the armies of another iron-willed German. Adolf Hitler bled his Wehrmacht to collapse by upholding his absolutist military doctrine of static defense at all cost. Could Ratzinger's policy of not giving an inch towards progress do the same to the Roman Church?

Rather than a brain drain the priesthood continues to suffer a youth drain so serious that, if not stanched by some dramatic change in faith or policy, the priesthood and auxiliary orders of nuns in many countries will simply disappear in a generation's time from attrition by old age.

Ratzinger and his pope will not allow a transfusion of tens of thousands of willing women to become Catholic priests. Since *Humanae vitae* slapped women's liberation in the face there has been a rise in pressure for the current pontiff to move from condescending testimonies about the virtues of women to granting the feminine members of his Church real power. Alas, God's special role for the celibate monk, placing him higher than the descendants of sexy Eve, is upheld by John Paul. He says that women are forbidden by divine law to become priests, even though a number of brilliant spokeswomen from the laity in today's Church cannot find a theological rule banning women from the priesthood or even from sitting on St. Peter's chair.

The pope who played a significant part in the fall of world communism at the end of the Cold War now bewails the new openness to the evils of the West inflicted upon his Polish home-land and the former communist bloc – thanks to what he believes is an unbridled and savage return of capitalism.

The champion against Godless communism faces a more subtle and alluring foe in the anti-God materialism and consumerism of the triumphant American superpower. The USA is the most powerful secular nation on Earth, usually led by Protestant heretic presidents. It is also, in this pope's view, one of the chief per-petrators of the culture of death, because it has made abortion legal. Perhaps this pope can now appreciate the stance of Iranian ayatollahs who view the USA as the great Satan.

The Vatican of John Paul is stressed over the need for more capital. The lack of funds is so serious that on two occasions he has called together the Sacred College of Cardinals to discuss the grave state of papal finances. This modern pope would not stoop to the long tradition of earlier popes who sold cardinal titles and bribed political leaders. One cannot fathom that this pope could ask for his cut in the earnings of the whores of Rome, as did many a Renaissance pope. Nor are modern Catholics unsophisticated enough to buy into indulgence taxes to save their souls – the scheme that built the dome of the grand basilica beneath which John Paul and his princes of the Church gather to hear mass and discuss the financial crises of his Church. But one way or another since the early 1990s the Vatican's bank balance has crawled, like a penitent on its knees, into the black each year.

Wrestling with Soviets was easy compared to wrestling with

sex. No issue rankles the righteousness of this pontiff more than any modern innovation that disturbs the sacred flow of man's semen from conception to birth to unassisted death. Contraception to him works like marijuana – it leads to more evil drugs. The rubber paves the way to the hell of abortion. A woman's right to choose when to bear a child leads straight to the evil of claiming one's right to die, euthanasia.

His autocratic stance on these issues has produced something like a second Protestant Reformation, which is overtaking even the staunchest Catholic bastions of South America such as Brazil. International Television Network reported in October 1997 that a majority of the faithful in the world's largest Catholic country are rejecting John Paul's conservative stance on abortion and contraception and are turning a deaf ear to his conservative appointees behind the pulpits. The 1990s have seen an exodus of around 33 per cent of the Catholic laity into the arms of evangelical Christianity.

Perhaps John Paul's difficulty in persuading a growing number of rebelling Catholics to abandon contraception comes from his habit of sidestepping a difficult issue. Take overpopulation. On the one hand he says in *Crossing the Threshold of Hope* that population growth cannot be irresponsible and the "rate of population growth must be taken into consideration." His answer to the world's exploding birth rate is to cite Paul VI's *Humanae vitae* and John XXIII's call for responsible parenthood. This is basically defined by the pope as a "necessary condition for human love, and it is also the necessary condition for authentic conjugal love, because love cannot be irresponsible."

Loving couples is not the point. It is too many couples, loving or otherwise, which cause the world to burst at the seams.

Within the next century, if this pope or his next two successors do not change their views on birth control, then even loving and responsible parents will become so numerous that they and their families break the back of this civilization with their demand on the Earth's dwindling food and water sources.

In December 1994, one hundred and eighty-five nations – including the Vatican State – gathered in Cairo for the first United Nations population conference. By the conclusion of the conference there was great hope, reflected in 90 per cent support for the motions of a draft agreement on population growth. If ratified, this agreement would commit 17 billion dollars annually to curb the population explosion by the year 2000. Clause 8.25, in part inspired by the Protestant American president, Bill Clinton, irritated the pope because it promoted the right of women all across planet Earth to have access to safe, legal and voluntary abortions. The pope, who was in constant contact with his delegates in Cairo, made sure that they kept the Latin American representatives in line. The Vatican delegates made alliances with those from baby-barraged Islamic nations to effectively grind the conference to a halt with nine days of protests and filibusters. Abortion, this culture-of-death-denouncing pope feared, threatened to become a global weapon against the population explosion. To salvage the first significant global effort to forestall what could become the 21st century's most pressing problem, the delegates struck paragraph 8.25 from the agreement. In turn the pope's delegates gave grudging and only partial consent to the document.

The pope's victory punctuated the move to make him *Time* magazine's Man of the Year for 1995. In Paul Gray's article on the matter entitled, "Empire of the Spirit," critics of John Paul's actions at Cairo generally reflected the same frustration – what Gray described as, "There he goes again . . . imposing his sectarian morality on a world already hungry and facing billions of new mouths to feed in the coming decades." Gray also cites a Spanish critic who called John Paul a "traveling salesman of demographic irrationality."

Catholic conservatives the world over sang his praises. The British Catholic weekly *The Tablet* said of his fight at Cairo, "Never has the Vatican cared less about being unpopular than under Pope John Paul II."

MOONIES FOR MARY?

The prophecies of Catholicism and the Virgin Mary sightings as they are generally interpreted call for some drastic and forceful effort to win back souls before the Millennium tribulations commence. Godless communists understood what a Polish pope fighting against them knows. A war for the hearts and minds of the masses is won by reprogramming the tender minds of youth. Christ's commune needs its own youth groups.

In war the end justifies the means, as long as that solution serves God, not the devil. If Hitler could revolutionize Germany overnight into a land of evil by winning the hearts of and instilling boundless fanaticism in its youth, so could this pontiff marshal millions of young people today into a global Catholic youth movement for the greater good. With his guidance they could transform the Church and the world with God's good news.

To date there are three charismatic movements which enjoy John Paul's patronage. They are Focolare, Communion and Liberation, and NC (Neocatechumenate). In the last decade these movements have grown to include over 30 million, mostly youthful, members. Some might say that the pope and his traditionalist insiders are preparing the Church for a spiritual war in the 21st century. John Paul would like to transform the simple barque of the Holy See into an armada of militant Catholic action groups poised to counter the infestation of godlessness in the modern world. Their zeal would also act as a warning shot lobbed across the bow of Protestant evangelical movements pirating away millions of Catholic followers.

Where the pope praises them as holy youth, their detractors and ex-members characterize them as something akin to Hitler Youth.

Gordon Urquhart, an ex-Focolare leader, has written a book, *The Pope's Armada* (Corgi), which recounts his nine years within the group. He has gathered witness confessions of dozens of ex-members of Focolare and other movements, painting the picture of a bizarre nether world of secret societies indoctrinating their gullible disciples to behave like cult followers. Urquhart records a long list of dubious psychotherapeutic practices, acts of ego-mortification and numerous sessions of moral and spiritual brainwashing. These are performed with the apparent blessing of the pontiff and his curia. The pope either does not know what is going on or does not want to know because he is too sympathetic to the ultra-traditional philosophies of the charismatic "gurus" who run these three movements.

Until an encyclical states otherwise, it must be taken for granted that before a new Catholic world order can put humanity right with God in the Third Christian Millennium, these charismatic movements must first win over enough local churches. Urquhart depicts parishes being infiltrated by agents of these movements. With time they exert pressure on the local priests or intimidate lay leaders in the parish until they surrender to the organization's authority. One could depict these movements as Rome's holy federalists waging a war against local church authority and resistance to the centralizing ambitions of John Paul II.

To the rare critic not censored by the curia who dares to complain directly to His Holiness in a private visit about the groups' heavy-handed tactics, Urquhart has been told that John Paul frowns and changes the subject. Perhaps his love is blind to the millions of young members of these charismatic groups who flock to his open-air masses and he does not want disturbing evidence of cult behavior to undermine his faith in them. With old age creaking shut its rusty iron door on his vitality and mobility this pope is clearly revitalized by their youth and support in mass rallies. He needs their hope in the Church's future as much as they need him to be their beloved shepherd into the new millennium.

Cardinal Ratzinger, the pope's theological confessor, adds his authority to the Catholic youth phenomenon. He calls them the "supra-territorial apostolic movements which rise up 'from below,' in which new charisms flower and which revive the life of the local church."

"Even today," says Ratzinger, "these movements, which cannot be derived from the episcopal principle, find their theological and practical support in the primacy [of the Pope]."

Perhaps this modern Grand Inquisitor is supporting the approved prophetic sequence of events. It must be remembered that before the last Judgment and return of Christ and Catholic world hegemony there must first arise visions and grass-roots movements of lay Catholics that galvanize the papal hierarchy.

The charismatics themselves brush off critics bewailing their take-no-prisoners invasion of local churches as the same kind of backslider's beef that new missionary movements like that of the Franciscans and the Jesuits endured with local bishops and laity in their own times. The minions of NC and Focolare indoctrinate their crusaders to expect a rocky road on their crusade towards dominance of Catholic life in the 21st century. They believe that they are God's agents to redeem the world.

After Ratzinger, Bishop Paul-Josef Cordes is perhaps the strongest defender within the pope's cabinet of the new movements. He defined their struggle with the mainstream Catholics as essentially an apocalyptic battle between the forces of light and the forces of evil within the Church.

"Therefore," declares this significant figure in the pope's inner circle, "he who takes part in it must grasp 'the sword of the spirit, i.e. the Word of God'; this means not leading a rearguard action, but facing the adversary eye to eye."

The pope has never tempered the bishop's public statements on the matter so one can only surmise that Cordes has his blessing.

PRUNING THE PAST WITH APOLOGIES

To his credit John Paul has done more to apologize for the crimes and errors committed in the name of the faith than any other pope in history. Where 29 popes over the course of 359 years stood by God's error in astronomy and condemned Galileo for saying that the Earth moved around the sun, John Paul took only 14 years to decide to publish his official regret about the Church's repression of the pioneering astronomer.

John Paul also voiced his regret for the persecution of the Protestants over the last four centuries, and he apologized to the Arabs for the crimes of the crusaders in the Holy Land. Next came a plea for forgiveness for the abuses of Europe's colonial-era proselytizing around the world.

This pope could forgive and apparently forget Archbishop Marcinkus' role in the Vatican Bank scandal and withhold granting Italian investigators access to important records to help them solve mafioso crimes. This is the same pope who later publicly condemned the Church's silence regarding Italy's history of Mafia slayings.

Rather than easing the pain, his apologies only prune the leaves of a bush full of unredeemed historical crimes, allowing more to sprout into view. In 1997 reporters heard him peevishly observe that it was always the pontiff and his Church that must apologize while others stay silent.

It is not easy to prune the leaves of ancient injustices. Your apology slices off a half-dozen leaves of a half-dozen crusades only to expose the unapologized-for leaves of the Albigensian holocaust. You pluck the twigs used to stake the Protestants for heresy and someone points out the stakes you left behind which impaled millions of tortured women condemned as witches.

And there is no end to the backlash.

You recognized the Jewish State of Israel where the Holy Sees of Pius XII, John XXIII, Paul VI and John Paul I did not, yet your pontificate must suffer the question of why it took over three decades to do so.

Even when you are the first pope in history to spend as much as 80 minutes in a synagogue, the people demand more. While making your historic visit of the Synagogue of Rome in 1986, you attempt a sad smile before you make your address to the assembled Jewish community. You begin to condemn the persecutions of the past against Jews "by anyone." And remember, you even repeated it more forcefully – "by anyone!" But it was not enough – they wanted you to be more specific.

You even dispensed with protocol and embraced the rabbi. You shared your sincere horror as a Pole from Cracow who had experienced the Nazi occupation which saw three million Jewish Poles slaughtered at the Nazi death camps.

The congregation cried, they applauded.

Still there are always more crimes to prune, more people saying that your apologies are not enough.

Why can not your sincere apology cut every weed of error for all the women burned, the Jews killed, the Galileos repressed and the Nazis squirreled away in Argentina?

Two years are left in the old millennium and pressure mounts for some ground-breaking encyclical or prayer of atonement for 20 centuries of Jewish persecution blessed and openly promoted by your infallible predecessors.

WAITING FOR GOLGOTHA

In 1979, on his first triumphal return to Poland as pontiff, John Paul made a pilgrimage to the soot-covered mausoleum of genocide at Auschwitz. There he referred to the Holocaust as the Golgotha of our century. This is the same century that a number of Catholic seers foresaw as being "consigned to the devil." Before it breeds its last bastard child of crimes against humanity, we await an official statement by the pope which will once and for all make a specific public accounting for the Church of Rome's actions – or lack thereof – during the Jewish Holocaust.

John Paul had appointed commissions and symposiums to help him gather findings for a pronouncement expected to be made sometime before the new millennium. This encyclical will be the most important and long-awaited since *Humanae vitae*. Indeed it may be the most significant paper on the Jews since AD 1179, when Alexander III codified all previous enactments against the Jews since the Council of Nicaea. The world is waiting to see if John Paul II will openly deny the authority of a vicious anti-Semitic Caraffa pope like the 16th-century Paul IV. Will John Paul write a public answer to the Caraffa pope's "faultless" contention in *Cum nimis absurdum* that Jews are a mongrel race of Christ-killers worthy of slavery? Perhaps John Paul's reckoning of the Church's part in programming and preparing Christians over 16 centuries for the Holocaust could become the most important encyclical ever written.

From what is known about the preparations being made in the Vatican, and from indications made in speeches by the pope, he apparently will not stand in judgment of Pius XII's silence and passivity during the Holocaust. In Celestine Bohlen's *New York Times* article, entitled "The Pope's in a Confessional And Jews Are Listening" (30 November 1997), she divulges a passage that the pope left out in a prepared speech criticizing detractors of Pius XII while on a visit to Germany in 1995. The pope avoided saying the following: "Those who don't limit themselves to cheap polemics know very well what Pius XII thought about the Nazi regime, and how much he did to help the countless victims persecuted by that regime."

Pius, to his merit, did save several hundred thousand Jews, but perhaps the pope left this statement out because it sidesteps what Pius did not do or say to stop the butchering of six million Jews. By brushing off all judgment of Pius this pope also plays dodge ball with a number of difficult issues. Among them are Pius' sympathy for Catholic Germans over other Catholics, and his public praise of the bloodiest invasion in history as a great Christian crusade – Hitler's war with Russia. Nor can we expect John Paul, the pope who assisted in the fall of communism, to pass judgment on Pius' efforts to hide, smuggle and protect thousands of Nazi war criminals from facing trial at Nuremberg because they were anti-communists.

John Paul may yet find a way to absolve the Catholic Church from bearing some responsibility for the Holocaust. He might proclaim that the crime was aided and abetted by a number of Catholic leaders who misinterpreted dogma, papal bulls and the New Testament. These mistaken followers of the Church might be defined as anti-Judaic rather than anti-Semitic in their mistake. In other words they were not really practicing genocide against another race, they were doing battle with the beliefs of another religion. They simply committed over a thousand years of crimes against humanity leading to what only looked like genocide simply because they were against the religion of the Jews.

Based upon what John Paul has already hinted he will say, I predict that if he lives until the Millennium you will witness him absolve the Roman Church of any crime against Jews. He will say that the Church has never lost its moral center. He will pass the buck of guilt to some of its followers and leaders. By the way, I doubt that he will name any pope in particular because declaring their errors would undermine his own infallibility. This pope will say that when encountering Hitler and the Holocaust certain unnamed Catholics shrank before their Christian duty to resist the Jewish genocide.

THE MARIAN PONTIFF

John Paul's passionate devotion to the Mother of Christ is legendary. Even the seal of his pontificate, his coat of arms, depicts an arcane letter *M* for her. Psychologists might explain this as the way in which a nine-year-old boy might fill the void left by the death of his mother at such a tender age. The absence of a beloved mother may have evolved, as did his spiritual quest, into a need to replace the woman of his birth with the holiest of mothers, the patron saint of his homeland. Even as I write this, CNN telecasts the frail frame of John Paul teetering down the stairs of his jet to stand upon Cuban soil. He no longer can bend down to kiss the earth. Children must hold up a pot of Cuban dirt for him to press upon a pair of partially paralyzed lips. He has made it clear that he comes to dedicate this land, one of the last under communism, to the Blessed Virgin Mary. He does this no doubt in part to fulfill the Mary apparition's prophecies of Fátima, who in the year of Bolshevism's creation (1917) foresaw the fall of communism if a pope would dedicate Russia to her immaculate heart.

John Paul's quest to love Mary may go beyond the doctrine of all of his predecessors since the Apostle Peter.

On 13 May 1981, on a sunny spring day in St. Peter's Square, the pope, standing in his popemobile, made his daily drive through the gathered worshipers to give blessings. A shot rang out and the pope, with arm outstretched in blessing, moved his hand to cover the bullet wound in his stomach and stop the flow of blood staining his cassock and vest.

Two more shots pierced his right arm and shattered his right hand.

The popemobile sped away to hospital with its martyr in the back seats crouched in a pool of blood. His assistants and bodyguards heard him whispering, "Madonna . . . Madonna . . ."

Mary's name was upon his lips when he lost consciousness from the anesthesia as Italian doctors worked desperately for hours to rebuild his shattered intestines and save his life.

In his book *Crossing the Threshold of Hope*, John Paul relates that the assassination attempt occurred on the anniversary of the Virgin Mary's appearance to the three Portuguese children for the first time, 64 years earlier in 1917. He admits that he had not given much thought to the Fátima prophecies until after the day of his near-assassination. Now he could recognize a "certain continuity" to the Mary sightings of La Salette, Lourdes, and Fátima "and in the distant past, [to] our Polish Jasna Góra."

After his recovery John Paul made a pilgrimage to visit the surviving messenger of the Fátima prophecies, Sister Lucia, and to pray in the great cathedral built over the spot where the beclouded feet of the Virgin apparition appeared above the little pine tree.

John Paul clearly believes that the synchronicity of his wounding on the feast day of the Lady of Fátima is not a coincidence but a sign that he become more directly involved in Catholic eschatology.

He believes that his beloved Mary, "spoke [to the children at Fátima] the words that now, at the end of this century, seem to be close to their fulfillment."

He has since proclaimed that the text from the Third Secret of Fátima leaked in 1963 to *Neues Europa* is authentic. The pope has put the weight of his papal authority behind interpretations of Marian prophecy that expect the new millennium to see God initiate through the mediation of the Virgin Mary a number of miraculous events and "happenings" to close the Second Christian millennium and prepare the Church and the world for the Second Coming of Christ.

THE DRIVE TO MAKE CHRIST'S MOTHER BLESSED AMONG MESSIAHS

If Christ is coming down to earth at this millennium's end his pope may require that he make some room for his mother as an equal partner in mediating your salvation.

In April 1997 John Paul said, "Having created man 'male and female,' the Lord also wants to place the New Eve beside the New Adam in the Redemption . . . Mary, the New Eve, thus becomes a perfect icon of the Church. . . . We can therefore turn to the Blessed Virgin, trustfully imploring her aid in the awareness of the singular role entrusted to her by God, the role of the co-operator in the Redemption."

Kenneth L. Woodward of *Newsweek* reports that in the last four years the pope has received over four million signatures on petitions from 157 countries requesting that he use his *ex cathedra* powers to make Mary Co-Redemptrix and Mediatrix of All Graces and Advocate for the People of God.

In other words, they want to make Jesus' mother, *She*-sus Christ.

It is a unique situation.

For the first time people from the highest of the papal hierarchy to the lowest of the laity around the world are pressing their pope with 100,000 letters a month to make an infallible statement. Among the lobbiers are the late Mother Teresa of Calcutta, around 500 bishops and 42 cardinals, including, Woodward says, Cardinal John O'Connor of New York, Cardinal Joseph Glemp of Poland and "half-a-dozen high ranking princes of the church at the Vatican itself."

Even dowdy 74-year-old Mother Angelica, Catholicism's own global televangelist, lobbies for Mary to become Co-Redemptrix. Woodward reports that in early August 1997 the good Mother interviewed the leader of the Marian drive, Professor Mark Miravale, in front of a worldwide television audience tuning in to her show, "Mother Angelica Live," from an estimated 55 million homes in 38 countries.

"If the Holy Father would define this dogma," she said, "it would save the world from great catastrophes and loosen God's mercy even more upon this world."

It was Ida Peerdeman, the Catholic seer from post-war Holland, who had galvanized interest in Mary as Co-Redemptrix and whose charismatic utterings may have contributed to Pope Pius XII's *ex cathedra* declaration on Mary's Assumption of "body and soul" into heaven in 1950. Before her death in 1995, Peerdeman predicted that just as Pius had used a Jubilee year of 1950 to declare his infallible statement about Mary, so will John Paul use the Jubilee year of 2000 to proclaim the "final dogma" of Mary's role as co-savior.

John Paul enjoys the greatest surge of Catholic interest in Christ's mother to ever overwhelm a pontiff. Even the Mary sightings of the 19th century, which began their upward surge after the 1830s, are dwarfed by sightings of the 20th century. John Dollison in his book *Pope-Pourri* reports that 250 sightings alone have been recorded between 1928 and 1994. (The Vatican confirms only six of these as authentic.) Mary's intrepid lobbier,

Miravalle, believes that there have been as many as 400 apparitions in the 20th century. Mary has allegedly been seen popping
up in the fields, descending from the sky, spectrally paper-hanging
her holy visage on walls, trees, burritos and on the wax finish of
cars, possessing auto shops and shedding tears and blood from
her statues on every continent except for that tread upon by the
emperor penguin pilgrims of Antarctica.

Beginning in June 1981, the month after John Paul was shot,
Mary was seen by six children from Medugorje, in Bosnia. They
say that she appeared to them as a beautiful young woman in
golden splendor, calling herself the Queen of Peace. She warned
of a coming apocalypse if people do not return to God and say
their prayers. Global Armageddon has not arrived, but the area
endured its third Balkan war in the 20th century in the 1990s.
Between 10 and 20 million pilgrims have visited the site since
1981.

The year 1981 also saw Mary sightings begin in Kibeho,
Rwanda. For the next eight years apparitions of Christ's desperate
mother revealed terrible visions of a coming plague of Rwandan
genocide. In the last apparition, on 28 November 1989, Mary is
said to have introduced herself as the "Mother of the World." She
pleaded with the Rwandans not to forget to pray to her and say
the rosary. Five years later the Rwandan version of Armageddon
did begin, with the massacre of nearly a million people. The
Church officially will not endorse Mary of Kibeho or Medugorje,
but the pontificate of John Paul pays very close attention to further
developments.

What if this pope were to yield to the temptation and place his
infallible "yes" to Mary's equal opportunity to mediate salvation
to the world?

Would not the pages of his edict fan the flames of new faith in
Catholics the world over to better keep out the godless cold of
modern civilizaton's "culture of death?" And if it turns out that
the Marian prophecies and their spectral emissaries are authentic,
maybe – just *maybe* – a strike of John Paul's God-driven pen on
encyclical paper could ease God's coming chastisement.

On the other hand his "ex" across the mouths of Catholic critics
of Mary's equality with her son could have a "cathedra" full of

dire karmic consequences for the Church's credibility in the new millennium.

Mary as Co-Redemptrix would find herself standing, as it were, clad in next to no theological clothing. She appears in fewer than a dozen anecdotes in the Gospels. The New Testament cites pretty skimpy details about her beyond the fact that she was a virgin and the mother of Christ.

Theological wolves in the Catholic faith as well as their ever tele-vigilant Protestant TV Bible-bashers are waiting to pounce on the pope if he dares press a scripturally unsound insult to God's son's unique mission on Earth. Unbelievers and atheist scholars would be poised to expose the historical weakness of Christian scripture in general if the Son of Man who would be Messiah is made equal to the mother Mary who would be Co-Christ. The world would be reminded that her immaculate conception and other holy attributes beyond simply being Christ's good mother may be embellishments as medieval and authentic as the Donation of Constantine.

THE FUTURE

I saw one of my successors taking to flight over the bodies of his brethren. He will take refuge in disguise somewhere; and after a short retirement he will die a cruel death. The present wickedness of the world is only the beginning of the sorrows which must take place before the end of the world.
St. Pius X (1909)

The time is coming when you will hear the noise of battle near at hand and the news of battles far away . . . For nation will make war upon nation, kingdom upon kingdom; there will be famines and earthquakes in many places. With all these things the birth-pangs of the new age begin.
Jesus Christ (Matthew:6–8)

ONE HUNDRED AND TEN

De labore solis
From the Sun's Eclipse

JOHN PAUL II AND HIS FUTURE

THE YEAR 1998 opened with renewed concern for Pope John Paul's health. Time, a grueling work and travel regimen for two decades, an assassination attempt and a series of injuries and accidents have all taken their toll on his body. He had a major operation in 1992. The following year he suffered two serious falls: the first dislocated his shoulder when he tripped over a carpet; the second was a fall in the bathroom that cracked his hip.

Some have labeled him accident prone. It might be more fair to say that the willing spirit of this energetic pope is having a hard time accepting the rapid decline of his weakening flesh.

In 1994 the second injury required the pope to undergo a serious bone-replacement operation. He did further harm to himself by being too impatient to follow doctor's advice and finish his physiotherapy. He now shuffles painfully, with an artificial femur in his right leg, and is required to use a cane, which he seems unwilling to learn how to use. In 1994 he was observed impatiently limping on his game right leg – with his cane dangling uselessly in his left hand. By 1998 one noticed him submitting to the pain and bearing some weight on the cane in the proper hand. On better days a wry smile touches his slackening lips and he twirls his cane to entertain his adoring followers, in defiance of his infirmities.

Since the early 1990s world attention and speculation about a new conclave in the near future increases like the tremor in the pope's left hand and arm. His shaking frame, the increasing bend of his dramatically stooped and rounded shoulders, along with the paralysis slacking the left side of his head are evidence of either a series of small strokes or the onset of Parkinson's disease. The Vatican denies any of it.

Ten days into 1998 the pope was seen on international

television performing baptisms having what appeared to be a dizzy spell. He swayed on his famous silver crosier designed by Lello Scorzelli, looking as sickly and worn as its stick-figured Christ. He would have lurched to the floor if a priest had not pulled on his robe to keep him steady. Following medieval protocol, Vatican officials denied that anything happened, apparently unconcerned about how silly this made them look.

John Paul privately grumbles at the attention his body receives; he does not want to be seen as an invalid pope. Often bad days are followed by vigorous ones that put the death-watch rumors to rest for a time. On better days he can apply his dry sense of humor to all the gossip:

"When I want to know what my health is like, I read a newspaper."

The same whimsical brush-off can be applied to growing whispers in the Vatican cardinalate about his death and replacement. Kevin Fedarko, in an article about the papal succession entitled "Who Will be First Among Us?" (*Time* Magazine, 2 January 1995), relates a story which may have some indirect association with my own work and the renewed interest in prophecy concerning the pope's future. Fedarko relates that one day an ebony-skinned bishop from Senegal was lunching with John Paul and said, "People are talking a lot about your succession. After you, they say there will be a black Pope."

"You seem very well informed," replied the pope.

"Yes," said the bishop cheerfully, "I read it in Nostradamus!"

The pope laughed.

At least some fuel for this joke in the Vatican hierarchy may have come from an interview I made in NBC's *Ancient Prophecies* series about St. Malachy and Nostradamus' prophecies concerning the future of John Paul and his successors. In the summer of 1994 the producer/director, Graeme Whifler, informed me that John Paul had personally ordered a video copy of the show. I think the pope was more interested in the segment that followed mine, which included a marvelous dramatization of the Fátima visitations by the Virgin Mary.

All seriousness aside, as we enter the Year of the Tiger, 1998 – the year that many Bible scholars believe is the true 2,000-year anniversary of the birth of Christ (2 BCE) – John Paul is soldiering his dwindling life forces to lead the Church of Rome into the new millennium. While working diligently to prepare the Church for the planned commemoration of the birth of Christ in the year 2000, his obsession with eschatology is intensifying, and his efforts and statements betray an increasingly apocalyptic nature. He is certain that some divine sign will descend upon the Earth in the year 2000. Perhaps he is privy to the date of the Lady of Garabandal's "great miracle" at that time. He believes that he has a divine mission to shepherd all Christians into the Third Millennium.

"He is in his last chapter," says Cardinal Achilli Silvestrini, a powerful member of John Paul's curia who is prefect of the Congregation for Oriental Churches as well as a prime candidate to succeed him.

No hair shirt like the one worn by a pope as recent as Paul VI is needed to mortify John Paul's flesh. It can be gathered from the current pope's statements on the virtue of suffering that he believes that his flesh is doing a good job of mortification on its own, encasing his sharp mind and steadfast will in a rapidly degrading and ever more painful corporeal container. It is safe to say that John Paul's prayers to the Virgin and to Jesus include a request for enough life force to brighten his sputtering candle so that it can cast its light a few years or even a few months into the next millennium.

His laundry list of goals for the year 2000 is impressive. He dreams of fulfilling the prophecy of his mentor, Stefan Cardinal Wyszynsky (the late archbishop of Warsaw), who saw him leading the Church into the Third Millennium. John Paul perceives himself in that year – God willing – still able to stand by hook or papal crook on the peak of Mt. Sinai celebrating a mass with Patriarch Aleksey II of Moscow to mark the final reconciliation of the ancient schism between Orthodox and Catholic Christendom. He expects to settle the controversy of Mary's role in dogma and will deliver a set of the most important encyclicals ever penned by a pope in which the Church may officially repent for a number of the terrible crimes listed in this book to the satisfaction of everyone.

If he can pull this off it would truly be a miracle!

At the time of this writing – in the 20th year of his pontificate,

700 days before the 20th century after his master's birth – the new historical currents of the Aquarian Age exert ever more pressure against the unbending bamboo of John Paul's conservatism. His unyielding will is strong enough to stand firm against the winds of change, but his flesh could crack, and soon.

Some indication of his own personal end time may be gleaned from an alternative interpretation of his motto DE LABORE SOLIS (from the sun's *eclipse*). The pope born on a solar eclipse in 1920 may die on or around the time of a portentous solar eclipse scheduled to darken most of Europe in the summer of 1999.

On 11 August 1999, a total eclipse will cast the shadow of night on the dome of St. Peter's Basilica as well as blacken England, France, Italy, Eastern Europe and Turkey. Prophets have always believed that eclipses are signs of omens of great change. Nostradamus frequently characterizes a great eclipse over Europe before the new millennium as the final warning initiating a great period of spiritual crisis and tribulation for planet Earth – otherwise described by him as the "twenty-seven-year war" of the "Third Antichrist." His prophecies can indicate that as many as 70 wars will rage across the planet, caused by the strains of our civilization trying to cope with the needs of too many people, unprecedented ecological and climatic disasters, global famines and plagues between 1999 and 2026.

Rather than the publication of encyclicals by John Paul that heal the wounds inflicted on humanity in the name of the Church, these "eclipse prophecies" seem to describe a Church under siege by the summer of 1999 due to either new scandals or new revelations of old scandals.

In previous books on Nostradamus I have introduced a number of controversial interpretations of dozens of prophecies which I believe describe three scandals foretold to mortally – and morally – wound the credibility of the Church of Rome. My take is that these will lead to its self-destruction around the end of this millennium or sometime in the first 30 years of the 21st century.

First, through its relationship with fascism and its silence in the face of the Holocaust, the papacy will collapse in forfeit of its spiritual integrity. Second: the Church would be further undermined by the murder, or rumor of murder, of a pope who is on the verge of revealing corruption. Third: the Catholic clergy would be decimated around the beginning of the new millennium by a new kind of plague. Nostradamus implies that this plague is of the "blood and substance" of the Church. One could speculate that he is foreseeing the devastating effect of AIDS and homosexual behavior in the clergy.[1]

One can not rule out that the "substance" of spiritual credibility is also "plagued" by some missed signal in the summer of 1999. John Paul may have produced his long-awaited atonement encyclicals by that time and their reception might be disastrous. The pope has a habit of sidestepping issues. He may find a way to shirk the Church's responsibility for its crimes and inherit a windstorm of protest and criticism from around the world.

Back to St. Malachy Another interpretation of the motto from the sun's eclipse has it stand for the eclipse of papal power in the world due to schisms over Church doctrine and scandals exposed during the reign of this pope.

The backlash against his encyclicals could bring on a theological fight that this pope has not the physical stamina to wage. Whether this future controversy happens or not, I sense that the pope is in danger of another serious health crisis by the summer of 1999. He may survive it and persevere, but his apparent battle with Parkinson's disease or a stroke at that time might turn him into something like a geriatric Soviet premier of the Vatican State – an invalid pope, long sequestered away in hospital from his pressing duties, leaving the church leadership adrift.

Vatican insiders have let it leak out that this pope would abdicate his throne and retire to spend his last days in a monastery in Poland if he found that he could no longer perform his duties because of failing health. Indeed the pontiff who broke tradition by being the first non-Italian pope since the year 1522 might close his reign as the first pontiff to retire since 1294.

But if he hung on to the Fisherman's ring it would not be the first time that the Church was run by a curia rallying around a crippled and perhaps mentally debilitated figurehead. If a conclave is not gathering to choose a new pontiff in August or in the final autumn of the old millennium, John Paul may lead his sheep into

---

[1] For a full accounting of Nostradamus' 14 prophecies for three papal scandals, see *Nostradamus: The Complete Prophecies* (Element Books, 1997).

the new millennium feet first and pierced by an IV needle in a hospital bed.

One thing is assured: whether the above speculation about his health is good prophecy, a good guess or is going to turn out different than anyone expects, the statements logged up to February of 1998 by John Paul and those in the Vatican speculating on his stamina betray a shared belief that his life candle is not expected to burn beyond the year 2000.

ONE HUNDRED AND ELEVEN

De gloria olivæ
(From the Glory of the Olive)[1]

JOHN PAUL III?
(c. 2000–c. 2020?)

WE ARE SOON to have a papal conclave to choose a new pontiff, perhaps as early as the summer of 1999 or as late as the year 2000. Papal watchers inside and outside the Vatican compound believe that when the voting princes of the Church gather in the Sacred College of Cardinals they will experience one of the longest and most challenging conclaves in modern times.

Modern comforts will be in part responsible for the expected Wagnerian-length election session. John Paul has taken care to streamline the conclave system, from procedural changes in the balloting all the way down to providing new lodgings for the men who will vote in his successor. Gone are the dank and gloomy rooms around the Sistine Chapel in which members of the college have traditionally been sealed away from the outside world. A new edifice now stands behind St. Peter's Basilica which some papal watchers have characterized as being like a modern hotel. It would be the envy of past conclaves for its 20th-century amenities.

[1]Alternative: *Of the Glory of the Olive Tree* [Dupont].

Experts think that the comfortable surroundings will allow the cardinals take more time to make this momentous decision.

At least 15 days after John Paul either retires to a Polish monastery or to heaven, the current 109 – but no more than 120 – voting cardinals will shuffle into the posh new lodgings for the conclave. Before they are sealed inside they will undergo something like a strip search. This indignity is a modern-day necessity – to catch bugging devices which could be planted by anyone from secret service agencies down to paparazzi employed by the *National Perspiror* or any other tabloid intent on getting the sacred scoop on who's next in line to be the most powerful Christian on Earth at the start of Christ's third millennium. Four times a day the cardinals will exit their comfortable   if Spartan – motel cells to pray and vote for a new pontiff.

A cardinal passes a silver collection plate, in which the ballots are placed; then the folded papers are tipped into a silver chalice. So that God will have His say in the proceedings, three cardinals are chosen by lottery to oversee the balloting ritual. The first reads the ballot, the second checks the name, the third reads the name aloud before he pierces the ballot with a needle and thread, adding it to the others so that they cannot be misplaced or reread in the counting. If a two-thirds majority is not achieved the ballots are tossed into a furnace and mixed with a chemical so that the world watching the chimney will know from the black sooty plume that the vote was unsuccessful.

The voting could go on indefinitely. The longest conclave, in the 13th century, lasted three years. To streamline the process John Paul has changed the rules so that if after 38 voting sessions (four ballots a day makes that around ten days) no successor is chosen by the two-thirds majority plus one, then the required ratio for electing a pope will fall to 50 per cent plus one. This requirement will remain for all subsequent sessions.

Once chosen as pope a cardinal is free to accept or deny his election. There is little chance that he will deny the will of the Holy Ghost, however, who is believed to be the real elector hiding behind the political intrigues and prayers of the college. When the elected one accepts, the ballots are burned and mixed with a chemical so that the chimney discharges white smoke. This will announce to the eager telephoto lenses of a hundred news agencies perched on neighboring rooftops outside the Vatican compound that the world has a new pope.

CANDIDATES FOR THE MILLENNIAL POPE

Believers can say that the Holy Spirit will move the Sacred College in every which way such that it is almost impossible to predict who will become the first new pope of the Third Christian Millennium. Only one thing is certain: the pope will not be a woman. Of all the potential candidates discussed, none could be said to be even sympathetic to women's issues.

Madeleine Bunting, a religious affairs journalist interviewed on Bill Kurtis' 1997 "Investigative Reports" documentary entitled "The Man Who Would Be Pope," said, "I can't think of a cardinal who has half the courage to come out and be perceived as being pro-women.

"A lot of cardinals make some very happy, nice sounds about wanting women to become more involved with the Church and praising women in terms of their wonderful child-rearing abilities, et cetera. Pope John Paul II himself has led the way in this; I mean, he's produced some amazing documents about how much he thinks women are completely, tremendously wonderful. But in terms of giving the women real powers – in terms of allowing women to become *priests* – no way. No way! No cardinal has ever, *ever* even hinted that he would be prepared to consider that. We're talking about a climate of fear. People don't like stepping out of line."

John Paul II has stuffed the college with so many traditionalists that many expect a righteously-winged pope cut in the same cassock. Where Paul VI appointed 19 voting cardinals, John Paul II has chosen 101 conservatives. He opened his 20th year as pontiff by appointing 23 new cardinals, the most traditionalist 19 among them having voting rights.

This would not be the first time that a pontiff hedged his bets for a clone successor of his own policies, only to have the mysteries of the sequestered conclave balloting blow out his candle of dreams with a surprise choice. Certainly if Cardinals Roncalli or Luciani had showed themselves to be runaway revolutionaries before they slipped on the Ring of the Fisherman as John XXIII and John Paul I, the voting cardinals might not have chosen them. As we have seen, the triple tiara and the crosier of maximum Vicar on Earth breaks down a conclave wall within many a cardinal's subconscious dreams, and what is freed from the confessional mask of a conservative cardinal is a closet liberal reformer.

Still, I believe that the mood within the Vatican is one of reaction against the changes of the new century, at least for the pontificate of the second to last in St. Malachy's mottoed line unto doomsday. At best the liberal Catholics can hope for a Clintonian pontiff – in other words, a centrist. Conservatives and liberals alike can pray for a peacemaker who will attempt to find a balance between the ever widening polarities within the Church.

Mainstream conclave watchers believe that the eventful and turbulent reigns of the John Pauls call for a less heroic and less charismatic man for the job. A more traditional pontiff, perhaps even an Italian, will be chosen, to give the Church a breather from the roller-coaster ride of controversy surrounding the choice of the first non-Italian pontiff.

With this in mind the conclave could toast the new millennium with a Martini – Carlo Maria Cardinal Martini, the archbishop of Milan to be exact. This suave and handsome biblical scholar and author of over 50 books speaks 11 languages, but he suffers from being tagged by the Italian press as "the one." Historically conclaves do not like to be told who to vote for. Martini, who is also known as Cardinal Clean, would bump his reverently bowed head against history's precedent that conclaves never choose a Jesuit as a pope. Statements that he has made implying that better communication of the Church's stance on contraception would make the policy "better understood and more adapted to reality" have earned him powerful opposition from the right wing of the Church as well as the pope's favorites outside of the curia, such as Cardinal Biffi of Bologna, another important Italian front runner.

Another obstacle against this cardinal is his past heart problems combined with his age. He will be 72 in the year 2000. With that said, popular pre-conclave candidates do often become pope. My own feeling is that he will be the next pope. But if Martini is not voted in then I believe that he will come very close to winning St. Peter's ring.

The election of the first Polish pope may have broken Italy's hold on the position of bishop of Rome forever. The axis shift of the Church to the Third World is in full lurch. John Paul has internationalized the College of Cardinals so that it currently represents 50 nations. There are just a little over 100 eligible voters, but this could be increased to up to a limit of 120. A European voting block of 50 or so will probably swing the vote toward a white European as the next pope. But the hushed conversations between balloting will no doubt reveal the voting cardinals debating their choice of a man less focused on First World Catholic controversies such as feminism, women in the priesthood and abortion. They will cogitate and argue over the merits of candidates who are more sensitive to Third-World issues such as social justice and poverty.

Poverty will be one of the defining issues in the choice of the next pope. That is why those cardinals from impoverished countries in Africa and especially Latin America will become prime candidates. I would add that another defining controversy for the man who would be *Glory of the Olive* will be a greater demand from the poor peoples of the Third World for reformed policy on birth control and contraception.

But will there be a black pontiff? Archbishop Stephen Neweke Ezeanya of Onishta, Nigeria, and curia Cardinal Bernadine Danteen, Prefect on the Congregation of Bishops are the best choices. A voting bloc of 17 African cardinals could swing such a vote for a man like Cardinal Francis Arinze, Prefect for the Council of Inter-Religious Dialogue. But Arinze's call for more dance, celebration and joy in Church rituals might find stiff opposition from white men in cardinalate cloth who are burdened with dogma and repressed racism.

Nostradamus' prophecies imply the potential of a future pontiff from Spain. The seer's 16th-century point of view, seen in the light of modern political realities, may include a South American cardinal coming from what were Spanish colonies in his day. The conclave members will have to wrestle with the prayers and political pull of half of the one billion Catholics on Earth in Latin America. The possibility of a Latino Vicar of Christ may steer John Paul's anti-communist appointees away from picking a man from the continent which gave the Church liberation theology –

a blending of Marxism with the mass. Watch for the two Brazilians: the Dominican Lucas Moreira Neves, archbishop of São Salvador da Bahia, and the Franciscan Evaristo Arns of São Paolo.

It is safe to say that any conclave watcher will eat his cap if a Canadian or an American cardinal makes it to St. Peter's chair. This Sacred College was put together by a pontiff who has not shown himself to be tolerant to the ideas of American-style democracy promoted by a majority of the 65 million American Catholics. At one point he called all the American archbishops to Rome to lecture them that the Church of Rome is not to be like America.

If in the next few years the aging pontiff withdraws from view, his curia will exert its ancient and traditional control over the future of the Church of Rome – with unprecedented powers. It is highly likely that the next pope will come from within its ranks. This brings to the forefront Italian cardinals such as Achille Silvistrini (Prefect for the Congregation for Oriental Churches) and Pio Laghi, the former nuncio for the USA and current Prefect for the Congregation for Catholic Education. If a curial member is not chosen the future pope could be a cardinal from the Sacred College who is a close ally outside the inner circle.

Like Archbishop Martini, these Italians will all be over 70 by the year 2000. In fact almost all the top contenders already mentioned will be in their 70s, except for Arinze. The only other important contender who we have not considered is Cardinal Daneels of Belgium. Although he will be a mere 67 at that time – in papal terms, a blushing young pontiff – his liberal views make him a very long shot. If GLORIA OLIVÆ should come from this graying stable of cardinals it is more than likely that he will not be as long-lived as John Paul II, who was 58.

If prophecy is to be our guide, then clues from the Malachy motto and interpretations of prophecies of Nostradamus augur good odds for the archbishop of Paris, Cardinal Jean-Marie Lustiger. This man, who will be 73 by the millennium, is a close friend and confidant of John Paul II. Some of his critics believe that he almost mimics John Paul II's views and styles. Lustiger is a French citizen, but he was born the son of Jewish Polish émigrés. Some of the more intolerant members of the race of Abraham would add that he also disavowed his heritage and religion. As a teenager he broke his parents' heart when he abandoned his name, Aaron, and converted to Catholicism. He, like John Paul, was a Pole who had his share of suffering at the hands of the Nazis. His mother died at Auschwitz.

One cannot deny the poetic juxtaposition – or karmic justice – of the Third Christian Millennium starting like the first, with a Jewish pope as bishop of Rome. Prophetically speaking, a Jew as pope has legs. The motto *Glory of the Olive* implies the olive branch, which is an ancient symbol of the Jewish race.

I was surprised to hear even Peter Stanford, a mainstream writer on Catholic issues, comment on the long-held interpretation of Nostradamus prophecy that if a Jew is elected, the end of the world is nigh.

However, in a quarter-century of study I have never found a clear allusion in Nostradamus to a Jew becoming pontiff. I do find more merit in interpretations of Nostradamus' quatrains which allude to the next pope after John Paul being a French citizen, which would lay out the carpet for Cardinal Lustiger.

When considering the Jew-as-pontiff prophecy Peter Stanford – who does not believe that the cardinals in the coming conclave have read Nostradamus – thinks that they just might find themselves put off when, as Stanford says, they are "sitting there in their little rooms reflecting on Nostradamus and saying, 'No, not that Lustiger, chap.' "

Anti-Semitism would be another block to his election, just as I imagine that the legacy of slavery in America would make a black president almost impossible to conceive at this time. Then there is the ancient wound that a converted Jew as pope might open. Stanford believes that just when some healing has begun between the Church and Jewish religious leaders around the world, a kosher Vicar of Christ would drag out the memories of pontiffs forcibly coercing Jews in the Roman ghetto to become Catholics. I might add that a Hebrew pope might rub Jewish noses into centuries of approved Catholic dogma on prophecy which promises that all Jews will be converted to the Church sometime after the new millennium.

Personally I see Lustiger having a better chance as the final pope on Malachy's list, *Petrus Romanus*, especially if his predecessor is short-lived enough. But even that is a real long shot. The cardinal himself would agree. When asked of his chances he replied, "Me? Totally excluded. Out of the question."

As said earlier, many Vatican watchers pray that the conclave will seek God's insight and pick a non-heroic, non-saintly or non-charismatic pope. They believe that pontiffs such as John Paul I and II suffer from people projecting on them their fantasies and expectations for an all-knowing demigod pontiff who will tell them what to do and believe. However, remarkable times may see the Church of Rome suffer in the reign of an unremarkable pontiff. Do those who hold this view wish St. Peter's chair to be occupied by a Czar Nicholas II as pope? The last czar of all the Russias was a handsome though unremarkable man who had not the charisma and force of personality to sustain the Romanoff dynasty in revolutionary times.

GLORIA OLIVAE: THE POPE OF THE MOUNT OF OLIVES PROPHECY

Two thousand years ago, it is recorded by the Apostle Matthew that Jesus took his disciples beyond what would become the future Wailing Wall of the Temple of Solomon to look upon Israel's greatest sacred compound.

One of his disciples – perhaps Matthew, the chronicler of this account – must have commented on the beauty of God's holiest house on Earth. Pointing to it Jesus replied, "Yes, look at it all, I tell you this: not one stone will be left upon another; all will be thrown down." (Matthew 24:1–2)

Jesus then took his disciples to sit upon the Mount of Olives. There he uttered one of his most detailed and far-reaching eschatological discourses on the future of Israel, his ministry, and his Second Coming.

I believe that either St. Malachy or his prescient forger intended the final climax of Christ's prophecy on the Mount of Olives (Matthew 24, 25) to be fulfilled some time during or at the end of the reign of Pope Gloria Olivae. Just as Christ promised the complete destruction of the Sacred Temple, so this motto from the prophet of the Malachy papal succession implies the toppling of St. Peter's dome and the resultant Diaspora of a pope and his cardinals from the Vatican. This could take place sometime in the first few decades of the Third Christian Millennium.

A new millennium warrants a fresh examination of some of the themes of the Mount of Olives prophecy to see how they might be applied to the reign of the next pope.

Matthew purportedly wrote down what Christ said around AD 90 – 57 years later. The fulfillment of Christ's prophecy about the destruction of the Temple therefore was put on record 20 years *after* the event took place in AD 70. This pivotal prophetic discourse – which is the basis for Christian prophetic dogma about the Rapture, the Second Coming and the foundation for the Catholic apocalyptic predictions of a divine warning followed by the Chastisement – was written down by an old man in his late 70s or early 80s, more than a half-century after Jesus uttered it.

As with so many important cornerstones of Christian dogma, we are asked to take it on faith that Matthew's memory was clear and that no hindsight embellishments were added to this prophecy. We are also asked by the Church to take it on faith that God's hand subsequently moved the hands of centuries of scribes in forgery-mongering Rome so that they would be unable to insert their additions.

With that said, this story, far removed from its original tongue, says that Jesus' disciples came privately to ask him when the temple would fall and what the signal would be for his coming again at "the end of the age." (Matthew 24:3)

Christ then offered a kind of instruction book on how to avoid being misled by false messiahs. Then he launched into a warning about the time of his Second Coming, which would be to the world plagued by numerous wars and rumors of wars:

> *The time is coming when you will hear the noise of battle near at hand and the news of battles far away; see that you are not alarmed. Such things are bound to happen; but the end is still to come. For nation will make war upon nation, kingdom upon kingdom; there will be famines and earthquakes in many places. With all these things the birth-pangs of the new age begin.* (Mt. 24:6–8)

Is this to occur during of the reign of Pope Gloria Olivæ? The pontiff of the first decade of a new Christian millennium will no doubt be faced with a worsening situation in the Middle East, which in a decade's time could see its peoples go to war as much over water rights as over religious and political differences. Over a hundred other nations, many of them Catholic bastions across Africa and South America, could go to war over water disputes and struggles for dwindling food resources.

Prophecies abound forewarning the period of 1998–2008 as a time of unprecedented earthquake activity. The prophecies of Nostradamus and other seers point to the spring of the year 2000 as a critical time. Not only must the conclave choose a new pope but the Earth's axis may shift drastically, causing the sinking of land masses and earthquakes off the scale. Modern seers believe that this shift is reflected in a grand alignment of planets which will take place at that time. All potential exaggeration of augurs aside, the last occurrence of a grand alignment of planets similar to the one in May 2000 was between 1958 and 1965. I do not recall the western USA sinking into the ocean or the axis tilting 40° then. This does not mean that in the next grand alignment mountains will not be sheared in half or coastlines altered by a few hundred acres, or that parts of towns and whole villages will not sink into the sea. Mt. Etna blew its top in 1958. The great Alaska quake of 1964 saw villages and hundreds of acres of coastline slide under or rise out of the ocean. In a few seconds the temblor split a mountain the size of Mt. Rushmore in half and sent it sliding into an Alaskan sound. In the late 1950s and early 1960s northern Japan, Sumatra and Peru suffered some of the most powerful killer quakes of the 20th century. The ocean floor off Morocco rose several thousand feet!

The Catholic relief organizations of the next pope could be stretched to the limit by a similar set of quakes and natural disasters across the world during the next planetary alignment. Los Angeles will not sink into the ocean, nor will there be beachcombers sunning themselves on the Pacific Coast of Nebraska. But from 1998 through to 2008 Los Angeles or the US plains states around St. Louis could suffer massive quakes of apocalyptic proportions without significantly altering the topography of the continents to satisfy some New Ager and his Earth changes map.

THE POPE OF THE FIRST WORLD WAR OF THE AQUARIAN AGE

Jesus predicted that his Second Coming will be announced not only by earthquakes but also by the infernal fanfare of many wars.

In *The Millennium Book of Prophecy* and in my series of Nostradamus books I have collected hundreds of shared prophetic visions from Judeo-Christian and non-Judeo-Christian traditions which describe the Third World War as unavoidable. It is supposed to take place after the Soviet Union falls and the Cold War ends. The only range of free movement that providence seems to permit us is this: we are at liberty to set into motion by our present actions what kind of war it will be.

Is it a world war free-for-all or global Balkanization of human civilization fighting over diminishing food and water resources by the 2020s?

Or is it a war that humanity fights against its own stupidity and its addiction to fossilized religious and social and economic traditions?

Nostradamus describes, in Century 9, Quatrain 55, a malevolent event that his astrological computations date for 23–27 February in the year 1998, just prior to the advent of the next pope.

> *The horrible war which is being prepared in the West,*
> *The following year the pestilence will come,*
> *So very horrible that young nor old nor animal* [may survive]:
> *Blood, fire, Mercury, Mars, Jupiter* [aspect for 23 February 1998] *in France.*

At that time the forces of "the West" will be preparing a great war which will unleash what may be the Iraqi genie-bottle of chemical and biological warfare, perhaps in a revenge attack of nuclear or biological terrorism in the summer 1999. This configuration of planets makes such a scenario also possible for 2004 and 2005. However, Nostradamus' dreadfully famous prediction for the summer of 1999 adds more weight to decisions made during the first time window:

In the year 1999 and seven months [July],
The great King of Terror will come from the sky.
He will bring back the great King of the Mongols [Genghis Khan].
Before and after Mars [the God of War] *rules.*

Perhaps in Century 10, Quatrain 72, Nostradamus foresees for July of 1999 a terrorist attack with weapons of mass destruction descending from the skies as the "King of Terror." A new and militant China may also be described in line two as the metaphorical resurrection of Genghis Khan, the "king of the Mongols." Other prophecies imply that China will negotiate a Sino/Pan-Islamic alliance with oil-rich Arab and Central Asian states so that it can control the weapon of oil. China will need to do this because in the future it will suffer from crippling famines which will only be exacerbated by the USA's weapon of withholding food. China will counterattack by trying to cut off the oil tap to the USA. Chinese astrology gives us a clue that this could lead to a Sino-American war by either the next year of the tiger, 2010, when oil reserves are expected to dramatically dry up, or in the year of the tiger set for 2022.

Nostradamus' "July 1999" prophecy ends by saying that before and after this date "Mars," the god of war, rules. This means that an incident in July 1999 may usher in Nostradamus' dreaded 27-year war of the "Third Antichrist."

His first Antichrist was identified by the anagram *Pau-Nay-Loron* or *Napaulon Roy* (Napoleon the King); the second was called *Hister* (Hitler). The third seems to be a man or even a weapon called *Mabus*. He comes from the Middle East or North Africa. He is not as easy to pinpoint as the first two. One thing is relatively clear: Nostradamus predicts that this Third Antichrist will be the first to fall in the war that he generated. It is the consequences surrounding his defeat that may cause the tribulation of a 27-year conflict between 1999 and 2026.

We should therefore know who he is talking about by the time Gloria Olivæ receives the Fisherman's ring from the cold and lifeless hand of John Paul II. Currently Saddam Hussein of Iraq is the prime candidate for the Third Antichrist. We might expect to see him killed in America's next Gulf War, which I have been dating since 1991 to take place as early as the week of 23 February 1998.

If Saddam survives, or war is averted by a stop-gap diplomatic solution at that time, then expect him or the real candidate for Nostradamus' Third Antichrist to fall in a Gulf War taking place later in 1998 or for the summer of 1999, around the time when a new conclave could meet to pick John Paul's successor. Saddam's death – or the death of a terrorist using weapons of mass destruction – somehow triggers a domino effect of many small wars and civil disruptions. Over the next two decades these will increase until – as Nostradamus warns elsewhere in his predictions – they reach a critical mass of 70 wars raging across the planet. At that time, either at the end of the rule of Gloria Olivae or at the onset of the pontificate of the last pope, the first world war of the Aquarian Age will go out of control.

Up to now our world wars have followed Piscean Age rules of engagement. This is why it may be hard for future popes and pundits to recognize the next one. The Piscean Age has trained us to expect clear definitions between the opposing forces, as well as fighting on traditional battlefields and following the commands of paternal father-figure leaders. But the wars of the next 20 centuries follow the collective influences of an age which celebrates the truth and freedom of the individual over the dogma and control of the collective or paternal leaders. In its darker side, the Aquarian Age pits the forces of rebellion and chaos against the establishment.

It will be an age that fights first and foremost on the battlefield of the human psyche. This inner war then blossoms in outer wars of social, religious and economic breakdown and revolution. The skirmishes of the coming world-war free-for-all are fought in the home and hearth where nuclear family values are besieged by change. Its major battles are the communal riots in India over religion and the urban street battles of South Central Los Angeles. Its platoons are gangs, its regiments are right-wing militias, its armies are Arab terrorists – all waging a new kind of conflict in which the capital weapons of war are placed in the hands of a few subversive individuals. It is a war in which the invader does not attack a country with its millions but strikes by the dozens. Death arrives not in tanks but in one rental truck full of chemical pesticides set off in Oklahoma. He is the hacker who shuts down the grid on all radars in airports with the stroke of a key. He is the solitary invader with a suitcase full of plutonium who takes the whole world hostage.

In the process of defeating such an enemy all aspects of human life will undergo revolutionary change in the next 30 years. In other books, I have collected a mountain of prophetic evidence that we cannot get to the future by repeating the past. The more a future pope or a president of the USA tries to restore the traditional concept of order in the future, the less order there will be. Thirty years into the 21st century, a significant segment of the suffering human population will understand that the past is not up to the challenges of the New Age.

There will be an axis shift, but it will not be of the Earth's crust. It is of the accepted crust of human perception. Where tradition and blind belief guided us for thousands of years, innovation will rule. There will grow over the next century a deep and collective urge to "know" God directly rather than have faith in Rome's reliance on pronouncements issued by any middle-man religious authority. While humanity in Aquarius' Age is threatened by the misuse of individual initiative, it is also an age in which creative and life-affirming individual initiative will eventually guide the human race to a golden age of peace.

The greatest casualties of the coming perception shift, first in war and later in a spiritual revolution, will be those icons of the former Piscean Age which were founded on the principle that belief supersedes science, as well as the dictates of a hierarchy which faces the future challenges with its mind buried in the sands of the past. Any organization – be it business or religiously oriented – will not survive long beyond the next 50 years if it clings to the wish that the future be more like the past, as pontiffs have done for centuries.

Thus we see Gloria Olivæ in the first decade of the next century trying his best to apply the lessons of the past to a new age that rejects that past. His motto implies that he will be drawn into the political and religious quagmire of the Middle East as the "glory" of the "olive branch" of a peacemaker. Perhaps, if the pope is the suave and brilliantly diplomatic Cardinal Martini, he might achieve some success as a third-party arbiter in the peace accords between Israel and the successor to the ailing leader of the Palestinians, Yasser Arafat – a man whom I believe will not see the new millennium.

Arafat and the Palestinian leadership are preparing for a defensive war that they cannot win, code-named Field of Thorns. The pope's role as peacemaker may be set in motion after Israeli troops get bogged down in bloody warfare and negative global public opinion when they fight an intifada of lead bullets rather than stones in street wars with West Bank Palestinian police. "It'll be much bigger than last September [1996]," says an Israeli commander to *Time* correspondent Lisa Beyer, "much crueler, much bloodier, much more complicated."

By the way, a prime candidate to replace Yasser Arafat as Chairman of the Palestinian State is named Abbas – a name which is a close approximation of that given by Nostradamus for the Third Antichrist, *Mabus*. Any solution that the peacemaker pope could achieve concerning a Palestinian state on the West Bank will have to cross over the political abyss of claims by Palestinians and Israelis to Jerusalem as their capital. Just beneath the surface of this challenge is the threat of a holy war over the Temple Mount.

In October 1997 I was informed by one of the foremost experts in cabalistic and Torah prophecy, Rabbi Ariel Bar Tzadok, that a cornerstone for the future third temple of Solomon had been lowered into the care- and history-worn earth of the Temple Mount in Jerusalem in 1997, just several dozen meters away from the third holiest shrine of Islam, the Dome of the Rock. Old Testament prophecy believes that when the Jewish people return to establish Israel and when the Temple is rebuilt, the "true" Messiah will return. This means that the dome must go. Rabbi Tzadok told me that his teachers in Jerusalem believe that an effort to rebuild the temple may be made as early as 2006. I am certain that this most serious crisis between Arab and Jew will arise to vex the aged heart of Pope Gloria Olivæ.

Because the olive branch is a symbol of Israel, the motto might imply that this pope will champion the cause of the Jews. Perhaps future history's standoff on Arab and Jewish holy ground might provide yet another opportunity for a pope to atone for the Church's anti-Semitic policies through his actions rather than through impotent words and encyclicals of apology. Perhaps a former Jew like Cardinal Lustiger, if he were pope, might initially insult the leadership of Israel with his crowning sometime in 1999 or 2000. Later on however, he could prove to be their greatest friend in a future holy war around 2006–2008, fought over the site of the temple that Jesus saw destroyed in his own near future.

The following excerpt from Christ's prophecy on the Mount of Olives may foresee the coming tribulation for the Catholic faithful of Gloria Olivæ's ministry:

> *You will then be handed over for punishment and execution; and men of all nations will hate you for your allegiance to me. Many will fall from their faith; they will betray one another and hate one another. Many false prophets will arise, and will mislead many; and as lawlessness spreads, men's love for one another will grow cold. But the man who holds out to the end will be saved. And this gospel of the Kingdom will be proclaimed throughout the earth as a testimony to all nations; and then the end will come.* (Matthew 24:9–14)

DYING DOGMAS DO NOT LET GO

What does Christ mean here? Be careful, we tread now upon a dangerous "mind-field." The vibe of the New Age dictates that you do not step upon this biblical path of prophecy with the heavy-foot of traditional Piscean Age assumptions. Do not be so ready to assume that this mystic Jew, Y'shua Bar Yoseph, whom we call Christ, is the fulfillment of all of our current gentile-correct interpretations – namely, that mainstream Christians are those toeing his correct line to the faith and therefore are grist for future punishment and persecution.

What if he was actually speaking of the allegiance of Jewish disciples to a Jewish spiritual revolution, and not a Church that would be mutated by *Imperial* Rome?

Then again, for argument's sake, what if the current pope and his successor are absolutely correct in assuming that their doctrine is in allegiance with Christ's religion? For a moment let us cool the blinding fires of faith and look at this prophecy as if we were visitors to the planet Earth, studying its religious evolution. One might uncover, between the lines of the prophecy above, the same syndrome of expected persecution foreseen in the prophecies of many mainstream religions. An examination of the scriptures and prophecies of other faiths which believe theirs to be the one and only understanding of God's plan shows that Hindus, the Muslims, the pagans and even native medicine men from fourth-world (native) cultures also foresee a threat coming from something new and unfamiliar, and therefore evil.

If one can put aside the blinders of 20 centuries of orthodoxy for a moment, let us look at the Sanhedrin rabbis of Jesus' time in a more sympathetic light. Would they not view the heretic from Galilee as their dreaded Antichrist? Or better, their Anti-Moses?

Let's go to Rome and the first pope, the Apostle Peter, and consider what the pagan priests of Isis and the cult of Mithras thought of this new and threatening cult of the crucified Jew. Would they not see its advent as a sign of their own foretold tribulation, in which the good and righteous pagan pantheist would face eventual persecution by an evil anti-pagan messiah?

It has happened before. It is happening again. The established religion always views the newcomers as a sign fulfilling their prophecies of future persecution. Historically they all believed that the devil of a new religion was the false prophet who would in the end be overcome. Whether the Messiah was Jesus, Mithras or the prophets upholding the Torah of Moses, they all urged their followers to clamp on their blinders to the new and hold on to their faith as they moved through future times of tempting new evils spun by false prophets. This tradition of fear continues. The faithful are promised that if they hang firm in their beliefs the evil ones will be destroyed and their mosque, their temple, their sacred teepee or their St. Peter's Basilica will rise again in glory.

That is not what usually happens.

Isis did not return. The warrior Messiah whom Caiaphas and the Sanhedrin expected to kick out the Romans and restore Israel did not arrive. Instead a false prophet named Y'shua caused all manner of problems. The Native Americans prophesied their persecution by the "white brother" and their medicine men promised their eventual triumph of Neolithic values over technology. Has the white man disappeared? Has his evil omen of the cross fallen as predicted? Have the buffalo returned from the dead?

Every established religion has its prophetic warnings, its great chastisement and its promise of eventual restoration in a golden age. And every religion's prophets have been generally accurate in foreseeing the signs of when tribulations and tests will come. The Aztec necromancers knew that Cortés was coming. The Tibetan astrologers calculated to the year the Chinese invasion and the onset of their apocalypse a century before it happened in 1950.

Religions always promise their own complete restoration, when in fact the coming tribulations usually bring death to established dogmas and sometimes rebirth into a form of new spiritual expression. The Dalai Lama may someday return to Tibet but he will find his religion and culture forever changed. The clock will not be turned back to pre-Columbian paradise in North America, even if the religion of the red man should overtake the white in the Aquarian Age, as some seers believe. A new synthesis will happen there as it will happen in Tibet. The buffalo herds will never return to their past glory on the American prairie, just as the broken stones of a thousand raised lamaseries will not rise again in a new hermit kingdom now crowded with millions of Chinese supplanting the re-educated Tibetan natives.

Today John Paul warns Catholics to stand strong in their faith against the evils and anti-Christian forces of the future. He tells Christians to prepare themselves for suffering and persecution on a level never before endured. The new supernation of the European Union is viewed by many Christian sects as the fulfillment of Bible prophecy. They believe that Christ will come soon after a new Rome and a new anti-Christian Nero rises to power to rule all of Europe.

Will it come to pass?

Or is this another example of the all-too-human habit of projecting as "anti" or evil all new visions of godliness and spirit?

The new requires the death of the old. How else can the old respond but with its fears and with its projections of survival when the end times come?

The Church of Gloria Olivae will endure the first significant pressures of new growth – a millennial religious rebellion – crowding it aside and overtaking the religious flower bed of the Aquarian Age. If prophecies are accurate because we are predictable, then this peacemaker pontiff will be a prisoner of his own dogma. Even if in his heart he is a liberal, this pontiff will be split apart by the pressure to sustain, in a new age ever more dominated by science and individualism, his authority which is based on Piscean Age values of faith and surrender to paternal authority figures.

A return to fundamentalism always rises and intensifies before old religious thinking is supplanted by the new. No institution is more vulnerable to this temptation than the papal succession, which has tried with rare exceptions to make the future look more like the past. It is all too predictable that drastic doctrinal declarations will be coming. Just as Pius IX, when faced with the end of a thousand years of secular power, declared himself infallible, so too will Gloria Olivæ fire away at the advance of spiritual progress threatening the Church's spiritual authority. Targeting the new, he may arm and train upon the world his weapon of doctrinal mass destruction: an *ex cathedra* statement.

Just as Eve was blamed for fouling up God's plan to have humans stay dumb and naked, eating grass in an earthly paradise, so too will the Aquarian Age – which is far more women-friendly than the Piscean – see Gloria Olivæ bend under the pressures to make the Virgin Mary Co-Redemptrix to Christ.

By the death of his predecessor, John Paul II, any hope of unity with the Christian Orthodox churches seemed remote, especially if Gloria Olivæ should pronounce Mary as equal to Jesus. Such an imperious and Roman gesture will make triumphant what most non-Catholic Christian sects find to be the Church of Rome's most repugnant habit: taking the religion's focus away from Christ and turning it towards the pronouncements of His Holiness, the pope. If he must make the Marian cultists happy the pronouncement by this pope might effectively wash away all attempts of the past 50 years among Anglican, Protestant and Orthodox Christians to unite with the Church of Rome. Indeed you will see the other Christian sects implicate this pope as the target of Christ's warning of false prophets and messiahs mentioned in his sermon on the Mount of Olives.

The next excerpt from the same prophecy could describe the closing years of Gloria Olivæ's besieged ministry:

> It will be a time of great distress; there has never been such a time

from the beginning of the world until now, and will never be again. If that time of troubles were not cut short, no living thing would survive; but for the sake of God's chosen it will be cut short. (Matthew 21, 22)

By 2008 the human race will begin feeling the full impact of changes, stretching to the breaking point the chrysalis of what it has known and believed. The transformation will be as frightening to us as it must be to the pupa, who has no idea of the butterfly it will become. The new seems to be the enemy because the pupa is afraid of the unknown. Still this mysterious force will prey upon us and push us through the birth channel of the next 30 years – whether we want to be free of the cozy womb of our dogmas and beliefs or not.

Around 2008 the peacemaking pope will probably leave this troubled Earth with his work unfinished, and unraveling. The besieged Church will then meet again to pick the Omega Pontiff of St. Malachy's list.

THE LAST POPE

Petrus Romanus (Peter of Rome)

IN PERSECUTIONE EXTREMA SACRÆ ROMANÆ ECCLESIÆ SEDEBIT PETRUS ROMANUS QUI PASCET OVES IN MULTIS TRIBULTIONIBUS; QUIBUS TRANSACTIS, CIVITAS SEPTICOLLIS DIRVETUR; ET JUDEX TREMENDUS JUDICABIT POPULUM.

During the last persecution of the Holy Roman Church, there shall sit Peter of Rome, who shall feed the sheep amidst many tribulations, and when these have passed, the City of the Seven Hills shall be utterly destroyed, and the awful Judge will judge the people.

The papal prophecy of St. Malachy ends with this Latin 25-word flourish containing some of the most frightening doomsday warnings written by any Catholic seer, be he a medieval saint or a prescient Renaissance forger.

One thing is certain about the last pope in this prophecy: he will never be called by the name Petrus Romanus (Peter of Rome). There is an ancient unwritten rule in the College of Cardinals that no successor to the first pope will dare use his name. Malachy prophecy watchers will have to seek other clues. Perhaps his Christian name will be Peter or his family or ecclesiastical armorial bearings will betray some evidence the Apostle whom Christ called "Rocky." Maybe the last pope's escutcheon will display a stone (a "peter"), or the apostle's fisherman boat or net will be seen. Maybe he will have some important posting at one of a thousand towns or cathedrals named after St. Peter, or he will take on a key post in St. Peter's Basilica itself.

The odds are better that his important deeds or the theme of his pontificate are the prophetic concern in this last of the post-Wion mottoes. Perhaps the name "Peter of Rome" signifies that the last pope's life will be similar to that of the first. He is the bishop of Rome at the birth of something new. He is also destined to die a martyr. One could expect the last man to sit upon St. Peter's chair to be a non-Italian just like the first – perhaps even born a Jew. One could expect that he would be an apostolic wanderer like his namesake. As Peter, the first bishop of Rome, saw the city destroyed by fire and himself persecuted and martyred, so too could the last bishop of Rome meet his ultimate martyrdom during the final destruction of Rome foreseen by so many Catholic seers – expected around or after the closing second Christian millennium.

If we are to conjure more details concerning this last pope we will have to move to the shared visions of other Catholic seers. Nostradamus published his mammoth history of the future four decades before Wion released the coda prophecy attributed to St. Malachy. Many of his prophecies (indexed below by their quatrain numbers for further reference) echo the "Pope Peter" theme, making it remotely possible that if the author was a forger prophet calling himself St. Malachy, then he had in his possession Nostradamus' *Les Prophéties*.

If one takes their similar views of the final pope as evidence of shared accuracy rather than as an attempt by the mystery author to flim-flam future readers, then Nostradamus in Century 5, Quatrain 75 (5 Q75) implies that the mystery-motto prophet's Petrus Romanus is a traditionalist burdened by many secrets. In 10 Q93 Nostradamus points to the shift of Rome's religious empire in the early 21st century to the Third World, perhaps implying that the last Holy Father will be picked from outside of Europe, maybe from a country in the Southern Hemisphere.

When foreseeing the end of the Vatican, Nostradamus describes the "fishing barque" of St. Peter, which this new pope will navigate or "rule" to "its greater detriment" (1 Q4). By emphasizing the fishing boat of the first pope, Nostradamus may be going beyond just describing the symbol of the Holy See. Perhaps he is indirectly clueing us in to the name of the last pope who will steer the ship of the Holy See into the rocks of the apocalypse in our near future.

Nostradamus foresees that at some time during the reign of Petrus Romanus the pope will be forced to abandon the Vatican, perhaps more than once. This involuntary exile will occur after the breakdown of a future alliance between Russia and America because of the deed of a terrorist from Libya or North Africa soon after the appearance of a great comet. Many scholars of Nostradamus believe that the passing of the comet Hale-Bopp in 1997 brackets the left side of this dreadful time window. As we have seen, the summer of 1999 is also mentioned as a time for added malevolence, when the world will experience the appearance of Nostradamus' third Antichrist, Mabus, a figure who will be one of the first casualties of a 27-year war of his own making.

If Hale-Bopp is the comet intended, then Russia and America will not be united in friendship for long. The Arab/North African terrorist and Antichrist will compel them to go to war within "thirteen years" (5 Q78). United States intelligence reports say that Saddam Hussein has squirreled away, in Qaddafi's Libya and in the Islamic fundamentally extreme states of Algeria and the Sudan, hundreds of his weapons of mass destruction and at least 400 Scud missiles to carry them. If war erupts in the spring of 1998 or again in the summer of 1999 these weapons may be used.

The tenor of Nostradamus' vision of the Antichrist's terror war implies that it is a conflict slow to spread around the world. One confrontation in the Gulf in 1998 leaves a nebulous political and diplomatic outcome which sets the stage for another violent and short war in the Gulf the following year, and so on. It may take 13 years, but eventually the conflicts affect the whole world and perhaps lead to war between Russia and America. If that is a correct reading of Nostradamus, then the war will unleash such a terrible loss of human and animal life that one prophecy says that one side will "bless the barque" of Peter and the "cape of the pope" (5 Q78) – in other words, the Christian nations of the Americas and Western Europe are generally fighting on the same side, perhaps against a set of Islamic nations, atheist Russians and China.

The 13-year countdown to doomsday starting from the appearance of Hale-Bopp could place these events in the reign of the last pope. He could be sitting on his throne as early as 2010–2012. Aside from Nostradamus there are many prophetic traditions from ancient times that pinpoint the year 2000 or a few decades afterwards as doomsday. The most accurate time clock for the end times comes from the ancient Mezo-American prophets and astrologers who invented the Mayan Calendar. Their system suffers a leap year miscalculation only once every 370,000 years. Their estimate could therefore be one of the most accurate calculations for the end of this current human epoch – the year 2012 – just two years after Nostradamus' 13-year countdown runs out, if Hale-Bopp is the starter-button.

In *Nostradamus: The Complete Prophecies* I argued that the year 2000 may pass with little apocalyptic fanfare. The French seer's astrological predictions, considered collectively, point to potential doomsday events being postponed for a few decades. The dark clouds of the latter days might not appear to us until 2005–2008. Things will certainly worsen by 2012 – the Mayan doomsday date – but I estimate that the worst is set to come by the 'roaring' 2020s. For that era Nostradamus and other seers forecast a world assaulted by civilization's breakdown from the stresses of overpopulation, pollution and ecological catastrophes which may include the rising tide of a dying ocean inundating much of the world's arable farmlands and 90 per cent of Asia's rice belts. All these runaway climatic disruptions due to global warming will lead to a global famine.

Nostradamus also describes a future pope during the apocalypse as the "great Roman" of the "Medusine" device (9 Q84). Medusine is an anagram for *Deus in Me*, St. Peter's motto. A number of Nostradamus' quatrains warn of a fish-like or serpentine weapon secreted to the mouth of the Tiber River by submarine (2 Q4). This weapon may be a nuclear device that terrorists intend to smuggle up the river to destroy Rome.

Perhaps these few pieces of Nostradamus' puzzle for our near future hint at a terrorist attack as the cause of the pope's desperate escape from the Vatican. To complete our mosaic of the life and deeds of the last pontiff, let us return again to the coda of St. Malachy's papal succession and see if the four major elements of its final testimony – persecution, tribulation, Rome's destruction and Judgment Day – find parallels in Nostradamus and other Catholic seers. The cross-section of shared visions on the following pages represent similar themes of hundreds of seers – both approved and disapproved by the Vatican.

STEP ONE: THE FINAL PERSECUTION

During the last persecution of the Holy Roman Church, there shall sit Peter of Rome. . . .

In the last days false prophets shall be multiplied, and such as corrupt the word, and the sheep shall be changed into wolves, and love into hatred: for through the abounding of iniquity the love of many shall wax cold. For men shall hate, and persecute, and betray one another.
Didache and Apostolic Constitutions (AD 90–100)

Toward the end of the world the tyrants and the hostile people will suddenly rob the prelates and clergy of the Church of all their possessions and grievously afflict and martyr them. The ones who heap the most abuse upon them will be held in high esteem. The clergy cannot escape these persecutions, but because of them all servants of the Church will be forced to lead an apostolic life.
Brother John of the Cleft Rock (1340)

I see the Lord as he will be scourging the world, and chastising it in a fearful manner so that few men and women will remain. The monks will have to leave their monasteries, and the nuns will be driven from their convents, especially in Italy. . . . The Holy Church will be persecuted. . . . Unless people obtain pardon through their prayers, the time will come when they will see the sword and death, and Rome will be without a shepherd.

Abbess Maria Steiner (d. 1862)

. . . Great errors will be spread through the world, giving rise to wars and persecutions against the Church; the good will suffer martyrdom and the Holy Father will have to suffer much; different nations will be destroyed . . .

The Prophecy of Fátima (13 July 1917)

Certainly a lot of books in the prophetic genre have described to the letter the effect of persecutions of Christians in the future, but today I would like to look deeper to unearth new insights into the cause. I would like to probe behind the usual account of the "future Christians wronged" theme.

Deep down people are trained to find something noble and ego-fulfilling in being persecuted. Perhaps that is why victimhood is as old as priestly hierarchies. A spiritual victimhood is a more subtle imprisonment – one in which the chains are carefully forged by indoctrination at a tender age so that by adulthood the victims are either unable to unlock their manacles or, perhaps worse, are blind to their existence.

Consider the dogma of Jesus on the cross dying for our sins.

Thanks to this act suffering and sacrifice have been glorified in the Piscean Age. But a new millennium is coming during which the dogma of mortified flesh and faith must pass away and be replaced by the Aquarian Age love of life and its use of science to understand the inner and outer mysteries of God's creation.

What if in the next century a majority of people demanded something more than faith before they would believe in Christ's crucifixion and resurrection? The advances in technology that popes of the last 200 years have generally condemned – and done their encyclical best to slow – have brought ordinary people face to face with information that puts pressure on centuries of unbending dogmatists to do some yielding and explaining.

Thanks to technology and new developments in sciences such as archaeology, Christians are learning that many of their most significant stories about the early years of their savior and his disciples are based on incorrect translations, shoddy ancient and medieval scholarship and in many cases bald-faced forgeries. The globalization of information in the past decades is making Christians far more aware of the beliefs of other religions than all the ecumenical efforts of popes in the last 500 years. The Information Age is waking Catholics up to the anti-Semitism and other crimes of popes, such as Innocent III and the Borgia Alexander VI. They can compare the myths and historical data of other faiths with their own and find many things in common. Now we discover not only that all religions have their share of myths mascarading as objective truth, but also that they share many universal truths of love, prayer, meditation and compassion. Access to this information will continue and its spread all over the world will make it harder for the priesthoods of all religions to insist that they have the monopoly on truth.

If the unique challenges that we face in the Aquarian Age require humanity to shift its axis from tradition to innovation in order to survive, then it seems to me that it is only natural that anyone or any organization which bases its raison d'être on the past and on retentive traditions will feel persecuted and abandoned.

Indeed the prophecies forewarning the persecution to come for Catholics and other Christians are not essentially incorrect, but perhaps they are misinterpreted by those who cannot see a life beyond their dogma-blindered eyes. The Church of Rome's prophets behold people losing their faith. They describe Christian sheep abandoning the cathedrals, not obeying the pope, and so on. And it seems that a lot of un-Christian people will get angry with the good Christian sheep who resist change. From the standpoint of the traditionalists the coming times when the old-time religion is criticized and abandoned must look like the end of the world.

Perhaps it is the end – of *their* world.

What the Church sees as its final persecution could actually be the next quantum awakening of human intelligence. It is as significant as the leap that Roman citizens took 20 centuries ago when they renounced pantheism to gather around the first Pope Peter and adopt the monotheism of Christ.

Once they were triumphant the missionaries and popes of Christ expected religious evolution to stand still. But this never happens. Humanity's search for religious truth always undergoes transmutations. The Adventists of one religion are supplanted by the Adventists of another, again and again, in humanity's eternal search for God.

Every religion believes that its faith is the omega punctuation point of eternity's journey. Anyone who challenges that belief will certainly be viewed as a threat, an enemy, even an Antichrist. A religion that cannot conceive of its eventual eclipse finds its prophets foreseeing the coming end correctly, but because of their bias they may misread the visions of the outcome. It is taken for granted that any vision of people abandoning their faith must be interpreted as a test from God instead of a sign that the religion has passed its prime and people are growing beyond its restricting tenets. Rather than encounter the unpalatable revelation that the apocalypse is pushing their religion aside to make way for a new spiritual revolution, the traditionalists reason that what is coming from God is a test of faith. God, therefore, wants his true believers to hold on to the tenets of his ancient commandments, whether or not they serve people's growth.

Of course it is expected that the faithful will face persecutions and temptations. And if your religion cannot tolerate change, then any criticism or new idea absolutely must be judged as evil and should be resisted; otherwise, when God's test is over and when he restores his old-time religion as the only truth on Earth, you who have yielded to the new sins will be weeded out of God's flock to meet eternal damnation alongside the persecutors.

If one becomes so fanatical and unbending to change is it not more than likely that other people might react in turn with persecution? For instance, if in the 2020s Pope Petrus Romanus commands all good Christians to abhor as an act of faith any means of contraception, a majority of the world suffering from the crushing catastrophe of overpopulation might condemn his ministry and his supporters. Demonstrations against the Catholic Church would be seen everywhere. The faithful themselves would choose sides and fight. The fundamentalist "victims" could say, "Look, our prophecies of persecution are being fulfilled."

Thus the unbending believer starts the vicious circle of prophetic self-fulfillment. He will not change, and because only *his* religious views are blessed by God he stands against others. And if those others are in the majority, and they betray the same lack of tolerance, persecution results. What is more, the persecution fulfills the traditional interpretation regarding the unbending believers' prophets. They feel special. They are martyrs, just like Christ. So the holier-than-thou victim will stand even more stubbornly against change, proclaiming his righteousness even louder, earning more punishment. And so it goes, *ad nauseam*.

If the pope of the most powerful bastion of Christianity in the world should choose to view detours from orthodoxy as the foreseen spiritual war against the Antichrist, he and his cardinals might fulfill many of the prophecies that we are examining in this chapter and suffer exile, persecution, massacres and even the destruction of Rome, just as the *pontifex maximus* of the Inca religion or the Aztec religion had to submit to destruction by the hands of the new Christian faith 500 years ago.

Personally I would pray that the worst persecution that any outmoded dogma or religion should suffer from unbelievers is crucifixion by laughter. Perhaps enlightenment is bright light and lightened meant. Therefore the worst pain of penance should come from nothing more violent than a bruised spiritual ego from taking ourselves and our religion too seriously rather than sincerely.

But in a way the seers who forecast persecution of the Church and its followers may be partially vindicated. The people of the future, caught in the fever of a new revolutionary period, may not be enlightened enough to forgive the long legacy of papal crimes. They will seek victims rather than understanding. That is why the following prophecies of many tribulations to come in the reign of the last pope may have their run in the near future. Innocent people calling themselves Christians will be victimized in part because they are identified with the intolerant dogmas which have contributed to the great unraveling of civilization in the next 30 years.

STEP TWO: FEEDING THE SHEEP

. . . [Peter of Rome] shall feed the sheep amidst many
tribulations. . . .

The great famine which I sense approaching, will often turn [up in
various places], then become universal. It will be so vast and long-
lasting that [people] will grab roots from the trees and children from
the breast. (1 Q67) . . . Bushels of wheat shall rise so high [yet] man
is eating his fellow man. (2 Q75)

Nostradamus (1555)

. . . The trees will not bear the usual quantity of fruit, fisheries will
become unproductive and the earth will not yield its usual abundance.
Inclement weather and famine will come and fishes will forsake the
rivers. The people, oppressed for want of food, will pine to death.
Dreadful storms and hurricanes will afflict them. Numberless diseases
will then prevail.

St. Columbcille (d. AD 597)

Hear thou, Thomas, the things which must come to pass in the last
times: there shall be famine and war and earthquakes in diverse places,
snow and ice and great drought shall there be, and many dissensions
among the peoples. At that time shall there be a very great rising of
the sea, so that no man shall tell news to any man.

The Apostle Thomas (1st century AD)

Is such a sacrifice not enough to satiate your wrath, O Lord? But no,
what then is this noise of arms? these cries of war and fear? What do
the four winds bring? Ah! the dragon [China?] has appeared in all
countries and has brought terrible confusion everywhere. There is war
everywhere. Men and people have risen up one against the other.
War, war, war – civil war and foreign war. What frightening onsets.
Everything is mourning and death; famine reigns in the fields.

Prophecy of Premol (AD 496)

Now I see that God will punish man with a severity that has not been
used since the Flood.

Third Secret of Fátima (1917)

If by the reign of Petrus Romanus there is a world war free-
for-all fought over a breakdown of nature and humanity's food

sustainability, part of the responsibility might be hurled at the Church of Rome and its long-standing battle to prevent birth control in the world.

By the 2020s its righteous policy of a culture of life – regardless of the cost in resources and suffering of an overcrowded world – could be considered a prime factor in bringing death to the current civilization. This stance alone, if it is not modified by John Paul's successors, could be enough to damn the Church of Rome in the eyes of the survivors for centuries to come. John Paul himself, who is so beloved today, may be viewed with equal contempt as a criminal against humanity tomorrow. Simply because he did not have the courage to alter birth control policies and prevent one billion Catholic faithful – the most fertile and baby-making members of any religion – from clogging the arteries of our food and resource flow with the overpopulative plaque of 30 more years of untempered birthrates.

The phrase "shall feed the sheep" implies that global famine is the mother of all the many tribulations that will rain on an overpopulated world. Today in 1998 there are less than 50 days of grain reserves to feed a human population of 6 billion souls. When there are 8 billion souls in the second and third decades of the 21st century, the superpower of China and more than 150 other nations will go to war, fighting over the last drops of unpolluted water and the last kernels of grain.

The equation of Armageddon by the 2020s combines two unsustainable factors: one is economic, the other religious. Factor one is a world indoctrinated by the USA, the victor of the Cold War, to consider unlimited economic growth and consumerism as good – no matter what the cost to finite resources. Worldwatch estimates that for everyone on Earth to live the wasteful, high-energy-consumptive life of the American dream there should be only 2.5 billion souls here, not the 8–10 billion people expected by the 2020s through to the 2040s. The second factor is a world indoctrinated by anti-contraception religions like Catholicism, Hinduism and Islam to believe that life is sacred and babies should not be prevented from crowding the planet in as many numbers as possible.

"Be fruitful and multiply:" the ancient creed.

Contraception is condemned because the popes, shankaracharyas and ayatollahs generally agree that God wants as many souls on the Earth as possible so that they can pass through the test of good and evil and stake their eternal destiny either in heaven, moksha or paradise, or burn in Christian, Islamic or Hindu hell. The two most fertile religions, Catholicism and Islam, have promoted a dogma now grooved deep into the human collective psyche for 2,000 years that the more wretchedly poor you are, the closer you are to God.

"I tell you this: a rich man will find it hard to enter the kingdom of Heaven . . . it is easier for a camel to pass through the eye of a needle than for a rich man to enter the kingdom of God." (Matthew 19:23–25)

Whether Jesus really said this, or it was added by the Council of Nicaea 300 years after his crucifixion is still under objective investigation, but the impact on history of this dogma that makes a virtue out of poverty is immense. And I might add that the impact that a love of poverty could have on near-future history could be apocalyptic. And I mean "apocalyptic" in both of its meanings: as a disaster and as a revelation that the dogma of the past glorifying poverty has betrayed us.

A religion that believes that poverty is holy cannot be expected to end poverty no matter how much it professes doing good deeds to relieve the suffering of the poor. A concerted effort to end poverty once and for all would ultimately have put many a saint of the past and a saint-to-be like Mother Teresa of Calcutta out of a heaven-merit-making job. Thus an opportunity to really end human suffering was hamstrung by the rise and ultimate dominance of Christianity in the world and later by the spread of Islam.

Both religions may see their prophecies of persecution fulfilled in the 2020s because the unprecedented number of people suffering the catastrophe of overpopulation and poverty will seek out the source of the crime and discover that it is their own fossilized religious view on poverty itself that has brought the world to ruin.

Because of the results of these two scourges Pope Petrus Romanus will be hard pressed to feed his flock with the dwindling reserves of food from Catholic relief foundations. The 70-plus wars that will plague the world will suck his relief foundations dry and break the Vatican Bank. The Vatican could be persecuted for its papal opulence and Petrus Romanus might face global pressure to sell off the vast wealth collected by unscrupulous and nepotistic popes to finance feeding the "blessed" poor.

Any progress towards peace on Earth that Pope Gloria Olivae will have achieved will be shattered during the reign of the last pope when he faces a world of a half-dozen billion people who are "the closest to God" that any poor wretch has ever been by virtue of their crushing numbers.

STEP THREE: ROME DESTROYED

. . . and when these [tribulations] *have passed, the City of the Seven Hills shall be utterly destroyed. . . .*

The kings of the earth and the princes and the captains shall be troubled, and no man shall speak freely. . . . In those days there shall be all manner of evils, even the death of the race of men from the east even unto Babylon [Iraq?]. *And thereafter death and famine and sword in the land of Canaan* [Israel/Palestine?] *even unto Rome.*

The Apostle Thomas (1st century AD)

And to you, Rome, what will happen? Ungrateful Rome, effeminate Rome, proud Rome! You have reached such a height that you search no further. You admire nothing else in your Sovereign except luxury, forgetting that you and your glory stand upon Golgotha. . . .

Rome! to you I shall come four times!

The first time, I shall strike your lands and the inhabitants thereof.

The second time, I shall bring the massacre and the slaughter even to your very walls. And will you not yet open your eyes?

I shall come a third time and I shall beat down to the ground your defenses and the defenders, and at the command of the Father, the reign of terror, of dreadful fear, and of desolation shall enter into your city.

But My wise men have now fled and My law is even now trampled under foot. Therefore I shall make a fourth visit. Woe to you if My law will still be considered as empty words. . . . War, pestilence, famine are the rods to scourge men's pride and wickedness. O wealthy men, where is your glory now, your estates, your palaces? They are the rubble on the highways and byways.

And you priests, why have you not run to "cry between the vestibule and the Altar," begging God to end these scourges? Why have you not, with the shield of faith, gone upon the rooftops, into the homes, along the highways and byways, into every accessible corner to carry the seed of My word? Know you not that this is the terrible two-edged sword that cuts down My enemies and that breaks the Anger of God and of men?

These things must come one after another. They are inexorable.

St. John Bosco (d. 1888)

The great star will blaze for seven days. The cloud will cause two suns to appear. . . .

[The sun in the sky and the solar flash of a nuclear explosion?]

. . . The great dog will howl all night when the great pontiff will change lands. (2 Q42)

[The *great dog* is Nostradamus' code name for Gog and Magog from the Book of Ezekiel: These are the northern powers that invade Israel during the battle of Armageddon.]

Very near the Tiber River the Goddess of Death threatens. Shortly after the great flood the head of the Church will be taken prisoner and cast out. The Castel [Sant'Angelo] *and the* [Vatican] *Palace in flames.* (2 Q93)

Nostradamus (1555)

. . . Priests shall be massacred, the churches shall be closed, but only for a short time; the Holy Father shall be obliged to abandon Rome.

Maria Taigi (d. 1837)

In the last great desolation of the world the last High Priest of the true God will reign. Criminal Rome will be destroyed and the terrible Judge, in glory, will judge all nations.

The Monk of Padua (1740)

There are hundreds of collective visions, both from pro- and anti-Catholic seers, which depict Rome's Wagnerian destruction in lurid terms to match the German composer's opera *Götter-dämmerung* (The Twilight of the Gods). Wagner's opera ends with the Vatican of the Nordic gods going down in a self-inflicted pyromania of glorious flames.

The twilight of the papal capital, or *Päpsterdämmerung*, might descend in a number of ways. There are the usual scenarios of flames falling from the skies in some form of nuclear terrorism, nuclear accident or atmospheric detonation from chemical or biological warheads. Nostradamus implies in his quatrains that the flames of Rome will be quenched by a great tidal wave mounting the Tiber River and the Pontine plain. The wave could come from a meteor strike in the Aegean which Nostradamus describes in 1 Q69 and 2 Q3 as "a great mountain 4,247 feet in circumference" falling out of the sky off the shore of Evvoea Island.

Other prophets see Rome's destruction as part of a global natural disaster wherein the skies of Earth are darkened for three days. Rome is destroyed and the pontiff must pick his way through mountains of his dead priests and parishioners to find a safe area. In St. Don Bosco's version the pontiff's ordeal lasts between 200 and 400 days.

The pope's exodus from Rome pops up in many interpretations of Nostradamus. Some believe that the pope and his surviving cardinals will establish the papacy in America, while others point to quatrains depicting Petrus Romanus returning to Southern France, the land of the last "Babylonian Captivity."

In 2 Q65 Nostradamus clues us in to potential astrological time windows for the papacy's next Diaspora. Look out for November 2015, late November 2017 and early November 2044. The last conjunction will be especially powerful, as Saturn and Mercury enter Sagittarius exactly at the same time. Given the longer life-spans of modern pontiffs, it is not out of the realm of possibility that the next two popes after John Paul could rule at least 20 years apiece and bring the final persecution and destruction of Rome as late as the early 2040s.

Some Nostradamians believe that the pope's predecessor, Gloria Olivæ, will have to flee Rome's destruction. They think that he will make his new Vatican in the more politically stable North American continent during the breakdown of civilization. Some interpreters believe that Gloria Olivæ, once in the USA, will come under the control of American cardinals who will eliminate the office of the Vatican as sole ruler of the Church. Gloria Olivæ is then assassinated and Petrus Romanus succeeds him as a puppet pope of the new order.

The view favored by radical interpreters and fundamentalist Protestant televangelists is that Petrus Romanus is an antipope in league with the Antichrist, if not the Antichrist himself.

The Nostradamian quatrains numbered 65 from Centuries 2, 3 and 10 share the themes of schisms and scandals that threaten the future of the Catholic Church. Quatrain 66 of Century 6 (no. 666) foretells the destruction of Rome and the birth of a new religion.

But generally speaking most seers perceive Rome's destruction as the final act of Armageddon and the Church's test from God. Rome must be destroyed to make way for the heavenly descent of New Jerusalem – the world's new spiritual capital for the Christian new world order.

STEP FOUR: THE AWFUL JUDGE

. . . and the awful Judge will judge the people.

When the persecution against the Church has spread like a wild raging fire, even to places where it was thought there was no danger, then the Lord, who knows how to draw glory out of everything, will suddenly command the mighty fire stream [war and global warming?] and Satan to halt. Then will a universal peace be proclaimed.

Jane Le Royer (d. 1798)

After this, Mary, all powerful, shall change all men into good wheat. All shall be good. The Pharisees will be the last to be converted; the great brigands will arrive beforehand. The Jews who have refused to receive Jesus Christ in his humiliation will acknowledge Him at the glorious arrival of Mary.

Venerable Magdalene Porzat (d. 1850)

There shall arise a righteous true and holy priest to reform the Church. The Greeks will return [to the Church], the Tartars will be converted, the Saracens destroyed, there will be one fold and one shepherd.

Roger Bacon (d. 1294)

Almost all unbelievers and the Jews will be converted and there will be one law, one faith, one baptism, one life. All people will love one another and peace will last a long time.

João de Vatiguerro (13th century)

Unbelievers are already judged and so will not come to the judgment.

Those who are not signed in faith, because they did not believe in God, will ... not come to this judgment. But they will see it all in obscurity and await its end, groaning deeply within themselves because they persevered in unbelief and did not know the true God. For they neither worshipped the living God in the Old Testament before the institution of baptism, nor received the remedy of baptism in the Gospel, but continued under the curse of Adam's fall, with its penalty of damnation. And therefore they are already judged, for the crime of infidelity.

When the judgment is finished, a great calm will arise.

And when the judgment is ended, the terrors of the elements, the lightnings and thunders and winds and tempests, will cease, and all that is fleeting and transitory will melt away and no longer be, like snow melted by the heat of the sun. And so, by God's dispensation, an exceedingly great calm will arise.

St. Hildegard von Bingen, *Scivias*: Vision 12:11,12 (12th century)

When I examine the prophecies of the Roman Catholic apocalypse or the other Christian Judgment Day scenarios I feel the chill of a shadow which has cast its fearful darkness wherever the love of Christ has passed. It has been my experience that wherever goes the graceful mystery of the Holy Trinity of God the Father, Christ the Son and the Holy Ghost, there follows the dark silhouette of an anti-Trinity – one which I believe has left the Church demonically possessed since its early Romanization:

Fear – the Father,
Sin – the Son,
And the Holy Ghost of Guilt.

The seers who promote God's "awful" and eternal death-dealing judgment of humanity in the future seem to me to exude a lust for revenge and punishment so perverse and cruel that I cannot imagine even Adolf Hitler being that mean to his enemies. I cannot conceive of any sin or crime, no matter how terrible, that would warrant someone like God kicking the transgressor, as it were, while he is down – forever. I cannot imagine that Innocent III, Torquemada, Alexander VI and even the Grand Inquisitor who became the infamous Carafa pope Paul IV deserve to spend eternity in a lake of fire for their mistakes. And mind you, these men are responsible for the torture and burning of hundreds of thousands of men, women and children in the name of Christ.

All I can say is, God forbid if the letter of these prophecies above is correct, because this means that even virtuous people who in their lives never knew Christ will be consigned to an eternal concentration camp of fire and brimstone. If Adam's or Eve's original sin is enough to get one eternally punished unless of course one accepts Christ as the Savior who has atoned for you as descendant of the original sinners, then God's justice is not any more reasonable than a Nazi racist who has no qualms about throwing law-abiding and virtuous Jews into the ovens of Auschwitz because they bore the sin of not being Aryans.

Can such an "awful Judge" be the same God which Christ said "is love"?

I do not think so. And I am happy to face the lake of fire for saying it.

If what I am about to declare has any truth, then the final outcome of the Judgment Day prophecies will be very different from what dogma and doctrine have ordained. To condemn others in prophecy because they have not measured up as spiritually pure enough (or spiritually Aryan enough) to live in God's final paradise will be seen in the future as one of prophecy's greatest goofs. Events in the future will show that Christian prophets were projecting an ancient misunderstanding onto what they feared would come during a new and unpredictable era in human history.

Perhaps the real Last Judgment is the day when judgments as such, not people, will be consigned to the eternal flames – along with fear, sin and guilt.

Taken in a different way, I can well imagine St. Hildegard's vision of the world when *judgment has ended* being a place of *exceedingly great calm* and silence. Once all that is *fleeting and transitory,* such as fear and guilt, *has melted away* and will *no longer be, like snow melted by the heat of the sun,* then we await a new humanity without judgments and fear. Human beings will exude silence and loving natures. Meditation – not meanness – will guide their hearts. Unconditional love and forgiveness, not fear, will be their new doctrine.

EPILOGUE

From Dogma to Divine Intimacy

We feel we must disagree with those prophets of gloom, who are always forecasting disaster, as though the end of the world was at hand.

In the present order of things, Divine Providence is leading us to a new order of human relations which, by men's own efforts and even beyond their very expectations, are directed towards the fulfillment of God's superior and inscrutable designs. And everything, even human differences, leads to the greater good of the church.

John XXIII (1962)
commenting on the 'Third Secret' of the prophecy of Fátima in his
opening speech at Vatican II

For the Church, too, the time of its greatest trial will come. . . . What is rotten will fall, never to rise again.

Third Secret of Fátima

The Lord showed me how beautiful the world will be after the awful chastisement. The people will be like the Christians of the primitive Church.

Abbess Maria Steiner (d. 1862)

The Church of Rome shall be destroyed in the Third State [Age of the Holy Spirit], *as the Synagogue of the Jews was destroyed in the Second State* [Age of the Son – Christ], *and the spiritual church shall from thenceforth succeed, to the end of the world.*

Joachim de Fiore (13th century)

A Vatican which could tame the revolution of John XXIII would not look kindly upon prophecies implying that their traditionalist survival into the new age of the spirit would not match what Pope John had called God's 'inscrutable designs.' Yet enough renegade visions from Catholic seers have survived to imply this eventuality.

The prophecies of Joachim de Fiore (c.1135–1202) best represent the unorthodox, small-c Catholic prophetic view. He believed that the 'Latin' or Catholic Church is only a pale, wan prologue of the coming spiritual civilization that people will enjoy in the Age of the Holy Spirit. In brief review, he believed that the evolution of God's Word on Earth could be divided into three epochs: the Era of the Old Testament; the Era of Christ's Church – that is, Catholicism and the New Testament; and, finally, the third era of a religiousness which is dispensed in every heart by the Holy Spirit. The third and future era is expected to follow a brief and violent apocalyptic period. Joachim's somewhat heretical view that the Church may be replaced just when the Golden Age that every pope has prayed for begins has probably survived in part because his views lost credibility when he miscalculated the date of the Third Era's beginning as 1260.

Still, his maverick eschatology endures. Over the centuries his prophecies keep resurfacing as if the Christian augury genre were desperate to find a counterbalancing future world view that accepts – and even looks forward to – a utopian vision of a third Christian millennium. It is a vision of a world that is not only thriving without war, but liberated from Vaticans, popes or the burden of a spiritual Mafia of any kind. Joachim's visions take the genre back to a future when Christianity returns to its early and humble roots before it became Roman.

The Joachite future does not condemn the past, any more than the dinosaur should condemn his ancient fish ancestors who slithered out of the sea to eventually walk the Earth as dominant thunder lizards. The fish lived on in the dinosaur, just as the thunder lizard may live on in some of the animals of our day. Thanks to new revelations in paleontology, animal anatomy and biology, scientists have entertained our Jurassic Park dreams with a new theory that dinosaurs have not completely died out, they just sprouted feathers and took flight as birds.

In the same way in which the lumbering and fundamentalist dinosaur called Catholicism, the T-Rex of all Christian religions, will not become extinct in Joachim's apocalypse, nor will any of the less thunderous Christian faiths. True, their mainstream expressions may die out in the coming apocalypse, but their religious essence will live on as birds of another faithful feather.

Joachim sees a world ruled not by popes but by a hierarchy of contemplative men. His medieval mind interpreted these to be monks, but if you catch hold of the essence rather than the medieval letter of his future sight, his vision closely resembles many non-Christian prophecies which forecast a new and meditative humanity born from the forge of a violent apocalyptic breakdown of current civilization and its religions. Seers from the East and many from the native peoples prophesy for that new era a world guided by the meritocracy of meditative people. Religion will take on a quality of divine intimacy. Rather than going to the church, the mosque, the synagogue or the Hindu or Buddhist temple to commune with God, each individual will become a living church, a mosque, synagogue or temple of the Holy Spirit. Each human being becomes a Buddha, a Vicar of Christ.

The new Aquarian Age is predicted as a time of unprecedented individual freedom. Likewise, Joachim de Fiore declared, "The third [epoch] will be the Age of the Holy Spirit, of whom the Apostle said: *Where there is the spirit of the Lord, there is liberty.*"

"The first epoch was that in which we were under the law," explained Joachim in his *Liber Concordie novi ac veteris Testamenti*. "The second [epoch] when we were under grace, the third [epoch of the Holy Spirit] when we will live in anticipation of even richer grace. . . ."

"The first epoch was in knowledge, the second in the authority of wisdom, the third in the perfection of understanding. The first in the chains of the slave, the second in the service of a son [Christ], the third in freedom. The first in the exasperation, the second in action, the third in contemplation [meditation]. The first in fear, the second in faith, the third in love. The first under slave bondage, the second in freedom, the third in friendship."

The third era, being in friendship, closely parallels Buddhist prophecies of the second coming of Buddha in the manifestation of the Lord Maitreya. Maitreya means "the Friend."

"The first age [was] of children," continues Joachim, "the second age of youth, the third that of the old [namely, it is an age of maturation]."

Humanity grows up.

In his *Expositio in Apocalypsim* Joachim explains how dogma will be transformed in three steps:

"The first of the three epochs spoken of existed during the age of the law [of Moses]. Then the Lord's people . . . were under the elements of this world. They were unable to attain the liberty of spirit spoken of by the one who said: *If the Son* [of God] *liberates you, you will be free indeed.*

"The second epoch was initiated under the Gospel. It remains to the present with some liberty considered from the perspective of the past but not with the freedom to be characterized in the future. . . ."

In other words, he may be saying that a Christian religion at this stage of its development – the Gospel stage – cannot help but be past-oriented. Its nature will not allow it to adapt to the new era or to correctly interpret the final outcome of its prophetic visions. The Era of the Gospel is destined to die as a seed dies so that a new flower of the Era of the Holy Spirit can be born. If it holds on to its dogma to fend off the coming changes it would be like a seed once blessed with fertile soil and water that fights to keep its shell sealed.

"The third epoch, therefore will be ushered in toward the close of the present age, no longer under the screen of the letter but in the spirit of complete freedom," concludes Joachim.

Then he goes on to side with more doctrinaire visions, such as the Jews being converted to Christianity of the Holy Spirit. This is not so righteous a propagation if the Era of the Holy Spirit is one that transcends the need for divisive religions and instead nourishes the religiousness in each living heart without the labels and dogmas that set people apart. The terms "Christian" or "Jew" will be irrelevant, at best utilitarian. God will speak through the Holy Spirit to each individual directly. You might say that in the Era of the Holy Spirit there are as many religions as there are living human beings. All equal in the law, all equally unique.

Thus we may hope that a better religious life is waiting for us when the label "Protestant," "Orthodox" or "Catholic" or the labels of 300 other religions are discarded and religion as we have known it comes to an end.

In its place all religious people will be reborn as catholic – with a small and unassuming *c*. They will be in "universal" union with God, they will be expressions of godliness.

Pope John Paul II declared in the closing days of the Second Christian Millennium, "Be not afraid."

The seers catching a glimpse of the glories to come in the Third Christian Millennium declare, "Be not afraid of a world without popes or priests."

The reign of the Holy Spirit will be the reign of the free.
Joachim de Fiore

APPENDIX

Post-Wion Prophecy Assessment

Clearly the skeptics are right. There is a dramatic change in the focus of the last 36 mottoes forecast for beyond the publication date of 1595 (See Table 1 below and Tables 2 and 3).

Table 1

74-Pre/36-Post	Pre	Post
Church posting/Church titles	33	7
Heraldry/symbols	30	13
Christian name/papal name	27	2
Birthplace	13	3
Family titles and Facts	9	3
Nationality	4	0
Key geographic location	4	4
Chief nemesis/outside influence	5	4
Character implied	5	7
Deeds, events of life	15	12

A ghost writer under Malachy's name is almost certain. But is the term con artist or forger fair? If we review the last 36 mottoes in the list, I believe that there is enough evidence for the open-minded that this mystery author of the Papal Prophecy of St. Malachy made some remarkably accurate predictions that go beyond chance.

75 Ex ANTIQUITATE URBIS (From the Oldness of a City)
   Gregory XIV: 1590–1591

   He served as Bishop of Cremona, which is the most ancient Latin settlement in the Po Valley.

76 PIA CIVITAS IN BELLO (A Dutiful State in War)
Innocent IX: 1591

The dutiful state was Venice. It helped Spain and her allies rout the Turkish fleet at the battle of Lepanto. The future pope was nuncio of Venice at that time and played an important part in convincing the city of sailors to join their fleet to the Christian armada.

77 CRUX ROMULEA (A Roman Cross)
Clement VIII: 1592–1605

Nothing specific here except that one could say that the Church of the "Roman Cross" was on the rebound during this pope's reign. With Protestantism checked the Church regained much of its territories and spiritual authority back from the Protestant Reformation.

78 UNDOSUS VIR (A Surging Man)
Leo XI: 1605

Perhaps a poetic – if not very objective – description of this short-lived pope. His pontificate surged and passed away with the speed of a wave.

79 GENS PERVERSA (A Perverse People)
Paul V: 1605–1621

A good post-Wion hit, for a pope's chief nemesis. In this case it is the perverse or heretical Protestants who went marching off to the Thirty Years War against the Catholics during Paul's reign.

80 IN TRIBULATIONE PACIS (In Tribulation of Peace)
Gregory XV: 1621–1623

Open to interpretation. Subjectively speaking one could apply this motto to Gregory, who on several occasions tried to undermine peace arrangements with the Protestants, which he viewed as burdensome. He pressured France to promote anti-Calvinist policies and therefore weaken the *tribulation*

Table 2.
PRE—WION DISCOVERY

Pope motto numbers	1	2	3	4	5	6	7	8	9	10	11	12	13	14	15	16	17	18	19	20	21	22	23	24	25
Church posting, Church titles						■	■	■	■	■	■	■	■			■	■	■	■	■	■			■	
Heraldry/symbols										■	■	■	■	■											
Christian name /papal name		■																	■	■					
Birthplace	■		■	■																■					
Family titles and facts																		■							
Nationality								■																	
Key geographical location																									
Chief nemesis /outside influence																				■					
Character implied																									
Deeds, events of life		■														■				■					

Pope motto numbers	26	27	28	29	30	31	32	33	34	35	36	37	38	39	40	41	42	43	44	45	46	47	48	49	50
Church posting, Church titles	■		■			■	■				■	■	■	■	■		■	■	■	■		■	■		
Heraldry/symbols	■	■		■								■						■							
Christian name /papal name	■																	■	■						
Birthplace				■					■																
Family titles and facts													■												
Nationality										■															
Key geographical location						■																			
Chief nemesis /outside influence										■			■												
Character implied									■									■						?	?
Deeds, events of life		?				■			■		■					■			■					?	?

Pope motto numbers	51	52	53	54	55	56	57	58	59	60	61	62	63	64	65	66	67	68	69	70	71	72	73	74
Church posting, Church titles	■	■				■		■							■									
Heraldry/symbols		■			■		■		■		■		■					■		■				
Christian name /papal name			■							■				■										
Birthplace				■																				
Family titles and facts									■			■							■					■
Nationality																								
Key geographical location																								
Chief nemesis /outside influence				?																				
Character implied																								
Deeds, events of life			■	?						■				■						?				

 **PROPHETIC SUCCESS**   ? **OPEN TO INTERPRETATION**

Table 3.
POST—WION DISCOVERY

Pope motto numbers	75	76	77	78	79	80	81	82	83	84	85	86	87	88	89	90	91	92	93	94	95	96	97	98	99
Church posting/Church titles	?						█	█		█	█									█		█			
Heraldry/symbols						█	█		█	█	█			█		█			█	█					
Christian name/papal name						█	█						█												
Birthplace						█	█												█						
Family titles and facts																?									
Nationality																									
Key geographical location	█							█												█					
Chief nemesis/outside influence			█									█									█				
Character implied																?		?						?	?
Deeds, events of life	█	?	?		?					█		?				█									

Pope motto numbers	100	101	102	103	104	105	106	107	108	109	110
Church posting/Church titles	█						█	█	?		
Heraldry/Symbols	█	█	█				█	█			
Christian name/papal name											
Birthplace											
Family titles and facts											█
Nationality											
Key geographical location							█				
Chief nemesis/outside influence	█										
Character implied						?					█
Deeds, events of life	█			█					█		

█ PROPHETIC SUCCESS   ? OPEN TO INTERPRETATION

of peace between the Christian communities decreed by the Edict of Nantes.

81 LILIUM ET ROSA (The Lily and the Rose)
Urban VIII: 1623–1644

A successful hit on many fronts. The motto describes the name of this future pontiff by describing the arms of an earlier pope to hold such a name, Urban IV. The rose was also the symbol of Umbria, where Urban VIII was posted as cardinal bishop of Spoleto. He was born in Florence, a city which uses a lily as its symbol.

82 JUCUNDITAS CRUCIS (The Pleasure of the Cross)
Innocent X: 1644–1655

Subjectively speaking, Innocent X and the Catholic *cross* would have the *pleasure* of seeing the Thirty Years War finally come to an end in 1648, along with the 80-year religious conflict in the Netherlands. Objectively speaking the post-Wion prophet may have visualized the engraved medallion which was issued by the pontiff. A caption stamped on its edge commemorated the *pleasure* of *the cross*. The medallion also shows two angels on bended knee on heavenly clouds above the Earth, worshipping the exalted cross of Christ glowing with rays emanating from its apex.

83 MONTIUM CUSTOS (Guardian of the Mountains)
Alexander VII: 1655–1667

The Chigi family crest of the future Alexander VII displays a gold sextuple mount (*mountains*) watched over by an eight-pointed *guardian* star.

84 SYDUS OLORUM (A Constellation of Swans)
Clement IX: 1667–1669

Abbé Maître says that the hall used in the conclave to pick the successor to Alexander was called the Chamber of the Swans.

85 DE FLUMINE MAGNO (From a Great River)
Clement X: 1670–1676

When Emilio Altieri, the future Clement X, was an infant the river Tiber flooded its banks and poured into the Albani household, nearly carrying off babe and cradle. The Altieri family identify their coat of arms with its six silver molets (of eight-pointed stars) in an azure background as representing the cosmic *magnum flumen* – the great river of stars flowing through the heavens as the Milky Way.

86 BELLUA INSATIABILIS (Insatiable Beast)
Innocent XI: 1676–1689

A much-mangled motto by skeptics and believers. The skeptics are right to trash the usual rationalization that this motto describes the "insatiable" appetite of this pope to consume counsel from a cardinal named after food (Cibo). However the skeptics overlook the obvious "chief nemesis" theme application. The insatiable beast is Louis XIV gobbling up control of the Catholic church in France during Innocent's reign. Detractors also look the other way about Innocent's coat of arms. Apparently they do not wish to address the fact that his arms depict a lion – an "insatiable beast."

87 PŒNITENTIA GLORIOSA (Glorious Penance)
Alexander VIII: 1689–1691

Maître and other sympathetic scholars are too abstract with their explainations that Alexander has exerted a glorious penance for the rehabilitated Jansenists. A less subjective rational would be that Alexander's lifetime love of the glorious penitent St. Bruno is depicted here. Because the usual pope has a whole miter cap full of favorite penitent saints to worship, this motto must be viewed as too general for a specific interpretation.

88 RASTRUM IN PORTA (The Rake at the Door)
Innocent XII: 1691–1700

Another clear success. Innocent's full Christian name was Antoinio Pignatelli del Rastello (Rastrum).

89 FLORES CIRCUMDATI (Flowers Set to Surround)
     Clement XI: 1700–1721

Abbé Maître points out that during Clement's pontificate an engraved medallion was fashioned commemorating the pope's birthplace. It shows the coat of arms and papal tiara of Innocent IX surrounded with a garland of luscious flowers. At the base of the medallion is the Latin inscription: "FLORES CIRCVM DATI"!

90 DE BONA RELIGIONE (Of Good Religion)
     Innocent XIII: 1721–1724

The skeptics say that too many popes come from too many good religious backgrounds to make this motto significant. But the sympathetic scholars point out that Innocent's House of Conti was particularly accomplished in being good and religious. This illustrious Roman family had already given the papacy three popes: Innocent III, Gregory IX and Alexander IV. Innocent XIII also showed good religious discipline by resisting the temptation to practice nepotism.

91 MILES IN BELLO (A Soldier in War)
     Benedict XIII: 1724–1730

A bit vague at best. Benedict did not lead the papacy in any war – except a moral war against the Jews of Rome and the licentiousness of its gentile citizens. Pro-Malachy motto scholars say that his clan, the Orsini, served with notable distinction as soldiers for the papacy.

92 COLUMNA EXCELSA (A Lofty Pillar)
     Clement XII: 1730–1740

He embellished Rome with beautiful buildings and restored the Andrea Corsini chapel and the lofty pillared façades of St. John Lateran. Page 260 of Abbé Maître's *La Prophétie des Papes* (1901) illustrates two medallions commemorating the renovation; one of them depicts the *lofty pillars* and high columnar facade of St. John Lateran.

93 ANIMAL RURALE (A Rustic Beast)
  Benedict XIV: 1740–1758

There seems to be little connection with this motto and the pope, except as an editorial commentary, and even then, it is pretty weak.

94 ROSA UMBRIÆ (A Rose of Umbria)
  Clement XIII: 1758–1769

Before becoming pope, he performed his duties in a number of posts, including a brief stint as governor of Rieti in Umbria.

95 URSUS VELOX (A Swift Bear)
  Clement XIV: 1769–1775

Clement XIV has no bears on his coat of arms; however, Maître relies on the revelation of the canon Ginzel to tell us that the future pontiff was born a short distance from Rimini. The arms of Rimini display a bear.

96 PEREGRINUS APOSTOLICUS (An Apostolic Wanderer)
  Pius VI: 1775–1799

An engraved medallion commemorating this pope's unique journey was foreseen in the motto. Beneath the profile of Pius VI reads the caption "Peregrinus Apostolic"! Pius would end his days a wandering prisoner of the French Revolutionary government.

97 AQUILA RAPAX (Rapacious Eagle)
  Pius VII: 1800–1823

The phrase *rapacious eagle* identifies the chief nemesis of Pius VII, Napoleon Bonaparte, who would adopt the imperial eagle of the classical fascist dictators of Rome as his symbol. Brass eagles could be seen on the standards of Napoleon's irresistible armies as they conquered most of continental Europe during the first nine years of Pius VII's reign.

98 CANIS ET COLUBER (A Dog and a Snake)
    Leo XII: 1823–1829

To many interpreters of these Latin epigraphs CANIS ET COLUBER is an adequate epithet for the negative character of this pope. That may be, but it is open to interpretation.

99 VIR RELIGIOSUS (A Religious Man)
    Pius VIII: 1829–1830

What pope is not a religious man? Oh well, the pro-Malachy camp can at least feel secure that this pope is safe and sound underneath a blanket of generality.

100 DE BALNEIS ETRURIÆ (From Balnea in Tuscany)
     Gregory XVI: 1831–1846

From two vague mottoes we jump into some objectively intriguing hits. Gregory would come from the strict Benedictine religious Order of the Camadolese, whose main headquarters was at Balnea, a town in the Tuscan hills a short distance from Florence, Tuscany.

101 CRUX DE CRUCE (The Cross from a Cross)
     Pius IX: 1846–1878

This motto is successful on two counts. First it describes the cross of Savoy of this pope's chief nemesis, King Victor-Emmanuel. Then it could be metaphorically applied. For instance the holder of the "cross" of Savoy forces the pope to bear the "cross" of persecution and loss of the Papal States, and the Church's secular powers to the modern world.

102 LUMEN IN CŒLO (A Light in the Sky)
     Leo XIII: 1878–1903

The arms of Leo show a comet.

103 IGNIS ARDENS (Burning Fire)
    St. Pius X: 1903–1914

The heraldic device of a "burning" star is correctly inferred. The Tunguska meteor blast in Eastern Siberia in 1908 is also implied. This cosmic display of unearthly light bathing the skies over most of North America and Eurasia at the mid-point in his reign stands here as one of the omens in Christian prophetic tradition forewarning a coming apocalypse. Another "burning fire" warns of doom: Halley's Comet, which appeared in 1912. The last visitation of a "burning fire" was World War I, which began a few days before this pope's death. All-in-all a good prophetic success.

104 RELIGIO DEPOPULATA (Religion Depopulated)
    Benedict XV: 1914–1922

During his reign 200 million Christians were converted to Bolshevism and 35 million Christians died during World War I and from the Spanish influenza. One of the best prophetic successes for the post-Wion mottoes.

105 FIDES INTREPIDA (Intrepid Faith)
    Pius XI: 1922–1939

Character themes are more open to opinion, but this motto aptly fits the character of this arch-traditionalist, anti-communist, anti-fascist pope.

106 PASTOR ANGELICUS (An angelic Pastor)
    Pius XII: 1939–1958

Another character theme but this time it is pretty weak. Though Pius' veneer was that of an "angelic" pastor, his pontificate is overshadowed in un-angelic controversy concerning his neutral and even somewhat sympathetic policies towards Hitler and Mussolini. He kept officially silent about the Jewish Holocaust, even though he gains some "angelic" merit for saving half a million Jews from the gas chambers. The strongest fact supporting the attribution "angelic pastor" would be Pius' ardent devotion and study of the teachings of the 13th-century Christian philosopher St. Thomas Aquinas, who was labeled the *Angelic* doctor.

107 PASTOR ET NAUTA (Shepherd and a Sailor)
John XXIII: 1958–1963

Poetically speaking the motto corresponds well with John's ministry as pope. He defined his pontificate as that of a good *shepherd*. The motto matches a number of objective details of John's life. Before becoming pope he was patriarch of Venice, an ancient maritime city famous for its sailors. He was Venice's *shepherd* and its *sailor*. Being a sailor also implies John's role as the spiritual *sailor* guiding the barque of St. Peter, the symbol of the Holy See. The badge of Vatican II displayed a cross and a ship.

108 FLOS FLORUM (A Flower of Flowers)
Paul VI: 1963–1978

The arms of Paul VI display three fleur-de-lys. He is the spiritual *flower* of the three-flowered coat of arms.

109 DE MEDIETATE LUNÆ (From the Half Moon)
John Paul I: 1978

His Christian name was Albino Luciani ("from the White Light") poetically describing the white light of the moon. He served as a priest in the town of Belluno ("good moon"). This pope died, or was poisoned, on the night of a waning half moon in third quarter phase.

110 DE LABORE SOLIS (From the Sun's Labor)
John Paul II: 1978–present

He was born on the day of a total eclipse. An eclipse is known as a sun's travail or labor in poetic medieval Latin.

Select Bibliography

━━━━━━━━━━━━━━━━━⇥ ⇤━━━━━━━━━━━━━━━━━

STUDIES ON THE PAPAL PROPHECIES OF ST. MALACHY AND RELATED WORKS

Boucher, Jean, *Corona Mystica*, Tournay, 1623

Carrière, *Historia chronologica Pontificum Romanorum cum praesignatione futurorum ex Sancto Malachia* (Second Edition) Lyon, 1663

Ciacconius, Alphonese Chacon, *Vitae et res gestae Pontificum Romanorum et Romanae Ecclesiae Cardinalium Romae*, 1601, in-folio (2ᵉ édition 1630, 2 vol. in-folio; 3ᵉ édition 1677, 4 vol. in folio. Cette dernière édition est la plus estimée: elle est accompagnée de notes importantes de *Victorelli, Ughelli* et *Oldoïn.*)

Cucherat, L'Abbé, *Revue du monde catholique* (Livraisons du 15 juin au 15 novembre 1871)

———, *La Prophétie de la succession des Papes*, par M. F. Cucherat, chanoine honoraire d'Autun et aumônier de l'hôpital de Paray-le-Monial

———, *Le grand Pape et le grand Roi, ou traditions historiques et dernier mot des prophéties*, 4ᵉ édition

Galbreath, Donald Lindsay, *A Treatise on Ecclesiastical Heraldry*, W. Heffer and Sons, Ltd, Cambridge, 1930

Grosjean, P., "La prophétie de S. Malachie sur l'Irlande,"*Anal. Boll.*, li, 1933, p. 318–24

Harnack, A., "Ueber den Verfasser und den Zweck der Prophetie Malachiae de Summis Pontificibus 1590," in Brieger, *Zeitschrift für Kirchengeschichte*, III, 1879

Lapide, Cornelius A., S. J. Comment. in Apocalypsim. XX. 5. Lyon, 1626

——, *Commentaires sur l'Ecriture Sainte (à l'exception des Psaumes)* publiés à Anvers de 1618 à 1642. Souvent réimprimés à Paris, à Lyon et à Venise

Luddy, Aible John, *Life of St Malachy*, M. H. Gill, Dublin, 1950

Maître, Abbé Joseph, *La Prophétie des Papes attribuée a St. Malachie*, Beaune, Librarie G. Loireau, 1901

——, *Les Papes et la Papauté*, Libraírie G. Loireau, Beaune 1903

Menestrier, S. J., *Réfutation des Prophélies faussement attribuées à S. Malachie sur les élections des Papes par le P. Cl. Fr. Menestrier*, Paris, 1689

Messingham, Thomas, *Florigelium insulae Sanctorum, seu vitae et aeta Sanctorum Hiberniae; quibus accesserunt non vulgaria monumenta, hoc est sancti Patritii Purgatorium, S. Malachiae prophetia de Summis Pontificibus ...*, omnia nun c primum partim in manuscriptis codicibus, partim typis editis collgeia et publicabat Thomas Messingham, 1624

Mollat, *Les Papes d'Avignon*, Paris, 1912

P. Papebroch (Papebrochius), S. J., *Acta Sanctorum, Propylaeum Maii*, Antwerp, 1668

Thurston, Herbert S. J., *The War & the Prophets: Notes on certain Popular Predictions Current in this Latter Age*, P. J. Kenedy & Sons, New York, 1915

Wion, Dom Arnold, *Lignum vitae, ornamentum et decus Ecclesiae*, 2 vol. in-4, Venice, 1595.

GENERAL HISTORY AND MISCELLANEOUS STUDIES

Aarons, Mark, *Unholy Trinity: The Vatican, The Nazis, and Soviet Intelligence*, St. Martin's Press, New York, 1991

Attwater, Donald, *The Penguin Dictionary of Saints*, Penguin Books, 1965 (reissued New York, 1983)

Auchincloss, Louis, *Richelieu*, Viking Press, New York, 1972

Baigent, Michael, Richard Leigh and Henry Lincoln, *The Messianic Legacy*, Corgi Books, London, 1987

Berlitz, Charles, *Doomsday 1999*, Doubleday, New York, 1981

Birch, Desmond A., *Trial, Tribulation & Triumph: Before, During and After Antichrist*, Queenship Publishing Co., Santa Barbara, 1996

Bobko, Jane (ed. with Barbara Newman and Michael Fox), *Vision: The Life and Music of Hildegard von Bingen*, Penguin Studio Book, New York, 1995

Brown, Michael H., *The Final Hour*, Faith Publishing Company, Milford, OH, 1992

Bunson, Matthew, *The Pope Encyclopedia: An A to Z of the Holy See*, Crown trade, New York, 1995

Castleden, Rodney, *World History: A Chronological Dictionary of Dates*, Shooting Star Press, New York, 1993

Cheetham, Nicolas, *Keepers of the Keys: A History of the Popes from St. Peter to John Paul II*, Charles Scribner & Sons, New York, 1982

Chitwood, Arlen L., *Prophecy on Mount Olivet*, The Lamp Broadcast, Inc., Norman, OK, 1989

Cournos, John, ed., *A Book of Prophecy: From the Egyptians to Hitler*, Bell Publishing Company, New York, 1942

Culleton, Rev. R. Gerald, *The Prophets and Our Times*, Tan Books, Rochford II, 1974

Dollison, John, *Pope-pourri: Little-known facts you may not remember from Sunday School, including why the Pope wears a pointy hat, the strange fate of the Singing Nun, what the Baltimore Catechism says, and why St. Lucy carries her eyeballs on a platter*, Simon and Schuster, New York, 1994

Dupont, Yves, *Catholic Prophecy: The Coming Chastisement*, Rochfort, Tan Books and Publishers Inc., IL, 1970, reprinted 1973

Ellerbe, Helen, *The Dark Side of Christian History*, Morningstar Books, San Rafael, 1995

Farmer, David Hugh, *The Oxford Dictionary of Saints*, Oxford University Press (third edition), New York, 1992

Fisher, Joe, *Predictions*, Collins, Toronto, 1980

Flynn, Ted and Maureen, *The Thunder of Justice: The Warning, The Miracle, The Chastisement, The Era of Peace*, Maxkol Communications, Sterling, VA, 1993

Forman, Henry James, *The Story of Prophecy in the Life of Mankind*, Tudor Publishing Company, New York, 1940

Gattey, Charles Neilson, *Prophecy and Prediction in the 20th Century*, Aquarian Press, Wellingborough, 1989

Glass, Justine, *They Foresaw the Future*, G. P. Putnam & Sons, New York, 1969

Gwynn, A., "St Malachy of Armagh," *I.E.R.*, lxx (1948), pp. 961–87; lxxi (1949), pp. 134–48, 317–31

Hall, Angus, *Signs of Things to Come*, Danbury Press/Aldus Books, London, 1975

Hall, Manly, P., *The Secret Teachings of All the Ages: An Encyclopedic Outline of Masonic, Hermetic, Qabbalistic and Rosicrucian Symbolical Philosophy. Being an Interpretation of the Secret Teachings concealed within the Rituals, Allegories and Mysteries of all Ages*, The Philosophical Research Society, Inc., Los Angeles, CA, 1977

——, *The Story of Astrology: The Belief in the Stars as a Factor in Human Progress*, The Philosophical Research Society, Inc., Los Angeles, CA, 1977

Hasler, August Bernard, *How the Pope Became Infallible*, Doubleday, New York, 1981

Hassell, Max, *Prophets without Honor*, Ace Books, New York, 1971

Haught, James A., *Holy Horrors: An Illustrated History of Religious Murder and Madness*, Prometheus Books, Buffalo, New York, 1990

Hildegard, St. (Mother Columba Hart and Jane Bishop Trs.), *Hildegard of Bingen: Scivias*, Paulist Press, New York, 1990

Hildegard, St. (Matthew Fox, ed.), *Hildegard of Bingen's Book of Divine Works: With Letters and Song*, Bear & Co., Santa Fe, 1987

Jochmans, J. R., *Rolling Thunder: The Coming Earth Changes*, Sun Books/Sun Publishing, Santa Fe, NM, 1986, tenth printing

John Paul II, Pope, *Crossing the Threshold of Hope*, Alfred A. Knopf, New York, 1995

Kelly, J. N. D., *The Oxford Dictionary of Popes*, Oxford University Press, London, 1989

Kingston, Jeremy (with David Lambert), *Catastrophe and Crisis*, Bloomsbury Books, London, 1979

Kohut, John J., (W. Roland Sweet: compilers) *Countdown to the Millennium*, Signet, New York, 1994

Küng, Hans, *Infallible? – An Inquiry*, Doubleday, New York, 1970

Lawlor, H. J., *St Malachy of Armagh*, 1920

Livesey, Anthony, *The Historical Atlas of World War I*, Henry Holt Reference Book, New York, 1994

Malachi, Martin, *The Keyes of This Blood: The Struggle for World Dominion Between Pope John Paul II, Mikhail Gorbachev, and the Capitalist West*, Simon & Schuster, New York, 1990

Parker, Geoffrey, *The Thirty Years' War*, Barnes & Noble, New York, 1987

Passelecq, Georges (with Bernard Suchecky), *The Hidden Encyclical of Pius XI: The Vatican's lost opportunity to oppose nazi policies that led to the Holocaust*, Harcort Brace & Company, New York, 1997

Reilly, Robert, *Irish Saints*, Wings Books, New York, 1964

Rosa, Peter de, *Vicars of Christ: The Dark Side of the Papacy*, Crown, New York, 1988

Schonfield, Dr. Hugh J., *The Passover Plot: A New Interpretation of the Life and Death of Jesus*, Bernard Geis Associates, New York, 1965

Stanford, Ray, *Fátima Prophecy: A psychic channels the controversial prophecy of Fátima for the New Age*, Ballantine, New York, 1988

Thomas, Gordon (w. Max Morgan-Witts), *Pontiff*, Doubleday & Company, Inc., New York, 1983

Wallechinsky, David, *The People's Almanac Presents, The Book of Predictions*, William Morrow & Co., Inc., New York, 1980

West, Delno C. (with Sandra L. Zimdars-Swarts), *Joachim of Fiore: A Study in Spiritual Perception and History*, Indiana University Press, Bloomington, IN, 1983

Urquhart, Gordon, *The Pope's Armada: The sensational exposure of brainwashing, intimidation and fanatical personality cults within the Catholic Church*, Corgi Books, London, 1995

Yallop, David A., *In God's Name: An Investigation into the Murder of Pope John Paul I*, Bantam Books, New York, 1985

Zimdars-Swartz, Sandra L., *Encountering Mary: Visions of Mary from La Salette to Medjugorje*, Avon Books, New York, 1991

Index

Contents at a Glance

My Kindle Fire HD

Table of Contents

2   Loading Your Kindle Fire   43

7 Watching Video on Your Kindle Fire — **177**

About the Author

Jim Cheshire has been writing about the Kindle since the very first Kindle device was released. Jim is an expert on technical devices such Amazon's Kindle, Windows Phone, and Windows 8, as well as Web design and programming. Jim has written a dozen books on these topics and also shares his passion and knowledge with readers via online columns and articles. Jim helps developers make the most of Microsoft technologies. When he's not working, Jim spends time enjoying his family and especially loves spending time outdoors.

Jennifer Kettell has written and contributed to dozens of books about software applications, web design, and digital photography. She also writes fiction. When Jenn isn't writing, she can usually be found with her Kindle, reading almost a book a day. Jenn has lived all over the United States but currently calls upstate New York home. Visit her website at www.jenniferkettell.com.

Dedication

To my extended "family" at Adirondack TKD for their love and support. My life is so much richer for having all of you in it.

Acknowledgments

My deepest gratitude and thanks to the many people at Que Publishing who have worked so hard to support me. I'm grateful to Loretta Yates for inviting me to write this book and making roadblocks seem like minor potholes. Huge thanks to Todd Brakke for his editing and sense of humor. Thanks also to Tonya Simpson and Krista Hansing for their production and copyediting expertise. Finally, I just can't put into words how much I appreciate Greg Kettell for reviewing the technical content of this book moments after I finished each chapter—and for pitching in with everything else around the house so I had more writing time.

We Want to Hear from You!

As the reader of this book, *you* are our most important critic and commentator. We value your opinion and want to know what we're doing right, what we could do better, what areas you'd like to see us publish in, and any other words of wisdom you're willing to pass our way.

We welcome your comments. You can email or write to let us know what you did or didn't like about this book—as well as what we can do to make our books better.

Please note that we cannot help you with technical problems related to the topic of this book.

When you write, please be sure to include this book's title and author as well as your name and e-mail address. We will carefully review your comments and share them with the author and editors who worked on the book.

Email: feedback@quepublishing.com

Mail: Que Publishing
        ATTN: Reader Feedback
        800 East 96th Street
        Indianapolis, IN 46240 USA

Reader Services

Visit our website and register this book at quepublishing.com/register for convenient access to any updates, downloads, or errata that might be available for this book.

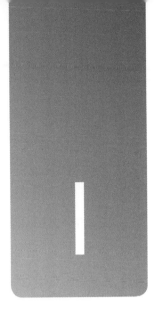

Introduction

You might have purchased your Kindle Fire primarily to read books, but the device you hold in your hands can do so much more. After you connect to the Internet and register the Kindle Fire with your Amazon.com account, you'll quickly fill it with books, music, videos, apps, and games. You'll use it to browse the Web. You'll even add your own photos and personal documents, making your Kindle Fire uniquely yours.

That's not to say that the Kindle Fire isn't good for reading. You'll have access to millions of books on Amazon.com and other websites, many of them free or less than $1.99. You can borrow books from your local library. When reading is inconvenient, such as when you're driving, you can even have your Kindle Fire read to you, either with an audiobook or using text-to-speech. You're also not limited to books; you can read magazines and newspapers as well.

The Kindle Fire is primarily intended for consuming content—that is, for reading, listening, or watching. Much of that content is stored in the *cloud*, on Amazon's servers, and you access it over a Wi-Fi or 4G connection. Even if you download content to your device, at which point it becomes device content, a copy stays in the cloud so that it remains accessible from other devices—or if you need to download a new copy. If that all that sounds a bit confusing right now, don't worry! Everything will become clear after you read this book.

An Overview of the Various Kindle Fire Models

Other Kindle devices are dedicated e-readers, but the Kindle Fire is also a multimedia entertainment device and a tablet computer. Four models of the Kindle Fire exist. All four have the same user interface and access to more than 22 million books, movies, songs, magazines, audiobooks, TV shows, games, and apps. Each model also offers free, unlimited cloud storage for your Amazon content. The processor, display, and storage vary for each model, however, as noted here:

Camera

View all your Amazon content from the Carousel.

Access Quick Links or similar content.

Click for Favorites.

- **Kindle Fire:** This is the second generation of the base Kindle Fire model. The new model is 40 percent faster than its predecessor, with twice the memory and longer battery life. It has a 7-inch LCD display with a resolution of 1024×600 pixels. (That's not quite HD.) The device offers 8GB of memory with a 1.2GHz dual-core processor. Unlike the other three models of the Kindle Fire, this device does not have a forward-facing camera. This base model also offers Wi-Fi connectivity but lacks the dual-band, dual-antenna of the higher-end models. The Kindle Fire's battery can handle up to 8.5 hours of continuous use. The Kindle Fire costs $159.

- **Kindle Fire HD:** Although it has the same 7-inch screen size as the base model, the Kindle Fire HD packs more power into its small space. It comes with an HD LCD display with 1280×800 resolution and up to 720p HD. It offers the same 1.2GHz dual-core processor, but it comes with either 16GB or 32GB of storage. The stereo speakers are better on the HD models, with Dolby Digital Plus audio, which automatically optimizes the audio based on whether you're listening to music or watching a movie. The Kindle Fire HD connects with dual-band, dual-antenna Wi-Fi for a faster and more reliable connection. The battery lasts for up to 11 hours of continuous use. The Kindle Fire HD costs $199 for the 16GB version and $249 for the 32GB model.

- **Kindle Fire HD 8.9-inch:** Want a larger display? As its name implies, this model comes with an 8.9-inch HD LCD display with 1920×1200 resolution and up to 1,080p HD. The other major difference is that the HD 8.9-inch model has a 1.5GHz processor. The Kindle Fire HD 8.9-inch costs $299 for the 16GB version and $369 for the 32GB version.

- **Kindle Fire HD 8.9-inch 4G:** As its name implies, this top-of-the-line model offers 4G LTE connectivity in addition to Wi-Fi. Amazon offers annual data plans through AT&T for $49.99 per year for 250MB of data per month (plans offering 3GB or 5GB data usage are also available). The Kindle Fire HD 8.9-inch 4G has the same 1.5GHz processor as the other 8.9-inch model, but it comes with either 32GB or 64GB of storage on the device and offers additional cloud storage for your personal documents and photos. The 32GB version of the Kindle Fire HD 8.9-inch 4G costs $499, and the 64GB model costs $599.

What's New on the Kindle Fire

No matter which Kindle Fire model you choose, you will find plenty to do with it. If you're upgrading from the first-generation Kindle Fire, you will be happy to discover many new features. In addition to the upgrades in display, processor, and other hardware enhancements, the new Kindle Fire offers many other improvements.

- Upgraded operating system. If you're of a technical bent, the Kindle Fire uses a proprietary version of Android 4.0 (Ice Cream Sandwich). For the rest of us, it's enough to know that the operating system is faster and smoother.

- Improved battery life in the base Kindle Fire model.

- Physical volume-control buttons on the device, to save you from having to navigate to the volume controls on the screen.

- A front-facing camera that enables video chat over Skype and other apps (not available on the base Kindle Fire).

- Integration with Facebook and Twitter.

- Kindle FreeTime, which provides parental control over what kids can do on the Kindle Fire and the hours during which they can do it.

- A micro-HDMI port to connect the Kindle Fire with an external display (not available on the base Kindle Fire).

All Kindle Fire models also come with a free month of Amazon Prime, if you don't already have an account. Amazon Prime offers unlimited streaming of more than 25,000 movies and TV shows, making it easy to watch a show wherever you have Wi-Fi (or 4G) access. Prime also lets you borrow one free title a month from the Kindle Owners' Lending Library. And if you shop on Amazon.com, you can get free two-day shipping on most items as part of your Prime membership.

What You'll Find in This Book

The Kindle Fire is a tablet computer for people who aren't necessarily computer geeks and who just want to be entertained, read a good book, or have fun—and might have the occasional need to get some work done. *My Kindle Fire* was written with that same mindset. I show you how to get the most fun out of your Kindle Fire, and teach you how to access your personal documents when you need to work. Of course, if you are a computer geek, this book can help you as well.

This book covers all the capabilities of your Kindle Fire. I cover each feature using a step-by-step approach, complete with figures that correspond to each step. You never have to wonder what or where to tap. Each task shows you how to interact with your Kindle Fire using simple symbols that illustrate what you should do.

This icon means that you tap and hold an object on the screen.

This icon means that you drag an item on the screen.

This icon indicates that you pinch on the screen.

This icon means that you spread your thumb and finger on the screen.

This icon indicates that you swipe on the screen.

Along the way, I add plenty of tips that help you better understand a feature or task. If you want to dig deeper, you'll appreciate the Go Further sidebars that provide a more in-depth look at certain features. I also warn you of problems and pitfalls with particular tasks with It's Not All Good sidebars.

How to Navigate This Book

There is a lot to discover about your Kindle Fire. The major functions might be visible to the naked eye, but a lot more hides beneath the surface. As you read this book, you might be surprised to find that your Kindle Fire does more than you ever imagined.

Here are the topics we'll cover in this book.

- Chapter 1, "Getting Started with the Kindle Fire," explains how to set up your device and access the most common settings. You also learn how to operate your Kindle Fire and use the onscreen keyboard. Finally, you learn how to set up external devices such as a Bluetooth keyboard and share your screen with an external display.

- Chapter 2, "Loading Your Kindle Fire," covers Amazon's cloud services and other ways to transfer content onto your Kindle Fire.

- Chapter 3, "Using Amazon's Manage Your Kindle Page," shows you how to access the Manage Your Kindle page on the Internet, where you can review your Kindle library, rename your Kindle Fire, manage all your Kindle devices and Kindle apps, and much more.

- Chapter 4, "Reading on the Kindle Fire," describes how to find reading material and take advantage of the Kindle Fire's powerful features for reading books, newspapers, magazines, and more.

- Chapter 5, "Managing Content with Calibre," introduces you to Calibre, a free application that helps you manage your eBook library, including books you get from sources other than directly through Amazon. It even helps you convert them to the proper format and transfer them onto your Kindle Fire.

- Chapter 6, "Accessing and Listening to Music," shows you how to use your Kindle Fire to play music in your music library (both on your device and in the cloud) and use Amazon's MP3 Store to add to your music collection. You also learn about using playlists and other, more advanced features.

- Chapter 7, "Watching Video on Your Kindle," covers using your Kindle Fire to stream and download videos from Amazon's video store. You also learn how to convert your own videos to play them on your Kindle Fire.

- Chapter 8, "Installing and Using Apps," introduces you to the world of apps that dramatically increase the functionality of your Kindle Fire. You learn how to find and install apps, as well as how to deal with misbehaving apps. You also discover some apps that you should definitely install on your Kindle Fire.

- Chapter 9, "Using Social Media and Chat," shows you how to access Facebook and Twitter to stay connected with your friends and how to video chat with them using the Skype app. You also learn how to connect to Game Circle to challenge your friends and compare scores.

- Chapter 10, "Reading and Sending E-mail," shows you how to use your Kindle Fire to read and send e-mail. You also learn how to handle attachments in e-mail.

- Chapter 11, "Managing Your Personal Documents and Data," covers loading, viewing, and editing your personal documents and photos on the Kindle Fire. You also learn how to add and manage contacts.

- Chapter 12, "Browsing the Web with Silk," walks you through using Silk, the web browser that comes with your Kindle Fire. You learn how to access websites, use bookmarks and tabs, and control Silk's behavior.

- Chapter 13, "Giving Your Kids a Kindle Fire," describes how to set up Kindle FreeTime to establish time limits and restrict the content your children can access from their Kindle Fire. I also recommend some good apps for kids.

Let's Light This Fire

If you've already gone through the initial setup of your Kindle Fire, you might be tempted to skip ahead to Chapter 2 at this point. I urge you to avoid the the rush and at least skim Chapter 1. You won't want to miss the hidden gems in Chapter 1.

Now that the stage is set, let's light up your Kindle Fire!

View content in each category

Swipe down to access Settings

View your Amazon content from the Carousel

Access Quick Links for Apps

Tap to see Favorites

In this chapter, you learn how to connect your Kindle Fire to your Wi-Fi network and register it with Amazon, and you discover the basics of navigating and using your tablet. Topics include the following:

Getting Started with the Kindle Fire

The Kindle Fire is unassuming at first glance. However, after you power it up, you soon realize that it opens up a new world of entertainment and information. Couple it with Amazon's wide range of services, and the Kindle Fire becomes a truly extraordinary device. In fact, in addition to being a great reading device, your Kindle Fire might replace your computer for some of the things you do on the Internet, especially when you're away from home.

The Kindle Fire is not difficult to use. Many of its features are intuitive, and you can easily discover many of the great tasks it can do just by playing with it. However, if this is your first tablet, you should be familiar with some essentials to get the most from the device. This chapter starts you on the right foot by teaching you about the basic operation of the Kindle Fire.

The Hardware

Your Kindle Fire is equipped with a power button on the top of the device when in portrait mode (holding the Kindle Fire with the camera on the left side). Press and release this button to power on your Kindle Fire. If the Kindle Fire is already turned on, a quick press of the power button puts it to sleep. Many Kindle Fire covers automatically turn on the device when opened and put it to sleep when closed. Pressing and holding the power button enables you to power off your Kindle Fire.

Should You Power Off?

The display on your Kindle Fire is the primary power consumer on the device. Therefore, your Kindle Fire uses much less power when it's in sleep mode. Obviously, turning it off completely uses even less power, but if you subscribe to a magazine or a newspaper, you won't get your subscription automatically when your Kindle Fire is turned off.

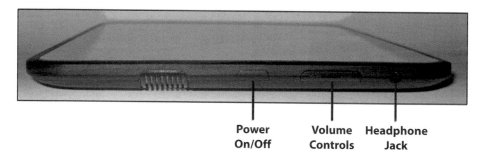

**Power
On/Off** **Volume
Controls** **Headphone
Jack**

To the left of the power button is the volume up/down button. Press the left side of the button to raise the volume, and press the right side to lower it. If you want to use headphones or external speakers while listening to music or video, plug them into the 1/4-inch audio plug to the right of the volume controls.

On the right side of the device (if you're holding it in portrait mode, with the camera on the left) is a micro-USB port for charging your Kindle Fire. The Kindle Fire comes with a cable to connect it to a computer so that you can charge the device from your computer's power. You can also separately purchase a wall charger, which charges the Kindle Fire faster and can be used when you're away from your computer.

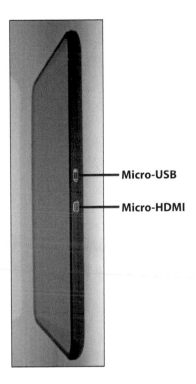

Micro-USB

Micro-HDMI

Below the micro-USB port is a micro-HDMI port. The micro-HDMI port is used to connect the Kindle Fire to a television or other display and is useful when you want to watch a movie or TV show on a larger screen. You learn how to make this connection later in this chapter.

At the top and bottom of your Kindle Fire are dual stereo speakers. If you hold your Kindle Fire in landscape position, the speakers are on either side of the device, making watching movies and TV shows a much more enjoyable audio experience.

It's Not All Good

Charging the Kindle Fire

The Kindle Fire ships with a micro-USB-to-USB cable. You can use this cable to connect your Kindle Fire to your computer so that you can transfer files and charge the device. Fully charging your Kindle Fire using this cable takes 11 hours. If you want to cut this to less than 5 hours, you must spend an extra $19.99 to purchase an Amazon Kindle PowerFast adapter. This charger plugs directly into a wall outlet instead of using your computer as a charging conduit.

Initial Setup

When you first turn on your Kindle Fire, you see the lock screen. This screen is usually an ad for a book or other form of Amazon content. Swipe your finger across the lock from right to left to unlock the device. You then go through a series of steps that get you started using your new device.

Kindle Fire Updates

It's possible that your Kindle Fire won't have the latest version of the Kindle operating system. If it doesn't, the latest version is downloaded and installed automatically when you set up your Kindle Fire for the first time.

Connecting to a Listed Wi-Fi Network

To access content on your Kindle Fire, you need to connect to a Wi-Fi network, which is where the initial setup process begins.

1. Tap the name of your Wi-Fi network.

2. Enter the password for your Wi-Fi network.

3. Tap Connect.

Manually Connecting to a Wi-Fi Network

If you need to return to the Wi-Fi setup or want to set up an additional Wi-Fi connection, first tap the time and pull down to open the Quick Settings and then tap Wi-Fi.

>>>Go Further

COMPLETE SETUP LATER

If you're anxious to play with your Kindle Fire without having to go through all the setup motions, use the Complete Setup Later option that appears at the bottom of the Connect to a Wi-Fi Network screen. Because this aborts the entire setup process, you must manually go into the My Account option in Settings to register your Kindle Fire with your Amazon account to gain access to the Amazon Cloud. You also must set up a connection in the Wireless option in Settings before you can connect to the Internet. My advice is to be patient and go through the entire setup procedure right away.

Connecting to an Unlisted Wi-Fi Network

If your network's name isn't listed, you might need to manually enter the information necessary to connect to your Wi-Fi network.

1. Tap Enter Other Wi-Fi Network at the bottom of the network list.

2. Enter the name (SSID) of your network.

3. Tap the type of security that your network uses.

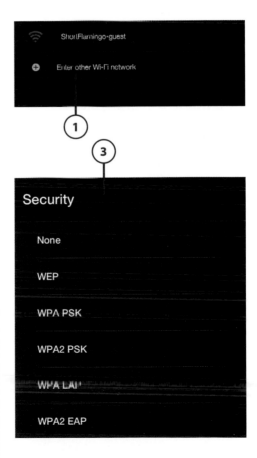

4. Enter the password for your network, if necessary.

5. Tap Save.

If you are fortunate enough to own a Kindle Fire HD 8.9-inch 4G, you can find instructions for setting up your 4G service at the website that accompanies this book. The URL for this site is www.informit.com/title/9780789750716.

Setting Your Time Zone

Your Kindle Fire doesn't have a GPS, so it can't determine your time zone automatically. You need to select your time zone during setup.

1. Tap your time zone.

2. If your time zone isn't listed, tap Select Another Time Zone to see a list of additional time zones.

3. Tap Continue.

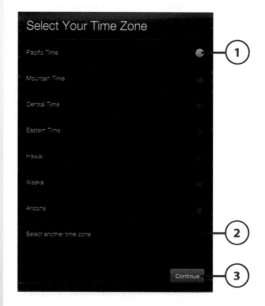

Registering with Amazon

Your Kindle Fire must be registered with an Amazon account so that you can access content. If your Kindle is not already registered to your Amazon account, you need to do that next.

Is Your Kindle Already Registered?

If you ordered your Kindle Fire from your own Amazon account, it will be preregistered before Amazon ships the device to you. If you received your Kindle Fire as a gift or purchased it at a retail store, you will need to register the device before you can access content.

1. Enter your e-mail address that is registered with Amazon.

2. Enter your Amazon password.

3. Tap Register.

Don't Have an Amazon Account?

If you don't already have an Amazon account, you can create one online at Amazon.com or you can tap Create Account at the bottom of the Register Your Kindle screen to create one.

4. Your Kindle confirms that it is now registered to your account. Tap Continue.

Connecting to Facebook and Twitter

Your Kindle Fire can help you stay connected to your social networks. If you enter your username and passwords during the initial setup, the Facebook and Twitter apps are automatically configured for you.

1. Select Connect Your Facebook Account.

2. Enter your e-mail address.

3. Enter your password.

4. Tap connect.

5. Repeat steps 1–4 for Twitter. Tap Get Started Now when you're done.

You've reached the end of the guided setup. Congratulations! After you complete the initial setup, the Kindle Fire guides you through a series of screens that describe some of the basic usability features of the tablet. And now you're ready to play.

Basic Usage of the Kindle Fire

By now, you're already familiar with tapping to select buttons and other items on your Kindle Fire. You can also use several other gestures to interact with your Kindle Fire.

Canceling a Tap

Taps are registered when you lift your finger from the screen. If you tap something by mistake and you want to cancel the tap, slide your finger onto another part of the screen before lifting it.

In addition to tapping to select items, you can double-tap to do things such as zoom in on a figure in a book or a website. To do this, tap your finger on the same point on the screen twice in quick succession.

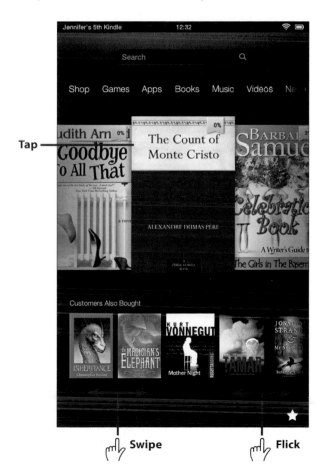

You can scroll through lists of items both horizontally and vertically by swiping your finger. Hold your finger on the list and move it up and down or left and right to scroll through items. To quickly scroll, flick your finger in the direction you want to scroll as you remove your finger from the screen.

To incrementally zoom in and out, you can use pinch and reverse pinch gestures. This is typically used on pictures, websites, and subscription content, but many applications also allow you to use this gesture.

To zoom in, place your thumb and index finger on the screen close together and move them apart (reverse pinching). To zoom out, place your thumb and index finger on the screen with some distance between them and move them together (pinching).

Zoom In

Zoom Out

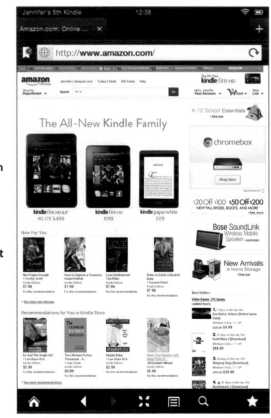

The Home Screen

After you complete the initial setup, press the Home button (the one that looks like a house) to get to the home screen. The Carousel contains thumbnails for your books and recently accessed content and websites. Swipe or flick across the Carousel to browse the items available there. Tapping an item opens that item. You can't change the order of items in the Carousel; the most recently accessed items always appear first.

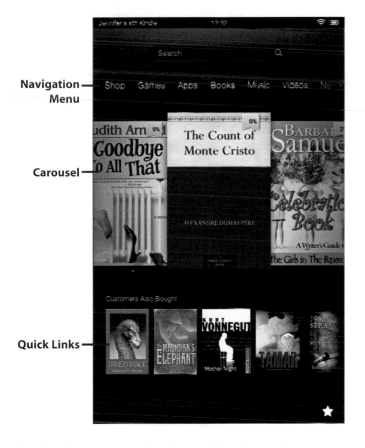

The Navigation menu provides quick access to the various content libraries available on the Kindle Fire. If you select a specific content library, the Carousel shows content from only that library. Swipe or flick across the Navigation menu to see additional categories of content.

The Quick Links bar provides thumbnails of content related to the content in the center of the Carousel. If the Carousel displays a book at the center, for example, the Quick Links show books that other readers of that book have purchased through Amazon. Some apps provide Quick Links to tasks within that app. If the Carousel is focused on the E-mail app, as shown here, the Quick Links provide options to send a new message or view your Favorite Contacts.

Application-Related Quick Links

Downloading Items

The Carousel displays both items on your Kindle Fire (called *device items*) and items that you've previously purchased that are in your online library (called *cloud items*). If you want to open a cloud item, you first need to download it to your device.

1. Swipe to the item you want to download.

2. Tap the item to download it to your device.

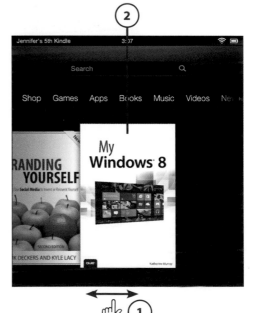

3. While the item is downloading, you can tap the X to cancel the download. After an item has been downloaded, it is a device item and can be accessed at any time, even when the Kindle Fire is not connected to Wi-Fi.

FINDING YOUR ITEMS

The Carousel on the home screen shows a mix of cloud and device items, but it shows only the most recently accessed items. If you are looking for content that is not visible on the Carousel, use the Navigation menu to access the type of content you're seeking (books, music, and so on), and then download the item you want from that screen.

Removing Downloaded Items from Your Kindle Fire

After an item is downloaded, it takes up some of the memory on your Kindle Fire. The amount of memory you have available varies by which model of the Kindle Fire you own. You can free up memory by removing unused items from your device. This removes only the device copy of the item; this content is still available to you in your cloud library, so you can download it again at a later date.

1. Tap and hold the item you want to remove.
2. Tap Remove from Device.

Cloud Versus Device

Cloud is a common buzzword in today's technology. If something is in the cloud, it means that it exists on a computer that you access via the Internet instead of on your local device. The Kindle Fire accesses a lot of its content on Amazon's computers in the cloud.

Many screens on the Kindle Fire enable you to choose whether you are viewing content on the device or in the cloud. Having content in the cloud makes sharing that content among multiple devices easy. You can read the same book or watch the same movie on your Kindle Fire, your computer, and your smartphone.

Adding an Item to Favorites

The Favorites drawer appears below the Carousel when you press the star icon in the lower-right corner. It provides a convenient way for you to access your most-often-used items. You can add any item to Favorites.

1. Tap and hold the item you want to add to Favorites.

2. Tap Add to Favorites.

3. Tap the Favorites icon.

4. Your Favorites appear on shelves below the carousel.

Adding Subscription Items to Favorites

If you add a subscription item to Favorites and that item isn't currently on your device, the item is downloaded immediately. If you remove that item from your device later, it is automatically removed from Favorites as well.

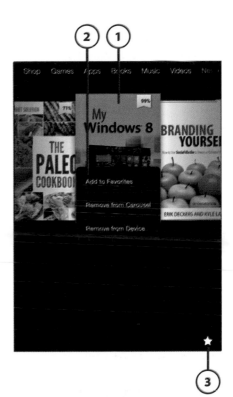

Removing an Item from Favorites

If you decide that you no longer want an item to be listed in Favorites, you can remove it.

1. Tap and hold the item in Favorites.
2. Tap Remove from Favorites.

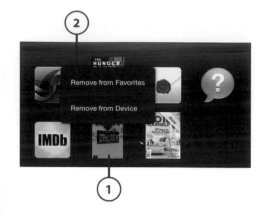

Rearranging Favorites

By default, items are listed in Favorites in the order in which you add them. If you want to rearrange your Favorites, you can easily do so.

1. Tap and hold the item you want to move. Don't lift your finger, even when you see the Remove from Favorites menu pop up.
2. Drag the item to the new location.
3. Release the item.

Changing the Screen Timeout

While you're learning how to use your Kindle Fire, particularly if you are doing each task as you follow along with this book, you might get frustrated if the device automatically goes into sleep mode just as you're about to reach for it. Your Kindle Fire's screen turns off automatically after 5 minutes without use. You can adjust the timeout or completely turn off the automatic timeout.

1. Tap the top of the screen (where the name of the device and time are displayed) and drag down.

2. Tap More.

3. Tap Sounds & Display.

4. Tap Screen Timeout.

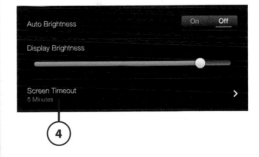

5.   Select a screen timeout period.

6.   Press the Home button to return to the home screen.

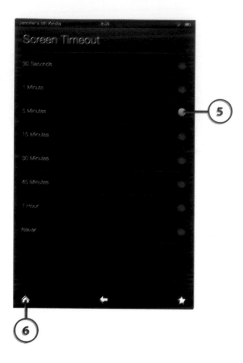

Notifications and Options

The status bar appears at the top of the Kindle Fire screen. It displays the name of your Kindle Fire, a notification indicator (if notifications are present), the clock, the Wi-Fi signal indicator, and the battery meter. If you have the Kindle Fire HD 8.9-inch 4G LTE, the status bar also displays your 4G signal strength.

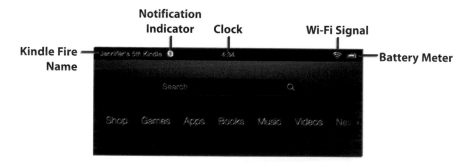

Notifications

Your Kindle Fire uses the notification indicator to inform you of the status of background tasks and let you know when you've received e-mail. When you see the notification indicator, you can tap it to get more information.

1. Swipe the status bar downward to open the notifications.

2. Tap a notification for more information or additional options.

Options

The Options bar appears at the bottom of many screens. The buttons on the Options bar are called icons and include a Home icon, a Back icon, a Menu icon, a Search icon, and the Favorites icon on most screens. The Home icon always takes you to the home screen. The Back icon takes you back one screen, the Menu icon displays a menu for the current screen, the Search icon displays the Search screen, and the Favorites icon opens the Favorites shelf.

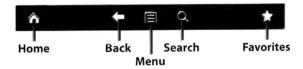

Home　　Back　　Search　　Favorites

Menu

Other Options Bar Icons

Depending on the screen, you might see additional icons on the Options bar. These are covered throughout the book, where applicable.

Settings

I cover many of the Kindle Fire's settings throughout the book as necessary, but you should be immediately familiar with some general settings.

Locking the Screen Orientation

Your Kindle Fire features an accelerometer that can sense the orientation of the device. When you turn the device while holding it, the screen rotates automatically to match the orientation of the device. In some cases, you might want to prevent the screen from rotating. For example, if you're reading a web page in portrait mode, setting your Kindle Fire on a table sometimes flips the orientation. You can lock the orientation to prevent this.

Orientation Isn't Always Your Choice

If you are watching videos, your Kindle Fire automatically switches to landscape orientation.

---

1. With the screen displaying the desired orientation, swipe the status bar down to open the Settings drawer.

2. Tap Unlocked to lock the orientation. The label on the icon changes to Locked.

Adjusting the Volume

A toggle button at the top of the device enables you to adjust the volume. When you press these buttons, a volume meter also appears on the screen to indicate the volume level. You can adjust the volume directly on the screen as well.

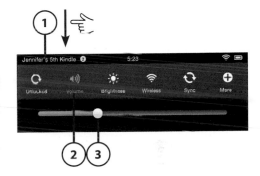

1. Swipe the status bar down to open the Settings drawer.

2. Tap Volume. The volume control appears.

3. Slide the volume control to the right to increase volume and to the left to decrease volume.

It's Not All Good

Using the Volume Toggle Switch

When you are holding your Kindle Fire in portrait mode, the volume toggles at the top of the device are counterintuitive. If you press the button to the right, the volume goes down. If you press the button to the left, the volume increases. Watch the volume control as you use these buttons, to adjust the volume to your liking.

Adjusting Screen Brightness

As mentioned earlier, the screen on the Kindle Fire uses more power than anything else, and the brighter the screen, the more battery power it uses. To increase battery life, you can lower the brightness of the display.

1. Swipe the status bar down to open the Settings drawer.

2. Tap Brightness.

3. Slide the brightness control to the right to increase brightness and to the left to decrease brightness.

Checking Device Information

The Device screen displays information about your Kindle Fire, such as the percentage of battery remaining, how much storage space you've used, the version of your operating system, and other useful information.

1. Swipe the status bar down to open the Settings drawer.

2. Tap More.

3. Tap Device.

4. The Device screen displays. If you want to check your storage space, tap Storage.

5. The Storage screen displays. Here you can see how much space you have used across various types of data and how much remains available for future use.

Turning Off Wi-Fi

Sometimes you need to turn off the Wi-Fi connection on your Kindle Fire, such as when you're traveling by air or in other sensitive areas. Turning off Wi-Fi also consumes less battery power when you don't need to access online content.

1. Swipe the status bar down to open the Settings drawer.

2. Tap Wireless.

3. Tap Off to turn off Wi-Fi. To reconnect, tap On.

Disconnecting from All Signals

If you are flying on a commercial airline, you will need to turn off Wi-Fi and all other wireless signals on your Kindle Fire, at least during takeoff and landing. Use the On/Off buttons for Airplane Mode on the Wireless screen to disable Wi-Fi, cellular (on the Kindle Fire HD 8.9-inch 4G LTE model), and Bluetooth signals.

Using the Keyboard

Your Kindle Fire's keyboard is much like the keyboard you use on your computer. However, unlike your computer's keyboard, this one has no physical keys. Instead, your Kindle Fire's keyboard uses touch, just like the rest of the interface.

At first, you might find the Kindle Fire's keyboard a bit hard to get used to, especially if you're typing a lengthy e-mail or document. After some time, however, you'll find it to be an easy way to enter data.

Entering Text

Entering text using your Kindle Fire's keyboard is a simple task, and a few convenient features make it easier.

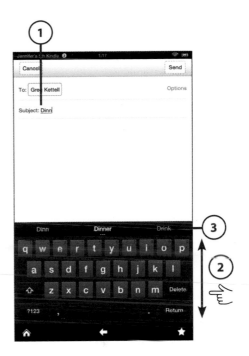

1. Tap an area where text entry is possible, such as an e-mail message.

2. Tap letters on the keyboard to enter your text.

3. Tap a suggested word to insert the word.

A Couple of Shortcuts

You can quickly add a period to the end of a sentence by double-tapping the space key.

You can activate caps lock by double-tapping the Shift key.

Positioning the Cursor

As you type, characters are added at the position of the cursor. You can reposition the cursor, if necessary.

1. Tap in the text entry area.

2. Tap a new position to move the cursor indicator.

Selecting and Editing Text

If you want to change or remove some of the text you've entered, you can select a block of text instead of deleting one character at a time.

1. Double-tap the entered text.

2. Drag the left indicator to the beginning of your desired selection.

3. Drag the right indicator to the end of your desired selection.

4. Press Backspace to delete the selection or type to replace the selection.

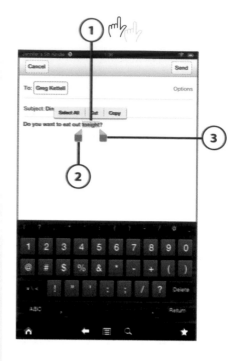

Selecting an Entire Block of Text

If you want to select everything you typed into a text area, such as the entire body of an e-mail message, tap Select All above the selection indicators.

Copying/Cutting and Pasting Text

You might want to copy or cut a selection of text and then paste it somewhere else. You can paste text either within the same message or document or into another message or document.

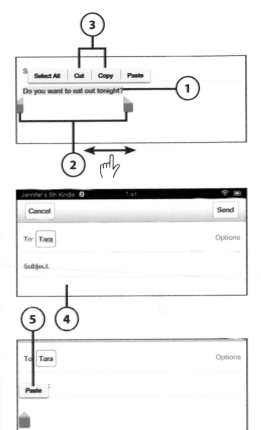

1. Double-tap the text you want to copy or cut.

2. Drag the indicators to make your selection, or tap Select All.

3. Tap Copy or Cut.

4. Tap and hold where you want to paste the text you copied or cut.

5. Tap Paste.

Entering Punctuation and Numbers

The most-often-used punctuation marks appear above the keyboard for easy access while you type. You can use the number keyboard to enter other punctuation, numbers, and symbols.

1. Tap the number key to change the keyboard so that it displays numbers and punctuation marks.

2. Tap the symbols key to change the keyboard so that it displays symbols.

3. Tap a number, punctuation mark, or symbol to enter it.

4. Tap the ABC key to return to the alphabet keyboard.

Adding Accent Marks and Diacriticals

If you are typing in a foreign language, you might need to add accent marks and diacriticals to certain letters. The letters that often require these marks are a, e, i, o, u, c, and n.

1. Tap and hold a letter that requires an accent.

2. Without lifting your finger from the keyboard, slide your finger to highlight the desired character and release.

Accessing Hidden Keyboard Features

As with adding accent marks, if you tap and hold the period (.) key, you can quickly slide your finger over additional punctuation marks without having to switch to the number keyboard.

If you tap and hold the comma (,) key and then slide your finger over the symbol that appears, you bring up the Keyboard options.

Connecting to Other Hardware

The Kindle Fire is a self-contained device. You can access your content directly from the Kindle Fire without connecting it to a computer or any other hardware. However, you might want to use accessories that will enhance the quality of your interaction with your Kindle Fire. You can pair the Kindle Fire with Bluetooth keyboards, headphones, or speakers. You can also use an HDMI cable to connect with a television or larger monitor so that you can view your movies on a larger screen.

Adding Bluetooth Accessories

Bluetooth keyboards and headsets can connect wirelessly to your device. With Bluetooth headphones, you can listen to your music without being attached to your Kindle Fire by a wire. A Bluetooth keyboard can help you type messages and documents faster. If you have Bluetooth speakers in your car, you can even play music from your Kindle Fire over your car stereo.

1. Swipe the status bar down to open the Settings drawer.

2. Select Wireless.

3. Select Bluetooth.

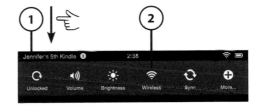

4. Tap the On button to enable Bluetooth.

5. After the Kindle Fire locates available devices, tap the device you want to pair with.

6. Follow additional instructions, which vary by device.

It's Not All Good

Bluetooth Has Limits

Although Bluetooth microphones and headsets are popular, particularly among gamers, the Kindle Fire does not support these devices. If you want to use voice chat, you must use the Kindle Fire's built-in microphone.

Go Further

SHARING YOUR SCREEN

The Kindle Fire comes with an HDMI port, located to the left of the mini-USB port. You can use a micro-HDMI-to-HDMI cable to connect to an external display or television. That display will then mirror the display on your Kindle Fire. You do not need to adjust any other settings or go through any menus to make this connection.

Searches

All the content in your Kindle library is indexed for easy searching. Search is more useful than it might seem at first. For example, when you're reading a novel, you can use search to find references to a particular character. This is especially helpful when you pick up a book that you haven't read in a while.

Search results include content both on your device and in the cloud.

Searching Within Content

You can also search within books and other content. I cover how to do that in the "Searching Content and Accessing Reference Materials" section of Chapter 4, "Reading on the Kindle Fire."

Searching Your Library

Searching your library returns results from books, periodicals, music, documents, and apps.

1. From the Home screen, tap inside the search box.

2. Tap Libraries to search your library.

3. Enter the text you want to search for using the keyboard that appears at the bottom of the screen. Results appear as you type.

4. Tap the item you want. If the item is on your device, it opens. If the item is stored on the Amazon cloud, it downloads to your Kindle Fire.

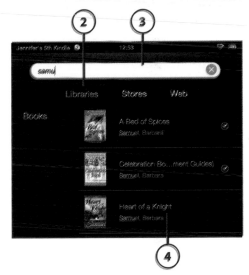

Searching the Web

In addition to searching for items in your libraries, you can search the Web quickly from the home screen.

1. From the home screen, tap inside the search box.

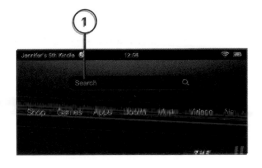

2. Tap Web to search the Web.

3. Enter the text you want to search for. Results appear as you type.

4. Tap an item in the results to open a search page using your default search engine. The preset default search engine is Bing.

Changing Your Web Search Engine

I cover how to set your default web search engine in Chapter 12, "Browsing the Web with Silk."

Searching Amazon Stores

You can search for items in the Amazon Stores from the Home screen. This is similar to performing a search on the Amazon website, but you can do it right from your Kindle Fire.

1. From the home screen, tap inside the search box.

2. Tap Stores to search Amazon Stores.

3. Enter the text you want to search for. Results appear as you type.

4. Tap an option in the results to get a list of items from a particular Amazon Store that match your search terms.

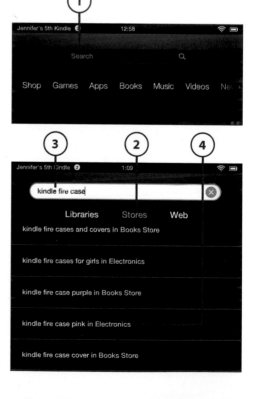

5. Tap the item you want to see from the list of items.

5

**Cloud Player
and Cloud
Drive**

**Instant
Video**

**Cloud
Reader**

In this chapter, you learn how to load Amazon and other content onto your Kindle Fire and use Amazon's Cloud to access content from your computer. Topics include the following:

→ Amazon Prime
→ Amazon Cloud Drive
→ Amazon Cloud Player
→ Amazon Instant Video
→ Kindle Reader Applications and Kindle Cloud Reader
→ Transferring files from your computer

Loading Your Kindle Fire

Amazon offers a collection of cloud services that augment the functionality of the Kindle Fire. In fact, your Kindle Fire is designed to be a handheld conduit into these cloud services. You can set up a cloud drive, add all your music, and have that music immediately available to you on your Kindle Fire anywhere you can connect to Wi-Fi (or 4G, if you have a Kindle Fire HD 8.9-inch 4G LTE). You can get a movie or TV show from Amazon on your computer or set-top box, watch part of it on your television, and then pick right up to watch the rest on your Kindle Fire while in bed or while traveling. You can also use Amazon's Cloud Services to load your personal photos and documents onto your Kindle Fire. Even if you leave your Kindle Fire behind, all your music, books, videos, and personal files are accessible from any computer with an Internet connection or from many mobile devices.

Amazon Prime

The key to accessing Amazon's Cloud Services is your Amazon account. A standard Amazon account enables you to manage your Kindle Fire device (more on that in Chapter 3, "Using Amazon's Manage Your Kindle Page") and to purchase books, music, and much more. To get the full value out of your Kindle Fire, however, consider upgrading to an Amazon Prime account.

An Amazon Prime account costs $79 per year. For that price, you get the following:

- **Prime Instant Videos:** Unlimited, instant streaming of thousands of movies and television shows, all commercial free. You can watch on your Kindle Fire or on any other Internet-connected TV or game machine you own.

- **Kindle Lending Library:** You can check out one book per month from the Kindle Lending Library catalog without any due dates and load it on your Kindle Fire. The Kindle Lending Library has more than 180,000 titles, so you're sure to find something to read each month.

- **Free two-day shipping:** When you shop for material goods on the Amazon site, you get free two-day shipping on most items. One-day shipping costs only $3.99 per item for eligible purchases. The Amazon Store sells everything from toys, to food, to clothing, so it's easy to see a return on your $79 Prime membership investment if you frequently shop online.

Extended Prime Benefits for Caregivers

If you are the primary caregiver (mom, dad, grandparent, and so forth) of a young child, you can get a 3-month subscription to Prime and 20 percent off diapers and wipes by joining Amazon Mom. Browse to www.amazon.com/prime for details.

Setting Up Amazon Prime

When you went through the setup process for your Kindle Fire, you either connected to an existing Amazon account or created a new one. You can set up a free trial of Prime on the same account. You do this on your Kindle Fire using the Silk browser or via the web browser on your computer.

1. Open a web browser and navigate to www.amazon.com.

2. Click Join Prime. If you are not already logged in to your Amazon account, enter your e-mail address and password.

3. Click Start Your One Month Free Trial.

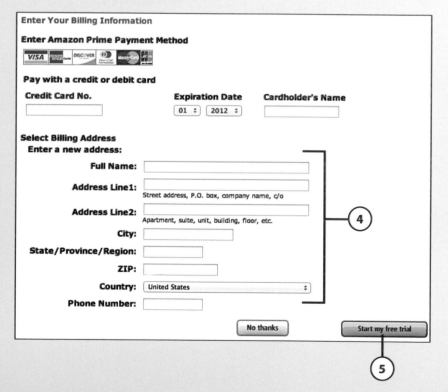

4. Enter your billing information.

5. Select Start My Free Trial.

Prime All the Time

At the end of your free trial, Amazon automatically bills you for $79 to extend your Prime membership for a full year. If you decide that you don't want to keep Prime, go to the Amazon.com site, select Your Account, and then select Do Not Upgrade sometime before the end of your 30-day trial.

Amazon Cloud Drive

Your computer has a hard drive in it where you can store your stuff. When you're sitting at your computer, that stuff is easy to access, but what about when you're not at your computer? The cloud is like having a hard drive available from anywhere you have Internet access.

Amazon provides 5GB of free storage that you can use for photos, personal documents, or anything else you want to store in the cloud. This space is in addition to the unlimited cloud storage Amazon provides for books, music, and videos you purchase directly from Amazon. If you need additional storage, Amazon offers plans from 20GB for $10 a year to 1,000GB for $500 a year. As a frame of reference, a typical HD movie is approximately 2GB. A single song is 3MB to 6MB, while a complete album is around 50MB. A high-quality photo is about 2MB to 3MB. As you see, if you start putting all these items onto your cloud storage, it can fill up quickly.

Go Further

WHY WOULD YOU NEED MORE SPACE?

You can use your Amazon Cloud Drive for more than just making your files accessible to your Kindle Fire. Your Cloud Drive can serve as a backup for important files in case of a crash. You can also use it to access your files from any other computer with Internet access, simply by logging in to your Amazon account.

Content you purchase on Amazon is automatically accessible from your Amazon Cloud account and, thus, from your Kindle Fire. But to access your personal photos and documents, you must upload them to your Cloud Drive.

Upload Files Button

File and Folder Management

Folders   **Amount of Used Storage**

Accessing Your Cloud Drive

You can access your Cloud Drive using Silk on your Kindle Fire or using the web browser on your computer.

1. Open your web browser and go to www.amazon.com.

2. Point to Shop All Departments. If you are using your computer's web browser and have a large enough window open, this menu might already be open when you navigate to the Amazon site.

3. Point to Amazon Cloud Drive.

4. Select Your Cloud Drive from the menu. You might get a prompt to install the desktop application, which I explain later in this chapter. You can install it at this time or click Continue to Your Cloud Drive. (Enter your e-mail address and Amazon password, if prompted.)

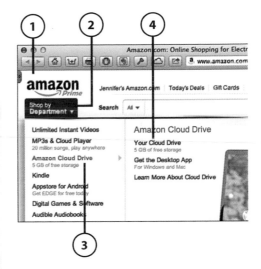

After you log in, you'll see your Cloud Drive and a big Upload button to get you started. I show you how to create folders and upload files next.

Creating Folders

By default, your Cloud Drive contains folders for the common file types. You'll see folders for pictures, documents, and videos. Those folders are a good starting point, but you might want to create additional folders. For example, if you're uploading pictures of your pets, you might want to first create a folder inside the Pictures folder called Pets and then upload those pictures there.

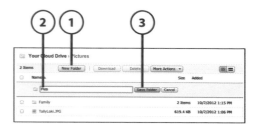

1. Click New Folder. If you want to place the new folder within another folder, first click that folder from the Folders sidebar.

2. Enter a name for the folder.

3. Click Save Folder.

More Actions

You can copy, move, and rename files and folders using the More Actions button.

Deleting Folders

You can delete folders from your Cloud Drive that you no longer need or to free up some space.

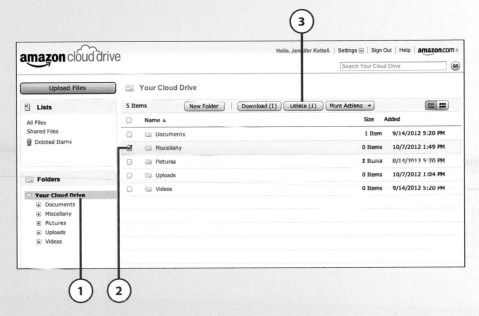

1. Click Your Cloud Drive so that your folders are visible.

2. Check the box to the left of the folder(s) you want to delete.

3. Click Delete. You will not see confirmation of this action, so be sure you choose your files correctly.

Recovering Deleted Items

If you accidentally delete your files, you can recover them. If you delete a folder that contains files, the files are deleted along with the folder. Recovering a folder also recovers the files that were originally inside the folder.

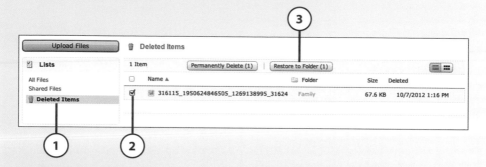

1. Click Deleted Items.
2. Check the box to the left of the files or folders you want to recover.
3. Click Restore to Folder.

Permanently Deleting Files

When you delete a file or folder, it is moved to a Deleted Items folder and continues to use space in your Cloud Drive. To permanently delete these items, click the Permanently Delete button in Deleted Items.

Adding Files to Your Cloud Drive

To add files to your Cloud Drive, you upload them to Amazon.

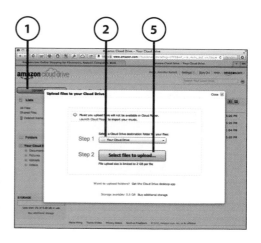

1. Click the Upload Files button near the top-left corner of the Cloud Drive screen.
2. Click the drop-down list to select a folder for your uploaded files.

3. Select your folder.

4. Click Select.

5. Click Select Files to Upload, locate the files on your computer, and select them.

After step 1, you might see a notice about the Amazon Cloud Drive application. You can choose to follow the prompts and download this application or proceed uploading your files using your web browser.

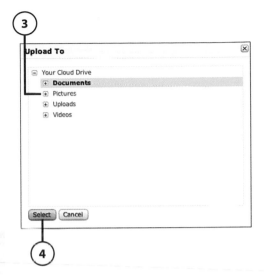

Downloading the Cloud Drive Application

If you use your Cloud Drive on a regular basis, you might find it easier to download and use the Amazon Cloud Drive application. You can download and install it when you see the prompt as you attempt to upload from your web browser, or you can install it at any other time.

1. On your computer, go to www.amazon.com.

2. If the Shop All Departments menu is not already open, hover over it.

3. Point to Amazon Cloud Drive.

4. Click Get the Desktop App.

5. On the page that appears, click Get the Desktop App. The application downloads to your computer. When the download is complete, double-click the file to initiate the installation procedure.

6. Follow the instructions to install the Amazon Cloud Drive application on your computer.

7. Enter your Amazon account username and password.

8. Click Sign In.

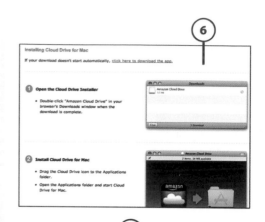

Using the Amazon Cloud Drive Application

After you sign in for the first time, the application provides a few screens with hints on how to get the most out of it. On a Mac, you can either drag files over the Amazon Cloud Drive icon in the menu bar or right-click a file and select Services | Upload to Amazon Cloud Drive (if you're uploading a picture) or simply Upload to Amazon Cloud Drive (if you're uploading a document). On a PC, you can drag files over the Amazon Cloud Drive icon in the taskbar or right-click a file and select Send To | Amazon Cloud Drive.

Accessing Cloud Drive Files from Your Kindle Fire

Your Kindle Fire automatically syncs with your Cloud Drive whenever you have a Wi-Fi connection. Files on your Cloud Drive are automatically sorted into the appropriate content library. If you want to view the photos you uploaded to your Cloud Drive, for example, you can find them in Photos. Personal documents are found in the Docs library.

1. Use the Navigation menu to access the library for the files you want to view. In this example, we access the Docs library.

2. Press the Cloud button if it's not already selected.

3. View a list of the files you have in the cloud for that library.

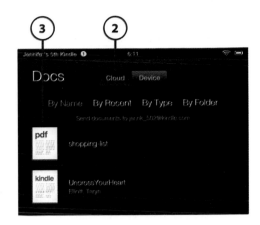

Folders and Subfolders

Folders and subfolders keep your documents organized. When you view your Docs library By Name, By Recent, or By Type, all of your documents are listed no matter how they're grouped in your Cloud Drive. View your docs By Folder to only see documents within a particular folder or subfolder.

Saving Files to Your Device

When you select a document from the Docs library, it is automatically saved onto your Kindle Fire, and you can then open it from either the Cloud or Device options. The process for transferring photos onto your device is a bit different.

1. Select Photos from the navigation bar.

2. Select a photo or folder from the Cloud library.

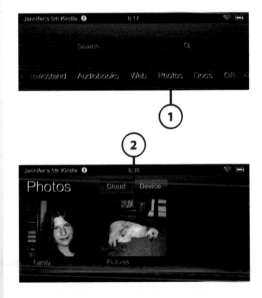

3. Tap the menu button.

4. Select Download.

DOWNLOADING FILES FROM YOUR CLOUD DRIVE TO A COMPUTER

You can also download files from your Cloud Drive onto a PC or Mac or even a tablet or smartphone. Use a web browser to navigate to www.amazon.com, and then sign into your account. Access your Cloud Drive, and then check the boxes to the left of the content you want to download. Click Download and select the folder where you want to save the file.

Amazon Cloud Player

Amazon Cloud Player is a convenient way to manage music on your Cloud Drive. You can also use it to listen to your music when you don't have your Kindle Fire with you, because it is available from any computer with Internet access or on most mobile devices.

Your Music   **Album**   **Songs**

Play Controls   **Now Playing**

Launching Cloud Player

You can access Amazon Cloud Player from your web browser.

1. Open your web browser and go to www.amazon.com.

2. Point to MP3s & Cloud Player on the menu.

3. Click Cloud Player for Web. If prompted, enter your e-mail address and Amazon password.

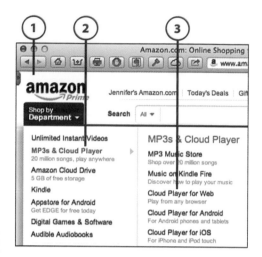

Amazon Cloud Player on the Kindle Fire

Although you can use Silk to access Cloud Player, doing so doesn't make sense. The Music screen on your Kindle Fire provides access to all your Cloud Drive music.

Importing Your Music

You can easily upload your music to Amazon Cloud Player. You can upload up to 250 songs for free or upgrade to a Premium account that stores up to 250,000 songs for $24.99 a year.

1. Open the Amazon Cloud Player.

2. Click Import Your Music.

3. Click the Download Now button to download the Amazon Music Importer application, and follow the installation instructions.

4. Open the Amazon Music Importer application.

5. Authorize your computer by giving the device a name.

6. Click Authorize Device.

7. Click Start Scan. The Amazon Music Importer application scans your hard drive, including your iTunes folders, for music.

8. After the scan is complete, you might be prompted to choose to upgrade to Cloud Player Premium for $24.99 a year or to select up to 250 songs free.

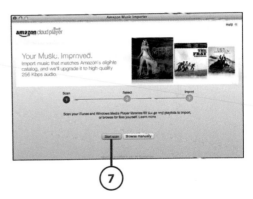

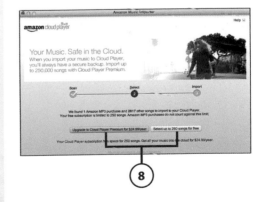

9. To select which songs to import into your Cloud Player, check the boxes to the left of the song, album, artist, or playlist title. You can also choose to import the 250 songs you most recently played on your computer.

10. Click Import Selected.

11. When the import is finished, click Close.

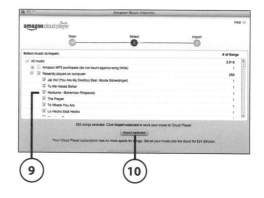

Music that you purchase directly from Amazon's MP3 Store is automatically added to your Amazon Cloud Player. It also does not count against your 250 song or Premium storage limitation.

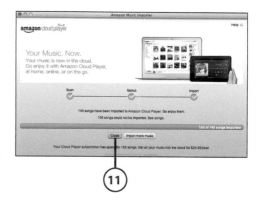

>>>Go Further

CONVERTING YOUR MUSIC

The Amazon Cloud Player can import music in either MP3 or unprotected AAC (iTunes) format. If your music is in some other format, you can find free converters by searching the Internet.

Playing Music on Your Computer

You can stream music from the Cloud Player without downloading the music to your computer.

1. Locate the music you want to play. You can browse by song, album, artist, or genre.

2. Click the check box next to one or more songs to select the songs to play. You can also check the box at the top of the list to select all songs that are displayed.

3. Click the Play button.

4. To go to the next song, click the Next button.

5. To go to the previous song, click the Previous button.

Shuffle and Repeat Songs

You can shuffle or repeat the songs you are playing by clicking the Repeat or Random button under the large Play button in the lower-left corner of Cloud Player.

Creating Playlists

You can create playlists of songs to play only the songs you want to hear. Playlists are a great way to make a song list for a party or special event. Playlists you create in Cloud Player are also available on your Kindle Fire.

1. Select the songs you want to add to your playlist.

2. Click the Add to Playlist button.

3. If you haven't created a playlist, enter a name for a new playlist. Otherwise, choose New Playlist or an existing playlist for the selected songs.

4. Browse to other songs, and add them to your playlist as desired.

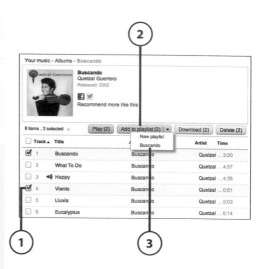

Refreshing Cloud Drive

Your Cloud Drive refreshes on your Kindle Fire every 10 minutes. Songs or playlists that you add appear after a refresh. If you're in a hurry to get your songs or playlists onto your Kindle Fire, swipe down from the status bar on your Kindle Fire to open the Settings drawer, and then choose Sync.

Downloading Songs to Your Kindle Fire

If you plan to be away from an Internet connection, you can still play your music by first downloading it to your Kindle Fire.

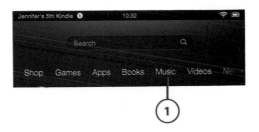

1. On the navigation bar of your Kindle Fire, press Music.

2. In the Cloud tab, select a playlist, artist, album, or song.

3. Click the Download All button.

4. If you want to exclude some songs for an artist or album from being downloaded, select the X to the right of the song title. When the download is complete, press Device to confirm that your music is now stored on your Kindle Fire.

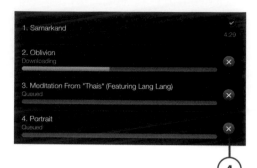

Downloading Songs to a Computer

If you want to download your music to a computer, use a web browser to access the Amazon Cloud Player. Select the songs you want to download and then click the Download button. You are prompted to download and install the Amazon MP3 Downloader if it hasn't previously been installed. After the MP3 Downloader is installed, clicking the Download button automatically downloads a link to the selected music to your computer. Double-click the downloaded file, and the MP3 Downloader imports the music into iTunes or Windows Media Player on your computer.

>>>Go Further
CHANGING MP3 DOWNLOADER OPTIONS

The MP3 Downloader detects whether you have iTunes installed. If you do, after it downloads a song, it automatically imports that song into iTunes. This saves you the trouble of importing your music to your iTunes library. If you don't like this behavior, however, you can change it. You can also change the folder where MP3 Downloader saves the songs you download.

To change MP3 Downloader options, click File | Preferences (on a Mac, click Amazon MP3 Downloader | Preferences). You can click the Save Downloads To option to save your songs to a different folder. You can also deselect the check box Add Downloaded Tracks to iTunes.

Changing these settings is best done before you start downloading songs. You can find the MP3 Downloader on your PC in the Amazon folder on your Start menu. On the Mac, you can locate it in your Applications folder.

Changing How Amazon Handles Purchased Music

You can choose whether Amazon automatically downloads your purchased music to your computer.

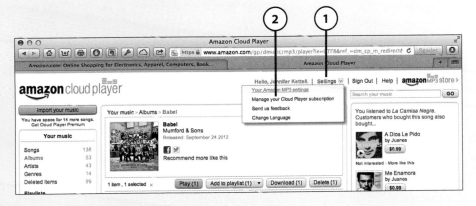

1. Click Settings from the Amazon Cloud Player.

2. Select Your Amazon MP3 Settings. Enter your e-mail address and password, if prompted.

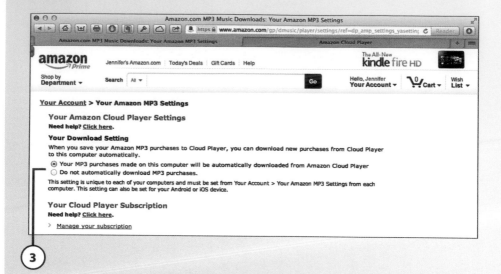

3. Choose whether music added to your Cloud Drive should be downloaded to your computer.

   This setting is computer dependent, not linked to your Amazon account. If you access your Amazon account from multiple computers, you need to change this setting on each computer.

Amazon Instant Video

Amazon has a huge selection of videos, including both movies and television programs, that you can watch on your Kindle Fire. You can also watch those videos on your computer. You can even purchase or rent videos on your computer and watch them on your Kindle Fire, or vice versa.

Getting Videos from Amazon Instant Video

You can use your computer to buy, rent, or stream Amazon Instant Video. Videos that you buy or rent are available on your computer, on your Kindle Fire, or on any other device that supports Amazon Instant Video.

1. Open your web browser and go to www.amazon.com/instantvideo. Or go to www.amazon.com and select Amazon Instant Video from the Shop by Department menu.

2. Select the movie or TV show that you want to watch.

3. Choose to purchase, rent, or watch your video. Not all options are available for all titles.

Choosing HD Movies

If you have one of the HD models of the Kindle Fire, you can choose to watch movies and TV shows in high definition. These are designated with a blue HD band when you choose a video. Videos that are available in multiple formats have links to access the other formats.

>>>Go Further

WHY RENT OR BUY INSTEAD OF STREAM FREE PRIME VIDEO?

If you're an Amazon Prime member, you might be able to watch a title free, but you still might want to rent it instead. Why? If you want to watch on your Kindle Fire and you don't have Wi-Fi access, such as on a long car trip, you need to first download the movie or TV show. You can download only videos that you've either purchased or rented.

If you rent a video, you have 30 days to begin watching it before it expires. After you begin watching it, you have 48 hours to complete it before the rental expires.

Kindle Reader Applications and Kindle Cloud Reader

In addition to reading on your Kindle Fire, Amazon offers free Kindle Reading apps for the PC, the Mac, and most mobile and tablet devices. All these applications enable you to access your Kindle books from the Amazon Cloud and save them to your computer or device to read offline. You can also access your Kindle books from the Kindle Cloud Reader on the Internet.

Accessing Kindle Reader Applications

Before you can read Kindle books on your computer, tablet, or smartphone, you must download and install the appropriate app.

1. In a web browser, go to www.amazon.com.

2. In the Shop By Department menu, choose Kindle, and then choose Free Kindle Reading Apps.

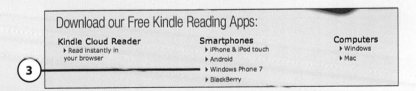

3. Select your computer or device and follow the directions for downloading and installing the appropriate app.

Downloading Smartphone and Tablet Apps

The information pages for each of the smartphone and tablet apps (iPhone and iPod Touch, Android, Windows Phone, BlackBerry, iPad, and Android Tablet) have links to the appropriate store or marketplace to download the required application.

Accessing Kindle Cloud Reader

The Kindle Cloud Reader makes it possible to read your Kindle books in your web browser from any location with Internet access. Kindle Cloud Reader requires a current version of either Google Chrome (www.google.com/chrome), Apple Safari (www.apple.com/safari), or Firefox (www.getfirefox.com).

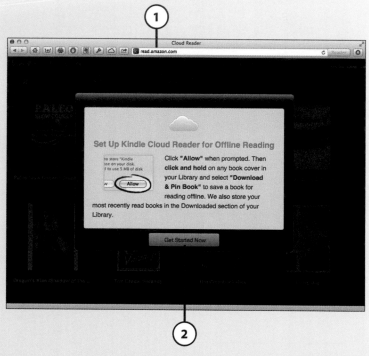

1. Browse to read.amazon.com using your web browser. You can also go to www.amazon.com, choose Kindle from the Shop by Department menu, and then select Kindle Cloud Reader.

2. Click the Get Started Now button.

3. Enter your e-mail address and Amazon password, if prompted.

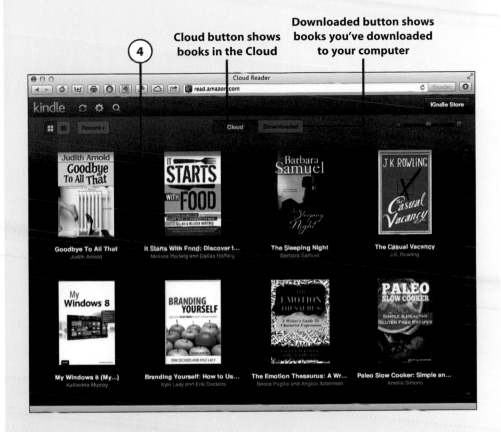

Cloud button shows books in the Cloud

Downloaded button shows books you've downloaded to your computer

4. View your Kindle Library in your browser window.

Opening and Downloading Books

When you select a book, the Kindle Reader apps or Amazon Cloud Reader automatically begin downloading it to your device or computer. This makes the book available even if you continue reading offline.

1. Locate the book you want to read. You can click the magnifying glass at the top of the screen to search for books, if necessary.

2. Click a book to start reading it. If you are using the Kindle Cloud Reader, the book begins downloading to your computer as you read. If you are using one of the other Kindle Reader apps, the book downloads to your device and then allows you to read it.

3. If you want to download a book without immediately beginning to read in the Kindle Cloud Reader and computer Kindle Reader apps, right-click the book and click Download & Pin book. In the smartphone Kindle Reader apps, press and hold the book until a Download button appears; then press that button.

Reading Books on the Kindle Cloud Reader

The Kindle Cloud Reader has many features to make reading a book more enjoyable. The other Kindle Reader applications are similar but might have slight differences in the location and method for accessing some features.

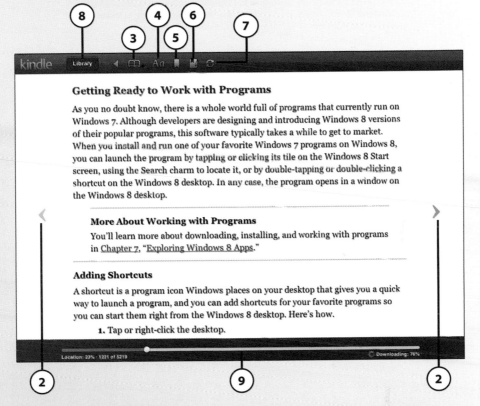

1. Open a book as described in the previous section. If the book has been opened previously on any Kindle device, it automatically opens at the farthest point read.

2. To turn pages, use the arrow keys on your keyboard or click the arrows on the left and right sides of the page.

3. Quickly access a part of the book using the Go To menu.

4. Change font size, margins, and color settings using the View Settings button.

5. Bookmark a page using the Bookmark button.

6. View notes and highlights using the Show Notes and Marks button.

7. Synchronize with your other Kindle devices using the Synchronize button.

8. Click the Library button to return to your library.

9. See where you are in the book using the location bar.

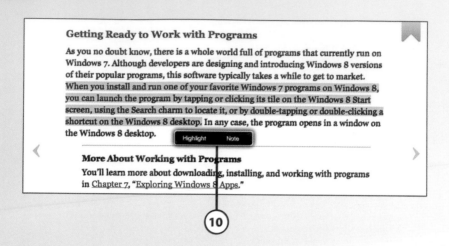

Getting Ready to Work with Programs

As you no doubt know, there is a whole world full of programs that currently run on Windows 7. Although developers are designing and introducing Windows 8 versions of their popular programs, this software typically takes a while to get to market. When you install and run one of your favorite Windows 7 programs on Windows 8, you can launch the program by tapping or clicking its tile on the Windows 8 Start screen, using the Search charm to locate it, or by double-tapping or double-clicking a shortcut on the Windows 8 desktop. In any case, the program opens in a window on the Windows 8 desktop.

More About Working with Programs

You'll learn more about downloading, installing, and working with programs in Chapter 7, "Exploring Windows 8 Apps."

10. To add Notes or Highlights, use your mouse to select the passage you want to mark; then right-click and choose to create a Note or Highlight.

Transferring Files from Your Computer

Most of the content you view on your Kindle Fire is available directly from Amazon and can be easily accessed from the Amazon Cloud. You can also transfer books, videos, music, and other files from other online sources or your personal library. This is known as *sideloading*. To get this content onto your Kindle Fire, transfer the files via the micro-USB cable that came with your device.

Kindle File Types

You can transfer the following types of files onto your Kindle Fire:

- **Books and documents:** AZW, TXT, PDF, MOBI, PRC, DOC, and DOCX formats

- **Audio (Music):** MP3, Non-DRM AAC (.m4a), MIDI, OGG, and WAV formats

- **Video:** MP4 format

- **Images:** JPEG, GIF, PNG, and BMP formats

The Kindle Fire cannot read Mobipocket files that utilize Digital Rights Management (DRM) protection. The Kindle Fire also does not support EPUB books. If you want to read EPUB books on your Kindle Fire, you must convert them to another format and then sideload them. You can find information about this in Chapter 5, "Managing Content with Calibre."

Transferring Files from a PC

If you're using Windows Vista or later, the Kindle Fire automatically shows up as an available external USB drive.

1. Connect your Kindle Fire to your PC using the micro-USB cable.

2. In Windows Explorer, click Computer.

3. Click Kindle.

4. Double-click Internal Storage.

5. Copy your files from their original location on your PC into the appropriate folders in the Internal Storage folder.

Using Windows XP

If you're using Windows XP, you need to update Windows Media Player to transfer files to your Kindle Fire. Windows Media Player 11 for Windows XP is located at www.microsoft.com/en-us/download/details.aspx?id=8163.

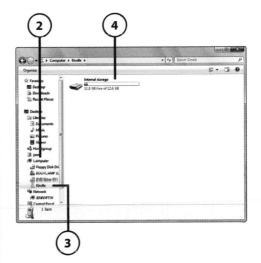

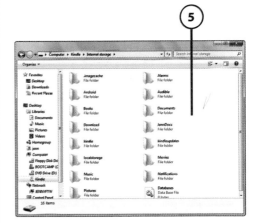

Transferring Files from a Mac

If you're using a Mac, you must download Android File Transfer, a free app, before you can transfer files using USB.

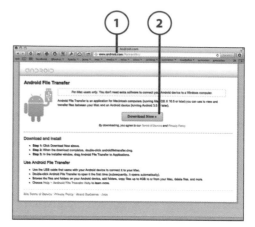

1. In your web browser, go to www.android.com/filetransfer.

2. Click the Download Now button, and follow the instructions to install Android File Transfer to your Applications folder.

3. Use the micro-USB cable to connect your Kindle Fire to your Mac.

4. Double-click the Android File Transfer app to open it. After you've opened it for the first time, it automatically opens whenever you connect your Kindle Fire to your Mac.

5. Copy your files from their original location on your Mac into the appropriate folders in the Android File Transfer app.

TRANSFERRING FILES FROM LINUX

If you're a Linux user, you can transfer files to your Kindle Fire using a Media Transfer Protocol (MTP) USB driver. You can find more information about connecting your device using MTP at http://research.jacquette.com/jmtpfs-exchanging-files-between-android-devices-and-linux/.

**Manage
Content**

**Manage
Devices**

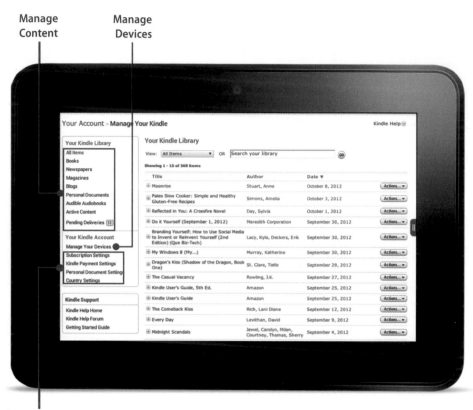

Your Account > **Manage Your Kindle**   Kindle Help ▼

Your Kindle Library

Your Kindle Library

All Items   View: All Items   ▼   OR   Search your library   GO
Books
Newspapers   Showing 1 – 15 of 368 items
Magazines
Blogs   Title   Author   Date ▼
Personal Documents   ⊞ Moonrise   Stuart, Anne   October 8, 2012   Actions... ▼
Audible Audiobooks   ⊞ Paleo Slow Cooker: Simple and Healthy   Simons, Amelia   October 3, 2012   Actions... ▼
Active Content   Gluten-Free Recipes
Pending Deliveries 11   ⊞ Reflected in You: A Crossfire Novel   Day, Sylvia   October 1, 2012   Actions... ▼

Your Kindle Account   ⊞ Do it Yourself (September 1, 2012)   Meredith Corporation   September 30, 2012   Actions... ▼

Manage Your Devices   Branding Yourself: How to Use Social Media
                         ⊞ to Invent or Reinvent Yourself (2nd   Lacy, Kyle, Deckers, Erik   September 30, 2012   Actions... ▼
Subscription Settings   Edition) (Que Biz-Tech)
Kindle Payment Settings ⊞ My Windows 8 (My....)   Murray, Katherine   September 30, 2012   Actions... ▼
Personal Document Settings
Country Settings   ⊞ Dragon's Kiss (Shadow of the Dragon, Book   St. Clare, Tielle   September 29, 2012   Actions... ▼
                            One)
                         ⊞ The Casual Vacancy   Rowling, J.K.   September 27, 2012   Actions... ▼
Kindle Support
                         ⊞ Kindle User's Guide, 5th Ed.   Amazon   September 25, 2012   Actions... ▼
Kindle Help Home
Kindle Help Forum   ⊞ Kindle User's Guide   Amazon   September 25, 2012   Actions... ▼
Getting Started Guide
                         ⊞ The Comeback Kiss   Rich, Lani Diane   September 12, 2012   Actions... ▼

                         ⊞ Every Day   Levithan, David   September 9, 2012   Actions... ▼

                         ⊞ Midnight Scandals   Jewel, Carolyn, Milan,   September 4, 2012   Actions... ▼
                                                            Courtney, Thomas, Sherry

**Manage Your
Account**

In this chapter, you learn how you can use Amazon's Manage Your Kindle page to keep track of your books and subscriptions, and manage your payment and device information. Topics include the following:

→ Managing your books and docs
→ Managing subscriptions
→ Updating Kindle payment information
→ Managing your Kindle devices

Using Amazon's Manage Your Kindle Page

Amazon's Manage Your Kindle page is a one-stop location for managing your Kindle content and your Kindle device. If you have multiple Kindle devices, the Manage Your Kindle Page is even more useful.

You can use the Manage Your Kindle page to send books from your Kindle library to any of your Kindle devices. You can also use it to see the periodicals you subscribe to, and you can manage those subscriptions as well. Links enable you to manage your method of payment to Amazon so that items you purchase on your Kindle Fire get charged to the right credit card. Finally, you can register and deregister Kindles and rename your devices from the Manage Your Kindle page.

Managing Your Books and Docs

You can view all the books and docs in your library using Manage Your Kindle. You can also transfer them to your Kindle. Books are eBooks that you have purchased from Amazon's Kindle store. Your docs can also be eBooks that you purchased from a source other than Amazon. Docs that you see listed in Manage Your Kindle have been e-mailed to your kindle.com e-mail address for document conversion. Manage Your Kindle doesn't list docs that you load to your Kindle Fire using the micro-USB cable (a process known as *sideloading*).

What's Up with Docs?

When I talk about "docs," I'm talking about Kindle Personal Documents. I use the term *docs* because the Kindle Fire uses the Docs screen for your Personal Documents.

Chapter 11, "Managing Your Personal Documents and Data," covers docs in detail.

Accessing Manage Your Kindle

Manage Your Kindle is a web page that you access using the web browser on your computer or using Silk on your Kindle Fire.

1. In your web browser, go to www.amazon.com.

2. Hover over the Your Account drop-down menu.

3. Choose Manage Your Kindle. If prompted, log in using your e-mail address and Amazon password.

A Faster Way to Manage Your Kindle

You can get to the Manage Your Kindle page directly by going to www.amazon.com/manageyourkindle in your web browser.

Viewing Books and Docs

Manage Your Kindle's default view lists your Kindle books, but you can view other content types as well. I talk about handling newspapers and magazines in the next section. This section covers just books and docs.

From the Manage Your Kindle page, you can select the type of content you want to view using the View drop-down list. You can sort content by title, author, or date by clicking one of the column headers. The first click of a column header sorts in descending order; clicking the same column header again sorts that column in ascending order.

If you want to see details on an item, click the plus sign next to the item title. If you have a lot of content and you want to search for a particular item, enter a search term and click Go.

Select the type of content you want to see from the View drop-down.

Search for an item by entering a search term.

Click a column header to order the list.

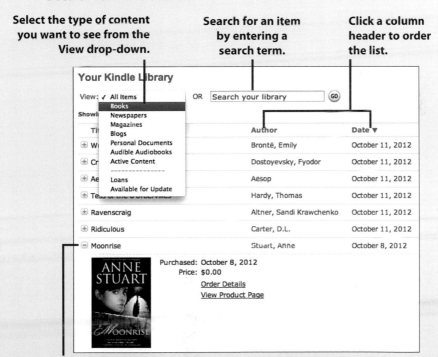

View item details by clicking the plus sign next to the title.

Why Use Manage Your Kindle?

A lot of the functionality in Manage Your Kindle, such as transferring a book from the Amazon cloud to your device, can be accomplished directly on your Kindle Fire. However, if you want to lend a book to another Kindle user, permanently delete a book from your Kindle Library, or deliver a book to another Kindle device, you accomplish those tasks through Manage Your Kindle. It's also a convenient way to manage content on multiple Kindle devices or to manage your account when someone else in the family is using your Kindle Fire.

Sending Books and Docs to Your Kindle

You can send books and docs to a Kindle device or to the Kindle apps for Android, iPad, iPhone, and iPod Touch. You can send books, but not docs, to the other Kindle apps. Content is delivered within a minute, assuming you are connected to Wi-Fi.

Kindle Apps

When I mention Kindle apps in this chapter, I'm not talking about apps installed on your Kindle Fire. I'm talking about the Kindle app that you can use on a computer, tablet, or smartphone to read Kindle eBooks.

1. Locate the book or doc that you want to send to your Kindle.

2. Point to the Actions drop-down list.

3. Click Deliver to My.

4. Select the device from the drop-down list. If the doc you are sending to your Kindle isn't in a format supported by a particular device, that device is not available in the drop-down list.

5. Click Deliver.

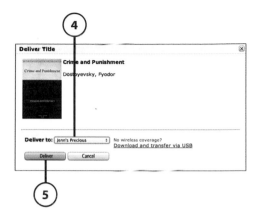

Downloading Books to a Computer

You can also download books (but not docs) to your computer. After you download a book, you can side-load it to your Kindle Fire using the micro-USB cable.

1. Point to the Actions drop-down list.

2. Click Download & Transfer via USB.

3. Select the Kindle to which you plan to transfer the book.

4. Click Download and save the book using your browser's download option.

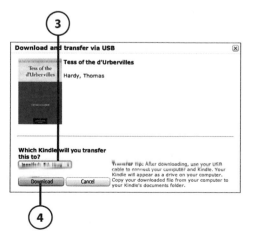

WHEN TO DOWNLOAD TO A COMPUTER

If you do not have access to Wi-Fi (or 4G) at home, you can still get content onto your Kindle Fire via USB. If you have a laptop, you can connect to Wi-Fi at a coffeeshop or library and follow the procedure just described to download books to your computer. Your books are then available for you to transfer onto your Kindle Fire via the micro-USB cable at your convenience. You can also sign onto a public computer at an Internet cafe or library, store the books on a flash drive, and then copy them onto your home computer. Transfer the books onto your Kindle Fire using the methods described in the "Transferring Files from Your Computer" section of Chapter 2, "Loading Your Kindle Fire."

Deleting Books and Docs

You can delete books and docs from your library if you do not want to reread them. Use this feature with caution because doing so removes the item permanently. If you delete a book that you purchased from Amazon, you have to buy it again if you change your mind.

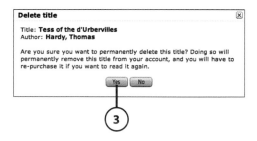

1. Point to the Actions drop-down list.

2. Click Delete from Library.

3. Click Yes to confirm that you want to permanently delete the book from your library.

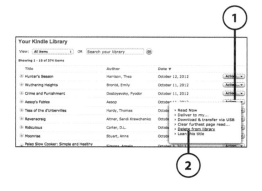

Changing Your Kindle E-mail Address

Use your Kindle e-mail address to send docs directly to your Kindle. You can change the e-mail address for your Kindle Fire on the Manage Your Kindle page.

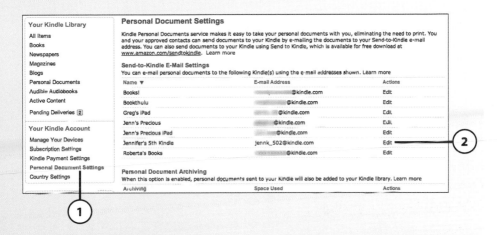

1. Click Personal Document Settings.
2. Click Edit next to the Kindle e-mail address you want to change.

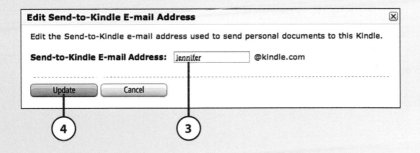

3. Enter the new e-mail address.
4. Click Update.

Adding an Approved E-mail for Docs

To prevent spam on your Kindle device, Amazon delivers only docs e-mailed from an approved list of senders. You can add an approved e-mail address using Personal Documents Settings.

1. From Personal Documents Settings, click Add a New Approved E-mail Address in the Approved Personal Document E-mail List section.

2. Enter the e-mail address you want to approve. You can also enter a partial e-mail address, such as *yourcompany*.com, to allow all senders from that particular domain.

3. Click Add Address.

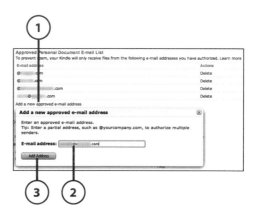

Deleting an Approved E-mail Address

You can delete an approved e-mail address by clicking Delete to the right of the e-mail address on the Approved Personal Document E-mail List.

PUTTING YOUR KINDLE E-MAIL ADDRESS TO WORK

Go Further

Some non-Amazon online bookstores, such as www.fictionwise.com, deliver purchases directly to your Kindle account if you provide them with your Kindle e-mail address. Be sure to add these providers to your approved e-mail list and follow the bookstore site's instructions about adding your Kindle address to your bookstore account before making a purchase.

Disabling Doc Archiving

By default, docs that are sent to your Kindle are also saved in your Kindle library. Amazon gives you 5GB of space for personal doc archiving. You can disable the archiving of personal docs.

1. From Personal Document Settings, click Edit in the Personal Document Archiving section.

2. Deselect the box to disable archiving.

3. Click Update.

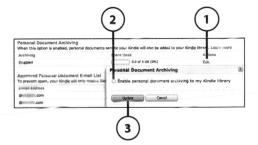

Double the Docs Space

The 5GB of personal doc storage in your Kindle library is separate from the 5GB of storage on your Amazon Cloud Drive, which you can also use for docs (among other files). I recommend saving the Kindle personal doc space for eBook purchases from other bookstores because it is e-mail accessible and using your Amazon Cloud Drive to store your other personal documents. This has the added benefit of keeping all your truly personal docs together on the Amazon Cloud Drive, which makes them easier to manage and organize.

Managing Subscriptions

You can also manage your subscriptions from the Manage Your Kindle page. You can choose which device gets your subscription automatically, send past issues to your Kindle Fire, or download past issues so that you can sideload them to your Kindle Fire. Finally, you can cancel your subscription altogether.

Changing Where a Subscription Is Delivered

You choose which device receives the automatic delivery of subscription content when you first subscribe. If you subscribe from your Kindle Fire, it automatically receives the subscription. You can change that choice from Manage Your Kindle. This option is available only if you have multiple Kindle devices registered.

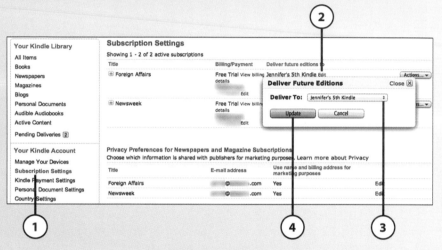

1. Click Subscription Settings.

2. Click Edit for the subscription you want to change.

3. Select a device to which new editions should be delivered.

4. Click Update.

Canceling a Subscription

Subscriptions are automatically charged on a monthly basis, even if the magazine arrives on your Kindle Fire on a different distribution schedule. If you want to cancel a subscription, you can do it from Manage Your Kindle.

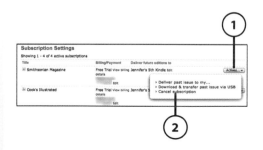

1. From Subscription Settings, click Actions for the subscription you want to cancel.

2. Click Cancel Subscription.

3. Select one or more reasons for canceling.

4. Enter a comment if you select Other.

5. Click Cancel Subscription.

Access to Past Issues for Canceled Subscriptions

If you cancel a subscription, any issues that have been download-ed to your Kindle Fire remain in your library. However, you won't be able to download any past issues. Be sure you've download-ed all the issues for which you've paid before you cancel.

Cancel your Kindle Subscription   Close ☒

Please confirm the cancellation of your Kindle Subscription to:

Subscription Title: **Smithsonian Magazine**

End Date: **Saturday, October 13, 2012**

Optional: **Please help us improve and let us know why you're canceling this subscription (select all that apply)**

☐ Did not have enough images
☐ Missing articles or sections
☐ Want a better way to find the articles I want to read
☐ Price is too high
☐ Do not have time to read
☐ Read it in other format
☐ Other

[Cancel Subscription]

Reactivating a Canceled Subscription

Amazon maintains a list of all your inactive subscriptions. You can use this list to easily reactivate a canceled subscription.

1. From Subscription Settings, click View Inactive Subscriptions.

2. Clilck Actions for the subscription you want to reactivate.

3. Click Reactivate Subscription.

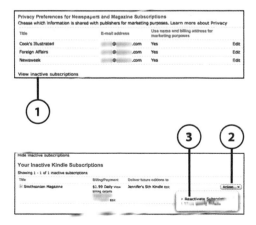

4. Click Reactivate Subscription in the confirmation dialog box.

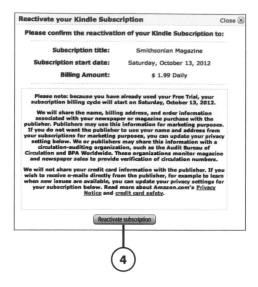

Reactivate your Kindle Subscription   Close ⊠

Please confirm the reactivation of your Kindle Subscription to:

Subscription title:	Smithsonian Magazine
Subscription start date:	Saturday, October 13, 2012
Billing Amount:	$ 1.99 Daily

Please note: because you have already used your Free Trial, your subscription billing cycle will start on Saturday, October 13, 2012.

We will share the name, billing address, and order information associated with your newspaper or magazine purchase with the publisher. Publishers may use this information for marketing purposes. If you do not want the publisher to use your name and address from your subscriptions for marketing purposes, you can update your privacy setting below. We or publishers may share this information with a circulation-auditing organization, such as the Audit Bureau of Circulation and BPA Worldwide. These organizations monitor magazine and newspaper sales to provide verification of circulation numbers.

We will not share your credit card information with the publisher. If you wish to receive e-mails directly from the publisher, for example to learn when new issues are available, you can update your privacy settings for your subscription below. Read more about Amazon.com's Privacy Notice and credit card safety.

[Reactivate subscription]

④

Why Is the Actions Button Missing?

If you have deregistered the Kindle to which an active subscription was being delivered, the Actions button is missing. Before you can reactivate the subscription, you first need to select a Kindle to which the subscription should be delivered.

It's Not All Good

Resubscribing During the Free Trial

Subscriptions typically begin with a free trial period, during which you receive one or more issues. If you do nothing after the free trial, you are automatically billed the monthly rate. If you cancel a subscription during the free trial and then resubscribe, however, you are billed immediately.

Changing Subscription Privacy Settings

Amazon does not share your e-mail address with content providers unless you explicitly give permission to do so. You can do that using subscription privacy settings.

1. From Subscription Settings, locate Privacy Preferences for Newspapers and Magazine Subscriptions.

2. Click Edit for the subscription you want to modify.

3. Check the box(es) for the information you want to share with the content provider.

4. If you want your settings to be the default for future subscriptions, check the appropriate box.

5. Click Update.

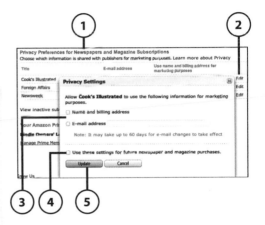

Updating Kindle Payment Information

You can change the credit card that Amazon uses for purchases and for current subscriptions.

Changing Amazon Purchases Credit Cards

When you buy Kindle books and MP3s, and rent or purchase Amazon videos, the credit card used for 1-Click purchases at Amazon.com is billed automatically. You can change this credit card information, add a new credit card, or choose a different credit card using Manage Your Kindle.

Multiple Credit Cards

Amazon can store several cards for your account, and you can choose which one is used for your 1-Click purchases on the Manage Your Kindle page. Keep in mind that changing your credit card does not change the credit card used for your subscriptions; you must change those separately.

1. Click Kindle Payment Settings.

2. Click Edit.

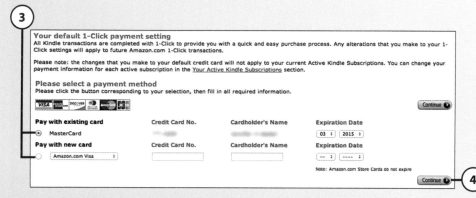

3. Enter your new credit card information, or select a different card.

4. Click Continue.

Changing Current Subscriptions Credit Cards

You must individually update payment options for current subscriptions.

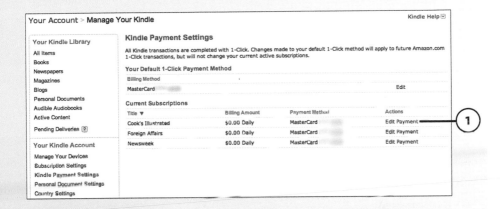

1. From Kindle Payment Settings, click Edit Payment for the subscription you want to change.

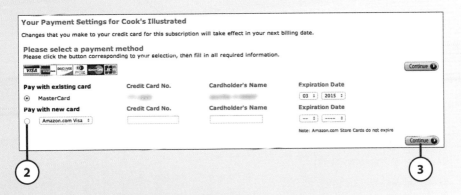

2. Enter the new credit card information.

3. Click Continue.

It's Not All Good

Updating Credit Card Information

Whenever you change your payment information, you need to remember to update each of your subscriptions as well. If you have multiple subscriptions, this can be a time-consuming process, and one easily forgotten when you change your 1-Click account.

Managing Your Kindle Devices

You can add multiple Kindles to your account. Having two or more Kindles registered to the same account is useful if you and other family members have the same tastes in books. If you buy a book on one Kindle, you can read it on another Kindle at the same time without having to buy it again.

The Manage Your Devices page lists all your Kindle devices (including the Kindle app installed on your computer, tablet, or phone). You can deregister a Kindle or change your Kindle's name.

It's Not All Good

Registering a Kindle at Amazon.com

You can also register a new Kindle from the Manage Your Kindle page, but to do so, you need the serial number of the Kindle you're registering. You can't find the serial number for a Kindle Fire without first starting the device and going through the initial setup, part of which is registering the device with Amazon. Therefore, it doesn't make sense to use the Manage Your Kindle page to register a Kindle Fire.

Deregistering a Kindle

If you decide to give away or sell your Kindle Fire, you should deregister it first. This removes the Kindle Fire's access to your account and prevents the new owner from using your credit card information.

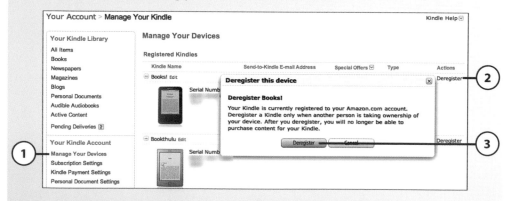

1. From the Manage Your Kindle page, click Manage Your Devices.

2. Locate the Kindle you want to deregister and click Deregister.

3. Click the Deregister button.

Renaming Your Kindle Fire

You can change the name of your Kindle device to make it unique and distinguish it from your other Kindles.

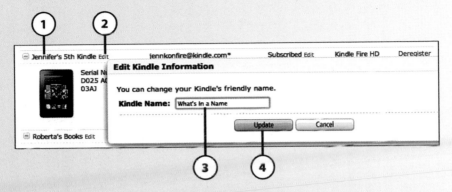

1. From Manage Your Devices, locate the Kindle whose name you want to change.

2. Click Edit next to the existing name.

3. Enter a new name for your Kindle.

4. Click Update.

Naming Your Kindle Fire

The name of your device appears on the Kindle Fire home screen. Unless you want to stare at something like "Jennifer's 2nd Kindle" every day, you might want to change it.

Deregistering a Kindle App

You can also deregister a Kindle app on your computer, tablet, or mobile phone.

1. From Manage Your Devices, locate the Registered Kindle Reading Apps section.

2. Click Deregister for the app you want to deregister.

3. Click the Deregister button.

Why Deregister an App?

If your computer, tablet, or mobile phone is lost or stolen, or if you sell or give it away, you should deregister the Kindle app. That way, no purchases can be made against your account without your knowledge.

Turning Off Whispersync

Whispersync keeps all your devices and Kindle apps synchronized. It synchronizes your reading position, notes, highlights, and more. If you personally use multiple devices or apps when reading a book, you might want to keep Whispersync turned on. If multiple people in your home read Kindles registered to the same account, disable Whispersync so that each device can maintain unique page positions, highlights, and notes for a book.

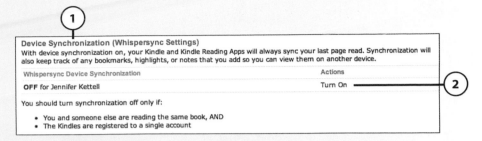

1. In Manage Your Devices, locate the Device Synchronization section.

2. Click Turn Off or Turn On to toggle Whispersync. This change takes effect immediately.

Turning Off Special Offers

Your Kindle Fire displays special offers, ads that appear on the screensaver, at the bottom of the screen, and in the Offers heading of the Navigation bar. You can pay a one-time fee to remove these offers.

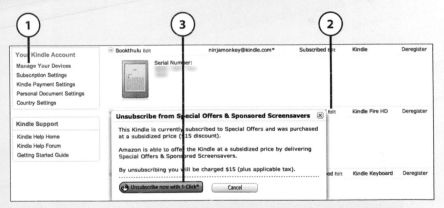

1. In Manage Your Devices, locate the device you want to unsubscribe from special offers.

2. Click Edit in the Special Offers column.

3. Click Unsubscribe Now with 1-Click. Your account is charged $15 to unsubscribe a Kindle Fire from these offers. The cost to unsubscribe other Kindle Devices varies.

Why Should I Have to Pay?

Amazon charges advertising fees for special offers, which they claim subsidizes the cost of the Kindle Fire. Thus, if you opt out, their rationale is that they expect you to pay the projected difference in cost. Many people are not disturbed by the placement of the offers, so I advise you to use your Kindle Fire for a while to see whether removing them is worth the additional cost.

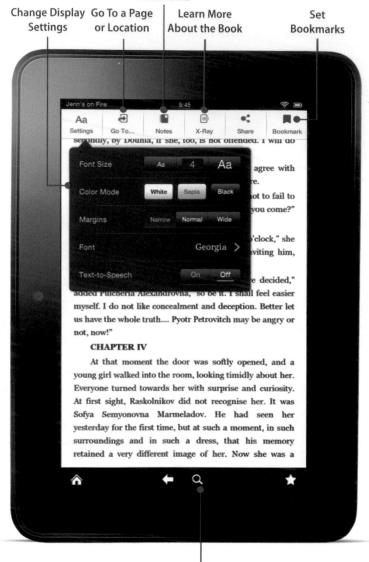

Change Display
Settings

Go To a Page
or Location

View
Notes &
Bookmarks

Learn More
About the Book

Set
Bookmarks

Search Your
Content

In this chapter, you learn about ways that you can find content for your Kindle Fire and how to read and interact with that content. You also discover how you can search your Kindle Fire libraries.

Reading on the Kindle Fire

Your Kindle Fire is a great tablet computer, but it's still a Kindle eBook reader at heart. Its size makes it convenient to carry with you so that you can read your books, magazines, newspapers, and other content no matter where you are. When it's inconvenient for you to look at the page, the Kindle Fire's audiobook immersion and text-to-speech features can even read for you.

Finding Content

Amazon's Kindle Store provides access to a huge assortment of reading content for your Kindle Fire. You can find just about any book you want to read for the Kindle. In addition to books, Amazon offers a wide array of newspapers and magazines. Because your Kindle Fire's screen is full color, reading periodicals can provide a similar experience to reading a glossy magazine. Reading has also become an audi tory experience as much as a visual one, and your Kindle Fire can play audiobooks. If you have both the eBook and audiobook copies of a title, you can immerse yourself in the reading experience, following along with the professional narration, and keep both books in sync.

Your source of great content doesn't stop with Amazon. You can also check out books from your local library, borrow books from friends and family, and even download books from other online eBook stores and websites, and then transfer them to your Kindle Fire.

Accessing Non-Amazon Books

Many other online bookstores deliver your books using your Kindle's e-mail address and the personal document delivery system. You can read more about setting up a unique Kindle e-mail address in Chapter 3, "Using Amazon's Manage Your Kindle Page," and about personal documents in Chapter 11, "Managing Your Personal Documents and Data."

Buying Books

Amazon's Kindle Store has more than 1 million books available for your Kindle Fire.

1. From the Home screen, tap Books.

2. Tap Store.

3. Tap a book that you want to read on your Kindle Fire. View books recommended by Amazon based on previous purchases, current bestsellers, or category.

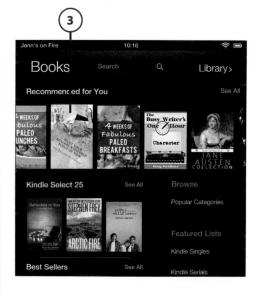

4. If you're trying out a new author or genre, download a free sample first. A free sample is generally the first chapter of a book, sometimes along with the table of contents and other introductory material.

5. Tap Buy to purchase the book and add it to your Kindle library.

Purchasing After Sampling

If you want to try out a new author or genre, download a free sample first. The length of samples varies based on the book. You can purchase the book if you want to continue reading.

1. At the end of the sample, click Buy Now.

2. Click the Buy button.

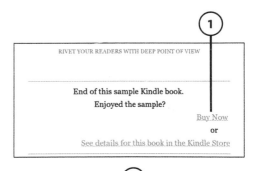

Using the Kindle Lending Library

If you are a Prime subscriber, you can borrow one book per month from the approximately 5,000 books in Amazon's Kindle Owners' Lending Library. You can keep borrowed books as long as you want, but you can borrow only one book in a calendar month.

Check Out Your Local Library

You can also check out Kindle books from thousands of local libraries. To find out if your local library offers this service, go to www.overdrive.com and enter your ZIP Code.

1. From the Home screen, tap Books.

2. Tap Store to open the Kindle Store and locate a book.

3. Locate a book. You can tap Kindle Owners' Lending Library to see a complete list of available titles.

4. If a book is available for borrowing, tap Borrow for Free to borrow the book and add it to your library.

Can't Borrow?

If a book is not available for borrowing, the Borrow for Free button isn't visible. If you've already borrowed a book during the past month, the Borrow for Free button is grayed out.

Only on Kindle Devices

You can borrow or read books from the Kindle Lending Library only on a Kindle device; you cannot borrow or read them from your web browser or any other Kindle app.

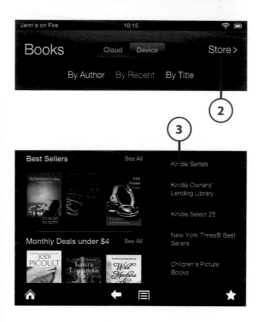

Lending Books to Friends and Family

You can loan some books to friends or family. Your friend or family member isn't required to have a Kindle device to read the book you lend. Loaned books can be read on a computer or other device with the free Kindle application.

1. Open your web browser and go to www.amazon.com/manageyourkindle.

2. Hover your mouse pointer over the Actions drop-down next to the title you want to lend.

3. Click Loan This Title.

4. Enter your friend or family member's information and a personal message.

5. Click Send Now.

What Happens Next?

When you lend a book, the recipient of the book receives an e-mail with a link to accept the request. That person needs an Amazon account to accept and access the book.

Books are loaned for 14 days, and you will not be able to read the book while it is loaned out to someone. You can see the status of the loan on the Manage Your Kindle page.

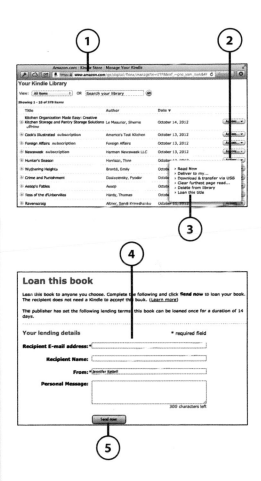

It's Not All Good

Why Can't I Lend My Book?

The publisher of a book decides whether an eBook can be loaned to others. If a publisher hasn't granted that right, the option to lend the book is not available.

You can determine whether a book can be loaned to others by reviewing the Product Details for the book on Amazon's website. If the book can be loaned, it displays "Lending: Enabled." Unfortunately, this information is not available from the Kindle Store listings on the Kindle Fire.

Subscribing to Periodicals

The Kindle Store offers a wide array of newspapers and magazines, including some that are optimized with multimedia content specifically for the Kindle Fire.

1. From the Home screen, tap Newsstand to open the Newsstand.

2. Tap Store to open the Kindle Newsstand.

3. Choose a magazine or newspaper you want to read.

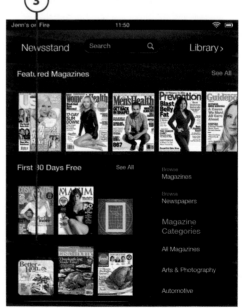

4. Tap Subscribe Now to download the latest edition to your Kindle Fire or Buy Issue to buy and download only the current issue.

Trial Subscriptions

Most periodicals provide a trial subscription, during which you are not charged. Unless you cancel your subscription within the trial period, you are charged the day after the trial concludes and monthly thereafter.

>>>Go Further

SIDELOADING BOOKS

Sources of eBooks abound, even beyond Amazon. After you download a Kindle-compatible eBook, you can transfer it to your Kindle using the micro-USB cable. Manually transferring files from your computer to your Kindle is called sideloading, and Chapter 2, "Loading Your Kindle Fire," covers it.

An easier way to sideload books, if you're using Windows or Linux, is to use Calibre. This application can organize your eBook library and even automatically convert eBooks in non-Kindle formats to a Kindle-compatible format. See Chapter 5, "Managing Content with Calibre," to learn more.

Organizing Your Books

The Kindle has always been a great device for reading. Instead of carrying around a pile of books, you can put everything you want to read on your Kindle. You can easily look up definitions with the integrated dictionary. You can search the Web when you want to read more about something you encounter in a book. You can even increase the size of a book's text to make it easier to read.

Browsing Your Library

After you buy or borrow a book or download a sample from the Kindle Store, it appears in the Books library and in the Carousel on the Home screen. You can view books on your device and in the cloud using the Books library.

1. From the Home screen, tap Books to access your Books library.

2. Tap Device to see content that has been downloaded to your Kindle Fire, or tap Cloud to see content that is in your online library.

3. Tap By Author, By Recent, or By Title to change the order in which your books are sorted.

Downloading a Book to Your Device

Before you can read a book, you must download it to your device.

1. From the Books library, tap Cloud to see the books in your online library.

2. Scroll to the book you want to download to your device.

3. Tap the book to download it to your device. You can also tap and hold the book and then tap Download.

Cloud and Device

When you are in Cloud view, you see books that are also on your device. That's because, even after you download a book to your device, it's still in the cloud so that you can download it to other Kindles or devices.

Books that you have downloaded to your device have a check mark in the lower-right corner.

Removing a Book from Your Device

You can remove downloaded books from your Kindle Fire to free up memory on the device. Your books will still be available in the cloud, so you can download them again at any time.

1. From the Books library, tap Device to see the books on your device.

2. Scroll to the book that you want to remove from your device.

3. Tap and hold the book.

4. Tap Remove from Device.

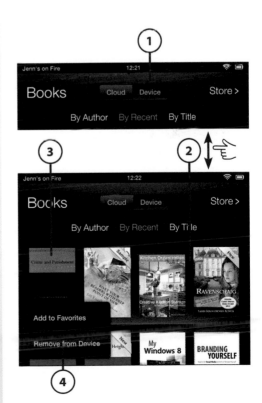

Reading on Your Kindle

The Kindle Fire is a great device for reading. Its backlit screen allows you to easily read in low-light conditions without a reading light. Your book always opens to the page you last read, so you don't have to worry about dog-earing pages or losing your place. If you don't know the meaning of a word, you can look up the definition on the spot.

My Book Doesn't Open on Page One

Kindle books open at the beginning of the book, but the beginning isn't necessarily page one. The publisher of an eBook can choose any page as the beginning of a book. eBooks frequently open at a point after the front matter—the cover, table of contents, foreword, and dedication. You can use the Go To button to access this material.

Reading a Book

Books appear in your Books library and on the Home screen Carousel. Reading a book on the Kindle Fire is as simple as tapping your finger.

1. From the Books library or the Carousel, tap a book to open it for reading.

2. Tap the right side of a page or swipe from right to left to move forward one page.

3. Tap the left side of a page or swipe from left to right to move back one page.

Where Are the Page Numbers?

Some eBooks use location numbers; others use traditional page numbers. Because text can be repaginated based on the text size you use, location numbers provide a better sense of where you are in the book.

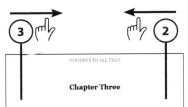

Navigating a Book

You can quickly access any page in a book, including the front matter.

1. Tap the center of the page.

2. Swipe the Location slider to move forward or backward within the book.

3. Tap the Go To button.

4. Tap the Go to Page or Location button to go to a specific location or page number.

5. Tap Sync to Furthest Page Read to return to the furthest page you've read in the book. If you have Whispersync turned on, as explained in Chapter 3, this button syncs to the furthest page you read on any of your Kindle devices or apps.

6. Tap Beginning to return to the first page of the book.

7. Tap Cover to see the book cover.

8. Tap Front Matter or a specific front matter element to see the table of contents, copyright page, and any other front matter the publisher chose to include.

9. Tap a chapter to go to the beginning of that chapter.

10. Tap the Back arrow to return to the page you were reading.

It's Not All Good

E Ink Versus LCD

Kindle devices have two types of displays: the E Ink on the Kindle e-readers and the LCD screen on the Kindle Fire. E Ink screens look very much like the printed page. They are very easy to read, and because they don't rely on a backlight, you can read an E Ink display in bright sunlight just as you can a printed page. The Kindle Paperwhite models shine light from above the E Ink, much like attaching a book light to your book or device, making it easy to read even in bed at night.

An LCD screen also has its own light source, but it's shined from the back of the display. Many people feel that reading an LCD screen is irritating to the eyes and can interfere with the body's circadian rhythm when viewed right before bed. However, because the Kindle Fire's screen is not as large as a computer monitor, it's generally less tiring to read on it.

Perhaps the biggest drawback to an LCD screen is that it can't be read comfortably in bright sunlight. Even the best LCD screens are washed out in bright daylight, and your Kindle Fire suffers from that same drawback. Don't expect to spend much time reading your Kindle Fire while relaxing on the beach. LCD screens also consume battery life faster, so if you take your Kindle Fire to the beach, plan to recharge by the end of the day.

Changing Font Styles

You can change the size of fonts, line spacing, page margins, and colors when reading Kindle content.

1. Tap the center of a page while you're reading.

2. Tap the Settings icon.

3. Tap the Font Size option to make the text larger or smaller. You can tap the appropriate button multiple times to get the size you want. The number between the larger and smaller buttons tells you the relative size of the font.

4. Tap a Color Mode to change the color of the page background and text.

5. Tap a Margins option to change the way the page is spread across the display.

6. Tap the Font option to select a different typeface.

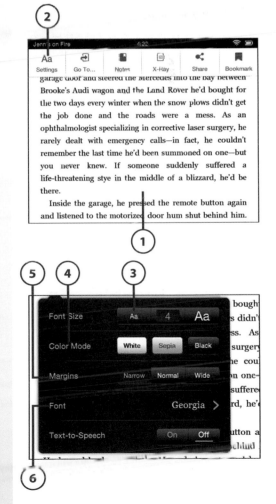

7. Choose a typeface from the options available.

Font Size and Typeface Are Not Just in Books

You can change font size and typeface settings in books, newspapers, personal documents, and magazines.

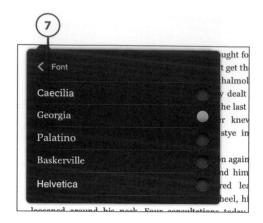

Looking Up Definitions

Your Kindle Fire comes with *The New Oxford American Dictionary* so that you can look up definitions of words while you're reading. Definitions are available from books, magazines, newspapers, and your personal documents.

1. Tap and hold the word you want to look up. A definition of the word displays.

2. Tap your book page to dismiss the pop-up definition.

3. Tap Full Definition to open the dictionary and see a more detailed definition.

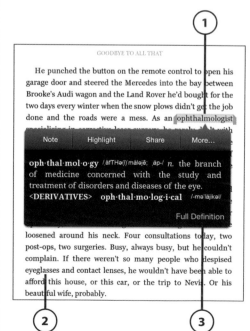

4. To return to your book after viewing a full definition, tap the center of the screen and then tap the Back icon.

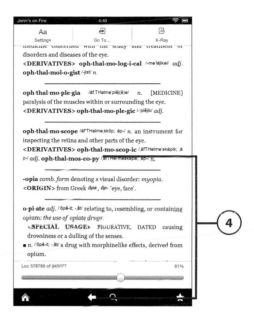

Working with Notes and Highlights

Just as when marking up a physical book, notes and highlights are a convenient way of annotating important passages. Notes are available in books and in personal documents that are in Mobi format. (Kindle files in Mobi format have either a .mobi or a .prc file extension.) Highlights are available in books and personal documents (that are in Mobi format), but you cannot highlight periodicals.

Notes enable you to visually locate a passage, along with personal comments that you attach to that passage. Highlights allow you to visually locate a passage again, but without personal comments.

Adding a Note

You can add a note to any book, whether you own the book or not. Notes that you add to a book are synchronized across all your Kindle devices and Kindle apps.

1. In an open book, tap and hold to begin selecting a passage to which you want to attach a note.

2. If necessary, tap and drag on the left and right of a selection to select more or fewer words.

3. Tap Note.

4. Enter the text for your note using the Kindle keyboard.

5. Tap Save to save the note.

6. To cancel a note, tap away from the Note pop-up.

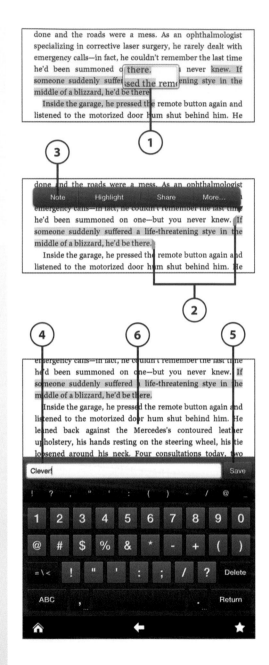

Viewing an Individual Note

Notes appear as highlighted text with a blue note icon. You can view an individual note by tapping it.

1. Tap the blue note icon that marks your note.

2. After reviewing your note, tap Close.

Editing a Note

You can easily edit notes, and any edits you make are synchronized across all your Kindle devices.

1. Tap the blue note icon that marks your note.

2. Tap Edit.

3. Enter the new text for your note.

4. Tap Save to commit your changes.

Deleting a Note

When you delete a note, you delete it across all your Kindle devices.

1. Tap the blue note icon that marks your note.

2. Tap Delete.

3. Tap Delete to confirm.

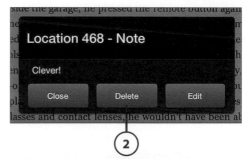

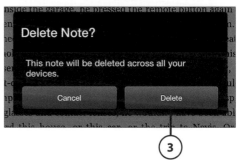

Adding a Highlight

As with the highlights in a physical book, a highlighted passage in a Kindle Fire book appears as yellow highlighted words.

1. Tap and hold to begin selecting a passage you want to highlight.

2. If necessary, tap and drag on the left and right of a selection to select more or fewer words.

3. Tap Highlight.

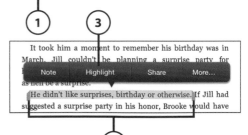

Viewing All Notes and Highlights

You can view a list of all your notes, highlights, and bookmarks for a particular book.

1. Tap the center of a page to access the Options bar.

2. Tap Notes to open the My Notes & Marks screen.

3. Scroll up and down to see all your notes and marks.

4. Tap a note or mark to go to that location in the book.

Deleting a Highlight

Unlike highlights in a physical book, you can delete a highlight in a Kindle book. The steps described here are also an alternative way to delete notes.

1. Tap the center of a page to access the Options bar.

2. Tap Notes to open the My Notes & Marks screen.

3. Locate the highlight (or note) you want to delete.

4. Tap and hold the highlight.

5. Tap Delete.

No Confirmation for Deleting Highlights

When you delete a highlight, you aren't asked whether you really want to delete it. If you think about it, this isn't a big deal because you can just highlight a passage again if you delete it in error.

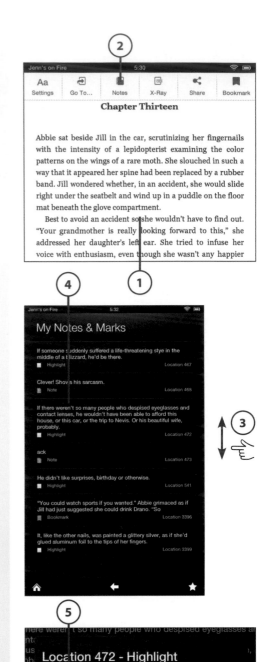

Working with Bookmarks

When you're reading a physical book, a bookmark enables you to mark your place so that you can easily return to it. The Kindle Fire marks your place automatically, but you still might want to add bookmarks on important pages so that you can easily locate them later. Think of these bookmarks as a dog-eared page. In fact, you can bookmark as many pages as you want in a book.

Bookmarks are available in books and in personal documents that are in Mobi format.

Adding a Bookmark

Adding a bookmark is easy. Bookmarks that you add are synchronized across all your Kindle devices and applications.

1. Move to the page where you want to add your bookmark.

2. Tap the middle of the page to bring up the Options bar.

3. Tap the Bookmark icon to add a bookmark.

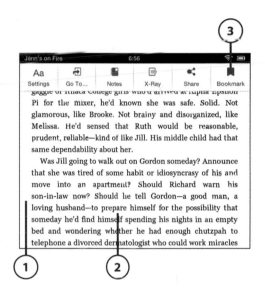

Removing a Bookmark

When you remove a bookmark, you remove it from all Kindle devices and applications.

1. Move to the page that is book-marked.

2. Tap the blue Bookmark icon to remove the bookmark.

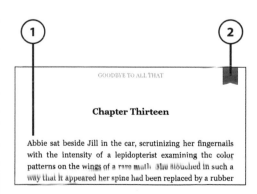

Easy Bookmark Removal

Bookmarks can also be deleted from the My Notes and Marks screen. Tap and hold the bookmark you want to remove and tap Delete.

Moving to a Bookmark

You can easily move to a page that you've bookmarked using the My Notes & Marks screen.

1. Tap the center of a page while reading your book.

2. Tap the Notes icon.

3. Scroll to the bookmark.

4. Tap the bookmark to move directly to the bookmarked page.

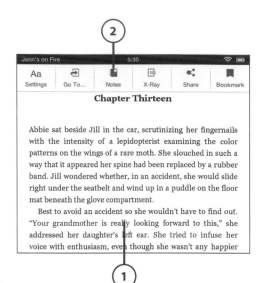

Reading Magazines and Newspapers

The Kindle Fire is a wonderful way to read magazines and newspapers. The full-color screen and the touch interface make the experience of reading periodicals similar to that of reading a physical magazine.

Reading a Page View–Enabled Magazine

Many magazines that are available in the Kindle Store are Page View–enabled, which means that they provide two views: Page View and Text View. Page View represents the look of the actual printed magazine. Text View reformats the article into pages, to enable you to more easily focus on the text of the article.

1. From Newsstand, tap a magazine that is Page View–enabled to open it.

2. Tap the center of a page to display page thumbnails.

3. Tap a page thumbnail to move to that page. The current page is outlined in blue.

4. Swipe across the thumbnails to quickly move through the pages.

5. Tap the Contents icon to see a list of articles.

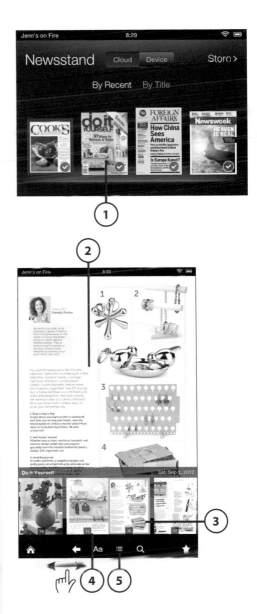

6. Tap an article to move directly to it.

7. Swipe left to move forward one page, or swipe right to move back one page. You can also tap the right edge of a page to page forward, and tap the left edge to page backward.

8. Reverse-pinch to zoom into a page.

9. Slide to move to a particular place on the page.

10. Pinch to zoom out.

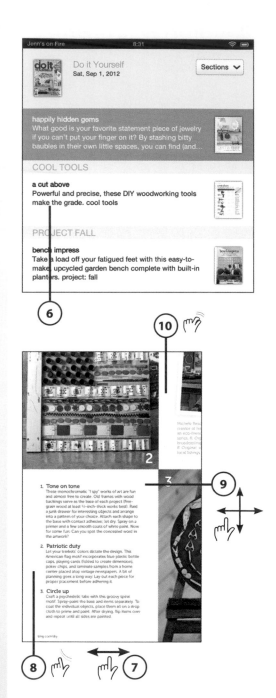

11. Double-tap a page to switch to Text View.

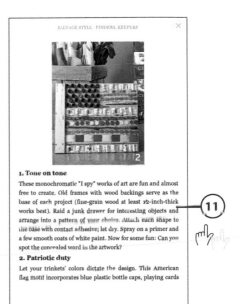

Reading in Text View and Reading Newspapers

Magazines that aren't Page View–enabled always display in Text View and do not offer the option of displaying in Page View. The experiences of reading a magazine in Text View and reading a newspaper are identical.

1. From the Newsstand, tap a magazine that is not Page View–enabled or tap a newspaper.

2. Tap the center of a page to show the Progress and Options bars.

3. Tap the arrows on the Progress bar to move forward and backward through articles.

4. Tap the Text icon to change text size, typeface, and color options.

5. Tap the Contents icon to display a list of articles and sections.

6. Tap an article to go to that article.

7. Swipe left to move forward one page, or swipe right to move back one page. You can also tap the right or left edges of a page to move forward or backward.

Magazine and Newspaper Sections

Many magazines and newspapers have a Sections button in the upper right of the contents page to make it easy to navigate quickly to a specific section.

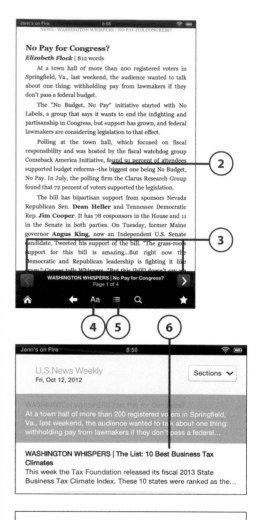

Listening to Audiobooks

Sometimes you want to read a good book, but perhaps you're driving or cooking and you don't have hands or eyes free to read it yourself. Audiobooks are audio editions of books, many of them read by celebrities or professional readers.

Not only can your Kindle Fire play audiobooks, but it can sync a bookmark across text and audio versions of the same book using Whispersync for Voice. You can also use Immersion Reading to follow along in the text while listening to the audiobook version.

Downloading Audiobooks

Audiobooks are sold in the Amazon Store through Audible. The first time you make an audiobook purchase, you're prompted to try a new Audible membership. If you already have an Audible account, you're asked to verify it.

1. Tap Audiobooks from the navigation bar.

2. Tap Store.

3. Select an audiobook.

4. Play a sample if you want to hear the reader's voice before purchasing.

5. If this is your first Audible purchase, you receive an option to sign up for an Audible membership and download two free audiobooks.

6. If you already have an Audible membership, tap the Buy button to purchase the audiobook.

7. If you have an Audible account, but you've never purchased Audible audiobooks through the Amazon Store, verify your account. This links your Audible and Amazon accounts.

8. Tap Listen Now if you want to start listening to your audiobook immediately. If you have both the eBook and the audiobook of a title, this button says Read & Listen Now.

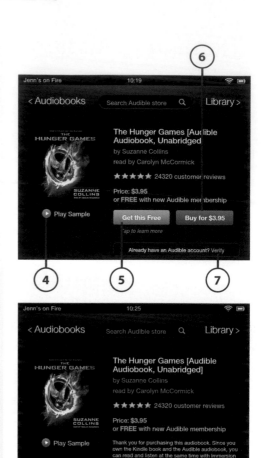

Listening to Audiobooks

Audiobooks are stored in the Amazon Cloud, available for download onto your device. Find your audiobooks in the Audiobooks library. Audiobooks are almost impossible to complete in one sitting, but don't worry about losing your place. Your Kindle Fire automatically syncs your audiobooks so you can start up again where you left off.

1. Tap Audiobooks in the navigation bar.

2. Tap an audiobook to play. If the audiobook has not yet been downloaded to your Kindle Fire, you must download it before you play it.

3. The audiobook automatically begins to play. Press Pause to temporarily stop the audio. Press Play to restart the audio.

4. Tap the Rewind 30 Seconds button to repeat the last 30 seconds of audio.

5. Tap Add Bookmark to add a bookmark to a point in the audio. Tap and hold to add a note.

6. Tap the Contents button to navigate to a specific chapter.

7. Swipe the location bar to play in a different location.

8. Choose the desired reading speed. Tap the turtle to decrease the reading speed, or tap the rabbit to increase it.

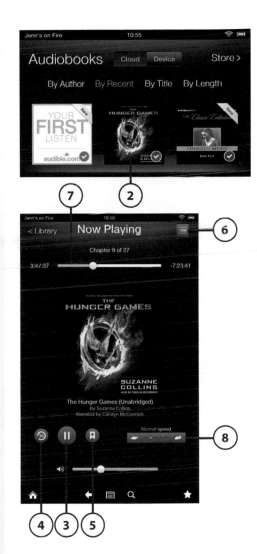

Viewing Bookmarks in Audiobooks

If you want to access bookmarks you set in an audiobook, tap the Menu icon in the Options bar and then tap View Bookmarks.

Setting a Sleep Timer

You can set a sleep timer to tell your Kindle Fire to automatically stop reading after a set amount of time.

1. Tap the Menu icon in the Options bar.

2. Tap Sleep Timer.

3. Set the amount of time you want the audiobook to play.

4. Tap End of Chapter if you want the audiobook to read to the end of the current chapter.

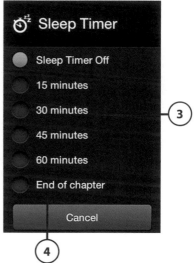

Immersion Reading

If you own both the eBook and audiobook versions of a book, you can use Immersion Reading to read along with the professional narrator.

1. Tap Books.

2. Tap the book you want to read and hear.

3. Tap the middle of the screen.

4. Tap Play to read with professional narration.

5. The gray highlights show the text the narrator is reading so you can follow along.

6. Tap Pause to pause the narration.

My Book Won't Sync

Immersion Reading is a new Kindle feature and is not without its flaws. Although it works well in most circumstances, it occasionally struggles to sync the eBook and audiobook, and you might have to tap the Play button several times to get it to work properly.

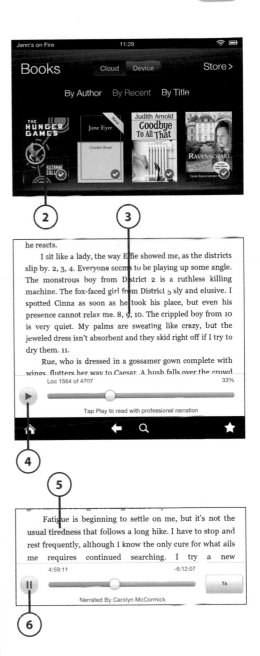

>>>Go Further

GETTING THE MOST OUT OF IMMERSION READING

Studies have shown that bimodal learning improves retention. If you're reading a book for academic purposes, such as Shakespeare, using Immersion Reading stimulates both your visual and your auditory senses, thereby helping you remember it later.

Using Text-to-Speech

Your Kindle Fire can read some books and periodicals even if you do not own the audiobook. Text-to-Speech reads in a very mechanical female voice, unlike the professional narration of audiobooks.

1. In a book, tap the middle of a page.

2. Tap Settings.

3. Tap the On button for Text-to-Speech.

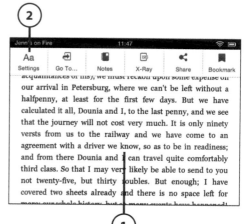

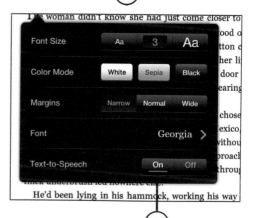

4. Tap the center of the page.

5. Tap Play to listen to Text-to-Speech. You can pause the narration with the same button.

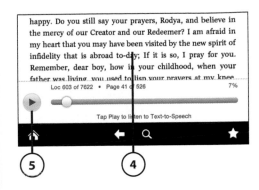

When Text-to-Speech Is Not Available

The publisher of a book determines whether the Text-to-Speech feature is available for that title.

Searching Content and Accessing Reference Materials

Your Kindle Fire provides several ways for you to get more information about your books. The device automatically maintains a searchable index of all the content in your libraries. You can also search in Wikipedia or Google. If you want to learn more about the book you're reading, X-Ray offers character breakdowns and other features.

Using X-Ray for Books

X-Ray shows you all the passages that refer to specific characters or terms. If you're reading a textbook, X-Ray can even act as a dynamic index.

1. Tap the middle of a page in the book you want to x-ray.

2. Tap X-Ray.

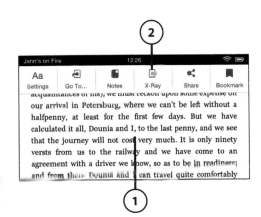

3. Examine the current page or chapter or the entire book.

4. Tap an entry to see a list of all references for that character or term.

5. Tap an entry to go to the source page for a reference.

Missing X-Rays

As with text-to-speech and certain other features, the availability of X-Ray is up to the publisher.

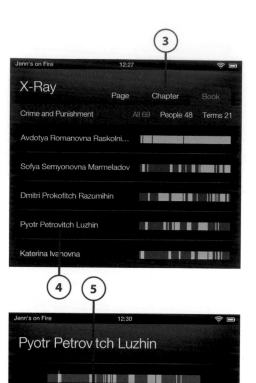

Searching the Current Item

You can search for one or more words in an item that you're reading.

1. While reading the item you want to search, tap the middle of a page.

2. Tap the Search icon.

3. Enter your search words in the Search box.

4. Tap Go.

5. Wait for the progress bar while the search completes.

6. Scroll to locate a specific search result.

7. Tap to move to the search result in the text.

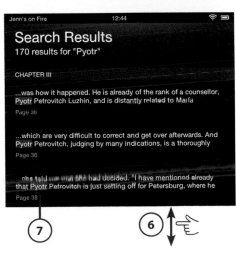

Searching Wikipedia or Google from Books

You can search the Web or Wikipedia for words that you select in books. If you select more than two words, these options aren't available.

1. Select one or two words you want to search for.

2. Tap More.

3. Tap Search Wikipedia to search for the selected word(s) in Wikipedia.

4. Tap Search the Web to search for the selected word(s) in your selected search engine.

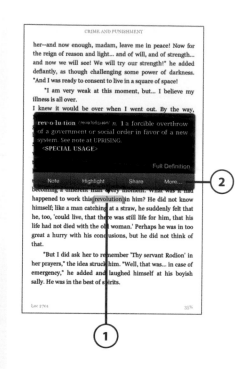

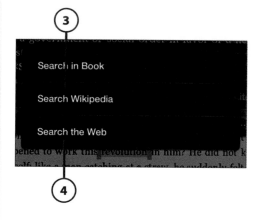

5. When you've finished reading the search results, tap the Back button to go back to your book.

Selecting a Search Engine

Your Kindle Fire uses Microsoft Bing as the default search engine. I explain how to change this in Chapter 12, "Browsing the Web with Silk."

Manage eBooks on your computer

Convert and transfer to your Kindle Fire

Edit author, title, and cover

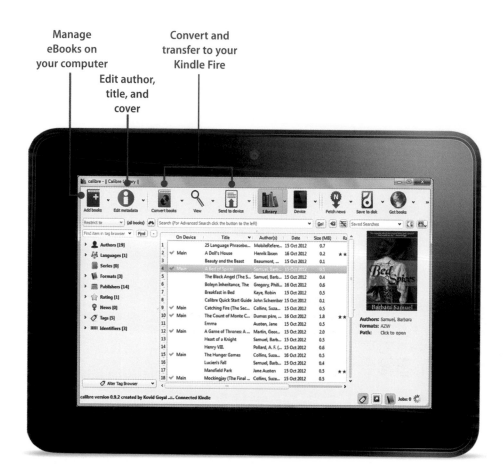

In this chapter, you learn how you can use a free tool called Calibre to manage eBooks that you download from sources other than Amazon.

→ Getting started with Calibre
→ Adding content to Calibre
→ Editing book information
→ Transferring eBooks to the Kindle Fire

5

Managing Content with Calibre

Amazon's Kindle Store offers millions of books that you can read on your Kindle Fire, but Amazon certainly doesn't have a corner on the eBook market. Sites such as www.feedbooks.com and www.fictionwise.com have plenty of eBooks that you can read on your Kindle.

Buying eBooks from Amazon gives you the benefit of having those eBooks stored in the cloud on Amazon's servers, an advantage that you don't get with third-party eBook vendors. However, by using a tool such as Calibre, you can easily manage your third-party eBooks.

Calibre Updates
Calibre is updated often, so by the time you read this chapter, the steps might have changed slightly. I wrote this chapter based on version 0.9.2 of Calibre.

Getting Started with Calibre

Calibre is a free eBook library management application for your computer. It organizes your eBook library, converts books into different formats, helps you locate books for purchase from dozens of eBook stores, and syncs your books onto all your eReader devices.

Calibre is available from www.calibre-ebook.com. Because you need to install Calibre on your computer, you must access the URL from your computer, not your Kindle Fire. Calibre is available for Windows, Mac OS X, and Linux. Go to the Download page on the Calibre website to access the version you need for your computer. Follow the download instructions for your operating system at the Calibre website.

It's Not All Good

Mac Users, Take Note

The Kindle Fire now uses Media Transfer Protocol (MTP) instead of USB Mass Storage. This might not sound like a big deal to most readers, but for Mac users, it's quite a blow. The Mac OS X does not recognize MTP, which means that transferring files to and from your Kindle Fire requires installation of a transfer app and extra steps that PC and Linux users do not have to undertake. Unfortunately, this also means that Mac users cannot use Calibre to sideload eBooks onto their Kindle Fire.

If you are a Mac user who already relies upon Calibre to maintain your eBook collection for an older Kindle device (including the first-generation Kindle Fire) or other eReader, this will undoubtedly cause frustration. You can e-mail your eBooks to the Kindle Fire, as explained at the end of this chapter, but your books will show up in the Docs library instead of your Books library. Another option is to run Calibre under Windows using Boot Camp, Parallels, or VMware Fusion, if you have one of those available. Taking this step, however, is outside the realm of this book.

Using the Welcome Wizard

After you've downloaded and installed Calibre, you can launch it and walk through the Welcome Wizard.

1. Choose your language.

2. Choose a folder for your Calibre library. If you've already downloaded eBooks to your computer that you want Calibre to manage, choose the folder that contains them. Otherwise, you can accept the default to create a new folder.

3. Click Next.

4. Select Amazon as the manufacturer and Kindle Fire as the device. (As you can see here, Calibre works with a host of eReader devices.)

5. Click Next.

6. Click Finish to start using Calibre.

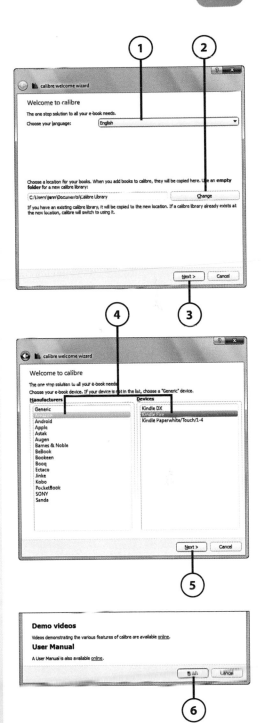

Adding Content to Calibre

If you already have eBooks in the folder you chose in the Welcome Wizard, Calibre should already be populated with your eBooks. Otherwise, you need to import any existing eBooks into Calibre.

Importing Books

You can import eBooks in any format into your Calibre library. If an eBook is in a format that your Kindle Fire doesn't recognize, Calibre can usually convert it for you.

1. Click Add Books.

2. Navigate to the folder on your computer that contains your eBooks.

3. Select one or more eBooks to add to your Calibre library.

4. Click the Open button to import the selected books into your library.

5. Wait until Calibre finishes importing your eBooks.

6. If Calibre notifies you that it found duplicates, click No so that they aren't imported.

Adding New Books

If you download new eBooks after you've built your Calibre library, you need to add them to Calibre using the Add Books button.

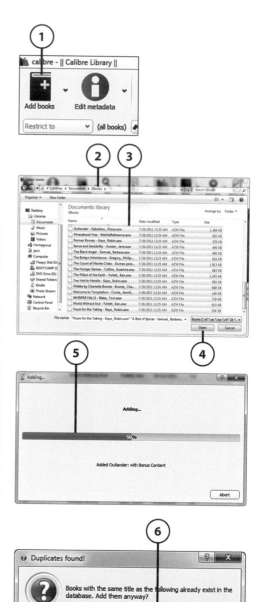

EBOOK FORMATS

eBooks come in many different formats. The most popular eBook format is called EPUB, and it's the format that libraries have used for the past several years. The Kindle is the only common eBook reader that does not support the EPUB format. Instead, the Kindle supports the MOBI format. eBooks that you purchase from the Kindle Store have an AZW extension, which is a form of MOBI that Amazon has modified to add its own digital rights management (DRM) so that you can't buy a book once and give it to a million Internet users. Other book formats might use a different form of DRM to protect against piracy.

Fortunately, converting books from EPUB and other formats into MOBI format is easy as long as the books are not protected with DRM, as I explain in this chapter. Unfortunately, if a book is protected with DRM, you need the correct type of eReader to view that book because it cannot legally be converted. Calibre warns you if you try to add a book to your Kindle Fire in an improper format.

Searching for New eBooks

Calibre has an integrated search engine that makes locating new eBooks easy. Calibre's search engine searches eBook stores on the Internet for the search term you enter, and many of these eBook stores sell books that are compatible with your Kindle Fire.

Calibre searches for either authors or titles. In other words, you can't enter "fantasy" to find fantasy books. Instead, you'll find books with "fantasy" in the title or books written by Mr. or Mrs. Fantasy.

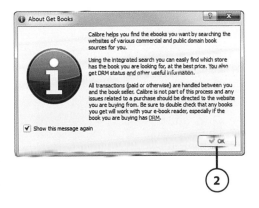

1. Click Get Books.

2. Click OK in the information dialog box.

3. Select the stores you want to search.

4. Enter your search query. Calibre searches using only the title and author.

5. Click Search.

6. Double-click a search result to view details in your web browser or to purchase the eBook. Online bookstores use various means to connect you to your purchases, so follow the site's instructions to complete your transaction and obtain your books.

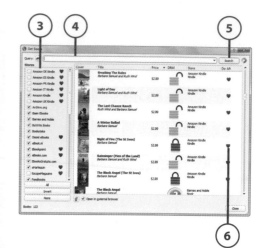

Pay Attention to DRM

Pay special attention to the DRM status of eBooks. If you see a red lock next to a search result, it means that the eBook is protected with DRM and can be read only on certain devices. Your Kindle Fire supports only Amazon Kindle DRM. If a book is DRM protected and it isn't from the Amazon Kindle Store, it won't open on your Kindle. Books with a green lock are not protected with DRM and can generally be converted to a format that will open on your Kindle. Books in Kindle AZW format also appear with a green lock because they can be viewed on your Kindle Fire, which you set as your device in the Welcome Wizard.

It's Not All Good

Use Caution When Searching

Some eBooks that you can find online might be copyrighted books that are being offered illegally. It's not a bad idea to search for eBooks only from sources that you know are legitimate. For example, if a site is offering an eBook for free and that same eBook costs $10 everywhere else, that's a good sign that something's not right. Downloading pirated books is a copyright infringement and keeps the author from being compensated for the work. It also leads to publishers putting further DRM restrictions on eBooks, which can limit your ability to lend books or access them in other formats.

Editing Book Information

Some of your eBooks might not display the correct author or title. The most common cause of this for Kindle users relates to personal docs e-mailed to your Kindle e-mail address. When Amazon converts these documents, it uses the sending e-mail for the author name. It's easy to use Calibre to edit the author, title, and other information about an eBook.

Downloading Metadata

Calibre can locate information about a particular eBook using well-known book sources such as Amazon and Google.

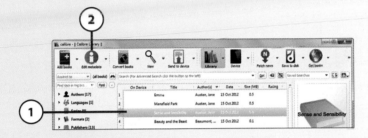

1. Select the book you want to edit.

2. Click Edit Metadata.

3. Click Download Metadata.

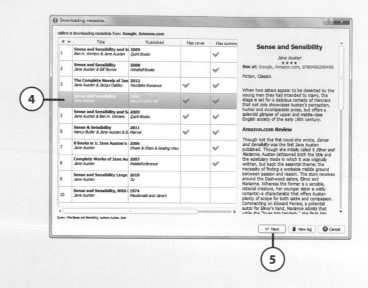

4. Click the title that matches your search.

5. Click Next.

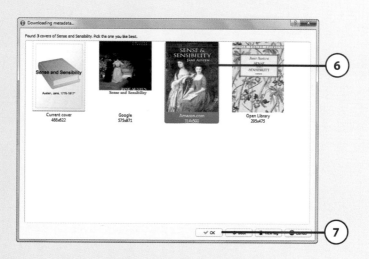

6. Click a cover picture for your book. Not all results include a book cover.

7. Click OK.

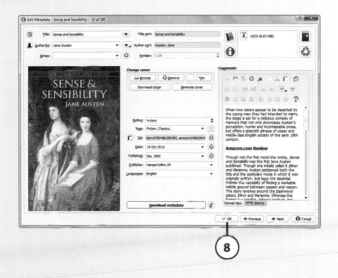

8. Click OK to add the new metadata to your eBook.

Better Metadata Searching

If you don't find a result when downloading metadata, try adding an ISBN number (you can get it by searching the Books section at Amazon) to the IDs text box and then clicking Download Metadata.

FINDING COVERS

Some eBooks, particularly those in the public domain, are not embedded with the same cover art that the print copies use. Calibre can usually locate a cover for your eBooks, but if it can't, an Internet search usually turns up a cover. When you locate one, save the image to your computer, edit the metadata for the book in Calibre, and use the Change Cover tools to browse to the image and attach it to your eBook.

Manually Editing Metadata

If Calibre can't find your eBook when you try to download metadata, you can edit the metadata manually. You can also enter additional metadata for a book. The more metadata is in a record, the easier it is to catalogue it and search for the book later.

1. Open the Metadata dialog box as described in the previous section.

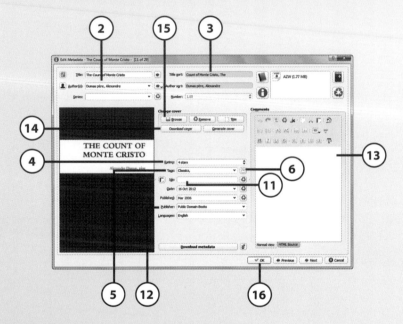

2. Correct the title or author's name, if necessary.

3. Correct the way the title or author's name appears when sorting by title or author. In the example, you can change the Author sort to "Dumas père, Alexandre" so that it appears in proper order by last name.

4. If you've already read the book, give it a rating.

5. Tag the book by genre or theme.

6. Open the Tag Editor to edit the list of tags.

7. Type the new tag. It can be a genre, a theme, or any other keyword you want.

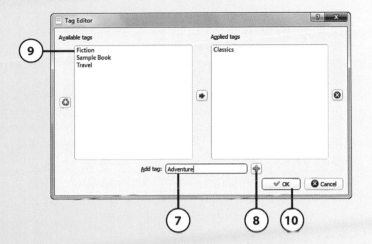

8. Click the plus sign to add the new tag.

9. Double-click an available tag to apply other tags to the book.

10. Click OK.

11. Add the ISBN for the book.

12. Change the publication and language information if it is incomplete or incorrect.

13. You can add your own comments or a review of the book. Use the formatting options to format your comments.

14. If you need to add a cover, click Download Cover.

15. If Calibre cannot locate a cover, but you downloaded one from another source, click Browse to locate the downloaded file, then navigate to the file and click OK.

16. Click OK to save your changes.

Transferring eBooks to the Kindle Fire

To use Calibre to sideload books onto your Kindle Fire, you first convert the eBook to a proper format, if necessary, and then transfer the file. The best format for transferring books onto your Kindle Fire is MOBI. If you follow the steps in the next section, your sideloaded books appear in the Books library along with your Kindle Store book purchases.

What About E-mailing Books?

If you e-mail books to your Kindle, they are stored in the Docs library, which means they're separated from your other books. This process is often less time consuming because you can usually provide your Kindle e-mail address to the online bookstore and have your purchases automatically e-mailed to your device. However, if you want to keep all your books together, sideloading through Calibre is the way to go. Instead of having books e-mailed directly to your Kindle, download your purchases onto your computer, add them to your Calibre library, and proceed from there.

Converting to MOBI Format

If your book is already in MOBI or EPUB format, this step is unnecessary. If your book is in any other format, however, you should convert the eBook to MOBI format before transferring it to your Kindle Fire.

Kindle Fire and EPUB Format

The Kindle Fire cannot read EPUB format, but Calibre can automatically convert books from EPUB to MOBI while uploading to the Kindle Fire. This conversion process still allows your books to show up correctly in your Books library.

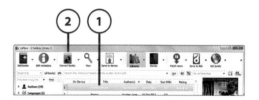

1. Select the book you want to convert.

2. Click Convert Books.

3. Change the Output Format to MOBI.

4. Check Use Cover from Source File.

5. Click MOBI Output.

6. Change the Personal Doc Tag to [EBOK].

7. Click OK. A jobs icon in the lower-right corner spins as Calibre processes the conversion.

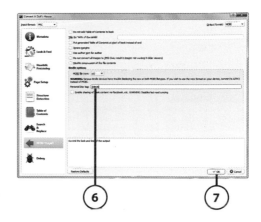

6   **7**

Deleting Non-MOBI Formats

If you intend to make the Kindle Fire your only eReader device, you need to keep only the MOBI format in your Calibre library. Save space by deleting unused formats.

1

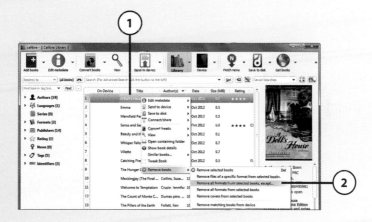

2

1. Right-click the book you just converted.

2. Point to Remove Books and click Remove All Formats from Selected Books, Except.

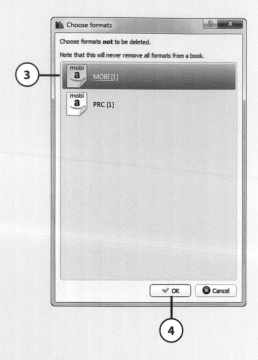

3. Select the MOBI format. This is the format you want to keep.
4. Click OK.

Transferring an eBook to Your Kindle

Now that you have a MOBI copy of your eBook in your Calibre library, you can transfer the eBook to your Kindle Fire. Before you complete these steps, make sure your Kindle Fire is connected to your computer with the mini-USB cable.

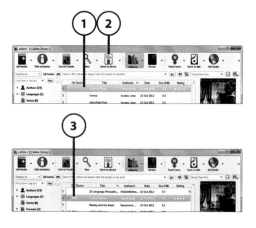

1. Select the eBook you want to transfer.

2. Click Send to Device.

3. Wait until Calibre shows that the eBook is on your device.

Transferring an EPUB Format eBook

If you choose to use EPUB-format eBooks, Calibre can automatically convert the EPUB format to one that is compatible with your Kindle Fire. After completing step 2, click Yes when asked whether you want to convert the eBook.

Finding the Sideloaded Book

You can find the book that you sideloaded to your Kindle Fire in your Books library. It also appears on the Carousel on the Home screen.

E-mailing eBooks to Your Kindle

Calibre can e-mail eBooks to your Kindle account. The eBook must already be in Microsoft Word (.doc or .docx), Rich Text, HTML, text, or MOBI format. Remember, e-mailed books show up in the Docs library, not the Books library, on your Kindle Fire.

Good News for Mac Users

This feature works for Mac users as well as PC and Linux users. At this time, this is the only way for Mac users to transfer books from Calibre to the Kindle Fire.

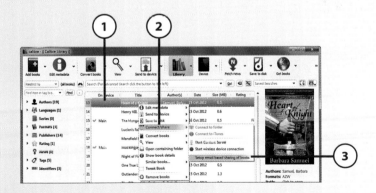

1. Right-click the book that you want to e-mail to your Kindle e-mail address.

2. Point to Connect/Share.

3. Select Setup E-mail Based Sharing of Books.

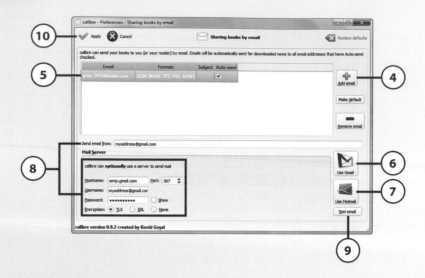

4. Click Add E-mail.

5. Enter your Kindle e-mail address. (Tap Docs on your Kindle Fire to find your Kindle e-mail address if you're not sure.)

6. Click Use Gmail and enter your Gmail information if you want to use a Gmail account to send the e-mail. This option automatically fills in the server information to send messages and eBooks through Gmail's servers.

7. Click Use Hotmail and enter your Hotmail information if you want to use a Hotmail account to send the e-mail. This option automatically fills in the server information.

8. If you don't want to use Hotmail or Gmail, enter your e-mail address and server information. If you don't know your e-mail server information, check with your Internet Service Provider.

9. Click Test E-mail to test your e-mail settings.

10. Click Apply.

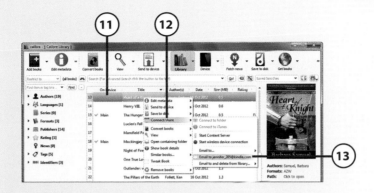

11.   Again, right-click the book you want to send.

12.   Point to Connect/Share.

13.   Select E-mail for the address you set up in steps 6–8.

Use an Approved E-mail

The e-mail address that you configure in Calibre needs to be an e-mail that is on your approved e-mail list for sending docs to your Kindle Fire. For details on adding an e-mail to the approved e-mail list, see "Adding an Approved E-mail for Docs" in Chapter 3, "Using Amazon's Manage Your Kindle Page."

>>>Go Further

EXTENDING YOUR CALIBRE KNOW-HOW

If you enjoy organizing your books in Calibre, you can get more out of this versatile app. In Calibre Preferences, you can get plug-ins to add new features. Look for the Goodreads Sync plug-in to link your library to your Goodreads account, Count Pages to estimate how many pages are in EPUB and MOBI files, and Reading List to organize your list of books to be read.

View Your Cloud
and Device Music

Use
Playlists

Browse
Music

Play
Music

In this chapter, you learn how to access and listen to music on your Kindle Fire. Topics include the following:

→ Browsing and downloading your music
→ Searching for music
→ Playing music
→ Managing playlists
→ Buying new music

Accessing and Listening to Music

The Kindle Fire is arguably the best way to play music that you have stored on Amazon's Cloud Player. Because it has a limited amount of user-accessible memory, you likely can't carry all your music on it when you're offline, but you can make playlists and download some of your music to enjoy when you're away from a Wi-Fi connection.

In addition to playing music, you can browse Amazon's extensive library of MP3s to add to your music collection.

Browsing and Downloading Your Music

Your Kindle Fire integrates directly into your Cloud Drive and provides a first-class interface into browsing and listening to your music. As soon as you start your Kindle Fire for the first time (after you've signed into your Amazon account on the device), it begins indexing the music on your Cloud Drive.

This chapter deals primarily with music in the cloud because that's likely the way you'll listen to music on your Kindle Fire. However, all the information presented also applies to interacting with music stored on your device.

Add Music to Your Cloud Drive

If you haven't added any music to your Cloud Drive, see Chapter 2, "Loading Your Kindle Fire," for information on how to do that.

Browsing Artists

Your Kindle Fire can provide you with a list of all artists in your music collection, in alphabetical order.

1. From the Home screen, tap Music.

2. Tap Cloud to view your Cloud Drive.

3. Tap Artists to display artists in your collection.

4. Scroll up and down to view artists.

5. Tap an artist to see a list of albums in your collection by the artist.

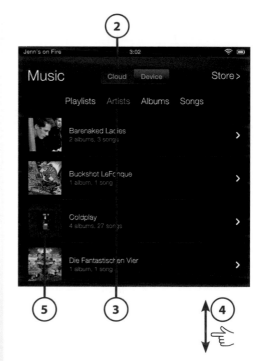
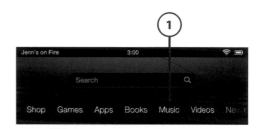

6. Tap Songs to see a list of all songs by the artist.

7. Tap Shop This Artist to open the Amazon MP3 Music Store, where you can buy songs and albums by the artist you are viewing.

8. Tap Download All to download all the songs by the artist you have stored in your Cloud Drive to your device.

9. Tap an album to see details on the album.

10. Tap Download All to download the album to your device.

11. Tap Music to quickly go back to a list of artists to choose a new artist.

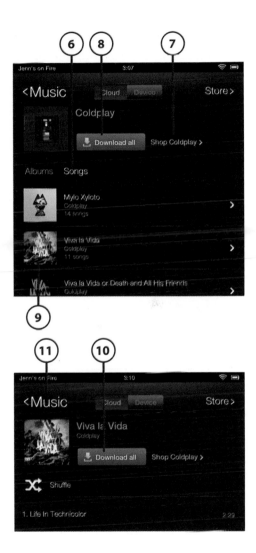

Browsing Albums and Songs

You can use the same technique to browse albums and songs on your Cloud Drive.

When you are viewing a list of albums from an artist, you can tap and hold an album and then tap Download Album to download it.

Scrolling Quickly in Music

Having a large number of artists, albums, or songs in your music collection is not uncommon. To more quickly find an item, you can scroll to items that begin with a particular letter of the alphabet.

This technique works in all lists in your Music library.

1. From a list of music items, tap and drag to begin scrolling.

2. As soon as the scroll handle appears, immediately tap and hold it.

3. Drag the scroll handle up and down to quickly browse by letter.

4. Release the scroll handle when the desired letter appears on the screen to jump to items that begin with that letter.

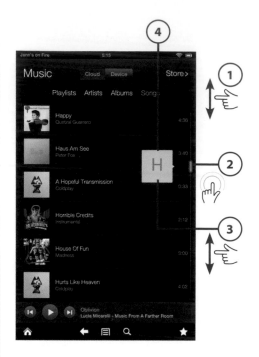

Monitoring Downloads from an Album

As your music tracks are being downloaded, you can monitor their progress and cancel the download, if necessary.

1. Locate an artist, album, or song you want to download.

2. Tap Download All.

3. Tap the X if you want to cancel the download for a particular song.

4. Tap Cancel Download.

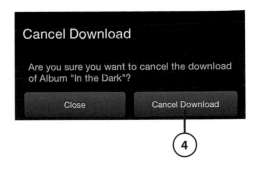

Monitoring All Music Downloads

If you're downloading music from several albums or artists, you can monitor the progress of all the downloads at once.

1. From any screen in your Music library, tap the Menu icon.

2. Tap Downloads.

3. Tap the Pause/Resume icon to pause or resume the current download.

4. Tap See Completed Downloads to see a list of tracks that have already been downloaded.

Latest Additions Playlist

When you view completed downloads, you're actually looking at an automatic playlist called Latest Additions. This playlist is also available on the Playlists screen.

Canceling Downloads

You can cancel pending downloads. Any tracks that have already downloaded remain on your device.

1. While viewing active downloads, tap and hold the item that's currently downloading.

2. Tap Cancel Download.

Searching for Music

Sometimes you have a burning desire to listen to a particular song. Of course, you can scroll through your song list on the Kindle Fire to find it, but if you have thousands of songs, it's often easier to search for what you want to hear.

Searching Your Music Collection

Your Kindle Fire can search both music that's on your device and music in the cloud. You can search for playlists, artists, albums, or songs.

1. In the Music app, tap the Search icon.

2. Enter your search term in the Search box. Results appear as you type.

3. Tap the item you seek. The search results list items from both the cloud and the device.

Sorting Through Search Results

If you are in the Music app when you begin your search, the first set of search results is from your Music library. These results are followed by a count of items matching your search term from other Kindle Fire apps.

Playing Music

Your Kindle Fire can play music you've downloaded to the device or stream music directly from your Cloud Drive. When you stream music, you need a Wi-Fi (or 4G) connection. If you're going to be in an area where you cannot connect to the Internet, plan ahead by downloading music so that it will be available no matter where you go.

Listening to Music

You can play music either through the speakers built into the Kindle Fire or through headphones or an external speaker system. After you begin playing music, you can do other tasks on your Kindle Fire, such as read a book or send an e-mail, while the music continues playing.

1. Locate and tap the song you want to hear. This brings up the Now Playing screen.

2. Tap or drag the location slider to move to a particular point in the song. As you drag it, an indicator displays your position in the song.

3. Tap Previous to move to the previous song.

4. Tap Next to move to the next song.

5. Tap or drag the Volume slider to adjust the volume of playback.

6. Tap the left side of the Volume slider to instantly mute the audio.

7. Tap the right side of the Volume slider to instantly change to full volume.

8. Tap Shuffle to randomly play the songs in the Now Playing queue. Tap it again to turn off shuffle playback.

9. Tap Repeat to repeat all the songs in the Now Playing queue. Tap Repeat again to repeat only the currently playing song.

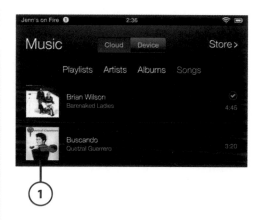

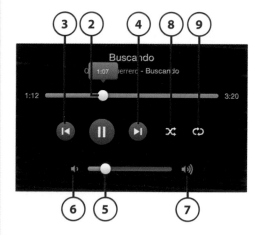

Accessing More Options

While viewing the Now Playing screen, tap and hold the album art for a menu of other ways you can interact with your music, including adding the song to a playlist, shopping for more music by the artist, and downloading the song (if you're currently streaming it) to your device.

Accessing Music Controls

You don't have to remain in the Music app while playing music. You can access playback controls or see the title and artist of the song that's currently playing while in any other app.

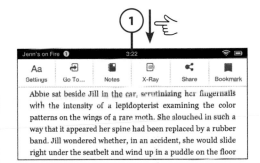

1. Swipe down from the status bar. If you're reading a book or periodical, tap the middle of the page first to display the status bar.

2. Tap the Pause button to pause the music.

3. Tap the Previous button to move to the previous song.

4. Tap the Next button to move to the next song.

5. Tap the name of the song to bring up the Now Playing screen.

6. Swipe up from the bottom of the screen to return to what you were doing.

Managing Playlists

Playlists enable you to create a list of tracks that you want to play. You can create playlists on your device or in the cloud. If you create a playlist in the cloud, that playlist can be accessed both from your computer and from another device that can access your Cloud Player.

Creating a Playlist

You create playlists on your device by first tapping the Device tab. If you tap the Cloud tab first, your playlist is created on your Cloud Player. Playlists that you create on your device can contain only songs that are downloaded to your device. Playlists that you create on your Cloud Player can contain any of your music that is on your Cloud Player.

1. From your Music library, tap Playlists.

2. Tap Cloud to create a playlist from tracks in your Cloud Player, or tap Device to create a playlist from tracks on your device.

3. Tap Create New Playlist.

4. Enter a name for your playlist.

5. Tap Save.

6. Add songs to your playlist by tapping the + sign next to the song.

7. Tap the Search Your Device Music field and enter a song, album, or artist name to search for tracks.

8. Tap Done when finished adding songs.

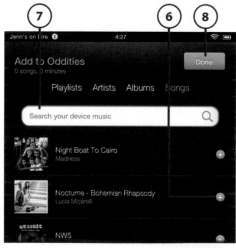

Cannot Move Device Playlist to the Cloud

When you create a playlist on your device, that playlist can contain only songs that are on your device. You cannot move a playlist created on your device to the cloud.

Editing a Playlist

After you've created a playlist and added your initial songs, you can add or remove songs by editing the playlist.

1. From the Playlists screen, tap your playlist.

2. Tap Edit.

3. Tap the minus sign to remove a song from the playlist.

4. Tap and hold the dots at the left edge of a song, and drag to a new position in the playlist to reorder songs.

5. Tap the Add Songs button to add new songs using the same interface you used when creating the playlist.

6. Tap Done to save your changes.

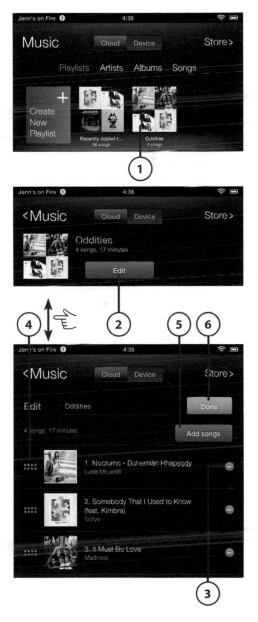

Adding Artists or Albums to a Playlist

You can add songs to a playlist when you edit the playlist, as I just explained, or whenever you come across music you want to add. Instead of adding songs one track at a time, you can also add all songs by an artist or in a particular album.

1. Tap and hold the song, artist, or album that you want to add to a playlist.

2. Tap Add to Playlist.

3. If you want to add the music to the most recent playlist, tap Add to (the name of the playlist).

4. Tap the playlist to which you want to add the music. Alternatively, tap Create New Playlist to create a new playlist.

5. If creating a new playlist, give it a name.

6. Tap Save to save the new playlist.

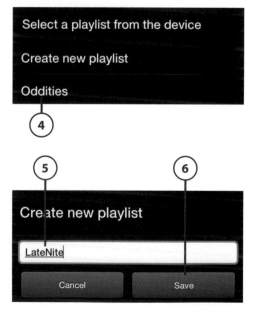

Playing a Playlist

Playlists that are on your device can
be played only on your Kindle Fire.
When you create playlists in the
cloud, you can play them on your
Kindle Fire or other devices that can
access your Cloud Player.

1. From your Music library, tap
   Playlists.

2. Tap Cloud to see playlists on your
   Cloud Drive, or tap Device to see
   playlists on your Kindle Fire.

3. Tap the playlist you want to play.

4. Tap a song in the playlist to start
   playing from that song onward.

5. Tap Shuffle to play the songs in
   random order.

Downloading a Playlist

You can't play playlists that you create in your Cloud Drive unless you
have an active Internet connection.
If you want to play the playlist when
you aren't connected, you first need
to download the playlist to your
device.

1. From the Playlists screen, tap
   Cloud.

2. Tap the playlist that you want to
   download.

3. Tap the Download All button to download the playlist to your device.

Downloaded Playlist

Downloaded playlists appear on the Device tab in the Playlists screen. Both the playlist and all songs in the playlist are downloaded.

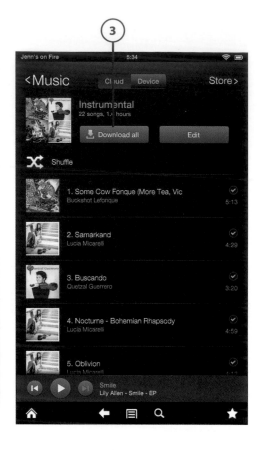

It's Not All Good

The Same Playlist, but Different

When you download a playlist from the cloud to your device, it is initially an identical match. In essence, however, you have created two different playlists. If you edit one playlist, your changes are not reflected in the other playlist. I recommend changing the name of one of the playlists after downloading it so you don't confuse them.

I also recommend creating and editing all your playlists in the cloud, even if you choose to also download them to your device. If you edit a playlist in the cloud, you can always download the updated playlist to your device again, whereas you can't upload a playlist you created or modified on your Fire back up to the cloud.

Renaming a Playlist

If you decide to change the name of a playlist, you can rename it from the Playlists screen.

1. From the Playlists screen, tap the playlist you want to rename.

2. Tap Edit.

3. Tap the current name of the play-list and enter a new name for the playlist.

4. Tap Done.

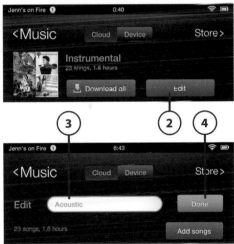

Deleting a Playlist

When you no longer want to keep a playlist, you can delete it. Deleting a playlist doesn't affect the songs themselves; it only removes the playlist.

When you delete a cloud playlist, it becomes inaccessible to all devices that access your Cloud Player.

1. From the Playlists screen, tap and hold the playlist you want to delete.

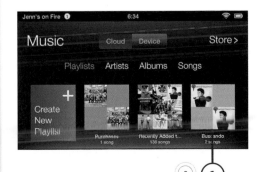

2. If you're deleting a cloud playlist, Tap Delete Playlist from Cloud. If you're deleting a device playlist, tap Remove Playlist from Device.

3. Tap Yes to confirm the deletion.

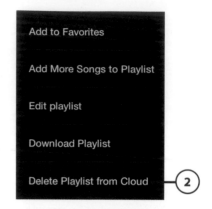

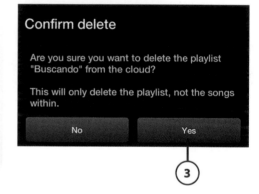

Buying New Music

You can purchase new music from Amazon's MP3 Music Store on your Kindle Fire. You can choose whether music that you purchase is added only to your Cloud Player or added to your Cloud Player and then automatically downloaded to your device.

Navigating the Music Store

The Music Store is accessible from your Music library.

1. From any screen in your Music library, tap Store to go to the Music Store.

2. Scroll through featured songs and albums.

3. Tap a category to see more music.

4. Tap See All to see more music of that type, such as the New Releases category, to see all new album releases.

5. Scroll through Recommended for You to see recommended music.

6. Tap Search to search for music.

7. Tap any item to see details, listen to sample tracks, and purchase music.

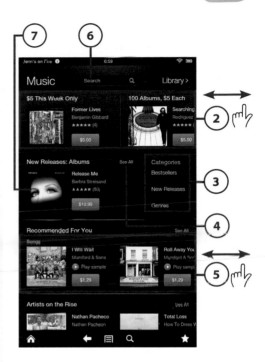

Sampling and Buying Music

As you're browsing the Music Store, you can sample 30 seconds of songs or purchase songs.

1. Tap a song or album.

2. Tap the Play Sample button to listen to a 30-second sample of a song.

3. Tap the song price to purchase the song.

4. Tap the album price to purchase the entire album.

5. Tap Shop Artist to see all music by that artist.

Sampling Multiple Songs

When a 30-second sample finishes for one song, your Kindle Fire automatically starts playing a 30-second sample of the next song in the album.

ALBUM ONLY

Some songs are listed as Album Only and cannot be purchased individually. This restriction most often appears on extra content, such as digital booklets, that accompany some albums. It might also appear on compilation albums in which particular songs are sold as part of the compilation and not individually. If you want to access this content, you must purchase the complete album.

Changing Music Delivery Preferences

When you purchase music, it is added to your Cloud Player. You can also choose to have your music automatically downloaded to your device.

1. Swipe down from the status bar to open Settings.

2. Tap More.

3. Tap Applications.

4. Scroll down and tap Music.

5. Tap the On button to automatically download music purchases to your device, or tap Off to store your music only on your Cloud Player.

Buy Now, Download Later

Of course, don't forget that you can always download music from your Cloud Player to your device at any time. Turning this setting to Off gives you more control over exactly which music is stored on your device at any given time.

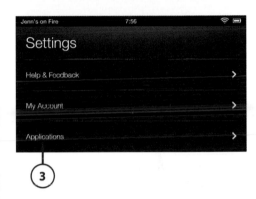

>>>Go Further

ACQUIRING MUSIC FROM OTHER SOURCES

Many other sources for digital music exist, including the iTunes Store and eMusic.com. Music must be in non-DRM AAC, MP3, MIDI, OGG, or WAV format to be accessible on the Kindle Fire. Use the Amazon Cloud Player website to add music to your Cloud Player, or sideload music from Windows Explorer (on the PC) or using the Android File Transfer app (on the Mac). You find instructions for using the Cloud Player and sideloading in Chapter 2.

Stream instantly
over Wi-Fi

Watch your
favorite movies
and TV shows

Watch Amazon Prime
videos for free

Create a Watchlist
for later viewing

In this chapter, you learn how to take advantage of the video capabilities of your Kindle Fire and explore how you can use your device to watch your own videos. Topics include the following:

→ Navigating the Video Store
→ Working with your video library
→ Sideloading videos

Watching Video on Your Kindle Fire

Your Kindle Fire is an excellent device for watching videos. The Kindle Fire HD provides high-definition (720p) video and Dolby Digital sound for a great theatrical experience that you can hold in your hands. Amazon offers more than 100,000 movies and TV shows that you can watch immediately on your Kindle Fire, and if you're a Prime member, you can find thousands of movies and TV shows that you can watch at no extra charge.

Navigating the Video Store

You can rent or purchase movies and TV shows from the Video Store. Amazon automatically synchronizes your playback location so you can start watching on one device and finish on another.

If you're an Amazon Prime member, you can instantly watch many movies or TV shows as part of your annual membership fee. These videos are streamed, so you can watch them only if you have a Wi-Fi (or 4G) connection.

You can also rent or purchase videos, which gives you the option of streaming or downloading the video to your Kindle Fire for offline viewing at your convenience. Keep in mind that even if a video is offered for free streaming with Amazon Prime, you still pay the rental or purchase fee if you prefer to download it to your device.

Video Store or Library

When you are connected to Wi-Fi (or 4G), tapping Videos on the home screen launches the Video Store. However, if you aren't connected to Wi-Fi, tapping Videos takes you to your video library.

Browsing the Video Store

Access the Video Store from your home screen.

1. Tap Videos to access the Video Store.

2. Tap in the Search box to search for videos.

3. Scroll to view recommended titles.

4. Tap See More to view all Prime Instant Videos.

5. Tap Movies or TV or see videos of that type.

6. Scroll to see Prime Instant Videos in other categories.

7. Tap All to view all videos, or tap Prime to view videos eligible for free streaming with a Prime membership.

8. Scroll down to see more categories of movies and TV shows for instant streaming, rental, or purchase.

Viewing Movie Details

The Movie Details screen provides viewing options, production information, and the duration of the movie. You might also find a plot overview and reviews of the film.

1. Tap a movie title in the Video Store.

2. Tap Watch Trailer to see the movie trailer.

3. Tap the name of the director to find other films he or she has made.

4. View the duration of the video.

5. View the rental terms if you choose to rent the movie.

6. Tap Rental & Purchase Details to view information about rental and purchase agreements from Amazon.

7. Scroll down to see recommended titles based on what other customers purchased and read customer reviews of the movie.

X-Ray for Movies

If a movie takes advantage of Amazon's new X-Ray for Movies feature, it's noted in the upper-right corner of the Movie Details screen. I cover this tool in more detail later in this chapter.

Renting or Purchasing a Movie

You can rent or purchase a movie on your Kindle Fire. A rental enables you to view the movie for a short period of time for a low price, similar to renting a movie from a RedBox kiosk. Purchasing a movie is more expensive, but you can watch the movie whenever you want without time restrictions, as when you purchase a movie at a retail store.

1. From the movie details screen, tap the price to rent or purchase the movie.

2. Tap the green Rent or Purchase button to complete your transaction.

Standard vs. High Definition

If you have a Kindle Fire HD (either the 7-inch or the 8.9-inch unit), rent or purchase the HD (high-definition) format to take full advantage of your device's display. The HD format is more expensive, but it's worth it.

If you have a base Kindle Fire model, you can rent or purchase the standard-definition format of the movie if you will be viewing the movie only on your Kindle Fire. If you have an HD-TV or other device, however, you might still want to purchase the HD format so you can watch it in higher quality on those devices. HD videos play fine on your Kindle Fire; they just display in SD.

It's Not All Good

Rented Movies Might Expire Sooner Than You Think

When you rent a movie, it typically expires 24 or 48 hours after you start watching it. However, if you initiate a download of the video to your Kindle Fire, that also starts the clock on the expiration period. Therefore, if you download a video to your Kindle Fire, pay careful attention to the expiration of the rental.

When you initiate a download, Amazon displays a notification informing you that you are about to start the rental period and telling you how many hours you have to watch the movie.

Viewing TV Show Details

Amazon carries hundreds of television shows, from sitcoms to mini-series.

1. Tap a TV show in the Video Store.

2. Scroll to see available seasons.

3. Scroll down to see additional information.

4. Tap an episode to see details on that episode.

5. Scroll down to see additional series details.

6. Tap the network name to see more TV shows from that network.

7. Scroll to see TV shows other customers bought.

8. Read reviews of the series from other customers.

9. Scroll to see the cast and other information about the series.

10. Tap a cast member's name to get more information about that person's career from the preinstalled IMDb app.

Missing Additional Show Details

Some movies and TV shows provide more information on their detail screens than others. If a listing falls short, you can always look up more information about a movie or TV show using the Silk browser on your Kindle Fire.

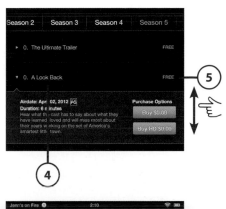

Buying TV Shows by Episode

Amazon offers the capability to purchase either single episodes or entire seasons of TV shows. Single episodes of a TV show are handy if you missed an episode of a favorite show on TV.

1. Tap a TV show from the Video Store.

2. Select a season.

3. Tap the episode you want to purchase.

4. Tap the price to purchase the episode.

5. Tap the green Buy button to complete your purchase.

No TV Show Rentals

Unlike movies, TV shows are not available as rentals. You can purchase a TV show (either a single episode or an entire series) or stream a TV show if it's currently available through Amazon Prime Instant Video.

Purchasing Complete TV Show Seasons

If you're catching up on previous seasons or want to complete your collection of a TV series, you can save a little money by purchasing the entire season at once.

1. Tap a TV show from the Video Store.

2. Tap the price to purchase the season.

3. Tap the green Buy button to complete your purchase.

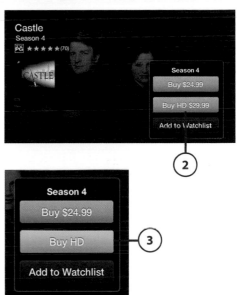

Purchasing a TV Show from Prime Instant Video

You can stream a TV show from Prime Instant Video, but if you want to download it to your device so you can watch without a Wi-Fi connection, you need to purchase it.

1. Tap a TV show from the Prime Instant Video listing.

2. Tap a season.

3. To purchase the complete season, tap Purchase Options.

4. Tap the Buy option.

5. If you change your mind, tap Close.

6. To purchase a single episode, tap the name of the episode.

7. Tap Additional Purchase Options.

8. Tap the Buy option.

9. If you change your mind, tap Close.

Not Everything Is in HD

Some TV shows, such as early seasons of *Doctor Who*, are available in only one format. If a TV show is for sale in multiple formats, the purchase options reflect those choices.

Buying a Season TV Pass

Amazon offers a "TV Pass" for some series. When you purchase a TV Pass, you immediately get the season's episodes that have already aired, and new episodes of the season are made available to you after they air, often the next day. Although you can view episodes on your Kindle Fire, TV Pass purchases must be made on the Amazon website through a browser.

1. In your web browser, go to www.amazon.com/Instant-Video to access the Video Store.

2. Click TV to browse all the available options.

3. Search for a particular series.

4. Click a current season of a series.

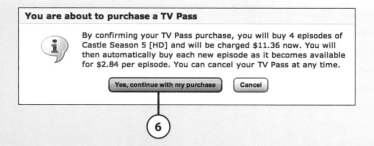

5. Click Buy TV Pass.

6. Click Yes, Continue with My Purchase.

Locating Your TV Pass Videos

Previously aired episodes of a series are immediately added to your Videos library. You can access them from Your Video Library on the Amazon site (www.amazon.com/gp/video/library) or from the Videos library on your Kindle Fire. New episodes automatically appear in your Videos library as they become available.

You can cancel a TV Pass at any time. If you decide to cancel a series, go to Your Video Library on the Amazon site. Click Passes and Preorders, and then click Cancel TV Pass.

Working with Your Video Library

Your video library contains video items that you own, as well as video rentals from the Video Store. Items that you own are always available in your video library unless you permanently delete them. Items that you rent appear in your video library only during the rental period, after which time they disappear.

Your Video Library

You can delete videos from your video library by visiting the Your Video Library page at www.amazon.com/gp/video/library. Simply click a video and then click the Delete link.

Watching a Movie or TV Show

You can stream movies and TV episodes from the cloud to your Kindle Fire as long as you have an active Wi-Fi connection. You can also watch videos that you've downloaded to your device.

1. From the Videos screen, tap Library.

2. Tap Movies or TV to locate the video you want to watch.

3. Tap Cloud to see movies in the cloud, or tap Device to see videos you've downloaded.

4. Tap the Menu button to bring up other options.

5. Tap Sort By to change how your videos are sorted, either by Recent or by Title.

6. Tap a video you want to watch.

7. Tap Watch Now to watch the video. You must remain connected to Wi-Fi while watching if you're streaming from the cloud.

8. Tap Download if you choose to download the video so that you can watch it even when you're not connected to Wi-Fi.

9. If the video is a rental, a warning appears to notify you that the rental period is beginning. Tap Start Rental to proceed.

10. While a video is playing, tap the middle of the screen to display the controls.

11. Tap Play/Pause to pause or resume the video.

12. Drag the slider to move to a specific point in the video.

13. Tap the Skip Back button to move backward 10 seconds.

14. Drag the volume slider to adjust the volume.

15. Tap the left side of the volume slider to mute the audio.

16. Tap the right side of the volume slider to increase the audio to the maximum setting.

17. Tap the X-Ray info to get more details about an actor in a scene.

18. Tap Back to return to the details screen for the video.

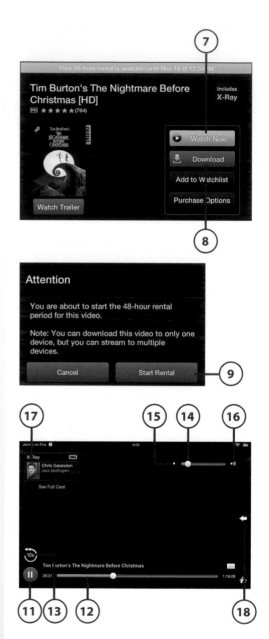

>>>Go Further

WATCHING AMAZON VIDEOS ON YOUR TV

After you rent or purchase a video, you can watch it on your Kindle Fire, your computer, or any compatible Internet-connected device. This includes your video game machine, Blu-ray player, Apple TV, or Internet-connected television. If you have an Amazon Prime account, you can also stream Amazon Instant Video titles over these devices.

You can also use a mini-HDMI cable to connect your Kindle Fire to your television and mirror your display on the TV.

Kindle Lending Library vs. Amazon Instant Video

Unlike the Kindle Lending Library for books, which can be utilized only directly from a Kindle device (not just any Kindle app), you can access Amazon Instant Video from your computer or other devices if you have an Amazon Prime account.

Using X-Ray for Video

Have you ever watched a movie and noticed a familiar actor, but you can't remember where you've seen him? X-Ray for Video tells you which actors are in each scene of a movie. If you want to learn more about an actor, you can get that person's complete film biography from IMDb, the Internet Movie Database.

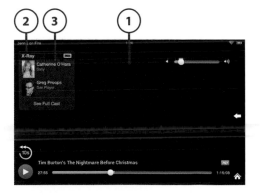

1. While watching a movie, tap the middle of the screen to bring up the video controls.

2. View the X-Ray for Video information on the screen.

3. Tap an actor's name to get more information.

4. Scroll to see more information about the actor.

5. Scroll to access other films in which the actor appears.

6. Tap and hold a film you want to remember to view in the future.

7. Tap Add to Watchlist.

8. Tap See Full Cast for a complete cast listing for the movie.

9. Tap Close to return to your movie.

Adding a Video to Your Watchlist

As you browse the Video Store, you're likely to find more movies and TV shows than you can possibly watch in one sitting. Instead of purchasing them all at once, add them to your Watchlist so you remember them later.

1. From the Video Store, tap a movie or TV show that interests you.

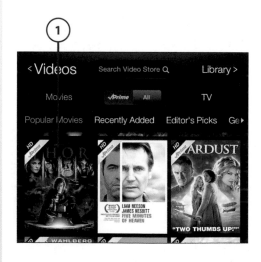

2. Tap Add to Watchlist.

3. Tap the Menu button.

4. Tap Your Watchlist.

Your Watchlist in the Video Store

Your Watchlist also appears on the main screen of the Video Store.

5. Tap Movies to view the movies in your Watchlist.

6. Tap TV to view the TV shows in your Watchlist.

7. Tap Prime to see videos on your Watchlist that are currently available for free streaming.

8. Tap a movie or TV show on your Watchlist to open the details screen.

Removing a Video from Your Watchlist

You can remove a video from your Watchlist by tapping the movie or TV show and then tapping the Remove from Watchlist button.

Downloading Movies

If you want to watch a video on a car trip, plane flight, or someplace else where you cannot get Wi-Fi access, you can plan ahead and download the video to your device in advance.

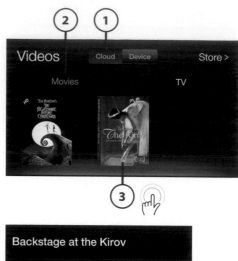

1. From your Videos library, tap Cloud.

2. Tap Movies.

3. Tap and hold the movie you want to download.

4. Tap Download to download the movie to your device.

5. Watch the progress bar while the movie downloads.

6. When the movie has finished downloading, an icon appears on its thumbnail.

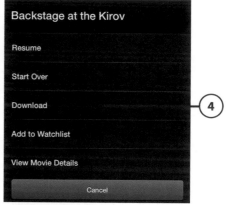

Managing Your Storage Space

Keep in mind that the average HD-quality movie is about 2GB, and the Kindle Fire HD comes with 16 or 32GB of storage (up to 64GB on the high-end models). By contrast, Amazon provides unlimited cloud storage for your Amazon purchases. It's best to store the majority of your movies in the cloud and download what you need only when you need it.

Downloading a TV Show

The process for downloading a TV show differs slightly from the process for movies because TV episodes are grouped by show.

1. From your Videos library, tap Cloud.

2. Tap TV.

3. Tap the TV show you want to download.

4. Tap the download icon for the episode you want to download.

5. Select the format you want to download. If you have a base-model Kindle Fire, choose SD format. If you have a Kindle Fire HD, you can choose HD for higher quality or choose SD to save time and storage.

6. Follow the progress of your download.

7. When the TV show has finished downloading, a check mark replaces the Download icon.

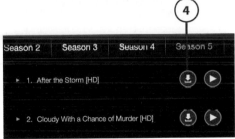

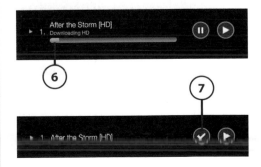

Removing a Downloaded Video

After you've watched a video, you might want to remove it from your device so that it doesn't take up space. If you own the video, you can download it again at any time.

1. From your Videos library, tap Device.

2. Tap and hold the video you want to delete from your device.

3. Tap Delete Download.

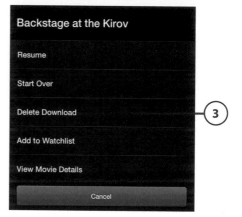

Sideloading Videos

Digital video comes in a wide assortment of formats. The Kindle Fire supports only one of them, MP4 (or MPEG 4). If you have video in other formats that you want to play on your Kindle Fire, you can convert it to an MP4 video using an app such as Handbrake on your PC or Mac. This free application and others like it convert into MP4 format any video that you download from the Internet or rip from DVDs.

Copying Video to Your Kindle Fire

Sideload videos onto your Kindle Fire using the instructions in Chapter 2, "Loading Your Kindle Fire."

1. Connect your Kindle Fire to your computer using a micro-USB cable.

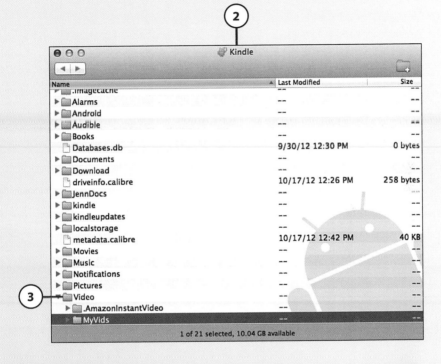

2. On a PC, open the drive for your Kindle Fire in Windows Explorer. On a Mac, open the Android File Transfer app.

3. Copy your video into the Video folder.

Organizing Your Personal Videos

You can create folders to organize your personal videos within the Kindle Fire's file system, but these folders do not appear when you view your videos on your Kindle Fire. The best use of a folder within the Video folder is simply to help distinguish your personal videos from any downloaded video content on your device.

Watching Sideloaded Videos

Sideloaded videos don't show up in your Videos library, even though they are stored in the Video folder. Instead, you need to use the Personal Video app on your Kindle Fire to watch them.

1. From your Home screen, tap Apps.

2. Tap the Personal Videos app.

3. Tap the video you want to watch.

4. Tap the middle of the screen to access the video controls.

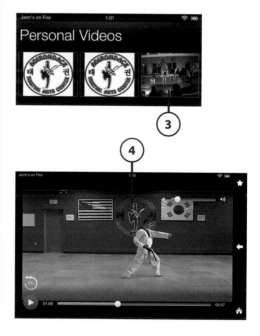

Deleting Sideloaded Videos

To delete sideloaded videos, you can simply delete the files from your Kindle Fire's Video folder using Windows Explorer (PC) or the Android File Transfer app (Mac). You can also delete them from within the Personal Videos app.

1. In Personal Videos, tap and hold the video you want to delete.

2. Tap Delete.

3. Tap OK to confirm the deletion.

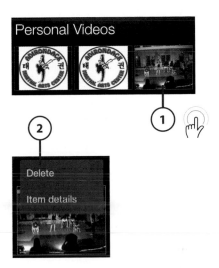

Turn your Kindle Fire
into a game machine

Get cool apps to enhance
the capabilities of your
Kindle Fire

In this chapter, you learn how to find and install apps from Amazon's Appstore for Android, as well as how to manage and use those apps. Topics include the following:

→ The Appstore
→ Your Apps library
→ Application Settings
→ Indispensable apps
→ Games for your Kindle Fire

Installing and Using Apps

You already know that your Kindle Fire is great for reading books, listening to music, and watching video. What you might not realize is that the Kindle Fire is capable of running apps that do a whole lot more. Your Kindle Fire comes with several apps already installed, and it provides access to Amazon's Appstore for Android so that you can get others. Apps that are available from the Appstore for Android on your Kindle Fire have been tested for compatibility with the Kindle Fire.

The Appstore for Android contains a wide assortment of apps for cooking, education, health and fitness, reference, productivity, shopping, sports, and games. Some of these apps are free; some are not. Unfortunately, you can't return an app for a refund after you buy it, so it's a good idea to read the reviews and look at the screenshots to decide whether an app is a good fit for you before you purchase it.

The Appstore

You purchase new apps for your Kindle Fire in the Appstore. When you browse the store from your Kindle Fire, all the apps listed are compatible with your device.

Appstore for Android from a Web Browser

You can also access the Appstore for Android on the Amazon website (www.amazon.com) on your computer using a web browser, but not all of the apps you see listed are compatible with your Kindle Fire. When you view an app from the Appstore for Android on a web browser, look for a check mark for the Kindle Fire, which indicates that the app is compatible.

An app compatible with the Kindle Fire.

Browsing Apps

The Appstore offers several tools to make shopping for apps easier.

1. From the Home screen, tap Apps to enter the Appstore.

2. Amazon offers a paid app for free every day. Tap to install the app.

3. Scroll to view highly rated apps.

4. Scroll to view apps that Amazon has recommended for you based on your previous browsing and purchasing history.

5. Scroll down to see new apps.

6. Tap to look for apps by category.

Returning to the Appstore

After you've opened the Apps library for the first time, tapping Apps from the Home screen puts you in the Apps library instead of the Appstore. To access the Appstore from the Apps library, tap Store at the top of the page.

Viewing and Purchasing Apps

You can view details of an app before you decide to purchase it.

1. Tap an app that interests you.

2. Scroll to view screenshots of the app.

3. Read a description of the app.

4. Scroll down to read reviews from other customers. You can also add your own review of the app.

5. Scroll down and read the permissions the app requires. These might have an impact on your privacy.

6. Read the product details, including the file size of the app, so you can control your storage.

7. Tap the price to purchase and install the app. If the app is free, the price button reads Free.

8. Tap the Save for Later button if you're interested in the app but not ready to purchase yet.

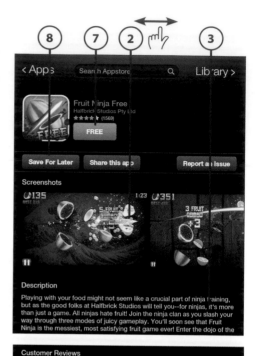

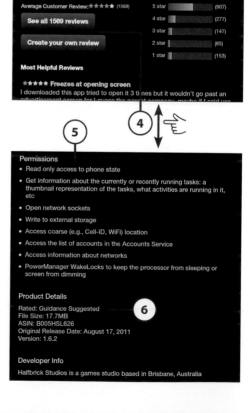

TEST-DRIVING AN APP

>>>Go Further

Most apps force you to make a purchasing decision based on a description, screenshots, and reviews. Some apps, however, offer a "test drive" mode on the Appstore for Android website. Use the web browser on your computer to go to the Appstore for Android, and then click the Test Drive Apps option. Choose an app to test. The app opens in a pop-up window with a replica of an Android device. Test drives are time-limited, and not all features might be available, but they generally offer a good idea of what the app has to offer. Remember to check whether the app is compatible with your Kindle Fire before purchasing from the Web.

Viewing Saved or Recently Viewed Apps

Your Saved for Later list is a wish list for apps. You can add to this list and access it at any time.

1. From anywhere in the Appstore, tap the menu icon.

2. Tap Saved for Later to view apps you've saved.

3. Tap an app in your list to open the details screen in the Appstore, where you can read more about it and purchase it if you're ready.

Removing Items from the Saved for Later List

Apps remain in the Saved for Later list until you remove them, even if you purchase the app. To remove an app from the list, tap it to open the details screen and then tap the Saved button.

Viewing Subscriptions

Some magazines are available for the Kindle Fire as apps. For example, the magazines *WIRED* and *The New Yorker* both have apps for accessing their content. The apps might offer additional features that aren't available from the Kindle Fire Newsstand. These magazines are typically offered as a free app, but to read the content, you must subscribe via the app. You can view the status and manage these subscriptions from the Appstore.

1. From the Appstore, tap the menu icon.

2. Tap My Subscriptions.

3. Tap a subscription to view details about it.

4. Tap Change Subscription Period if you want to change from a monthly subscription to an annual basis.

5. Tap a new subscription period.

6. Tap Save Changes.

7. If you want to turn off autorenewal so that your subscription is not automatically renewed when it's due to expire, tap Turn Off Auto-Renewal.

8. Tap Turn off Auto-Renewal.

Reactivating Auto-Renewal

After you've turned off auto-renewal, you can turn it back on by tapping Turn On Auto-Renewal in the subscription details.

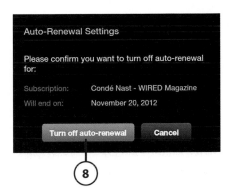

Auto-Renewal Settings

Please confirm you want to turn off auto-renewal for:

Subscription: Condé Nast - WIRED Magazine

Will end on: November 20, 2012

Turn off auto-renewal   Cancel

⑧

Your Apps Library

Your Apps library contains applications that you have downloaded to your device, as well as applications that you have purchased but not downloaded. When you purchase an app from the Appstore directly on your Kindle Fire, the app is added to your Apps library and installed on your device.

Included Free Apps

Amazon includes some free apps in your Apps library, but not all of them are preinstalled on your Kindle Fire. You'll see them when you tap the Cloud tab in your Apps library.

Browsing Your Apps Library

All your apps are available by browsing your Apps library.

1. From the Home screen, tap Apps. The Appstore opens.

2. Tap Library.

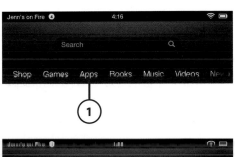

Jenn's on Fire

Search

Shop   Games   Apps   Books   Music   Videos   New

①

Apps   Search Appstore   Library >

②

3. Tap Cloud to see all the apps you've purchased, both on your device and in the cloud.

4. Tap Device to see only the apps that are installed on your device.

5. Tap By Recent to sort your apps according to when they were added to your library.

6. Tap By Title to sort your apps by title.

7. Scroll to see more apps.

8. Tap the Search icon to search your Apps library.

Installing a Purchased App

When you purchase an app from the Appstore for Android using your web browser, the app is stored in the cloud. You need to download and install it before you can use it. Installed apps appear in the Cloud listing with a check mark.

1. From the Cloud list in the Apps library, tap the app that you want to install.

2. Wait for your app to download and install. You can tap several apps at a time, and each is queued for download. A checkmark appears on the icon when the app is downloaded.

3. Tap an app to open it.

Accessing Your Apps

Aside from the Apps library, newly installed apps appear on the Carousel on your home screen.

It's Not All Good

Installing Apps from Unknown Sources

Your Kindle Fire provides the capability to sideload third-party apps from sources other than the Appstore. However, I advise against doing so, for a couple reasons. First, many of the apps I tested crashed my Kindle Fire or caused unpredictable behavior. The Kindle Fire version of the Android operating system is highly customized, so features that work well on an Android phone or tablet might not work on the Kindle Fire. Second, Android apps are a common source of Android viruses, and because the Kindle Fire is directly tied to your Amazon account, the risk of installing apps from unkown sources is simply too great to ignore.

Adding an App to Favorites

You can add an app to your Favorites shelf for easier access. Find more information on using and organizing your Favorites in Chapter 1, "Getting Started with the Kindle Fire."

1. Tap Device to see only the apps that you've installed.

2. Tap and hold the app that you want to add to Favorites.

3. Tap Add to Favorites.

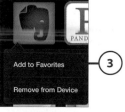

Uninstalling an App

Uninstalling an app removes it from your device, but it remains stored in the cloud. You can reinstall the app later without having to pay for it again.

1. Tap Device to see only the apps you've installed.

2. Tap and hold the app that you want to uninstall.

3. Tap Remove from Device to uninstall the app.

Cannot Uninstall Preinstalled Apps

Contacts, E-mail, Help & Feedback, IMDb, OfficeSuite, Personal Videos, Shop Amazon, Silk, and Calendar are all preinstalled apps that you cannot uninstall from your Kindle Fire. Each of these apps serves a purpose on the device. For example, the X-Ray for Movies feature uses IMDb.

Updating an Application

Your Kindle Fire automatically updates apps as new versions are released. You can change your update settings to turn off automatic updates or to receive a notice when an app is updated.

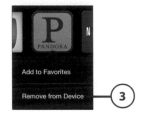

1. Swipe down from the status bar to open Settings.

2. Tap More.

3. Tap Applications.

4. Tap Appstore.

5. Tap Automatic Updates.

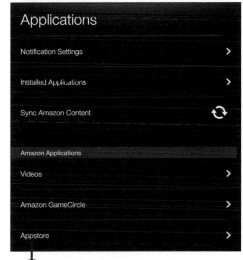

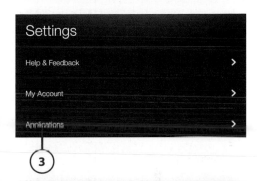

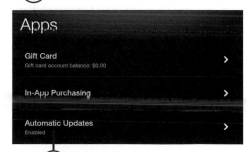

6. Enable Automatic Updates is selected by default. Deselect this option if you don't want your Kindle Fire to update apps automatically.

7. Tap Notify Me When Updates Are Installed if you want your Kindle Fire to display a notification whenever a new version of an app is installed. Notifications appear in the status bar.

Application Settings

Apps are prone to bugs that can cause them to become unresponsive or crash. This is why apps get updated so often, to fix the problems that become obvious only when a large number of users interact with the app.

In some cases, you might need to force an application to close if it's misbehaving. If an app is behaving unpredictably even after you force-close it and relaunch it, the app might have some corrupted data in its cache or database. You can force-close apps and delete app data from the Application Settings screen.

Force-Stopping an Application

If an app is causing problems on your Kindle Fire, or if it hangs and becomes unresponsive, you can force the app to close. This is called *force-stopping* an app.

1. Swipe down from the status bar.

2. Tap More.

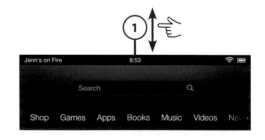

3. Tap Applications.

4. Tap Installed Applications.

5. Scroll to locate the app you want to stop, and then tap the app that's frozen.

6. Tap Force Stop to stop the app.

7. Tap OK in the confirmation dialog box to force-stop the app.

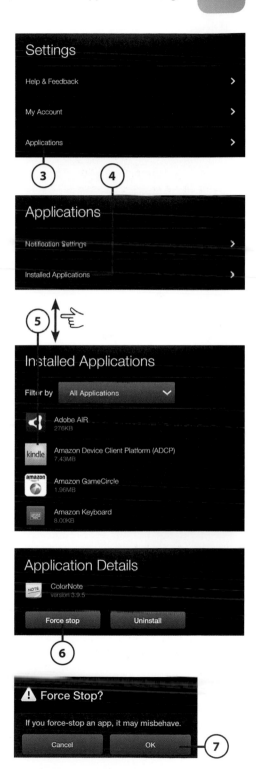

>>>Go Further

SHOULD YOU CLOSE YOUR APPS?

When you finish with an app on your Kindle Fire, you tap the Home button to get back to the home screen. When you do this, the app remains running in the background. After awhile, you might have dozens of apps running in the background on your Kindle Fire.

On a laptop or desktop computer, you don't want to have a large number of applications running when you're not using them because they can slow your computer. However, the Kindle Fire's operating system is designed to account for many apps running that aren't currently in use. When you switch away from an app, it enters a state in which it doesn't do anything. Some apps are designed to periodically check for content or perform some other task, but they go back to sleep after that task is completed. So although you can close apps you're not using, it's unnecessary.

Clearing Application Data

If an app is not working properly even after you force-stop it, the app's data might be corrupt. You can clear an app's data in Application settings.

1. While viewing the Installed Application settings, tap the app whose data you want to clear.

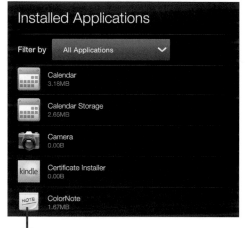

2. Tap Clear Data.

3. Tap OK in the confirmation dialog box.

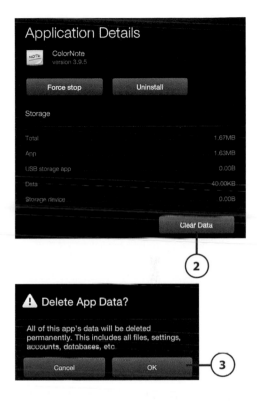

It's Not All Good

Clearing Data Clears Everything

When you clear data for an app, you clear all settings and any other data that the app has stored. The next time you launch the app, it starts with the default settings. Don't clear data unless you're sure that you don't need any information that the app is storing.

Indispensable Apps

Amazon includes several apps on your Kindle Fire when it ships. Some of these, such as the E-mail app, you might use every day. Other apps available in the Appstore are equally indispensable. These are merely my recommendations; you'll undoubtedly develop your own list of must-have apps as you use your Kindle Fire.

Evernote

Evernote is a notetaking app that enables you to store notes, photos, lists, and all the other scraps of data that cross your path. You can share notebooks with your computer, your smartphone, and even other Evernote users.

1. Launch Evernote.

2. Sign in or create a new Evernote account.

3. Add a new note.

4. Enter a note title.

5. Enter the note's content.

6. Add tags, audio, and photos to the note.

7. Tap Done to save the note.

8. Create different notebooks to organize your ideas.

Pandora

Pandora Internet Radio is a service that enables you to enter the name of a song or artist to get recommendations from Pandora for other songs you'll almost certainly like. It's a great way to discover new music.

1. Launch Pandora.

2. Sign in or create a new Pandora account.

3. To create a new station, enter an artist, genre, or composer. You can also view existing stations sorted by genre.

4. While a station is playing, tap Pause to pause playback. Tap Play to resume.

5. Tap Next to skip to a new song.

6. Tap the thumbs-up to tell Pandora that you like the current song.

7. Tap the thumbs-down to tell Pandora that you don't like the current song and to skip to the next song.

8. Tap the menu icon to see more options.

9. Tap Buy Track if you want to purchase the current song or album. This takes you to the Music Store on your Kindle Fire to complete the transaction.

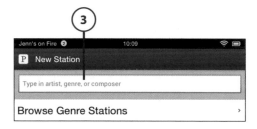

It's Not All Good

Finding Ads in Your Apps

Many free apps, such as Pandora, are ad supported. You get to use the app for free, but in return, you're presented with ads on the screen. Some apps offer an upgrade to an ad-free version, for a price. If the ads are unobtrusive, you hardly notice them after awhile. In the case of an app such as Pandora, however, with static ads displaying on the screen during every song and video ads appearing after every other song, upgrading is well worth the price if you use the app frequently.

ES File Explorer

The ES File Explorer app provides a convenient way to view files that are stored on your Kindle Fire. It's the easiest way I've found to locate files you downloaded from the Internet, attachments you've saved from e-mails, and other files stored on your Kindle Fire's internal memory.

Be Careful When Deleting or Renaming Files

Because ES File Explorer enables you to see the files that are part of your Kindle Fire's operating system, it's possible for you to corrupt your Kindle Fire if you delete or rename a system file. Be careful!

1. Launch ES File Explorer.

2. Tap a folder to see the contents of the folder.

3. Tap a file to open it, and then select an app capable of viewing it.

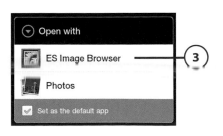

ES File Explorer and Viewing Files

ES File Explorer includes ES Image Browser and other mini-apps that can view certain file types. If you attempt to open a file type in ES File Explorer that isn't supported on your Kindle Fire, ES File Explorer typically displays a black screen instead of the file. In these cases, just tap Back to return to the interface.

Go Further

MORE APPS FOR YOUR CONSIDERATION

With more than 10,000 apps in the Appstore, this chapter could be endless. Other apps I use that you might want to explore include Weather+, Netflix, CalenGoo, Timers4Me, iTranslate, Pinterest, and Pocket (formerly Read It Later).

Games for Your Kindle Fire

No tablet device is complete without games, and the Kindle Fire is no exception. You can purchase and install games on your Kindle Fire from the Appstore for Android. They appear in the Apps library along with all your other apps.

Games also appear in the Games library. This screen makes it faster to access your games and provides access to certain game-specific features, such as tracking achievements and comparing scores with your friends using GameCircle.

Is GameCircle Necessary?

GameCircle adds a social element to your gameplay, but if that's not your thing, it's easily ignored. Learn more about GameCircle in Chapter 9, "Using Social Media and Chat."

Accessing Games

The Games library contains all apps that the Kindle Fire identifies as games. Developers identify the category of an app when they submit it to the Appstore.

1. From the home screen, tap Games.

2. Tap to download and install the app if it hasn't already been installed, or tap to play the game.

3. Tap Store to enter a special area in the Appstore for games.

4. Scroll to locate a game.

5. Choose a category of games to hone in on what you like to play.

6. Tap a game to view the details page.

7. Tap the price to purchase the game. This button reads Free if there is no charge for the app.

8. Tap Get App.

GAME RECOMMENDATIONS

Every game enthusiast has a favorite type of games. If you enjoy action games, try Temple Run, Fruit Ninja, and Doodle Jump. If you like physics-based games, any variation of Angry Birds fits the bill. Mystery Manor is a hidden-object game that's constantly expanding. If you want to play turn-based social games with your friends, consider Draw Something or Words with Friends. The Appstore has several sudoku apps for puzzle enthusiasts, or try Unblock Me. If you're feeling nostalgic for the board games of your youth, download The Game of Life.

>>>Go Further

Make video calls

Update your
Facebook status

Compare game
scores with
your friends

In this chapter, you learn how to interact with your friends using your Kindle Fire. Topics include the following:

→ Sharing with Facebook, Twitter, and the Kindle community
→ Video chatting over Skype
→ Sharing game achievements with GameCircle

Using Social Media and Chat

Your Kindle Fire provides several ways for you to connect with friends and family. Share notes, highlights, and final thoughts about the books you read on Facebook and Twitter. Import your Facebook photos onto your Kindle Fire. Make free video chat calls using the Skype app and the camera on your Kindle Fire. Compare achievements and high scores in your games with friends on GameCircle.

If you add some free apps to your Kindle Fire, you can also keep up with what your friends are doing on Facebook and Twitter.

Sharing with Facebook, Twitter, and the Kindle Community

When you initially set up your Kindle Fire, you are prompted to provide your Facebook and Twitter logins. Your Kindle Fire makes use of this information in several ways. Whenever you create a note or highlight in a book, you can quickly share it with your Facebook friends and Twitter followers.

Amazon also maintains its own social network, called the Kindle community. The Kindle community shares comments, reviews, and rankings of Kindle books.

It's Not All Good

Social Network Integration Does Not Equal Full Interaction

Adding your Facebook and Twitter information to your Kindle Fire settings enables you to post updates about your Kindle books but does not give you full access to Facebook and Twitter. If you want to post other updates or access your newsfeed, you need to download an app from the Appstore for Android. These apps are not preinstalled on the Kindle Fire.

Setting Up Your Social Networks

The initial setup sequence for your Kindle Fire asks for your Facebook and Twitter account information. If you did not provide that information initially, you can add it later.

1. Swipe down from the status bar.

2. Tap More from the settings options.

3. Tap My Account.

4. Tap Manage Social Network Accounts.

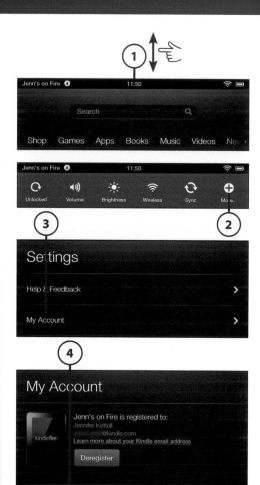

5. Tap Facebook if you want to link a Facebook account to your Kindle Fire.

6. Tap Log In. If you don't already have an account, tap Sign Up. Follow the prompts to authorize Amazon to link to your Facebook account.

7. Tap Twitter if you want to link a Twitter account to your Kindle Fire.

8. Enter your account info

9. If you don't already have a Twitter account, tap Sign Up.

10. Tap Authorize App and then follow the prompts to authorize Amazon to link to your Twitter account.

11. After linking your accounts, you can unlink them, if necessary, by tapping Unlink.

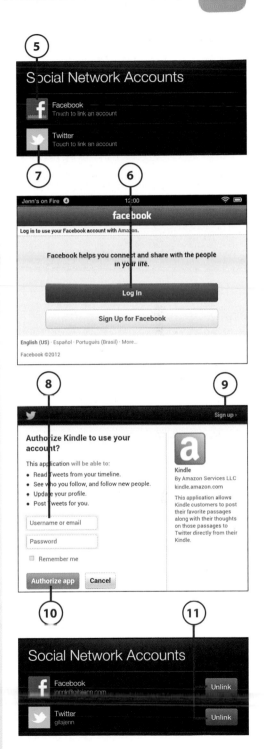

Sharing General Comments About Books

As you read a book on your Kindle Fire, you can share your thoughts with the Kindle community and your friends on Facebook and Twitter.

1. Tap the middle of a page in a book.

2. Tap Share.

3. Enter a comment.

4. Share with Twitter and Facebook, or choose just one of these services. Both services are selected by default if you have linked your Kindle Fire to those accounts.

5. Tap Share.

6. Your comment appears in the general thread for the book on the Kindle community. You can delete your comment by tapping the X button.

7. Scroll to read other readers' comments.

8. Press the Back button to return to your book.

Seeing Your Twitter and Facebook Posts

When you share your comments, you see the post as it appears in the Kindle community, but not your Facebook or Twitter updates. To see those, you need to access Facebook and Twitter. You can do this on your Kindle Fire using Silk to browse to the Facebook and Twitter sites or using a Facebook or Twitter app downloaded from the Appstore. You can also use a web browser on your computer.

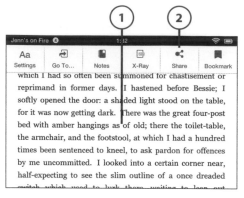

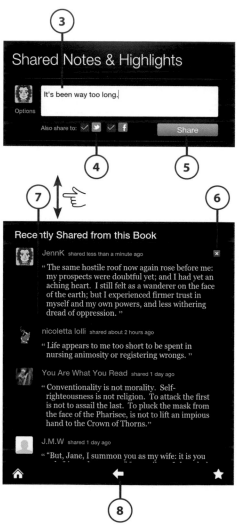

Sharing Highlights from Books

You can highlight key passages in a book to share with the Kindle community and your friends on Twitter and Facebook.

Adding Highlights

Learn how to mark up your books with highlights in the "Working with Notes and Highlights" section of Chapter 4, "Reading on the Kindle Fire."

1. In a book, tap and hold while moving over a passage to select it.

2. Tap Share.

3. Add an optional note.

4. Share with Twitter and Facebook, or choose just one of these services. Both services are selected by default if you have linked your Kindle Fire to those accounts.

5. Tap Share.

6. Press the Back button to return to your book.

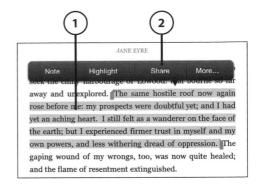

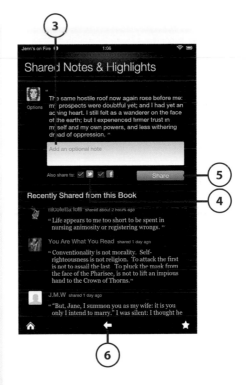

THE KINDLE COMMUNITY

When you share highlights and notes, rate a book, or generally comment on a Kindle book, those insights are automatically posted to the Kindle community, as well as to Twitter or Facebook (if you opted to share with those services). To access more of the Kindle community and follow other readers with similar reading tastes, use your web browser to go to kindle.amazon.com.

Before You Go in Books

When you reach the end of a book, the Before You Go page appears. Rate and review the book you just read, and share your comments with the Kindle community, your Facebook friends, and your Twitter followers.

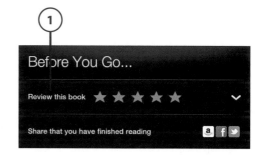

1. From the Before You Go page, tap Review This Book.

2. Tap the stars to give the book a rating.

3. Type a headline for your review.

4. Enter a review. Your review must be at least 20 words, but it can be quite lengthy, if you prefer.

5. Tap Submit.

6. Tap Share That You Have Finished Reading.

7. Enter your comments.

8. Share with Twitter and Facebook, or choose just one of these services. Both services are selected by default if you have linked your Kindle Fire to those accounts.

9. Tap Share.

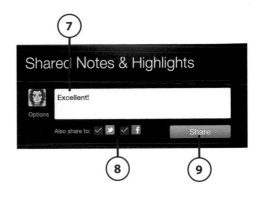

Importing Your Facebook Photos

If you linked your Facebook account to your Kindle Fire, you can import your Facebook photo gallery into the Photos library. Imported photos are stored in the cloud. You can then download them onto your device, if you want.

1. From the Home screen, tap Photos.

2. Tap the menu button.

3. Tap Import.

4. Tap OK to continue. It might take a minute for your import to begin.

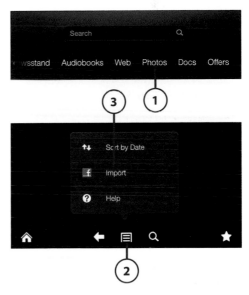

5. Tap OK to confirm the import.

6. The Kindle Fire imports your photos into the same folders in which they were organized on Facebook. Tap a folder to view the photos in that gallery.

Storing Photos on Your Cloud Drive

Imported Facebook photos are stored on your Cloud Drive. For more information about how to use your Cloud Drive, see the "Amazon Cloud Drive" section of Chapter 2, "Loading Your Kindle Fire." Remember, you have 5GB of free space on your Cloud Drive. If you're importing a lot of photos, purchase additional cloud storage, if necessary.

Using the Facebook App

If you want to post status updates or read your newsfeed on Facebook, you need to install a Facebook app. The Appstore offers several apps that can connect to Facebook, including the official Facebook app.

Downloading and Installing the Facebook App

To learn how to locate, download, and install an app from the Appstore for Android, see Chapter 8, "Installing and Using Apps."

1. Download and install the Facebook app from the Appstore, and then tap the app to open it.

2. The Facebook app automatically uses your account information if you linked your Facebook account to your Kindle Fire. Scroll down to read your newsfeed.

3. Tap the menu button to open the side menu.

4. Tap Messages to view your private messages.

5. Tap Events to respond to events to which you've been invited.

6. Tap Friends to access a list of all your Facebook friends and any pages you've Liked.

7. Tap a group to access the group's newsfeed.

8. Swipe from right to left to close the menu and return to your newsfeed.

9. Tap the Friends icon to respond to friend requests.

10. Tap the Messages icon to read and send private messages.

11. Tap the Notifications icon to view your notifications.

12. Tap Status to post a status update.

13. Tap Photo to upload a photo from your Photos library.

14. Tap the menu icon to access settings for the Facebook app.

Some Features Are Not for the Kindle Fire

The Facebook app is designed for all Android devices, including smartphones, so some of the features do not work on the Kindle Fire. The Check In feature cannot pinpoint your location, and most of the Settings options are designed for Android smartphone notifications, not the Kindle Fire.

>>>Go Further

USING TWITTER FROM YOUR KINDLE FIRE

At this time, no official Twitter app exists for the Kindle Fire. If you want to view your timeline and tweet from your Kindle Fire, you need to install a third-party app from the Appstore. Tweetcaster is a popular choice that displays your newsfeed, allows you to compose tweets, shows you trending topics, and enables you to manage your account and followers.

Some apps consolidate all your social media networks in one place. HootSuite connects to Twitter, Facebook, FourSquare, and LinkedIn. Seesmic accesses Twitter and Facebook. Scope, an app still in beta, brings together Facebook, Twitter, FourSquare, Instagram, and Tumblr.

Video Chatting over Skype

Your Kindle Fire has a front-facing camera to facilitate video chat. Skype is a free app that makes video calls to anyone around the world. Put the two together, and you have everything you need to video chat with your friends and family. You can also use it to make free voice calls to other Skype users or buy Skype credits to make regular domestic and international voice calls.

Skype is available for the Kindle Fire, other Android tablets and smartphones, iPhone and iPad, Windows, and Mac. If you want to video chat with someone, chances are, she can install the Skype app to facilitate it.

Setting Up Skype

Amazon adds the Skype account to your cloud account when you register your Kindle Fire, so it's already available for you to download and install.

1. From the Home screen, tap Apps.

2. Tap Cloud to access your apps in the cloud.

3. Tap Skype to download and install the app. After the app is installed, tap it again to open it.

4. Tap Continue. When asked to accepts Skype's terms and conditions, tap Accept.

5. If you've used Skype in the past, enter your Skype name and password; then tap Sign In.

6. If you are new to Skype, tap Create an Account.

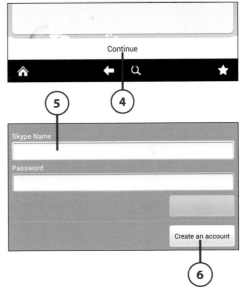

7. To sign up for an account, enter your contact information.

8. Tap Next. Tap Continue to progress through the information screens.

9. Tap Contacts to view and create Skype contacts.

10. Tap Call Phones to dial a number that's not in your contacts.

11. Tap Recent to call someone you've recently contacted.

12. Tap Profile to access your account information.

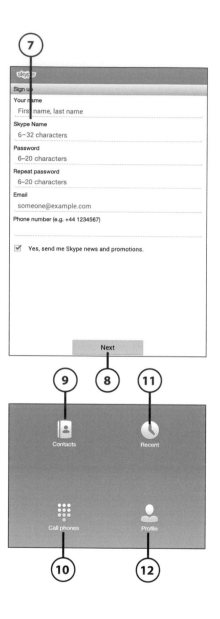

13. Tap Skype Credit to purchase credits to use on voice calls to landlines and mobile phones that don't have Skype.

14. Tap Skype Number to obtain a phone number where you can be reached by friends and family who do not have Skype.

15. Update your status for all your Skype contacts.

16. Tap Profile to add or edit your personal information, email address, location, and contact info.

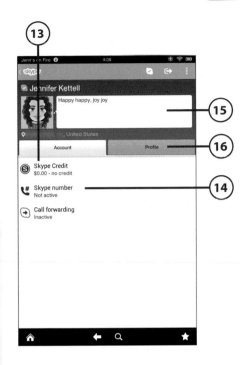

Adding Skype Contacts

Before making a call, add your friends and family to your Skype contacts list.

1. From the Skype home screen, tap Contacts.

2. Tap the menu button.

3. Tap Add Contacts.

4. Enter your friend's name, email address, or Skype name.

5. Tap the name you want to add.

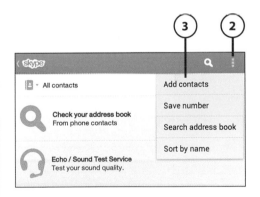

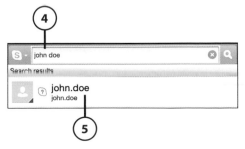

6. Tap Add.

7. Tap Add Contacts.

Making a Call with Skype

After your contact request has been accepted, tap the name of the contact to open that person's profile.

1. Tap Video Call to video chat.

2. Skype initiates a call. Tap the Disconnect button if the contact doesn't answer.

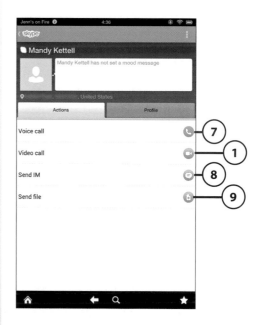

3. When the call connects, your contact's image appears. Tap the video camera to turn your own video image on or off.

4. Tap the microphone to mute the sound so that the person on the call can't hear you. Tap it again to restore the sound.

5. Tap the plus sign to add another caller to the video chat.

6. Tap the phone to disconnect the call.

7. Tap Voice Call to make a voice-only call.

8. Tap Send IM to send an instant message.

9. Tap Send File to send a file from your Docs, Videos, or Photos libraries.

10. To receive a call, tap the green phone button to respond only by voice.

11. Tap the green video camera to respond by voice and video.

12. Tap the red phone to reject the call.

Sharing Game Achievements with GameCircle

Gaming on your Kindle Fire can become a social experience. Although you cannot play a multiplayer game on the Fire and interact with your friends in real time, you can share your achievements in certain games and challenge your friends to see who can get the highest score.

GameCircle brings this social interaction to your Kindle Fire games. Although you don't have to use GameCircle to play any game on the Kindle Fire, if you want to work to earn trophies or show up your friends, this is a great way to do it.

Identifying GameCircle Games

Not every game can interact with GameCircle. The game developer decides whether to include these features in an app.

1. From the Home screen, tap Games.

2. Tap Device to locate games that are installed on your Kindle Fire.

3. Select a game that shows a series of blue icons to the right of the name. These are GameCircle games.

4. Tap to see which GameCircle friends are playing this game.

5. Tap to see which achievements you've reached in the game.

6. Tap to see the leaderboard for the game.

7. Tap to see a summary for the game.

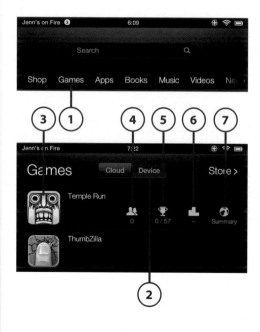

Buying and Installing Apps

If you need help finding and installing apps, see Chapter 8, "Installing and Using Apps."

It's Not All Good

Finding GameCircle Games

Locating GameCircle games is not easy. If you're shopping in the Appstore (whether from the Apps or Games pages), no designation in the game details lets you know whether a game is GameCircle enabled. You can tell only after you've installed downloaded the game and see the GameCircle details appear next to the game's listing in your Games library.

If you want to find out in advance whether a game utilizes GameCircle, you need to use a web browser to visit the Appstore for Android on the Amazon site. There you can click the Amazon GameCircle link to browse for games with this feature. Even on the website, however, the details page for the games themselves does not indicate whether they're powered by GameCircle. Let's hope that, as this feature becomes more popular, Amazon decides to promote it better.

Creating a GameCircle Profile

The first time you play a GameCircle-enabled game, your Kindle Fire automatically creates a nonsensical username and profile for you. Fortunately, you can update and customize it to your liking.

1. In the Games library, tap the menu icon.

2. Tap Profile to see your current GameCircle nickname and avatar.

3. Tap Edit.

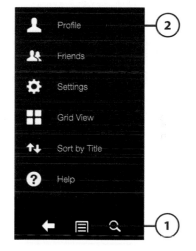

4. Swipe to choose a different avatar.

5. Tap to enter a new nickname.

6. Tap Update.

7. Tap the Back button to return to your Games library.

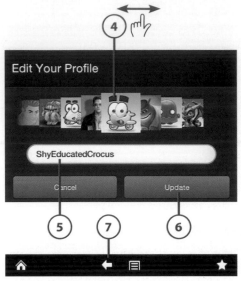

Adding Friends on GameCircle

Share your GameCircle nickname with your friends so they can find your name on the leaderboards.

1. From the Games library, tap the menu icon.

2. Tap Friends.

3. Tap Add Friends.

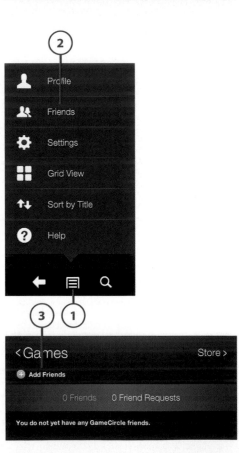

4. Enter the GameCircle nickname of a friend.

5. Tap the Search key.

6. When you find the friend you're looking for, tap Friend.

Accessing Game Achievements

Games in GameCircle offer trophies for achievments as you play. An achievement might be to collect a certain number of points or reach a particular level.

1. In the Games library, tap the trophy icon for a GameCircle game.

2. Scroll through the possible achivements.

3. Track your progress toward an achievement by viewing the completion percentage.

4. See the date when you completed a goal.

5. Tap Play to play the game.

Accessing Leaderboards

The leaderboard shows current high scores for a game. Some games don't have a leaderboard; others have multiple leaderboards for different goals in the game.

1. In the Games library, tap the leaderboard icon for a GameCircle game.

2. Tap a leaderboard to see the gamers who have reached the top of that chart.

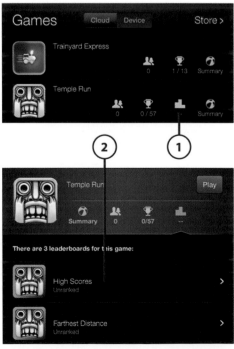

3. Tap Top 100 to see more rankings.

4. Tap a timeframe to see top scorers for that period.

5. Tap Play to play the game.

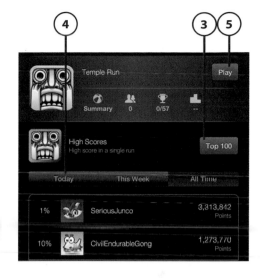

FINDING FRIENDS ON THE LEADERBOARDS

If you don't know anyone who plays games on a Kindle Fire, you can find GameCircle friends by checking the leaderboards for the games you play. Tap a nickname, and then tap Friend. The players with the highest scores are the most avid gamers and generally the most willing to make friends in a game.

Viewing Game Summaries

The game summary provides an overview of the leaderboards, achievements, and top players for a game.

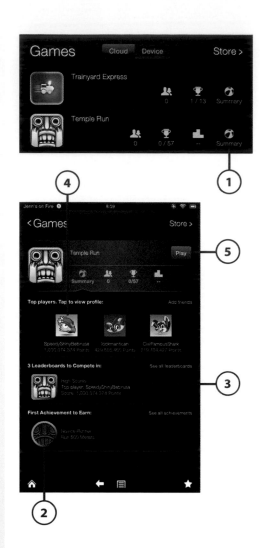

1. In the Games library, tap the Summary icon for a GameCircle game.

2. Review the next achievement you need to earn.

3. See how many points the high scorer has in the game.

4. Tap a top player's avatar to view that profile.

5. Tap Play to play the game.

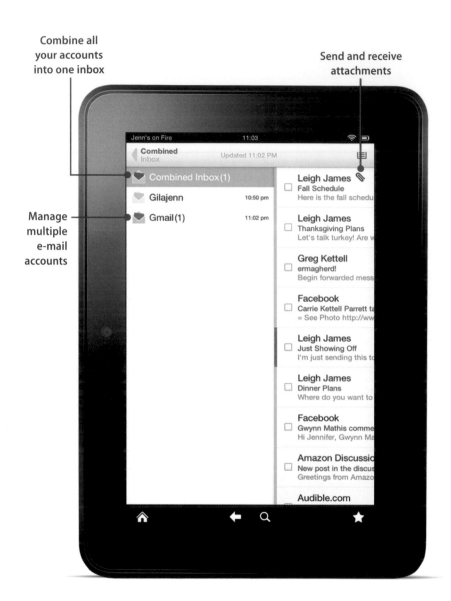

Combine all your accounts into one inbox

Send and receive attachments

Manage multiple e-mail accounts

In this chapter, you learn how to set up e-mail accounts on your Kindle Fire, how to check your e-mail, and how to send e-mail. You also learn how to deal with e-mail attachments. Topics include the following:

→ E-mail accounts
→ Managing your e-mail inbox
→ Reading e-mail

Reading and Sending E-mail

Your Kindle Fire comes with an app for e-mail. You can read your e-mail, send mail, and even view attachments. The Kindle Fire supports various e-mail services, including Gmail, Hotmail, Yahoo!, and POP3 and IMAP servers.

E-mail Accounts

The first step in using e-mail on your Kindle Fire is setting up your e-mail account. You can set up multiple e-mail accounts on your Kindle Fire. You can then either access each inbox individually or use the combined inbox to see all your messages from all accounts on one screen.

Accessing the Add Account Page

The Kindle Fire makes adding your e-mail accounts easy, whether it's from a service such as Gmail, a Microsoft Exchange account, or a POP3/IMAP account.

1. Swipe down from the status bar to open the settings.

2. Tap More.

3. Tap Applications.

4. Tap E-mail, Contacts, Calendars.

5. Tap Add Account.

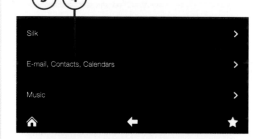

Adding a Gmail, Hotmail, AOL, or Yahoo! Account

If you have an account with a web-mail provider—Gmail, Hotmail, AOL, or Yahoo!—all you need is your e-mail address and password to set up your account on your Kindle Fire.

1. From the Add Account screen, tap the type of account you want to add.

2. Enter your name as you want it to appear on messages you send.

3. Enter your e-mail address. Use the full address, yourname@gmail.com (or yourname@aol.com, and so on).

4. Enter the password for your e-mail account.

5. Swipe down to continue.

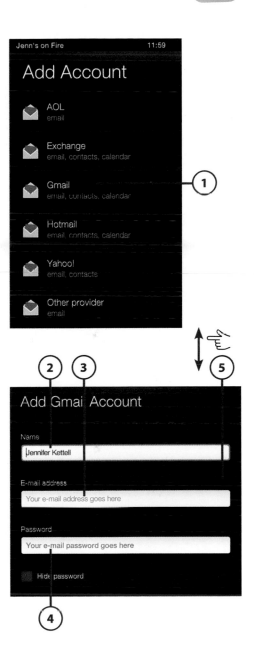

6. The Description field is automatically filled in with the name of the host, but you can change this. If you have more than one account with a host, you should customize this field to distinguish your account inboxes.

7. Tap Next.

8. If your host offers integration with a calendar or contact-management service, you can select to synchronize those with your Kindle Fire.

9. Tap Save.

10. If you want to immediately access your e-mail, tap View Inbox.

11. To view or change your account settings, tap Go to Account Settings. (I talk more about this page in the "Modifying Your Account Settings" section.)

12. Tap Add Another Account if you have additional e-mail accounts.

13. Tap the Home button to return to your Home screen.

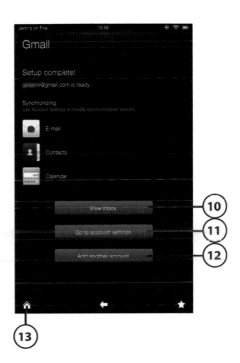

Using Your Contacts and Calendar

Many services enable you to synchronize the contacts and calendars you have stored on their site with your Kindle Fire's Contacts and Calendar apps. Learn more about these apps in Chapter 11, "Managing Your Personal Documents and Data."

Adding a POP3 or IMAP Account

If your e-mail account is through your Internet service provider (ISP) or a private domain, you need to gather more information before setting up your account. Be sure to have your e-mail address, password, IMAP or POP3 (incoming mail) server name, and SMTP (outgoing mail) server name. You also need to know what type of security is used on the mail servers (usually SSL.)

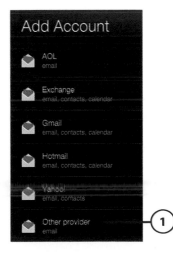

1. From the Add Account screen, tap Other Provider.

2. Type your name as you want it to appear on your messages.

3. Enter your e-mail address.

4. Type your password.

5. Swipe down to continue.

6. The Description field uses the domain name of your e-mail address by default. You can change this if you want.

7. Tap Next.

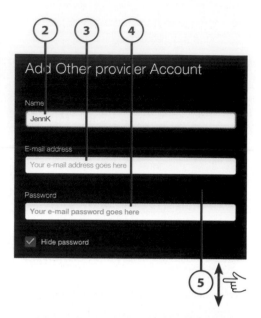

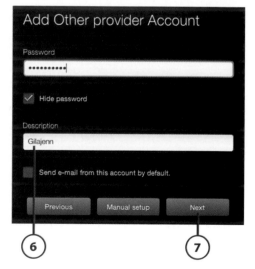

8. Choose an account type, either IMAP or POP3.

9. Confirm your username. This is usually your e-mail address, but if your host uses a different username, enter it here.

10. Confirm your password.

11. Swipe down to continue.

12. Enter your IMAP (or POP3) server name.

13. Select the security type of your server.

14. Change the port number, if necessary.

15. Swipe down to continue.

16. Enter your outgoing (SMTP) server. In some cases, this is the same as the IMAP server name.

17. Select the security type for the SMTP server.

18. Change the port number, if necessary.

19. Swipe down to continue.

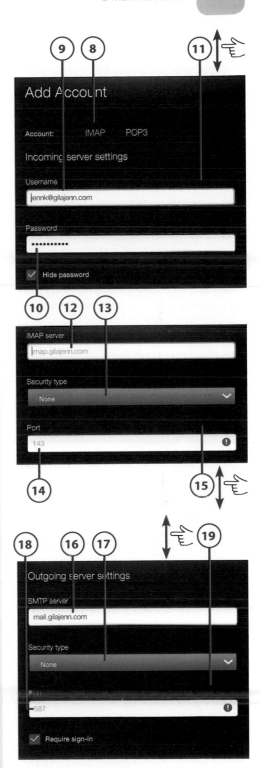

20. If your SMTP server requires you to log in, enter the username and password here.

21. Tap Next. If any of your settings has an error, you will not be able to move forward until you correct it.

22. Tap Save.

23. Tap View Inbox to immediately access your e-mail.

24. Tap Go to Account Settings to view or change your settings.

25. Tap Add Another Account if you have additional e-mail addresses you want to use with your Kindle Fire.

26. Tap the Home button to return to the Home screen.

Adding a Microsoft Exchange Account

If you use a Microsoft Exchange account, a type used in many corporate settings, you need to know your host server name and your domain name. If you don't know this information, ask your network administrator to help you set up your account.

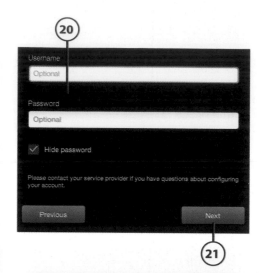

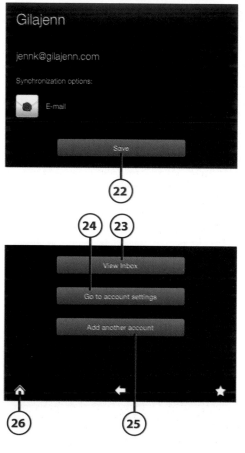

WHAT'S THE DIFFERENCE BETWEEN IMAP AND POP3?

The POP3 protocol downloads your e-mail onto your Kindle Fire (or your computer or other device). The advantage to this is that your e-mail is available even if you don't have an Internet connection. If you reply to a message, however, it is saved on your device, which means you cannot access it from your other computers and devices. And if your device crashes, your messages are lost. You can optionally configure POP3 to leave messages on the server, but if you read your mail on multiple devices, they are flagged as new on each device. Reading the same messages multiple times is sure to get annoying.

The IMAP protocol connects you directly to the server and keeps your e-mail on the server. This keeps it available from any device you use to access your mail, and all your replies remain available as well. Even if your device crashes, your messages are safe on the server. IMAP also lets you create folders to organize your messages. The only disadvantage to IMAP is that your mail is not available if you cannot connect to the Internet.

If your e-mail provider offers a choice of connecting to your e-mail server through either POP3 or IMAP, I recommend IMAP, especially if you're accessing your messages on multiple devices, such as your Kindle Fire, your computer, and a smartphone.

Modifying Your Account Settings

When you have your e-mail account set up, you can modify the default settings to automatically check mail less frequently or append a text signature to your outgoing messages.

1. Swipe down from the status bar to open Settings.

2. Tap More.

3. Tap Applications.

4. Tap E-mail, Contacts, Calendars.

5. Tap an e-mail account to modify its account settings.

6. Turn syncing of e-mail, the calendar, or contacts on or off.

7. Tap to change the frequency with which your Kindle Fire checks for e-mail.

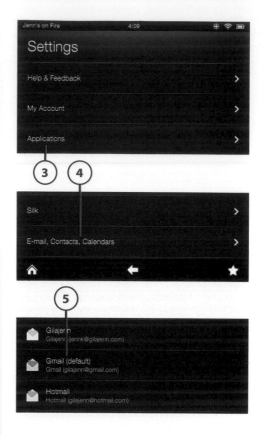

8. Choose a new setting for Inbox Check Frequency.

9. Tap to change how long your Kindle Fire stores old e-mail messages.

10. Select a new duration for storing messages.

11. Tap to create a signature line that's automatically appended to every message you send from this e-mail account.

12. Type a signature line and then tap OK. This is usually your name and title or a message stating that you're typing on your Kindle Fire (which can serve as a warning to recipients that you're not fully responsible for typos).

13. Tap to change the server settings. This opens the account setup screen so that you can change the password or server information for your account.

CHANGING E-MAIL GENERAL SETTINGS

Aside from the settings specific to each account, you can modify the general settings for the E-mail app. To do this, choose E-mail General Settings from the E-mail, Contacts, Calendars page. From the General Settings page, you can change the text size of messages, instruct the Kindle Fire to show or hide images embedded in the messages you receive, and decide whether to quote the original message when you reply to an e-mail.

You can also tell the Kindle Fire to automatically download attachments. I recommend leaving this option set to the default, which is not to automatically download attachments. This protects you against downloading a virus and keeps you in control of how your storage is used on your Kindle Fire. You can always manually download the attachments you want to keep on your device.

Removing an Account

If you change e-mail providers or no longer want your Kindle Fire to check an account for e-mail, you can remove it from your Kindle Fire.

1. From the E-mail, Contacts, Calendars page, type the account you want to remove.

2. Scroll to the bottom of the account settings screen.

3. Tap Remove Account.

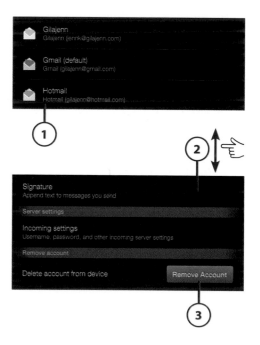

4. Tap OK to confirm the deletion of the account.

Deleting an Account Deletes Your Data

When you remove an account from your Kindle Fire, all the e-mail, contacts, and calendars associated with that account are deleted. If you remove a POP3 account and did not have your messages saved on the server, those messages are gone forever.

Managing Your E-mail Inbox

The E-mail app is preinstalled in the Apps library on your Kindle fire. It is also automatically added to your Favorites drawer. When you open it the first time, the app also appears on your home screen Carousel.

Your inbox is where you can view all the e-mail messages you have received. Without opening a mail message, you can see who sent the mail, the subject of the e-mail, and a brief snippet of the message. You can also flag your mail, sort it, and delete messages you aren't interested in.

Choosing an Inbox

Your inbox can display e-mail messages from a single account or in a combined account view that shows all messages from all accounts.

1. From your inbox, tap an account name.

2. Select a different account to view the inbox for that account.

3. Select Combined Inbox to view the inbox for all the accounts at once.

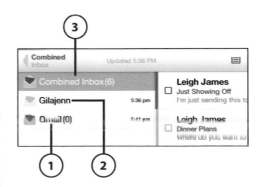

Determining the Source of a Message

Each e-mail account is color-coded when you add it to your Kindle Fire. As you scroll through your combined inbox, the color of the bar to the left of the message identifies which account it came from.

Choosing a Folder

Most e-mail providers enable you to create folders so that you can organize e-mail that you want to keep. You can choose which folder is displayed when viewing an account's inbox.

1. From your account inbox, tap the Inbox button to open the account menu.

2. Tap Show Folders.

3. Select a folder to display the messages in that folder.

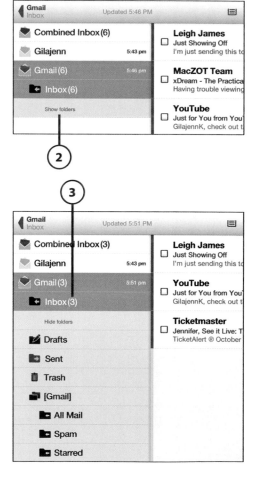

It's Not All Good

Creating Folders

You can use folders on your Kindle Fire, but you can't create them on the device. To create folders for your e-mail account, you have to use an e-mail program on your computer or in your web browser. Those folders are then synced with your Kindle Fire the next time it checks your e-mail.

Searching E-mail

You can search your e-mail messages.

1. Tap the Search icon.

2. Enter the text you want to search for.

3. Tap the part of the message you want to search.

4. Tap a message from your search results to open the message. You can search the subject, the To field, and the From field for all message types. You can search the entire message for IMAP and POP3 accounts.

5. Tap the back arrow to exit the search.

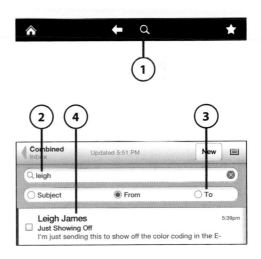

You Can't Search the Text of a Message

The search function in e-mail is very limited. You cannot search the text of a message unless the e-mail account type supports it. If you use the combined inbox and one of the accounts doesn't support searching the text of a message, that type of search is unavailable for all messages in the combined inbox. IMAP supports full message search, but Gmail does not.

Synchronizing E-mail and Loading More Messages

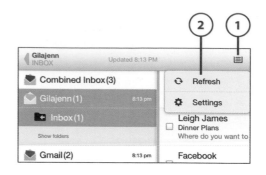

Your Kindle Fire automatically checks for mail with the frequency you selected in the account settings. You can manually synchronize at any time to check for new messages between update intervals. The Kindle Fire downloads 25 messages at a time, but you can request more.

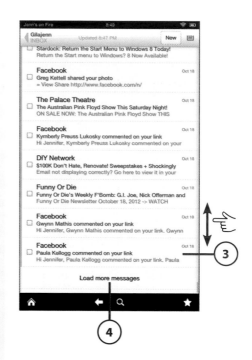

1. From your inbox, tap the menu icon.

2. Tap Refresh.

3. To load additional messages, scroll to the bottom of your inbox.

4. Tap Load More Messages.

Requesting Additional Messages

The Load More Messages option appears only on POP3 and IMAP accounts.

Selecting and Managing Multiple Messages

You can select one or more messages in your inbox and then choose to delete them, move them to another folder, or mark them as read or unread.

1. Tap the check box next to the messages you want to select.

2. Tap Delete to delete the messages.

3. Tap Move to move the messages to another folder.

4. Choose a folder to move the messages into.

5. Tap Mark to open the Mark menu.

6. Mark the messages as read or unread. This menu item is a toggle, based on whether the selected messages are currently read or unread.

7. Tap Star to flag a message as important. Flagged messages appear with a star under the date and time received.

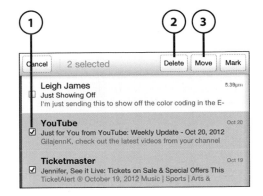

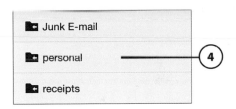

Reading E-mail

Having e-mail on your Kindle Fire is a great convenience. Not only is it nice to browse your mail while you relax on the couch, but it's also easy to triage your e-mail from the Kindle Fire. By that, I mean that you can quickly peruse your inbox and delete junk mail or other mail you're not interested in, move mail to another folder, mark important mail for follow-up later, and so forth. Then when you sit down at your computer, you know exactly which messages are worth your attention.

Reading a Message

While reading a message, you can view address details, delete the message, move it to another folder, or flag it with a star.

1. Tap a message in your inbox to open it.

2. Tap Details/Hide Details to display or hide the recipients of the message, including the Cc: list.

3. Tap Newer to read the next message up in your inbox.

4. Tap Older to read the next-oldest message in your inbox.

5. Tap Delete to delete the message.

6. Tap Respond to reply to the message.

7. Tap Reply to reply to the sender.

8. Tap Reply All to reply to the sender and everyone on the To: or Cc: list.

9. Tap Forward to forward the message and any attachments to a new recipient.

10. Tap New to compose a new message.

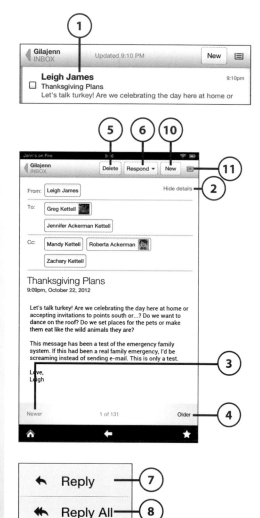

11. Tap the menu button for more options.

12. Tap Move to move the message into another folder.

13. Tap Star to flag the message as important.

14. Tap Mark Unread to mark the message as unread in your inbox.

15. Tap Settings to go to the E-mail, Contacts, Calendars page to change either account settings or general settings for your e-mail.

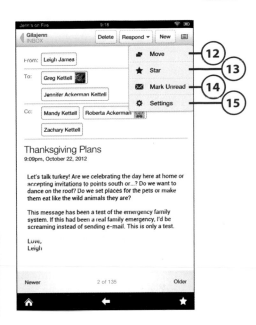

Viewing Attachments

Your Kindle Fire comes with apps that can view many file types, including images, videos in MP4 format, PDF files, and Microsoft Office documents. If you receive attachments in these formats, you can download and access them on your Kindle Fire.

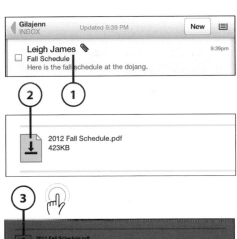

1. Tap a mail message containing an attachment. A paperclip appears on messages with attachments in the inbox.

2. Tap the attachment. The file downloads, and the icon changes to show the format of the file.

3. Tap and hold the attachment to open the attachment menu.

4. Tap Open to open the attachment in an appropriate app.

5. Tap Save to save the attachment onto your Kindle Fire.

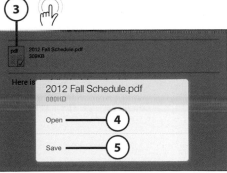

Opening Saved Attachments

When you save an attachment, your Kindle Fire automatically puts the file in the appropriate library. PDFs are stored in your Docs library, for example.

Composing a New E-mail Message

You can compose a new e-mail either while viewing your inbox or while viewing a message.

1. Tap the New icon.

2. Enter the e-mail address of the recipient of your message. Separate multiple e-mail addresses with a comma.

3. Tap the plus (+) sign to select a contact from your Contacts app. For more information on the Contacts app, see Chapter 11, "Managing Your Personal Documents and Data."

4. Tap Options.

5. Enter one or more e-mail addresses in the Cc: field if you want additional people copied on your message.

6. Enter one or more e-mail addresses in the Bcc: field if you want to copy additional people on your message without the other recipients seeing their address(es).

7. Tap your e-mail address in the From: field if you want to change which account sends the message.

8. Enter a subject for your message.

9. Enter the text of the message.

10. Tap Attach to attach a file to your message.

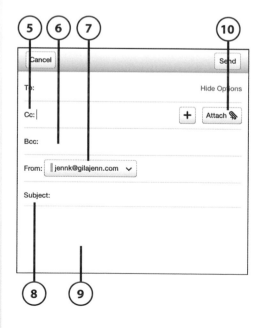
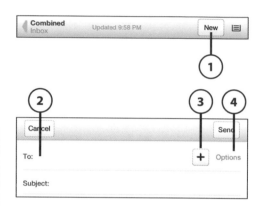

11. Choose an app to use for browsing to the file you want to attach.

12. Select the file you want to attach using the app you selected.

13. Tap the X to remove an attached file.

14. Tap Send to send your message.

15. Tap Cancel if you decide not to send your message right away.

16. Tap Save Draft if you want to save the message to edit and send later.

17. Tap Delete Draft to cancel and delete the message.

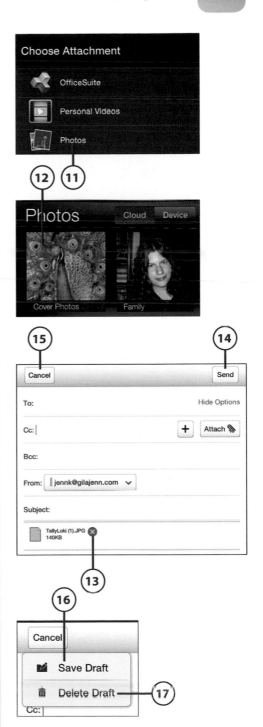

Schedule events

Manage
your
contacts

Read and
edit your
personal
documents

Jenn's on Fire   11:00

Search   Q

Shop   Games   Apps   Books   Music   Videos   Ne

pdf
shopping-li

TUE

23

Quick Links

New Message   This Week   Favorite Contacts

Quick access
to contacts
and your
calendar

In this chapter, you learn how to maintain the documents and contact information that convert your Kindle Fire from a content viewer into a personal management tool. Topics include the following:

→ Managing personal documents
→ Using the contacts app

Managing Your Personal Documents and Data

Life is messy. You accumulate all manner of bits and pieces of information, phone numbers, and appointments just going about your day. You learned in earlier chapters how to use your Kindle Fire to view content and access some apps to help you connect with friends and manage your e-mail. Until you understand how to use your Kindle Fire to organize those other aspects of your life, though, it won't be a truly reliable companion.

The Kindle Fire provides tools to organize and retrieve your personal documents, including spreadsheets and Word .doc and .docx files. The Contacts app keeps track of all the people in your life and integrates with the E-mail app to make reaching them easy.

Managing Personal Documents

In Chapter 2, "Loading Your Kindle Fire," you learned how to use your Cloud Drive and how to sideload to get personal documents onto your Kindle Fire. In Chapter 3, "Using Amazon's Manage Your Kindle

Page," you learned how to e-mail personal documents to your Kindle Fire. No matter which of these techniques you use to transfer documents onto your device, when your documents are in your library, you can easily access them.

Viewing PDF Documents

Your experience in reading personal documents differs depending on what type of file the document is. The Kindle Fire can read PDFs with the built-in Adobe PDF reader.

1. From the Home screen, tap Docs.

2. The format of files in your Docs library is evident from the color-coding and the format name on the icon. Tap a PDF document.

3. Double-tap to zoom in on the page.

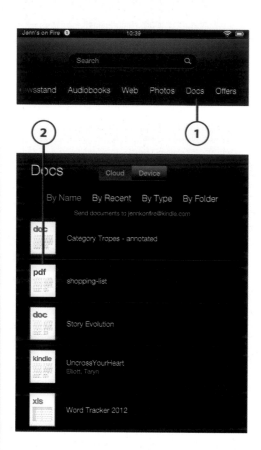

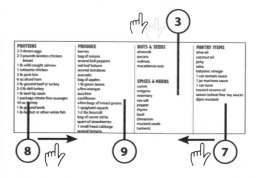

4. Reverse-pinch to enlarge a particular area.

5. Pinch to zoom out.

6. Tap and slide to move around the page.

7. Tap the right side of the page or swipe from right to left to advance one page.

8. Tap the left side of the page or swipe from left to right to go back one page.

9. Tap the middle of the page to display the PDF controls.

10. Slide the location bar to quickly move to another page in the document.

11. Tap the Back button to return to your Docs library.

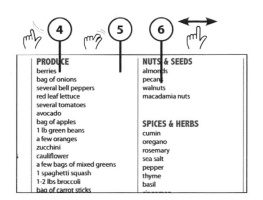

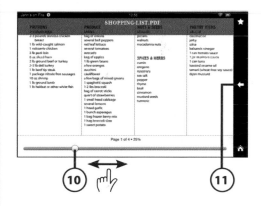

Rotating Landscape-Formatted PDFs

PDF documents open full-screen, depending on the orientation of your Kindle Fire and the document layout. Rotate your Kindle Fire to landscape orientation for better viewing of landscape-layout documents.

Viewing Word Documents

Personal documents in .txt, .doc, .docx, and .rtf formats open in OfficeSuite. This preinstalled app enables you to view your files and get a word count, but it does not allow you to edit the files.

1. In your Docs library, tap a DOC-formatted file.

2. Double-tap the page to quickly zoom in or out.

3. Scroll down to continue reading the document. Word processing documents are not paginated in the same way as PDFs, so your file will scroll as one long page.

4. Tap Word Count to see how many words, characters, and paragraphs are in the document.

5. Tap OK to return to the document.

6. Tap Find to search the document.

7. Enter your search criteria.

8. Tap Next to see the next occurrence of your search term.

9. Tap Previous to see the previous occurrence of your search term.

10. Tap Done to exit the search.

11. Tap the menu icon to access the View options.

12. Tap View to navigate through your document.

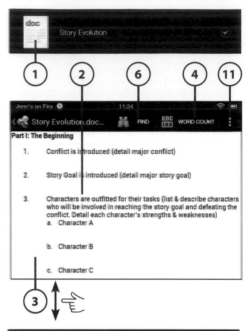

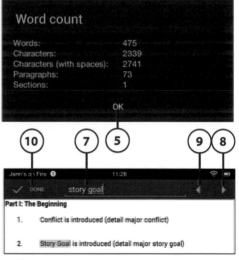

13. Tap Go to Top to jump to the top of the document.

14. Tap Go to Bottom to jump to the bottom of the document.

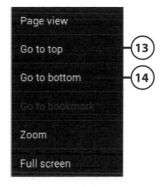

Viewing Spreadsheets

OfficeSuite also enables you to view spreadsheets. Again, you can look at the file and open charts, but you cannot edit the spreadsheet.

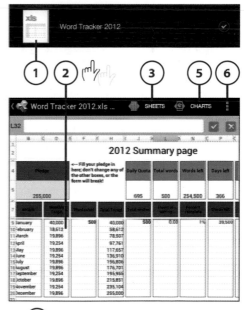

1. From the Docs library, tap to open an .xls- or .xlsx-formatted spreadsheet.

2. Double-tap the page to quickly zoom in or out. Use the same gestures to navigate through the spreadsheet as you would a document.

3. Tap Sheets to see a list of all the sheets in the worksheet.

4. Choose a sheet. (Not all spreadsheets have multiple worksheets.)

5. Tap Charts to see any charts that are embedded in the spreadhseet.

6. Tap the menu button to access additional options.

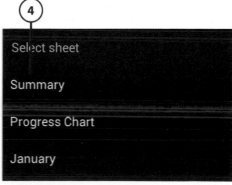

7. Tap Go To to find a specific cell.

8. Enter the cell coordinates.

9. Tap Go.

Can't Edit Spreadsheets

When you navigate through the cells of a spreadsheet, you can see the formulas that were used to calculate each cell, but you cannot edit them.

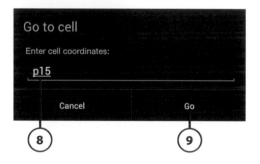

>>>Go Further

EDITING WORD DOCUMENTS AND SPREADSHEETS

If you want to edit documents and spreadsheets on your Kindle Fire, you can purchase one of several Office suites available in the Appstore. OfficeSuite Pro extends the capabilities of the preinstalled OfficeSuite to allow you to edit files. You might want to compare the features in OfficeSuite Pro with those of Documents to Go or Quickoffice Pro. Each of these apps costs $14.99, but occasionally you can find one listed as the Free App of the Day in the Appstore.

Using the Contacts App

Your Kindle Fire's Contacts app makes it easy to maintain a list of contacts for e-mail messages or for reference. You can easily import contacts from another source into your Kindle Fire. If you make changes to your contacts on the Kindle Fire and want to apply those changes to your contact list in another e-mail application, you can export your Kindle Fire contacts so that you can use them elsewhere.

Viewing Contacts

You can view your contacts from the Contacts app.

1. Open the Contacts app. You can access it from the Apps library, your Carousel, or the Quick Links.

2. Tap All to view all your contacts.

3. Tap Favorites to view contacts that you've marked as your favorites.

4. Tap and hold the scrollbar to quickly scroll through the alphabet.

5. Tap a contact to view contact details.

Favorite Contacts

You can add a contact to your favorites list by viewing the entry's contact details and then tapping the star.

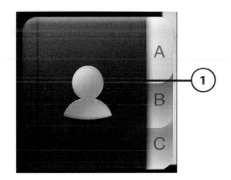

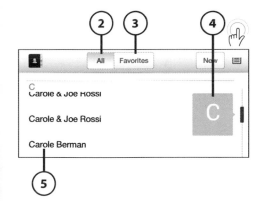

Adding a Contact

When you meet someone new, add that person's contact information to the Contacts app.

1. Tap the New button.

2. Select which account you want to use to synchronize your contacts. If you did not already set up your accounts in Chapter 10, "Reading and Sending E-mail," tap Add New Account to link your Kindle Fire with your webmail account.

3. Enter the name information for your contact.

4. Enter the phone number.

5. Select the type of phone number you entered.

6. Enter the e-mail address and select the type.

7. Enter the address and select the type.

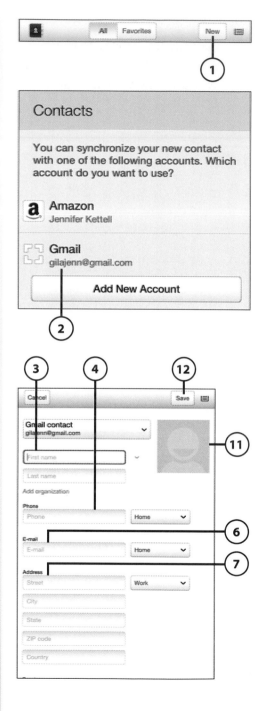

8. Enter your contact's birthday.

9. Tap Add Another Field to enter more information.

10. Choose the type of information you want to add to the contact record.

11. Tap the picture icon to add a picture of the contact. The picture must already be on your Kindle Fire.

12. Tap Save.

Synchronizing Contacts

You can synchronize your contacts with only one account. If you use Gmail or another webmail service to manage your contacts and calendars on your other devices, choose the same account here so that your data stays in sync.

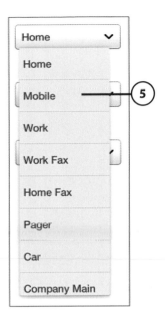

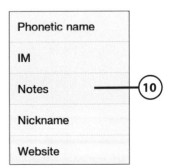

Editing a Contact

You can edit existing contacts.

1. On the contact details screen, tap Edit.
2. Edit the information as necessary and tap Save.

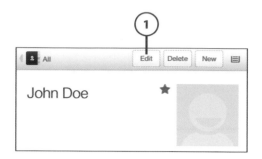

Changing Contact Sort Order and Name Display

By default, contacts are sorted by first name, which can make it difficult to easily locate the contact you seek. You can change the sort order of your contacts and how names are displayed.

1. From your contact list, tap the menu icon and then tap Settings.
2. Tap Contacts General Settings.

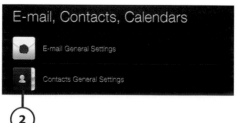

3. Tap Sort Order of Contact Name.

4. Tap Last, First to sort your contacts list by last name.

5. Tap Display Order of Contact Name, and then choose how you want names to be displayed in the contacts list.

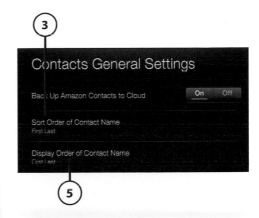

Contacts General Settings

Back Up Amazon Contacts to Cloud   On   Off

Sort Order of Contact Name
First Last

Display Order of Contact Name
First Last

Sort Order of Contact Name

First Last

Last, First

Cancel

Use tabs to browse
multiple sites

Bookmark your
favorite sites

Browse
websites

See what
sites other
Kindle Fire
users are
viewing
most

In this chapter, you learn how to use Silk, the web browser that's included with your Kindle Fire. Topics include the following:

→ Browsing the web
→ Working with tabs
→ Using bookmarks and history
→ Downloading files
→ Configuring Silk settings

Browsing the Web with Silk

Your Kindle Fire includes a web browser called Silk. Silk is a full-featured browser with support for most of today's modern web standards.

You'll likely find that browsing on a tablet device is a mixed bag. Some sites look and work great; others might not work as well. Tapping a specific link can be difficult when hyperlinks on a page appear too close to each other. (You can solve that problem by zooming in on the page.) Even with these drawbacks, though, having the ability to browse the Internet easily from your favorite chair is a great convenience.

Browsing the Web

Silk works similarly to the web browser that you use on your computer. One major difference is that, instead of using a mouse, you use touch to navigate with Silk.

In this section, you learn the basics of using Silk. In the sections that follow, I explain additional features, such as using favorites and tabs, to help you get the most out of Silk.

Using the Starter Page

When you first open Silk, the Starter page opens. The Starter page suggests websites based on three different criteria.

1. From the Home screen, tap Web to launch Silk. Silk is also added to your Favorites drawer by default.

2. Swipe through Most Visited to see the sites you visit most frequently. The pages that appear in this area change as you use Silk.

3. Swipe through Trending Now to see sites visited by other Silk users, as tracked by Amazon from users' page views.

4. Swipe through Selected Sites to see sites of general interest, such as shopping, entertainment, and information sites.

5. Tap a site to open the page.

Returning to the Starter Page

You can return to the Starter page from any other site by tapping the menu icon at the bottom of the page and then tapping Starter Page.

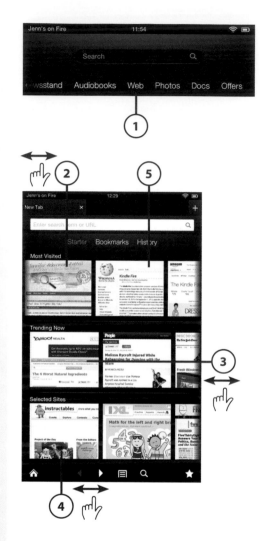

It's Not All Good

Opting Out of Trending Now

Trending Now suggestions appear on the Starter page in Silk and below the carousel on the Home page. These pages are compiled by Amazon's tracking of pages viewed by Kindle Fire users. If the privacy implications of this bother you, there is a way to opt out. If you select Optional Encryption in the Silk Settings, Amazon no longer caches your browser history, thus disabling the Trending Now feature. The downside is that pages might load slower. I explain how to access Silk Settings later in this chapter.

Browsing to a Website

You can enter a URL and browse directly to a website.

1. In the browser, tap inside the address bar.

2. Enter a URL. As you type, Silk attempts to home in on the URL you seek.

3. Tap one of the suggested entries when your destination appears. You can also type a complete URL and tap the Go button on the keyboard.

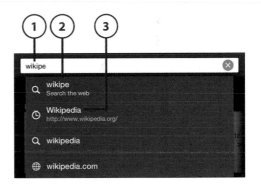

Navigating a Page

Web pages open full screen. You can navigate the page using zoom and pan techniques.

1. Browse to a URL.

2. Double-tap an area to zoom in.

3. Drag to move around the page.

4. Reverse-pinch to zoom in on the page.

5. Pinch to zoom out on the page.

6. Tap a link to follow the link.

7. Double-tap to zoom back to full-page view.

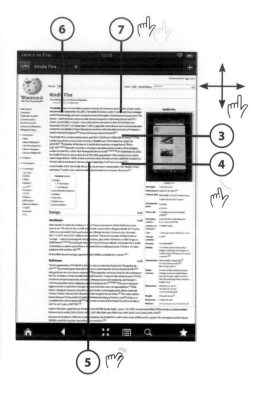

It's Not All Good

No Support for Flash

Some web pages cannot be viewed properly in Silk because they use Flash, which is a method of adding animation and interactivity to websites. The Kindle Fire HD does not support Flash. If you've upgraded from a first-generation Kindle Fire, the loss of this feature might be disappointing, but it's not Amazon's fault. Adobe, the creator of Flash, has decided to no longer support Flash on any tablet or smartphone devices.

Sharing Pages on Facebook

When you find a page that you want to share with your Facebook friends, you can do it easily.

1. From the page that you want to share, tap the menu icon.

2. Tap Share Page.

3. Tap Facebook.

4. Enter a comment about the page.

5. Tap Share to post the page and your comment on your Wall.

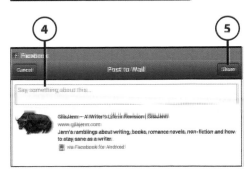

Sharing Pages with E-mail

You can also share a page by sending a link through e-mail.

1. From the Share Via menu, tap E-mail.

2. Enter one or more e-mail addresses.

3. Add a message, if you want.

4. Tap Send to send from your default e-mail account.

Sharing with Other Apps

Many other apps have the capability to share links from Silk. Installed apps with this feature also appear in the Share Via menu.

Copying a Link to the Current Page

You can copy a link to the current page so that you can paste it into a document.

1. Scroll to the top of the page so that the URL is visible.

2. Tap and hold the URL in the address bar.

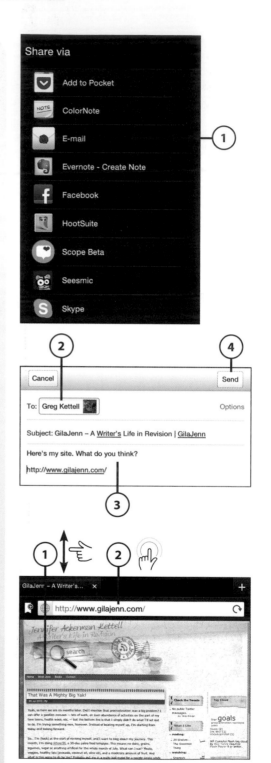

3. Tap Copy to copy the URL so that you can paste it elsewhere. You can paste the URL on another page within Silk or even in another app.

Pasting URLs

To paste a URL, tap and hold, and then tap Paste. You can paste into the address bar in Silk, the subject or text of an e-mail message, or in many other apps.

Copying a Hyperlink on a Page

You can also copy a hyperlink that appears on a page.

1. Tap and hold a hyperlink.
2. Tap Copy Link URL.

Saving Images

If you tap and hold an image on a web page, you have the option to save the image in your Photos library.

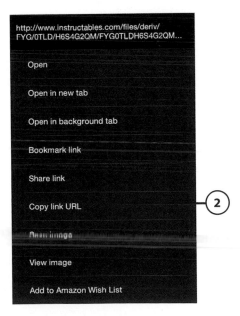

Searching in the Current Page

You can search for text within the current page.

1. While viewing the page, tap the menu icon.

2. Tap Find in Page.

3. Enter your search term. As you type, search results are highlighted on the page.

4. Tap Done to close the keyboard so that you can see more of the page.

5. Tap the Next Result icon to highlight the next result.

6. Tap the Previous Result icon to highlight the previous result.

7. Tap Done to stop searching.

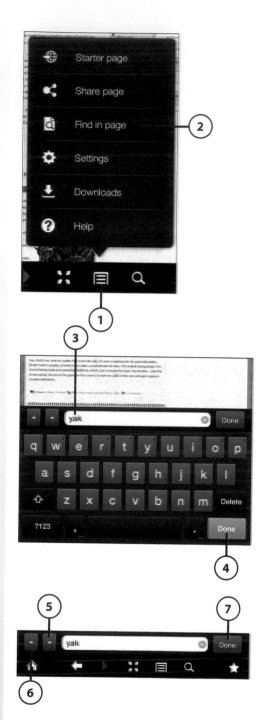

Searching the Web

Whenever you begin typing in the
address bar, Silk offers the option to
search for the term you enter.

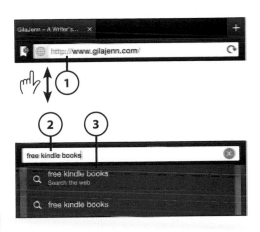

1. Scroll to the top of the page so
   that the address bar is visible, and
   tap the address bar.

2. Enter your search term. The URL
   that was in the address bar is
   replaced with what you type.

3. Tap Go (on the keyboard) or tap a
   search suggestion to search using
   your configured search engine.

Your Search Engine

The default search engine is Bing,
but you can change it in Silk's settings, if you want. I show you how
later in this chapter.

Working with Tabs

After you tap a link on a website, you can always tap the Back button to
return to the previous page, but using tabs is much more convenient. Tabs
enable you to have more than one web page open at the same time. You can
flip between pages by tapping the tab that contains the page you want to
view.

Because each tab is using resources on your Kindle Fire, Silk limits you to a
total of 10 open tabs at a time.

Opening Links in a New Tab

When you tap a link, the new page opens in the same tab by default. However, you can choose to open a link in a new tab so that you can have both the original page and the new page open at the same time. You can also open a new tab in the background so that you can view it when you're done with the current page.

1. Tap and hold a link that you want to follow. Zoom in on the page, if necessary, to accurately tap the link.

2. Tap Open in New Tab to open the page in a new tab and immediately make it the active tab.

3. Tap Open in Background Tab to open the page in a new tab but remain on the current tab as the active tab.

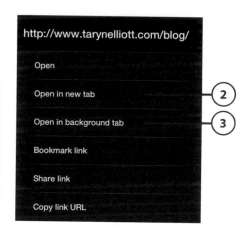

Navigating Tabs

You can add a new tab so that you can browse to a new page while leaving the current page open in a different tab. You can then close a single tab or multiple tabs.

1. Tap the Add Tab icon to add a new tab.

2. Tap the Close icon to close a tab.

3. If you have too many tabs open to see at once, swipe to locate a desired tab.

4. Tap and hold a tab to close multiple tabs.

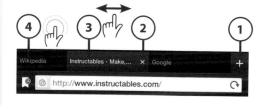

5. Tap Close Other Tabs to close all tabs except for the active tab.

6. Tap Close All Tabs to close all the tabs and return to the Starter page.

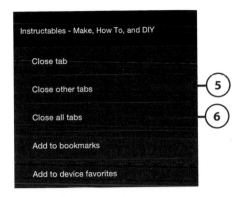

Always One Tab

Even if you tap Close All Tabs, one tab remains open and displays the Starter page. If you tap the Close icon on this tab, Silk closes and returns you to the Home screen.

Using Bookmarks and History

Bookmarks are an easy way to return to a page at any time. Bookmarks aren't just convenient for saving your favorite sites. You can also use them to temporarily save links to websites while you are researching a particular topic. For example, you can save bookmarks to product reviews so that you can easily refer back to them when deciding which item to purchase.

Bookmarking the Current Page

You can bookmark any page that you are currently viewing.

1. Scroll to the top of the page you want to bookmark.

2. Tap the Add Bookmark button to the left of the address bar.

3. Edit the name of the bookmark (or you can just go with the default).

4. Tap OK to save the bookmark.

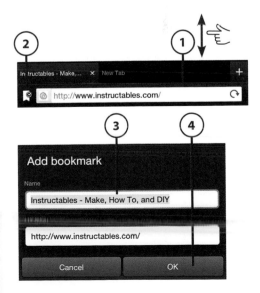

Bookmarking a Hyperlink

You can bookmark a hyperlink with-out following the link.

1. Tap and hold the hyperlink that you want to bookmark.

2. Tap Bookmark Link.

3. Enter a name for the bookmark.

4. Edit the URL, if desired. You can shorten a link to a specific page on a site to the main URL for the site, for example.

5. Tap OK to save your bookmark.

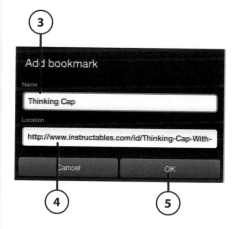

Viewing and Following Bookmarks

You can view all your bookmarks on one page and then tap to follow one.

1. On the Starter page, tap Bookmarks.

2. Tap a bookmark to go to that page.

3. Tap the menu button to change the view of the bookmarks.

4. Tap List View to view the bookmarks in a list. Tap Grid View to return to the default view.

5. Tap Add Bookmark to create a new bookmark without first navigating to the URL.

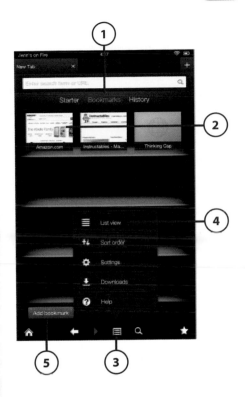

Editing a Bookmark

You can edit the name or location of a bookmark.

1. From the Bookmarks screen, tap and hold the bookmark you want to edit.

2. Tap Edit Bookmark.

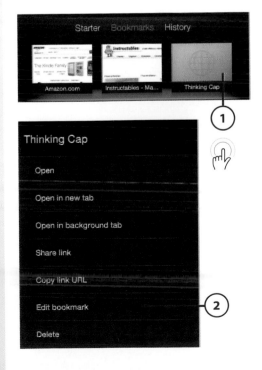

3. Make the desired changes to your bookmark.

4. Tap OK to save the bookmark.

Deleting a Bookmark

The process to delete a bookmark is much the same. Tap and hold the bookmark you want to delete, and then tap Delete from the menu.

Viewing History

As you browse the Web, Silk keeps a record of where you've been. You can view your browsing history for the last seven days so that you can return to a page you've previously visited.

1. From the Starter or Bookmarks page, tap History.

2. Tap a section to expand or collapse the history by that date.

3. Tap an entry to browse to that page.

4. Tap and hold an entry to bring up the options to open the page in a new tab, share the link, copy the link URL, or add a bookmark.

5. Tap the X to delete that page from your history.

6. Tap Clear All to delete the entire history.

Downloading Files

You can download files using Silk. Files that are downloaded are available on the Downloads screen. You can access the Downloads screen by tapping the menu icon while browsing and then tapping Downloads.

Although it doesn't make sense to download some types of files (executable files that install software on a computer, for example), you might want to download eBook files, PDF files, .doc or .docx files (Microsoft Word), pictures, or MP4 videos.

It's Not All Good

Be Cautious of Downloading Files

The Internet isn't always a safe place. Before you download a file, make sure you trust the source of the file. Numerous Android viruses can infect your Kindle Fire, and a common source of Android viruses is infected apps and files. You can keep yourself safe by downloading files from only known, reputable websites. For example, if you're downloading a PDF manual of your new TV set from the manufacturer's website, you'll be fine. If you locate what appears to be a PDF manual from a different website, you're better off getting it from the manufacturer's site.

When you download a file, your Kindle Fire uses the file's extension (the letters after the period in the filename) to determine which one of your apps can handle opening the file. If you have more than one app installed that can open the file, you're prompted to select an app to use. You can also choose an app as the default app for that particular file type.

Starting and Monitoring Downloads

After starting a download, you can see a list of your downloads and monitor it easily.

1. Tap a downloadable link to start the download.

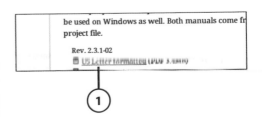

2. To monitor your download, tap the menu icon.

3. Tap Downloads.

4. Tap a download that has completed.

Identifying File Types

If the Kindle Fire can identify which app supports the downloaded file, it opens immediately. Otherwise, you're prompted to choose an application to open the downloaded file.

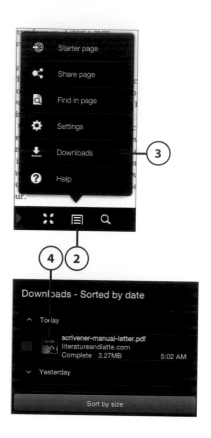

Sharing Downloaded Files

You can share downloaded files as e-mail attachments, via Skype, and with other apps, such as Evernote, that utilize this feature.

1. From the Downloads screen, tap the check box to select the file or files you want to share.

2. Tap the Share button.

3. Tap the app you want to use to share the downloaded file, such as E-mail.

4. Enter the name of the person you want to send the downloaded file to.

5. Enter a subject for the message.

6. Enter additional text to the message, if necessary.

7. Tap Send to send the e-mail from your default account.

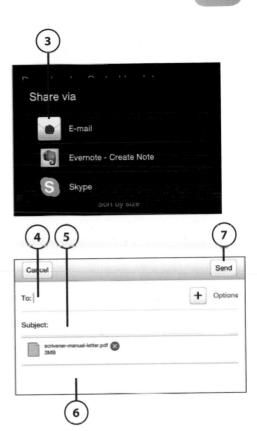

Deleting Downloaded Files

You can delete downloaded files to free up space on your Kindle Fire.

1. From the Downloads screen, tap the check box to select the file or files you want to delete.

2. Tap the Trash button.

Be Sure Before Deleting Downloaded Files

No confirmation or warning appears before you delete a downloaded file, so be certain you're deleting the correct file before you tap the Trash button.

Configuring Silk Settings

Several settings in Silk help you get the most out of your Kindle Fire. I don't cover all the settings here, but here are a couple that are useful.

All of Silk's settings are on the Settings screen. To access the Settings screen, tap the menu icon while browsing and then tap the Settings icon. The Silk Settings are grouped into General, Saved Data, and Advanced settings to help you navigate the lengthy menu.

Setting Your Search Engine

Silk uses Bing as the default search engine. If you have a different favorite, you can select it.

1. From the Silk Settings, tap Search Engine.
2. Select a search engine. Choose from Bing, Yahoo!, or Google.

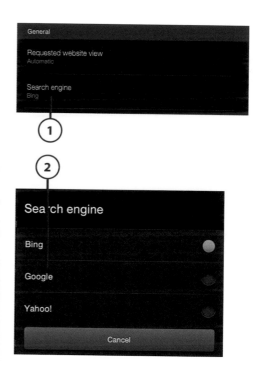

Enable Location

Some sites request access to your
location so that they can tag your
messages with location data or show
you ads specific to your region. You
can deny sites access to this data.

1. From the Silk Settings, tap Enable
   Location to clear the check box
   and disable this feature.

2. Tap the check box again if you
   change your mind and want to
   allow Silk to share location data.

A blue background lets you see at a glance that your child is in FreeTime

Search is limited to the child's content

Each child has a separate Carousel and content

Locate content by character or theme for nonreaders

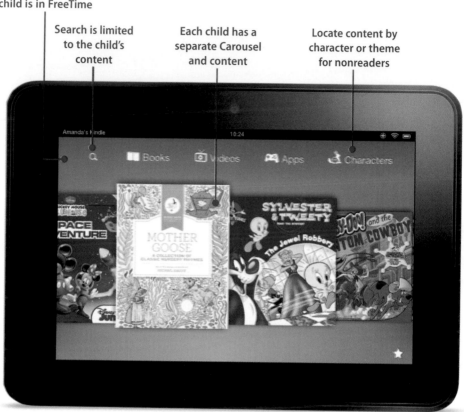

In this chapter, you learn how to configure parental controls and Kindle FreeTime to create a safe environment for your child to enjoy the Kindle Fire. Topics include these:

→ Setting up Kindle FreeTime

→ Teaching your kids how to use Kindle FreeTime

→ Parental controls for older children

Giving Your Kids a Kindle Fire

The Kindle Fire is perfect for kids. The device itself is solid, with a display that's 30 times harder than plastic, so accidental drops and bangs aren't likely to do major damage.

The Kindle Fire offers two types of parental controls. Kindle FreeTime is a brand new service for families with young children. FreeTime provides a child-friendly customized interface and allows parents to customize the specific books, music, videos, and apps children can view. The standard parental controls are for older children who are mature enough for the regular Kindle Fire interface and who do not require time restrictions but aren't yet ready to be given free rein over the content they use.

Setting Up Kindle FreeTime

Kindle FreeTime is a preinstalled app that turns your Kindle Fire into a kid-friendly device. FreeTime blocks access to Silk and the Amazon Store. It disables GameCircle and sharing to the Kindle Community,

Facebook, and Twitter. In-app purchases require a password, which prevents your child from making unexpected purchases on your credit card.

You can create a separate profile for each child and give each profile access to specific content. You can set limits on how much screen time each child is allowed on the Kindle Fire. FreeTime also provides a kid-friendly interface for your children, with a blue background and larger font size for text, and a search feature for nonreaders.

FreeTime requires setup before you put the Kindle Fire into your young child's hands.

Accessing Kindle FreeTime

The parent account provides password-protected access to the Kindle FreeTime settings.

1. From the Apps library, tap Kindle FreeTime.

2. The intro screen explains the basic steps to get started. Tap Next.

3. Enter your parental controls password. If you have not yet set a password for parental controls, you are prompted to create one.

4. Tap OK.

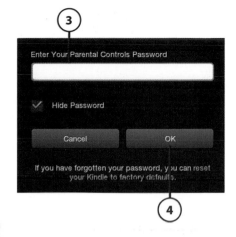

Setting Up Child Profiles

Each child in your family can have an individual profile on Kindle FreeTime.

1. After you enter your parental controls password, you're immediately prompted to create a child profile. Enter your child's name.

2. Select your child's gender.

3. Tap to enter your child's date of birth.

4. Use the sliders to set your child's birthdate.

5. Tap Set.

6. Tap to set a photo for the profile.

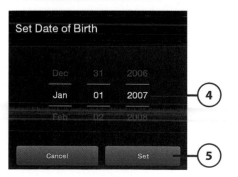

7. Tap an avatar your child can use to identify the profile.

8. Tap Next if you want to set up FreeTime for one child.

9. Tap Add Another Child to set up additional profiles, and then tap Next when you are finished entering profiles. You can create up to six profiles on your Kindle Fire.

Completing Profile Setup

After you set up child profiles, the Kindle FreeTime app opens to the start page whenever you open the app in the future. If you need to change a profile or add another child, tap Manage Child Profiles on the start page.

Manage Content on FreeTime

After creating a profile for each child, you can customize the settings so your children each have access to the content you think is appropriate.

Shop First, Add Content Later

Kindle FreeTime does not have access to the Amazon Store, so purchase content for your children before opening FreeTime to manage content. Of course, you can always add more content to your child's profile when you make future purchases.

1. From the Kindle FreeTime start page, tap Manage Content.

2. Enter your parental controls password.

3. Tap OK.

4. Tap Add Titles to [Your Child's] Library.

5. Tap Books, Videos, or Apps to select a type of content.

6. Tap the box to the right of each title you want to add to the profile.

7. Tap Save.

8. Tap the Back button to return to the FreeTime start page.

Adding Videos to FreeTime

You must purchase videos for use with FreeTime. You cannot add video rentals or content from Prime Instant Video to child profiles.

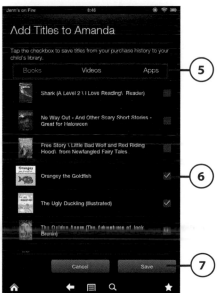

Setting Daily Time Limits

You can set time limits for how long your child can use the Kindle Fire. Alternatively, you can define different limits for each type of content, such as allowing unlimited reading time but only one hour for apps.

1. From the FreeTime start page, tap Daily Time Limits.

2. Enter your parental controls password.

3. Tap OK.

4. Tap a child's profile.

5. Tap On. The screen expands to open the time limit controls.

6. Use the slider to set a total daily usage limit for the Kindle Fire.

7. Tap Content Activity Time to set limits based on type of content.

8. Use the slider to set a time limit for Reading Books.

9. Use the slider to set a time limit for Watching Videos. The slider adjusts in 15-minute increments.

10. Use the slider to set a time limit for Using Apps. This setting does not distinguish between educational apps and games.

11. Tap the Back button.

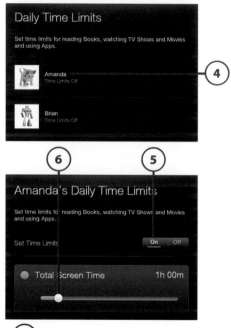

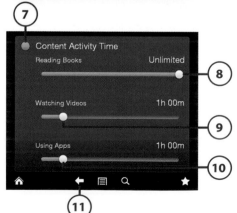

12. Tap another profile to set time limits or tap the Back button to return to the start page.

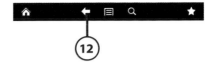

SHOULD I SET A LIMIT ON READING BOOKS?

Most parents want to encourage their children to read, so the default setting for Reading Books on FreeTime is Unlimited. If your child has vision problems, however, you might want to limit overall screen time, to foster time away from the screen. Also, studies have shown that backlit screen time just before bed can affect a child's sleep, so you might want to encourage reading traditional paper books (or E Ink–based devices such as Kindle Paperwhite) at bedtime.

Changing the Parental Controls Password

You can change your parental controls password.

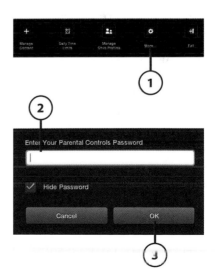

1. From the FreeTime start page, tap More.

2. Enter your current parental controls password.

3. Tap OK.

4. Tap Change Parental Controls Password.

5. Enter your current password.

6. Type a new password.

7. Reenter the new password.

8. Tap Finish.

It's Not All Good

Remember Your Password

If you forget your parental controls password, you need to restore your Kindle Fire to factory settings. This wipes out all your Amazon account information, downloaded content, and personal documents, photos, and videos.

If you need to restore your Kindle Fire to factory settings, swipe down from the status bar to open Settings and then tap More. Tap Device and then tap Reset to Factory Defaults. Be sure you've first backed up any personal content you want to keep to your Cloud Drive or computer.

Teaching Your Kids How to Use Kindle FreeTime

After setting up FreeTime, tap a child's profile from the start page to enter that child's FreeTime account. The Kindle Fire interface changes to a controlled, kid-friendly environment. The content that you have added to the child's profile is available in the appropriate Books, Videos, and Apps categories. Content also appears on the Carousel.

It's Not All Good

Preinstalled Content on FreeTime

In addition to the content you put on your child's profile, Amazon has made some of its own selections. FreeTime comes with several books and apps preinstalled. Some parents might not appreciate Amazon choosing content for their children. Unfortunately, you need to individually download each book or app within the child's account before you can choose to remove it from the device (tap and hold the item, and then choose Remove from Device). If you object to any of the preinstalled content, you should download and remove it before giving the Kindle Fire to your child.

Using the FreeTime Interface

Although children seem to inherently know how to operate electronic devices, and the FreeTime interface is very intuitive, here are some tips for you to help your child get started.

1. Swipe along the Carousel to browse new or recently used books, apps, and videos.

2. Tap Books, Videos, or Apps to see what's available.

3. Tap a book, video, or app to open it.

4. If the item has not yet been downloaded, follow the orange progress bar as it downloads the book, video, or app to the Kindle Fire. If the item has a check mark, it's ready to be used.

5. The Back button takes you back to where you were.

6. The Search button lets you look for a book, app, or video on your account.

7. Tap and hold a book, video, or app to add it to your Favorites drawer.

8. Tap Add to Favorites.

9. Tap the star to see your Favorites drawer.

10. Tap an icon in your Favorites drawer to open it.

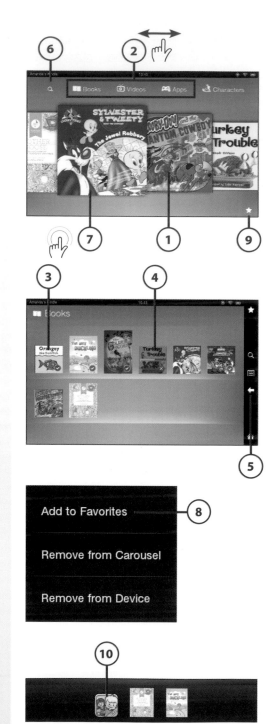

Removing Content

Although it seems illogical in such an otherwise controlled environment, your child can remove content from the Kindle Fire by tapping and holding an item and then choosing Remove from Device. If your child inadvertently does this, you must add the content to the profile again for your child to have access to it.

Navigation for Nonreaders

If your child is not yet reading, the Characters option on the Home screen lets your child choose books, videos, and apps based on the characters or theme of the content.

1. From the Home screen, tap Characters.

2. Choose a character or theme.

3. Choose a book or app to open.

You Can't Choose How Content Is Categorized

The Characters groupings are not perfect. Content is sorted by Amazon, not by the parent, so you cannot control which characters and themes appear or whether a book, video, or app is included or excluded from that grouping. This feature should improve over time.

Exiting FreeTime

When it's your turn to use your Kindle Fire, you can exit FreeTime.

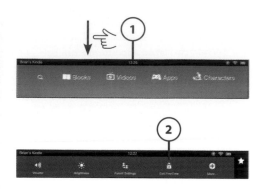

1. Swipe down from the status bar to open Settings.

2. Tap Exit FreeTime.

3. Enter your parental controls password.

4. Tap OK.

Changing Settings

Your child can access Settings to change the volume on the Kindle Fire and adjust the brightness of the display. If your child attempts to exit FreeTime or access any other settings or parental controls, the Kindle Fire prompts your child for a password.

Parental Controls for Older Children

If you have slightly older children, they might be ready to use the standard Kindle Fire interface and have more freedom over how much time they spend using the Kindle Fire. As a parent, however, you might still want to limit your child's access to the Internet, e-mail, and other content.

The Kindle Fire's regular parental controls are much less restrictive than those of Kindle FreeTime. In addition to blocking types of content or apps, you can password-protect access to the Amazon Store and Instant Video, to prevent your child from making unauthorized purchases or downloading inappropriate content.

It's Not All Good

You Cannot Control Content by Rating

You can disable access to an entire content library, such as Videos or Books. However, you cannot control access to content by rating. If your child has access to the Videos library, for example, he or she can watch any video you have purchased on the Kindle Fire. If your child has access to the Books library, he or she can read that copy of *50 Shades of Gray* you purchased for your morning train commute. If you share your Kindle Fire with your children and worry about them accessing your content, consider limiting them to a FreeTime profile.

Setting a Parental Controls Password

Parental controls are password protected.

1. Swipe down from the status bar to open Settings.

2. Tap More.

3. Tap Parental Controls.

4. Tap On to turn on parental controls.

5. Create a parental controls password. If you've already created a password while setting up FreeTime for a younger child, use it here.

6. Type the password again to confirm it.

7. Tap Finish.

Managing Parental Controls Settings

After you enter your password, the Parental Controls screen displays several options to limit your child's use of the Kindle Fire.

1. Tap Web Browser to block or unblock access to Silk.

2. Tap E-mail, Contacts, Calendars to control access to those apps.

3. Tap the On or Off button for the Password Protect Purchases option. When this is On, purchases from the Amazon Store or the Amazon Shop app require a password. This includes in-app purchases.

4. Tap the On or Off button to password protect video playback. When On, this option requires a password to play Amazon Instant Video and Prime Instant Video.

5. Tap Block and Unblock Content Types to control access to content libraries.

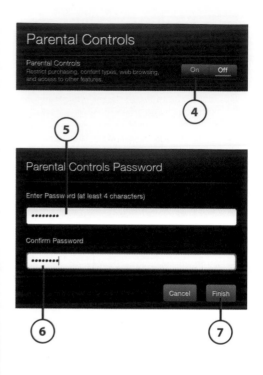

6. Tap the Unblocked button to the right of any content type to toggle the button and block access to that content library.

7. Tap Back to return to the Parental Controls screen.

8. Tap Change Password to change the parental controls password.

9. Enter your current password.

10. Enter a new password.

11. Re-enter the new password to confirm it.

12. Tap Finish.

13. Tap the On or Off button to Password Protect Wi-Fi. When On, this setting requires the parental controls password to turn on Wi-Fi in order to download or stream content.

Turning Off Parental Controls

If you want to turn off parental controls, return to the Parental Controls screen and tap the Off button.

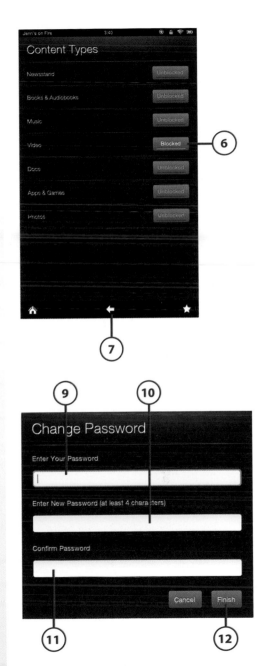

Index

C

G

O

P

X-Y-Z

My Kindle Fire HD

COVERS
Kindle Fire HD and
2nd-Generation
Kindle Fire

FREE
Online Edition

Safari
Books Online

Jim Cheshire and Jennifer Kettell

Your purchase of *My Kindle Fire HD* includes access to a free online edition for 45 days through the **Safari Books Online** subscription service. Nearly every Que book is available online through **Safari Books Online**, along with thousands of books and videos from publishers such as Addison-Wesley Professional, Cisco Press, Exam Cram, IBM Press, O'Reilly Media, Prentice Hall, Sams, and VMware Press.

Safari Books Online is a digital library providing searchable, on-demand access to thousands of technology, digital media, and professional development books and videos from leading publishers. With one monthly or yearly subscription price, you get unlimited access to learning tools and information on topics including mobile app and software development, tips and tricks on using your favorite gadgets, networking, project management, graphic design, and much more.

Activate your FREE Online Edition at
informit.com/safarifree

STEP 1: Enter the coupon code: EACVHFH.

STEP 2: New Safari users, complete the brief registration form. Safari subscribers, just log in.

If you have difficulty registering on Safari or accessing the online edition, please e-mail customer-service@safaribooksonline.com

---